Java for the Web with Servlets, JSP, and EJB: A Developer's Guide to J2EE Solutions

Contents At a Glance

Java for the Web with Servlets, JSP, and EJB

Budi Kurniawan

www.newriders.com
201 West 103rd Street, Indianapolis, Indiana 46290
An Imprint of Pearson Education
Boston • Indianapolis • London • Munich • New York • San Francisco

Java for the Web with Servlets, JSP, and EJB

FIRST EDITION: April, 2002

International Standard Book Number: 0-7357-1195X

Library of Congress Catalog Card Number: *2001093802*

06 05 04 03 7 6 5 4

Interpretation of the printing code: The rightmost double-digit number is the year of the book's printing; the rightmost single-digit number is the number of the book's printing. For example, the printing code 02-1 shows that the first printing of the book occurred in 2002.

Trademarks

All terms mentioned in this book that are known to be trademarks or service marks have been appropriately capitalized. New Riders Publishing cannot attest to the accuracy of this information. Use of a term in this book should not be regarded as affecting the validity of any trademark or service mark.

Warning and Disclaimer

This book is designed to provide information about Java for the web working with servlets, jsp, and ejb. Every effort has been made to make this book as complete and as accurate as possible, but no warranty of fitness is implied.

The information is provided on an as-is basis. The authors and New Riders Publishing shall have neither liability nor responsibility to any person or entity with respect to any loss or damages arising from the information contained in this book or from the use of the discs or programs that may accompany it.

Publisher
David Dwyer

Associate Publisher
Stephanie Wall

Production Manager
Gina Kanouse

Managing Editor
Kristy Knoop

Acquisitions Editor
Deborah Hittel-Shoaf

Development Editor
Grant Munroe

Product Marketing Manager
Kathy Malmloff

Publicity Manager
Susan Nixon

Copy Editor
Kathy Murray

Indexer
Chris Morris

Manufacturing Coordinator
Jim Conway

Book Designer
Louisa Klucznik

Cover Designer
Brainstorm Design, Inc.

Cover Production
Aren Howell

Proofreader
Sossity Smith

Composition
Jeff Bredensteiner

Media Developer
Jay Payne

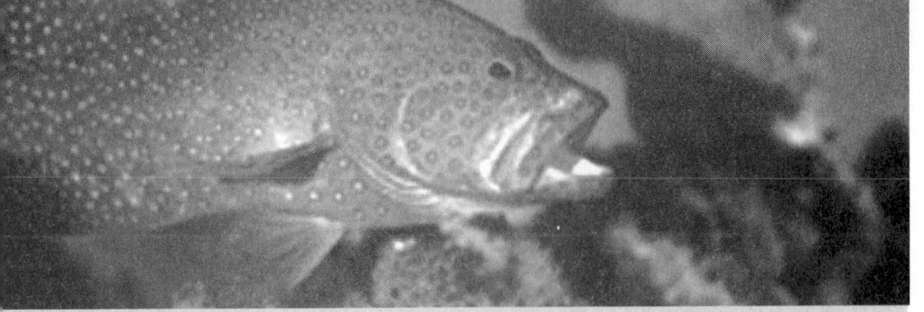

Table of Contents

About the Author

Budi Kurniawan is an IT consultant specializing in Internet and object-oriented programming and has taught both Java and Microsoft technologies. He is the author of the most popular Java Upload bean from BrainySoftware.com, which is licensed by Commerce One
(NASDAQ: CMRC) and purchased by major corporations, such as Saudi Business Machine Ltd (`www.sbm.com.sa`), Baxter Healthcare Corporation (`www.baxter.com`), and others.

Budi has a Masters of Research degree in Electrical Engineering from Sydney University, Australia. His research topic was on digital image processing. Budi has written a number of computer books, as well as published articles for more than 10 publications—including prestigious Java magazines, such as *Java-Pro*, *JavaWorld*, *JavaReport*, and O'Reilly's `www.onjava.com`. Budi is now the weekly contributor for the Servlets/JSP section of *Java Insight* and can be contacted at `budi@brainysoftware.com`.

About the Technical Reviewers

These reviewers contributed their considerable hands-on expertise to the entire development process for *Java for the Web with Servlets, JSP, and EJB*. As the book was being written, these dedicated professionals reviewed all the material for technical content, organization, and flow. Their feedback was critical to ensuring that *Java for the Web with Servlets, JSP, and EJB* fits our reader's need for the highest-quality technical information.

Chris Crane is currently teaching at Memorial University of Newfoundland, where he offers programming courses covering a wide range of programming concepts and languages, such as desktop application development using Visual Basic, C++, and Java to Distributed Enterprise Applications using EJB, and Microsoft .Net Web Services. Outside of his teaching duties, Chris runs his own consulting company, developing Enterprise-level applications for companies throughout Canada and the U.S. He is also certified as an MCP, MCSD, MCT, CCNA, CCAI and SCP/Java2.

Lan Wu joined Persistence Software in Silicon Valley after receiving her Master's Degree in Computer Science. Lan's efforts at Persistence were focused on Java with EJBs. Later, she moved on to myCFO Corporation, where she is involved with the designing and developing of the automation system. She is now with Blue Martini Software and responsible for automation with Java and web programming.

Acknowledgments

So many people are involved in the process of delivering this book, without whom this book would never be a reality.

First and foremost I'd like to thank Deborah Hittel-Shoaf, my Acquisitions Editor, for her professionalism and flexibility. Really, she takes care of her authors.

Thanks also go to Grant Munroe, my Development Editor, for his patience and for getting all the chapters together.

Two excellent editors helped me with technical review and provided invaluable feedback and made the content much, much better: Lan Wu and Chris Crane. I would also like to thank them.

Finally, all the folks at New Riders who helped me with the diagrams, proofreading, index, layout, and so on. Thank you.

Special thanks go to my best friend Ken for providing me with excellent accommodation (and Internet access) during my Christmas visit to Vancouver, BC—after being knocked out exhausted in the middle of the writing of this book. His party and the tours refreshed me.

Tell Us What You Think

As the reader of this book, you are the most important critic and commentator. We value your opinion and want to know what we're doing right, what we could do better, what areas you'd like to see us publish in, and any other words of wisdom you're willing to pass our way.

As the Associate Publisher for New Riders Publishing, I welcome your comments. You can fax, email, or write me directly to let me know what you did or didn't like about this book—as well as what we can do to make our books stronger.

Please note that I cannot help you with technical problems related to the topic of this book, and that due to the high volume of mail I receive, I might not be able to reply to every message.

When you write, please be sure to include this book's title and author as well as your name and phone or fax number. I will carefully review your comments and share them with the author and editors who worked on the book.

Fax: 317-581-4663

Email: `stephanie.wall@newriders.com`

Mail: Stephanie Wall
Associate Publisher
New Riders Publishing
201 West 103rd Street
Indianapolis, IN 46290 USA

Introduction

The Internet is still young and vulnerable. Therefore, its history is not a lengthy one. The web started when everything was just static pages. Unless you are a six-year-old whiz kid reading this book because you are more interested in Java web programming than PlayStation2, it is most likely that you experienced the time when a web site was no more than HTML pages. In the earlier days, a web site had at most one page and it more often than not was called a home page.

The terms "Internet application" or "web application" were coined when dynamic content was introduced. Loosely interpreted, a web application is a web site whose contents are generated dynamically before being sent to the browser. You should first understand how the Internet works before learning how a web application works.

When you surf the Internet, you basically request for a certain file located in a particular computer in the location you specify in the Uniform Resource Locator (URL). The computer where the file is stored is called the web server. This computer's main function is to serve anybody on the Internet who requests files it hosts. Because you never know when a user will visit and use your web application, your web server must be up and running all the time.

When you click or type in a URL in the Location or Address box of your browser, the following things happen:

- The client browser establishes a TCP/IP connection with the server.
- The browser sends a request to the server.
- The server sends a response to the client.
- The server closes the connection.

Note that after sending the requested page to the browser, the server always closes the connection, whether or not the user requests other pages from the server.

What Is Happening in the Industry

Since the emergence of the Internet, web technologies have become more and more important, and web applications are more and more common. The use of a web browser is no longer restricted to surfing static pages on the Internet. It is now very commonplace to see a web browser used as an application's client.

What this means is, some people believe, whoever controls the Internet controls the future of computing—or even the future itself. At the very least, the evidence has been demonstrated by the struggles of a few companies to grab the web browsers' domination in the late 1990s. As the best example, Microsoft Corporation—still the number one player in the software business up until now—felt it was important to have everyone on the planet using its Internet Explorer browser. That's why it exerted its overwhelming power in software technology to create the fastest and smartest browser ever and distribute it for free. With the surrender of Netscape, Microsoft has won the battle of browsers. In the next five years, it is still hard to imagine how any browser could surpass the popularity of Microsoft Internet Explorer.

On the server side, it's a different story, though. The war is far from over. Microsoft can't push its server technology as easily as it forced Netscape to give up. In fact, the most popular server technology is Java. To be precise, it's Sun Microsystems' Java 2, Enterprise Edition (J2EE). Microsoft is still trying to catch up with its new .NET initiative that is a replacement of its previous Distributed interNet Applications (DNA) platform for developing enterprise applications. Released in early 2002, .NET will collide head-on with J2EE. The next few years will still see J2EE and .NET as the two competing server technologies. Right now, it's still too premature to predict who will come out the winner.

Strategy-wise, Microsoft takes a far different approach from Sun in trying to win. Microsoft provides a single-vendor solution, selling from the operating system to the database server. J2EE, on the other hand, is supported by the entire industry. (For a list of vendors who provide J2EE compliant servers, see Appendix G, "Related Resources.") Analysts have tried to compare J2EE and .NET in many white papers published on the Internet. Unfortunately, the conclusions vary a great deal. To find out more about how J2EE and .NET compare, you can consult the following articles, which are available online:

- Microsoft .NET vs. J2EE: How Do They Stack Up?, `http://java.oreilly.com/news/farley_0800.html`
- Java 2 Enterprise Edition (J2EE) versus The .NET Platform: Two Visions for eBusiness, `http://www.objectwatch.com/FinalJ2EEand DotNet.doc`
- J2EE vs. Microsoft.NET: A Comparison of Building XML-Based Web Services, `http://www.theserverside.com/resources/article.jsp?l=J2EE-vs-DOTNET`
- Compare Microsoft .NET to J2EE Technology, `http://msdn.microsoft.com/net/compare/default.asp`
- "The Great Debate: .NET vs. J2EE" `http://www.javaworld.com/javaworld/jw-03-2002/jw-0308-j2eenet.html`

At this point, you should have gotten the big picture of what is happening in the industry. You can find out more about .NET at `http://msdn.microsoft.com`. J2EE is presented in the section, "Java 2, Enterprise Edition (J2EE)."

Also note that the term web server can also be used to refer to the software package used in the web server computer to handle requests and respond to them. In fact, throughout this book, the term web server is used to refer to this software.

The first popular web server—NCSA HTTPd—was created by Rob McCool at the National Center for Supercomputing Applications. And, McCool's invention was really cool because it helped the Internet revolutionize our lives and went on to become the foundation for the Apache web server—the most used web server on the Internet today.

The Hypertext Transfer Protocol (HTTP)

HTTP is the protocol that allows web servers and browsers to exchange data over the Internet. It is a request and response protocol. The client requests a file and the server responds to the request. HTTP uses reliable TCP connections—by default on TCP port 80. HTTP (currently at version 1.1 at the time of this writing) was first defined in RFC 2068. It was then refined in RFC 2616, which can be found at `http://www.w3c.org/Protocols/`.

In HTTP, it's always the client who initiates a transaction by establishing a connection and sending an HTTP request. The server is in no position to contact a client or make a callback connection to the client. Either the client or the server can prematurely terminate a connection. For example, when using a web browser you can click the Stop button on your browser to stop the download process of a file, effectively closing the HTTP connection with the web server.

HTTP Requests

An HTTP transaction begins with a request from the client browser and ends with a response from the server. An HTTP request consists of three components:

- Method——URI—Protocol/Version
- Request headers
- Entity body

An example of an HTTP request is the following:

```
GET /servlet/default.jsp HTTP/1.1
Accept: text/plain; text/html
Accept-Language: en-gb
Connection: Keep-Alive
Host: localhost
Referer: http://localhost/ch8/SendDetails.htm
User-Agent: Mozilla/4.0 (compatible; MSIE 4.01; Windows 98)
Content-Length: 33
Content-Type: application/x-www-form-urlencoded
Accept-Encoding: gzip, deflate

LastName=Franks&FirstName=Michael
```

The method—URI—protocol version appears as the first line of the request.

```
GET /servlet/default.jsp HTTP/1.1
```

where `GET` is the request method, `/servlet/default.jsp` represents the URI and `HTTP/1.1` the Protocol/Version section.

The request method will be explained in more details in the next section, "HTTP request Methods."

The URI specifies an Internet resource completely. A URI is usually interpreted as being relative to the server's root directory. Thus, it should always begin with a forward slash /. A URL is actually a type of URI (see `http://www.ietf.org/rfc/rfc2396.txt`). The Protocol version represents the version of the HTTP protocol being used.

The request header contains useful information about the client environment and the entity body of the request. For example, it could contain the language the browser is set for, the length of the entity body, and so on. Each header is separated by a carriage return/linefeed (CRLF) sequence.

Between the headers and the entity body, there is a blank line (CRLF) that is important to the HTTP request format. The CRLF tells the HTTP server where the entity body begins. In some Internet programming books, this CRLF is considered the fourth component of an HTTP request.

In the previous HTTP request, the entity body is simply the following line:

```
LastName=Franks&FirstName=Michael
```

The entity body could easily become much longer in a typical HTTP request.

HTTP request Methods

Each HTTP request can use one of the many request methods as specified in the HTTP standards. The HTTP 1.1 request methods and the descriptions of each method are given in Table I.1.

Table I.1 **HTTP 1.1 request Methods**

Method	Description
GET	GET is the simplest, and probably, most used HTTP method. GET simply retrieves the data identified by the URL. If the URL refers to a script (CGI, servlet, and so on), it returns the data produced by the script.
HEAD	The HEAD method provides the same functionality as GET, but HEAD only returns HTTP headers without the document body.
POST	Like GET, POST is also widely used. Typically, POST is used in HTML forms. POST is used to transfer a block of data to the server in the entity body of the request.
OPTIONS	The OPTIONS method is used to query a server about the capabilities it provides. Queries can be general or specific to a particular resource.
PUT	The PUT method is a complement of a GET request, and PUT stores the entity body at the location specified by the URI. It is similar to the PUT function in FTP.

DELETE	The DELETE method is used to delete a document from the server. The document to be deleted is indicated in the URI section of the request.
TRACE	The TRACE method is used to trace the path of a request through firewall and multiple proxy servers. TRACE is useful for debugging complex network problems and is similar to the traceroute tool.

Warning

HTTP 1.0 only has three request methods: GET, HEAD, and POST.

Of the seven methods, only GET and POST are commonly used in an Internet application.

HTTP Responses

Similar to requests, an HTTP response also consists of three parts:

- Protocol—Status code——Description
- Response headers
- Entity body

The following is an example of an HTTP response:

```
HTTP/1.1 200 OK
Server: Microsoft-IIS/4.0
Date: Mon, 3 Jan 1998 13:13:33 GMT
Content-Type: text/html
Last-Modified: Mon, 11 Jan 1998 13:23:42 GMT
Content-Length: 112

<HTML>
<HEAD>
<TITLE>HTTP Response Example</TITLE></HEAD><BODY>
Welcome to Brainy Software
</BODY>
</HTML>
```

The first line of the response header is similar to the first line of the request header. The first line tells you that the protocol used is HTTP version 1.1, the request succeeded (200 = success), and that everything went okay.

The response headers contain useful information similar to the headers in the request. The entity body of the response is the HTML content of the response itself. The headers and the entity body are separated by a sequence of CRLFs.

System Architecture

This section is meant to give you the big picture of a software application system utilizing Java or other technologies. This section takes the common approach of introducing software system architecture by observing how it has evolved.

A well-designed software application is partitioned into separate logical parts called layers. Each layer has a different responsibility in the overall architecture. These layers are purely abstractions, and do not correspond to physical distribution.

Typical layers in a software system are as follows:

- **Presentation layer**. In this layer are parts that handle the user interface and user interaction.
- **Business logic layer**. This layer contains components that handle the programming logic of the application.
- **Data layer**. This layer is used by the business logic layer to persist state permanently. This layer normally consists of one or more databases where data is stored. However, other types of datastore could also be used. For example, it is now very common to use XML documents as storage to keep data.

The Two-Tier Architecture

A two-tiered application is a simple client-server application in which the processing workload falls onto the client computer's shoulders and the server simply acts as a traffic controller between the client and the data. The term "fat client" for this type of architecture is due to the bulk of processing requirements at the client side. In this architecture, the presentation layer and the business logic layer are hosted in one tier and the data layer is on another tier. Figure I.1 shows a two-tier architecture.

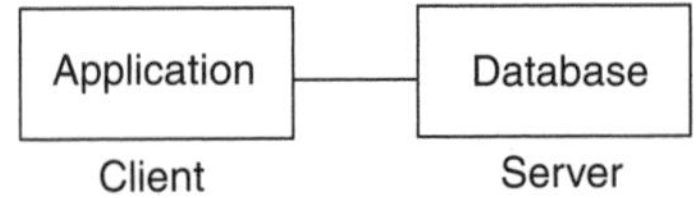

Figure I.1 A two-tiered application.

The drawback of this type of architecture is that it starts to pose problems as the number of clients increases. The first problem is due to the fact that all processing happens at the client side. There is increased network traffic because each client has to make multiple requests for data from the server—even before presenting anything to the user.

Another problem is cost because each client needs a machine with sufficient processing power. As the number of clients increases, the cost for providing client machines alone could be astronomical.

However, the most severe problem that this type of architecture can cause is probably a maintenance problem. Even a tiny change to the processing logic might require a complete rollout to the entire organization. Even though the process can be automated, there are always problems with larger organizations because some users may not be ready for an upgrade, whereas others insist it be performed immediately.

The Three-Tier Architecture

To overcome the problems in many two-tiered applications, an application is broken up into three separate tiers, instead of two. The first tier contains the presentation layer, the second tier, or the middle tier, consists of the business logic layer, and the third tier contains the data layer. Figure I.2 shows a three-tier architecture.

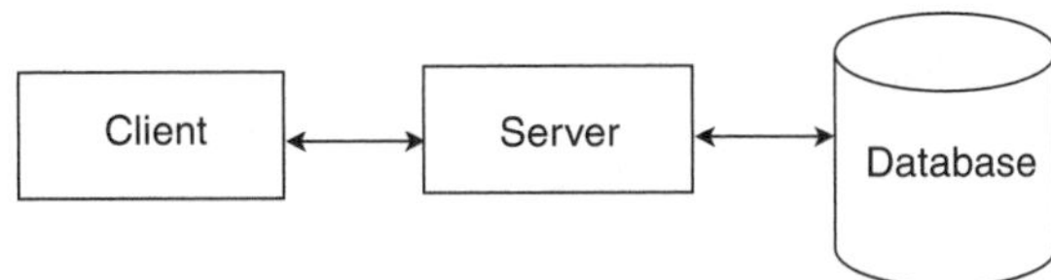

Figure I.2 A three-tiered application.

The *n*-Tier Architecture

To achieve more flexibility, the three tiers in the three-tiered application can be segregated even further. An application with this type of architecture is called an *n*-tiered application. In this architecture, the business logic layer is divided by function instead of being physically divided. It breaks down like the following:

- **A user interface.** This handles the user interaction with the application. In an Internet application, this is usually a web browser used to render HTML tags.
- **Presentation logic.** This defines what the user interface displays and how user requests are handled.
- **Business logic.** This models the application business logic.
- **Infrastructure services.** These provide additional functionality required by the application components.
- **The data layer.** Hosts the application data.

Java 2, Enterprise Edition (J2EE)

First of all, J2EE is not a product. Rather, it is a specification that defines the contract between applications and the container. The container here refers to a standardized runtime environment, which provides specific services for components deployed in it. J2EE is described in more detail in Part III, "Developing Scalable Applications with EJB," of this book.

Developing Web Applications in Java

You normally adopt two main architectures when developing web applications in Java. The first architecture utilizes servlets and JSP in the middle tier to serve clients and process the business logic. This architecture is depicted in Figure I.3. The middle tier is discussed during the servlets and JSP coverage in this book.

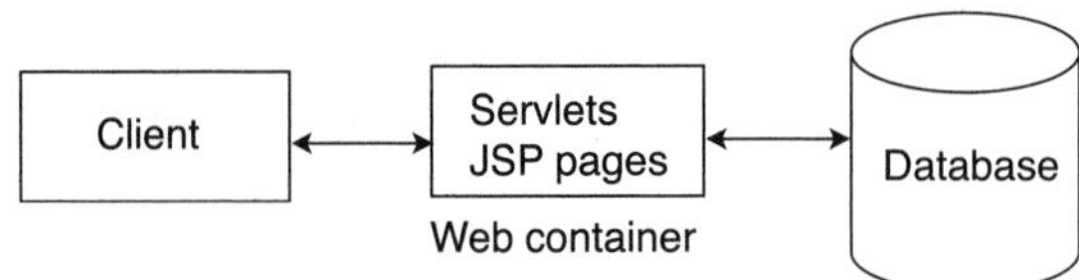

Figure I.3 A servlets/JSP application architecture.

Small to medium-size applications use this design model.

The second architecture includes the use of J2EE server and Enterprise JavaBeans (EJB) and this is especially useful for large enterprise applications that need scalability. The architecture is shown in Figure I.4, and EJB is discussed in Part III of this book.

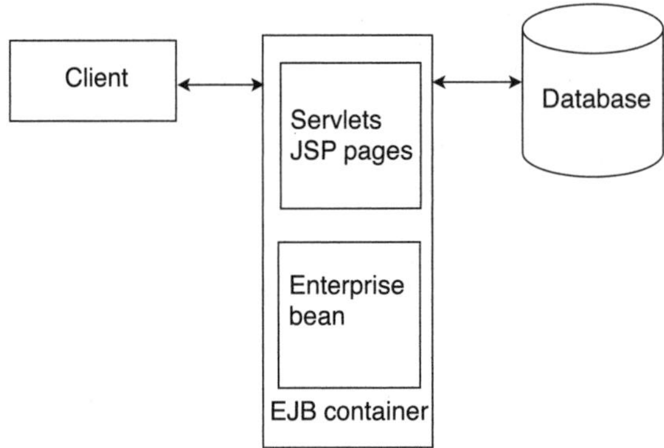

Figure I.4 A J2EE application architecture.

Overview of Parts and Chapters

This book consists of four parts, including the appendixes.

Part I: Building Java Web Applications

This part is comprised of 20 chapters on servlets and JavaServer Pages (JSP).

Chapter 1, "The Servlet Technology," introduces you to the servlet technology and compares it with other existing web technologies. More importantly, this chapter prepares you to write servlets, including the step-by-step instructions on quickly configuring the servlet container, compiling your servlet, and deploying it in the container. If you follow the instructions correctly, you will be able to view your servlet in action with your web browser.

Chapter 2, "Inside Servlets," discusses the nuts and bolts of the latest release of the Java Servlet specification Application Programming Interface (API), version 2.3. This chapter explains the first of the two packages available for servlet programmers: javax.servlet. This package contains basic classes and interfaces that you can use to write servlets from scratch. Important concepts, such as a servlet's life cycle, a servlet's context, requests, responses, and how to write thread-safe servlets are discussed in this chapter.

Chapter 3, "Writing Servlet Applications," explains the classes and interfaces in the javax.servlet.http package. Compared to the javax.servlet package, javax.servlet.http offers more advanced classes and interfaces that extend classes and interfaces in javax.servlet. This chapter also demonstrates the use of several techniques, such as obtaining values sent by the user, using different HTTP methods, response buffering, request dispatching, and including other resources in a servlet.

Chapter 4, "Accessing Databases with JDBC," shows how you can access and manipulate data in a database using Java Database Connectivity (JDBC). This chapter starts with a look at the object model in the java.sql package and explains how to connect to a database in detail. After a few examples, this chapter concludes with a multipurpose tool that enables you to type your SQL statement in the browser, get it executed on the server, and have the result displayed in the browser.

Chapter 5, "Session Management," explains the importance of being able to manage user session and retain state from previous requests. Several techniques are introduced, such as URL rewriting, hidden fields, and cookies. However, the servlet container offers its own automatic session management, a great feature that makes managing user session easy and straightforward.

Chapter 6, "Application and Session Events," discusses the new feature in the Servlet 2.3 specification, as well as several events that have been available since the previous versions of the specification. This chapter provides examples on how to listen and capture the application and session events and configure the deployment descriptor.

Chapter 7, "Servlet Filtering," explains another new feature in the Servlet 2.3 specification. This chapter shows you how you can make full use of servlet filtering to achieve some important tasks, such as preprocessing an HTTP request.

Chapter 8, "JSP Basics," introduces the second Java web technology that should be used in conjunction with servlets. This chapter explains situations where you want to use JSP, and discusses the relation between servlets and JSP.

Chapter 9, "JSP Syntax," presents the complete syntax for JavaServer Pages. In particular, it discusses directives, scripting elements, and action elements. Wherever possible, examples are given to illustrate how to use each item.

Chapter 10, "Developing JSP Beans," introduces the component-centric approach for writing JSP applications using JavaBeans. Using this approach, division of labor is possible. The Java programmer writes and compiles JavaBeans that incorporate all the functionality needed in an application and the page designer works with the page design at the same time. When the JavaBeans are ready, the page designer uses tags to call methods and properties of the beans from the JSP page.

Chapter 11, "Using JSP Custom Tags," explains what custom tags are and how to use them to perform custom actions from a JSP page. This chapter explores the great features of custom tags and begins with writing a JSP page that uses custom tags. It then explains the classes and interfaces in the javax.servlet.jsp.tagext package.

Chapter 12, "Programmable File Download," discusses a technique that allows you to programmatically send a file to a browser. Using this technique, you, the programmer, have full control over the downloaded file. This chapter offers an example of how to do programmable file download from a JSP page.

Chapter 13, "File Upload," explains all you need to know about file upload, including the underlying theory of HTTP requests. Knowledge of the HTTP request is critical because when you process an uploaded file, you work with raw data not obtainable from simply querying the HTTP Request object. The last section of the chapter talks about the File Upload Bean from Brainysoftware.com, included on the accompanying CD.

Chapter 14, "Security Configuration," presents the technique for securing your web application by configuring the deployment descriptor to instruct the web container to restrict access to some, or all, of the resources. The configuration means that you only need to modify your deployment descriptor file—no coding is needed.

Chapter 15, "Caching," offers two caching techniques to enhance the application performance: caching data in a text file and caching data in memory. The first solution writes frequently accessed but hardly changed data into text files. When your application needs the data from the database, instead of hitting the database server, the application can just include a text file. The second technique can boost performance more dramatically by caching data in memory. This chapter will show you how you can use these two techniques to improve your application performance.

Chapter 16, "Application Deployment," discusses the process of deploying a servlet and JSP application. To understand how to properly display your web application, you need to first understand the directory structure of an application. Therefore, this chapters starts with a review of the directory structure. The next topic is the deployment descriptor where you can configure each application.

Chapter 17, "Architecting Java Web Applications," presents the two models in servlets/JSP applications and discusses how to select the right architecture for your applications.

Chapter 18, "Developing E-Commerce Applications," demonstrates an online store application that uses Model 2 architecture, which is discussed in Chapter 17. This is a complete application that covers most of the features in an e-commerce application.

Chapter 19, "XML-Based E-Books" presents a project that can be used as an online help system whose table of contents is based on an XML document.

Chapter 20, "Web-Based Document Management," offers the complete solution to a document management tool. The user interface looks like Windows Explorer inside a web browser. You can explore the database structure that manages all objects representing your documents and extend the functionality to suit your needs.

Part II: Client-Side Programming with JavaScript

This part contains seven chapters on how to use JavaScript as the client-side programming language in your web application.

Chapter 21, "JavaScript Basics," presents an introduction to JavaScript and prepares you to program the client-side of your web application.

Chapter 22, "Client-Side Programming Basics," offers the discussion on the benefits of client-side programming. These benefits not only contribute to the level of scalability of your web application, but also to user satisfaction. In this chapter you will learn the sort of problems that you will encounter when programming for the client side, problems that you should be aware of even before you write your first line of code.

Chapter 23, "Redirection," discusses various techniques to redirect users to another resource. Redirection is a commonly used in many web applications, and it is important to be able to select the right technique for the redirection.

Chapter 24, "Client-Side Input Validation," provides you with techniques to do input validation on the client-side. When you apply client-side validation, you ensure that the values of form elements are valid before the form is submitted. From the server's perspective, this means reduced workload because it does not have to return the user to the form to correct a value. For users, this means they receive a much faster response because they get an instant warning when a form entry is not correct. This chapter discusses the two types of input validation: at the form level and at the form element level.

Chapter 25, "Working with Client-Side Cookies," looks at cookies in detail, especially how to manipulate cookies at the client-side (for example, on the browser). This chapter presents tips for working with cookies, including how to create, delete, and edit a cookie both on the server side and the client side.

Chapter 26, "Working with Object Trees," offers the technique to work with objects in a hierarchy. The technique described in this chapter is used for the XML-based online help and document management projects in Chapter 19 and Chapter 20.

Chapter 27, "Controlling Applets," does not discuss how to write applets. Instead, it discusses a different aspect of working with applets: how you can control applets from an HTML page using JavaScript. Controlling an applet includes running an applet's methods, reading its properties, and passing a value to it for further processing.

Part III: Developing Scalable Applications with EJB

This part offers six chapters on Enterprise JavaBeans to help you develop scalable applications.

Chapter 28, "Enterprise JavaBeans," serves as the introduction to Enterprise JavaBeans (EJB). It starts with defining what EJB is and presenting some of the benefits of using EJB—most of which are not available in servlet/JSP. Then, it discusses the architecture and the distinct roles in the EJB application and deployment life cycle. It then provides a sample application and some technical insights by presenting a review of the javax.ejb package. Lastly, two client applications are presented to test the sample application.

Chapter 29, "The Session Bean," presents the first type of enterprise bean: session bean. It starts with an overview of what a session bean is and explains two types of session beans: stateful and stateless. After a discussion of the API, it offers an example that demonstrates the use of session beans and how to write a client application that uses the bean.

Chapter 30, "Entity Beans," explains the two types of entity beans: entity beans with bean-managed persistence (BMP) and entity beans with container-managed persistence (CMP).

Chapter 31, "EJB Query Language," presents the language added to the EJB 2.0 specification: the Enterprise JavaBeans Query Language (EJB QL). EJB QL is similar to Structured Query Language (SQL) and is used by bean developers to select data for finder methods of CMP entity beans.

Chapter 32, "Java Message Service," offers an introduction to messaging and the JMS API. This chapter also provides several examples that use JMS to send and receive messages. This chapter should provide the basic knowledge for working with the third type of Enterprise JavaBeans (EJB): message-driven beans (MDB).

Chapter 33, "Message-Driven Beans," begins with an overview of what a message-driven bean is and a close look at the object model. It then continues with an example of a message-driven bean and instruction on how to deploy it in JBoss.

Appendixes

The last part of this book comprises of seven appendixes, all of which are self-explanatory. The seven appendixes are as follows:

Appendix A, "Tomcat Installation and Configuration"
Appendix B, "The javax.servlet Package Reference"
Appendix C, "The javax.servlet.http Package Reference"
Appendix D, "The javax.servlet.jsp Package Reference"
Appendix E, "The javax.servlet.jsp.tagext Package Reference"
Appendix F, "JBoss Installation and Configuration"
Appendix G, "Related Resources"
Appendix H, "What's On the CD-ROM?"

I

Building Java Web Applications

1

The Servlet Technology

THE SERVLET TECHNOLOGY IS THE FOUNDATION of web application development using the Java programming language. It is one of the most important Java technologies, and it is the underlying technology for another popular Java technology for web application development: JavaServer Pages (JSP). Therefore, understanding the servlet technology and its architecture is important if you want to be a servlet developer. Even if you plan to develop your Java web application using JSP pages alone, understanding the servlet technology helps you build a more efficient and effective JSP application.

The aim of this chapter is to introduce the servlet technology and make you comfortable with it by presenting step-by-step instructions that enable you to build and run a servlet application.

In particular, this chapter discusses the following topics:

- The benefits of servlets
- Servlet application architecture
- How a servlet works
- How to write and run your first servlet application

Throughout this book, Tomcat 4.0 is used as both the servlet container and JSP container. In this chapter, you learn how to configure Tomcat quickly so that you can run your first servlet application.

> **Note**
> For a complete reference on how to configure your application, see Chapter 16, "Application Deployment." You can find more detail on Tomcat installation in Appendix A, "Tomcat Installation and Configuration."

The Benefits of Servlets

When it first emerged, this great thing we call the Internet consisted of only static contents written using Hypertext Markup Language (HTML). At that time, anyone who could author HTML pages was considered an Internet expert.

This did not last long, however.

Soon dynamic web contents were made possible through the Common Gateway Interface (CGI) technology. CGI enables the web server to call an external program and pass HTTP request information to that external program to process the request. The response from the external program is then passed back to the web server, which forwards it to the client browser. CGI programs can be written in any language that can be called by the web server. Over the course of time, Perl became the most popular language to write CGI programs.

As the Internet became more and more popular, however, the number of users visiting a popular web site increased exponentially, and it became apparent that CGI had failed to deliver scalable Internet applications. The flaw in CGI is that each client request makes the web server spawn a new process of the requested CGI program. As we all know, process creation is an expensive operation that consumes a lot of CPU cycles and computer memory.

Gradually, new and better technologies will replace CGI as the main technology for web application development. The world has witnessed the following technologies trying to dominate web development:

- **ColdFusion.** Allaire's ColdFusion provides HTML-like custom tags that can be used to perform a number of operations, especially querying a database. This technology had its glamorous time in the history of the World Wide Web as the main technology for web application programming. Its glorious time has since gone with the invention of other technologies.
- **Server-side JavaScript (SSJS).** SSJS is an extension of the JavaScript language, the scripting language that still rules client-side web programming. SSJS can access Java classes deployed at the server side using the LiveWire technology from Netscape.

- **PHP**. PHP is an exciting open-source technology that has matured in recent years. The technology provides easy web application development with its session management and includes some built-in functionality, such as file upload. The number of programmers embracing PHP as their technology of choice has risen sharply in recent years.
- **Servlet**. The servlet technology was introduced by Sun Microsystems in 1996. This technology is the main focus of this book and will be explained in more detail in this and coming chapters.
- **JavaServer Pages (JSP)**. JSP is an extension of the servlet technology. This, too, is the center of attention in this book.
- **Active Server Pages (ASP)**. Microsoft's ASP employs scripting technologies that work in Windows platforms, even though there have been efforts to port this technology to other operating systems. Windows ASP works with the Internet Information Server web server. This technology will soon be replaced by Active Server Pages.NET.
- **Active Server Pages.NET (ASP.NET)**. This technology is part of Microsoft's .NET initiative. Interestingly, the .NET Framework employs a runtime called the Common Language Runtime that is very similar to Java Virtual Machine and provides a vast class library available to all .NET languages and from ASP.NET pages. ASP.NET is an exciting technology. It introduced several new technologies including state management that does not depend on cookies or URL rewriting.

In the past, ASP and servlet/JSP have been the main technologies used in web application development. With the release of ASP.NET, it is not hard to predict that this technology will become the servlet/JSP's main competitor. ASP (and ASP.NET) and servlet/JSP each have their own fans, and it is not easy to predict which one will come out the winner. The most likely outcome is that neither will be an absolute winner that corners the market; instead the technologies will probably run head-to-head in the coming years.

Servlet (and JSP) offers the following benefits that are not necessarily available in other technologies:

- **Performance**. The performance of servlets is superior to CGI because there is no process creation for each client request. Instead, each request is handled by the servlet container process. After a servlet is finished processing a request, it stays resident in memory, waiting for another request.
- **Portability**. Similar to other Java technologies, servlet applications are portable. You can move them to other operating systems without serious hassles.

- **Rapid development cycle.** As a Java technology, servlets have access to the rich Java library, which helps speed up the development process.
- **Robustness.** Servlets are managed by the Java Virtual Machine. As such, you don't need to worry about memory leak or garbage collection, which helps you write robust applications.
- **Widespread acceptance.** Java is a widely accepted technology. This means that numerous vendors work on Java-based technologies. One of the advantages of this widespread acceptance is that you can easily find and purchase components that suit your needs, which saves precious development time.

Servlet Application Architecture

A servlet is a Java class that can be loaded dynamically into and run by a special web server. This servlet-aware web server is called a *servlet container*, which also was called a *servlet engine* in the early days of the servlet technology.

Servlets interact with clients via a request-response model based on HTTP. Because servlet technology works on top of HTTP, a servlet container must support HTTP as the protocol for client requests and server responses. However, a servlet container also can support similar protocols, such as HTTPS (HTTP over SSL) for secure transactions.

Figure 1.1 provides the architecture of a servlet application.

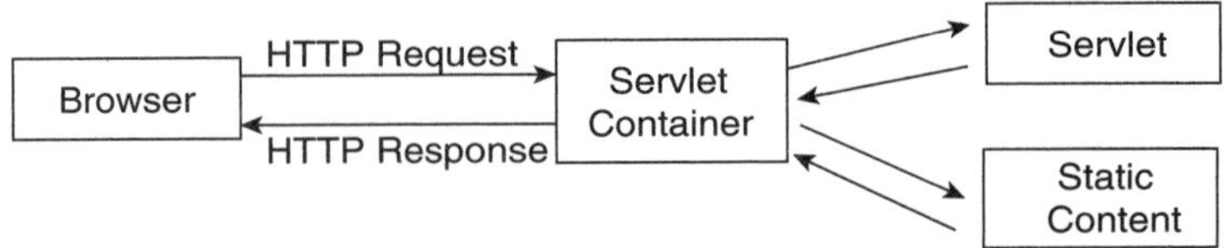

Figure 1.1 The servlet application architecture.

In a JSP application, the servlet container is replaced by a JSP container. Both the servlet container and the JSP container often are referred to as the *web container* or *servlet/JSP container*, especially if a web application consists of both servlets and JSP pages.

> **Note**
> You will learn more about servlet and JSP containers in Chapter 8, "JSP Basics."

As you can see in the Figure 1.1, a servlet application also can include static content, such as HTML pages and image files. Allowing the servlet container to serve static content is not preferable because the content is faster if served by a more robust HTTP server, such as the Apache web server or Microsoft Internet Information Server. As such, it is common practice to put a web server at the front to handle all client requests. The web server serves static content and passes to the servlet containers all client requests for servlets. Figure 1.2 shows a more common architecture for a servlet application.

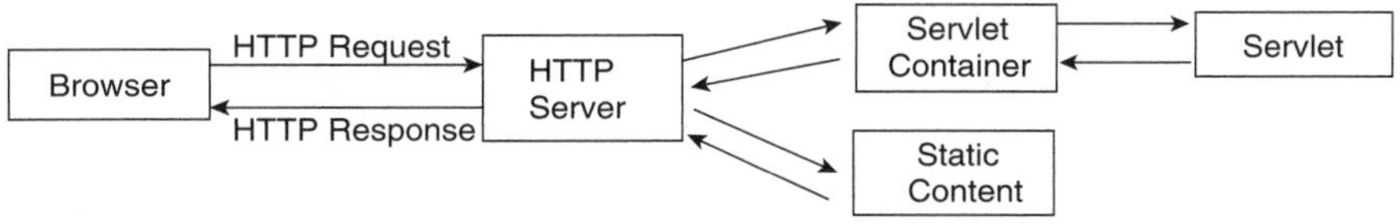

Figure 1.2 The servlet application architecture employing an HTTP server.

> **Caution**
> A Java web application architecture employing a J2EE server is different from the diagrams in Figures 1.1 and 1.2. This is discussed in Chapter 28, "Enterprise JavaBeans."

How a Servlet Works

A servlet is loaded by the servlet container the first time the servlet is requested. The servlet then is forwarded the user request, processes it, and returns the response to the servlet container, which in turn sends the response back to the user. After that, the servlet stays in memory waiting for other requests—it will not be unloaded from memory unless the servlet container sees a shortage of memory. Each time the servlet is requested, however, the servlet container compares the timestamp of the loaded servlet with the servlet class file. If the class file timestamp is more recent, the servlet is reloaded into memory. This way, you don't need to restart the servlet container every time you update your servlet.

The way in which a servlet works inside the servlet container is depicted in the diagram in Figure 1.3.

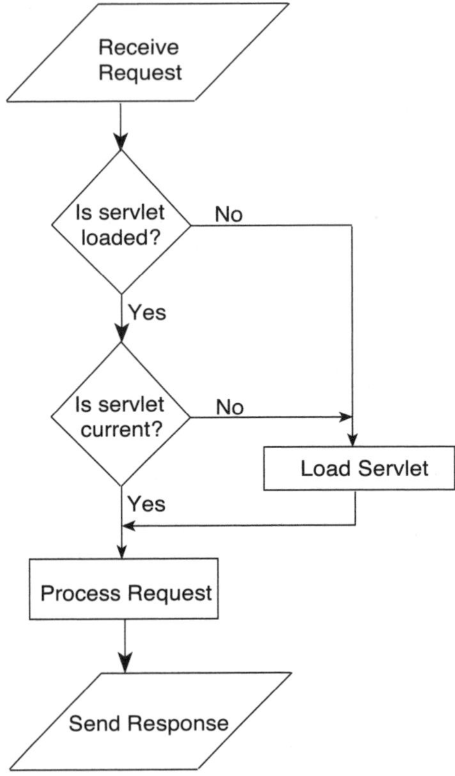

Figure 1.3 How a servlet works.

The Tomcat Servlet Container

A number of servlet containers are available today. The most popular one—and the one recognized as the official servlet/JSP container—is Tomcat. Originally designed by Sun Microsystems, Tomcat source code was handed over to the Apache Software Foundation in October 1999. In this new home, Tomcat was included as part of the Jakarta Project, one of the projects of the Apache Software Foundation. Working through the Apache process, Apache, Sun, and other companies—with the help of volunteer programmers worldwide—turned Tomcat into a world-class servlet reference implementation. Two months after the handover, Tomcat version 3.0 was released. Tomcat went through several 3.*x* releases until version 3.3 was introduced.

The successor of version 3.3 is the current version, version 4.0. The 4.0 servlet container (Catalina) is based on a completely new architecture and has been developed from the ground up for flexibility and performance. Version 4.0 implements the Servlet 2.3 and JSP 1.2 specifications, and it is this version you will be using in this book.

Another popular servlet container is JRun from Allaire Corporation. JRun is available in three editions: Developer, Professional, and Enterprise. The Developer edition is free but not licensed for deployment. The Professional and Enterprise editions grant you the license for deployment with a fee. You can download JRun from `http://commerce.allaire.com/download`.

Tomcat by itself is a web server. This means that you can use Tomcat to service HTTP requests for servlets, as well as static files (HTML, image files, and so on). In practice, however, since it is faster for non-servlet, non-JSP requests, Tomcat normally is used as a module with another more robust web server, such as Apache web server or Microsoft Internet Information Server. Only requests for servlets or JSP pages are passed to Tomcat.

To write a servlet, you need at least version 1.2 of the Java Development Kit. If you have not already downloaded one, you can download JDK 1.2 from `http://java.sun.com/j2se`. The reference implementation for both servlets and JSP are not included in J2SE, but they are included in Tomcat. Tomcat is written purely in Java.

If you haven't yet installed and configured Tomcat, now's the time to do it. If you need help with these tasks, refer to Appendix A for specific steps.

Six Steps to Running Your First Servlet

After you have installed and configured Tomcat, you can put it into service. Basically, you need to follow six steps to go from writing your servlet to running it. These steps are summarized as follows:

1. Create a directory structure under Tomcat for your application.
2. Write the servlet source code. You need to import the javax.servlet package and the javax.servlet.http package in your source file.
3. Compile your source code.
4. Create a deployment descriptor.
5. Run Tomcat.
6. Call your servlet from a web browser.

The sections that follow walk you through each of these steps.

Step 1: Create a Directory Structure Under Tomcat

> **Note**
> The directory where Tomcat is installed is often referred to as %CATALINA_HOME%. In previous versions of Tomcat, this directory was called %TOMCAT_HOME%.

When you install Tomcat, several subdirectories are automatically created under the Tomcat home directory (%CATALINA_HOME%). One of the subdirectories is webapps. The webapps directory is where you store your web applications. A *web application* is a collection of servlets and other content installed under a specific subset of the server's URL namespace. A separate directory is dedicated for each servlet application. Therefore, the first thing to do when you build a servlet application is create an application directory. To create a directory structure for an application called myApp, follow these steps:

1. Create a directory called myApp under the webapps directory. The directory name is important because this also appears in the URL to your servlet.
2. Create the WEB-INF directories under myApp, and create a directory named classes under WEB-INF. The directory structure is shown in Figure 1.4. The directory classes under WEB-INF is for your Java classes. If you have HTML files, put them directly under the myApp directory. You may also want to create a directory called images under myApp for all your image files.

   Note that the examples, manager, ROOT, tomcat-doc, and webdav directories are for applications that are created automatically when you install Tomcat.

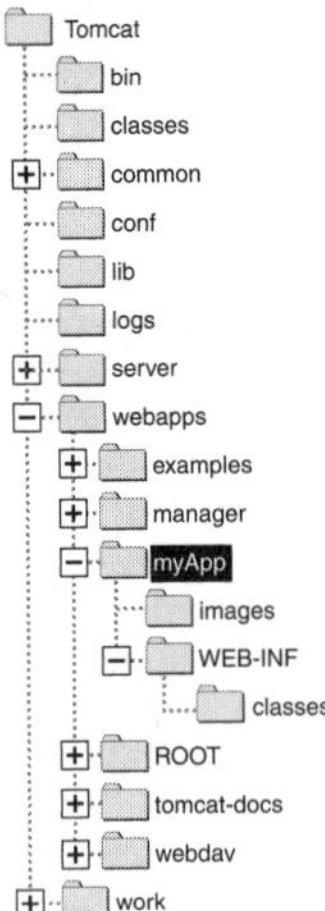

Figure 1.4 Tomcat application directory structure.

Step 2: Write the Servlet Source Code

In this step, you prepare your source code. You can write the source code yourself using your favorite text editor or copy it from the accompanying CD.

> **Tip**
> The source code for all examples in this book are also available on the book's web site. Check out `www.newriders.com` to download the files you need.

The code in Listing 1.1 shows a simple servlet called TestingServlet. The file is named TestingServlet.java. The servlet sends a few HTML tags and some text to the browser. For now, don't worry if you haven't got a clue about how it works.

Listing 1.1 **TestingServlet.java**

```
import javax.servlet.*;
import javax.servlet.http.*;
import java.io.*;
import java.util.*;

public class TestingServlet extends HttpServlet {

  public void doGet(HttpServletRequest request,
    HttpServletResponse response)
    throws ServletException, IOException {

    PrintWriter out = response.getWriter();
    out.println("<HTML>");
    out.println("<HEAD>");
    out.println("<TITLE>Servlet Testing</TITLE>");
    out.println("</HEAD>");
    out.println("<BODY>");
    out.println("Welcome to the Servlet Testing Center");
    out.println("</BODY>");
    out.println("</HTML>");
  }
}
```

Now, save your TestingServlet.java file to the WEB-INF/classes directory under myApp. Placing your source code here will make it inaccessible from a web browser. Static files, such as HTML files and image files, should be placed directly under the myApp directory or a directory under it.

> **Warning**
> Placing your source code files outside the WEB-INF directory will make them viewable from a browser.

Step 3: Compile Your Source Code

For your servlet source code to compile, you need to include the path to the servlet.jar file in your CLASSPATH environment variable. The servlet.jar is located in the common\lib\ subdirectory under %CATALINA_HOME%.

For example, if you installed Tomcat under the C:\drive on Windows and you named the install directory tomcat, type the following command from the directory where TestingServlet.java resides.

```
javac-classpath C:\tomcat\common\lib\servlet.jar TestingServlet.java
```

Alternatively, to save you typing the class path every time you compile your source code, you can add the complete path to the servlet.jar file to your CLASSPATH environment variable. Again, if you have installed Tomcat under C:\and named the install directory tomcat, you must add C:\tomcat\common\lib\servlet.jar to the CLASSPATH environment variable. Afterward, you can compile your source by simply typing the following.

```
javac TestingServlet.java
```

> **Note**
> If you have forgotten how to edit the CLASSPATH environment variable, refer to Appendix A.

If you are using Windows, remember that the new environment variable takes effect only for new console windows. In other words, after changing a new environment variable, open a new console window for typing in your command lines.

Step 4: Create the Deployment Descriptor

A deployment descriptor is an optional component in a servlet application. The descriptor takes the form of an XML document called web.xml and must be located in the WEB-INF directory of the servlet application. When present, the deployment descriptor contains configuration settings specific to that application. Deployment descriptors are discussed in detail in Chapter 16.

To create the deployment descriptor, you now need to create a web.xml file and place it under the WEB-INF directory under myApp.

The web.xml for this example application must have the following content.

```
<?xml version="1.0" encoding="ISO-8859-1"?>

<!DOCTYPE web-app
  PUBLIC "-//Sun Microsystems, Inc.//DTD Web Application 2.3//EN"
  "http://java.sun.com/dtd/web-app_2_3.dtd">

<web-app>
  <servlet>
```

```
    <servlet-name>Testing</servlet-name>
    <servlet-class>TestingServlet</servlet-class>
  </servlet>
</web-app>
```

The web.xml file has one element—web-app. You should write all your servlets under <web-app>. For each servlet, you have a <servlet> element and you need the <servlet-name> and <servlet-class> elements. The <servlet-name> is the name for your servlet, by which it is known by Tomcat. The <servlet-class> is the compiled file of your servlet without the .class extension.

Having more than one servlet in an application is very common. For every servlet, you need a <servlet> element in the web.xml file. For example, the following shows you how web.xml looks if you add another servlet called Login:

```
<?xml version="1.0" encoding="ISO-8859-1"?>

<!DOCTYPE web-app
  PUBLIC "-//Sun Microsystems, Inc.//DTD Web Application 2.3//EN"
  "http://java.sun.com/dtd/web-app_2_3.dtd">

<web-app>
  <servlet>
    <servlet-name>Testing</servlet-name>
    <servlet-class>TestingServlet</servlet-class>
  </servlet>
  <servlet>
    <servlet-name>Login</servlet-name>
    <servlet-class>LoginServlet</servlet-class>
  </servlet>
</web-app>
```

Step 5: Run Tomcat

If Tomcat is not already running, you need to start it. See Appendix A for information on how to start or run Tomcat.

Step 6: Call Your Servlet from a Web Browser

Now, you can call your servlet from a web browser. By default, Tomcat runs on port 8080 in the myApp virtual directory under the servlet subdirectory. The servlet that you wrote in the preceding steps is named Testing. The URL for that servlet has the following format:

```
http://domain-name/virtual-directory/servlet/servlet-name
```

Any static file can be accessed using the following URL:

```
http://domain-name/virtual-directory/staticFile.html
```

For example, a Logo.gif file under the myApp/images/ directory can be accessed using the following URL.

```
http://domain-name/virtual-directory/images/Logo.gif
```

If you run the web browser from the same computer as Tomcat, you can replace the *domain-name* part with "localhost". In that case, the URL for your servlet is

```
http://localhost:8080/myApp/servlet/Testing
```

In the deployment descriptor you wrote in Step 4, you actually mapped the servlet class file called TestingServlet with the name "Testing," so that your servlet can be called by specifying its class file (TestingServlet) or its name (Testing). Without a deployment descriptor, you must call the servlet by specifying its class name; that is, TestingServlet. This means that if you did not write a deployment descriptor in Step 4, you need to use the following URL to call your servlet:

```
http://localhost:8080/myApp/servlet/TestingServlet
```

Typing the URL in the Address or Location box of your web browser will give you the string "Welcome to the Servlet Testing Center," as shown in Figure 1.5.

Figure 1.5 The Testing servlet.

Congratulations. You have just written your first servlet.

If you don't want to type the port number each time, you can change the default port of Tomcat so that it runs on port 80, the default port for a web server. (Details on how to change the port number can be found in Appendix A.) However, the rest of the book will use Tomcat's default port 8080.

> **Note**
>
> You will find code for various servlets in this chapter and the next. To run each individual servlet, you need to repeat these six steps. To avoid repetition, I do not mention these steps for every servlet presented in this book. You don't need to worry about these steps if you are using a Java development tool, such as Borland's JBuilder or IBM's VisualAge, because those steps are taken care of by the RAD program.

Summary

This chapter has given you the big picture of how to build a servlet application. Specifically, you learned about the benefits of servlets, explored servlet application architecture, and discovered how a servlet works inside the servlet container. You also have been shown how to configure Tomcat and followed the six steps you need to build your own servlets. The next chapter digs deeper into the servlet technology by presenting the Java Servlet specification Application Programming Interface (API) version 2.3

2

Inside Servlets

WATCHING YOUR SERVLET IN ACTION, as you did in Chapter 1, "The Servlet Technology," should bring you confidence. And, as some people say, having confidence is half the battle in learning anything. To be an expert, however, you need to understand the nuts and bolts of the Java Servlet specification Application Programming Interface (API). This book has been written using the latest release of the servlet specification API—version 2.3. Two packages are available for servlet programmers: javax.servlet and javax.servlet.http. The first one contains basic classes and interfaces that you can use to write servlets from the scratch. The second package, javax.servlet.http, offers more advanced classes and interfaces that extend classes and interfaces from the first package. It is much more convenient to program using the second package.

When you learn something, it is best to start with the basics and build a strong foundation. For example, understanding the javax.servlet.Servlet interface is very important because it encapsulates the life cycle methods of a servlet and it is the interface that all servlets must implement. You also need to know the servlet's context, which represents a servlet's environment, and the servlet's configuration. Because of the importance of these items, this chapter introduces you to members of the javax.servlet package. In this chapter, you also will see that oftentimes several ways exist to do the same thing.

After a few examples, I will introduce you to the GenericServlet class, a member of the javax.servlet package that acts as a wrapper for the javax.servlet.Servlet interface. Extending this class makes your code simpler because you need to provide implementations only for methods that you need to use.

To run each example in this chapter, you need to compile the source code and copy the resulting class file into the classes directory under the WEB-INF directory of your application. Refer to Chapter 1 if you have forgotten the six steps you need to run your servlet.

The rest of this chapter explains and uses the interfaces and classes of the javax.servlet package. The chapters that follow focus more on the second package.

The javax.servlet Package

The javax.servlet package contains seven interfaces, three classes, and two exceptions. Instead of using the conventional approach by explaining each interface and class in alphabetical order—thus making the book feel like a dictionary—I present the discussions based on functions and offer examples that demonstrate each function.

Nevertheless, mastering all the members of this package is important. To help you, a complete reference is given in Appendix B, "The java.servlet Package Reference."

The seven interfaces are as follows:

- RequestDispatcher
- Servlet
- ServletConfig
- ServletContext
- ServletRequest
- ServletResponse
- SingleThreadModel

The three classes are as follows:

- GenericServlet
- ServletInputStream
- ServletOutputStream

And, finally, the exception classes are these:

- ServletException
- UnavailableException

The object model of the javax.servlet package is shown in Figure 2.1.

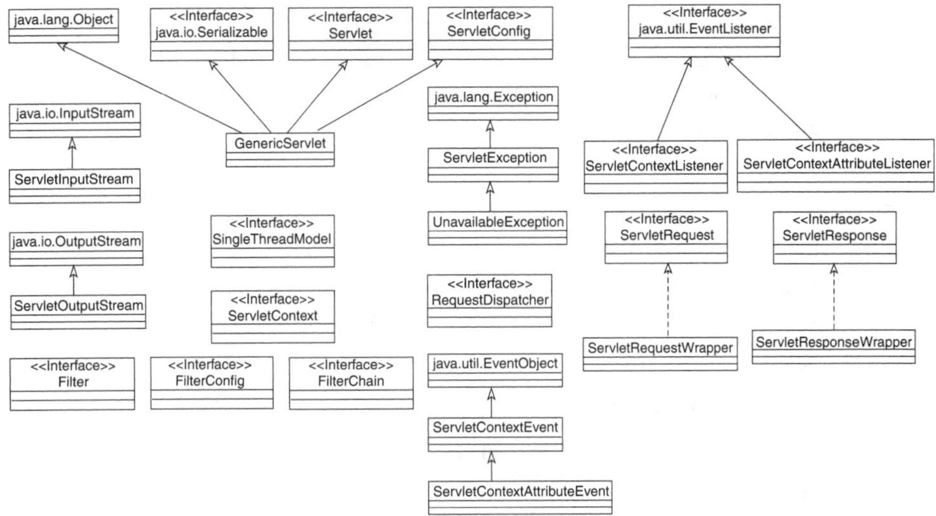

Figure 2.1 The javax.servlet package object model.

A Servlet's Life Cycle

Let there be Servlet. This interface in the javax.servlet package is the source of all activities in servlet programming. Servlet is the central abstraction of the Java servlet technology. Every servlet you write must implement this javax.servlet.Servlet interface, either directly or indirectly. The life cycle of a servlet is determined by three of its methods: init, service, and destroy.

The init( ) Method

The init method is called by the servlet container after the servlet class has been instantiated. The servlet container calls this method exactly once to indicate to the servlet that the servlet is being placed into service. The init method must complete successfully before the servlet can receive any requests.

You can override this method to write initialization code that needs to run only once, such as loading a database driver, initializing values, and so on. In other cases, you normally leave this method blank.

The signature of this method is as follows:

```
public void init(ServletConfig config) throws ServletException
```

The init method is important also because the servlet container passes a ServletConfig object, which contains the configuration values stated in the web.xml file for this application. More on ServletConfig can be found later in this chapter, in the section, "Obtaining Configuration Information."

This method also can throw a ServletException. The servlet container cannot place the servlet into service if the init method throws a ServletException or the method does not return within a time period defined by the web server.

> **Note**
> ServletException is the most important exception in servlet programming. In fact, a lot of methods in the javax.servlet and javax.servlet.http packages can throw this exception when a problem exists in a servlet.

The service( ) Method

The service method is called by the servlet container after the servlet's init method to allow the servlet to respond to a request.

Servlets typically run inside multithreaded servlet containers that can handle multiple requests concurrently. Therefore, you must be aware to synchronize access to any shared resources, such as files, network connections, and the servlet's class and instance variables. For example, if you open a file and write to that file from a servlet, you need to remember that a different thread of the same servlet also can open the same file. See the section, "Creating Thread-Safe Servlet," for more on the topic of multithreading and synchronization.

This method has the following signature:

```
public void service(ServletRequest request, ServletResponse response)
  throws ServletException, java.io.IOException
```

The servlet container passes a ServletRequest object and the ServletResponse object. The ServletRequest object contains the client's request and the ServletResponse contains the servlet's response. These two objects are important because they enable you to write custom code that determines how the servlet services the client request.

The service method throws a ServletException if an exception occurs that interferes with the servlet's normal operation. The service method also can throw a java.io.IOException if an input or output exception occurs during the execution of this method.

service method exists so that you can write code
tion the way it is supposed to.

d

the destroy method before removing a servlet
normally happens when the servlet container is
ontainer needs some free memory.
nly after all threads within the servlet's service
er a timeout period has passed. After the servlet
d, it will not call the service method again on

ves the servlet an opportunity to clean up any
eld (for example, memory, file handles, and threads)
ersistent state is synchronized with the servlet's cur-

nethod is as follows:

```
public void destroy()
```

Demonstrating the Life Cycle of a Servlet

Listing 2.1 contains the code for a servlet named PrimitiveServlet, a very simple servlet that exists to demonstrate the life cycle of a servlet. The PrimitiveServlet class implements javax.servlet.Servlet (as all servlets must) and provides implementations for all the five methods of Servlet. What it does is very simple. Each time any of the init, service, or destroy methods is called, the servlet writes the method's name to the console.

Listing 2.1 **PrimitiveServlet.java**

```
import javax.servlet.*;
import java.io.IOException;

public class PrimitiveServlet implements Servlet {

  public void init(ServletConfig config) throws ServletException {
    System.out.println("init");
  }

  public void service(ServletRequest request, ServletResponse response)
    throws ServletException, IOException {
    System.out.println("service");
  }
```

continues

Listing 2.1 **Continued**

```
    public void destroy() {
      System.out.println("destroy");
    }

    public String getServletInfo() {
      return null;
    }
    public ServletConfig getServletConfig() {
      return null;
    }

  }
```

After you compile the source code into the myApp\WEB-INF\classes directory, add the servlet to the web.xml under the name Primitive, as shown in Listing 2.2.

Listing 2.2 **The web.xml File for PrimitiveServlet**

```
<?xml version="1.0" encoding="ISO-8859-1"?>

<!DOCTYPE web-app
  PUBLIC "-//Sun Microsystems, Inc.//DTD Web Application 2.3//EN"
  "http://java.sun.com/dtd/web-app_2_3.dtd">

<web-app>
  <servlet>
    <servlet-name>Primitive</servlet-name>
    <servlet-class>PrimitiveServlet</servlet-class>
  </servlet>
</web-app>
```

You should then be able to call this servlet from your browser by typing the following URL:

```
http://localhost:8080/myApp/servlet/Primitive
```

The first time the servlet is called, the console displays these two lines:

```
init
service
```

This tells you that the init method is called, followed by the service method. However, on subsequent requests, only the service method is called. The servlet adds the following line to the console:

```
service
```

This proves that the init method is called only once.

What are the getServletInfo and getServletConfig doing in Listing 2.1? Nothing. They can be useful, but in the PrimitiveServlet class, they are just there to meet the specification that a class must provide implementations for all methods in the interface it implements.

You can return any string in the getServletInfo method, such as your company name or the author name or other information deemed necessary. Other people might extend your servlet class and might want to know what useful information the designer of the servlet has provided.

The getServletConfig is more important. We will see how it can be of use next.

Obtaining Configuration Information

The servlet specification allows you to configure your application. You'll find more information on this topic in the discussion of the deployment descriptor in Chapter 16, "Application Deployment." In this chapter, I present an example that demonstrates how you can retrieve configuration information from the application web.xml file.

For each servlet registered in the web.xml file, you have the option of specifying a set of initial parameter name/value pairs that you can retrieve from inside the servlet. The following web.xml file contains a servlet called ConfigDemo whose class is named ConfigDemoServlet.class. The servlet has two initial parameter name/value pairs. The first parameter is named adminEmail and its value is `admin@brainysoftware.com`. The second parameter is named adminContactNumber and the value for this parameter is 04298371237.

```
<?xml version="1.0" encoding="ISO-8859-1"?>
<!DOCTYPE web-app
    PUBLIC "-//Sun Microsystems, Inc.//DTD Web Application 2.2//EN"
    "http://java.sun.com/j2ee/dtds/web-app_2.2.dtd">

<web-app>
  <servlet>
    <servlet-name>ConfigDemo</servlet-name>
    <servlet-class>ConfigDemoServlet</servlet-class>
    <init-param>
      <param-name>adminEmail</param-name>
      <param-value>admin@brainysoftware.com</param-value>
    </init-param>
    <init-param>
      <param-name>adminContactNumber</param-name>
      <param-value>04298371237</param-value>
    </init-param>
  </servlet>
</web-app>
```

Why would you want to use an initial parameter? For practicality. Hardcoding information in the servlet code means that you have to recompile the servlet if the information changes. A web.xml file is plain text. You can edit its content easily using a text editor.

Note

You need to restart Tomcat for the changes in the deployment descriptor (the web.xml file) to take effect.

The code that retrieves the initial parameter name and values is given in Listing 2.3.

To retrieve initial parameters, you need the ServletConfig object passed by the servlet container to the servlet. After you get the ServletConfig object, you then can use its getInitParameterNames and getInitParameter methods. The getInitParameterNames does not take an argument and returns an Enumeration containing all the parameter names in the ServletConfig object. The getInitParameter takes a String containing the parameter name and returns a String containing the value of the parameter.

Because the servlet container passes a ServletConfig object to the init method, it is easiest to write the code in the init method. The code in Listing 2.3 loops through the Enumeration object called parameters that is returned from the getInitParameterNames method. For each parameter, it outputs the parameter name and value. The parameter value is retrieved using the getInitParameter method.

Listing 2.3 **Retrieving Initial Parameters**

```
import javax.servlet.*;
import java.util.Enumeration;
import java.io.IOException;

public class ConfigDemoServlet implements Servlet {

  public void init(ServletConfig config) throws ServletException {
    Enumeration parameters = config.getInitParameterNames();
    while (parameters.hasMoreElements()) {
      String parameter = (String) parameters.nextElement();
      System.out.println("Parameter name : " + parameter);
      System.out.println("Parameter value : " +
        config.getInitParameter(parameter));
    }
  }

  public void destroy() {
  }

  public void service(ServletRequest request, ServletResponse response)
    throws ServletException, IOException {
```

```
  }

  public String getServletInfo() {
    return null;
  }

  public ServletConfig getServletConfig() {
    return null;
  }
}
```

The output of the code in the console is as follows:

```
Parameter name : adminContactNumber
Parameter value : 04298371237
Parameter name : adminEmail
Parameter value : admin@brainysoftware.com
```

Preserving the ServletConfig

The code in Listing 2.3 shows how you can use the ServletConfig object in the init method. Sometimes, however, you may want more flexibility. For example, you may want to have access to the ServletConfig object from the service method, when you are servicing the user. In this case, you need to preserve the ServletConfig object to a class level variable. This task is not difficult. You need to create a ServletConfig object variable and set it to the ServletConfig object returned by the servlet container in the init method.

Listing 2.4 gives the code that preserves the ServletConfig object for later use. First, you need a variable for the ServletConfig object.

```
ServletConfig servletConfig;
```

Then, in the init method, you write the following code:

```
servletConfig = config;
```

Now the servletConfig variable references the ServletConfig object returned by the servlet container. The getServletConfig method is provided to do just that: return the ServletConfig object.

```
public ServletConfig getServletConfig() {
  return servletConfig;
}
```

If you extend the ReserveConfigServlet class, you can still retrieve the ServlerConfig object by calling the getServletConfig method.

Listing 2.4 **Preserving the ServletConfig Object**

```
import javax.servlet.*;
import java.io.IOException;

public class ReserveConfigServlet implements Servlet {
  ServletConfig servletConfig;

  public void init(ServletConfig config) throws ServletException {
    servletConfig = config;
  }

  public void destroy() {
  }

  public void service(ServletRequest request, ServletResponse response)
    throws ServletException, IOException {
  }

  public String getServletInfo() {
    return null;
  }

  public ServletConfig getServletConfig() {
    return servletConfig;
  }

}
```

The Servlet Context

In servlet programming, the servlet context is the environment where the servlet runs. The servlet container creates a ServletContext object that you can use to access information about the servlet's environment.

A servlet also can bind an object attribute into the context by name. Any object bound into a context is available to any other servlet that is part of the same web application.

How do you obtain the ServletContext object? Indirectly, from the ServletConfig object passed by the servlet container to the servlet's init method. The ServletConfig interface has a method called getServletContext that returns the ServletContext object. You then can use the ServletContext interface's various methods to get the information you need. These methods include the following:

- **getMajorVersion.** This method returns an integer representing the major version for the servlet API that the servlet container supports. If the servlet container supports the servlet API version 2.3, this method will return 2.
- **getMinorVersion.** This method returns an integer representing the minor version of the servlet API that the servlet container supports. For the servlet API version 2.3, this method will return 3.
- **getAttributeNames.** This method returns an enumeration of strings representing the names of the attributes currently stored in the ServletContext.
- **getAttribute.** This method accepts a String containing the attribute name and returns the object bound to that name.
- **setAttribute.** This method stores an object in the ServletContext and binds the object to the given name. If the name already exists in the ServletContext, the old bound object will be replaced by the object passed to this method.
- **removeAttribute.** This method removes from the ServletContext the object bound to a name. The removeAttribute method accepts one argument: the name of the attribute to be removed.

The code in Listing 2.5 shows a servlet named ContextDemoServlet that retrieves some of the servlet context information, including attribute names and values, minor and major versions of the servlet container, and the server info.

Listing 2.5 **Retrieving Servlet Context Information**

```
import javax.servlet.*;
import java.util.Enumeration;
import java.io.IOException;

public class ContextDemoServlet implements Servlet {
  ServletConfig servletConfig;

  public void init(ServletConfig config) throws ServletException {
    servletConfig = config;
  }

  public void destroy() {
  }

  public void service(ServletRequest request, ServletResponse response)
    throws ServletException, IOException {
```

continues

Listing 2.5 **Continued**

```
    ServletContext servletContext = servletConfig.getServletContext();
    Enumeration attributes = servletContext.getAttributeNames();
    while (attributes.hasMoreElements()) {
      String attribute = (String) attributes.nextElement();
      System.out.println("Attribute name : " + attribute);
      System.out.println("Attribute value : " +
        servletContext.getAttribute(attribute));
    }

    System.out.println("Major version : " +
servletContext.getMajorVersion());
    System.out.println("Minor version : " +
servletContext.getMinorVersion());
    System.out.println("Server info : " + servletContext.getServerInfo());
  }

  public String getServletInfo() {
    return null;
  }
  public ServletConfig getServletConfig() {
    return null;
  }

}
```

The output of the code is as follows. This output may be different on your computer, depending on the version of Tomcat you are using, the operating system, and so on.

```
Attribute name : javax.servlet.context.tempdirAttribute value :
..\work\localhost\myApp
Attribute name : org.apache.catalina.resources
Attribute value : org.apache.naming.resources.ProxyDirContext@24e2e3
Attribute name : org.apache.catalina.WELCOME_FILES
Attribute value : [Ljava.lang.String;@2bb7e0
Attribute name : org.apache.catalina.jsp_classpath
Attribute value : C:\tomcat4\webapps\myApp\WEB-INF\classes;
.
.
.
Major version : 2
Minor version : 3
Server info : Apache Tomcat/4.0-b5
```

Sharing Information Among Servlets

For some applications, you want to make certain types of information available to all the servlets. You can share this information—such as a database connection string or a page count—among the servlets by using attributes in the ServletContext object.

The following example uses two servlets: AttributeSetterServlet and DisplayAttributesServlet. The AttributeSetterServlet servlet, shown in Listing 2.6, binds the name password to a String object containing the word "dingdong". The servlet does this by first obtaining the ServletContext object from the ServletConfig object passed by the servlet container to the init method. Then the servlet uses the setAttribute method to bind "password" with "dingdong".

Listing 2.6 **The AttributeSetterServlet**

```
import javax.servlet.*;
import java.io.IOException;

public class AttributeSetterServlet implements Servlet {

  public void init(ServletConfig config) throws ServletException {
    // bind an object that is to be shared among other servlets
    ServletContext servletContext = config.getServletContext();
    servletContext.setAttribute("password", "dingdong");
  }

  public void service(ServletRequest request, ServletResponse response)
    throws ServletException, IOException {
  }

  public void destroy() {
  }

  public String getServletInfo() {
    return null;
  }
  public ServletConfig getServletConfig() {
    return null;
  }
}
```

The code in Listing 2.7 is the servlet that retrieves all attribute name/value pairs in the ServletContext object. The init method of this servlet preserves the ServletConfig object into servletConfig. The service method then uses the ServletConfig interface's getServletContext method to obtain the ServletContext object. After you get the ServletContext object, you can then use its getAttributeNames method to get an Enumeration of all attribute names and loop through it to obtain each attribute's value, which it outputs to the console along with the attribute name.

Listing 2.7 **DisplayAttributesServlet**

```
import javax.servlet.*;
import java.io.IOException;
import java.util.Enumeration;

public class DisplayAttributesServlet implements Servlet {
  ServletConfig servletConfig;

  public void init(ServletConfig config) throws ServletException {
    servletConfig = config;
  }

  public void destroy() {
  }

  public void service(ServletRequest request, ServletResponse response)
    throws ServletException, IOException {

    ServletContext servletContext = servletConfig.getServletContext();
    Enumeration attributes = servletContext.getAttributeNames();
    while (attributes.hasMoreElements()) {
      String attribute = (String) attributes.nextElement();
      System.out.println("Attribute name : " + attribute);
      System.out.println("Attribute value : " +
        servletContext.getAttribute(attribute));
    }
  }

  public String getServletInfo() {
    return null;
  }
  public ServletConfig getServletConfig() {
    return null;
  }

}
```

```
Enumeration attributes = servletContext.getAttributeNames();
  while (attributes.hasMoreElements()) {
    String attribute = (String) attributes.nextElement();
    System.out.println("Attribute name : " + attribute);
    System.out.println("Attribute value : " +
      servletContext.getAttribute(attribute));
  }
```

To see the servlets work, first you need to call the AttributeSetterServlet servlet to set the attribute "password". You then call the DisplayAttributesServlet to get an Enumeration of the names of all attributes and display the values.

The output is given here:

```
Attribute name : javax.servlet.context.tempdir
Attribute value : C:\123data\JavaProjects\JavaWebBook\work\localhost_8080
Attribute name : password
Attribute value : dingdong
Attribute name : sun.servlet.workdir
Attribute value : C:\123data\JavaProjects\JavaWebBook\work\localhost_8080
```

Requests and Responses

Requests and responses are what a web application is all about. In a servlet application, a user using a web browser sends a request to the servlet container, and the servlet container passes the request to the servlet.

In a servlet paradigm, the user request is represented by the ServletRequest object passed by the servlet container as the first argument to the service method. The service method's second argument is a ServletResponse object, which represents the response to the user.

The ServletRequest Interface

The ServletRequest interface defines an object used to encapsulate information about the user's request, including parameter name/value pairs, attributes, and an input stream.

The ServletRequest interface provides important methods that enable you to access information about the user. For example, the getParameterNames method returns an Enumeration containing the parameter names for the current request. To get the value of each parameter, the ServletRequest interface provides the getParameter method.

The getRemoteAddress and getRemoteHost methods are two methods that you can use to retrieve the user's computer identity. The first returns a string representing the IP address of the computer the client is using, and the second method returns a string representing the qualified host name of the computer.

The following example, shown in Listings 2.8 and 2.9, shows a ServletRequest object in action. The example consists of an HTML form in a file named index.html that you need to put in the application directory—that is, under myApp—and a servlet called RequestDemoServlet.

Listing 2.8 **index.html**

```
<HTML>
<HEAD>
<TITLE>Sending a request</TITLE>
</HEAD>
<BODY>
<FORM ACTION=servlet/RequestDemoServlet METHOD="POST">
<BR><BR>
Author: <INPUT TYPE="TEXT" NAME="Author">
<INPUT TYPE="SUBMIT" NAME="Submit">
<INPUT TYPE="RESET" VALUE="Reset">
</FORM>
</BODY>
</HTML>
```

Listing 2.9 **RequestDemoServlet**

```
import javax.servlet.*;
import java.util.Enumeration;
import java.io.IOException;

public class RequestDemoServlet implements Servlet {

  public void init(ServletConfig config) throws ServletException {
  }

  public void destroy() {
  }

  public void service(ServletRequest request, ServletResponse response)
    throws ServletException, IOException {

    System.out.println("Server Port: " + request.getServerPort());
    System.out.println("Server Name: " + request.getServerName());
    System.out.println("Protocol: " + request.getProtocol());
    System.out.println("Character Encoding: " +
      request.getCharacterEncoding());
    System.out.println("Content Type: " + request.getContentType());
    System.out.println("Content Length: " + request.getContentLength());
    System.out.println("Remote Address: " + request.getRemoteAddr());
    System.out.println("Remote Host: " + request.getRemoteHost());
    System.out.println("Scheme: " + request.getScheme());
    Enumeration parameters = request.getParameterNames();
    while (parameters.hasMoreElements()) {
      String parameterName = (String) parameters.nextElement();
      System.out.println("Parameter Name: " + parameterName);
      System.out.println("Parameter Value: " +
        request.getParameter(parameterName));
    }
```

```
    Enumeration attributes = request.getAttributeNames();
    while (attributes.hasMoreElements()) {
      String attribute = (String) attributes.nextElement();
      System.out.println("Attribute name: " + attribute);
      System.out.println("Attribute value: " +
        request.getAttribute(attribute));
    }
  }

  public String getServletInfo() {
    return null;
  }

  public ServletConfig getServletConfig() {
    return null;
  }

}
```

To run the example, first request the index.html file by using the following URL:

```
http://localhost:8080/myApp/index.html
```

Figure 2.2 shows the index.html file in which "haywood" has been typed in as the value for author.

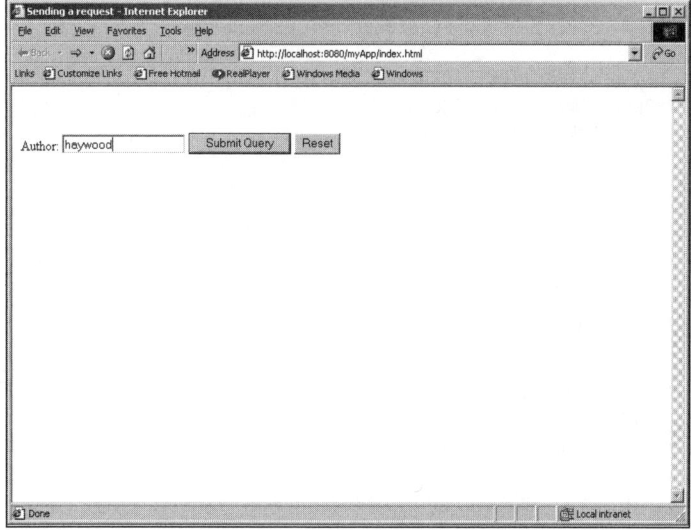

Figure 2.2 The index.html file.

When you submit the form, you should see the list of attribute names and values in your console.

The ServletResponse Interface

The ServletResponse interface represents the response to the user. The most important method of this interface is getWriter, from which you can obtain a java.io.PrintWriter object that you can use to write HTML tags and other text to the user.

The code in Listings 2.10 and 2.11 offer an HTML file named index2.html and a servlet whose service method is overridden with code that outputs some HTML tags to the user. This servlet modifies the example in Listings 2.8 and 2.9 that retrieves various information about the user. Instead of sending the information to the console, the service method sends it back to the user.

Note that the code in Listing 2.10 is similar to the code in Listing 2.8, except that in Listing 2.10 the value for the form's ACTION attribute is servlet/ResponseDemoServlet.

Listing 2.10 **index2.html**

```
<HTML>
<HEAD>
<TITLE>Sending a request</TITLE>
</HEAD>
<BODY>
<FORM ACTION=servlet/ResponseDemoServlet METHOD="POST">
<BR><BR>
Author: <INPUT TYPE="TEXT" NAME="Author">
<INPUT TYPE="SUBMIT" NAME="Submit">
<INPUT TYPE="RESET" VALUE="Reset">
</FORM>
</BODY>
</HTML>
```

Listing 2.11 **The ResponseDemoServlet**

```
import javax.servlet.*;
import java.io.PrintWriter;
import java.io.IOException;
import java.util.Enumeration;

public class ResponseDemoServlet implements Servlet {

  public void init(ServletConfig config) throws ServletException {
  }
```

```
  public void destroy() {
  }

  public void service(ServletRequest request, ServletResponse response)
    throws ServletException, IOException {

    PrintWriter out = response.getWriter();
    out.println("<HTML>");
    out.println("<HEAD>");
    out.println("<TITLE>");
    out.println("ServletResponse");
    out.println("</TITLE>");
    out.println("</HEAD>");
    out.println("<BODY>");
    out.println("<B>Demonstrating the ServletResponse object</B>");
    out.println("<BR>");

    out.println("<BR>Server Port: " + request.getServerPort());
    out.println("<BR>Server Name: " + request.getServerName());
    out.println("<BR>Protocol: " + request.getProtocol());
    out.println("<BR>Character Encoding: " + request.getCharacterEncoding());
    out.println("<BR>Content Type: " + request.getContentType());
    out.println("<BR>Content Length: " + request.getContentLength());
    out.println("<BR>Remote Address: " + request.getRemoteAddr());
    out.println("<BR>Remote Host: " + request.getRemoteHost());
    out.println("<BR>Scheme: " + request.getScheme());
    Enumeration parameters = request.getParameterNames();
    while (parameters.hasMoreElements()) {
      String parameterName = (String) parameters.nextElement();
      out.println("<br>Parameter Name: " + parameterName);
      out.println("<br>Parameter Value: " +
        request.getParameter(parameterName));
    }
    Enumeration attributes = request.getAttributeNames();
    while (attributes.hasMoreElements()) {
      String attribute = (String) attributes.nextElement();
      out.println("<BR>Attribute name: " + attribute);
      out.println("<BR>Attribute value: " + request.getAttribute(attribute));
    }
    out.println("</BODY>");
    out.println("</HTML>");
  }

  public String getServletInfo() {
    return null;
  }

  public ServletConfig getServletConfig() {
    return null;
  }

}
```

To run the example, first request the index2.html file by using the following URL:

```
http://localhost:8080/myApp/index2.html
```

Figure 2.3 shows the index2.html file in which "haywood" has been typed in as the value for author.

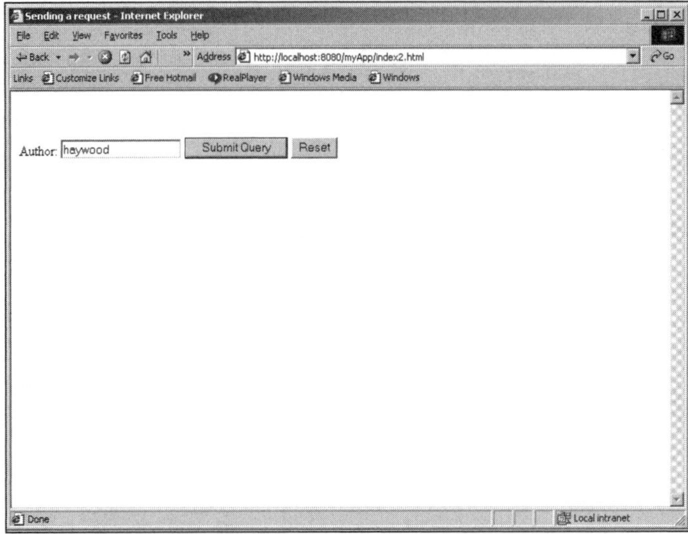

Figure 2.3 The index2.html file.

When you submit the form, the ResponseDemoServlet is invoked and your browser should display an image similar to Figure 2.4.

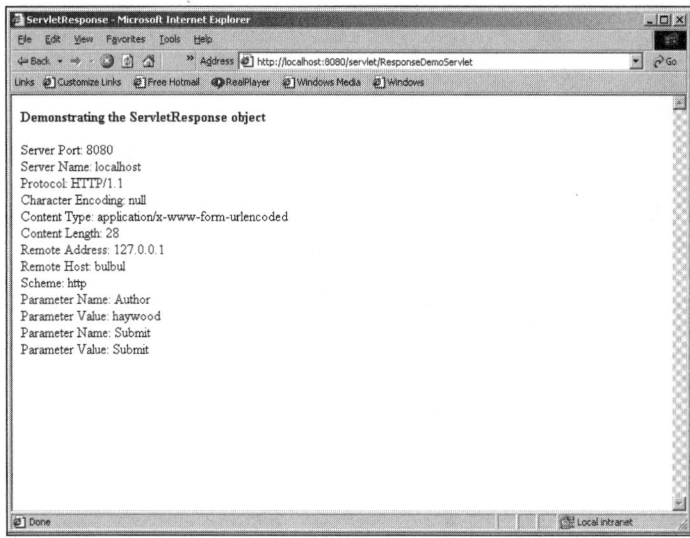

Figure 2.4 Utilizing the ServletResponse object.

The GenericServlet Wrapper Class

Throughout this chapter, you have been creating servlet classes that implement the javax.servlet.Servlet interface. Everything works fine, but there are two annoying things that you've probably noticed:

1. You have to provide implementations for all five methods of the Servlet interface, even though most of the time you only need one. This makes your code look unnecessarily complicated.
2. The ServletConfig object is passed to the init method. You need to preserve this object to use it from other methods. This is not difficult, but it means extra work.

The javax.servlet package provides a wrapper class called GenericServlet that implements two important interfaces from the javax.servlet package: Servlet and ServletConfig, as well as the java.io.Serializable interface. The GenericServlet class provides implementations for all methods, most of which are blank. You can extend GenericServlet and override only methods that you need to use. Clearly, this looks like a better solution.

The code in Listing 2.12 is a servlet called SimpleServlet that extends GenericServlet. The code provides the implementation of the service method that sends some output to the browser. Because the service method is the only method you need, only this method needs to appear in the class. Compared to all servlet classes that implement the javax.servlet.Servlet interface directly, SimpleServlet looks much cleaner and clearer.

Listing 2.12 **Extending GenericServlet**

```
import javax.servlet.*;
import java.io.IOException;
import java.io.PrintWriter;

public class SimpleServlet extends GenericServlet {

  public void service(ServletRequest request, ServletResponse response)
    throws ServletException, IOException {

    PrintWriter out = response.getWriter();
    out.println("<HTML>");
    out.println("<HEAD>");
    out.println("<TITLE>");
    out.println("Extending GenericServlet");
    out.println("</TITLE>");
    out.println("</HEAD>");
    out.println("<BODY>");
    out.println("Extending GenericServlet makes your code simpler.");
    out.println("</BODY>");
    out.println("</HTML>");
  }
}
```

The output from the SimpleServlet servlet is shown in Figure 2.5.

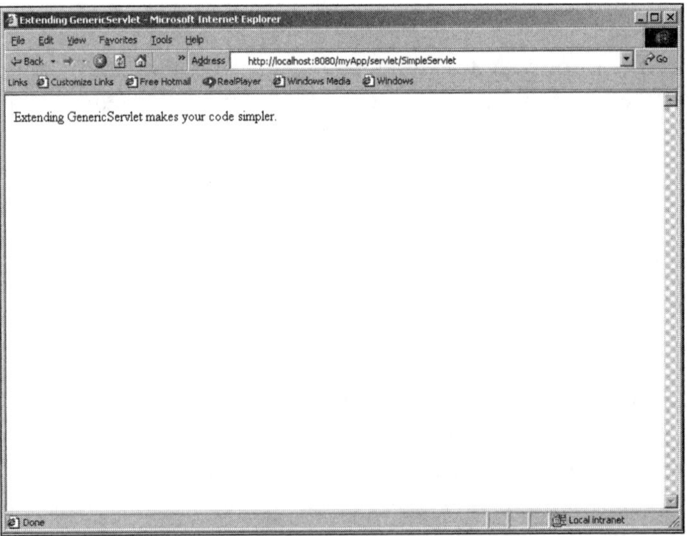

Figure 2.5 Extending GenericServlet.

Creating Thread-Safe Servlets

A servlet container allows multiple requests for the same servlet by creating a different thread to service each request. In many cases, each thread deals with its own ServletRequest and ServletResponse objects that are isolated from other threads. Problems start to arise, however, when your servlet needs to access an external resource. To understand the problem introduced by multi-threaded servlets, consider the following "playing dog" illustration.

Imagine a servlet accessing an external resource as a dog who enjoys moving tennis balls from one box to another. Each box can hold ten balls, no matter how the balls are arranged. The boxes and the balls are an external resource to the dog. To play, the dog needs two boxes and ten balls. Initially, those ten balls are placed in the first box. The dog moves all balls from the first box to the second, one ball at a time. The dog is smart enough to count to ten. Therefore, it knows when it's finished.

Now imagine a second thread of the same servlet as a second dog that plays the same game. Because there are only two boxes and ten balls for both dogs, the two dogs share the same "external resource." The game goes like this:

1. The first dog starts first (the servlet receives a call from a user).
2. After the first dog moves three balls, the second dog starts to play (the servlet is invoked by the second user). What will happen?

The two dogs sharing the same balls are illustrated in Figure 2.6.

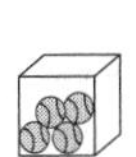

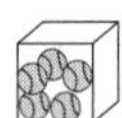
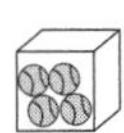

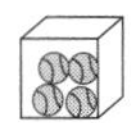

Figure 2.6 Understanding multi-threaded code.

The first dog and the second dog will not find enough balls to finish the game, and both will be confused.

If somehow the second dog can be queued to wait to start until the first dog finishes, however, the two dogs are happy.

That's what happens when two threads of the same servlet need to access an external resource, such as opening a file and writing to it. Consider the following example, which reflects a real-world situation.

The code in Listing 2.13 presents a page counter servlet. What it does is simple. The servlet overrides the service method to do the following:

1. Open the counter.txt file using a BufferedReader, read the number into a counter, and close the file.
2. Increment the counter.
3. Write the counter back to the counter.txt file.
4. Display the counter in the web browser.

Imagine what happens if there are two users, Boni and Bulbul, who request the servlet. First Boni requests it, and then a couple of nanoseconds after Boni, Bulbul requests the same servlet. The scenario probably looks like this:

1. The service method executes Steps 1 and 2, and then gets distracted by the other request.
2. The method then does Step 1 from Bulbul before continuing to do Step 3 and 4 for Boni.

What happens next? Boni and Bulbul get the same number, which is not how it is supposed to be. The servlet has produced an incorrect result. As you can see in Listing 2.13, the servlet is an unsafe multithreaded servlet.

Listing 2.13 **Unsafe Multi-Threaded Servlet**

```
import javax.servlet.*;
import java.io.*;

public class SingleThreadedServlet extends GenericServlet
 {

  public void service(ServletRequest request, ServletResponse response)
    throws ServletException, IOException {
    int counter = 0;

    // get saved value
    try {
      BufferedReader reader = new BufferedReader(
        new FileReader("counter.txt"));
```

```
        counter = Integer.parseInt( reader.readLine() );
        reader.close();
      }
      catch (Exception e) {
      }

      // increment counter
      counter++;

      // save new value
      try {
        BufferedWriter writer = new BufferedWriter(
          new FileWriter("counter.txt"));
        writer.write(Integer.toString(counter));

        writer.close();
      }
      catch (Exception e) {
      }

      try {
        PrintWriter out = response.getWriter();
        out.println("You are visitor number " + counter);
      }
      catch (Exception e) {
      }
    }
  }
```

To solve the problem, remember the solution to the "playing dog" illustration: When the second dog waited until the first dog finished playing, both dogs could complete the game successfully.

This is exactly how you solve the problem in a servlet needing to service two users at the same time: by making the second user wait until the first servlet finishes serving the first user. This solution makes the servlet single-threaded.

This solution is very easy to do because of the marker SingleThreadedServlet interface. You don't need to change your code; you need only to implement the interface.

The code in Listing 2.14 is the modification of the code in Listing 2.13. Nothing changes, except that the SingleThreadedServlet class now implements SingleThreadModel, making it thread safe.

Listing 2.14 **Safe Multi-Threaded Servlet**

```
import javax.servlet.*;
import java.io.*;

public class SingleThreadedServlet extends GenericServlet
  implements SingleThreadModel {

  public void service(ServletRequest request, ServletResponse response)
    throws ServletException, IOException {
    int counter = 0;

    // get saved value
    try {
      BufferedReader reader = new BufferedReader(
        new FileReader("counter.txt"));
      counter = Integer.parseInt( reader.readLine() );
      reader.close();
    }
    catch (Exception e) {
    }

    // increment counter
    counter++;

    // save new value
    try {
      BufferedWriter writer = new BufferedWriter(
        new FileWriter("counter.txt"));
      writer.write(Integer.toString(counter));

      writer.close();
    }
    catch (Exception e) {
    }

    try {
      PrintWriter out = response.getWriter();
      out.println("You are visitor number " + counter);
    }
    catch (Exception e) {
    }
  }
}
```

Now, if a user requests the service of the servlet while the servlet is servicing another user, the user who comes later will have to wait.

If you want to experience erroneous multi-threading yourself, the code in Listing 2.15 provides the SingleThreadedServlet with a delay of 6 seconds. Open two browsers and request the same servlet quickly. Notice that you get the same number for both browsers.

Listing 2.15 **Demonstrating an Unsafe Multi-Threaded Servlet**

```
import javax.servlet.*;
import java.io.*;

public class SingleThreadedServlet extends GenericServlet {

  public void service(ServletRequest request, ServletResponse response)
    throws ServletException, IOException {
    int counter = 0;

    // get saved value
    try {
      BufferedReader reader = new BufferedReader(
        new FileReader("counter.txt"));
      counter = Integer.parseInt( reader.readLine() );
      reader.close();
    }
    catch (Exception e) {
    }

    // increment counter
    counter++;

    // delay for 6 seconds to make observation possible
    try {
      Thread thread = new Thread();
      thread.sleep(6000);
    }
    catch (InterruptedException e) {
    }

    // saved new value
    try {
      BufferedWriter writer = new BufferedWriter(
        new FileWriter("counter.txt"));
      writer.write(Integer.toString(counter));

      writer.close();
    }
    catch (Exception e) {
    }

    try {
      PrintWriter out = response.getWriter();
      out.println("You are visitor number " + counter);
    }
    catch (Exception e) {
    }
  }
}
```

What the code does is simple: It opens the counter.txt file, reads the value, increments the value, and writes the incremented value back to the file.

However, between the line of code that increments the value and the line of code that writes the incremented value back to the user, we inserted the following code:

```
try {
  Thread thread = new Thread();
  thread.sleep(6000);
}
catch (InterruptedException e) {
}
```

Now you have time to request the same servlet from the second browser. The value shown in both browsers will be the same if the second request comes before the first thread of the servlet has the time to update the value in the counter.txt file.

> **Warning**
>
> The code in listing 2.15 might give you an unexpected result because implementing the SingleThreadModel interface only guarantees that no two threads will concurrently execute the service () method within the same servlet instance. Since the servlet container may instantiate multiple instances of a servlet class to handle a heavy request load, the SingleThreadModel interface is left useless.

An inexperienced programmer would wonder whether a good solution might be to make every servlet implement the SingleThreadModel interface. The answer is no. If a servlet never accesses an external resource, queuing the second request will create unnecessary delay to the subsequent user after the first. Also, if the external resource is accessed but there is no need to update its value, you don't need to implement the SingleThreadModel interface. For example, if the service method of a servlet needs only to read a static value from a file, you can let multiple threads of the servlet open and read the file at the same time.

Summary

This chapter introduced you to most of the interfaces and classes of the javax.servlet package, one of the two packages provided for servlet programming. This package contains basic classes and interfaces that are extended by members of the second package: javax.servlet.http. Understanding the basic classes and interfaces in javax.servlet is important, even though you use them less often than the javax.servlet.http package members in real-world applications. This chapter also showed you how to implement theSingleThreadModel interface to solve the problem multi-threaded servlets can have when accessing the same external resource.

The next chapter shows you how to write servlets that use the members of the second Servlet API package, javax.servlet.http.

3

Writing Servlet Applications

IN THE PREVIOUS CHAPTERS, YOU HAVE learned how to write servlets, run them in the servlet container, and invoke them from a web browser. You also have studied various classes and interfaces in the javax.servlet package and learned how to solve the problem introduced by a multi-threaded servlet.

When you are programming servlets, however, you will work with another package called javax.servlet.http. The classes and interfaces in this package derive from those in javax.servlet; however, the members of the javax.servlet.http package are much richer and more convenient to use. In this package, the HttpServlet class represents a servlet, extending javax.servlet.GenericServlet and bringing a great number of methods of its own. The javax.servlet.http package also has interfaces that are equivalent to javax.servlet.ServletRequest and javax.servlet.ServletResponse interfaces—the HttpServletRequest and the HttpServletResponse, respectively. It is not a coincidence that HttpServletRequest extends the javax.servlet.ServletRequest interface, and HttpServletResponse is derived from the javax.servlet.ServletResponse interface.

Additional classes exist that are not available in the javax.servlet package. For example, you can use a class called Cookie to work with cookies. In addition, you will find session-related methods in the HttpServlet class that enable you to deal with user sessions. Both cookies and sessions are explained in detail in Chapter 5, "Session Management."

Let's now begin with an overview of the HttpServlet class, a class that you almost always extend when developing servlets.

The HttpServlet Class

As mentioned previously, the HttpServlet class extends the javax.servlet.GenericServlet class. The HttpServlet class also adds a number of interesting methods for you to use. The most important are the six do*xxx* methods that get called when a related HTTP request method is used. The six methods are doPost, doPut, doGet, doDelete, doOptions and doTrace. Each do*xxx* method is invoked when a corresponding HTTP method is used. For instance, the doGet method is invoked when the servlet receives an HTTP request that was sent using the GET method.

Note

If you are familiar with the HTTP 1.1 protocol, you will notice that the HEAD method does not have a corresponding do method in the servlet. You are right. Actually, there is a doHead method in the HttpServlet class, but it is a private method.

Of the six do*xxx* methods, the doPost and the doGet methods are the most frequently used.

The doPost method is called when the browser sends an HTTP request using the POST method. The POST method is one of the two methods that can be used by an HTML form. Consider the following HTML form at the client side:

```
<FORM ACTION="Register" METHOD="POST">
<INPUT TYPE=TEXT Name="firstName">
<INPUT TYPE=TEXT Name="lastName">
<INPUT TYPE=SUBMIT>
</FORM>
```

When the user clicks the Submit button to submit the form, the browser sends an HTTP request to the server using the POST method. The web server then passes this request to the Register servlet and the doPost method of the servlet is invoked. Using the POST method in a form, the parameter name/value pairs of the form are sent in the request body. For example, if you use the preceding form as an example and enter Ann as the value for firstName and Go as the value for lastName, you will get the following result in the request body:

```
firstName=Ann
lastName=Go
```

An HTML form can also use the GET method; however, POST is much more often used with HTML forms.

The doGet method is invoked when an HTTP request is sent using the GET method. GET is the default method in HTTP. When you type a URL, such as `www.yahoo.com`, your request is sent to Yahoo! using the GET method. If you use the GET method in a form, the parameter name/value pairs are appended to the URL. Therefore, if you have two parameters named firstName and lastName in your form, and the user enters *Ann* and *Go*, respectively, the URL to your servlet will become something like the following:

```
http://yourdomain/myApp/Register?firstName=Ann&lastName=Go
```

Upon receiving a GET method, the servlet will call its doGet method.

Note

You may wonder how a servlet knows what do*xxx* method to invoke. You can find the answer by reading the source code of the HttpServlet class. This class inherits the service method from the javax.servlet.Servlet interface that gets called by the servlet container. Remember that its signature is as follows:

```
public void service(ServletRequest request,
  ServletResponse response)
  throws ServletException, IOException
```

The method tries to downcast request to HttpRequest and response to HttpResponse, and pass both as arguments to the second service method that has the following signature:

```
protected void service(HttpServletRequest request,
  HttpServletResponse response)
  throws ServletException, IOException
```

The HttpServletRequest interface has a method named getMethod that returns a String containing the HTTP method used by the client request. Knowing the HTTP method, the service method simply calls the corresponding do*xxx* method.

The servlet in Listing 3.1 demonstrates the doGet and the doPost methods.

> **Note**
> If an HTML form does not have the ACTION attribute, the default value for this attribute is the current page.

Listing 3.1 **The doGet and doPost Methods**

```
import javax.servlet.*;
import javax.servlet.http.*;
import java.io.*;

public class RegisterServlet extends HttpServlet {
  public void doGet(HttpServletRequest request,
    HttpServletResponse response)
    throws ServletException, IOException {
    response.setContentType("text/html");
    PrintWriter out = response.getWriter();
    out.println("<HTML>");
    out.println("<HEAD>");
    out.println("<TITLE>The GET method</TITLE>");
    out.println("</HEAD>");
    out.println("<BODY>");
    out.println("The servlet has received a GET. " +
      "Now, click the button below.");
    out.println("<BR>");
    out.println("<FORM METHOD=POST>");
    out.println("<INPUT TYPE=SUBMIT VALUE=Submit>");
    out.println("</FORM>");
    out.println("</BODY>");
    out.println("</HTML>");

  }
  public void doPost(
    HttpServletRequest request, HttpServletResponse response)
    throws ServletException, IOException {
    response.setContentType("text/html");
    PrintWriter out = response.getWriter();
    out.println("<HTML>");
    out.println("<HEAD>");
    out.println("<TITLE>The POST method</TITLE>");
    out.println("</HEAD>");
    out.println("<BODY>");
    out.println("The servlet has received a POST. Thank you.");
    out.println("</BODY>");
    out.println("</HTML>");
  }
}
```

When the servlet is first called from a web browser by typing the URL to the servlet in the Address or Location box, GET is used as the request method. At the server side, the doGet method is invoked. The servlet sends a string saying "The servlet has received a GET. Now, click the button below." plus an HTML form. The output is shown in Figure 3.1.

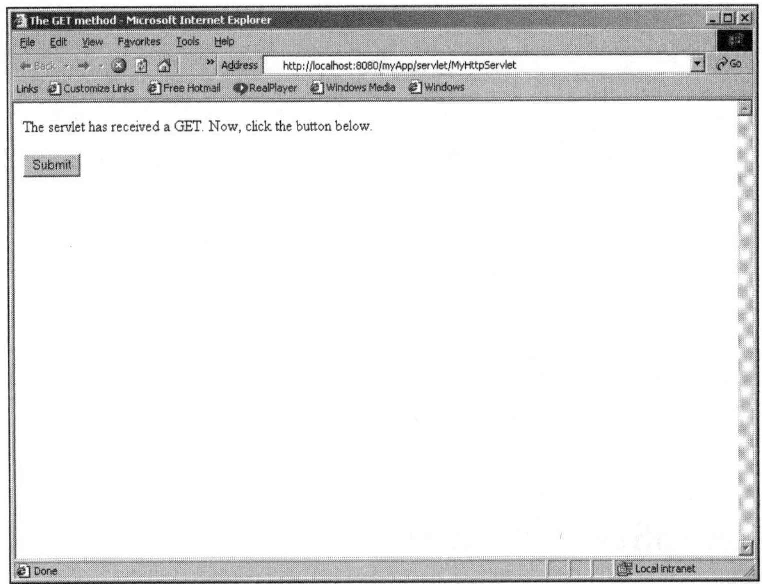

Figure 3.1 The output of the doGet method.

The form sent to the browser uses the POST method. When the user clicks the button to submit the form, a POST request is sent to the server. The servlet then invokes the doPost method, sending a String saying, "The servlet has received a POST. Thank you," to the browser. The output of doPost is shown in Figure 3.2.

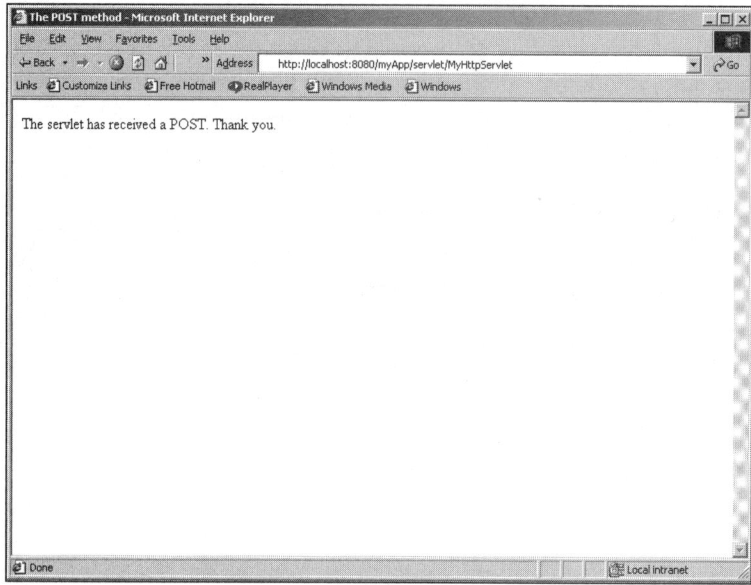

Figure 3.2 The output of the doPost method.

The HttpServletRequest Interface

In addition to providing several more protocol-specific methods in the HttpServlet class, the javax.servlet.http package also provides more sophisticated request and response interfaces. The request interface, HttpServletRequest, is described in this section. The response interface, HttpServletResponse, is explained in the next section.

Obtaining HTTP Request Headers from HttpServletRequest

The HTTP request that a client browser sends to the server includes an HTTP request header with important information, such as cookies and the referer. You can access these headers from the HttpServletRequest object passed to a do*xxx* method.

> **Note**
> The list of all HTTP request headers is given in Chapter 13, "File Upload."

The following example demonstrates how you can use the HttpServletRequest interface to obtain all the header names and sends the header name/value pairs to the browser. The code is given in Listing 3.2.

Listing 3.2 **Obtaining HTTP request Headers**

```
import javax.servlet.*;
import javax.servlet.http.*;
import java.io.*;
import java.util.*;

public class RegisterServlet extends HttpServlet {
  public void doGet(HttpServletRequest request, HttpServletResponse response)
    throws ServletException, IOException {

    response.setContentType("text/html");
    PrintWriter out = response.getWriter();
    Enumeration enumeration = request.getHeaderNames();
    while (enumeration.hasMoreElements()) {
      String header = (String) enumeration.nextElement();
      out.println(header + ": " + request.getHeader(header) + "<BR>");
    }
  }
}
```

The RegisterServlet in Listing 3.2 uses the getHeaderNames and the getHeader methods. The getHeaderNames is first called to obtain an Enumeration containing all the header names found in the client request. The value of each header then is retrieved by using the getHeader method, passing a header name.

The output of the code in Listing 3.2 depends on the client environment, such as the browser used and the operating system of the client's machine. For example, some browsers might send cookies to the server. Also, whether the servlet is requested by the user typing the URL in the Address/Location box or by clicking a hyperlink also accounts for the presence of an HTTP request header called referer.

The output of the code in Listing 3.2 is shown in Figure 3.3.

Some other methods of the HttpServletRequest interface provide information about paths. The getPathInfo method returns—following the servlet path but preceding the query string—a String containing any additional path information, or returns null if there is no additional path information. The getPathTranslated method returns the same information as the getPathInfo method, but translates the path to its physical path name before returning it, or returns null if there is no additional path information. Additional information comes after the servlet name and before the query string. The servlet name and the additional information is separated by the forward slash character (/).

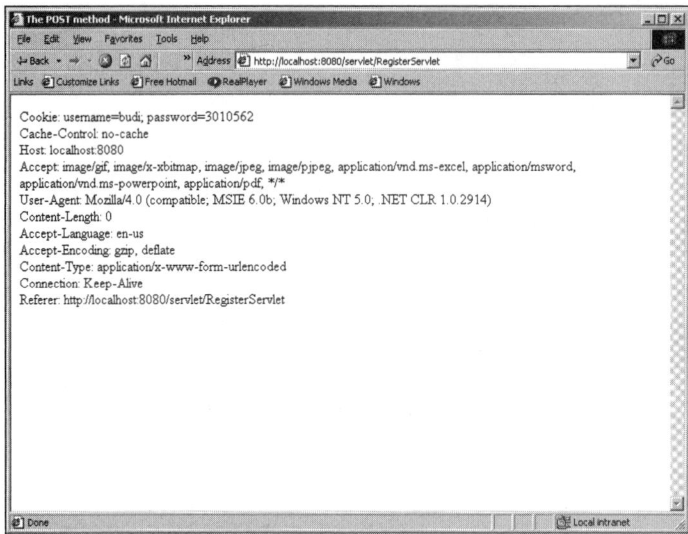

Figure 3.3 Obtaining HTTP request headers.

For example, consider a request to a servlet called PathInfoDemoServlet, made with the following URL:

```
http://localhost:8080/myApp/servlet/PathInfoDemoServlet/AddInfo?id=2
```

This URL contains additional info "/AddInfo" after the servlet name. The getPathInfo method will return the String "/AddInfo", the getQueryString method will return "id=2", and the getPathTranslated method returns "C:\App\Java\AddInfo". The return value of getPathTranslated depends on the location of the servlet class file.

Next, the getRequestURI method returns the first line of the request's Uniform Resource Identifier (URI). This is the part of the URI that is found to the left of the query string. The getServletPath method returns the part of the URI that refers to the servlet being invoked. Figure 3.4 shows the path information of a servlet called HttpRequestDemoServlet.

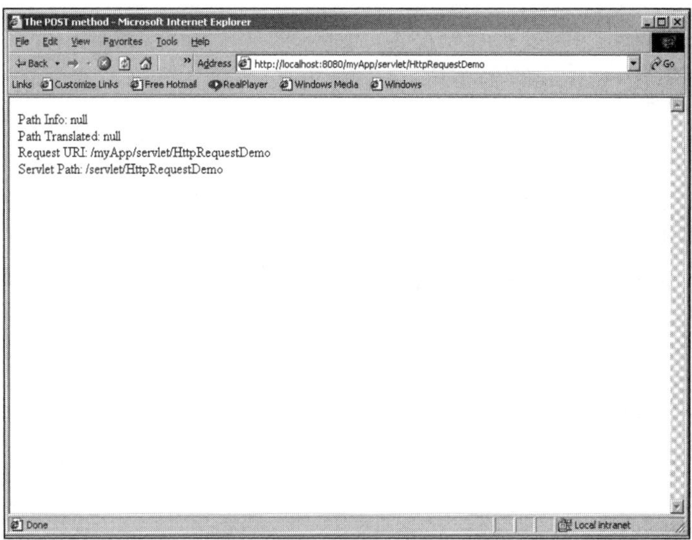

Figure 3.4 The path information of HttpRequestDemoServlet.

Obtaining the Query String from HttpServletRequest

The next important method is the getQueryString method, which is used to retrieve the query string of the HTTP request. A query string is the string on the URL to the right of the path to the servlet. The following example helps you see what a query string looks like.

As mentioned previously, if you use the GET method in an HTML form, the parameter name/value pairs will be appended to the URL. The code in Listing 3.3 is a servlet named HttpRequestDemoServlet that displays the value of the request's query string and a form.

Listing 3.3 **Obtaining the Query String**

```
import javax.servlet.*;
import javax.servlet.http.*;
import java.io.*;
import java.util.*;

public class HttpRequestDemoServlet extends HttpServlet {
  public void doGet(HttpServletRequest request, HttpServletResponse response)
    throws ServletException, IOException {
```

continues

Listing 3.3 **Continued**

```
      response.setContentType("text/html");
      PrintWriter out = response.getWriter();
      out.println("<HTML>");
      out.println("<HEAD>");
      out.println("<TITLE>Obtaining the Query String</TITLE>");
      out.println("</HEAD>");
      out.println("<BODY>");
      out.println("Query String: " + request.getQueryString() + "<BR>");
      out.println("<FORM METHOD=GET>");
      out.println("<BR>First Name: <INPUT TYPE=TEXT NAME=FirstName>");
      out.println("<BR>Last Name: <INPUT TYPE=TEXT NAME=LastName>");
      out.println("<BR><INPUT TYPE=SUBMIT VALUE=Submit>");
      out.println("</FORM>");
      out.println("</BODY>");
      out.println("</HTML>");
    }
  }
```

When the user enters the URL to the servlet in the web browser and the servlet is first called, the query string is null, as shown in Figure 3.5.

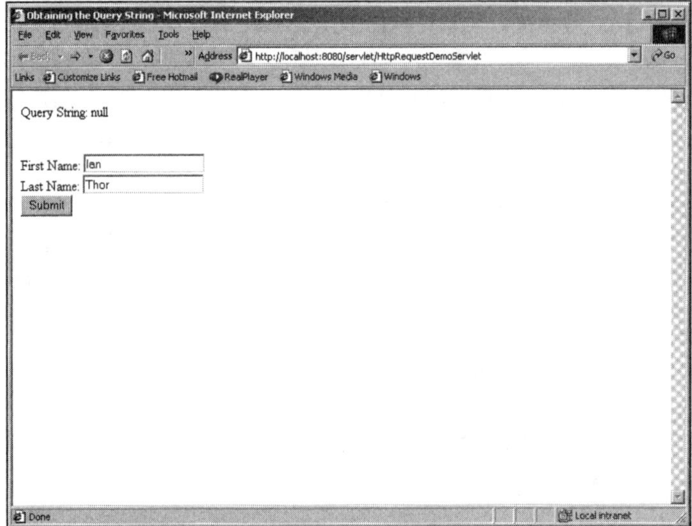

Figure 3.5 The query string is null.

After you enter some values into the HTML form and submit the form, the page is redisplayed. Note that now there is a string added to the URL. The query string has a value of the parameter name/value pairs separated by an ampersand (&). The page is shown in Figure 3.6.

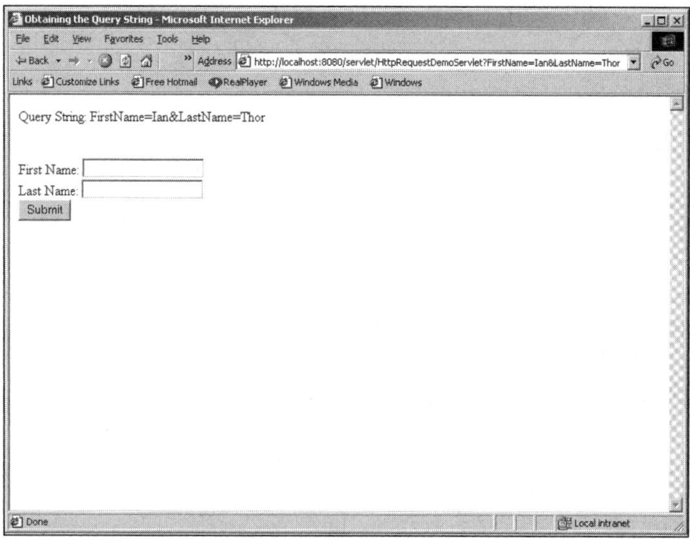

Figure 3.6 The query string with a non-null value.

Obtaining the Parameters from HttpServletRequest

You have seen that you can get the query string containing a value. This means that you can get the form parameter name/value pairs or other values from the previous page. You should not use the getQueryString method to obtain a form's parameter name/value pairs, however, because this means you have to parse the string yourself. You can use some other methods in HttpServletRequest to get the parameter names and values: the getParameterNames and the getParameter methods.

The getParameterNames method returns an Enumeration containing the parameter names. In many cases, however, you already know the parameter names, so you don't need to use this method. To get a parameter value, you use the getParameter method, passing the parameter name as the argument.

The following example demonstrates how you can use the getParameterNames and the getParameter methods to display all the parameter names and values from the HTML form from the previous page. The code is given in Listing 3.4.

Listing 3.4 **Obtaining the Parameter Name/Value Pairs**

```
import javax.servlet.*;
import javax.servlet.http.*;
import java.io.*;
import java.util.*;

public class HttpRequestDemoServlet extends HttpServlet {
  public void doGet(HttpServletRequest request, HttpServletResponse response)
  throws ServletException, IOException {

    response.setContentType("text/html");
    PrintWriter out = response.getWriter();
    out.println("<HTML>");
    out.println("<HEAD>");
    out.println("<TITLE>Obtaining the Parameter</TITLE>");
    out.println("</HEAD>");
    out.println("<BODY>");
    out.println("The request's parameters are:<BR>");

    Enumeration enumeration = request.getParameterNames();
    while (enumeration.hasMoreElements()){
      String parameterName = (String) enumeration.nextElement();
      out.println(parameterName + ": " +
        request.getParameter(parameterName) + "<BR>" );
    }

    out.println("<FORM METHOD=GET>");
    out.println("<BR>First Name: <INPUT TYPE=TEXT NAME=FirstName>");
    out.println("<BR>Last Name: <INPUT TYPE=TEXT NAME=LastName>");
    out.println("<BR><INPUT TYPE=SUBMIT VALUE=Submit>");
    out.println("</FORM>");
    out.println("</BODY>");
    out.println("</HTML>");
  }
}
```

When the servlet is first called, it does not have any parameter from the previous request. Therefore, the no parameter name/value pair is displayed, as shown in Figure 3.7.

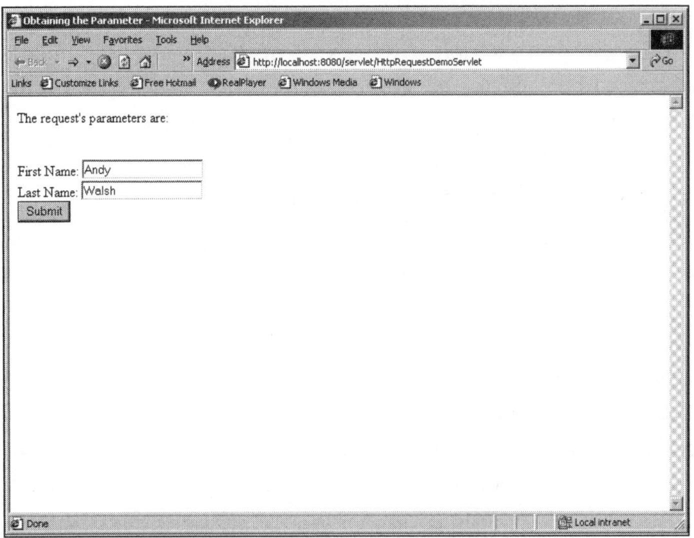

Figure 3.7 The first request does not have a parameter.

On subsequent requests, the user should enter values for both the firstName and lastName parameters. This is reflected on the next page, which is shown in Figure 3.8.

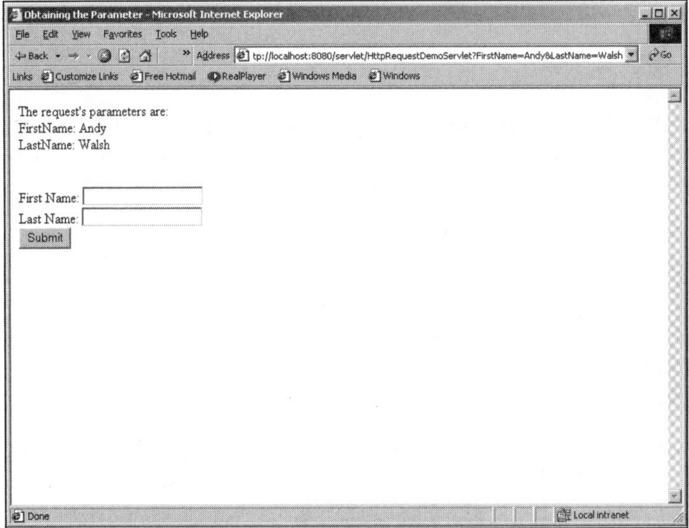

Figure 3.8 The parameter name/value pairs.

The code in Listing 3.4 also can be used without any modification if the form uses the POST method, which is what you normally use for a form. There are numerous cases, however, where you need to pass non-form values in the URL. This technique is reviewed in Chapter 5.

Manipulating Multi-Value Parameters

You may have a need to use parameters with the same name in your form. This case might arise, for example, when you are using check box controls that can accept multiple values or when you have a multiple-selection HTML select control. In situations like these, you can't use the getParameter method because it will give you only the first value. Instead, you use the getParameterValues method.

The getParameterValues method accepts one argument: the parameter name. It returns an array of string containing all the values for that parameter. If the parameter of that name is not found, the getParameterValues method will return a null.

The following example illustrates the use of the getParameterValues method to get all favorite music selected by the user. The code for this servlet is given in Listing 3.5.

Listing 3.5 **Obtaining Multiple Values from a Parameter**

```
import javax.servlet.*;
import javax.servlet.http.*;
import java.io.*;
import java.util.*;

public class HttpRequestDemoServlet extends HttpServlet {
  public void doGet(HttpServletRequest request, HttpServletResponse response)
  throws ServletException, IOException {

    response.setContentType("text/html");
    PrintWriter out = response.getWriter();
    out.println("<HTML>");
    out.println("<HEAD>");
    out.println("<TITLE>Obtaining Multi-Value Parameters</TITLE>");
    out.println("</HEAD>");
    out.println("<BODY>");

    out.println("<BR>");
    out.println("<BR>Select your favorite music:");
    out.println("<BR><FORM METHOD=POST>");
    out.println("<BR><INPUT TYPE=CHECKBOX " +
      "NAME=favoriteMusic VALUE=Rock>Rock");
    out.println("<BR><INPUT TYPE=CHECKBOX " +
      "NAME=favoriteMusic VALUE=Jazz>Jazz");
    out.println("<BR><INPUT TYPE=CHECKBOX " +
      "NAME=favoriteMusic VALUE=Classical>Classical");
```

```
    out.println("<BR><INPUT TYPE=CHECKBOX " +
      "NAME=favoriteMusic VALUE=Country>Country");
    out.println("<BR><INPUT TYPE=SUBMIT VALUE=Submit>");
    out.println("</FORM>");
    out.println("</BODY>");
    out.println("</HTML>");
  }

  public void doPost(HttpServletRequest request, HttpServletResponse
response)
    throws ServletException, IOException {

    String[] values = request.getParameterValues("favoriteMusic");
    response.setContentType("text/html");
    PrintWriter out = response.getWriter();
    if (values != null ) {
      int length = values.length;
      out.println("You have selected: ");
      for (int i=0; i<length; i++) {
        out.println("<BR>" + values[i]);
      }
    }
  }
}
```

When the servlet is first called, the doGet method is invoked and the method sends a form to the web browser. The form has four check box controls with the same name: favoriteMusic. Their values are different, however. This is shown in Figure 3.9.

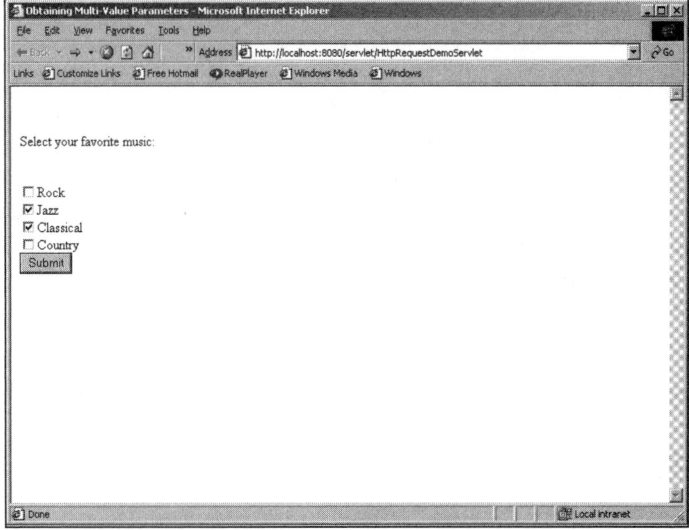

Figure 3.9 A form with multiple value check boxes.

When the user selects the value(s) of the check boxes, the browser sends all selected values. In the server side, you use the getParameterValues to retrieve all values sent in the request. This is shown in Figure 3.10

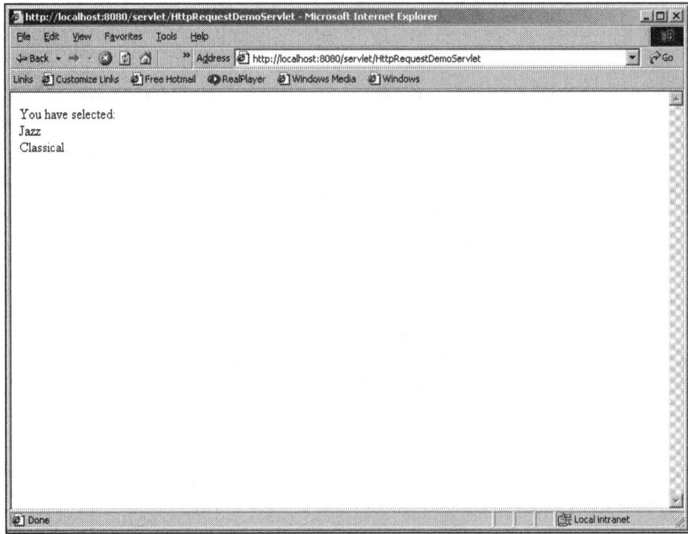

Figure 3.10 Displaying the selected values.

Note that you use the POST method for the form; therefore, the parameter name/value pairs are retrieved in the doPost method.

HttpServletResponse

The HttpServletResponse interface provides several protocol-specific methods not available in the javax.servlet.ServletResponse interface.

The HttpServletResponse interface extends the javax.servlet.ServletResponse interface. In the examples in this chapter so far, you have seen that you always use two of the methods in HttpServletResponse when sending output to the browser: setContentType and getWriter.

```
response.setContentType("text/html");
PrintWriter out = response.getWriter();
```

There is more to it, however. The addCookie method sends cookies to the browser. You also use methods to manipulate the URLs sent to the browser. These methods are explored further in the section on user session management in Chapter 5.

Another interesting method in the HttpServletResponse interface is the setHeader method. This method allows you to add a name/value field to the response header.

You can also use a method to redirect the user to another page: sendRedirect. When you call this method, the web server sends a special message to the browser to request another page. Therefore, there is always a round trip to the client side before the other page is fetched. This method is used frequently and its use is illustrated in the following example. Listing 3.6 shows a Login page that prompts the user to enter a user name and a password. If both are correct, the user will be redirected to a Welcome page. If not, the user will see the same Login page.

When the servlet is first requested, the servlet's doGet method is called. The doGet method then outputs the form. The user can then enter the user name and password, and submit the form. Note that the form uses the POST method, which means that at the server side, the doPost method is invoked and the user name and password are checked against some predefined values. If the user name and password match, the user is redirected to a Welcome page. If not, the doPost method outputs the Login form again along with an error message.

Listing 3.6 **A Login Page**

```
import javax.servlet.*;
import javax.servlet.http.*;
import java.io.*;
import java.util.*;

public class LoginServlet extends HttpServlet {

  private void sendLoginForm(HttpServletResponse response,
    boolean withErrorMessage)
    throws ServletException, IOException {
    response.setContentType("text/html");
    PrintWriter out = response.getWriter();
    out.println("<HTML>");
    out.println("<HEAD>");
    out.println("<TITLE>Login</TITLE>");
    out.println("</HEAD>");
    out.println("<BODY>");

    if (withErrorMessage)
      out.println("Login failed. Please try again.<BR>");

    out.println("<BR>");
    out.println("<BR>Please enter your user name and password.");
```

continues

Listing 3.6 **Continued**

```
    out.println("<BR><FORM METHOD=POST>");
    out.println("<BR>User Name: <INPUT TYPE=TEXT NAME=userName>");
    out.println("<BR>Password: <INPUT TYPE=PASSWORD NAME=password>");
    out.println("<BR><INPUT TYPE=SUBMIT VALUE=Submit>");
    out.println("</FORM>");
    out.println("</BODY>");
    out.println("</HTML>");

  }
  public void doGet(HttpServletRequest request, HttpServletResponse response)
    throws ServletException, IOException {
    sendLoginForm(response, false);
  }

  public void doPost(HttpServletRequest request,
    HttpServletResponse response)
    throws ServletException, IOException {
    String userName = request.getParameter("userName");
    String password = request.getParameter("password");
    if (userName!=null && password!=null &&
      userName.equals("jamesb") && password.equals("007")) {
      response.sendRedirect("http://domain/app/WelcomePage");
    }
    else {
      sendLoginForm(response, true);
    }

  }
}
```

Note

Note that if you are redirecting to a resource in the same application, you don't need to specify the complete URL; that is, you can just write, in the previous example, response.sendRedirect ("/app/WelcomePage"). For efficiency, however, you don't normally use the sendRedirect method to redirect a user to another resource in the same application. Instead, you forward the user, as you will see in the section, "Request Dispatching," later in this chapter.

In the code in Listing 3.6, I wrote a private method called sendLoginForm that accepts an HttpServletResponse object and a boolean that signals whether an error message be sent along with the form. This sendLoginForm method is called both from the doGet and the doPost methods. When called from the doGet method, no error message is given, because this is the first time the user requests the page. The withErrorMessage flag is therefore false. When called from the doPost method, this flag is set to true because the sendLoginForm method is only invoked from doPost if the user name and password did not match.

The Login page, when it is first requested, is shown in Figure 3.11. The Login page, after a failed attempt to log in, is shown in Figure 3.12.

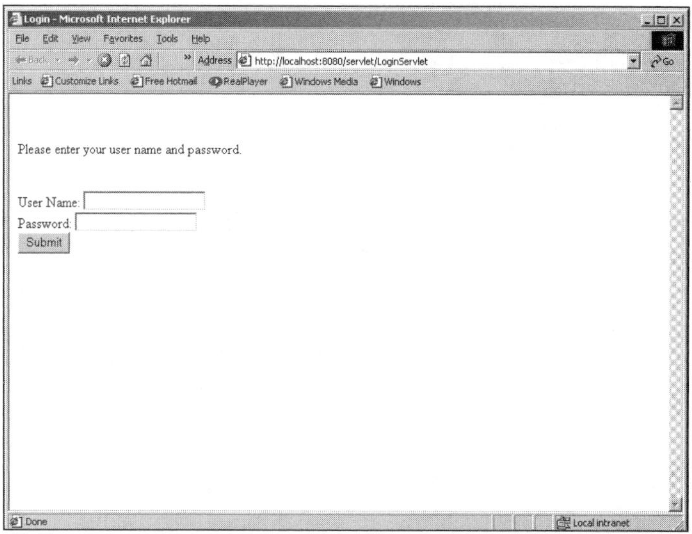

Figure 3.11 The Login page when first requested.

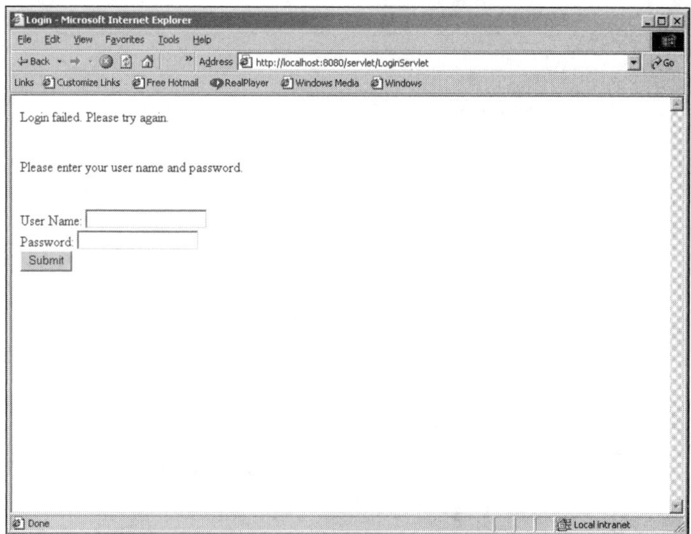

Figure 3.12 The Login page after a failed login.

After seeing the example, an experienced reader may ask, "If we can go to the Welcome page by just typing its URL in the web browser, why do we have to log in?"

This is true. The user can bypass the Login page, and this issue has to do with session management and will be addressed in Chapter 5.

Sending an Error Code

The HttpServletResponse also allows you to send pre-defined error messages. The interface defines a number of public static final integers that all start with SC_. For example, SC_FORBIDDEN will be translated into an HTTP error 403.

Along with the error code, you also can send a custom error message. Instead of redisplaying the Login page when a failed login occurs, you can send an HTTP error 403 plus your error message. To do this, replace the call to the sendLoginForm in the doPost method with the following:

```
response.sendError(response.SC_FORBIDDEN, "Login failed.");
```

The user will see the screen in Figure 3.13 when a login fails.

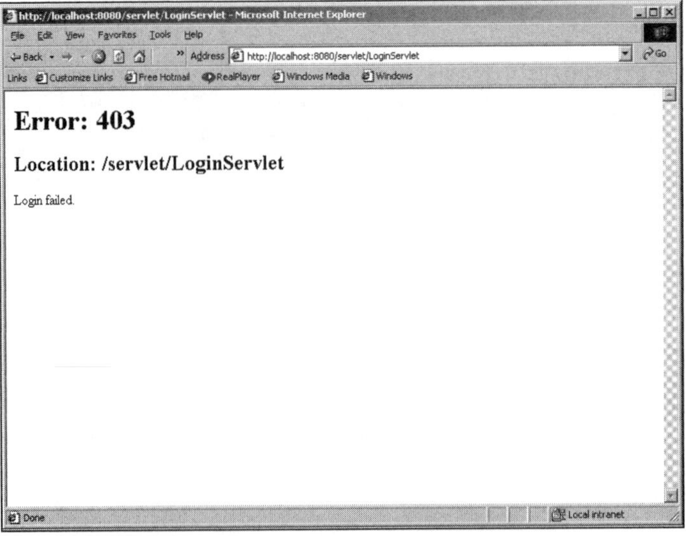

Figure 3.13 Sending an HTTP Error 403.

> **Note**
> The complete list of status codes can be found in Appendix C, "The javax.servlet.http Package Reference."

Sending Special Characters

Several characters have a special meaning in HTML. For instance, the less-than character (<) is used as the opening character of an HTML tag, and the greater-than character (>) is the closing character of an HTML tag.

When sending these characters to be displayed in the browser, you need to encode them so that they will be rendered correctly. For example, consider the code in Listing 3.7.

The doGet method of the SpecialCharacterServlet is very simple. It is intended to send a string that will be rendered as the following text in the browser:

```
In HTML, you use <BR> to change line.
```

Listing 3.7 **Incorrect Rendering of Special Characters**

```
import javax.servlet.*;
import javax.servlet.http.*;
import java.io.*;
import java.util.*;

public class SpecialCharacterServlet extends HttpServlet {
  public void doGet(HttpServletRequest request, HttpServletResponse response)
  throws ServletException, IOException {

    response.setContentType("text/html");
    PrintWriter out = response.getWriter();
    out.println("<HTML>");
    out.println("<HEAD>");
    out.println("<TITLE>HTML Tutorial — Changing Line</TITLE>");
    out.println("</HEAD>");
    out.println("<BODY>");
    out.println("In HTML, you use <BR> to change line.");
    out.println("</BODY>");
    out.println("</HTML>");
  }
}
```

This code produces a problem, however. To see what went wrong, take a look at the output of the doGet method in a browser, as shown in Figure 3.14.

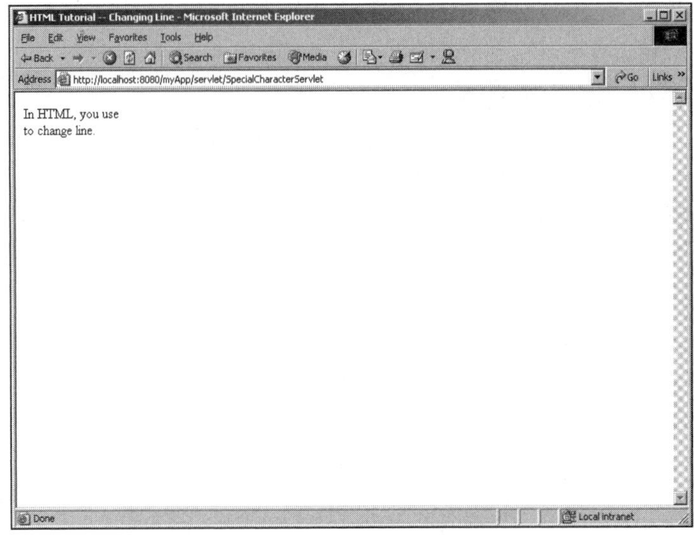

Figure 3.14 Special characters are not displayed correctly.

Because <BR> means change line in HTML, the intended string is not displayed correctly. Instead, it was interpreted as a command to cut the original string into two and the output was displayed in two lines.

To get around this, every time you want to display a special character, you need to encode it. The less-than character (<) is encoded as "<" and the greater-than character (>) as ">". Other special characters are the ampersand (&) and double quotation mark (") characters. You replace the ampersand (&) with "&" and the double quotation marks (") with """. Additionally, two or more white spaces are always displayed as a single space, unless you convert each individual space to " ".

Converting every occurrence of a special character is a tedious task, however. That's why you need a function that will do it automatically. Such a function is called encodeHtmlTag and is given in Listing 3.8. Now, if you suspect that the String you want to send to the browser contains a special character, just pass it to the encodeHtmlTag function.

Listing 3.8 **The encodeHtmlTag Function**

```
public static String encodeHtmlTag(String tag) {
    if (tag==null)
      return null;
    int length = tag.length();
    StringBuffer encodedTag = new StringBuffer(2 * length);
    for (int i=0; i<length; i++) {
      char c = tag.charAt(i);
      if (c=='<')
        encodedTag.append("&lt;");
      else if (c=='>')
        encodedTag.append("&gt;");
      else if (c=='&')
        encodedTag.append("&amp;");
      else if (c=='"')
        encodedTag.append("&quot;");
      else if (c==' ')
        encodedTag.append(" ");
      else
        encodedTag.append(c);

    }
    return encodedTag.toString();
  }
```

Listing 3.9 demonstrates a servlet that includes the encodeHtmlTag method and uses it to encode any String with special characters.

Listing 3.9 **Using the encodeHtmlTag Method in a Servlet**

```
import javax.servlet.*;
import javax.servlet.http.*;
import java.io.*;
import java.util.*;

public class SpecialCharacterServlet extends HttpServlet {
  public void doGet(HttpServletRequest request, HttpServletResponse response)
  throws ServletException, IOException {

    response.setContentType("text/html");
    PrintWriter out = response.getWriter();
    out.println("<HTML>");
    out.println("<HEAD>");
    out.println("<TITLE>HTML Tutorial — Changing Line</TITLE>");
    out.println("</HEAD>");
    out.println("<BODY>");
    out.println(encodeHtmlTag("In HTML, you use <BR> to change line."));
    out.println("</BODY>");
    out.println("</HTML>");
```

continues

Listing 3.9 **Continued**

```
  }

  /**
   * Encode an HTML tag so it will be displayed
   * as it is on the browser.
   * Particularly, this method searches the
   * passed in String and replace every occurrence
   * of the following character:
   * '<' with "&lt;"
   * '>' with "&gt;"
   * '&' with "&amp;"
   * //'"' with "&quot;"
   * ' ' with " "
   */
  public static String encodeHtmlTag(String tag) {
    if (tag==null)
      return null;
    int length = tag.length();
    StringBuffer encodedTag = new StringBuffer(2 * length);
    for (int i=0; i<length; i++) {
      char c = tag.charAt(i);
      if (c=='<')
        encodedTag.append("&lt;");
      else if (c=='>')
        encodedTag.append("&gt;");
      else if (c=='&')
        encodedTag.append("&amp;");
      else if (c=='"')
        encodedTag.append("&quot;");  //when trying to output text as tag's
value as in
        // values="???".
      else if (c==' ')
        encodedTag.append(" ");
      else
        encodedTag.append(c);

    }
    return encodedTag.toString();
  }
}
```

Figure 3.15 shows the output of sending the string, "In HTML, you use <BR> to change line". If you look at the HTML source code, you will notice that the < character has been converted to < and the > character to >.

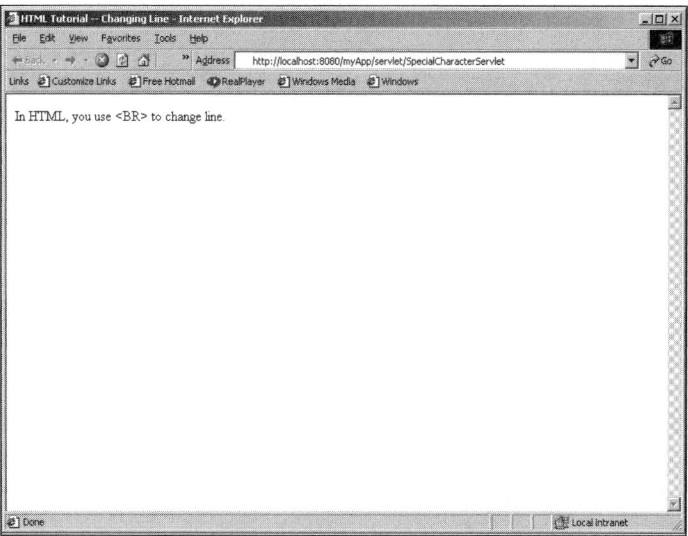

Figure 3.15 Encoding special characters.

Buffering the Response

If response buffering is enabled, the output to the browser is not sent until the servlet processing is finished or the buffer is full. Buffering enhances the performance of your servlet because the servlet needs to send the string output only once, instead of sending it every time the print or println method of the PrintWriter object is called. By default, buffering is enabled and the buffer size is 8,192 characters. You can change this value by using the HttpServletResponse interface's setBufferSize method. This method can be called only before any output is sent.

Populating HTML Elements

One of the tasks that you will perform often is populating the values of HTML elements. This is a straightforward task that can be tricky if you are not cautious. To do it correctly, pay attention to the following two rules:

1. Always enclose a value with double quotation marks ("). This way, white spaces will be rendered correctly.
2. If the value contains a double quotation mark character, you need to encode the double quotation marks (").

The servlet in Listing 3.10 contains an HTML form with two elements: a Textbox and a Password box. The Textbox element is given the value, Duncan "The Great" Young, and the password is lo&&lita.

Listing 3.10 **Populating HTML Elements**

```
import javax.servlet.*;
import javax.servlet.http.*;
import java.io.*;
import java.util.*;

public class PopulateValueServlet extends HttpServlet {
  public void doGet(HttpServletRequest request, HttpServletResponse response)
  throws ServletException, IOException {

    String userName = "Duncan \"The Great\" Young";
    String password = "lo&&lita";
    response.setContentType("text/html");
    PrintWriter out = response.getWriter();
    out.println("<HTML>");
    out.println("<HEAD>");
    out.println("<TITLE>Populate HTML elements</TITLE>");
    out.println("</HEAD>");

    out.println("<H3>Your user name and password.</H3>");
    out.println("<FORM METHOD=POST>");
    out.println("<BR>User name: <INPUT TYPE=TEXT NAME=userName VALUE=\"" +
      userName + "\">");
    out.println("<BR>Password: <INPUT TYPE=PASSWORD NAME=password VALUE=\"" +
      password + "\">");

    out.println("<BODY>");
    out.println("</BODY>");
    out.println("</HTML>");

  }
}
```

As you can see in Figure 3.16, however, the value in the Textbox element is truncated because the first double quotation mark character—in "The Great"—fools the browser into thinking that it is the end of the value. To overcome this problem, use the encodeHtmlTag method.

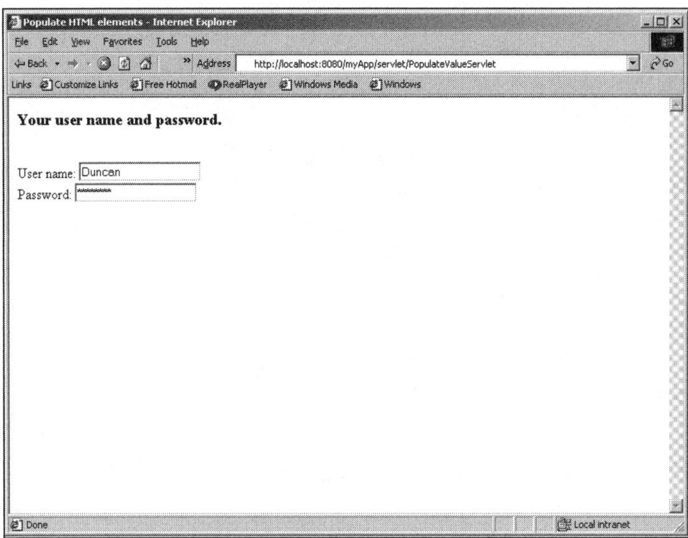

Figure 3.16 Truncated value.

Request Dispatching

In some circumstances, you may want to include the content from an HTML page or the output from another servlet. Additionally, there are cases that require that you pass the processing of an HTTP request from your servlet to another servlet. The current servlet specification responds to these needs with an interface called RequestDispatcher, which is found in the javax.servlet package. This interface has two methods, which allow you to delegate the request-response processing to another resource: include and forward. Both methods accept a javax.servlet.ServletRequest object and a javax.servlet.ServletResponse object as arguments.

As the name implies, the include method is used to include content from another resource, such as another servlet, a JSP page, or an HTML page. The method has the following signature:

```
public void include(javax.servlet.ServletRequest request,
  javax.servlet.ServletResponse response)
  throws javax.servlet.ServletException, java.io.IOException
```

The forward method is used to forward a request from one servlet to another. The original servlet can perform some initial tasks on the ServletRequest object before forwarding it. The signature of the forward method is as follows:

```
public void forward(javax.servlet.ServletRequest request,
  javax.servlet.ServletResponse response)
  throws javax.servlet.ServletException, java.io.IOException
```

The Difference Between sendRedirect and forward

Both the sendRedirect and forward methods bring the user to a new resource. There is a fundamental difference between the two, however, and understanding this can help you write a more efficient servlet.

The sendRedirect method works by sending a status code that tells the browser to request another URL. This means that there is always a round trip to the client side. Additionally, the previous HttpServletRequest object is lost. To pass information between the original servlet and the next request, you normally pass the information as a query string appended to the destination URL.

The forward method, on the other hand, redirects the request without the help from the client's browser. Both the HttpServletRequest object and the HttpServletResponse object also are passed to the new resource.

To perform a servlet include or forward, you first need to obtain a RequestDispatcher object. You can obtain a RequestDispatcher object three different ways, as follows:

- Use the getRequestDispatcher method of the javax.servlet.ServletContext interface, passing a String containing the path to the other resource. The path is relative to the root of the ServletContext.
- Use the getRequestDispatcher method of the javax.servlet.ServletRequest interface, passing a String containing the path to the other resource. The path is relative to the current HTTP request.
- Use the getNamedDispatcher method of the javax.servlet.ServletContext interface, passing a String containing the name of the other resource.

When programmers new to servlet programming are writing code for request dispatching, they often make the common mistake of passing an incorrect path to the getRequestDispatcher method. A big difference exists between the getRequestDispatcher method of the ServletContext interface and that belonging to the ServletRequest interface. The one you use depends on the location of the resource to be included or forwarded to. If you use the getRequestDispatcher method of the javax.servlet.ServletContext interface, you pass a path that is relative to the root of the ServletContext. If you use the getRequestDispatcher method of the javax.servlet.ServletRequest interface, you pass a path that is relative to the current HTTP request.

When you are creating a RequestDispatcher object from a servlet named FirstServlet to include or forward the request to another servlet called SecondServlet, the easiest way is to place the class files of both FirstServlet and SecondServlet in the same directory. This way, FirstServlet can be invoked from the URL `http://domain/VirtualDir/servlet/FirstServlet` and SecondServlet can be called from the URL `http://domain/VirtualDir/servlet/SecondServlet`. You then can use the getRequestDispatcher from the ServletRequest interface, passing the name of the second servlet. In FirstServlet, you can write the following code:

```
public void doGet(HttpServletRequest request, HttpServletResponse response)
  throws ServletException, IOException {

  RequestDispatcher rd = request.getRequestDispatcher("SecondServlet");
  rd.include(request, response);
}
```

or

```
public void doGet(HttpServletRequest request, HttpServletResponse response)
  throws ServletException, IOException {

  RequestDispatcher rd = request.getRequestDispatcher("SecondServlet");
  rd.forward(request, response);
}
```

Because both FirstServlet and SecondServlet are in the same directory, you don't need to include the forward slash (/) character before SecondServlet. In this case, you don't need to worry about the paths of both servlets.

Another option is to do it the harder way by passing the following String to the getRequestDispatcher of ServletRequest:

```
"/servlet/SecondServlet"
```

If you are to use the getRequestDispatcher from the ServletContext, you must pass "/VirtualDir/servlet/SecondServlet" as the path argument, such as the following:

```
public void doGet(HttpServletRequest request, HttpServletResponse response)
  throws ServletException, IOException {

  RequestDispatcher rd =
    getServletContext().getRequestDispatcher("/servlet/SecondServlet");
  rd.include(request, response);
}
```

or

```
public void doGet(HttpServletRequest request, HttpServletResponse response)
  throws ServletException, IOException {
```

```
    RequestDispatcher rd =
      getServletContext().getRequestDispatcher("/servlet/SecondServlet");
    rd.forward(request, response);
  }
```

To use the getNamedDispatcher method, your code would become

```
public void doGet(HttpServletRequest request, HttpServletResponse response)
  throws ServletException, IOException {

  RequestDispatcher rd =
    getServletContext().getNamedDispatcher("SecondServlet");
  rd.include(request, response);
}
```

or

```
public void doGet(HttpServletRequest request, HttpServletResponse response)
  throws ServletException, IOException {

  RequestDispatcher rd =
    getServletContext().getNamedDispatcher("SecondServlet");
  rd.forward(request, response);
}
```

Of course, when you use the getNamedDispatcher method, you must register the second servlet in your deployment descriptor. Here is an example:

```
<?xml version="1.0" encoding="ISO-8859-1"?>
<!DOCTYPE web-app
  PUBLIC "-//Sun Microsystems, Inc.//DTD Web Application 2.3//EN"
  "http://java.sun.com/dtd/web-app_2_3.dtd">

<web-app>
  <servlet>
    <servlet-name>FirstServlet</servlet-name>
    <servlet-class>FirstServlet</servlet-class>
  </servlet>
  <servlet>
    <servlet-name>SecondServlet</servlet-name>
    <servlet-class>SecondServlet</servlet-class>
  </servlet>
</web-app>
```

If you are including from a doPost method, the doPost method of the second servlet will be invoked. If including from a doGet method, the doGet method of the second servlet will be called.

Warning

If you change the resource included in your servlet, you need to restart Tomcat for the change to take effect. This is required because the included servlet is never invoked directly. After the included servlet is loaded, its timestamp is never compared again.

The following sections give you a closer look at the use of the RequestDispatcher interface.

Note

Note that in the olden days (which are not so long ago, of course), servlet chaining was the technique used to perform what RequestDispatcher can do. Servlet chaining is not part of the J2EE specification, however, and its use is dependent on specific servlet containers. You may still find this term in old literature on servlets.

Including Other Resources

On many occasions, you may want to include other resources inside your servlet. For example, you may have a collection of JavaScript functions that you want to include in the response to the user. Separating non-servlet content makes sure that modularity is maintained. In this case, a JavaScript programmer can work independently of the servlet programmer. The page containing the JavaScript functions can then be included using the include method of a RequestDispatcher.

Another time you may want to include other resources in your servlet might be when you want to include the output of a servlet whose output is a link to a randomly selected advertisement banner. By separating into a separate servlet the code that selects the banner, the same code can be included in more than one servlet, and formatting can be done by modifying the included servlet solely.

The include method of the RequestDispatcher interface may be called at any time. The target servlet has access to all aspects of the request object, but can only write information to the ServletOutputStream or Writer object of the response object. The target servlet also can commit a response by either writing content past the end of the response buffer or explicitly calling the flush method of the ServletResponse interface. The included servlet cannot set headers or call any method that affects the header of the response.

When a servlet is being called from within an include method, it is sometimes necessary for that servlet to know the path by which it was invoked. The following request attributes are set and accessible from the included servlet via the getAttribute method on the request object:

- javax.servlet.include.request_uri
- javax.servlet.include.context_path
- javax.servlet.include.servlet_path
- javax.servlet.include.path_info
- javax.servlet.include.query_string

These attributes are not set if the included servlet was obtained by using the getNamedDispatcher method.

Including Static Content

Sometimes you need to include static content, such as HTML pages or image files that are prepared by a web graphic designer. You can do this by using the same technique for including dynamic resources that you've been reading about in this chapter.

The following example shows a servlet named FirstServlet that includes an HTML file named AdBanner.html. The servlet class file is located in the WEB-INF\classes directory, whereas the AdBanner.html file, like other HTML files, resides in the application directory. In other words, using the myApp application, the AdBanner.html file resides in the myApp directory, whereas the servlet class file is in myApp/WEB-INF/classes directory. The servlet is given in Listing 3.11 and the HTML file is given in Listing 3.12.

Listing 3.11 **Including Static Content**

```
import javax.servlet.*;
import javax.servlet.http.*;
import java.io.*;
import java.util.*;

public class FirstServlet extends HttpServlet {

  public void doGet(HttpServletRequest request, HttpServletResponse response)
    throws ServletException, IOException {

    RequestDispatcher rd = request.getRequestDispatcher("/AdBanner.html");

    rd.include(request, response);
  }
}
```

Listing 3.12 **The AdBanner.html File**

```
<HTML>
<HEAD>
<TITLE>Banner</TITLE>
</HEAD>
<BODY>
<IMG SRC=myApp/images/banner.jpg>
</BODY>
</HTML>
```

Including Another Servlet

The second example shows a servlet (FirstServlet) that includes another servlet (SecondServlet). The second servlet simply sends the included request parameter to the user. The FirstServlet is given in Listing 3.13 and the SecondServlet is presented in Listing 3.14. The output of the example is given in Figure 3.17.

Listing 3.13 **FirstServlet**

```
import javax.servlet.*;
import javax.servlet.http.*;
import java.io.*;
public class FirstServlet extends HttpServlet {

  public void doGet(HttpServletRequest request, HttpServletResponse response)
    throws ServletException, IOException {

    response.setContentType("text/html");
    PrintWriter out = response.getWriter();
    out.println("<HTML>");
    out.println("<HEAD>");
    out.println("<TITLE>Included Request Parameters</TITLE>");
    out.println("</HEAD>");
    out.println("<BODY>");
    out.println("<B>Included Request Parameters</B><BR>");
    RequestDispatcher rd =
      request.getRequestDispatcher("/servlet/SecondServlet?name=budi");
    rd.include(request, response);
    out.println("</BODY>");
    out.println("</HTML>");
  }
}
```

Listing 3.14 **SecondServlet**

```
import javax.servlet.*;
import javax.servlet.http.*;
import java.io.*;
import java.util.*;

public class SecondServlet extends HttpServlet {

  public void doGet(HttpServletRequest request, HttpServletResponse response)
    throws ServletException, IOException {
    response.setContentType("text/html");
    PrintWriter out = response.getWriter();
    Enumeration enum = request.getAttributeNames();
    while (enum.hasMoreElements()) {
      String attributeName = (String) enum.nextElement();
      out.println(attributeName + ": " +
        request.getAttribute(attributeName) + "<BR>");
    }
  }
}
```

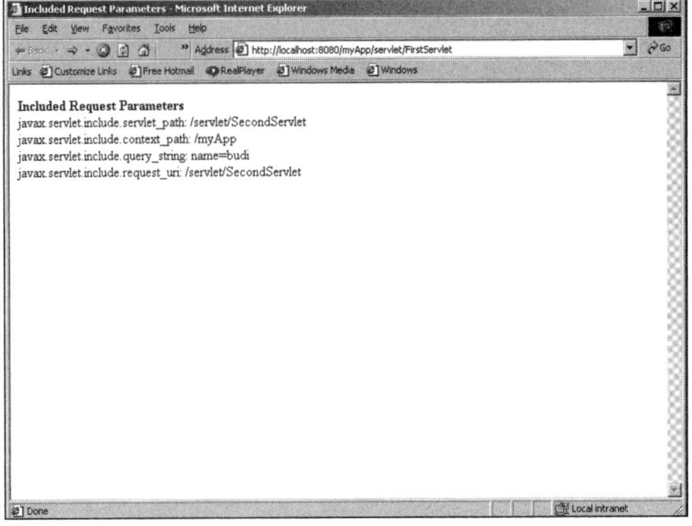

Figure 3.17 The included request parameters.

Forwarding Processing Control

Unlike the include method, the forward method of the RequestDispatcher interface may be called only by the calling servlet if no output has been committed to the client. If output exists in the response buffer that has not been committed, the buffer must be cleared before the target servlet's service method is called. If the response has been committed prior to calling the forward method, an IllegalStateException will be thrown. For example, the servlet in Listing 3.15 will raise an error because the flushBuffer method is called before the forward method.

Listing 3.15 **Forwarding Control After the Buffer Is Flushed**

```
import javax.servlet.*;
import javax.servlet.http.*;
import java.io.*;

public class FirstServlet extends HttpServlet {

  public void doGet(HttpServletRequest request,
  HttpServletResponse response)
  throws ServletException, IOException {

    response.setContentType("text/html");
    PrintWriter out = response.getWriter();
    out.println("<HTML>");
    out.println("<HEAD>");
    out.println("<TITLE>Included Request Parameters</TITLE>");
    out.println("</HEAD>");
    out.println("<BODY>");
    out.println("<B>Included Request Parameters</B><BR>");
    response.flushBuffer();
    RequestDispatcher rd =
      request.getRequestDispatcher("/servlet/SecondServlet");
    rd.forward(request, response);
    out.println("asdfaf</BODY>");
    out.println("</HTML>");
  }
}
```

The forward method also can be used to forward the request to a static content. Again, the flushBuffer method must not be called beforehand.

The forward method is also a good replacement for the sendRedirect method of the HttpServletResponse interface. You may recall that with the sendRedirect method there is a round trip to the client. If you are redirecting the user to a servlet or a page in the current application, you can use the forward method instead. There is no round trip to the browser when using the forward method; therefore, this gives the user a faster response.

The following example rewrites the Login servlet from Listing 3.6. Instead of using the sendRedirect method, the servlet uses a RequestDispatcher to forward the request to the WelcomeServlet servlet when the login was successful. The code for the modified Login servlet is given in Listing 3.16 and the code for the WelcomeServlet servlet is shown in Listing 3.17.

Listing 3.16 **The LoginServlet Servlet**

```
import javax.servlet.*;
import javax.servlet.http.*;
import java.io.*;
import java.util.*;

public class LoginServlet extends HttpServlet {

  private void sendLoginForm(HttpServletResponse response,
    boolean withErrorMessage)
    throws ServletException, IOException {
    response.setContentType("text/html");
    PrintWriter out = response.getWriter();
    out.println("<HTML>");
    out.println("<HEAD>");
    out.println("<TITLE>Login</TITLE>");
    out.println("</HEAD>");
    out.println("<BODY>");

    if (withErrorMessage)
      out.println("Login failed. Please try again.<BR>");

    out.println("<BR>");
    out.println("<BR>Please enter your user name and password.");
    out.println("<BR><FORM METHOD=POST>");
    out.println("<BR>User Name: <INPUT TYPE=TEXT NAME=userName>");
    out.println("<BR>Password: <INPUT TYPE=PASSWORD NAME=password>");
    out.println("<BR><INPUT TYPE=SUBMIT VALUE=Submit>");
    out.println("</FORM>");
    out.println("</BODY>");
    out.println("</HTML>");

  }
  public void doGet(HttpServletRequest request, HttpServletResponse response)
    throws ServletException, IOException {
    sendLoginForm(response, false);
  }

  public void doPost(HttpServletRequest request,
    HttpServletResponse response)
    throws ServletException, IOException {
    String userName = request.getParameter("userName");
```

```
    String password = request.getParameter("password");
    if (userName!=null && password!=null &&
      userName.equals("jamesb") && password.equals("007")) {
      RequestDispatcher rd = request.getRequestDispatcher("WelcomeServlet");
      rd.forward(request, response);
    }
    else {
      sendLoginForm(response, true);
    }

  }
}
```

Listing 3.17 **The WelcomeServlet Servlet**

```
import javax.servlet.*;
import javax.servlet.http.*;
import java.io.*;

public class WelcomeServlet extends HttpServlet {
  public void doPost(HttpServletRequest request,
    HttpServletResponse response) throws ServletException, IOException {
    response.setContentType("text/html");
    PrintWriter out = response.getWriter();
    out.println("<HTML>");
    out.println("<HEAD>");
    out.println("<TITLE>Welcome</TITLE>");
    out.println("</HEAD>");
    out.println("<BODY>");
    out.println("<P>Welcome to the Bulbul's and Boni's Web Site.</P>");
    out.println("</BODY>");
    out.println("</HTML>");
  }
}
```

> **Note**
> If a request is dispatched from doGet, the doGet method of the destination servlet will be invoked. If it is from doPost, the doPost method of the destination servlet will be invoked.

Summary

In this chapter, you have learned how to use some of the classes and interfaces from the javax.servlet.http package. You have been shown a number of examples that demonstrate the use of HttpServlet, HttpServletRequest and HttpServletResponse.

In addition, this chapter introduced you to the RequestDispatcher interface. This interface is useful for including other resources and forwarding the request to another resource.

The next chapter discusses database access using the Java Database Connectivity (JDBC) technology. This is an important chapter considering that almost all non-trivial web applications involve accessing data in a database.

4

Accessing Databases with JDBC

MOST WEB APPLICATIONS USE A DATABASE. Database accessing and programming therefore play a significant role in web development. In this chapter, you examine how data can be stored, retrieved, and manipulated. In Java, the technology that enables database access and manipulation is called Java Database Connectivity (JDBC).

JDBC has two parts: the JDBC Core Application Programming Interface (API) and the JDBC Optional Package API. The JDBC Core API is the main part of JDBC and when people talk about JDBC, they often are referring to this part.

The JDBC Core API is part of the Java 2, Standard Edition (J2SE) and takes the form of the classes and interfaces in the java.sql package. At the time of writing, the most recent version is 3.0. You use the members of the java.sql package primarily for basic database programming.

The JDBC Optional Package API is specified in the javax.sql package and is currently in version 2.0. The javax.sql package supports connection pooling, distributed transactions, rowsets, and so on. Of these, connection pooling is the most important in servlet programming; it is therefore explored in this chapter. You can download this package from `http://java.sun.com/products/jdbc/download.html`.

JDBC is a broad topic, and a complete discussion of its object model requires a book of its own. This chapter starts with a look at the object model in the java.sql package, but does not attempt to explain JDBC thoroughly. Some of the features in JDBC do not even suit our needs in web programming. For example, JDBC supports cursors that can scroll back, but using this type of cursor in a servlet is not tolerable for efficiency reasons. If you want to know more about JDBC, refer to the JDBC web site, `http://java.sun.com/products/jdbc/index.html`.

With the exception of the section, "Connection Pooling," toward the end of this chapter, the examples use the interfaces and classes of the java.sql package. A discussion of this package at the beginning of this chapter provides the uninitiated reader with enough JDBC knowledge to build database-enabling servlets. However, the discussion assumes familiarity with Structured Query Language (SQL). After the initial discussion, this chapter provides an easy passage to database programming in servlets in the section, "Four Steps to Getting to the Database." (If you are already a JDBC expert, you may want to skip that section.)

The java.sql Package

The java.sql package provides the API for accessing and processing data in a data source. The most important members of the java.sql package are as follows:

- The DriverManager class
- The Driver interface
- The Connection interface
- The Statement interface
- The ResultSet interface
- The PreparedStatement interface
- The ResultSetMetaData interface

Each of the types is briefly discussed in the following sections.

The DriverManager Class

The DriverManager class provides static methods for managing JDBC drivers. Each JDBC driver you want to use must be registered with the DriverManager. The JDBC driver of the database to which you want to connect is supplied either by the database vendor or a third party. You use different

JDBC drivers for different database servers. For example, the JDBC driver for Microsoft SQL Server is different from the one used to access Oracle databases. JDBC drivers are discussed in more detail in the section, "Four Steps to Getting to the Database."

To load a JDBC driver from a servlet or JSP page, you copy the JDBC driver file for a particular database server (normally a .jar file) to the WEB-INF\lib directory under your application directory. Create the lib directory, if it doesn't exist, and then use the following code:

```
try {
  Class.forName("JDBC.driver");
}
catch (ClassNotFoundException e) {
  // driver not found
}
```

In this case, *JDBC.driver* is the fully qualified name of the JDBC driver class. This name can be found in the documentation accompanying the JDBC driver.

The DriverManager class's most important method is getConnection that returns a java.sql.Connection object. This method has three overloads whose signatures are as follows:

```
public static Connection getConnection(String url)
public static Connection getConnection(String url, Properties info)
public static Connection getConnection(String url, String user, String
password)
```

The Driver Interface

The Driver interface is implemented by every JDBC driver class. The driver class itself is loaded and registered with the DriverManager, and the DriverManager can manage multiple drivers for any given connection request. In the case where there are multiple drivers registered, the DriverManager will ask each driver in turn to try to connect to the target URL.

The Connection Interface

The Connection interface represents a connection to the database. An instance of the Connection interface is obtained from the getConnection method of the DriverManager class.

close

The close method immediately closes and releases a Connection object instead of waiting for it to be released automatically. Its signature is as follows:

```
public void close() throws SQLException
```

isClosed

You use this method to test whether the Connection object is closed. The signature of this method is as follows:

```
public boolean isClosed() throws SQLException
```

createStatement

The createStatement method is used to create a Statement object for sending SQL statements to the database. If the same SQL statement is executed many times, it is more efficient to use a PreparedStatement object.

This method has two overloads with the following signatures:

```
public Statement createStatement() throws SQLException
public Statement createStatement
(int resultSetType,
int resultSetConcurrency) throws SQLException
```

prepareStatement

You use the prepareStatement method to create a PreparedStatement object. Its signature is as follows:

```
public PreparedStatement prepareStatement()throws SQLException
```

getAutoCommit

The getAutoCommit method returns a boolean specifying the current auto-commit state. The signature of this method is as follows:

```
public boolean getAutoCommit() throws SQLException
```

This method returns true if auto-commit is enabled and false if auto-commit is not enabled. By default, auto-commit is enabled.

setAutoCommit

The setAutoCommit method sets the auto-commit state of the Connection object. Its signature is as follows:

```
public void setAutoCommit(boolean autocommit) throws SQLException
```

commit

You use the commit method to commit a transaction. The signature of this method is as follows:

```
public void commit() throws SQLException
```

rollback

You use the rollback method to roll back a transaction. Its signature is as follows:

```
public void rollback() throws SQLException
```

The Statement Interface

You use the statement interface method to execute an SQL statement and obtain the results that are produced. The two most important methods of this interface are executeQuery and executeUpdate.

executeQuery

The executeQuery method executes an SQL statement that returns a single ResultSet object. Its signature is as follows:

```
public ResultSet executeQuery(String sql) throws SQLException
```

executeUpdate

The executeUpdate method executes an insert, update, and delete SQL statement. The method returns the number of records affected by the SQL statement execution, and its signature is as follows:

```
public int executeUpdate(String sql)
```

The ResultSet Interface

The ResultSet interface represents a table-like database result set. A ResultSet object maintains a cursor pointing to its current row of data. Initially, the cursor is positioned before the first row. The following are some important methods of the ResultSet interface.

isFirst

The isFirst method indicates whether the cursor points to the first record in the ResultSet. Its signature is as follows:

```
public boolean isFirst() throws SQLException
```

isLast

The isLast method indicates whether the cursor points to the last record in the ResultSet. Its signature is as follows:

```
public boolean isLast() throws SQLException
```

next

The next method moves the cursor to the next record, returning true if the current row is valid and false if there are no more records in the ResultSet object. The method's signature is as follows:

```
public boolean next() throws SQLException
```

getMetaData

The getMetaData method returns the ResultSetMetaData object representing the meta data of the ResultSet. The signature of the method is as follows:

```
public ResultSetMetaData getMetaDate() throws SQLException
```

In addition to the previous methods, you can use several get*XXX* methods to obtain the value of the specified column in the row pointed by the cursor. In this case, *XXX* represents the data type returned by the method at the specified index, and each get*XXX* method accepts the index position of the column in the ResultSet. The column index 1 indicates the first column. The signature of this method is as follows:

```
public XXX getXXX(int columnIndex) throws SQLException
```

For example, the getString method has the following signature and returns the specified cell as String:

```
public String getString(int columnIndex) throws SQLException
```

The PreparedStatement Interface

The PreparedStatement interface extends the Statement interface and represents a precompiled SQL statement. You use an instance of this interface to execute efficiently an SQL statement multiple times.

The ResultSetMetaData Interface

The ResultSetMetaData interface represents the meta data of a ResultSet object. The following sections introduce the most important methods.

getColumnCount

The getColumnCount method returns the number of columns in the ResultSet whose meta data is represented by the ResultSetMetaData object. Its signature is as follows:

```
public int getColumnCount() throws SQLException
```

getColumnName

The getColumnName method returns the column name as the specified column index. Its signature is as follows:

```
public String getColumnName(int columnIndex) throws SQLException
```

The first column is indicated by index number 1.

Four Steps to Getting to the Database

This section explains what it takes to access a database and manipulate data in it.

Before you can manipulate data in a database, you need to connect to that database server. After you get the connection, you can communicate with the database server. You can send an SQL query to retrieve data from a table, update records, insert new records, or delete data you no longer need. You also can do more than manipulate data: You can invoke a stored procedure, create a table, and more.

Accessing a database with JDBC can be summarized in the following four steps:

1. Load the JDBC database driver.
2. Create a connection.
3. Create a statement.
4. Create a resultset, if you expect the database server to send back some data.

The discussion of each of these steps can be found in the following sections.

Step 1: Load a JDBC Database Driver

Database servers have their own proprietary "languages" for communication. This means that if you want to communicate with a database server, you need to understand its language. Fortunately, there are "translators" that can interface Java code with these database servers. These translators take the form of JDBC drivers. In other words, if you want to access a particular database, you need to get the JDBC driver for that database.

JDBC Drivers are available for most popular databases today. Oracle, Sybase, DB2, Microsoft SQL Server, MySQL—you name it. Drivers are even available for Open Database Connectivity (ODBC), which means that if you can't find a JDBC driver for a certain database but that database can be connected through ODBC, you still can access the database through ODBC.

These JDBC drivers come at various prices and quality. Some are free and some are pricey. Some are slow, and some are lightning fast. The list of JDBC drivers can be found at `http://industry.java.sun.com/products/jdbc/drivers`.

Driver Types

Not all JDBC drivers are created equal. As mentioned previously, some are fast and some are slow. Slower drivers are not necessarily inefficient code. Some drivers are slower than others due to their architectural limitation. Depending on the architecture, a JDBC driver can fall into one of four types: Type 1, Type 2, Type 3, and Type 4.

JDBC started with Type 1 drivers. Today this type is normally the slowest, used only when you have no other alternative. Type 1 drivers are drivers that provide access to ODBC drivers and also are called the *JDBC-ODBC Bridge* driver. This driver is included in the J2SE and J2EE distribution and originally played an important role to help JDBC gain market acceptance. Why the bridge? At the moment JDBC was conceived, ODBC had already ruled the database connectivity world. Sun played a good strategy by enabling Java programmers to access any database server that could be accessed through ODBC.

As previously mentioned, you don't use Type 1 drivers in production, unless you can't find other drivers for that database. For rapid prototyping, however, these drivers are acceptable. For example, if you need to prove a concept and a Microsoft Access database is all you have, the JDBC-ODBC Bridge can allow access to it in no time.

Note that you need to set up an ODBC Data Source Name (DSN) on the computer you use to connect to the database. Some ODBC native code and, in many cases, native database client code must be loaded on each machine that uses this type of driver. Hence, this kind of driver is generally most appropriate when automatic installation and downloading of a Java technology application is not important.

Setting Up an ODBC Data Source Name

To set up an ODBC data source name, follow these steps:

1. Open the ODBC Data Source Administration dialog box from the Control Panel.
2. Click the System DSN tab.
3. Click the Add button.
4. Select a driver name from the list of ODBC drivers.
5. Enter the needed information in the Setup dialog box that appears.
6. Click OK to close the dialog box.

Type 2 drivers are drivers written in part Java and part native API to convert JDBC calls into calls on the client API for Oracle, Sybase, Informix, DB2, or other DBMS. Note that, like the bridge driver, this style of driver requires that some binary code be loaded on each client machine.

Type 3 drivers are drivers written to use the network protocol to translate JDBC API calls into a DBMS-independent net protocol, which is then translated to a DBMS protocol by a server. This net server middleware is able to connect all of its Java technology-based clients to many different databases. The specific protocol used depends on the vendor. In general, this is the most flexible JDBC API alternative—and most likely, all vendors of this solution will provide products suitable for Intranet use. In order for these products also to support Internet access, they must handle the additional requirements for security, access through firewalls, and so forth, that the web imposes. Several vendors are adding JDBC technology-based drivers to their existing database middleware products.

Type 4 drivers are pure Java. They are written to use the native protocol to convert JDBC technology calls into the network protocol directly used by DBMSs. This allows a direct call from the client machine to the DBMS server and is a practical solution for Intranet access. Because many of these protocols are proprietary, the database vendors themselves will be the primary source for this style of driver.

Note

For the list of JDBC drivers for various databases, see `http://industry.java.sun.com/products/jdbc/drivers`.

Installing JDBC Drivers

Because JDBC drivers normally come in a .jar file, the first thing you need to do after you get the driver is tell Tomcat where to find it by copying the .jar file into the WEB-INF\lib directory under your application directory. Create the lib directory if it doesn't exist.

Note

If you are using the JDBC-ODBC bridge, you do not need to install the driver because it's already included in your Java Development Kit (JDK).

Now that the driver is within reach, you can create an instance of it using the static forName method of the Class class, passing the driver's fully qualified class name. The following is the code:

```
Class.forName(driverName)
```

For example, for a MySQL database, the most popular driver is the Type 4 driver developed by Mark Matthews of Purdue University and downloadable from `http://www.worldserver.com/mm.mysql/`. This driver is available under the GNU General Public License. Assuming that you have downloaded it and made it available to your Java code, you can load it using the following code:

```
Class.forName("org.gjt.mm.mysql.Driver");
```

Of course, the *driverName* argument will be different if you are using a different driver for MySQL.

For an ODBC database, the code that loads the driver is the following:

```
Class.forName("sun.jdbc.odbc.JdbcOdbcDriver");
```

Or, if you are using the FreeTds Type 4 JDBC driver to connect to a Microsoft SQL Server, you use this code to load the driver:

```
Class.forName("com.internetcds.jdbc.tds.Driver");
```

Your JDBC driver should come with documentation that tells you the driver class name to use.

> **Note**
>
> Microsoft SQL Server 2000 has its own Type 4 JDBC Driver, downloadable from `http://www.microsoft.com/sql/downloads/2000/jdbc.asp`.

If you plan to connect to different database servers in your code, you need to load all JDBC drivers for every database. For example, if you need to connect to an ODBC database as well as a MySQL database, you load both drivers by using the following code:

```
Class.forName("sun.jdbc.odbc.JdbcOdbcDriver");
Class.forName("org.gjt.mm.mysql.Driver");
```

Step 2: Creating a Connection

After you register a JDBC driver with the DriverManager, you can use it to get a connection to the database. In JDBC, a database connection is represented by the java.sql.Connection interface. You use the DriverManager class's getConnection method to obtain a Connection object.

As mentioned in the previous section, the getConnection method has three overloads, two of which are normally used. The first overload takes three arguments: url, userName, and password. Its signature is as follows:

```
public static Connection getConnection(String url,
  String user, String password)
  throws SQLException
```

The url part is the trickiest element in this method. The url is of this syntax:

```
jdbc:subprotocol:subname
```

The subprotocol and subname parts depend on the database server you use. The documentation of the JDBC driver should tell you the subprotocol and subname to use.

If you are using a JDBC-ODBC bridge driver, the subprotocol is "odbc" and the subname is the Data Source Name (DSN) for that database. For instance, for a DSN called MarketingData, your URL will be:

```
jdbc:odbc:MarketingData
```

If you want to connect to a MySQL database, the subprotocol part is "mysql" and the subname part should be given the name of the machine and the database. For example, for a database named Fred, use the following:

```
jdbc:mysql///Fred
```

If one of the drivers you loaded recognizes the JDBC URL passed to the getConnection method, that driver will try to establish a connection to the database specified in the URL. For example, the following code shows how you obtain a Connection object to a MySQL database named Fred in a server called robusta. You also pass the user "admin" and the password "secret" to the getConnection method.

```
Connection connection =
  DriverManager.getConnection("jdbc:mysql///robusta/Fred", "admin", "secret");
```

You use the following code to get access to an ODBC database whose DSN is MarketingData, using the user name "sa" and password "1945":

```
Connection connection =
  DriverManager.getConnection("jdbc:odbc:MarketingData", "sa", "1945");
```

If the connection does not require you to login, you can pass null as arguments for the user and password parts.

The other overload of the getConnection method allows you to pass the user and password information in the URL. Its signature is as follows:

```
public static Connection getConnection(String url)
  throws SQLException
```

For example, you can use the following URL to connect to a MySQL database named Fred in robustathat requires the user name "me" and password "pwd":

```
DriverManager.getConnection("jdbc:mysql://robusta/Fred?user=me&password=pwd");
```

Or, to connect to an ODBC database named MarketingData that is accessible without a login name and password, you use the following:

```
Connection connection =
  DriverManager.getConnection("jdbc:odbc:MarketingData");
```

If one of the drivers you loaded recognizes the JDBC URL supplied to the method DriverManager.getConnection, that driver will establish a connection to the DBMS specified in the JDBC URL.

The getConnection method is probably the first and the last method of the DriverManager class you need to know to write Java programs that access databases. Other methods are needed only if you are writing a JDBC driver yourself.

The Connection object obtained through the DriverManager class's getConnection method is an open connection you can use to pass your SQL statements to the database server. As such, you do not need to have a special method to open a Connection.

Let's see what we can do with it in the next subsection: "Step 3 Creating a Statement."

Step 3: Creating a Statement

After you have a Connection object, your SQL skill takes over. Basically, you can pass any SQL statement that your database server understands. The level of understanding is different from one server to another. For example, an Oracle database is comfortable with subqueries, whereas a MySQL server is not. Also, whether your SQL statement will be executed successfully on the database server depends on the permission level of the user who passed the query to the database. If the user has the permission to view all the tables in the database, you can pass an SQL SELECT statement to it and expect some return. If the user has the permission to update records but not to delete records, you can only update, not delete, records. You should understand these factors before you program your JDBC code.

After you have a Connection object from the DriverManage.getConnection method, you are ready to pass a SQL statement. To do this, you need to create another JDBC object called Statement. You can do this using the createStatement method of the Connection interface. Although there are two overloads of this method, the one that you almost always use is the no-argument overload. Its signature is as follows:

```
public Statement createStatement() throws SQLException
```

Therefore, to create a Statement object from an open Connection object, you write the following:

```
// connection is an open Connection object
Statement statement = connection.createStatement();
```

Next, use the methods in the Statement class interface to manipulate your data or data structure. You will use two important methods: executeUpdate and executeQuery. The signatures for both methods are as follows:

```
public int executeUpdate(String sql) throws SQLException
public ResultSet executeQuery(String sql) throws SQLException
```

The executeUpdate and executeQuery Methods

Both executeUpdate and executeQuery methods accept a String containing an SQL statement. The SQL statement does not end with a DBMS statement terminator, which can vary from DBMS to DBMS. For example, Oracle uses a semicolon (;) to indicate the end of a statement, and Sybase uses the word go. The driver you are using will automatically supply the appropriate statement terminator, and you will not need to include it in your JDBC code.

The executeUpdate method executes an SQL INSERT, UPDATE, or DELETE statement and also data definition language (DDL) statements to create, drop, and alter tables. This method returns the row count for INSERT, UPDATE, or DELETE statements or returns 0 for SQL statements that return nothing.

The executeQuery method executes an SQL SELECT statement that returns data. This method returns a single ResultSet object that is discussed next. The ResultSet object contains the data produced by the given query. This method never returns a null.

For example, to create a table named Addresses with two fields, you can use the following code:

```
String sql = "CREATE TABLE Addresses " +
  "(FirstName VARCHAR(32), LastName VARCHAR(32)";
statement.executeUpdate(sql);
```

And, to insert a record in the Addresses table, you use the following code:

```
String sql = "INSERT INTO Addresses " +
"VALUES ('Don', 'Bradman')";
statement.executeUpdate(sql);
```

You use executeQuery when you expect a ResultSet object. You learn about the ResultSet interface in the next section.

> **Tip**
>
> The close method of Statement releases immediately this Statement object's database and JDBC resources instead of waiting for this to happen when it is automatically closed at garbage collection. Releasing resources as soon as you are finished with them is good practice—that way, you avoid tying up database resources.

Step 4: Creating a ResultSet

A ResultSet is the representation of a database table that is returned from a Statement object. A ResultSet object maintains a cursor pointing to its current row of data. When the cursor is first returned, it is positioned before the first row. To access the first row of the ResultSet, you need to call the next() method of the ResultSet interface.

The next() method moves the cursor to the next row and can return either a true or false value. It returns true if the new current row is valid; it returns false if there are no more rows. Normally, you use this method in a while loop to iterate through the ResultSet object.

To get the data from the ResultSet, you can use one of many the get*XXX* methods of ResultSet, such as getInt, getLong, and so on. getShort You use the getInt method, for example, to obtain the value of the designated column in the current row of this ResultSet object as an int in the Java programming language. The getLong gets the cell data as a long, etc. The most commonly used method is getString, which returns the cell data as a String. Using getString is preferable in many cases because you don't need to worry about the data type of the table field in the database.

The getString method, similar to other get*XXX* methods, has two overloads that allow you to retrieve a cell's data by passing either the column index or the column name. The signatures of the two overloads of getString are as follows:

```
public String getString(int columnIndex) throws SQLException
public String getString(String columnName) throws SQLException
```

The following example illustrates the use of the next() method as well as the getString method. The code is used to retrieve the FirstName and LastName columns from a table called Users. It then iterates the returned ResultSet and prints to the console all the first names and last names in the format "first name:last name". As you consider the following code, assume that you already have a Statement object called statement:

```
String sql = "SELECT FirstName, LastName FROM Users";
ResultSet resultSet = statement.executeQuery(sql);
```

```
while (resultSet.next()) {
  System.out.println(resultSet.getString(1) + ":" +
resultSet.getString("LastName") );
}
```

The first column is retrieved by passing its column index, which is 1 for the first column. The second column is obtained by passing its column name.

Another important method is the close method that closes the ResultSet object when it is no longer used. The close method releases this ResultSet object's database and JDBC resources immediately instead of waiting for this to happen when it is automatically closed. A ResultSet object will be closed automatically when it is garbage collected or when the Statement object that generated it is closed, re-executed, or used to retrieve the next result from a sequence of multiple results. Always call the close method to explicitly close the ResultSet object. Completing your example code, you should put the following code right after you finish accessing the ResultSet object:

```
resultSet.close();
```

Note that if an SQL query results in zero row, the Statement object will return a ResultSet object containing no row, not a null.

Putting It All Together

This section summarizes the four steps just discussed by presenting an example that uses the FreeTds Type 4 JDBC driver to access the Users table in a Microsoft SQL Server database named Registration. The database server is called Lampoon and you need to pass the user name "sa" and password "s3m1c0nduct0r" to login to the database server. The SQL statement queries two columns: FirstName and LastName. Upon retrieving the ResultSet, the statement will loop through it to print all the first names and last names in the ResultSet. The code is given in Listing 4.1.

Listing 4.1 **Accessing a Database**

```
try {
  Class.forName("com.internetcds.jdbc.tds.Driver");
  Connection con = DriverManager.getConnection(
    "jdbc:freetds:sqlserver://Lampoon/Registration",
    "sa", " s3m1c0nduct0r");
  System.out.println("got connection");

  Statement s = con.createStatement();
  String sql =
    "INSERT INTO UserReg VALUES ('a', 'b', '12/12/2001', 'f')";
  s.executeUpdate(sql);
```

continues

Listing 4.1 **Continued**

```
    sql = "SELECT FirstName, LastName FROM Users";
    ResultSet rs = s.executeQuery(sql);
    while (rs.next()) {
      System.out.println(rs.getString(1) + " " + rs.getString(2));
    }
    rs.close();
    s.close();
    con.close();
  }
  catch (ClassNotFoundException e1) {
    System.out.println(e1.toString());
  }
  catch (SQLException e2) {
    System.out.println(e2.toString());
  }
  catch (Exception e3) {
    System.out.println(e3.toString());
  }
```

On my machine, the code returns the following at the console. The result displayed depends on the data stored in your table, of course.

```
Jimmy Barnes
Richard Myers
George Lucas
```

A Database-Based Login Servlet

As your first example of connecting a database from a servlet, I would like to present the type of servlet that is probably built most often: a Login servlet. Unlike the Login servlet in Chapter 3, "Writing Servlet Applications," in which you hard-coded the user name and password that log in a user, this servlet matches the entered user name and password against the values of the UserName and Password columns in a table called Users. This table may have other columns, but those other columns are not relevant here.

When the user types the URL in the Location or Address box and first calls the servlet, its doGet method is invoked. The servlet then does what a login servlet should do—challenges the user to type in a user name and password. What the doGet does is call the private method sendLoginForm, which sends the HTML page for the user to login.

```
sendLoginForm(response, false);
```

The sendLoginForm method accepts two arguments: a HttpServletResponse object that the method can use to send output to the browser, and a boolean. This boolean is a flag to indicate whether an error message should be sent along with the form. The error message tells the user that the previous login has failed. When the servlet is first called, of course, no error message is sent; thus the false value is given for the second argument of the sendLoginForm method called from doGet. The sendLoginForm method is given in Listing 4.2. The Login page is shown in Figure 4.1.

Listing 4.2 **The LoginServlet's sendLoginForm Method**

```
private void sendLoginForm(HttpServletResponse response,
    boolean withErrorMessage)
    throws ServletException, IOException {

    response.setContentType("text/html");
    PrintWriter out = response.getWriter();
    out.println("<HTML>");
    out.println("<HEAD>");
    out.println("<TITLE>Login</TITLE>");
    out.println("</HEAD>");
    out.println("<BODY>");
    out.println("<CENTER>");

    if (withErrorMessage)
      out.println("Login failed. Please try again.<BR>");

    out.println("<BR>");
    out.println("<BR><H2>Login Page</H2>");
    out.println("<BR>");
    out.println("<BR>Please enter your user name and password.");
    out.println("<BR>");
    out.println("<BR><FORM METHOD=POST>");
    out.println("<TABLE>");
    out.println("<TR>");
    out.println("<TD>User Name:</TD>");
    out.println("<TD><INPUT TYPE=TEXT NAME=userName></TD>");
    out.println("</TR>");
    out.println("<TR>");
    out.println("<TD>Password:</TD>");
    out.println("<TD><INPUT TYPE=PASSWORD NAME=password></TD>");
    out.println("</TR>");
    out.println("<TR>");
    out.println("<TD ALIGN=RIGHT COLSPAN=2>");
    out.println("<INPUT TYPE=SUBMIT VALUE=Login></TD>");
    out.println("</TR>");
    out.println("</TABLE>");
    out.println("</FORM>");
    out.println("</CENTER>");
    out.println("</BODY>");
    out.println("</HTML>");
  }
```

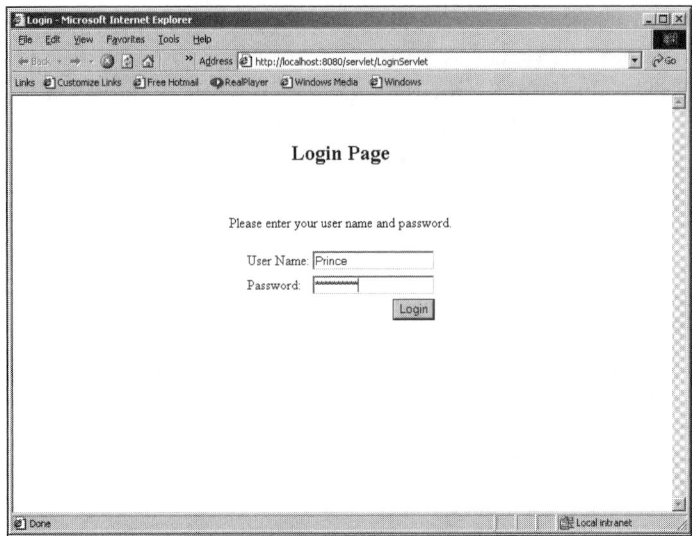

Figure 4.1 The database-based Login servlet.

The user can then type the user name and password to login and click the Submit button. Upon submit, the doPost method is invoked. The first thing it does is obtain the userName and password from the HttpServletRequest object, as follows:

```
String userName = request.getParameter("userName");
String password = request.getParameter("password");
```

Then, the method passes the userName and password to the login method. This method returns true if the user name and password are correct; otherwise, it returns false. On successful login, the request is dispatched to another servlet, as follows:

```
RequestDispatcher rd =
  request.getRequestDispatcher("AnotherServlet");
rd.forward(request, response);
```

If the login failed, the doPost calls the sendLoginForm method again, this time with an error message, as follows:

```
sendLoginForm(response, true);
```

The doPost method is given in Listing 4.3.

Listing 4.3 **The LoginServlet's doPost Method**

```
public void doPost(HttpServletRequest request,
    HttpServletResponse response)
    throws ServletException, IOException {

    String userName = request.getParameter("userName");
    String password = request.getParameter("password");
    if (login(userName, password)) {
      RequestDispatcher rd =
        request.getRequestDispatcher("AnotherServlet");
      rd.forward(request, response);
    }
    else {
      sendLoginForm(response, true);
    }
  }
```

Here is the part that does the authentication: the login method. The method tries to authenticate the user by trying to retrieve a record whose UserName field is userName and Password field is the same as password. If a record is found, the login succeeds; otherwise, the login fails.

The login method first loads the JDBC driver, as follows:

```
Class.forName("sun.jdbc.odbc.JdbcOdbcDriver");
```

This example uses a JDBC-ODBC driver; however, as you learned in the previous section, you can use any other driver without changing the rest of your code.

With a JDBC driver, you can create a Connection object and call its createStatement method to create a Statement object, as follows:

```
Connection con =
  DriverManager.getConnection("jdbc:odbc:JavaWeb");
Statement s = con.createStatement();
```

Note that you use the getConnection method overload that accepts an argument—the URL.

When a Statement object is available, you can call its executeQuery method, passing an SQL statement of the following syntax:

```
SELECT UserName FROM Users
WHERE UserName=userName
AND Password=password
```

To determine whether there is any record in the ResultSet object, you can call its next() method. This method returns true if there is a record; otherwise, it returns false. On true, the login method returns a true, indicating a successful login. A false return value indicates otherwise. The login method is given in Listing 4.4, and the complete code for LoginServlet is given in Listing 4.5.

Listing 4.4 **The LoginServlet's login Method**

```
boolean login(String userName, String password) {
  try {
    Class.forName("sun.jdbc.odbc.JdbcOdbcDriver");
    Connection con =
      DriverManager.getConnection("jdbc:odbc:JavaWeb");
    System.out.println("got connection");

    Statement s = con.createStatement();
    String sql = "SELECT UserName FROM Users" +
      " WHERE UserName='" + userName + "'" +
      " AND Password='" + password + "'";
    ResultSet rs = s.executeQuery(sql);
    if (rs.next()) {
      rs.close();
      s.close();
      con.close();
      return true;
    }
    rs.close();
    s.close();
    con.close();
  }
  catch (ClassNotFoundException e) {
    System.out.println(e.toString());
  }
  catch (SQLException e) {
    System.out.println(e.toString());
  }
  catch (Exception e) {
    System.out.println(e.toString());
  }
  return false;
}
```

Listing 4.5 **The LoginServlet Servlet**

```
import javax.servlet.*;
import javax.servlet.http.*;
import java.io.*;
import java.util.*;
import java.sql.*;

public class LoginServlet extends HttpServlet {

  public void doGet(HttpServletRequest request,
```

```
    HttpServletResponse response)
    throws ServletException, IOException {
    sendLoginForm(response, false);
  }

  private void sendLoginForm(HttpServletResponse response,
    boolean withErrorMessage)
    throws ServletException, IOException {

    response.setContentType("text/html");
    PrintWriter out = response.getWriter();
    out.println("<HTML>");
    out.println("<HEAD>");
    out.println("<TITLE>Login</TITLE>");
    out.println("</HEAD>");
    out.println("<BODY>");
    out.println("<CENTER>");

    if (withErrorMessage)
      out.println("Login failed. Please try again.<BR>");

    out.println("<BR>");
    out.println("<BR><H2>Login Page</H2>");
    out.println("<BR>");
    out.println("<BR>Please enter your user name and password.");
    out.println("<BR>");
    out.println("<BR><FORM METHOD=POST>");
    out.println("<TABLE>");
    out.println("<TR>");
    out.println("<TD>User Name:</TD>");
    out.println("<TD><INPUT TYPE=TEXT NAME=userName></TD>");
    out.println("</TR>");
    out.println("<TR>");
    out.println("<TD>Password:</TD>");
    out.println("<TD><INPUT TYPE=PASSWORD NAME=password></TD>");
    out.println("</TR>");
    out.println("<TR>");
    out.println("<TD ALIGN=RIGHT COLSPAN=2>");
    out.println("<INPUT TYPE=SUBMIT VALUE=Login></TD>");
    out.println("</TR>");
    out.println("</TABLE>");
    out.println("</FORM>");
    out.println("</CENTER>");
    out.println("</BODY>");
    out.println("</HTML>");
  }

  public void doPost(HttpServletRequest request,
    HttpServletResponse response)
    throws ServletException, IOException {
```

continues

Listing 4.5 **Continued**

```
    String userName = request.getParameter("userName");
    String password = request.getParameter("password");
    if (login(userName, password)) {
      RequestDispatcher rd =
        request.getRequestDispatcher("AnotherServlet");
      rd.forward(request, response);
    }
    else {
      sendLoginForm(response, true);
    }
  }

  boolean login(String userName, String password) {
    try {
      Class.forName("sun.jdbc.odbc.JdbcOdbcDriver");
      Connection con =
        DriverManager.getConnection("jdbc:odbc:JavaWeb");
      System.out.println("got connection");

      Statement s = con.createStatement();
      String sql = "SELECT UserName FROM Users" +
        " WHERE UserName='" + userName + "'" +
        " AND Password='" + password + "'";
      ResultSet rs = s.executeQuery(sql);
      if (rs.next()) {
        rs.close();
        s.close();
        con.close();
        return true;
      }
      rs.close();
      s.close();
      con.close();
    }
    catch (ClassNotFoundException e) {
      System.out.println(e.toString());
    }
    catch (SQLException e) {
      System.out.println(e.toString());
    }
    catch (Exception e) {
      System.out.println(e.toString());
    }
    return false;
  }
}
```

The Single Quote Factor

The LoginServlet servlet in the previous section works fine, but not perfectly. The servlet passes the user name and password to the login method and the SQL statement is composed on the fly. For example, for user name equals "jeff" and password "java", the SQL statement is as follows:

```
SELECT UserName
FROM Users
WHERE UserName='jeff'
AND Password='java'
```

The values for the user name and the password are enclosed in the single quote pairs, as in 'jeff' and 'java'. A username can be anything, including a name that includes an apostrophe, such as *o'connor*. This is also true for passwords. If the username is "o'connor" and password is "java," the SQL statement will become the following:

```
SELECT UserName
FROM Users
WHERE UserName='o'connor'
AND Password='java'
```

The database engine will encounter a single quote character after the o in "o'connor," and think it sees the end of the value for UserName, and expect a space after it. The engine finds a c instead, and this is confusing to the database server. An error will be thrown.

Does this mean you can't let users have a username that contains an apostrophe? Fortunately, there is a work around. If a string value in an SQL statement contains an apostrophe, you just need to prefix the apostrophe with another apostrophe, resulting in the following SQL statement:

```
SELECT UserName
FROM Users
WHERE UserName='o''connor'
AND Password='java'
```

Now everything works correctly. The LoginServlet servlet in the previous example should be fixed by passing all values entered by the user to a method called fixSQLFieldValue, which accepts a String. This method will replace every occurrence of a single quote character in the String with two single quote characters. The fixSQLFieldValue takes a String whose value may contain a single quote character and doubles every occurrence of it.

The fixSQLFieldValue method uses a StringBuffer with an initial capacity of 1.1 times the length of the argument passed in String object. The 1.1 is based on the estimate that the resulting SQL statement will be at most 10 percent longer. Here is the code:

```
StringBuffer fixedValue = new StringBuffer((int) (length* 1.1));
```

The statement then tests each character of the String in a for loop. If a character is a single quote, it appends two single quote characters to the StringBuffer; otherwise, the character itself is appended, as you see here:

```
for (int i=0; i<length; i++) {
  char c = value.charAt(i);
  if (c=='\'')
    fixedValue.append("''");
  else
    fixedValue.append(c);
}
```

The fixSqlFieldValue method is given in Listing 4.6.

Listing 4.6 **The fixSqlFieldValue Method**

```
public static String fixSqlFieldValue(String value) {
  if (value==null)
    return null;
  int length = value.length();
  StringBuffer fixedValue =
    new StringBuffer((int) (length * 1.1));
  for (int i=0; i<length; i++) {
    char c = value.charAt(i);
    if (c=='\'')
      fixedValue.append("''");
    else
      fixedValue.append(c);
  }
  return fixedValue.toString();
}
```

The login method in Listing 4.5 and Listing 4.6 must pass the userName and password values before composing the SQL statement. With the fixSqlFieldValue method included in the LoginServlet servlet, the part that forms the SQL statement should be modified into the following line:

```
String sql = "SELECT UserName FROM Users" +
  " WHERE UserName='" + fixSqlFieldValue(userName) + "'" +
  " AND Password='" + fixSqlFieldValue(password) + "'";
```

Clearly, the fixSqlFieldValue method should be called every time you compose an SQL statement that includes a value from the user input. The method has been included in the StringUtil class that is part of the com.brainysoftware.java.package included in the CD of this book. The use of this method in the next sample code will be from this package. This at least saves having to write the same code in all classes that need it. This method in the StringUtil class is made static so that you can just call it with the following code:

```
import com.brainysoftware.java.StringUtil
StringUtil.fixSqlFieldValue(string)
```

To use this class, you need to create a directory structure under the /WEB-INF/classes directory under your application directory; that is, you need to create a directory called com under the classes directory, the brainysoftware directory under com, the java directory under the brainysoftware directory, and copy the StringUtil.class there.

Inserting Data into a Table with RegistrationServlet

Inserting a record into a table is a common database task. An example of this is a servlet named RegistrationServlet that takes user input to insert a record into a Users table. The table itself has columns as described in Table 4.1.

Table 4.1 **The Users Table**

Column Name	Column Type	Description
Id	Numeric	An autonumber that serves as the primary key and is auto-incremented by the database.
FirstName	String	The first name of the user.
LastName	String	The last name of the user.
UserName	String	The user name for the user to login. No duplicate allowed.
Password	String	The password for the user to login.

To insert a record containing a user's details, you need to retrieve the values entered by the user and compose an SQL Statement, such as the following:

```
INSERT INTO Users
(FirstName, LastName, UserName, Password)
VALUES
(firstName, lastName, userName, password)
```

The Id column is not included because it's an autonumber. A new unique number will be generated by the database server automatically for the Id column when you insert a new record into the table. Also note that the UserName column value must be unique. No two users can have the same user name.

When first called, the RegistrationServlet displays an HTML form with four text boxes, as shown in Figure 4.2.

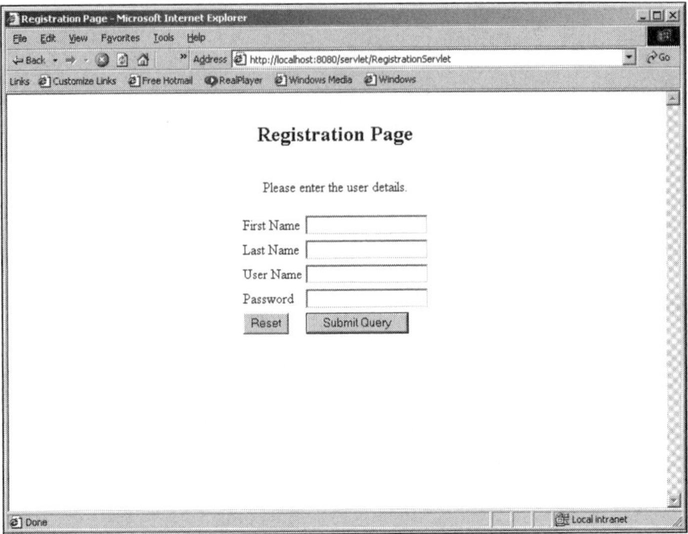

Figure 4.2 The RegistrationServlet.

The user can then fill in the necessary details: first name, last name, and a self-chosen user name and password. The user name must be unique. If the user enters a user name that's already taken, the servlet will display an error message and present the same form again, with the previously typed in values retained (see Figure 4.3).

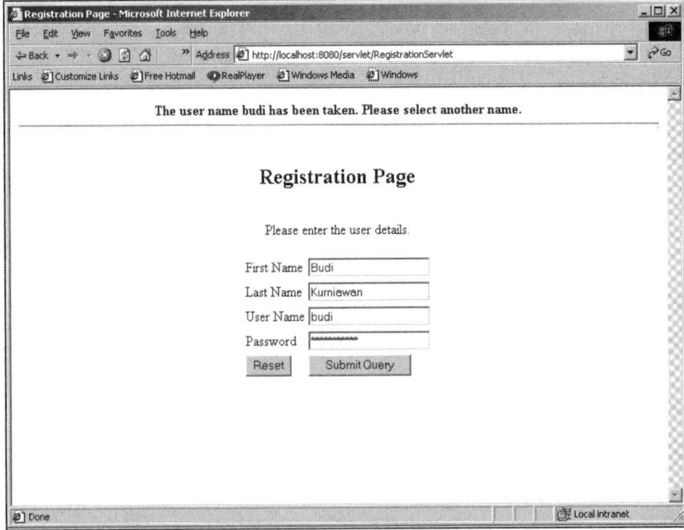

Figure 4.3 Failed registration because the user name has been taken.

If the servlet encounters an unexpected error, the error also will be displayed and the previously entered values retained.

On successful registration, the servlet will display the message "Successfully added one user." and present a clean form. The user then can enter another user's details if desired.

In the RegistrationServlet, the method to display the form is called sendRegistrationForm. The method accepts three arguments: an HttpServletRequest object, an HttpServletResponse object, and a boolean. The boolean indicates whether the previously entered values, if any, should be displayed. The sendRegistrationForm method is given in Listing 4.7. Note that when you need to display a value in an HTML input box, you need to call the encodeHtmlTag method (which is also part of the com.brainysoftware.java.StringUtil class) just in case the value contains one of the four HTML special characters, as described in Chapter 3. The RegistrationServlet therefore imports the com.brainysoftware.java.StringUtil class.

Listing 4.7 **The sendRegistrationForm Method**

```
private void sendRegistrationForm(HttpServletRequest request,
    HttpServletResponse response, boolean displayPreviousValues)
    throws ServletException, IOException {

    PrintWriter out = response.getWriter();
    out.println("<BR><H2>Registration Page</H2>");
    out.println("<BR>Please enter the user details.");
    out.println("<BR>");
    out.println("<BR><FORM METHOD=POST>");
    out.println("<TABLE>");
    out.println("<TR>");
    out.println("<TD>First Name</TD>");
    out.print("<TD><INPUT TYPE=TEXT Name=firstName");

    if (displayPreviousValues)
      out.print(" VALUE=\"" +
      StringUtil.encodeHtmlTag(firstName) + "\"");

    out.println("></TD>");
    out.println("</TR>");
    out.println("<TR>");
    out.println("<TD>Last Name</TD>");
    out.print("<TD><INPUT TYPE=TEXT Name=lastName");

    if (displayPreviousValues)
      out.print(" VALUE=\"" +
      StringUtil.encodeHtmlTag(lastName) + "\"");
```

continues

Listing 4.7 **Continued**

```
    out.println("></TD>");
    out.println("</TR>");
    out.println("<TR>");
    out.println("<TD>User Name</TD>");
    out.print("<TD><INPUT TYPE=TEXT Name=userName");

    if (displayPreviousValues)
      out.print(" VALUE=\"" +
      StringUtil.encodeHtmlTag(userName) + "\"");

    out.println("></TD>");
    out.println("</TR>");
    out.println("<TR>");
    out.println("<TD>Password</TD>");
    out.print("<TD><INPUT TYPE=PASSWORD Name=password");

    if (displayPreviousValues)
      out.print(" VALUE=\"" +
      StringUtil.encodeHtmlTag(password) + "\"");

    out.println("></TD>");
    out.println("</TR>");
    out.println("<TR>");
    out.println("<TD><INPUT TYPE=RESET></TD>");
    out.println("<TD><INPUT TYPE=SUBMIT></TD>");
    out.println("</TR>");
    out.println("</TABLE>");
    out.println("</FORM>");
    out.println("<BR>");
    out.println("<BR>");
  }
```

Unlike the form in the LoginServlet, however, the registration form does not include the <HTML> tag, the head section of the HTML, and the opening <BODY> tag. Nor does it contain the closing </BODY> and </HTML> tags. Page headers can be sent to the browser by calling the sendPageHeader method, whose code is given in Listing 4.8.

Listing 4.8 **The sendPageHeader Method**

```
private void sendPageHeader(HttpServletResponse response)
    throws ServletException, IOException {
    response.setContentType("text/html");
    PrintWriter out = response.getWriter();
    out.println("<HTML>");
    out.println("<HEAD>");
    out.println("<TITLE>Registration Page</TITLE>");
```

```
    out.println("</HEAD>");
    out.println("<BODY>");
    out.println("<CENTER>");
  }
```

The page footer can be sent by calling the sendPageFooter method, listed in Listing 4.9.

Listing 4.9 **The sendPageFooter Method**

```
  private void sendPageFooter(HttpServletResponse response)
    throws ServletException, IOException {
    PrintWriter out = response.getWriter();
    out.println("</CENTER>");
    out.println("</BODY>");
    out.println("</HTML>");
  }
```

When first called, the servlet invokes its doGet method to send the registration form plus all necessary HTML tags to the browser. The doGet method is given in Listing 4.10.

Listing 4.10 **The doGet Method**

```
public void doGet(HttpServletRequest request, HttpServletResponse
  response) throws ServletException, IOException {
    sendPageHeader(response);
    sendRegistrationForm(request, response, false);
    sendPageFooter(response);
  }
```

When the user submits the form, the doPost method is invoked. The doPost method first retrieves the values from the users, as follows:

```
firstName = request.getParameter("firstName");
lastName = request.getParameter("lastName");
userName = request.getParameter("userName");
password = request.getParameter("password");
```

After opening a Connection object and creating a Statement object, the method needs to determine whether the user name has already been taken. It does so by trying to retrieve a record whose UserName field value is userName, as follows:

```
Connection con =
  DriverManager.getConnection("jdbc:odbc:JavaWeb");
Statement s = con.createStatement();
```

```
String sql = "SELECT UserName FROM Users" +
  " WHERE userName='" +
  StringUtil.fixSQLFieldValue(userName) + "'";
ResultSet rs = s.executeQuery(sql);
```

If the ResultSet object returned by the Statement interface's executeQuery method has a record, its next method will return true, indicating that the user name has already been taken; otherwise, false is returned.

If the user name has been taken, a message of "The user name... has been taken" is assigned to the message String and the error flag is set. If not, an SQL statement will be composed on the fly and the executeUpdate method of the Statement object will be called to insert a new record into the Users table, as seen in Figure 4.4.

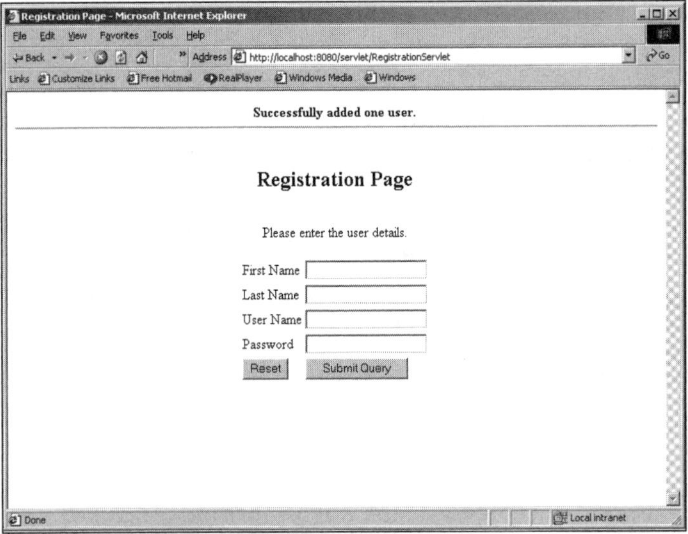

Figure 4.4 Successful registration.

```
if (rs.next()) {
  rs.close();
  message = "The user name <B>" +
    StringUtil.encodeHtmlTag(userName) +
    "</B> has been taken. Please select another name.";
  error = true;
}
else {
  rs.close();
  sql = "INSERT INTO Users" +
```

```
        " (FirstName, LastName, UserName, Password)" +
        " VALUES" +
        " ('" +  StringUtil.fixSQLFieldValue(firstName) + "'," +
        " '" +  StringUtil.fixSQLFieldValue(lastName) + "'," +
        " '" +  StringUtil.fixSQLFieldValue(userName) + "'," +
        " '" +  StringUtil.fixSQLFieldValue(password) + "')";
      int i = s.executeUpdate(sql);
      if (i==1) {
        message = "Successfully added one user.";
      }
    }
```

The last part of the doPost method checks whether the message is null and whether the error flag has been set. If the message is not null, it is sent to the browser, as you see here:

```
    if (message!=null) {
      PrintWriter out = response.getWriter();
      out.println("<B>" + message + "</B><BR>");
      out.println("<HR><BR>");
    }
```

If the error is set, the registration form is sent with the last argument equal to true, indicating the sendRegistrationForm to display the previously entered values. Otherwise, the sendRegistrationForm method is sent with the false value for the last argument, as you see here:

```
  if (error==true)
      sendRegistrationForm(request, response, true);
    else
      sendRegistrationForm(request, response, false);
    sendPageFooter(response);
  }
```

The doPost method is given in Listing 4.11.

Listing 4.11 **The doPost Method**

```
public void doPost(HttpServletRequest request,
    HttpServletResponse response)
    throws ServletException, IOException {
    sendPageHeader(response);

    firstName = request.getParameter("firstName");
    lastName = request.getParameter("lastName");
    userName = request.getParameter("userName");
    password = request.getParameter("password");

    boolean error = false;
    String message = null;
    try {
```

```
      Connection con = DriverManager.getConnection("jdbc:odbc:JavaWeb");
      System.out.println("got connection");

      Statement s = con.createStatement();

      String sql = "SELECT UserName FROM Users" +
        " WHERE userName='" + StringUtil.fixSQLFieldValue(userName) + "'";
      ResultSet rs = s.executeQuery(sql);
      if (rs.next()) {
        rs.close();
        message = "The user name <B>"
          ➥+ StringUtil.encodeHtmlTag(userName) +
          "</B> has been taken. Please select another name.";
        error = true;
      }
      else {
        rs.close();
        sql = "INSERT INTO Users" +
          " (FirstName, LastName, UserName, Password)" +
          " VALUES" +
          " ('" +  StringUtil.fixSQLFieldValue(firstName) + "'," +
          " '" +  StringUtil.fixSQLFieldValue(lastName) + "'," +
          " '" +  StringUtil.fixSQLFieldValue(userName) + "'," +
          " '" +  StringUtil.fixSQLFieldValue(password) + "')";
        int i = s.executeUpdate(sql);
        if (i==1) {
          message = "Successfully added one user.";
        }
      }
      s.close();
      con.close();
    }
    catch (SQLException e) {
      message = "Error." + e.toString();
      error = true;
    }
    catch (Exception e) {
      message = "Error." + e.toString();
      error = true;
    }
    if (message!=null) {
      PrintWriter out = response.getWriter();
      out.println("<B>" + message + "</B><BR>");
      out.println("<HR><BR>");
    }
    if (error==true)
      sendRegistrationForm(request, response, true);
    else
      sendRegistrationForm(request, response, false);
    sendPageFooter(response);
  }
```

You may have noticed that the code that loads the JDBC driver is missing from the doPost method. Instead, it has been moved to the init method of the servlet. The JDBC driver needs to be loaded only once, so it is appropriate to put it in the init method, which is only called once during the life cycle of the servlet. The init method is given in Listing 4.12.

Listing 4.12 **The init Method of the RegistrationServlet**

```
public void init() {
    try {
      Class.forName("sun.jdbc.odbc.JdbcOdbcDriver");
      System.out.println("JDBC driver loaded");
    }
    catch (ClassNotFoundException e) {
      System.out.println(e.toString());
    }
  }
```

The complete code of the RegistrationServlet servlet is given in Listing 4.13.

Listing 4.13 **The RegistrationServlet**

```
import javax.servlet.*;
import javax.servlet.http.*;
import java.io.*;
import java.util.*;
import java.sql.*;
import com.brainysoftware.java.StringUtil;

public class RegistrationServlet extends HttpServlet {

  private String firstName = "";
  private String lastName = "";
  private String userName = "";
  private String password = "";

  public void init() {
    try {
      Class.forName("sun.jdbc.odbc.JdbcOdbcDriver");
      System.out.println("JDBC driver loaded");
    }
    catch (ClassNotFoundException e) {
      System.out.println(e.toString());
    }
  }

  /**Process the HTTP Get request*/
  public void doGet(HttpServletRequest request, HttpServletResponse response)
➥throws ServletException,IOException {
```

continues

Listing 4.13 **Continued**

```
    sendPageHeader(response);
    sendRegistrationForm(request, response, false);
    sendPageFooter(response);
  }

  /**Process the HTTP Post request*/
  public void doPost(HttpServletRequest request,
    HttpServletResponse response)
    throws ServletException, IOException {
    sendPageHeader(response);

    firstName = request.getParameter("firstName");
    lastName = request.getParameter("lastName");
    userName = request.getParameter("userName");
    password = request.getParameter("password");

    boolean error = false;
    String message = null;
    try {
      Connection con = DriverManager.getConnection("jdbc:odbc:JavaWeb");
      System.out.println("got connection");

      Statement s = con.createStatement();

      String sql = "SELECT UserName FROM Users" +
        " WHERE userName='" + StringUtil.fixSQLFieldValue(userName) + "'";
      ResultSet rs = s.executeQuery(sql);
      if (rs.next()) {
        rs.close();
        message = "The user name <B>"
          ➥+ StringUtil.encodeHtmlTag(userName) +
          "</B> has been taken. Please select another name.";
        error = true;
      }
      else {
        rs.close();
        sql = "INSERT INTO Users" +
          " (FirstName, LastName, UserName, Password)" +
          " VALUES" +
          " ('" +  StringUtil.fixSQLFieldValue(firstName) + "'," +
          " '" +  StringUtil.fixSQLFieldValue(lastName) + "'," +
          " '" +  StringUtil.fixSQLFieldValue(userName) + "'," +
          " '" +  StringUtil.fixSQLFieldValue(password) + "')";
        int i = s.executeUpdate(sql);
        if (i==1) {
          message = "Successfully added one user.";
        }
      }
```

```
      s.close();
      con.close();
    }
    catch (SQLException e) {
      message = "Error." + e.toString();
      error = true;
    }
    catch (Exception e) {
      message = "Error." + e.toString();
      error = true;
    }
    if (message!=null) {
      PrintWriter out = response.getWriter();
      out.println("<B>" + message + "</B><BR>");
      out.println("<HR><BR>");
    }
    if (error==true)
      sendRegistrationForm(request, response, true);
    else
      sendRegistrationForm(request, response, false);
    sendPageFooter(response);
  }

  /**
   * Send the HTML page header, including the title
   * and the <BODY> tag
   */
  private void sendPageHeader(HttpServletResponse response)
    throws ServletException, IOException {
    response.setContentType("text/html");
    PrintWriter out = response.getWriter();
    out.println("<HTML>");
    out.println("<HEAD>");
    out.println("<TITLE>Registration Page</TITLE>");
    out.println("</HEAD>");
    out.println("<BODY>");
    out.println("<CENTER>");
  }

  /**
   * Send the HTML page footer, i.e. the </BODY>
   * and the </HTML>
   */
  private void sendPageFooter(HttpServletResponse response)
    throws ServletException, IOException {
    PrintWriter out = response.getWriter();
    out.println("</CENTER>");
    out.println("</BODY>");
    out.println("</HTML>");
  }
```

continues

Listing 4.13 **Continued**

```
/**Send the form where the user can type in
 * the details for a new user
 */
private void sendRegistrationForm(HttpServletRequest request,
  HttpServletResponse response, boolean displayPreviousValues)
  throws ServletException, IOException {

  PrintWriter out = response.getWriter();
  out.println("<BR><H2>Registration Page</H2>");
  out.println("<BR>Please enter the user details.");
  out.println("<BR>");
  out.println("<BR><FORM METHOD=POST>");
  out.println("<TABLE>");
  out.println("<TR>");
  out.println("<TD>First Name</TD>");
  out.print("<TD><INPUT TYPE=TEXT Name=firstName");

  if (displayPreviousValues)
    out.print(" VALUE=\"" + StringUtil.encodeHtmlTag(firstName) + "\"");

  out.println("></TD>");
  out.println("</TR>");
  out.println("<TR>");
  out.println("<TD>Last Name</TD>");
  out.print("<TD><INPUT TYPE=TEXT Name=lastName");

  if (displayPreviousValues)
    out.print(" VALUE=\"" + StringUtil.encodeHtmlTag(lastName) + "\"");

  out.println("></TD>");
  out.println("</TR>");
  out.println("<TR>");
  out.println("<TD>User Name</TD>");
  out.print("<TD><INPUT TYPE=TEXT Name=userName");

  if (displayPreviousValues)
    out.print(" VALUE=\"" + StringUtil.encodeHtmlTag(userName) + "\"");

  out.println("></TD>");
  out.println("</TR>");
  out.println("<TR>");
  out.println("<TD>Password</TD>");
  out.print("<TD><INPUT TYPE=PASSWORD Name=password");

  if (displayPreviousValues)
    out.print(" VALUE=\"" + StringUtil.encodeHtmlTag(password) + "\"");
```

```
    out.println("></TD>");
    out.println("</TR>");
    out.println("<TR>");
    out.println("<TD><INPUT TYPE=RESET></TD>");
    out.println("<TD><INPUT TYPE=SUBMIT></TD>");
    out.println("</TR>");
    out.println("</TABLE>");
    out.println("</FORM>");
    out.println("<BR>");
    out.println("<BR>");
  }
}
```

Displaying All Records

Displaying data is inevitable when you program with a database. You can achieve this task easily with the knowledge of JDBC you have learned so far. Which data you need to display depends on your application. In this section and the next, you will display data and format it in an HTML table. This section displays all records in the Users table, and the next section implements a Search Page that displays data selectively.

Displaying all records could not be simpler. You need only to open a Connection, create a Statement object, and execute a query to produce a ResultSet object. You then iterate each record in a while loop. The code is very straightforward and is given in Listing 4.14. The output of this servlet is shown in Figure 4.5.

Listing 4.14 **Displaying All Records in the Users Table**

```
import javax.servlet.*;
import javax.servlet.http.*;
import java.io.*;
import java.sql.*;
import com.brainysoftware.java.StringUtil;

public class DataViewerServlet extends HttpServlet {
  /**Load JDBC driver*/
  public void init() {
    try {
      Class.forName("sun.jdbc.odbc.JdbcOdbcDriver");
      System.out.println("JDBC driver loaded");
    }
    catch (ClassNotFoundException e) {
      System.out.println(e.toString());
    }
```

continues

Listing 4.14 **Continued**

```
  }
  /**Process the HTTP Get request*/
  public void doGet(HttpServletRequest request, HttpServletResponse response)
➥throws ServletException, IOException {
    response.setContentType("text/html");

    PrintWriter out = response.getWriter();
    out.println("<HTML>");
    out.println("<HEAD>");
    out.println("<TITLE>Display All Users</TITLE>");
    out.println("</HEAD>");
    out.println("<BODY>");
    out.println("<CENTER>");
    out.println("<BR><H2>Displaying All Users</H2>");
    out.println("<BR>");
    out.println("<BR>");
    out.println("<TABLE>");
    out.println("<TR>");
    out.println("<TH>First Name</TH>");
    out.println("<TH>Last Name</TH>");
    out.println("<TH>User Name</TH>");
    out.println("<TH>Password</TH>");
    out.println("</TR>");

    String sql = "SELECT FirstName, LastName, UserName, Password" +
      " FROM Users";
    try {
      Connection con = DriverManager.getConnection("jdbc:odbc:JavaWeb");
      System.out.println("got connection");

      Statement s = con.createStatement();
      ResultSet rs = s.executeQuery(sql);

      while (rs.next()) {
        out.println("<TR>");
        out.println("<TD>" + StringUtil.encodeHtmlTag(rs.getString(1))
➥+ "</TD>");
        out.println("<TD>" + StringUtil.encodeHtmlTag(rs.getString(2))
➥+ "</TD>");
        out.println("<TD>" + StringUtil.encodeHtmlTag(rs.getString(3))
➥+ "</TD>");
        out.println("<TD>" + StringUtil.encodeHtmlTag(rs.getString(4))
➥+ "</TD>");
        out.println("</TR>");
      }
      rs.close();
      s.close();
      con.close();
    }
```

```
        catch (SQLException e) {
        }
        catch (Exception e) {
        }
        out.println("</TABLE>");
        out.println("</CENTER>");
        out.println("</BODY>");
        out.println("</HTML>");
    }

    public void doPost(HttpServletRequest request, HttpServletResponse
  ➥response)
        throws ServletException, IOException {
        doGet(request, response);
    }
}
```

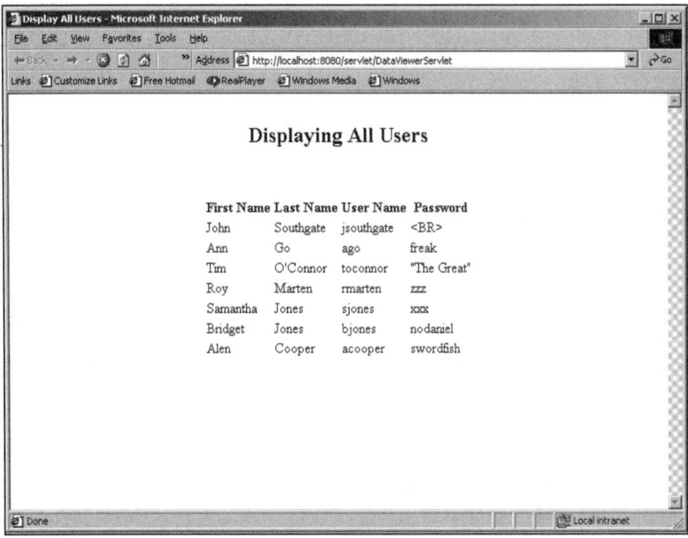

Figure 4.5 Displaying all records from a table.

Search Page

In many cases, displaying all records is not preferable. More often than not, you need only to display data selectively. For example, someone might try to find the details of a person called Jones without knowing the person's first name. Displaying all the users does not help much, especially if you have a large number of records in the table. The page is more useful if you can let the user specify a keyword and display all records that match the keyword.

In this example, you will write a SearchServlet that lets the user enter a keyword that could be the first name, the last name, or even part of the first name or last name. The appearance of this servlet output is shown in Figure 4.6.

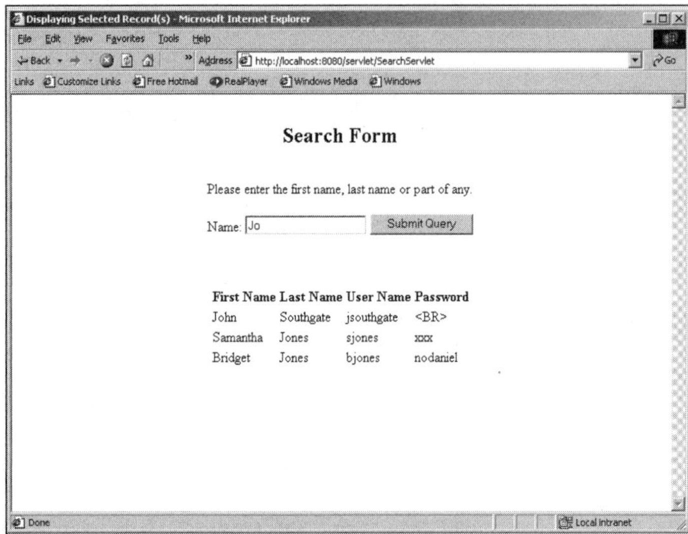

Figure 4.6 The SearchServlet.

The main part of this servlet is the sendSearchResult method that connects to the database, executes the following SQL statement, and sends the result to the browser.

```
SELECT FirstName, LastName, UserName, Password
FROM Users
WHERE FirstName LIKE '%keyword%'
OR LastName LIKE '%keyword%'
```

The code is given in Listing 4.15.

Listing 4.15 **The SearchServlet Servlet**

```
import javax.servlet.*;
import javax.servlet.http.*;
import java.io.*;
import java.util.*;
import java.sql.*;
import com.brainysoftware.java.StringUtil;

public class SearchServlet extends HttpServlet {
```

```
  private String keyword = "";

  public void init() {
    try {
      Class.forName("sun.jdbc.odbc.JdbcOdbcDriver");
      System.out.println("JDBC driver loaded");
    }
    catch (ClassNotFoundException e) {
      System.out.println(e.toString());
    }
  }

  /**Process the HTTP Get request*/
  public void doGet(HttpServletRequest request,
➥HttpServletResponse response) throws ServletException,
➥IOException {
    sendPageHeader(response);
    sendSearchForm(response);
    sendPageFooter(response);
  }

  /**Process the HTTP Post request*/
  public void doPost(HttpServletRequest request,
➥HttpServletResponse response) throws ServletException,
➥IOException {

    keyword = request.getParameter("keyword");
    sendPageHeader(response);
    sendSearchForm(response);
    sendSearchResult(response);
    sendPageFooter(response);
  }

  void sendSearchResult(HttpServletResponse response)
    throws IOException {
    PrintWriter out = response.getWriter();
    try {
      Connection con = DriverManager.getConnection("jdbc:odbc:JavaWeb");
      System.out.println("got connection");

      Statement s = con.createStatement();

      out.println("<TABLE>");
      out.println("<TR>");
      out.println("<TH>First Name</TH>");
      out.println("<TH>Last Name</TH>");
      out.println("<TH>User Name</TH>");
      out.println("<TH>Password</TH>");
      out.println("</TR>");
      String sql = "SELECT FirstName, LastName, UserName, Password" +
```

continues

Listing 4.15 **Continued**

```
        " FROM Users" +
        " WHERE FirstName LIKE '%"
➥+ StringUtil.fixSqlFieldValue(keyword) + "%'" +
        " OR LastName LIKE '%" + StringUtil.fixSqlFieldValue(keyword)
➥+ "%'";
      ResultSet rs = s.executeQuery(sql);
      while (rs.next()) {
        out.println("<TR>");
        out.println("<TD>" + StringUtil.encodeHtmlTag(rs.getString(1))
➥+ "</TD>");
        out.println("<TD>" + StringUtil.encodeHtmlTag(rs.getString(2))
➥+ "</TD>");
        out.println("<TD>" + StringUtil.encodeHtmlTag(rs.getString(3))
➥+ "</TD>");
        out.println("<TD>" + StringUtil.encodeHtmlTag(rs.getString(4))
➥+ "</TD>");
        out.println("</TR>");
      }
      s.close();
      con.close();
    }
    catch (SQLException e) {
    }
    catch (Exception e) {
    }
    out.println("</TABLE>");
  }

  /**
   * Send the HTML page header, including the title
   * and the <BODY> tag
   */
  private void sendPageHeader(HttpServletResponse response)
    throws ServletException, IOException {
    response.setContentType("text/html");
    PrintWriter out = response.getWriter();
    out.println("<HTML>");
    out.println("<HEAD>");
    out.println("<TITLE>Displaying Selected Record(s)</TITLE>");
    out.println("</HEAD>");
    out.println("<BODY>");
    out.println("<CENTER>");
  }

  /**
   * Send the HTML page footer, i.e. the </BODY>
   * and the </HTML>
   */
  private void sendPageFooter(HttpServletResponse response)
```

```
    throws ServletException, IOException {
    PrintWriter out = response.getWriter();
    out.println("</CENTER>");
    out.println("</BODY>");
    out.println("</HTML>");
  }

  /**Send the form where the user can type in
   * the details for a new user
   */
  private void sendSearchForm(HttpServletResponse response)
    throws IOException {

    PrintWriter out = response.getWriter();
    out.println("<BR><H2>Search Form</H2>");
    out.println("<BR>Please enter the first name, last name or
    ➥part of any.");
    out.println("<BR>");
    out.println("<BR><FORM METHOD=POST>");
    out.print("Name: <INPUT TYPE=TEXT Name=keyword");
    out.println(" VALUE=\"" + StringUtil.encodeHtmlTag(keyword) + "\"");
    out.println(">");
    out.println("<INPUT TYPE=SUBMIT>");
    out.println("</FORM>");
    out.println("<BR>");
    out.println("<BR>");
  }

}
```

An Online SQL Tool

When working with a database, you may want to change data in a database for testing. When connecting to a database from a servlet, however, it is often the case that the database resides somewhere beyond your physical reach. Oftentimes, the only way to connect to the database is through the database client program. Of course, the client program needs to be installed on the computer you are using to connect to the database. This is not good if you need to be mobile, or if you need to be able to connect to the database from different locations. Because the database is available to a servlet, you can also make it available online.

The program given in this application is an online SQL tool that lets you manipulate your data or data structure by using a web browser. You can type in any SQL statement and send it to the server to be executed by the database server. If the database server returns a ResultSet, the tool displays it in the form of a table. If the database server sends an error message, that also is displayed in the form. The form is shown in Figure 4.7.

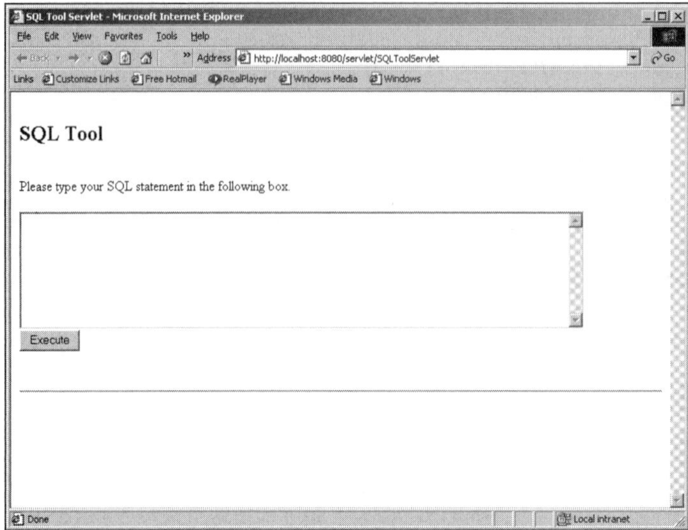

Figure 4.7 The online SQL Tool.

The user can type an SQL statement in the box. Figures 4.8 and 4.9 show how the form looks when the database server returns a ResultSet and when it notifies the user that it has successfully executed an SQL that affects one record.

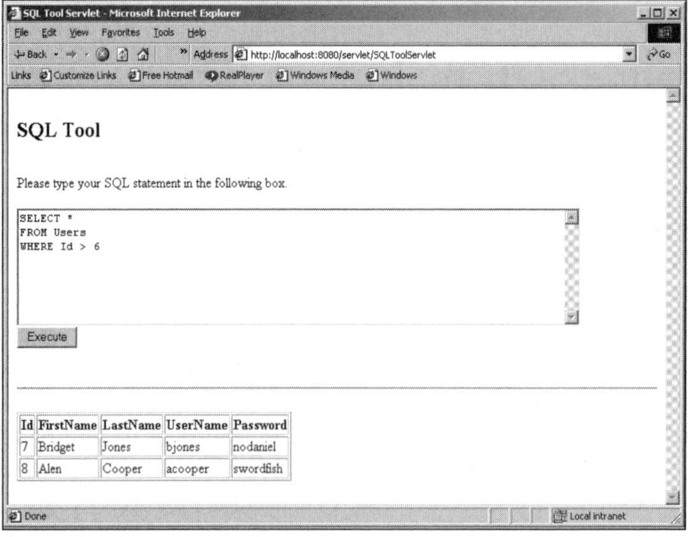

Figure 4.8 The SQL Tool with a returned ResultSet.

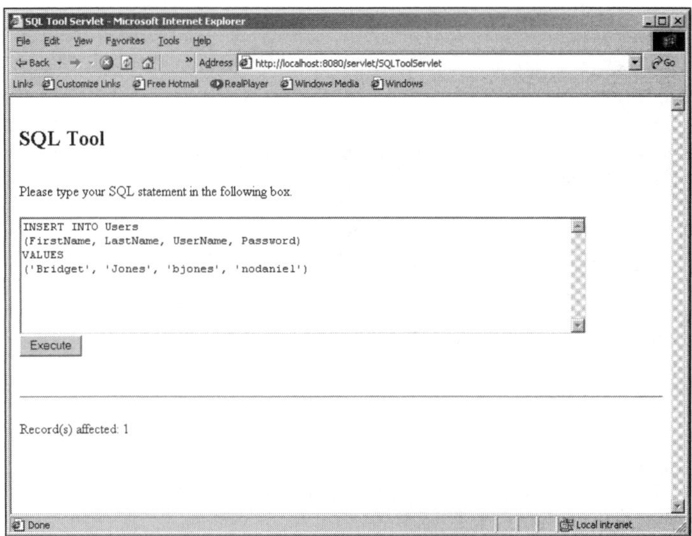

Figure 4.9 The SQL Tool after inserting a new record.

When first called, the servlet will invoke the doGet method that calls the sendSqlForm. The latter sends the SQL form to the browser. The doGet method is given in Listing 4.16.

Listing 4.16 **The doGet Method of the SQLToolServlet**

```
public void doGet(HttpServletRequest request,
  HttpServletResponse response)
throws ServletException, IOException {
  sendSqlForm(request, response);
}
```

The sendSqlForm method does what its name implies: it sends the SQL form. The method is given in Listing 4.17.

Listing 4.17 **The sendSqlForm Method**

```
private void sendSqlForm(HttpServletRequest request,
    HttpServletResponse response)
    throws ServletException, IOException {

    response.setContentType("text/html");
    PrintWriter out = response.getWriter();
    out.println("<HTML>");
    out.println("<HEAD>");
    out.println("<TITLE>SQL Tool Servlet</TITLE>");
```

continues

Listing 4.17 **Continued**

```
    out.println("</HEAD>");
    out.println("<BODY>");
    out.println("<BR><H2>SQL Tool</H2>");
    out.println("<BR>Please type your SQL statement in
➥the following box.");
    out.println("<BR>");
    out.println("<BR><FORM METHOD=POST>");
    out.println("<TEXTAREA NAME=sql COLS=80 ROWS=8>");
    String sql = request.getParameter("sql");

    // Reprint the previously entered SQL in the TextArea
    if (sql!=null)
      out.println(sql);

    out.println("</TEXTAREA>");
    out.println("<BR>");
    out.println("<INPUT TYPE=SUBMIT VALUE=Execute>");
    out.println("</FORM>");
    out.println("<BR>");
    out.println("<HR>");
    out.println("<BR>");

    if (sql!=null) {
      executeSql(sql.trim(), response);
    }

    out.println("</BODY>");
    out.println("</HTML>");
  }
```

The sendSqlForm method retrieves the sql value from the HttpServletRequest object. When this method is called from the doGet method, the sql parameter is null. When called from the doPost method, however, the sql parameter is not null. When the latter is the case, the executeSql method is called.

The executeSql method accepts a String containing the SQL statement, which it tries to execute, and a HttpServletResponse object that it can write to for sending text to the browser. The executeSql method is given in Listing 4.18.

Listing 4.18 **The executeSql Method**

```
public void executeSql(String sql, HttpServletResponse response)
    throws ServletException, IOException {

    PrintWriter out = response.getWriter();
    try {
      //Class.forName("sun.jdbc.odbc.JdbcOdbcDriver");
```

```
      Connection con = DriverManager.getConnection("jdbc:odbc:JavaWeb");
      System.out.println("got connection");

      Statement s = con.createStatement();

      if (sql.toUpperCase().startsWith("SELECT")) {
        out.println("<TABLE BORDER=1>");
        ResultSet rs = s.executeQuery(sql);
        ResultSetMetaData rsmd = rs.getMetaData();
        // Write table headings
        int columnCount = rsmd.getColumnCount();
        out.println("<TR>");
        for (int i=1; i<=columnCount; i++) {
          out.println("<TD><B>" + rsmd.getColumnName(i)
➥+ "</B></TD>\n");
        }
        out.println("</TR>");
        while (rs.next()) {
          out.println("<TR>");
          for (int i=1; i<=columnCount; i++) {
            out.println("<TD>"
➥+ StringUtil.encodeHtmlTag(rs.getString(i)) + "</TD>" );
          }
          out.println("</TR>");
        }
        rs.close();
        out.println("</TABLE>");
      }
      else {
        int i = s.executeUpdate(sql);
        out.println("Record(s) affected: " + i);
      }
      s.close();
      con.close();
      out.println("</TABLE>");
    }
    catch (SQLException e) {
      out.println("<B>Error</B>");
      out.println("<BR>");
      out.println(e.toString());
    }
    catch (Exception e) {
      out.println("<B>Error</B>");
      out.println("<BR>");
      out.println(e.toString());
    }
  }
}
```

The complete code of the SQLToolServlet is given in Listing 4.19.

Listing 4.19 **The SQLToolServlet Servlet**

```
import javax.servlet.*;
import javax.servlet.http.*;
import java.io.*;
import java.util.*;
import java.sql.*;
import com.brainysoftware.java.StringUtil;

public class SQLToolServlet extends HttpServlet {

  /**Load the JDBC driver*/
  public void init() {
    try {
      Class.forName("sun.jdbc.odbc.JdbcOdbcDriver");
      System.out.println("JDBC driver loaded");
    }
    catch (ClassNotFoundException e) {
      System.out.println(e.toString());
    }
  }
  /**Process the HTTP Get request*/
  public void doGet(HttpServletRequest request,
    HttpServletResponse response)
  throws ServletException, IOException {
    sendSqlForm(request, response);
  }

  /**Process the HTTP Post request*/
  public void doPost(HttpServletRequest request,
➥HttpServletResponse response) throws ServletException,
➥IOException {
    sendSqlForm(request, response);
  }

  /**Send the form where the user can type in
   * an SQL statement to be processed
   */
  private void sendSqlForm(HttpServletRequest request,
    HttpServletResponse response)
    throws ServletException, IOException {

    response.setContentType("text/html");
    PrintWriter out = response.getWriter();
    out.println("<HTML>");
    out.println("<HEAD>");
    out.println("<TITLE>SQL Tool Servlet</TITLE>");
    out.println("</HEAD>");
    out.println("<BODY>");
```

```
    out.println("<BR><H2>SQL Tool</H2>");
    out.println("<BR>Please type your SQL statement in
Âthe following box.");
    out.println("<BR>");
    out.println("<BR><FORM METHOD=POST>");
    out.println("<TEXTAREA NAME=sql COLS=80 ROWS=8>");
    String sql = request.getParameter("sql");

    // Reprint the previously entered SQL in the TextArea
    if (sql!=null)
      out.println(sql);

    out.println("</TEXTAREA>");
    out.println("<BR>");
    out.println("<INPUT TYPE=SUBMIT VALUE=Execute>");
    out.println("</FORM>");
    out.println("<BR>");
    out.println("<HR>");
    out.println("<BR>");

    if (sql!=null) {
      executeSql(sql.trim(), response);
    }

    out.println("</BODY>");
    out.println("</HTML>");
  }

  /**execute the SQL */
  public void executeSql(String sql, HttpServletResponse response)
    throws ServletException, IOException {

    PrintWriter out = response.getWriter();
    try {
      //Class.forName("sun.jdbc.odbc.JdbcOdbcDriver");
      Connection con = DriverManager.getConnection("jdbc:odbc:JavaWeb");
      System.out.println("got connection");

      Statement s = con.createStatement();

      if (sql.toUpperCase().startsWith("SELECT")) {
        out.println("<TABLE BORDER=1>");
        ResultSet rs = s.executeQuery(sql);
        ResultSetMetaData rsmd = rs.getMetaData();
        // Write table headings
        int columnCount = rsmd.getColumnCount();
        out.println("<TR>");
        for (int i=1; i<=columnCount; i++) {
          out.println("<TD><B>" + rsmd.getColumnName(i)
➥+ "</B></TD>\n");
        }
```

continues

Listing 4.19 **Continued**

```
          out.println("</TR>");
          while (rs.next()) {
            out.println("<TR>");
            for (int i=1; i<=columnCount; i++) {
              out.println("<TD>"
➥+ StringUtil.encodeHtmlTag(rs.getString(i)) + "</TD>" );
            }
            out.println("</TR>");
          }
          rs.close();
          out.println("</TABLE>");
        }
        else {
          int i = s.executeUpdate(sql);
          out.println("Record(s) affected: " + i);
        }
        s.close();
        con.close();
        out.println("</TABLE>");
      }
      catch (SQLException e) {
        out.println("<B>Error</B>");
        out.println("<BR>");
        out.println(e.toString());
      }
      catch (Exception e) {
        out.println("<B>Error</B>");
        out.println("<BR>");
        out.println(e.toString());
      }
    }
  }
```

Should I Keep the Connection Open?

All the examples given up to this point in this chapter have closed the Connection object after the servlet services the request. However, you might ask the following question: If the servlet is called more than once and it opens a Connection object with the same arguments (url, user, and password) each time, wouldn't it better to leave the Connection object open for future use; that is, for when the servlet is called again?

In fact, opening a Connection object is one of the most expensive operations in database programming. Being able to save CPU cycles by keeping the Connection object is very tempting. In many reference books, however, including those of non-Java web programming, you are always told to close the Connection object as soon as it's no longer needed. The recommendation is so intense that some people have the impression that keeping the connection open is forbidden. Why?

Actually, an open connection is not taboo. Whether to leave the Connection object open really depends on the application you are building. First, however, you should consider that it is true that the response time will be faster if you can access the database without having to open a Connection object. For example, you can make the object variable of the Connection object class level so that it can be accessed from anywhere in the servlet and put the code that opens the Connection object in the init method. This way, the Connection object will be opened when the servlet first initializes. On subsequent requests, the Connection is already open, so the user will experience faster response.

A servlet can be accessed by multiple users at the same time, however. The bad news is that the underlying architecture of the Connection object will allow only one query to be processed at a time. As a result, only one user can use the connection at a time. The others will have to queue. Considering that modern databases allow multiple connections, this is really a waste.

The conclusion is that if your servlet is accessed only by a single user at a time, leaving the Connection object open makes the response time faster. If you can't guarantee that there will not be simultaneous accesses to the servlet, however, response time will start to decrease because the second and subsequent users have to wait until the first user gets serviced.

That's why, except in some rare cases, you should always close your Connection object. Rather than having the Connection object open, a technique called *connection pooling* is implemented by the driver to manage the Connection objects to a database so that multiple connections can be pooled. A connection can be used and, when finished, returned to the pool to be used by another request.

Transactions

A *transaction* is a unit of work that can comprise one or more SQL operations. In the examples you have seen so far, every SQL operation is executed and the change is committed (made permanent) on the database right after the SQL statement is executed.

In some cases, however, a set of SQL operations must succeed or fail as a whole. If one of the SQL statements fails, the other SQL statements in the group must also be rolled back. Consider the following scenario.

In an online store a customer purchases several books. When the customer checks out and pays using a credit card, the following things must happen:

1. A record must be added to the Orders table specifying the order, including the delivery address and the credit card details. This operation results in an OrderId used to identify each item in the OrderDetails table.
2. A record must be inserted into the OrderDetails table for each purchase item. Each item is linked to the Orders table using the OrderId value returned by the previous SQL operation.

Now, if everything goes smoothly, both SQL statements will be executed successfully in the database. Things can go wrong, however. Say, for example, the first operation is committed successfully but the second SQL statement fails. In this case, the order details are lost and the customer won't get anything. The customer's credit card will still be debited by the amount of the purchase, however, because a record is added to the Orders table.

In this case, you want both SQL statements to succeed or fail as a whole. You can do this using a transaction. Upon a failed transaction, you can notify the customer so that he or she can try to check out again.

By default, a Connection object's auto-commit state is true, meaning that the database is updated when an SQL statement is executed. If you want to group a set of SQL statements in one transaction, you must first tell the Connection object not to update the change until it is explicitly notified to do so. You do this by calling the setAutoCommit method and passing false as its argument, as follows:

```
connection.setAutoCommit(false);
```

Then, you can execute all the SQL statements in the group normally, using the executeQuery and the updateQuery methods. After the last call to the executeQuery or the updateQuery method, you call the commit method of the Connection object to make the database changes permanent, such as

```
connection.commit();
```

If you don't call the commit method within a specified time, all SQL statements will be rolled back after calling the setAutoCommit method. Alternatively, you can roll back the transaction explicitly by calling the Connection object's rollback method:

```
connection.rollback();
```

> **Note**
>
> You learn how to use transactions further when you build a shopping cart in Chapter 18, "Developing E-Commerce Applications."

Connection Pooling

Creating a Connection object is one of the most expensive operations in database programming. This is especially true when the Connection object is used for only one or two SQL operations, as demonstrated in the servlets discussed in this chapter.

To make the use of Connection objects more efficient, those objects are not pooled. When the application starts, a certain number of Connection objects are created and stored in a pool. When a database client, such as a servlet, needs to use a Connection object, it does not create the object but instead requests one from the pool. When the client is finished with it, the Connection object is returned to the pool.

You can create a pool of Connection objects programmatically; however, there is an easier and more robust way: by using the connection pooling feature of the JDBC Optional Package. The good thing about this feature is that the connection pooling is transparent. There is no single line of code that the programmer needs to change to use it.

To use the connection pooling feature in the javax.sql package, you need to connect to the data source using the javax.sql.DataSource interface. The code for getting a connection utilizes JNDI, which is briefly discussed in Chapter 28, "Enterprise JavaBeans." The code is as follows:

```
Context context = new InitialContext();
DataSource ds = (DataSource)context.lookup("jdbc/myDB");
Connection connection = ds.getConnection(user, password)
```

Summary

Database access is one of the most important aspects of web programming. Java has its own technology for this called JDBC, whose functionality is wrapped in a package called java.sql. In this chapter, you have seen various members of this package and learned how to use them. You also have learned how to create servlets that access a database. A couple of servlets have been created that illustrate various real-life applications.

5 Session Management

The Hypertext Transfer Protocol (HTTP) is the network protocol that web servers and client browsers use to communicate with each other. HTTP is the language of the web. HTTP connections are initiated by a client browser that sends an HTTP request. The web server then responds with an HTTP response and closes the connection. If the same client requests another resource from the server, it must open another HTTP connection to the server. The server always closes the connection as soon as it sends the response, whether or not the browser user needs some other resource from the server.

This process is similar to a telephone conversation in which the receiver always hangs up after responding to the last remark/question from the caller. For example, a call goes something like this:

Caller dials. Caller gets connected.
Caller: "Hi, good morning."
Receiver: "Good morning."
Receiver hangs up.
Caller dials again. Caller gets connected.
Caller: "May I speak to Dr. Zeus, please?"
Receiver: "Sure."
Receiver hangs up.
Caller dials again, and so on, and so on.

Putting this in a web perspective, because the web server always disconnects after it responds to a request, the web server does not know whether a request comes from a user who has just requested the first page or from a user who has requested nine other pages before. As such, HTTP is said to be *stateless*.

Being stateless has huge implications. Consider, for example, a user who is shopping at an online store. As usual, the process starts with the user searching for a product. If the product is found, the user then enters the quantity of that product into the shopping cart form and submits it to the server. But, the user is not yet checking out—she still wants to buy something else. So she searches the catalog again for the second product. The first product order has now been lost, however, because the previous connection was closed and the web server does not remember anything about the previous connection.

The good news is that web programmers can work around this, and this chapter discusses techniques for that. The solution is called *user session management*. The web server is forced to associate HTTP requests and client browsers.

What Is Session Management?

You know that HTTP statelessness has a deep impact on web application programming. To see the problem more clearly, consider the LoginServlet in Chapter 3, "Writing Servlet Applications," and Chapter 4, "Accessing Databases with JDBC." The skeleton is presented here:

```
public void doGet(HttpServletRequest request,
  HttpServletResponse response)
  throws ServletException, IOException {
  sendLoginForm(response, false);
}

public void doPost(HttpServletRequest request,
  HttpServletResponse response)
  throws ServletException, IOException {

  String userName = request.getParameter("userName");
  String password = request.getParameter("password");
  if (login(userName, password)) {
    // login successful, display the information
  }
  else {
    // login failed, re-send the Login form
    sendLoginForm(response, true);
  }
}
```

The Login servlet is used to require users to enter a valid user name and password before they can see some information. When a user first requests the servlet, the Login form is displayed. The user then can enter a user name and password and submit the form. Assuming that the form uses the POST method, the user information is captured in the doPost method, which does the authentication by calling the login method. If the login was successful, the information is displayed. If not, the Login form is sent again.

What if you have another servlet that also only allows authorized users to view the information? This second servlet does not know whether the same user has successfully logged in to the first servlet. Consequently, the user will be required to log in again!

This is, of course, not practical. Every time a user goes to request a protected servlet, he or she has to login again even though all the servlets are part of the same application. This easily pushes the user to the edge of frustration and most likely results in a lost customer.

Fortunately, there are ways to get around this, using techniques for remembering a user's session. Once users have logged in, they do not have to login again. The application will remember them. This is called *session management*.

Session management, also called *session tracking*, goes beyond simply remembering a user who has successfully logged in. Anything that makes the application remember information that has been entered or requested by the user can be considered session management. Session management does not change the nature of HTTP statelessness—it simply provides a way around it.

By principle, you manage a user's session by performing the following to servlets/pages that need to remember a user's state:

1. When the user requests a servlet, in addition to sending the response, the servlet also sends a token or an identifier.
2. If the user does not come back with the next request for the same or a different servlet, that is fine. If the user does come back, the token or identifier is sent back to the server. Upon encountering the token, the next servlet should recognize the identifier and can do a certain action based on the token. When the servlet responds to the request, it also sends the same or a different token. This goes on and on with all the servlets that need to remember a user's session.

You will use four techniques for session management. They operate based on the same principle, although what is passed and how it is passed is different from one to another. The techniques are as follows:

- URL rewriting
- Hidden fields
- Cookies
- Session objects

Which technique you use depends on what you need to do in your application. Each of the techniques is discussed in the sections below. The section, "Knowing Which Technique to Use," concludes the chapter.

URL Rewriting

With URL rewriting, you append a token or identifier to the URL of the next servlet or the next resource. You can send parameter name/value pairs using the following format:

```
url?name1=value1&name2=value2&…
```

A name and a value is separated using an equal sign (=); a parameter name/value pair is separated from another parameter name/value pair using the ampersand (&). When the user clicks the hyperlink, the parameter name/value pairs will be passed to the server. From a servlet, you can use the HttpServletRequest interface's getParameter method to obtain a parameter value. For instance, to obtain the value of the second parameter, you write the following:

```
request.getParameter(name2);
```

The use of URL rewriting is easy. When using this technique, however, you need to consider several things:

- The number of characters that can be passed in a URL is limited. Typically, a browser can pass up to 2,000 characters.
- The value that you pass can be seen in the URL. Sometimes this is not desirable. For example, some people prefer their password not to appear on the URL.
- You need to encode certain characters—such as & and ? characters and white spaces—that you append to a URL.

As an example, you will build an application that you can use to administer all registered persons in a database. The application uses the Users table created in Chapter 4 and allows you to do the following:

1. Enter a keyword that will become the search key for the first name and the last name columns of the Users table.
2. Display all persons that match the keyword.
3. In addition to the data for each record, there are Delete and Update hyperlinks. The user id is included in the hyperlinks.
4. If the Delete hyperlink is clicked, the corresponding person will be deleted from the Users table.
5. If the Update hyperlink is clicked, the corresponding person's details will be displayed in a form. You then can change the data and submit the form to update that person's record.

The Administration application is shown in Figures 5.1, 5.2, and 5.3.

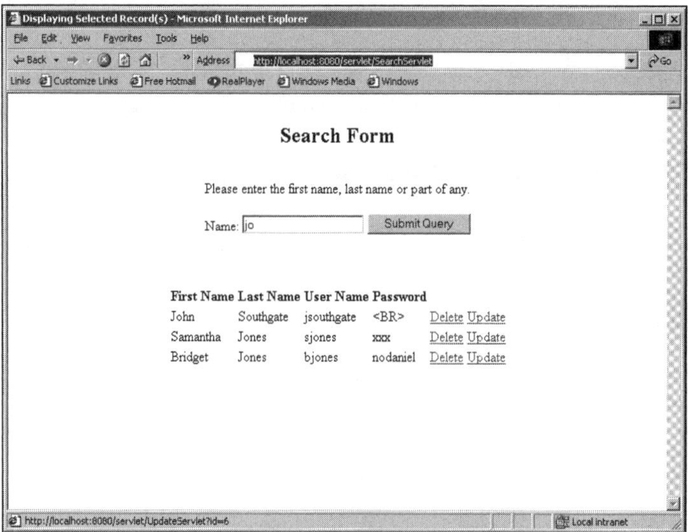

Figure 5.1 The Administration's Search page.

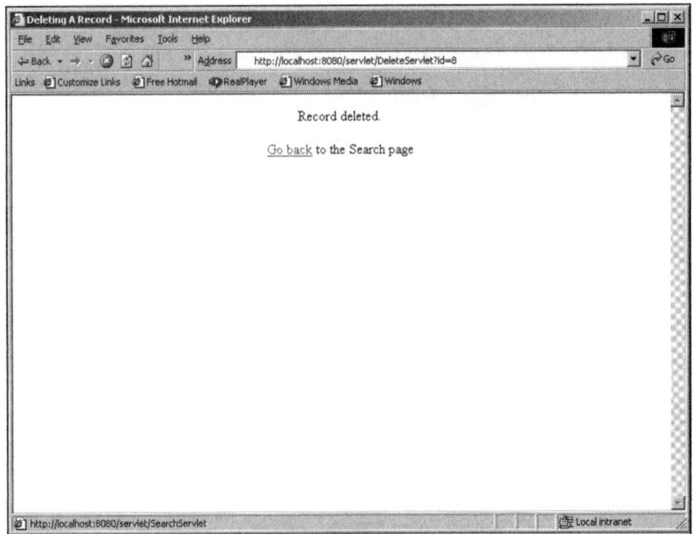

Figure 5.2 The Administrations Delete page.

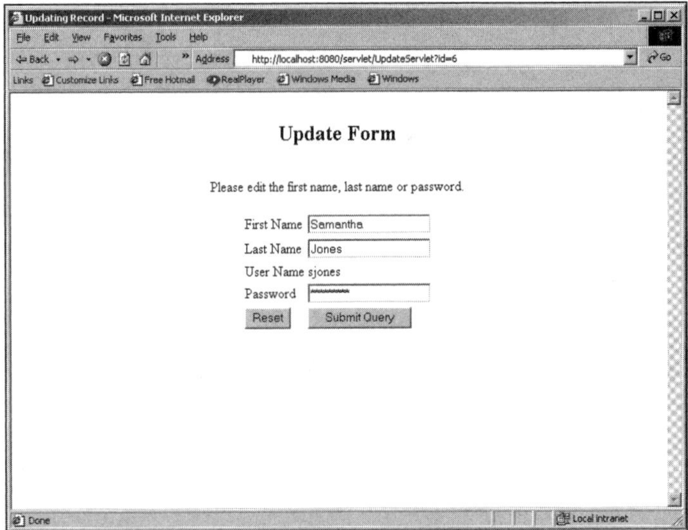

Figure 5.3 The Administration's Update page.

The first servlet, the SearchServlet, is similar to the one in Chapter 4. The doGet method sends the form for the user to type in a keyword. This keyword could be a first name, a last name, or part of a first name or a last name. To allow more flexibility, this example separates the form from the rest of the page. Therefore, you send the page header and page footer separately. The doGet method is given in Listing 5.1.

Listing 5.1 **The doGet Method of the SearchServlet**

```
public void doGet(HttpServletRequest request,
  HttpServletResponse response)
  throws ServletException, IOException {
    sendPageHeader(response);
    sendSearchForm(response);
    sendPageFooter(response);
  }
```

The page header contains the head part of the HTML page, including the page title and the opening <BODY> tag. To send the page header, you call the sendPageHeader method. The page footer contains the bottom part of the page, that is, the closing </BODY> and </HTML> tags. Calling the sendPageFooter method will send the page footer.

The sendSearchForm method sends the HTML form. This form uses the POST method and, when submitted, this form will send the keyword to the server. The server then invokes the doPost method whose code is given in Listing 5.2.

Listing 5.2 **The doPost Method of the SearchServlet**

```
public void doPost(HttpServletRequest request,
  HttpServletResponse response)
  throws ServletException, IOException {

  keyword = request.getParameter("keyword");
  sendPageHeader(response);
  sendSearchForm(response);
  sendSearchResult(response);
  sendPageFooter(response);
}
```

The first thing doPost does is retrieve the keyword from the HttpServletRequest object and store it in a class-level variable keyword. It then sends the page header, the search form, the search result, and the page footer to the browser.

The sendSearchResult method forms an SQL select statement that incorporates the keyword, in the following syntax:

```
SELECT Id, FirstName, LastName, UserName, Password
FROM Users
WHERE FirstName LIKE '%keyword%'
OR LastName LIKE '%keyword%'
```

Note that the % character represents any text of zero length or more. This means that jo% will find jo, john, jones, and so on. Note, however, that this wildcard character is different from one database server to another and you should consult your database server documentation before using it.

Because the value entered by the user as the keyword can contain a single quote character, you use the StringUtil class's fixSqlFieldValue method to "fix" the keyword. StringUtil class is part of the com.brainysoftware.java package that can be found on the accompanying CD. You need to copy the StringUtil.java file into the com/brainysoftware/java/ directory under the directory where you put your source files. See Chapter 3 for more information on how to use the StringUtil class.

You compose the SQL statement using the following code:

```
String sql =
  "SELECT Id, FirstName, LastName, UserName, Password" +
  " FROM Users" +
  " WHERE FirstName LIKE '%" +
  StringUtil.fixSqlFieldValue(keyword) + "%'" +
  " OR LastName LIKE '%" +
```

Once the SQL statement is executed, the returned ResultSet can be looped through to get its cell data. Of particular interest is the call to the getString method passing the integer 1. This returns the Id for that person. The Id is important because it is used as the token for that person. The Id is passed in the URL to the DeleteServlet as well as to the UpdateServlet, as follows:

```
out.println("<TD><A HREF=DeleteServlet?id=" + id +
  ">Delete</A></TD>");
out.println("<TD><A HREF=UpdateServlet?id=" + id +
  ">Update</A></TD>");
```

Therefore, for a person with an Id of 6, the hyperlink to the DeleteServlet will be:

```
<A HREF=DeleteServlet?id=6>Delete</A>
```

And for a person with an Id of 8, the hyperlink to the UpdateServlet is

```
<A HREF=UpdateServlet?id=8>Delete</A>
```

See how information has been added to the URL?

The complete listing of the SearchServlet is presented in Listing 5.3.

Listing 5.3 **The SearchServlet**

```
import javax.servlet.*;
import javax.servlet.http.*;
import java.io.*;
import java.util.*;
import java.sql.*;
import com.brainysoftware.java.StringUtil;

public class SearchServlet extends HttpServlet {

  private String keyword = "";

  public void init() {
    try {
      Class.forName("sun.jdbc.odbc.JdbcOdbcDriver");
      System.out.println("JDBC driver loaded");
    }
    catch (ClassNotFoundException e) {
      System.out.println(e.toString());
    }
  }

  /**Process the HTTP Get request*/
  public void doGet(HttpServletRequest request,
➥HttpServletResponse response) throws ServletException,
➥IOException {
    sendPageHeader(response);
    sendSearchForm(response);
    sendPageFooter(response);
  }

  /**Process the HTTP Post request*/
  public void doPost(HttpServletRequest request,
➥HttpServletResponse response) throws ServletException,
➥IOException {

    keyword = request.getParameter("keyword");
    sendPageHeader(response);
    sendSearchForm(response);
    sendSearchResult(response);
    sendPageFooter(response);
  }

  void sendSearchResult(HttpServletResponse response)
    throws IOException {
    PrintWriter out = response.getWriter();
    try {
      Connection con =
```

continues

Listing 5.3 **Continued**

```
        DriverManager.getConnection("jdbc:odbc:JavaWeb");
      System.out.println("got connection");

      Statement s = con.createStatement();

      out.println("<TABLE>");
      out.println("<TR>");
      out.println("<TH>First Name</TH>");
      out.println("<TH>Last Name</TH>");
      out.println("<TH>User Name</TH>");
      out.println("<TH>Password</TH>");
      out.println("<TH></TH>");
      out.println("<TH></TH>");
      out.println("</TR>");
      String sql =
        "SELECT Id, FirstName, LastName, UserName, Password" +
        " FROM Users" +
        " WHERE FirstName LIKE '%" +
        StringUtil.fixSqlFieldValue(keyword) + "%'" +
        " OR LastName LIKE '%" +
        StringUtil.fixSqlFieldValue(keyword) + "%'";
      ResultSet rs = s.executeQuery(sql);
      while (rs.next()) {
        String id = rs.getString(1);
        out.println("<TR>");
        out.println("<TD>" + StringUtil.encodeHtmlTag(rs.getString(2))
➥+ "</TD>");
        out.println("<TD>" + StringUtil.encodeHtmlTag(rs.getString(3))
➥+ "</TD>");
        out.println("<TD>" + StringUtil.encodeHtmlTag(rs.getString(4))
➥+ "</TD>");
        out.println("<TD>" + StringUtil.encodeHtmlTag(rs.getString(5))
➥+ "</TD>");
        out.println("<TD><A HREF=DeleteServlet?id=" + id
➥+ ">Delete</A></TD>");
        out.println("<TD><A HREF=UpdateServlet?id=" + id
➥+ ">Update</A></TD>");
        out.println("</TR>");
      }
      s.close();
      con.close();
    }
    catch (SQLException e) {
    }
    catch (Exception e) {
    }
    out.println("</TABLE>");
  }

  /**
   * Send the HTML page header, including the title
```

```
   * and the <BODY> tag
   */
  private void sendPageHeader(HttpServletResponse response)
    throws ServletException, IOException {
    response.setContentType("text/html");
    PrintWriter out = response.getWriter();
    out.println("<HTML>");
    out.println("<HEAD>");
    out.println("<TITLE>Displaying Selected Record(s)</TITLE>");
    out.println("</HEAD>");
    out.println("<BODY>");
    out.println("<CENTER>");
  }

  /**
   * Send the HTML page footer, i.e. the </BODY>
   * and the </HTML>
   */
  private void sendPageFooter(HttpServletResponse response)
    throws ServletException, IOException {
    PrintWriter out = response.getWriter();
    out.println("</CENTER>");
    out.println("</BODY>");
    out.println("</HTML>");
  }

  /**Send the form where the user can type in
   * the details for a new user
   */
  private void sendSearchForm(HttpServletResponse response)
    throws IOException {

    PrintWriter out = response.getWriter();
    out.println("<BR><H2>Search Form</H2>");
    out.println("<BR>Please enter the first name, last name or part of any.");
    out.println("<BR>");
    out.println("<BR><FORM METHOD=POST>");
    out.print("Name: <INPUT TYPE=TEXT Name=keyword");
    out.print(" VALUE=\"" + StringUtil.encodeHtmlTag(keyword) + "\"");
    out.println(">");
    out.println("<INPUT TYPE=SUBMIT>");
    out.println("</FORM>");
    out.println("<BR>");
    out.println("<BR>");
  }
}
```

The DeleteServlet takes the value of id appended to the URL and deletes the record of the person having that id.

Retrieving the id is achieved by using the getParameter method of the HttpServletRequest interface:

```
String id = request.getParameter("id");
```

After you get the id, an SQL statement can be composed, as follows:

```
String sql = "DELETE FROM Users WHERE Id=" + id;
```

Next, you can create a Connection object and a Statement object, and use the latter to execute the SQL statement:

```
Connection con = DriverManager.getConnection("jdbc:odbc:JavaWeb");
Statement s = con.createStatement();
recordAffected = s.executeUpdate(sql);
```

The code for the DeleteServlet is given in Listing 5.4. Note that in the DeleteServlet, and in the UpdateServlet, there is no code for loading the JDBC driver. This has been done in the SearchServlets and the driver stays on for other servlets that need to connect to the same database.

Listing 5.4 **The DeleteServlet**

```
import javax.servlet.*;
import javax.servlet.http.*;
import java.io.*;
import java.util.*;
import java.sql.*;

public class DeleteServlet extends HttpServlet {
  /**Process the HTTP Get request*/
  public void doGet(HttpServletRequest request,
➥HttpServletResponse response) throws ServletException,
➥IOException {
    int recordAffected = 0;
    try {
      String id = request.getParameter("id");
      String sql = "DELETE FROM Users WHERE Id=" + id;
      Connection con =
        DriverManager.getConnection("jdbc:odbc:JavaWeb");

      Statement s = con.createStatement();
      recordAffected = s.executeUpdate(sql);
      s.close();
      con.close();
    }
    catch (SQLException e) {
    }
    catch (Exception e) {
```

```
      }
      response.setContentType("text/html");
      PrintWriter out = response.getWriter();
      out.println("<HTML>");
      out.println("<HEAD>");
      out.println("<TITLE>Deleting A Record</TITLE>");
      out.println("</HEAD>");
      out.println("<BODY>");
      out.println("<CENTER>");
      if (recordAffected==1)
        out.println("<P>Record deleted.</P>");
      else
        out.println("<P>Error deleting record.</P>");
      out.println("<A HREF=SearchServlet>Go back</A> to the Search page");
    }
  }
```

The UpdateServlet gets the id passed in the URL and sends a form containing the user details of the person with that id. The user can update the first name, the last name, or the password for that person, but not the user name. Therefore, the first name, last name, and the password are represented in text boxes, whereas the user name is displayed as HTML text.

The business rule for this servlet states that the user name cannot be changed because it's been guaranteed unique at the time of data insertion. Allowing this value to change can break this restriction. Of course, how you implement a servlet depends on your own requirement and business rules. The UpdateServlet is called by clicking the URL in the SearchServlet. The URL always carries an id for the person whose details are to be changed. This request invokes the UpdateServlet's doGet method that sends the page header, the update form, and the page footer. The doGet method is presented in Listing 5.5.

Listing 5.5 **The doGet Method of the UpdateServlet**

```
public void doGet(HttpServletRequest request,
  HttpServletResponse response)
  throws ServletException, IOException {
    sendPageHeader(response);
    sendUpdateForm(request, response);
    sendPageFooter(response);
  }
```

sendUpdateForm first retrieves the id from the URL using the getParameter method, as follows:

```
String id = request.getParameter("id");
```

The method then connects to the database to retrieve the details from the Users table. The SQL statement for that is simply the following:

```
SELECT FirstName, LastName, UserName, Password
FROM Users
WHERE Id=id
```

Then the method will send the details in an HTML form, similar to the one shown earlier in Figure 5.3.

The interesting part of the code is when the <FORM> tag is sent:

```
out.println("<BR><FORM METHOD=POST ACTION=" +
  request.getRequestURI() + "?id=" + id + ">");
```

Normally, you won't have an ACTION attribute in your form because the form is to be submitted to the same servlet. This time, however, you need to append the value of the id to the URL. Therefore, you use the getRequestURI method to get the current Uniform Resource Identifier (URI) and append the following information, such as

```
?id=6
```

for the user with an id of 6.

When the user submits the form, the doPost method of the UpdateServlet will be invoked. The doPost method is given in Listing 5.6.

Listing 5.6 **The doPost Method of the UpdateServlet**

```
public void doPost(HttpServletRequest request,
  HttpServletResponse response)
  throws ServletException, IOException {

  sendPageHeader(response);
  updateRecord(request, response);
  sendPageFooter(response);
}
```

The important method called from doPost is the updateRecord method. The updateRecord method first retrieves the values of id, firstName, lastName, and password using the getParameter method. Note that the id is retrieved from the URL and the others from the request body, as follows:

```
String id = request.getParameter("id");
String firstName = request.getParameter("firstName");
String lastName = request.getParameter("lastName");
String password = request.getParameter("password");
```

With these values, you can compose the SQL that will update the record. It has the following syntax:

```
UPDATE Users
SET FirstName=firstName,
LastName=lastName,
Password=password
WHERE Id=id
```

Then you can execute the SQL as usual:

```
Connection con = DriverManager.getConnection(dbUrl);
Statement s = con.createStatement();
int i = s.executeUpdate(sql);
```

Now, the executeUpdate should return the number of records affected by the SQL statement. Because the id is unique, it should return 1 as the number of records affected. If it is 1, you simply send a message saying, "Record updated". If it is not 1 because an unexpected error occurred, say, "Error updating record".

```
if (i==1)
  out.println("Record updated");
else
  out.println("Error updating record");
```

The complete code for the UpdateServlet is given in Listing 5.7.

Listing 5.7 **The UpdateServlet**

```
import javax.servlet.*;
import javax.servlet.http.*;
import java.io.*;
import java.util.*;
import java.sql.*;
import com.brainysoftware.java.StringUtil;

public class UpdateServlet extends HttpServlet {
  private String dbUrl = "jdbc:odbc:JavaWeb";

  /**Process the HTTP Get request*/
  public void doGet(HttpServletRequest request,
➥HttpServletResponse response) throws ServletException,
➥IOException {
    sendPageHeader(response);
    sendUpdateForm(request, response);
    sendPageFooter(response);
  }

  /**Process the HTTP Post request*/
  public void doPost(HttpServletRequest request,
➥HttpServletResponse response) throws ServletException,
➥IOException {
```

continues

Listing 5.7 **Continued**

```
    sendPageHeader(response);
    updateRecord(request, response);
    sendPageFooter(response);
  }


  /**
   * Send the HTML page header, including the title
   * and the <BODY> tag
   */
  private void sendPageHeader(HttpServletResponse response)
    throws ServletException, IOException {
    response.setContentType("text/html");
    PrintWriter out = response.getWriter();
    out.println("<HTML>");
    out.println("<HEAD>");
    out.println("<TITLE>Updating Record</TITLE>");
    out.println("</HEAD>");
    out.println("<BODY>");
    out.println("<CENTER>");
  }

  /**
   * Send the HTML page footer, i.e. the </BODY>
   * and the </HTML>
   */
  private void sendPageFooter(HttpServletResponse response)
    throws ServletException, IOException {
    PrintWriter out = response.getWriter();
    out.println("</CENTER>");
    out.println("</BODY>");
    out.println("</HTML>");
  }

  /**Send the form where the user can type in
   * the details for a new user
   */
  private void sendUpdateForm(HttpServletRequest
➥request, HttpServletResponse response)
    throws IOException {
    String id = request.getParameter("id");
    PrintWriter out = response.getWriter();
    out.println("<BR><H2>Update Form</H2>");
    out.println("<BR>Please edit the first name,
➥last name or password.");
    out.println("<BR>");
    try {
      String sql = "SELECT FirstName, LastName," +
        " UserName, Password" +
        " FROM Users" +
        " WHERE Id=" + id;
```

```
      Connection con = DriverManager.getConnection(dbUrl);
      Statement s = con.createStatement();
      ResultSet rs = s.executeQuery(sql);
      if (rs.next()) {
        String firstName = rs.getString(1);
        String lastName = rs.getString(2);
        String userName = rs.getString(3);
        String password = rs.getString(4);

        out.println("<BR><FORM METHOD=POST ACTION=" +
          request.getRequestURI() + "?id=" + id + ">");
        out.println("<TABLE>");
        out.println("<TR>");
        out.println("<TD>First Name</TD>");
        out.print("<TD><INPUT TYPE=TEXT Name=firstName");
        out.print(" VALUE=\"" + StringUtil.encodeHtmlTag(firstName)
➥+ "\"");
        out.println("></TD>");
        out.println("</TR>");
        out.println("<TR>");
        out.println("<TD>Last Name</TD>");
        out.print("<TD><INPUT TYPE=TEXT Name=lastName");
        out.print(" VALUE=\"" + StringUtil.encodeHtmlTag(lastName)
➥+ "\"");
        out.println("></TD>");
        out.println("</TR>");
        out.println("<TR>");
        out.println("<TD>User Name</TD>");
        out.print("<TD>" + StringUtil.encodeHtmlTag(userName)
➥+ "</TD>");
        out.println("</TR>");
        out.println("<TR>");
        out.println("<TD>Password</TD>");
        out.print("<TD><INPUT TYPE=PASSWORD Name=password");
        out.print(" VALUE=\"" + StringUtil.encodeHtmlTag
➥(password) + "\"");
        out.println("></TD>");
        out.println("</TR>");
        out.println("<TR>");
        out.println("<TD><INPUT TYPE=RESET></TD>");
        out.println("<TD><INPUT TYPE=SUBMIT></TD>");
        out.println("</TR>");
        out.println("</TABLE>");
        out.println("</FORM>");
      }
      s.close();
      con.close();
    }
    catch (SQLException e) {
      out.println(e.toString());
    }
```

continues

Listing 5.7 **Continued**

```
    catch (Exception e) {
      out.println(e.toString());
    }
  }

  void updateRecord(HttpServletRequest request,
➥HttpServletResponse response)
    throws IOException {
    String id = request.getParameter("id");
    String firstName = request.getParameter("firstName");
    String lastName = request.getParameter("lastName");
    String password = request.getParameter("password");
    PrintWriter out = response.getWriter();
    try {
      String sql = "UPDATE Users" +
        " SET FirstName='" + StringUtil.fixSqlFieldValue(firstName)
➥+ "'," +
        " LastName='" + StringUtil.fixSqlFieldValue(lastName) + "'," +
        " Password='" + StringUtil.fixSqlFieldValue(password) + "'" +
        " WHERE Id=" + id;
      Connection con = DriverManager.getConnection(dbUrl);
      Statement s = con.createStatement();
      int i = s.executeUpdate(sql);
      if (i==1)
        out.println("Record updated");
      else
        out.println("Error updating record");
      s.close();
      con.close();
    }
    catch (SQLException e) {
      out.println(e.toString());
    }
    catch (Exception e) {
      out.println(e.toString());
    }
    out.println("<A HREF=SearchServlet>Go back</A> to the Search Page");
  }
}
```

Hidden Fields

Another technique for managing user sessions is by passing a token as the value for an HTML hidden field. Unlike the URL rewriting, the value does not show on the URL but can still be read by viewing the HTML source code. Although this method also is easy to use, an HTML form is always required.

Using Hidden Fields

As the first example to illustrate the use of this technique, you will modify the sendUpdateForm method in the UpdateServlet in Listing 5.7. To try this example, you need to change the sendUpdateForm method in the UpdateServlet. This servlet should still be used with the SearchServlet and the DeleteServlet, given in Listings 5.3 and 5.4. The two servlets are not modified, and the code won't be repeated here.

The new sendUpdateForm method is given in Listing 5.8.

Listing 5.8 **The Modified sendUpdateForm Method in UpdateServlet**

```
private void sendUpdateForm(HttpServletRequest request,
➥HttpServletResponse response)
    throws IOException {
    String id = request.getParameter("id");
    PrintWriter out = response.getWriter();
    out.println("<BR><H2>Update Form</H2>");
    out.println("<BR>Please edit the first name,
➥last name or password.");
    out.println("<BR>");
    try {
      String sql = "SELECT FirstName, LastName," +
        " UserName, Password" +
        " FROM Users" +
        " WHERE Id=" + id;
      Connection con = DriverManager.getConnection(dbUrl);
      Statement s = con.createStatement();
      ResultSet rs = s.executeQuery(sql);
      if (rs.next()) {
        String firstName = rs.getString(1);
        String lastName = rs.getString(2);
        String userName = rs.getString(3);
        String password = rs.getString(4);

        out.println("<BR><FORM METHOD=POST>");
        out.print("<INPUT TYPE=HIDDEN Name=id VALUE=" + id + ">");
        out.println("<TABLE>");
        out.println("<TR>");
        out.println("<TD>First Name</TD>");
        out.print("<TD><INPUT TYPE=TEXT Name=firstName");
        out.print(" VALUE=\"" + StringUtil.encodeHtmlTag(firstName)
➥+ "\"");
        out.println("></TD>");
        out.println("</TR>");
        out.println("<TR>");
        out.println("<TD>Last Name</TD>");
        out.print("<TD><INPUT TYPE=TEXT Name=lastName");
        out.print(" VALUE=\"" + StringUtil.encodeHtmlTag(lastName)
```

continues

Listing 5.8 **Continued**

```
➥+ "\"");
          out.println("></TD>");
          out.println("</TR>");
          out.println("<TR>");
          out.println("<TD>User Name</TD>");
          out.print("<TD>" + StringUtil.encodeHtmlTag(userName)
➥+ "</TD>");
          out.println("</TR>");
          out.println("<TR>");
          out.println("<TD>Password</TD>");
          out.print("<TD><INPUT TYPE=PASSWORD Name=password");
          out.print(" VALUE=\"" + StringUtil.encodeHtmlTag(password)
➥+ "\"");
          out.println("></TD>");
          out.println("</TR>");
          out.println("<TR>");
          out.println("<TD><INPUT TYPE=RESET></TD>");
          out.println("<TD><INPUT TYPE=SUBMIT></TD>");
          out.println("</TR>");
          out.println("</TABLE>");
          out.println("</FORM>");
        }
        s.close();
        con.close();
      }
      catch (SQLException e) {
        out.println(e.toString());
      }
      catch (Exception e) {
        out.println(e.toString());
      }
    }
```

If you run this application in a web browser, you will be able to see that the id is not appended to the URL. Therefore, you don't need the ACTION attribute in the form. The id is now written to a HIDDEN field as follows:

```
out.print("<INPUT TYPE=HIDDEN Name=id VALUE=" + id + ">");
```

When the form is submitted, the hidden field is sent along with the other input elements' values of the form. On the servlet, the id still can be retrieved using the getParameter method.

Splitting Forms

The second example of the use of the hidden field occurs when you want to split a large form into several smaller ones for the sake of user-friendliness. Again, for this example, you will use the now familiar Users table. You will write an application that the user can use to insert a new record to the Users table, similar to the one in Chapter 4. Instead of having one form in which the user can enter the first name, the last name, the user name, and the password at the same time, however, the form is split into two smaller forms. The first form will accept the first name and the last name. The user name and password can be entered on the second form. When the second form is submitted, all four values must be sent to a third servlet that composes and executes an SQL insert statement.

In this example, you will use three servlets for each page in the process. They are simply called Page1Servlet, Page2Servlet, and Page3Servlet. Page1Servlet does not do much except send an HTML form with two text fields. You can replace this servlet with a static HTML file if you want. Page1Servlet is shown in Figure 5.4.

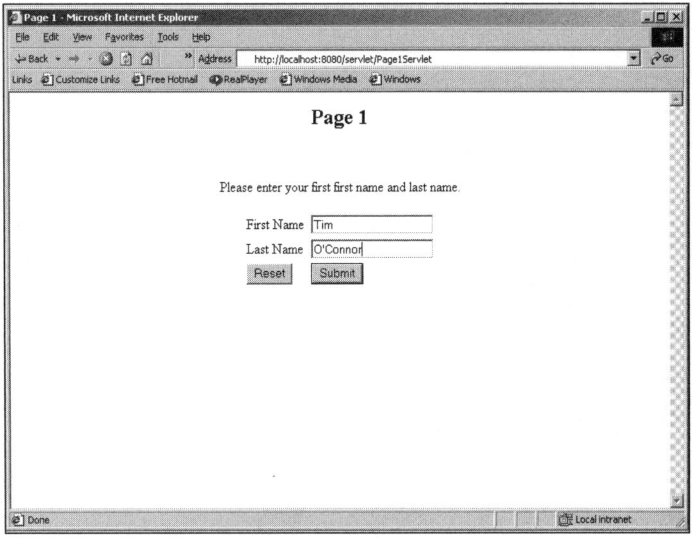

Figure 5.4 Page 1.

When the form sent by Page1Servlet is submitted, it goes to Page2Servlet. Page2Servlet sends the second form as well as the values from the first form. It is shown in Figure 5.5.

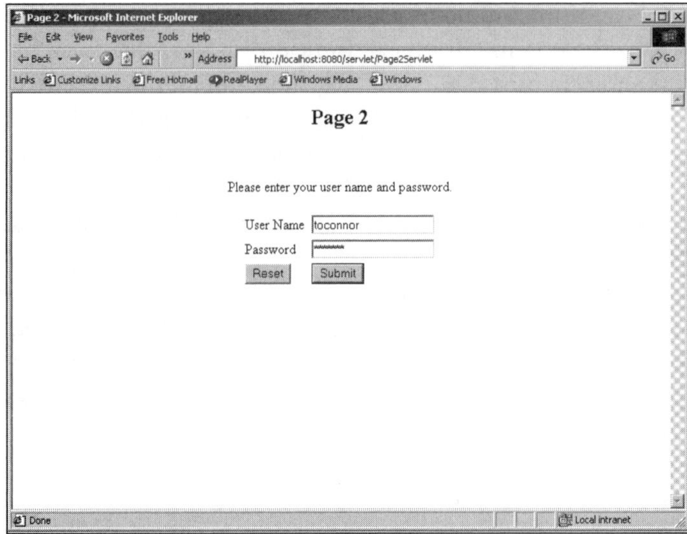

Figure 5.5 Page 2.

When the second form is submitted, all four values go to Page3Servlet. You could insert a new record to the database. For brevity, however, you will simply display the values without trying to access any database. The result from the Page3Servlet is shown in Figure 5.6.

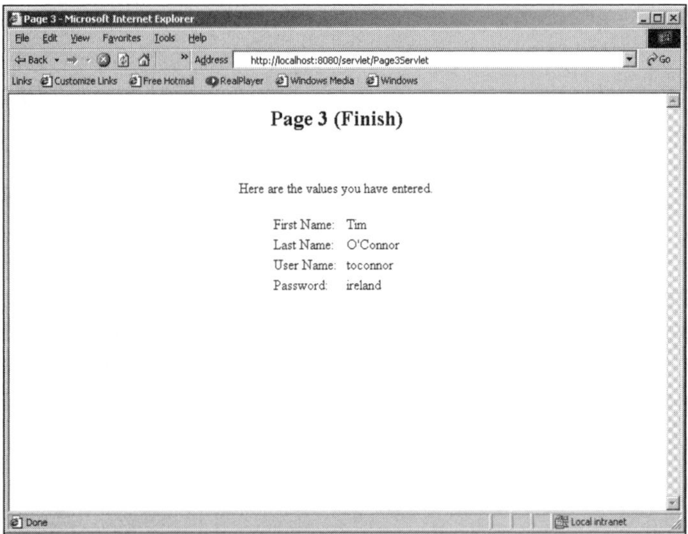

Figure 5.6 Page 3.

Now, let's dissect the code.

As mentioned, Page1Servlet is a simple HTML form. It is given in Listing 5.9.

Listing 5.9 **Page1Servlet**

```
import javax.servlet.*;
import javax.servlet.http.*;
import java.io.*;
import java.util.*;

public class Page1Servlet extends HttpServlet {
  /**Process the HTTP Get request*/
  public void doGet(HttpServletRequest request,
➥HttpServletResponse response) throws ServletException,
➥IOException {
    sendPage1(response);  }

  /**Process the HTTP Post request*/
  public void doPost(HttpServletRequest request,
➥HttpServletResponse response) throws ServletException,
➥IOException {
    sendPage1(response);
  }

  void sendPage1(HttpServletResponse response)
    throws ServletException, IOException {
    response.setContentType("text/html");
    PrintWriter out = response.getWriter();
    out.println("<HTML>");
    out.println("<HEAD>");
    out.println("<TITLE>Page 1</TITLE>");
    out.println("</HEAD>");
    out.println("<BODY>");
    out.println("<CENTER>");
    out.println("<H2>Page 1</H2>");
    out.println("<BR>");
    out.println("<BR>");
    out.println("Please enter your first first name and last name.");
    out.println("<BR>");
    out.println("<BR>");
    out.println("<FORM METHOD=POST ACTION=Page2Servlet>");
    out.println("<TABLE>");
    out.println("<TR>");
    out.println("<TD>First Name </TD>");
    out.println("<TD><INPUT TYPE=TEXT NAME=firstName></TD>");
    out.println("</TR>");
    out.println("<TR>");
    out.println("<TD>Last Name </TD>");
    out.println("<TD><INPUT TYPE=TEXT NAME=lastName></TD>");
```

continues

Listing 5.9 **Continued**

```
        out.println("</TR>");
        out.println("<TR>");
        out.println("<TD><INPUT TYPE=RESET></TD>");
        out.println("<TD><INPUT TYPE=SUBMIT VALUE=Submit></TD>");
        out.println("</TR>");
        out.println("</TABLE>");
        out.println("</FORM>");
        out.println("</CENTER>");
        out.println("</BODY>");
        out.println("</HTML>");
    }
}
```

One thing to note is that you use the ACTION attribute for the form, as you see here:

```
out.println("<FORM METHOD=POST ACTION=Page2Servlet>");
```

The value for the ACTION attribute is Page2Servlet, which makes sure that the form will be submitted to Page2Servlet.

Page2Servlet retrieves the first name and last name from the form in Page1Servlet and retains them in hidden fields. These hidden fields are included in a form that also sends the two text input for user name and password. The code for this servlet is given in Listing 5.10.

Listing 5.10 **Page2Servlet**

```
import javax.servlet.*;
import javax.servlet.http.*;
import java.io.*;
import java.util.*;
import com.brainysoftware.java.StringUtil;

public class Page2Servlet extends HttpServlet {
  String page1Url = "Page1Servlet";
  String firstName;
  String lastName;

  /**Process the HTTP Get request*/
  public void doGet(HttpServletRequest request,
➥HttpServletResponse response)
    throws ServletException, IOException {
    response.sendRedirect(page1Url);
  }

  /**Process the HTTP Post request*/
  public void doPost(HttpServletRequest request,
➥HttpServletResponse response) throws ServletException,
```

```
➥IOException {
    firstName = request.getParameter("firstName");
    lastName = request.getParameter("lastName");
    if (firstName==null || lastName==null)
      response.sendRedirect(page1Url);

    sendPage2(response);
  }

  void sendPage2(HttpServletResponse response)
    throws ServletException, IOException {
    response.setContentType("text/html");
    PrintWriter out = response.getWriter();
    out.println("<HTML>");
    out.println("<HEAD>");
    out.println("<TITLE>Page 2</TITLE>");
    out.println("</HEAD>");
    out.println("<BODY>");
    out.println("<CENTER>");
    out.println("<H2>Page 2</H2>");
    out.println("<BR>");
    out.println("<BR>");
    out.println("Please enter your user name and password.");
    out.println("<BR>");
    out.println("<BR>");
    out.println("<FORM METHOD=POST ACTION=Page3Servlet>");
    out.println("<INPUT TYPE=HIDDEN NAME=firstName VALUE=\"" +
      StringUtil.encodeHtmlTag(firstName) + "\">");
    out.println("<INPUT TYPE=HIDDEN NAME=lastName VALUE=\"" +
      StringUtil.encodeHtmlTag(lastName) + "\">");
    out.println("<TABLE>");
    out.println("<TR>");
    out.println("<TD>User Name </TD>");
    out.println("<TD><INPUT TYPE=TEXT NAME=userName></TD>");
    out.println("</TR>");
    out.println("<TR>");
    out.println("<TD>Password </TD>");
    out.println("<TD><INPUT TYPE=PASSWORD NAME=password></TD>");
    out.println("</TR>");
    out.println("<TR>");
    out.println("<TD><INPUT TYPE=RESET></TD>");
    out.println("<TD><INPUT TYPE=SUBMIT VALUE=Submit></TD>");
    out.println("</TR>");
    out.println("</TABLE>");
    out.println("</FORM>");
    out.println("</CENTER>");
    out.println("</BODY>");
    out.println("</HTML>");
  }
}
```

If you enter "Tim" and "O'Connor" as the first name and last name into the first form, the HTML source code passed back to Page 2 is as follows (look at the lines in bold where the values of the previous form are passed back to the browser):

```
<HTML>
<HEAD>
<TITLE>Page 2</TITLE>
</HEAD>
<BODY>
<CENTER>
<H2>Page 2</H2>
<BR>
<BR>
Please enter your user name and password.
<BR>
<BR>
<FORM METHOD=POST ACTION=Page3Servlet>
<INPUT TYPE=HIDDEN NAME=firstName VALUE="Tim">
<INPUT TYPE=HIDDEN NAME=lastName VALUE="O'Connor">
<TABLE>
<TR>
<TD>User Name </TD>
<TD><INPUT TYPE=TEXT NAME=userName></TD>
</TR>
<TR>
<TD>Password </TD>
<TD><INPUT TYPE=PASSWORD NAME=password></TD>
</TR>
<TR>
<TD><INPUT TYPE=RESET></TD>
<TD><INPUT TYPE=SUBMIT VALUE=Submit></TD>
</TR>
</TABLE>
</FORM>
</CENTER>
</BODY>
</HTML>
```

Finally, Listing 5.11 presents the Page3Servlet that retrieves all the values from the second form.

Listing 5.11 **Page3Servlet**

```
import javax.servlet.*;
import javax.servlet.http.*;
import java.io.*;
import java.util.*;
import com.brainysoftware.java.StringUtil;
```

```
public class Page3Servlet extends HttpServlet {
  String page1Url = "Page1Servlet";
  String firstName;
  String lastName;
  String userName;
  String password;

  /**Process the HTTP Get request*/
  public void doGet(HttpServletRequest request,
➥HttpServletResponse response)
    throws ServletException, IOException {
    response.sendRedirect(page1Url);
  }

  /**Process the HTTP Post request*/
  public void doPost(HttpServletRequest request,
➥HttpServletResponse response) throws ServletException,
➥IOException {
    firstName = request.getParameter("firstName");
    lastName = request.getParameter("lastName");
    userName = request.getParameter("userName");
    password = request.getParameter("password");
    if (firstName==null || lastName==null ||
      userName==null || password==null)
      response.sendRedirect(page1Url);
    // display all the values from the previous forms
    displayValues(response);
  }

  void displayValues(HttpServletResponse response)
    throws ServletException, IOException {
    response.setContentType("text/html");
    PrintWriter out = response.getWriter();
    out.println("<HTML>");
    out.println("<HEAD>");
    out.println("<TITLE>Page 3</TITLE>");
    out.println("</HEAD>");
    out.println("<BODY>");
    out.println("<CENTER>");
    out.println("<H2>Page 3 (Finish)</H2>");
    out.println("<BR>");
    out.println("<BR>");
    out.println("Here are the values you have entered.");
    out.println("<BR>");
    out.println("<BR>");
    out.println("<TABLE>");
    out.println("<TR>");
    out.println("<TD>First Name:  </TD>");
    out.println("<TD>" + StringUtil.encodeHtmlTag(firstName) + "</TD>");
    out.println("</TR>");
    out.println("<TR>");
```

continues

Listing 5.11 **Continued**

```
    out.println("<TD>Last Name:  </TD>");
    out.println("<TD>" + StringUtil.encodeHtmlTag(lastName) + "</TD>");
    out.println("</TR>");
    out.println("<TR>");
    out.println("<TD>User Name:  </TD>");
    out.println("<TD>" + StringUtil.encodeHtmlTag(userName) + "</TD>");
    out.println("</TR>");
    out.println("<TR>");
    out.println("<TD>Password:  </TD>");
    out.println("<TD>" + StringUtil.encodeHtmlTag(password) + "</TD>");
    out.println("</TR>");
    out.println("</TABLE>");
    out.println("</CENTER>");
    out.println("</BODY>");
    out.println("</HTML>");
  }
}
```

Multiple Forms in One Servlet

The previous example demonstrated how you could retain values in hidden fields in three servlets. Using more than one servlet is probably the last thing you want to do for a simple application, considering the maintenance involved for each servlet. This example shows the same application using only one servlet.

The problem with using one servlet is that each form will submit to the same servlet and the same doPost method will be invoked. How do you know which form to display next? The solution is simply done by incorporating a hidden field called page with a value of the form number. In the first form, the page field will have the value of 1, and in the second form this field will have the value of 2.

When the servlet is first called, the doGet method is invoked. What it does is very predictable: send the first form to the browser using the sendPage1 method:

```
sendPage1(response);
```

When the first form is submitted, it will invoke the doPost method because the form uses the POST method. The doPost method will retrieve the value of the parameter called page using the getParameter method. It should always find a value. However, if for some reason it does not, the method simply sends the first form and returns, as you see here:

```
String page = request.getParameter("page");
if (page==null) {
  sendPage1(response);
  return;
}
```

If a value for page is found, it could be 1 or 2. If 1 is returned, the previous request is from the first page; therefore Page 2 should be sent. The request that submits the first form must be accompanied by the parameters firstName and lastName, however. In other words, both the getParameter("firstName") and getParameter("lastName") must not return null. The values themselves could be blank strings, as is the case if the user does not type anything in the text boxes. However, a valid request from the first page must carry these parameters:

```
if (page.equals("1")) {
  if (firstName==null || lastName==null)
    sendPage1(response);
  else
    sendPage2(response);
  }
```

If either firstName or lastName is not found, the sendPage1 is called again because the request is not valid.

If the first page is okay, the doPost method calls the sendPage2 method, which sends the second form as well as the previous values from the first form.

If the value for page is 2, the previous page must come from the second page and four parameters must be present in the request: firstName, lastName, userName, and password. Missing one of the values is a sufficient reason to resend the first page, as shown here:

```
else if (page.equals("2")) {
  if (firstName==null || lastName==null ||
    userName==null || password==null)
    sendPage1(response);
  else
    displayValues(response);
}
```

If the value for page is 2 and all the other values are found, the displayValues method is called and it displays all the four values from the first and second forms.

The complete code is given in Listing 5.12.

Listing 5.12 **MultipleFormsServlet**

```
import javax.servlet.*;
import javax.servlet.http.*;
import java.io.*;
import java.util.*;
import com.brainysoftware.java.StringUtil;
```

continues

Listing 5.12 **Continued**

```
public class MultipleFormsServlet extends HttpServlet {
  String firstName;
  String lastName;
  String userName;
  String password;

  /**Process the HTTP Get request*/
  public void doGet(HttpServletRequest request,
➥HttpServletResponse response)
    throws ServletException, IOException {
    sendPage1(response);
  }

  /**Process the HTTP Post request*/
  public void doPost(HttpServletRequest request,
➥HttpServletResponse response) throws ServletException,
➥IOException {
    String page = request.getParameter("page");
    firstName = request.getParameter("firstName");
    lastName = request.getParameter("lastName");
    userName = request.getParameter("userName");
    password = request.getParameter("password");
    if (page==null) {
      sendPage1(response);
      return;
    }
    if (page.equals("1")) {
      if (firstName==null || lastName==null)
        sendPage1(response);
      else
        sendPage2(response);
    }
    else if (page.equals("2")) {
      if (firstName==null || lastName==null ||
        userName==null || password==null)
        sendPage1(response);
      else
        displayValues(response);
    }
  }

  void sendPage1(HttpServletResponse response)
    throws ServletException, IOException {
    response.setContentType("text/html");
    PrintWriter out = response.getWriter();
    out.println("<HTML>");
    out.println("<HEAD>");
    out.println("<TITLE>Page 1</TITLE>");
    out.println("</HEAD>");
    out.println("<BODY>");
    out.println("<CENTER>");
```

```
    out.println("<H2>Page 1</H2>");
    out.println("<BR>");
    out.println("<BR>");
    out.println("Please enter your first first name and last name.");
    out.println("<BR>");
    out.println("<BR>");
    out.println("<FORM METHOD=POST>");
    out.println("<INPUT TYPE=HIDDEN NAME=page VALUE=1>");
    out.println("<TABLE>");
    out.println("<TR>");
    out.println("<TD>First Name </TD>");
    out.println("<TD><INPUT TYPE=TEXT NAME=firstName></TD>");
    out.println("</TR>");
    out.println("<TR>");
    out.println("<TD>Last Name </TD>");
    out.println("<TD><INPUT TYPE=TEXT NAME=lastName></TD>");
    out.println("</TR>");
    out.println("<TR>");
    out.println("<TD><INPUT TYPE=RESET></TD>");
    out.println("<TD><INPUT TYPE=SUBMIT VALUE=Submit></TD>");
    out.println("</TR>");
    out.println("</TABLE>");
    out.println("</FORM>");
    out.println("</CENTER>");
    out.println("</BODY>");
    out.println("</HTML>");
  }

  void sendPage2(HttpServletResponse response)
    throws ServletException, IOException {
    response.setContentType("text/html");
    PrintWriter out = response.getWriter();
    out.println("<HTML>");
    out.println("<HEAD>");
    out.println("<TITLE>Page 2</TITLE>");
    out.println("</HEAD>");
    out.println("<BODY>");
    out.println("<CENTER>");
    out.println("<H2>Page 2</H2>");
    out.println("<BR>");
    out.println("<BR>");
    out.println("Please enter your user name and password.");
    out.println("<BR>");
    out.println("<BR>");
    out.println("<FORM METHOD=POST>");
    out.println("<INPUT TYPE=HIDDEN NAME=page VALUE=2>");
    out.println("<INPUT TYPE=HIDDEN NAME=firstName VALUE=\"" +
      StringUtil.encodeHtmlTag(firstName) + "\"></TD>");
    out.println("<INPUT TYPE=HIDDEN NAME=lastName VALUE=\"" +
      StringUtil.encodeHtmlTag(lastName) + "\"></TD>");
    out.println("<TABLE>");
```

continues

Listing 5.12 **Continued**

```
    out.println("<TR>");
    out.println("<TD>User Name </TD>");
    out.println("<TD><INPUT TYPE=TEXT NAME=userName></TD>");
    out.println("</TR>");
    out.println("<TR>");
    out.println("<TD>Password </TD>");
    out.println("<TD><INPUT TYPE=PASSWORD NAME=password></TD>");
    out.println("</TR>");
    out.println("<TR>");
    out.println("<TD><INPUT TYPE=RESET></TD>");
    out.println("<TD><INPUT TYPE=SUBMIT VALUE=Submit></TD>");
    out.println("</TR>");
    out.println("</TABLE>");
    out.println("</FORM>");
    out.println("</CENTER>");
    out.println("</BODY>");
    out.println("</HTML>");
  }

  void displayValues(HttpServletResponse response)
    throws ServletException, IOException {
    response.setContentType("text/html");
    PrintWriter out = response.getWriter();
    out.println("<HTML>");
    out.println("<HEAD>");
    out.println("<TITLE>Page 3</TITLE>");
    out.println("</HEAD>");
    out.println("<BODY>");
    out.println("<CENTER>");
    out.println("<H2>Page 3 (Finish)</H2>");
    out.println("<BR>");
    out.println("<BR>");
    out.println("Here are the values you have entered.");
    out.println("<BR>");
    out.println("<BR>");
    out.println("<TABLE>");
    out.println("<TR>");
    out.println("<TD>First Name:  </TD>");
    out.println("<TD>" + StringUtil.encodeHtmlTag(firstName) + "</TD>");
    out.println("</TR>");
    out.println("<TR>");
    out.println("<TD>Last Name:  </TD>");
    out.println("<TD>" + StringUtil.encodeHtmlTag(lastName) + "</TD>");
    out.println("</TR>");
    out.println("<TR>");
    out.println("<TD>User Name:  </TD>");
    out.println("<TD>" + StringUtil.encodeHtmlTag(userName) + "</TD>");
    out.println("</TR>");
    out.println("<TR>");
    out.println("<TD>Password:  </TD>");
    out.println("<TD>" + StringUtil.encodeHtmlTag(password) + "</TD>");
```

```
        out.println("</TR>");
        out.println("</TABLE>");
        out.println("</CENTER>");
        out.println("</BODY>");
        out.println("</HTML>");
    }
}
```

Cookies

The third technique that you can use to manage user sessions is by using cookies. A *cookie* is a small piece of information that is passed back and forth in the HTTP request and response. Even though a cookie can be created on the client side using some scripting language such as JavaScript, it is usually created by a server resource, such as a servlet. The cookie sent by a servlet to the client will be passed back to the server when the client requests another page from the same application.

Cookies were first specified by Netscape (see `http://home.netscape.com/newsref/std/cookie_spec.html`) and are now part of the Internet standard as specified in RFC 2109: The HTTP State Management Mechanism. Cookies are transferred to and from the client in the HTTP headers.

In servlet programming, a cookie is represented by the Cookie class in the javax.servlet.http package. You can create a cookie by calling the Cookie class constructor and passing two String objects: the name and value of the cookie. For instance, the following code creates a cookie object called c1. The cookie has the name "myCookie" and a value of "secret":

```
Cookie c1 = new Cookie("myCookie", "secret");
```

You then can add the cookie to the HTTP response using the addCookie method of the HttpServletResponse interface:

```
response.addCookie(c1);
```

Note that because cookies are carried in the request and response headers, you must not add a cookie after an output has been written to the HttpServletResponse object. Otherwise, an exception will be thrown.

The following example shows how you can create two cookies called userName and password and illustrates how those cookies are transferred back to the server. The servlet is called CookieServlet, and its code is given in Listing 5.13.

When it is first invoked, the doGet method of the servlet is called. The method creates two cookies and adds both to the HttpServletResponse object, as follows:

```
Cookie c1 = new Cookie("userName", "Helen");
Cookie c2 = new Cookie("password", "Keppler");
response.addCookie(c1);
response.addCookie(c2);
```

Next, the doGet method sends an HTML form that the user can click to send another request to the servlet:

```
response.setContentType("text/html");
    PrintWriter out = response.getWriter();
    out.println("<HTML>");
    out.println("<HEAD>");
    out.println("<TITLE>Cookie Test</TITLE>");
    out.println("</HEAD>");
    out.println("<BODY>");
    out.println("Please click the button to see the cookies sent to you.");
    out.println("<BR>");
    out.println("<FORM METHOD=POST>");
    out.println("<INPUT TYPE=SUBMIT VALUE=Submit>");
    out.println("</FORM>");
    out.println("</BODY>");
    out.println("</HTML>");
```

The form does not have any element other than a submit button. When the form is submitted, the doPost method is invoked. The doPost method does two things: It iterates all the headers in the request to show how the cookies are conveyed back to the server, and it retrieves the cookies and displays their values.

To display all the headers in the HttpServletRequest method, it first retrieves an Enumeration object containing all the header names. The method then iterates the Enumeration object to get the next header name and passes the header name to the getHeader method to display the value of that header, as you see here:

```
Enumeration enum = request.getHeaderNames();
while (enum.hasMoreElements()) {
  String header = (String) enum.nextElement();
  out.print("<B>" + header + "</B>: ");
  out.print(request.getHeader(header) + "<BR>");
}
```

To retrieve cookies, you use the getCookies method of the HttpServletRequest interface. This method returns a Cookie array containing all cookies in the request. It is your responsibility to loop through the array to get the cookie you want, as follows:

```
Cookie[] cookies = request.getCookies();
int length = cookies.length;
for (int i=0; i<length; i++) {
  Cookie cookie = cookies[i];
  out.println("<B>Cookie Name:</B> " +
    cookie.getName() + "<BR>");
  out.println("<B>Cookie Value:</B> " +
    cookie.getValue() + "<BR>");
}
```

The headers and cookies are displayed in Figure 5.7.

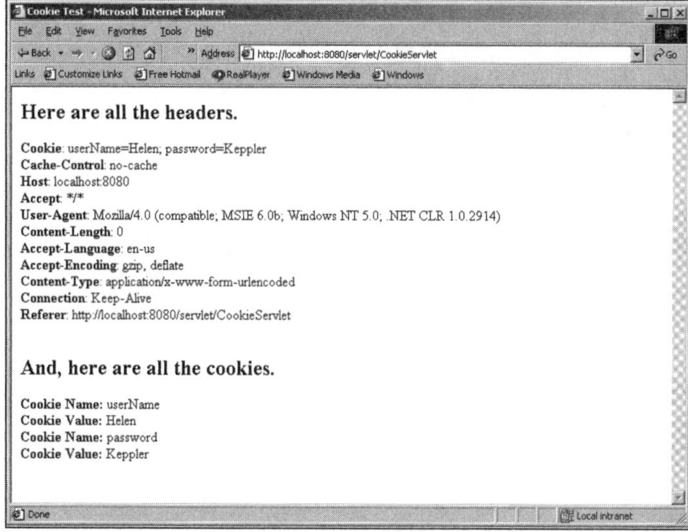

Figure 5.7 The headers containing cookies and the cookies' values.

Listing 5.13 **Sending and Receiving Cookies**

```
import javax.servlet.*;
import javax.servlet.http.*;
import java.io.*;
import java.util.*;

public class CookieServlet extends HttpServlet {

  /**Process the HTTP Get request*/
  public void doGet(HttpServletRequest request, HttpServletResponse response)
    throws ServletException, IOException {
```

continues

Listing 5.13 **Continued**

```
    Cookie c1 = new Cookie("userName", "Helen");
    Cookie c2 = new Cookie("password", "Keppler");
    response.addCookie(c1);
    response.addCookie(c2);

    response.setContentType("text/html");
    PrintWriter out = response.getWriter();
    out.println("<HTML>");
    out.println("<HEAD>");
    out.println("<TITLE>Cookie Test</TITLE>");
    out.println("</HEAD>");
    out.println("<BODY>");
    out.println("Please click the button to see the cookies
➥sent to you.");
    out.println("<BR>");
    out.println("<FORM METHOD=POST>");
    out.println("<INPUT TYPE=SUBMIT VALUE=Submit>");
    out.println("</FORM>");
    out.println("</BODY>");
    out.println("</HTML>");
  }
  /**Process the HTTP Post request*/
  public void doPost(HttpServletRequest request,
➥HttpServletResponse response) throws ServletException,
➥IOException {
    response.setContentType("text/html");
    PrintWriter out = response.getWriter();
    out.println("<HTML>");
    out.println("<HEAD>");
    out.println("<TITLE>Cookie Test</TITLE>");
    out.println("</HEAD>");
    out.println("<BODY>");
    out.println("<H2>Here are all the headers.</H2>");

    Enumeration enum = request.getHeaderNames();
    while (enum.hasMoreElements()) {
      String header = (String) enum.nextElement();
      out.print("<B>" + header + "</B>: ");
      out.print(request.getHeader(header) + "<BR>");
    }

    out.println("<BR><BR><H2>And, here are all the cookies.</H2>");
    Cookie[] cookies = request.getCookies();
    int length = cookies.length;
    for (int i=0; i<length; i++) {
      Cookie cookie = cookies[i];
      out.println("<B>Cookie Name:</B> " + cookie.getName() + "<BR>");
      out.println("<B>Cookie Value:</B> " + cookie.getValue() + "<BR>");
    }
```

```
        out.println("</BODY>");
        out.println("</HTML>");
    }
}
```

Another example of a servlet that uses cookies is a Login servlet that utilizes cookies to carry the user name and password information. The use of cookies is more appropriate than both URL rewriting and hidden values. First, unlike URL rewriting, the values of the cookies are not directly visible (you don't want this sensitive information to be seen by anyone). Second, you don't need to use any form, which is the requirement of using hidden fields.

Using cookes has a disadvantage, however: The user can choose not to accept them. Even though browsers leave the factories with the cookie setting on, any user can (accidentally) change this setting. The normal practice is therefore to use cookies with warnings to the user if the application does not work as expected. The warning could be a simple message telling the user to activate his cookie setting, or it could be a hyperlink to a page that thoroughly describes how to set the cookie setting in various browsers.

So, here it is: the CookieLoginServlet that modifies the previous LoginServlet in Chapter 4. The complete code is given in Listing 5.14. If the cookie setting is not on, the servlet will send a message. The servlet also will send a message if the authentication fails (see Figure 5.8).

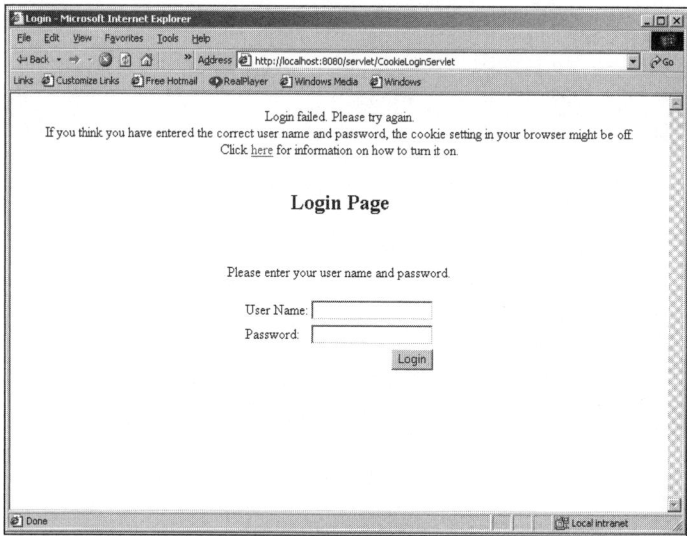

Figure 5.8 CookieLoginServlet.bmp.

An important part of the listing that deserves an explanation is the part that redirects the user to another resource when the login is successful. First, you need to create two cookies called userName and password and add them to the HttpServletResponse object. The cookies will always go back to the server when the user gets redirected to another resource. This resource can then retrieve the cookies and do the authentication again against the same database. This way, the user does not have to log in more than once.

Next, you need the code that redirects the user. Normally, to redirect a user, you would use the sendRedirect method. When you need to send cookies at the same time, however, redirecting using the sendRedirect method will not make the cookies get passed back to the server. As an alternative, you use a META tag of the following syntax:

```
<META HTTP-EQUIV=Refresh CONTENT=x;URL=ContentServlet>
```

This META tag will make the browser request another resource as indicated in the URL part. x indicates the number of seconds the browser will wait before the redirection occurs.

The code that does these two things is given here:

```
    if (login(userName, password)) {
      //send cookie to the browser
      Cookie c1 = new Cookie("userName", userName);
      Cookie c2 = new Cookie("password", password);
      response.addCookie(c1);
      response.addCookie(c2);
      response.setContentType("text/html");
      PrintWriter out = response.getWriter();
      //response.sendRedirect does not work here.
      // use a Meta tag to redirect to ContentServlet
      out.println(
"<META HTTP-EQUIV=Refresh CONTENT=0;URL=ContentServlet>");
    }
```

Listing 5.14 **CookieLoginServlet**

```
import javax.servlet.*;
import javax.servlet.http.*;
import java.io.*;
import java.util.*;
import java.sql.*;
import com.brainysoftware.java.StringUtil;

public class CookieLoginServlet extends HttpServlet {

  public void doGet(HttpServletRequest request,
➥HttpServletResponse response)
```

```
    }
    catch (Exception e) {
      System.out.println(e.toString());
    }
    return false;
  }
}
```

The second resource (such as another servlet) has to check the presence of the two cookies before displaying its supposedly important content. A servlet called ContentServlet is created to demonstrate this. The CookieLoginServlet will redirect the user to this servlet upon a successful login. The ContentServlet is given in Listing 5.15.

Listing 5.15 **ContentServlet**

```
import javax.servlet.*;
import javax.servlet.http.*;
import java.io.*;
import java.util.*;

public class ContentServlet extends HttpServlet {

  public String loginUrl = "CookieLoginServlet";

  /**Process the HTTP Get request*/
  public void doGet(HttpServletRequest request, HttpServletResponse response)
  ➥throws ServletException, IOException {
    String userName = null;
    String password = null;
    Cookie[] cookies = request.getCookies();
    if (cookies!=null) {
      int length = cookies.length;
      for (int i=0; i<length; i++) {
        Cookie cookie = cookies[i];
        if (cookie.getName().equals("userName"))
          userName = cookie.getValue();
        else if (cookie.getName().equals("password"))
          password = cookie.getValue();
      }
    }
    if (userName==null || password==null ||
    ➥!CookieLoginServlet.login(userName, password))
      response.sendRedirect(loginUrl);

    // This is an authorized user, okay to display content
    response.setContentType("text/html");
```

continues

Listing 5.15 **Continued**

```
    PrintWriter out = response.getWriter();
    out.println("<HTML>");
    out.println("<HEAD>");
    out.println("<TITLE>Welcome</TITLE>");
    out.println("</HEAD>");
    out.println("<BODY>");
    out.println("Welcome.");
    out.println("</BODY>");
    out.println("</HTML>");
  }

  /**Process the HTTP Post request*/
  public void doPost(HttpServletRequest request, HttpServletResponse
➥response) throws ServletException, IOException {
    doGet(request, response);
  }
}
```

After studying the previous example, you might wonder why you need to create two cookies that hold the value for the user name and password, respectively. Can't you just use a cookie that contains the value of true to indicate a previous successful login? The ContentServlet can just find this cookie and doesn't have to authenticate the user name and password again, hence saving a database manipulation.

This might sound better; however, a clever user can create a cookie at the client side. Knowing that a successful cookie carries a special flag, the user can create the cookie and get authenticated without having to know a valid user name and password.

Anticipating a Failed Redirection

When you need to do redirection while using cookies for managing user sessions—even when everything looks perfect—a redirection might fail. In the code that is supposed to redirect the user, you should provide a link that the user can manually click should the automatic redirection fail.

> **Note**
>
> If you are testing a cookie and find that the code does not work as expected, close your browser to delete the cookie.

Persisting Cookies

The cookies you created in the previous example last as long as the browser is open. When the browser is closed, the cookies are deleted. You can choose to persist cookies so that they last longer. The javax.servlet.http.Cookie class has the setMaxAge method that sets the maximum age of the cookie in seconds.

In the next example, you will create a Login servlet that uses a cookie that persists for 10,000 seconds. If the user closes the browser but comes back within 10,000 seconds, he or she does not have to enter a user name again. Figure 5.9 shows the Login page in which the user name has been supplied by the server.

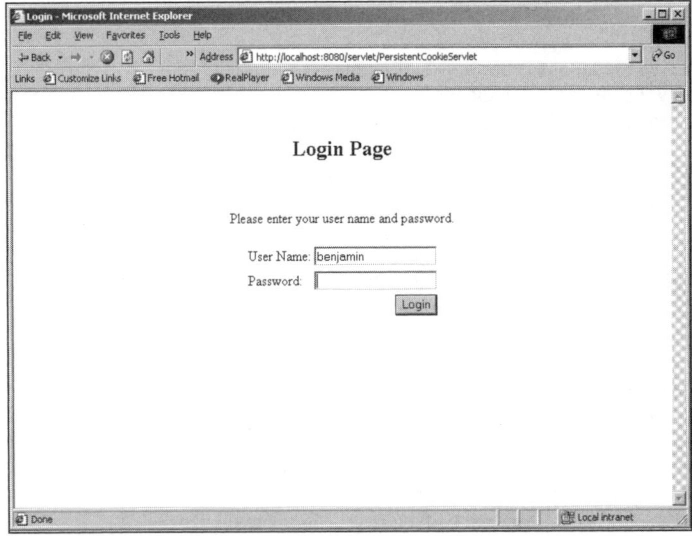

Figure 5.9 Persistent Cookie servlet.

The servlet is called PersistentCookieServlet and is given in Listing 5.16.

Listing 5.16 **PersistentCookieServlet**

```
import javax.servlet.*;
import javax.servlet.http.*;
import java.io.*;
import java.util.*;
import java.sql.*;
import com.brainysoftware.java.StringUtil;

public class PersistentCookieServlet extends HttpServlet {
```

continues

Listing 5.16 **Continued**

```
  String persistedUserName;

  public void doGet(HttpServletRequest request,
➥HttpServletResponse response)
    throws ServletException, IOException {
    Cookie[] cookies = request.getCookies();
    int length = cookies.length;
    for (int i=0; i<length; i++) {
      Cookie cookie = cookies[i];
      if (cookie.getName().equals("userName"))
        persistedUserName = cookie.getValue();
    }
    sendLoginForm(response, false);
  }

  public void doPost(HttpServletRequest request,
➥HttpServletResponse response)
    throws ServletException, IOException {

    String userName = request.getParameter("userName");
    String password = request.getParameter("password");
    if (login(userName, password)) {
      //send cookie to the browser
      Cookie c1 = new Cookie("userName", userName);
      Cookie c2 = new Cookie("password", password);
      c1.setMaxAge(10000);

      response.addCookie(c1);
      response.addCookie(c2);
      response.setContentType("text/html");
      PrintWriter out = response.getWriter();
      //response.sendRedirect does not work here.
      // use a Meta tag to redirect to ContentServlet
      out.println("<META HTTP-EQUIV=Refresh
➥CONTENT=0;URL=ContentServlet>");
    }
    else {
      sendLoginForm(response, true);
    }
  }

  private void sendLoginForm(HttpServletResponse response,
➥boolean withErrorMessage)
    throws ServletException, IOException {
    response.setContentType("text/html");
    PrintWriter out = response.getWriter();
    out.println("<HTML>");
    out.println("<HEAD>");
    out.println("<TITLE>Login</TITLE>");
    out.println("</HEAD>");
    out.println("<BODY>");
```

```
    out.println("<CENTER>");

    if (withErrorMessage) {
      out.println("Login failed. Please try again.<BR>");
      out.println("If you think you have entered the correct
➥user name" +
        " and password, the cookie setting in your browser
➥might be off." +
        "<BR>Click <A HREF=InfoPage.html>here</A> for information" +
        " on how to turn it on.<BR>");
    }
    out.println("<BR>");
    out.println("<BR><H2>Login Page</H2>");
    out.println("<BR>");
    out.println("<BR>Please enter your user name and password.");
    out.println("<BR>");
    out.println("<BR><FORM METHOD=POST>");
    out.println("<TABLE>");
    out.println("<TR>");
    out.println("<TD>User Name:</TD>");
    out.print("<TD><INPUT TYPE=TEXT NAME=userName");

    if (persistedUserName!=null)
      out.print(" VALUE=\"" + persistedUserName + "\"");
    out.print("></TD>");
    out.println("</TR>");
    out.println("<TR>");
    out.println("<TD>Password:</TD>");
    out.println("<TD><INPUT TYPE=PASSWORD NAME=password></TD>");
    out.println("</TR>");
    out.println("<TR>");
    out.println("<TD ALIGN=RIGHT COLSPAN=2>");
    out.println("<INPUT TYPE=SUBMIT VALUE=Login></TD>");
    out.println("</TR>");
    out.println("</TABLE>");
    out.println("</FORM>");
    out.println("</CENTER>");
    out.println("</BODY>");
    out.println("</HTML>");
  }

  public static boolean login(String userName, String password) {
    try {
      Class.forName("sun.jdbc.odbc.JdbcOdbcDriver");
      Connection con = DriverManager.getConnection("jdbc:odbc:JavaWeb");
      Statement s = con.createStatement();
      String sql = "SELECT UserName FROM Users" +
        " WHERE UserName='" + StringUtil.fixSqlFieldValue(userName)
➥+ "'" +
        " AND Password='" + StringUtil.fixSqlFieldValue(password) + "'";
```

continues

Listing 5.16 **Continued**

```
        ResultSet rs = s.executeQuery(sql);

        if (rs.next()) {
          rs.close();
          s.close();
          con.close();
          return true;
        }
        rs.close();
        s.close();
        con.close();
      }
      catch (ClassNotFoundException e) {
        System.out.println(e.toString());
      }
      catch (SQLException e) {
        System.out.println(e.toString());
      }
      catch (Exception e) {
        System.out.println(e.toString());
      }
      return false;
    }
  }
```

When a user requests the PersistentCookieServlet, either the first time or a subsequent time, the doGet method is invoked. What this method does is browse through the Cookie collection obtained from the getCookies() method of the javax.servlet.http.HttpServletResponse interface. For each Cookie, the code tests whether the cookie name is "userName". If it is, the cookie value is assigned to the persistentUserName field as follows:

```
Cookie[] cookies = request.getCookies();
int length = cookies.length;
for (int i=0; i<length; i++) {
  Cookie cookie = cookies[i];
  if (cookie.getName().equals("userName"))
    persistedUserName = cookie.getValue();
}
```

Then, the doGet method calls the sendLoginForm method to send the Login form that the user can use to log in:

```
sendLoginForm(response, false);
```

When the user submits the Login form, the doPost method in the PersistentCookieServlet is invoked. The doPost method first tries to retrieve the userName and password values entered by the user, as you see here:

```
String userName = request.getParameter("userName");
String password = request.getParameter("password");
```

It then sends the userName and password values to the login method. This method will return true if the userName and password are valid. Upon successful login, two cookies, c1 and c2, will be created. c1 is called userName, and c2 is named password:

```
if (login(userName, password)) {
  //send cookie to the browser
  Cookie c1 = new Cookie("userName", userName);
  Cookie c2 = new Cookie("password", password);
```

The c1 cookie is set to last for 10,000 seconds using the setMaxAge method, as follows:

```
c1.setMaxAge(10000);
```

Then, the doPost method sends both c1 and c2 to the browser and redirects the browser to another servlet, as the following code shows:

```
response.addCookie(c1);
response.addCookie(c2);
response.setContentType("text/html");
PrintWriter out = response.getWriter();
//response.sendRedirect does not work here.
// use a Meta tag to redirect to ContentServlet
out.println(
  "<META HTTP-EQUIV=Refresh CONTENT=0;URL=ContentServlet>");
```

If the user comes back within 10,000 seconds, the browser will send the userName cookie back to the server and the cookie will be found in the doGet method.

The login method called from the doPost method sets up a database connection and sends the following SQL statement:

```
SELECT UserName FROM Users
WHERE UserName='userName'
AND Password='password'
```

If the SQL statement execution returns a non-empty ResultSet object, a user account by that name and password is found and the login method returns true:

```
public static boolean login(String userName, String password) {
    try {
      Class.forName("sun.jdbc.odbc.JdbcOdbcDriver");
      Connection con = DriverManager.getConnection("jdbc:odbc:JavaWeb");
      Statement s = con.createStatement();
      String sql = "SELECT UserName FROM Users" +
        " WHERE UserName='" + StringUtil.fixSqlFieldValue(userName)
➥+ "'" +
        " AND Password='" + StringUtil.fixSqlFieldValue(password) + "'";
```

```
        ResultSet rs = s.executeQuery(sql);

        if (rs.next()) {
          rs.close();
          s.close();
          con.close();
          return true;
        }
        rs.close();
        s.close();
        con.close();
      }
      catch (ClassNotFoundException e) {
        System.out.println(e.toString());
      }
      catch (SQLException e) {
        System.out.println(e.toString());
      }
      catch (Exception e) {
        System.out.println(e.toString());
      }
      return false;
    }
  }
```

Checking Whether Cookie Setting Is On

All the cookie-related examples assume that the user browser's cookie setting is on. Even though browsers leave the factory with this setting on, the user can turn this off. One approach to solving this problem is to send a warning message if the application does not work as expected. The other option is to check this setting automatically. This option can be explained with an example of a servlet called CheckCookieServlet.

What the servlet does is simple enough. It sends a response that forces the browser to come back for the second time. With the first response, it sends a cookie. When the browser comes back for the second time, the servlet checks whether the request carries the cookie sent previously. If the cookie is there, it can be concluded that the browser setting for cookies is on. Otherwise, it could be that the user is using a very old browser that does not recognize cookies at all, or the cookie support for that browser is off.

The CheckCookieServlet is given in Listing 5.17.

Listing 5.17 **CheckCookieServlet**

```
import javax.servlet.*;
import javax.servlet.http.*;
import java.io.*;
import java.util.*;

public class CheckCookieServlet extends HttpServlet {
  /**Process the HTTP Get request*/
  public void doGet(HttpServletRequest request,
➥HttpServletResponse response) throws ServletException,
➥IOException {
    response.setContentType("text/html");
    PrintWriter out = response.getWriter();
    if (request.getParameter("flag")==null) {
      // the first request
      Cookie cookie = new Cookie("browserSetting", "on");
      response.addCookie(cookie);
      String nextUrl = request.getRequestURI() + "?flag=1";
      out.println("<META HTTP-EQUIV=Refresh CONTENT=0;URL="
➥+ nextUrl +">");
    }
    else {
      // the second request
      Cookie[] cookies = request.getCookies();
      if (cookies!=null)  {
      int length = cookies.length;
      boolean cookieFound = false;
      for (int i=0; i<length; i++) {
        Cookie cookie = cookies[i];
        if (cookie.getName().equals("browserSetting") &&
          cookie.getValue().equals("on")) {
          cookieFound = true;
          break;
        }
      }
      if (cookieFound) {
        out.println("Your browser's cookie setting is on.");
      }
      else {
        out.println("Your browser does not support cookies or" +
          " the cookie setting is off.");
      }
    }
  }
  /**Process the HTTP Post request*/
  public void doPost(HttpServletRequest request, HttpServletResponse
 response) throws ServletException, IOException {
    doGet(request, response);
  }
}
```

Session Objects

Of the four techniques for session management covered in this chapter, the Session object, represented by the javax.servlet.http.HttpSession interface, is the easiest to use and the most powerful. For each user, the servlet can create an HttpSession object that is associated with that user only and can only be accessed by that particular user. The HttpSession object acts like a Hashtable into which you can store any number of key/object pairs. The HttpSession object is accessible from other servlets in the same application. To retrieve an object previously stored, you need only to pass the key.

An HttpSession object uses a cookie or URL rewriting to send a token to the client. If cookies are used to convey session identifiers, the client browsers are required to accept cookies.

Unlike previous techniques, however, the server does not send any value. What it sends is simply a unique number called the *session identifier*. This session identifier is used to associate a user with a Session object in the server. Therefore, if there are 10 simultaneous users, 10 Session objects will be created in the server and each user can access only his or her own HttpSession object.

The way an HttpSession object is created for a user and retrieved in the next requests is illustrated in Figure 5.10.

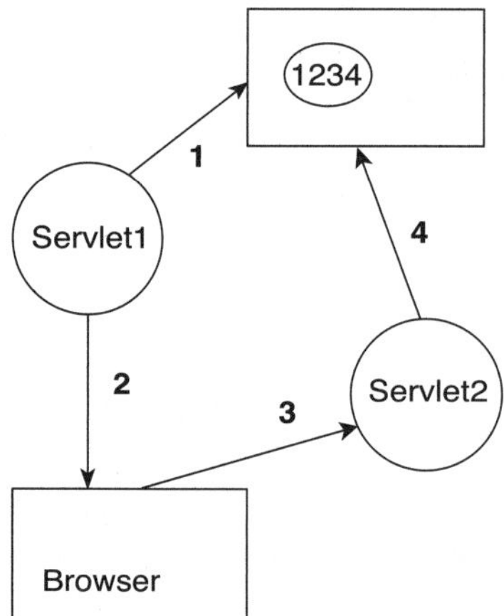

Figure 5.10 How session tracking works with the HttpSession object.

Figure 5.10 shows that there are four steps in session tracking using the HttpSession object:

1. An HttpSession object is created by a servlet called Servlet1. A session identifier is generated for this HttpSession object. In this example, the session identifier is 1234, but in reality, the servlet container will generate a longer random number that is guaranteed to be unique. The HttpSession object then is stored in the server and is associated with the generated session identifier. Also the programmer can store values immediately after creating an HttpSession.
2. In the response, the servlet sends the session identifier to the client browser.
3. When the client browser requests another resource in the same application, such as Servlet2, the session identifier is sent back to the server and passed to Servlet2 in the javax.servlet.http.HttpServletRequest object.
4. For Servlet2 to have access to the HttpSession object for this particular client, it uses the getSession method of the javax.servlet.http.HttpServletRequest interface. This method automatically retrieves the session identifier from the request and obtains the HttpSession object associated with the session identifier.

Note

What if the user never comes back after an HttpSession object is created? Then the servlet container waits for a certain period of time and removes that HttpSession object. One worry about using Session objects is scalability. In some servlet containers, Session objects are stored in memory, and as the number of users exceeds a certain limit, the server eventually runs out of memory.

One solution to this memory problem when using Session objects is to save Session objects to the database or disk. However, the Servlet 2.3 Specification does not clearly state how a servlet container should do this. If you are using Tomcat 4, however, your Session objects will be moved to secondary storage once the number of Session objects has exceeded some value.

The getSession method of the javax.servlet.http.HttpServletRequest interface has two overloads. They are as follows:

- HttpSession getSession()
- HttpSession getSession(boolean create)

The first overload returns the current session associated with this request, or if the request does not have a session identifier, it creates a new one.

The second overload returns the HttpSession object associated with this request if there is a valid session identifier in the request. If no valid session identifier is found in the request, whether a new HttpSession object is created depends on the create value. If the value is true, a new HttpSession object is created if no valid session identifier is found in the request. Otherwise, the getSession method will return null.

Now that you know how session management works using the HttpSession object, let's have a look at the javax.servlet.http.HttpSession interface in more detail.

The javax.servlet.http.HttpSession Interface

This interface has the following methods:

- getAttribute
- getAttributeNames
- getCreationTime
- getId
- getLastAccessedTime
- getMaxInactiveInterval
- getServletContext
- getSessionContext
- getValue
- getValueNames
- invalidate
- isNew
- putValue
- removeAttribute
- removeValue
- setAttribute
- setMaxInactiveInterval

Each of the methods is discussed below.

getAttribute

This method retrieves an attribute from the HttpSession object. The return value is an object of type Object; therefore you may have to downcast the attribute to its original type. To retrieve an attribute, you pass the name associated with the attribute. This method returns an IllegalStateException if it is called upon an invalidated HttpSession object.

The signature for this method is as follows:

```
public Object getAttribute(String name) throws IllegalStateException
```

getAttributeNames

The getAttributeNames method returns a java.util.Enumeration containing all attribute names in the HttpSession object. This method returns an IllegalStateException if it is called upon an invalidated HttpSession object.

The signature is as follows:

```
public java.util.Enumeration getAttributeNames()
➥throws IllegalStateException
```

getCreationTime

The getCreationTime method returns the time that the HttpSession object was created, in milliseconds since January 1, 1970 00:00:00 GMT. This method returns an IllegalStateException if it is called upon an invalidated HttpSession object.

The signature for this method is as follows:

```
public long getCreationTime() throws IllegalStateException
```

getId

The getID method returns the session identifier. The signature for this method is as follows:

```
public String getId()
```

getLastAccessedTime

The getLastAccessedTime method returns the time the HttpSession object was last accessed by the client. The return value is the number of milliseconds lapsed since since January 1, 1970 00:00:00 GMT. The following is the method signature:

```
public long getLastAccessedTime()
```

getMaxInactiveInterval

The getMaxInactiveInterval method returns the number of seconds the HttpSession object will be retained by the servlet container after it is last accessed before being removed. The signature of this method is as follows:

```
public int getMaxInactiveInterval()
```

getServletContext

The getServletContext method returns the javax.servlet.ServletContext object the HttpSession object belongs to. The signature is as follows:

```
public javax.servlet.ServletContext getServletContext
```

getSessionContext

This method is deprecated.

getValue

This method is deprecated.

getValueNames

This method is deprecated.

invalidate

The invalidate method invalidates the HttpSession object and unbinds any object bound to it. This method throws an IllegalStateException if this method is called upon an already invalidated HttpSession object. The signature is as follows:

```
public void invalidate() throws IllegalStateException
```

isNew

The isNew method indicates whether the HttpSession object was created with this request and the client has not yet joined the session tracking. This method returns an IllegalStateException if it is called upon an invalidated HttpSession object.

Its signature is as follows:

```
public boolean isNew() throws IllegalStateException
```

putValue

This method is deprecated.

removeAttribute

The removeAttribute method removes an attribute bound to this HttpSession object. This method returns an IllegalStateException if it is called upon an invalidated HttpSession object.

Its signature is as follows:

```
public void removeAttribute(String name) throws IllegalStateException
```

removeValue

This method is deprecated.

setAttribute

The setAttribute method adds a name/attribute pair to the HttpSession object. This method returns an IllegalStateException if it is called upon an invalidated HttpSession object. The method has the following signature:

```
public void setAttribute(String name, Object attribute) throws
IllegalStateException
```

setMaxInactiveInterval

The setMaxInactiveInterval method sets the number of seconds from the time the HttpSession object is accessed the servlet container will wait before removing the HttpSession object. The signature is as follows:

```
public void setMaxInactiveInterval(int interval)
```

Passing a negative number to this method will make this HttpSession object never expire.

Using HttpSession Object

The following example modifies the previous Login page and uses HttpSession objects. You don't need to create two cookies for both the user name and password. Because only the server can store and retrieve values from a HttpSession object, you can create a key called loggedIn with the value of "true" if the user has successfully logged in before.

The code is given in Listing 5.18.

Listing 5.18 **The SessionLoginServlet**

```
import javax.servlet.*;
import javax.servlet.http.*;
import java.io.*;
import java.util.*;
import java.sql.*;
import com.brainysoftware.java.StringUtil;

public class SessionLoginServlet extends HttpServlet {
```

continues

Listing 5.18 **Continued**

```
  public void doGet(HttpServletRequest request,
➥HttpServletResponse response)
    throws ServletException, IOException {
    sendLoginForm(response, false);
  }

  public void doPost(HttpServletRequest request,
➥HttpServletResponse response)
    throws ServletException, IOException {

    String userName = request.getParameter("userName");
    String password = request.getParameter("password");
    if (login(userName, password)) {
      //send cookie to the browser
      HttpSession session = request.getSession(true);
      session.setAttribute("loggedIn", new String("true"));
      response.sendRedirect("Content2Servlet");
    }
    else {
      sendLoginForm(response, true);
    }
  }

  private void sendLoginForm(HttpServletResponse response,
➥boolean withErrorMessage)
    throws ServletException, IOException {
    response.setContentType("text/html");
    PrintWriter out = response.getWriter();
    out.println("<HTML>");
    out.println("<HEAD>");
    out.println("<TITLE>Login</TITLE>");
    out.println("</HEAD>");
    out.println("<BODY>");
    out.println("<CENTER>");

    if (withErrorMessage) {
      out.println("Login failed. Please try again.<BR>");
      out.println("If you think you have entered the correct
➥user name" +
        " and password, the cookie setting in your browser
➥might be off." +
        "<BR>Click <A HREF=InfoPage.html>here</A> for information" +
        " on how to turn it on.<BR>");
    }
    out.println("<BR>");
    out.println("<BR><H2>Login Page</H2>");
    out.println("<BR>");
    out.println("<BR>Please enter your user name and password.");
    out.println("<BR>");
    out.println("<BR><FORM METHOD=POST>");
    out.println("<TABLE>");
    out.println("<TR>");
```

```
    out.println("<TD>User Name:</TD>");
    out.println("<TD><INPUT TYPE=TEXT NAME=userName></TD>");
    out.println("</TR>");
    out.println("<TR>");
    out.println("<TD>Password:</TD>");
    out.println("<TD><INPUT TYPE=PASSWORD NAME=password></TD>");
    out.println("</TR>");
    out.println("<TR>");
    out.println("<TD ALIGN=RIGHT COLSPAN=2>");
    out.println("<INPUT TYPE=SUBMIT VALUE=Login></TD>");
    out.println("</TR>");
    out.println("</TABLE>");
    out.println("</FORM>");
    out.println("</CENTER>");
    out.println("</BODY>");
    out.println("</HTML>");
  }

  public static boolean login(String userName, String password) {
    try {
      Class.forName("sun.jdbc.odbc.JdbcOdbcDriver");
      Connection con = DriverManager.getConnection("jdbc:odbc:JavaWeb");
      Statement s = con.createStatement();
      String sql = "SELECT UserName FROM Users" +
        " WHERE UserName='" + StringUtil.fixSqlFieldValue(userName)
➥+ "'" +
        " AND Password='" + StringUtil.fixSqlFieldValue(password) + "'";

      ResultSet rs = s.executeQuery(sql);

      if (rs.next()) {
        rs.close();
        s.close();
        con.close();
        return true;
      }
      rs.close();
      s.close();
      con.close();
    }
    catch (ClassNotFoundException e) {
      System.out.println(e.toString());
    }
    catch (SQLException e) {
      System.out.println(e.toString());
    }
    catch (Exception e) {
      System.out.println(e.toString());
    }
    return false;
  }
}
```

Listing 5.19 **Content2Servlet**

```
import javax.servlet.*;
import javax.servlet.http.*;
import java.io.*;
import java.util.*;

public class Content2Servlet extends HttpServlet {

  public String loginUrl = "SessionLoginServlet";

  /**Process the HTTP Get request*/
  public void doGet(HttpServletRequest request,
➥HttpServletResponse response) throws ServletException,
➥IOException {
    HttpSession session = request.getSession();
    if (session==null)
      response.sendRedirect(loginUrl);
    else {
      String loggedIn = (String) session.getAttribute("loggedIn");
      if (!loggedIn.equals("true"))
        response.sendRedirect(loginUrl);
    }
    // This is an authorized user, okay to display content
    response.setContentType("text/html");

    PrintWriter out = response.getWriter();
    out.println("<HTML>");
    out.println("<HEAD>");
    out.println("<TITLE>Welcome</TITLE>");
    out.println("</HEAD>");
    out.println("<BODY>");
    out.println("Welcome.");
    out.println("</BODY>");
    out.println("</HTML>");
  }

  /**Process the HTTP Post request*/
  public void doPost(HttpServletRequest request,
➥HttpServletResponse response) throws ServletException,
➥IOException {
    doGet(request, response);
  }
}
```

Session Tracking with URL-Rewriting

As mentioned previously, by default a session identifier is sent to the client browser and back to the server using a cookie. This means that the client browser must have its cookie support enabled. Therefore, you need to perform browser cookie testing as explained in the previous section, "Checking Whether Cookie Setting Is On."

Alternatively, you can avoid the use of cookies by sending session identifiers in the URL using the URL-rewriting technique. Fortunately, the Servlet API provides an easy way to append session identifier to the URL—using the encodeURL method of the javax.servlet.http.HttpServletResponse interface.

To use the URL-rewriting technique, pass any URL referenced to in a servlet into the encodeURL method of the javax.servlet.http.HttpServletResponse interface. For example, the following code:

```
out.println("<a href=Servlet2>Click here</a>");
```

must be changed into the following:

```
out.println("<a href=" + response.encodeURL("Servlet2") +
  ">Click here</a>");
```

This will add the session identifier to the end of the string, resulting in a URL similar to the following:

```
http://localhost:8080/myApp/servlet/Servlet2;jsessionid=AB348989283429489234At
```

where the number after jsessionid= is the session identifier.

One disadvantage of using URL rewriting as opposed to cookies in sending your session identifiers is that URL rewriting does not survive static pages. For example, if the user has to browse through some HTML page during his or her session, the session identifier will be lost.

The not-so-practical solution is of course to convert all static pages into servlets or JSP pages.

Knowing Which Technique to Use

Having learned the four techniques for managing user sessions, you may be wondering which one you should choose to implement.

Clearly, using Session objects is the easiest and you should use this if your servlet container supports swapping Session objects from memory to secondary storage. If you are using Tomcat 4, this feature is available to you.

One concern when using the Session objects is whether cookie support is enabled in the user browser. If it is, you have two options:

- You can test the cookie support setting by using the technique described in the section “Checking Whether Cookie Setting Is On.”
- You can use URL-rewriting.

Appending your session identifier to the URL is a good technique, even though this creates some additional work for the programmer. However, this relieves you of having to rely on cookies.

Using cookies is not as flexible as using Session objects. However, cookies are the way to go if you don't want your server to store any client-related information or if you want the client information to persist when the browser is closed.

Finally, hidden fields are probably the least-often-used technique. If you need to split a form into several smaller ones, however, using hidden fields is the cheapest and most efficient method. You don't need to consume server resources to temporarily store the values from the previous forms, and you don't need to rely on cookies. I would suggest hidden fields over Session objects, URL-rewriting, or cookies in this case.

Summary

In this chapter, you have learned that HTTP is a stateless protocol. You also have been shown the implications of this statelessness. Additionally you learned about four techniques you can use to manage user sessions. Each technique has been described, and examples have been built to demonstrate the technique.

6

Application and Session Events

In Chapter 3, "Writing Servlet Applications," you learned how to use the ServletContext object to share information among all the servlets in a web application. You also learned how to obtain this object so that you can use its methods. The ServletContext object is created by the servlet container, and, among other things, it has a method called setAttribute. That method causes the object to act like a Hashtable, where you can store an object that is identified by a key and later retrieve the object by passing the key.

In Chapter 5, "Session Management," you learned how to create and invalidate the HttpSession object. You also learned how to use an HttpSession object to store user session information. Similar to the ServletContext object, an Httpsession enables you to store key/object pairs. Unlike the ServletContext, which is accessible by all the servlets, an HttpSession object is linked to a particular user and is available only to that user.

In this chapter, you see a new feature in the Servlet 2.3 API Specification that has to do with both the ServletContext and HttpSession objects. This new feature supports application and session-level events. If you use Tomcat 4, this new feature is available to you.

The concept is very simple, so let me provide you an overview.

In relation to the ServletContext object, the Servlet 2.3 API enables you to get notifications when the ServletContext object is created and destroyed, or when an attribute (a key/object pair) is created, removed, or replaced. The moments these things occur have now become Java events that you can listen to.

The question is, why would you want to know when these things happen? Surely you can live without these events; however, they can be very useful because you can write code that gets called automatically when one of the events happens. For example, you know that the ServletContext object is created by the servlet container when it initializes. You can therefore do certain things in response to this event, such as loading a JDBC driver or creating a database connection object. Or, you probably want to initialize a connection URL and store it as a variable in the ServletContext object so that it is accessible from all the servlets in the web application.

For events that get triggered when the ServletContext is destroyed, you can write code that does some cleanup, such as closing files or ending a database connection.

The same applies to events related to ContextServlet's attributes. For example, you can make a persistent page counter whose value gets written to a file every time the value is changed. Assuming that you store this counter value as an attribute in the ServletContext object, you can write some I/O code that automatically executes when the ServletContext's attribute gets replaced, thus allowing for an accurate count.

Additionally, with an HttpSession object, you also can get notified when an HttpSession object is created or invalidated or when an attribute of a HttpSession object is added, removed, or replaced.

In this chapter, you will see various event classes and listener interfaces that support event notification for state changes in the ServletContext and the HttpSession objects.

Listening to Application Events

At the application level, the javax.servlet package provides two listener interfaces that support event notifications for state changes in the ServletContext object: the ServletContextListener interface and the ServletContextAttributesListener interface.

The ServletContextListener Interface

You can use the ServletContextListener interface to listen to the ServletContext life cycle events. Its signature is given as follows:

```
public interface ServletContextListener extends java.util.EventListener
```

Your listener class must implement this interface to listen to ServletContext life cycle events. The ServletContextListener interface has two methods: contextInitialized and contextDestroyed. The signatures for these methods are the following:

```
public void contextInitialized(ServletContextEvent sce)
public void contextDestroyed(ServletContextEvent sce)
```

The contextInitialized method is called when the web application is ready to service requests. The method is called automatically by the servlet container when its own initialization process is finished. You can write code that needs to get executed when the application initializes, such as loading a JDBC driver, creating a database Connection object, or assigning initialization values to global variables.

The contextDestroyed method is invoked when the servlet context is about to be shut down. You can use this method to write code that needs to run when the application shuts down, such as closing a database connection or writing to the log.

Utilizing the contextInitialized method is similar to writing code in a servlet's init( ) method, and the contextDestroyed method has a similar effect as a servlet's destroy( ) method. However, using application events make the codes available throughout the whole application, not only from inside a servlet.

The ServletContextEvent Class

As you have seen, both methods of the ServletContextListener interface pass a ServletContextEvent class. This class has the following signature:

```
public class ServletContextEvent extends java.util.EventObject
```

The ServletContextEvent has only one method: getServletContext. This method returns the ServletContext that is changed.

Deployment Descriptor

To use application events and include a servlet listener class, you must tell the servlet container by registering the listener class in the deployment descriptor. The <web-app> element must contain a <listener> element like the following:

```
<web-app>
  <listener>
    <listener-class>
      AppLifeCycleEvent
    </listener-class>
  </listener>
</web-app>
```

The <listener> element must come before the <servlet> part.

An Example: AppLifeCycleEvent Class

The following is a simple listener class that listens to the life cycle events of the ServletContext. It simply prints the string "Application initialized" when the ServletContext is initialized and "Application destroyed" when the ServletContext is destroyed. The code for the program is given in Listing 6.1.

Listing 6.1 **The AppLifeCycleEvent Class**

```
import javax.servlet.ServletContextListener;
import javax.servlet.ServletContextEvent;

public class AppLifeCycleEvent implements ServletContextListener {

  public void contextInitialized(ServletContextEvent cse) {
    System.out.println("Application initialized");
  }

  public void contextDestroyed(ServletContextEvent cse) {
    System.out.println("Application shut down");
  }
}
```

For the AppLifeCycleEvent class to work, you must register it in the deployment descriptor. The deployment descriptor is given in Listing 6.2.

Listing 6.2 **The Deployment Descriptor for the AppLifeCycleEvent Class**

```
<?xml version="1.0" encoding="ISO-8859-1"?>

<!DOCTYPE web-app
  PUBLIC "-//Sun Microsystems, Inc.//DTD Web Application 2.3//EN"
  "http://java.sun.com/dtd/web-app_2_3.dtd">

<web-app>
  <listener>
    <listener-class>
      AppLifeCycleEvent
    </listener-class>
  </listener>
</web-app>
```

Now, restart Tomcat and watch the console window. You should be able to see the string "Application initialized" at the console.

If you want, you can have more than one listener class. To do this, list all the listener classes in the deployment descriptor, as follows:

```
<?xml version="1.0" encoding="ISO-8859-1"?>

<!DOCTYPE web-app
  PUBLIC "-//Sun Microsystems, Inc.//DTD Web Application 2.3//EN"
  "http://java.sun.com/dtd/web-app_2_3.dtd">

<web-app>
  <listener>
    <listener-class>
      AppLifeCycleEvent1
    </listener-class>
  </listener>
  <listener>
    <listener-class>
      AppLifeCycleEvent2
    </listener-class>
  </listener>
</web-app>
```

With a deployment descriptor like this, when Tomcat starts, it will call the contextInitialized method in the AppLifeCycleEvent1 class and then call the same method in the AppLifeCycleEvent2 class.

Another Example: Loading a JDBC Driver and Setting a ServletContext Attribute

The following example uses the contextInitialized method in the ServletContextListener interface to load a JDBC driver and set a ServletContext attribute named "dbUrl" with a value of "jdbc:mysql///Fred". Loading the JDBC driver here makes it available for the next access to the database.

The example has two classes: a listener class called AppLifeCycleEventDemo and a servlet named ApplicationEventDemoServlet. The listener class provides a method (contextInitialized) that will be called automatically when the ServletContext object is initialized. This is where you put the code that loads the JDBC driver and sets a ServletContext attribute. The servlet is used to display the attribute value. The AppLifeCycleEventDemo class is given in Listing 6.3, and the ApplicationEventDemoServlet in Listing 6.4.

Listing 6.3 **AppLifeCycleEventDemo**

```
import javax.servlet.ServletContext;
import javax.servlet.ServletContextListener;
import javax.servlet.ServletContextEvent;

public class AppLifeCycleEventDemo implements ServletContextListener {

  public void contextInitialized(ServletContextEvent sce) {
    System.out.println("Initializing Application ...");
    // Load the JDBC driver
    try {
      Class.forName("org.gjt.mm.mysql.Driver ");
    }
    catch (ClassNotFoundException e) {
      System.out.println(e.toString());
    }

    // Get the ServletContext object
    ServletContext servletContext = sce.getServletContext();

    // Set a ServletContext attribute
    servletContext.setAttribute("dbUrl", "jdbc:mysql///Fred");
    System.out.println("Application initialized");
  }

  public void contextDestroyed(ServletContextEvent cse) {
    System.out.println("Application shut down");
  }
}
```

Note that before you can set a ServletContext attribute, you first need to obtain the ServletContext object using the getServletContext method of the ServletContextEvent class. This is shown in the following line of code from Listing 6.3.

```
ServletContext servletContext = sce.getServletContext();
```

In the servlet, to get an attribute from the ServletContext object, you need first to obtain the ServletContext object. In a servlet that extends the javax.servlet.http.HttpServlet class, you can use the getServletContext method to achieve this, as demonstrated in the code in Listing 6.4.

Listing 6.4 **The ApplicationEventDemoServlet Servlet**

```
import javax.servlet.*;
import javax.servlet.http.*;
import java.io.*;

public class ApplicationEventDemoServlet extends HttpServlet {

  public void doGet(HttpServletRequest request, HttpServletResponse response)
    throws ServletException, IOException {
    response.setContentType("text/html");
    PrintWriter out = response.getWriter();
    out.println("<HTML>");
    out.println("<HEAD>");
    out.println("<TITLE>Application Event Demo Servlet</TITLE>");
    out.println("</HEAD>");
    out.println("<BODY>");
    out.println("Your database connection is ");

    // get the ServletContext object
    ServletContext servletContext = getServletContext();
    // display the "dbUrl" attribute
    out.println(servletContext.getAttribute("dbUrl"));

    out.println("</BODY>");
    out.println("</HTML>");
  }
}
```

Listing 6.5 gives you the deployment descriptor you need for the application to work.

Listing 6.5 **The Deployment Descriptor for the Example**

```
<?xml version="1.0" encoding="ISO-8859-1"?>
<!DOCTYPE web-app
  PUBLIC "-//Sun Microsystems, Inc.//DTD Web Application 2.3//EN"
  "http://java.sun.com/dtd/web-app_2_3.dtd">

<web-app>
  <listener>
    <listener-class>
      AppLifeCycleEventDemo
    </listener-class>
  </listener>
  <servlet>
    <servlet-name>
      ApplicationEventDemo
    </servlet-name>
    <servlet-class>
      ApplicationEventDemoServlet
    </servlet-class>
  </servlet>
</web-app>
```

After you compile both classes, restart Tomcat and direct your browser to the servlet URL.You should see something similar to Figure 6.1.

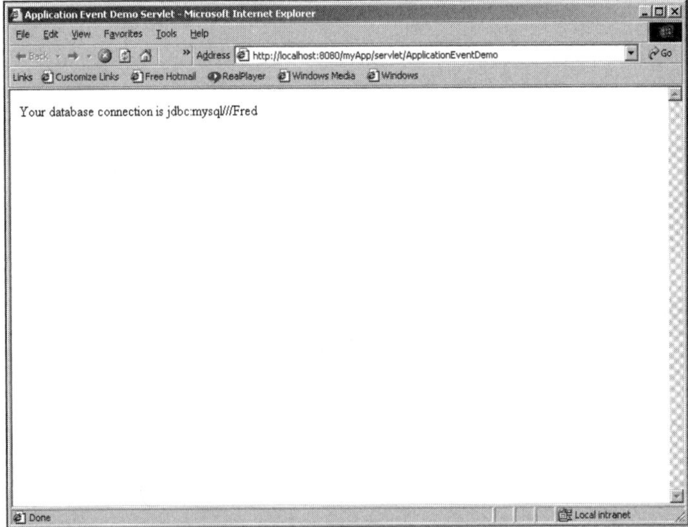

Figure 6.1 Obtaining an attribute value set when the application initializes.

Listening to ServletContextAttributeListener

In addition to a life cycle listener, you also can implement the ServletContextAttributeListener class to be notified when any attribute is added to the ServletContext or if any of the ServletContext's attributes are changed or removed. Implementing this interface, you must provide implementations for its three methods: attributeAdded, attributeRemoved, and attributeReplace. The signatures for those methods are as follows:

```
public void attributeAdded(ServletContextAttributeEvent scae)
public void attributeRemoved(ServletContextAttributeEvent scae)
public void attributeReplaced(ServletContextAttributeEvent scae)
```

The attributeAdded method is called when a new attribute is added to the ServletContext object. The attributeRemove method is called when an attribute is removed from the ServletContext object, and the attributeReplaced method is invoked when an attribute in the ServletContext object is replaced.

Note that attribute changes may occur concurrently. It is your responsibility to ensure that accesses to a common resource are synchronized.

Another Example: PageCounterServlet

As another example, consider the following application that provides a page counter for a servlet. The servlet increments a counter every time it is requested, thus the name *page counter.* The value of the counter is stored as an attribute of the ServletContext object so that it can be accessed from any servlet in the application. However, if the servlet container crashes, you will not lose this value because the value is also written to a text file called counter.txt. Clearly, this is a type of application you can use to measure the popularity of your site.

The application consists of two classes. The first is a listener class named AppAttributeEventDemo and the second is a servlet called PageCounterServlet.

The AppAttributeEventDemo implements both ServletContextListener interface and ServletContextAttributeListener interface. In the contextInitialized method, you write the code that will read the counter value from the counter.txt file and use this value to initialize a ServletContext attribute named pageCounter. As in the previous example, you need to obtain the ServletContext object from the ServletContextEvent object passed to the contextInitialized method.

Every time the PageCounterServlet servlet is requested, it will increment the value of pageCounter. When this happens, the attributeReplaced method of the listener class will be triggered. In this method, you write the code that writes the value of pageCounter to the counter.txt file.

Because the servlet can be called simultaneously by multiple users, the method writeCounter, called from the attributeReplaced method, is synchronized. Here is where you write the code to write pageCounter to the file.

The listener class is given in Listing 6.6 and the PageCounterServlet in Listing 6.7. After you compile these two classes, open your browser and type the URL for the servlet. You should see something similar to Figure 6.2.

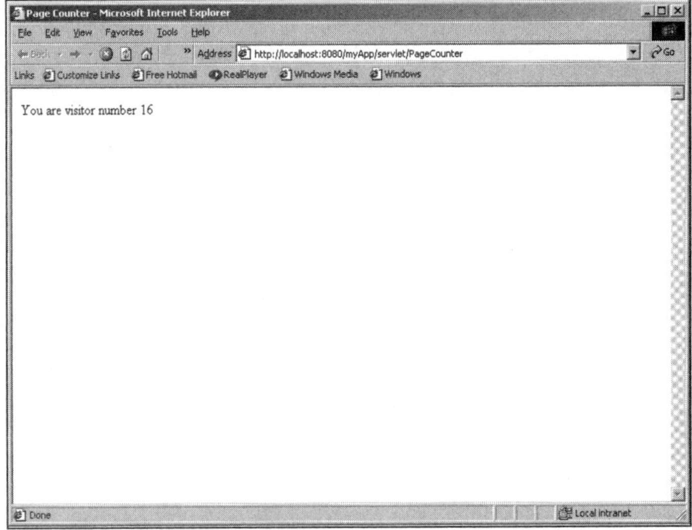

Figure 6.2 PageCounterServlet.

Listing 6.6 **The AppAttributeEventDemo class**

```
import javax.servlet.ServletContext;
import javax.servlet.ServletContextListener;
import javax.servlet.ServletContextEvent;
import javax.servlet.ServletContextAttributeListener;
import javax.servlet.ServletContextAttributeEvent;
import java.io.*;

public class AppAttributeEventDemo
  implements ServletContextListener, ServletContextAttributeListener {
```

```
int counter;
String counterFilePath = "C:\\counter.txt";

public void contextInitialized(ServletContextEvent cse) {
  try {
    BufferedReader reader = new
      BufferedReader(new FileReader(counterFilePath));
    counter = Integer.parseInt( reader.readLine() );
    reader.close();
     System.out.println("Reading" + counter);

  }
  catch (Exception e) {
     System.out.println(e.toString());
  }

  ServletContext servletContext = cse.getServletContext();

  servletContext.setAttribute("pageCounter", Integer.toString(counter));
  System.out.println("Application initialized");
}

public void contextDestroyed(ServletContextEvent cse) {
  System.out.println("Application shut down");
}

public void attributeAdded(ServletContextAttributeEvent scae) {
  System.out.println("ServletContext attribute added");
}

public void attributeRemoved(ServletContextAttributeEvent scae) {
  System.out.println("ServletContext attribute removed");
}


public void attributeReplaced(ServletContextAttributeEvent scae) {
  System.out.println("ServletContext attribute replaced");
  writeCounter(scae);
}

synchronized void writeCounter(ServletContextAttributeEvent scae) {
  ServletContext servletContext = scae.getServletContext();

  counter = Integer.parseInt((String)
    servletContext.getAttribute("pageCounter"));

  try {
    BufferedWriter writer = new
      BufferedWriter(new FileWriter(counterFilePath));
    writer.write(Integer.toString(counter));
    writer.close();
```

continues

Listing 6.6 **Continued**

```
        System.out.println("Writing");
      }
      catch (Exception e) {
        System.out.println(e.toString());
      }

    }
  }
```

Listing 6.7 **The PageCounterServlet Servlet**

```
import javax.servlet.*;
import javax.servlet.http.*;
import java.io.*;

public class PageCounterServlet extends HttpServlet {

  public void doGet(HttpServletRequest request, HttpServletResponse response)
    throws ServletException, IOException {
    response.setContentType("text/html");
    PrintWriter out = response.getWriter();
    out.println("<HTML>");
    out.println("<HEAD>");
    out.println("<TITLE>Page Counter</TITLE>");
    out.println("</HEAD>");
    out.println("<BODY>");
    ServletContext servletContext = getServletContext();
    int pageCounter = Integer.parseInt((String)
      servletContext.getAttribute("pageCounter"));
    pageCounter++;
    out.println("You are visitor number " + pageCounter);
    servletContext.setAttribute("pageCounter",
      Integer.toString(pageCounter));

    out.println("</BODY>");
    out.println("</HTML>");
  }
}
```

The deployment descriptor for the example is given in Listing 6.8.

Listing 6.8 **The Deployment Descriptor for the PageCounter Example**

```
<?xml version="1.0" encoding="ISO-8859-1"?>

<!DOCTYPE web-app
  PUBLIC "-//Sun Microsystems, Inc.//DTD Web Application 2.3//EN"
```

```
    "http://java.sun.com/dtd/web-app_2_3.dtd">

  <web-app>
    <listener>
      <listener-class>
        AppAttributeEventDemo
      </listener-class>
    </listener>
    <servlet>
      <servlet-name>
        PageCounter
      </servlet-name>
      <servlet-class>
        PageCounterServlet
      </servlet-class>
    </servlet>
  </web-app>
```

Note that the attributeReplaced also is called when the attributeAdded is triggered.

Listening to HttpSession Events

The javax.servlet.http package provides two interfaces that you can implement to listen to HttpSession events: HttpSessionListener and HttpSessionAttributeListener. The first enables you to listen to a session's life cycle events, that is, the event that gets triggered when an HttpSession object is created and the event that is raised when an HttpSession object is destroyed. The second interface, HttpSessionAttributeListener, provides events that get raised when an attribute is added to, removed from, or modified in the HttpSession object.

The two interfaces are explained next.

The HttpSessionListener Interface

The HttpSessionListener interface has two methods: sessionCreated and sessionDestroyed. The signatures of the two methods are given here:

```
public void sessionCreated(HttpSessionEvent se)
public void sessionDestroyed(HttpSessionEvent se)
```

The sessionCreated method is automatically called when an HttpSession object is created. The sessionDestroyed method is called when an HttpSession object is invalidated. Both methods will be passed in an HttpSessionEvent class that you can use from inside the method.

The HttpSessionEvent class is derived from the java.util.EventObject class. The HttpSessionEvent class defines one new method called getSesssion that you can use to obtain the HttpSession object that is changed.

An Example: User Counter

The following example is a counter that counts the number of different users currently "in session." It creates an HttpSession object for a user the first time the user requests the servlet. If the user comes back to the same servlet, no HttpSession object will be created the second time. Therefore, the counter is incremented only when an HttpSession object is created.

An HttpSession object can also be destroyed, however. When this happens, the counter must be decremented. For the counter to be accessible to all users, it is stored as an attribute in the ServletContext object.

The example has two classes: the listener class and a servlet class that displays the counter value. The listener class is named SessionLifeCycleEventDemo and implements both the ServletContextListener interface and the HttpSessionListener interface. You need the first interface so that you can create a ServletContext attribute and assign it an initial value of 0. As you can guess, you put this code in the contextInitialized method, as in the following:

```
public void contextInitialized(ServletContextEvent sce) {
  servletContext = sce.getServletContext();
  servletContext.setAttribute(("userCounter"), Integer.toString(counter));
}
```

Notice that the ServletContext object is assigned to a class variable servletContext, making the ServletContext object available from anywhere in the class.

The counter must be incremented when an HttpSession is created and decremented when an HttpSession is destroyed. Therefore, you need to provide implementations for both sessionCreated and sessionDestroyed methods, as you see here:

```
public void sessionCreated(HttpSessionEvent hse) {
  System.out.println("Session created.");
  incrementUserCounter();
}
public void sessionDestroyed(HttpSessionEvent hse) {
  System.out.println("Session destroyed.");
  decrementUserCounter();
}
```

The sessionCreated method calls the synchronized method

incrementUserCounter and the sessionDestroyed method calls the synchronized method decrementUserCounter.

The incrementUserCounter method first obtains an attribute called userCounter from the ServletContext object, increments the counter, and stores the counter back to the userCounter attribute.

```
synchronized void incrementUserCounter() {
  counter = Integer.parseInt(
    (String)servletContext.getAttribute("userCounter"));
  counter++;
  servletContext.setAttribute(("userCounter"), Integer.toString(counter));
  System.out.println("User Count: " + counter);
}
```

The decrementUserCounter method does the opposite. It first obtains the userCounter attribute from the ServletContext object, decrements the counter, and stores the counter back to the userCounter attribute, as you see here:

```
synchronized void decrementUserCounter() {
  int counter = Integer.parseInt(
    (String)servletContext.getAttribute("userCounter"));
  counter--;
  servletContext.setAttribute(("userCounter"), Integer.toString(counter));
  System.out.println("User Count: " + counter);
}
```

The listener class is given in Listing 6.9.

Listing 6.9 **The SessionLifeCycleEventDemo Class**

```
import javax.servlet.http.HttpSession;
import javax.servlet.http.HttpSessionListener;
import javax.servlet.http.HttpSessionEvent;
import javax.servlet.ServletContextListener;
import javax.servlet.ServletContext;
import javax.servlet.ServletContextEvent;

public class SessionLifeCycleEventDemo
  implements ServletContextListener, HttpSessionListener {
  ServletContext servletContext;
  int counter;
  public void contextInitialized(ServletContextEvent sce) {
    servletContext = sce.getServletContext();
    servletContext.setAttribute(("userCounter"), Integer.toString(counter));
  }

  public void contextDestroyed(ServletContextEvent sce) {
  }
```

continues

Listing 6.9 **Continued**

```
  public void sessionCreated(HttpSessionEvent hse) {
    System.out.println("Session created.");
    incrementUserCounter();
  }
  public void sessionDestroyed(HttpSessionEvent hse) {
    System.out.println("Session destroyed.");
    decrementUserCounter();
  }

  synchronized void incrementUserCounter() {
    counter = Integer.parseInt(
      (String)servletContext.getAttribute("userCounter"));
    counter++;
    servletContext.setAttribute(("userCounter"), Integer.toString(counter));
    System.out.println("User Count: " + counter);
  }

  synchronized void decrementUserCounter() {
    int counter = Integer.parseInt(
      (String)servletContext.getAttribute("userCounter"));
    counter—;
    servletContext.setAttribute(("userCounter"), Integer.toString(counter));
    System.out.println("User Count: " + counter);
  }
}
```

The second class of the application is the UserCounterServlet. This servlet displays the value of the userCounter ServletContext attribute whenever someone requests the servlet. The code that does this is written in the doGet method.

When the doGet method is invoked, you obtain the ServletContext object by calling the getServletContext method.

```
ServletContext servletContext = getServletContext();
```

Then, the method tries to obtain an HttpSession object from the HttpServletRequest object and creates one if no HttpSession object exists, as follows:

```
HttpSession session = request.getSession(true);
```

Next, you need to get the userCounter attribute from the ServletContext object:

```
int userCounter = 0;
userCounter = Integer.parseInt(
  (String)servletContext.getAttribute("userCounter"));
```

The complete code for the servlet is given in Listing 6.10.

Listing 6.10 **The userCounterServlet Servlet**

```
import javax.servlet.*;
import javax.servlet.http.*;
import java.io.*;

public class UserCounterServlet extends HttpServlet {

  public void doGet(HttpServletRequest request, HttpServletResponse response)
    throws ServletException, IOException {
    ServletContext servletContext = getServletContext();
    HttpSession session = request.getSession(true);
    int userCounter = 0;
    userCounter =
      Integer.parseInt((String)servletContext.getAttribute("userCounter"));

    response.setContentType("text/html");
    PrintWriter out = response.getWriter();
    out.println("<HTML>");
    out.println("<HEAD>");
    out.println("<TITLE>User Counter</TITLE>");
    out.println("</HEAD>");
    out.println("<BODY>");

    out.println("There are " + userCounter + " users.");
    out.println("</BODY>");
    out.println("</HTML>");
  }
}
```

For the example to work, you need to create a deployment descriptor as given in Listing 6.11.

Listing 6.11 **The Deployment Descriptor for the UserCounter Example**

```
<?xml version="1.0" encoding="ISO-8859-1"?>

<!DOCTYPE web-app
  PUBLIC "-//Sun Microsystems, Inc.//DTD Web Application 2.3//EN"
  "http://java.sun.com/dtd/web-app_2_3.dtd">

<web-app>
  <listener>
    <listener-class>
      SessionLifeCycleEventDemo
    </listener-class>
  </listener>
  <servlet>
    <servlet-name>
      UserCounter
    </servlet-name>
```

continues

Listing 6.11 **Continued**

```
    <servlet-class>
      UserCounterServlet
    </servlet-class>
  </servlet>
</web-app>
```

After you compile the two classes, open your browser and type in the URL for the servlet. You should see something similar to Figure 6.3.

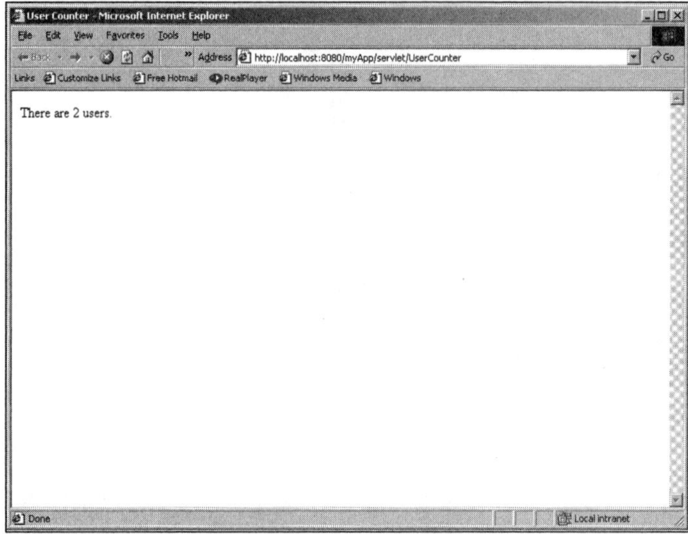

Figure 6.3 The user counter.

The HttpSessionAttributeListener Interface

The second session event listener interface is HttpSessionAttributeListener. You can implement this interface if you need to listen to events related to session attributes. The interface provides three methods: attributeAdded, attributeRemoved, and attributeReplaced. The signatures of the three methods are as follows:

```
public void attributeAdded(HttpSessionBindingEvent sbe)
public void attributeRemoved(HttpSessionBindingEvent sbe)
public void attributeReplaced(HttpSessionBindingEvent sbe)
```

The attributeAdded method is called when an attribute is added to an HttpSession object. The attributeRemoved and attributeReplaced methods are called when an HttpSession attribute is removed or replaced, respectively.

All the methods receive an HttpSessionBindingEvent object whose class is described next.

The HttpSessionBindingEvent is derived from the HttpSessionEvent class so it inherits the getSession method. In addition, the HttpSessionBindingEvent class has two methods: getName and getValue. The signatures of the two methods are as follows:

```
public String getName()
public Object getValue()
```

The getName method returns the name of the attribute that is bound to an HttpSession or unbound from an HttpSession. The getValue method returns the value of an HttpSession attribute that has been added, removed, or replaced.

Summary

This chapter introduced application and session events and described the use of those events with a few examples. The ability to listen to these events are not very critical, however they can be very useful as shown in the examples in this chapter.

7 Servlet Filtering

Filters are new in the Servlet 2.3 specification, enabling you to intercept a request before it reaches a resource. In other words, a filter gives you access to the HttpServletRequest and the HttpServletResponse objects before they are passed in to a servlet.

Filters can be very useful. For example, you can write a filter that records all incoming requests and logs the IP addresses of the computers from which the requests originate. You also can use a filter as an encryption and decryption device. Other uses include user authentication, data compression, user input validation, and so on.

For a filter to intercept a request to a servlet, you must declare the filter with a <filter> element in the deployment descriptor and map the filter to the servlet using the <filter-mapping> element. Sometimes you want a filter to work on multiple servlets. You can do this by mapping a filter to a URL pattern so that any request that matches that URL pattern will be filtered.

You also can put a set of filters in a chain. The first filter in the chain will be called first and then pass control to the second filter, and so on. Filter chaining ensures that you can write a filter that does a specific task but adds some functionality in another filter.

This chapter starts with javax.servlet.Filter, an interface that a filter class must implement. The chapter then moves on to building various filters and along the way introduces other relevant classes and interfaces.

An Overview of the API

When writing a filter, you basically deal with the following three interfaces in the javax.servlet package:

- Filter
- FilterConfig
- FilterChain

These three interfaces are described in the next sections.

The Filter Interface

javax.servlet.Filter is an interface that you must implement when writing a filter. The life cycle of a filter is represented by this interface's three methods: init, doFilter, and destroy. Their signatures are given here:

```
public void init(FilterConfig filterConfig)
public void doFilter(HttpServletRequest request,
  HttpServletResponse response, FilterChain chain)
public void destroy()
```

A filter starts its life when its init method is called by the servlet container. The servlet container calls a filter's init method only once, when it finishes instantiating the filter. The servlet container will pass in the FilterConfig object that represents the filter configuration. Normally, you assign this object to an object variable so that the FilterConfig object will be available from other methods. Compare the init method with the init method of the Servlet interface.

The doFilter method is where the filtering is performed. The servlet container calls the doFilter method every time a user requests a resource, such as a servlet, to which the filter is mapped. When doFilter is invoked, the servlet container passes in the HttpServletRequest object, the HttpServletResponse object, and a FilterChain object. The HttpServletRequest and HttpServletResponse objects are the same objects that will get passed to a servlet. You can manipulate these two objects. For example, you can add an attribute to the HttpServletRequest using the setAttribute method, or you can obtain the PrintWriter object of the HttpServletResponse and write to it. The FilterChain object is useful here so that you can pass control to the next resource. It will be explained in more detail when we discuss the FilterChain later in this chapter.

The doFilter method is analogous to the service method of the Servlet interface. The servlet container calls the destroy method to tell the filter that it will be taken out of service. The filter can then do some clean-up, if necessary. For instance, it can close a resource that it opened at initialization. The destroy method in the Filter interface is similar to the destroy method in the Servlet interface.

The FilterConfig Interface

A FilterConfig object represents the configuration for the filter. This object allows you to obtain the ServletContext object and pass initialization values to the filter through its initial parameters, which you define in the deployment descriptor when declaring the filter.

The FilterConfig interface has four methods: getFilterName, getInitParameter, getInitParameterNames, and getServletContext. The signatures for these methods are as follows:

```
public String getFilterName()
public String getInitParameter(String parameterName)
public java.util.Enumeration getInitParameterNames()
public ServletContext getServletContext()
```

The getFilterName method returns the name of the filter and the getServletContext method returns the ServletContext object. The getInitParameterNames gives you an Enumeration containing all parameter names of the filter. You then can retrieve the value of each individual initial parameter using the getInitParameter, passing the parameter name.

The FilterChain Interface

As mentioned previously, a FilterChain object is passed in by the servlet container to the doFilter method of the filter class. Filters use the FilterChain object to invoke the next filter in the chain, or, if the filter is the last in the chain, to invoke the next resource (servlet).

The FilterChain interface has only one method: doFilter, whose signature is given as follows:

```
public void doFilter(HttpServletRequest request, HttpServletResponse
response)
```

> **Note**
>
> Don't confuse this method with the doFilter method of the Filter interface. The latter has three arguments.

You should always call the FilterChain interface's doFilter method to pass control over to the next filter. If you are using only one filter, the doFilter method passes control to the next resource, which can be a servlet you want to filter. Failure to call this method will make the program flow stop.

A Basic Filter

As an example of your first filter, I will present here a very basic filter that does nothing other than show its life cycle by printing a message to the console every time its method is invoked. This filter also declares a FilterConfig object reference called filterConfig. In the init method, you pass the FilterConfig object to this variable. Notice that the filter's doFilter method calls the doFilter method of the FilterChain object at the last line of the method. You can find the code for the filter, appropriately named BasicFilter, in Listing 7.1.

Listing 7.1 **The BasicFilter Class**

```
import java.io.IOException;
import javax.servlet.Filter;
import javax.servlet.FilterChain;
import javax.servlet.FilterConfig;
import javax.servlet.ServletException;
import javax.servlet.ServletRequest;
import javax.servlet.ServletResponse;

public class BasicFilter implements Filter {
  private FilterConfig filterConfig;


  public void init(FilterConfig filterConfig) throws ServletException {
    System.out.println("Filter initialized");
    this.filterConfig = filterConfig;
  }

  public void destroy() {
    System.out.println("Filter destroyed");
    this.filterConfig = null;
  }

  public void doFilter(ServletRequest request, ServletResponse response,
    FilterChain chain)
    throws IOException, ServletException {
    System.out.println("doFilter");
    chain.doFilter(request, response);
  }
}
```

For the filter to work, you need to decide which servlet or servlets you want to filter and tell the servlet container by declaring the filter in the deployment descriptor using the <filter> element and the <filter-mapping> element. These two elements must come before any <listener> and <servlet> elements. The deployment descriptor for this example is given in Listing 7.2.

Listing 7.2 **The Deployment Descriptor for this Example**

```
<?xml version="1.0" encoding="ISO-8859-1"?>

<!DOCTYPE web-app
  PUBLIC "-//Sun Microsystems, Inc.//DTD Web Application 2.3//EN"
  "http://java.sun.com/dtd/web-app_2_3.dtd">

<web-app>
  <!-- Define servlet-mapped and path-mapped filters -->
  <filter>
    <filter-name>
      Basic Filter
    </filter-name>
    <filter-class>
      BasicFilter
    </filter-class>
  </filter>


  <!-- Define filter mappings for the defined filters -->
  <filter-mapping>
    <filter-name>
      Basic Filter
    </filter-name>
    <servlet-name>
      FilteredServlet
    </servlet-name>
  </filter-mapping>
  <listener>
    <listener-class>
      SessionLifeCycleEventDemo
    </listener-class>
  </listener>
  <servlet>
    <servlet-name>
      FilteredServlet
    </servlet-name>
    <servlet-class>
      FilteredServlet
    </servlet-class>
  </servlet>
</web-app>
```

You can see that the filter name is Basic Filter and its class is BasicFilter. You also find a <filter-mapping> element that maps the filter to a servlet called FilteredServlet. You need to create a servlet (that does anything) called FilteredServlet to see the example work.

After you compile the filter and servlet classes and modify your deployment descriptor, restart the servlet container. You should see the message sent from the filter's init method in the console.

Open your browser and type the URL to the FilteredServlet servlet. You should see more messages in the console that show how the filter is invoked before the servlet.

If you want to apply the filter to more than one servlet, you need only to repeat the <filter-mapping> element for each servlet. For example, the filter applies to both FilteredServlet and FilteredServlet2 in the following deployment descriptor in Listing 7.3.

Listing 7.3 **The Deployment Descriptor that Applies the Filter to More than One Servlet**

```
<?xml version="1.0" encoding="ISO-8859-1"?>

<!DOCTYPE web-app
  PUBLIC "-//Sun Microsystems, Inc.//DTD Web Application 2.3//EN"
  "http://java.sun.com/dtd/web-app_2_3.dtd">

<web-app>
  <!-- Define servlet-mapped and path-mapped filters -->
  <filter>
    <filter-name>
      Basic Filter
    </filter-name>
    <filter-class>
      BasicFilter
    </filter-class>
  </filter>


  <!-- Define filter mappings for the defined filters -->
  <filter-mapping>
    <filter-name>
      Basic Filter
    </filter-name>
    <servlet-name>
      FilteredServlet
    </servlet-name>
  </filter-mapping>
  <filter-mapping>
    <filter-name>
```

```
      Basic Filter
    </filter-name>
    <servlet-name>
      FilteredServlet2
    </servlet-name>
  </filter-mapping>


  <servlet>
    <servlet-name>
      FilteredServlet
    </servlet-name>
    <servlet-class>
      FilteredServlet
    </servlet-class>
  </servlet>
  <servlet>
    <servlet-name>
      FilteredServlet2
    </servlet-name>
    <servlet-class>
      FilteredServlet2
    </servlet-class>
  </servlet>
</web-app>
```

Mapping a Filter with a URL

In addition to mapping a filter to a servlet or a number of servlets, you can map the filter to a URL pattern so all requests that match that pattern will invoke the filter.

Consider a servlet whose URL is similar to the following:

```
http://localhost:8080/myApp/servlet/FilteredServlet
```

To map a filter to a URL pattern, you use the <filter-mapping> element of your deployment descriptor similar to the following:

```
<!-- Define filter mappings for the defined filters -->
<filter-mapping>
  <filter-name>
    Logging Filter
  </filter-name>
  <url-pattern>/servlet/FilteredServlet</url-pattern>
</filter-mapping>
```

As an alternative, you can use /* to make the filter work for all static and dynamic resources, as follows:

```
<!-- Define filter mappings for the defined filters -->
<filter-mapping>
  <filter-name>
    Logging Filter
  </filter-name>
  <url-pattern>/*</url-pattern>
</filter-mapping>
```

A Logging Filter

Here is another simple example of a filter that logs user IP addresses to the log file. The location of the log file is servlet container implementation specific. (See Appendix A, "Tomcat Installation and Configuration," for more information.)

The filter class is given in Listing 7.4.

Listing 7.4 **The Logging Filter**

```
import java.io.IOException;
import javax.servlet.Filter;
import javax.servlet.FilterChain;
import javax.servlet.FilterConfig;
import javax.servlet.ServletContext;
import javax.servlet.ServletException;
import javax.servlet.ServletRequest;
import javax.servlet.ServletResponse;

public class LoggingFilter implements Filter {
  private FilterConfig filterConfig = null;
  public void destroy() {
    System.out.println("Filter destroyed");
    this.filterConfig = null;
  }

  public void doFilter(ServletRequest request, ServletResponse response,
    FilterChain chain)
    throws IOException, ServletException {
    System.out.println("doFilter");

    // Log user's IP address.
    ServletContext servletContext = filterConfig.getServletContext();
    servletContext.log(request.getRemoteHost());
    chain.doFilter(request, response);
  }
```

```
  public void init(FilterConfig filterConfig) throws ServletException {
    System.out.println("Filter initialized");
    this.filterConfig = filterConfig;
  }
}
```

Not much difference exists between this filter and the BasicFilter, except that the doFilter method obtains the ServletContext object and uses its log to record the client IP address obtained from the getRemoteHost method of the HttpServletRequest object. The following code shows this action:

```
// Log user's IP address.
ServletContext servletContext = filterConfig.getServletContext();
servletContext.log(request.getRemoteHost());
```

The deployment descriptor of this example is given in Listing 7.5.

Listing 7.5 **The Deployment Descriptor for the LoggingFilter**

```
<?xml version="1.0" encoding="ISO-8859-1"?>

<!DOCTYPE web-app
  PUBLIC "-//Sun Microsystems, Inc.//DTD Web Application 2.3//EN"
  "http://java.sun.com/dtd/web-app_2_3.dtd">

<web-app>
  <!-- Define servlet-mapped and path-mapped filters -->
  <filter>
    <filter-name>
      Logging Filter
    </filter-name>
    <filter-class>
      LoggingFilter
    </filter-class>
  </filter>


  <!-- Define filter mappings for the defined filters -->
  <filter-mapping>
    <filter-name>
      Logging Filter
    </filter-name>
    <servlet-name>
      FilteredServlet
    </servlet-name>
  </filter-mapping>

  <servlet>
```

continues

Listing 7.5 **Continued**

```
    <servlet-name>
      FilteredServlet
    </servlet-name>
    <servlet-class>
      FilteredServlet
    </servlet-class>
  </servlet>
</web-app>
```

Practically, any servlet named FilteredServlet will invoke the filter. Listing 7.6 gives you an example of such a servlet.

Listing 7.6 **A Servlet to Be Used with LoggingFilter**

```
import javax.servlet.*;
import javax.servlet.http.*;
import java.io.*;

public class FilteredServlet extends HttpServlet {

  public void doGet(HttpServletRequest request, HttpServletResponse response)
throws ServletException, IOException {

    response.setContentType("text/html");
    PrintWriter out = response.getWriter();
    out.println("<HTML>");
    out.println("<HEAD>");
    out.println("<TITLE>User Counter</TITLE>");
    out.println("</HEAD>");
    out.println("<BODY>");
    out.println("IP:" + request.getRemoteHost());
    out.println("</BODY>");
    out.println("</HTML>");
  }
}
```

Filter Configuration

You can pass some initial parameters to a filter in a FilterConfig object that gets passed into the init method of the Filter interface. The initial parameters are declared in the deployment descriptor using the <init-param> element under the <filter> element. For example, the following deployment descriptor in Listing 7.7 describes a filter called MyFilter with two initial parameters: adminPhone and adminEmail.

Listing 7.7 **The Deployment Descriptor with a Filter with Two Initial Parameters**

```
<!DOCTYPE web-app
  PUBLIC "-//Sun Microsystems, Inc.//DTD Web Application 2.3//EN"
  "http://java.sun.com/dtd/web-app_2_3.dtd">

<web-app>
  <!-- Define servlet-mapped and path-mapped filters -->
  <filter>
    <filter-name>
      MyFilter
    </filter-name>
    <filter-class>
      MyFilter
    </filter-class>

    <init-param>
      <param-name>
        adminPhone
      </param-name>
      <param-value>
        0414789098
      </param-value>
    </init-param>

    <init-param>
      <param-name>
        adminEmail
      </param-name>
      <param-value>
        admin@labsale.com
      </param-value>
    </init-param>

  </filter>
</web-app>
```

You then can retrieve the values of the AdminPhone and AdminEmail parameters using the following code, which you should put under the doFilter method of a filter:

```
String adminPhone = filterConfig.getInitParameter("adminPhone");
String adminEmail = filterConfig.getInitParameter("adminEmail");
```

A Filter that Checks User Input

When you receive input from a user, the first thing you should do is to check whether the input is valid. If the input is invalid, you normally send an error message, telling the user that a correct entry is needed.

Sometimes the input is not totally invalid; it only contains leading or trailing empty spaces. In this case, you don't need to send an error message, but you can make the correction yourself; that is, when you ask users to enter their first names into the firstName box in an HTML form, you need to make sure that they type in something like "John" or "George", not " John" or "George " (with blank spaces). Normally in situations like this, you use the trim function of the String class when you obtain a parameter value, as follows:

```
String firstName = request.getParameter("firstName");
if (firstName!=null)
  firstName = firstName.trim();
```

If you have quite a large number of input boxes in the HTML form, however, you have to call the trim method for every parameter. Additionally, you need to do this in every servlet that accepts user input. A filter can help make this task easier.

You can write a filter that trims every parameter value in the HttpServletRequest object before the HttpServletRequest object reaches a servlet. This way, you don't need to trim anything in your servlet. You need to write only one filter to serve all servlets that need this service. In the example that follows, you get a chance to write a filter that trims all parameter values.

To ensure that the filter is able to trim all parameters in a HttpServletRequest object, do not hard-code the name of the parameter. Instead, use the getParameterNames method to obtain an Enumeration containing all the parameter names. Next, you need to loop through the Enumeration to get the parameter values and call the trim method.

You can't change a parameter value, however, which means that it is not possible to trim it directly. A closer look at the HttpServletRequest reveals that you can set its attribute. What you can do is to put trimmed parameter values as attributes. The parameter names become attribute names. Later, in the servlet, instead of retrieving user input from HttpServletRequest parameters, you can obtain the trimmed versions of the input from the HttpServletRequest attributes, as shown here:

```
Enumeration enum = request.getParameterNames();
while (enum.hasMoreElements()) {
  String parameterName = (String) enum.nextElement();
```

```
    String parameterValue = request.getParameter(parameterName);
    request.setAttribute(parameterName, parameterValue.trim());
  }
```

In your servlet, do the following to get a trimmed input value:

```
request.getAttribute(parameterName);
```

Instead of retrieving a value using the getParameter method of the HttpServletRequest, you use its getAttribute method.

The filter that does this service is called TrimFilter and its code is given in Listing 7.8.

Listing 7.8 **The TrimFilter**

```
import java.io.*;
import javax.servlet.Filter;
import javax.servlet.FilterChain;
import javax.servlet.FilterConfig;
import javax.servlet.ServletContext;
import javax.servlet.ServletException;
import javax.servlet.ServletRequest;
import javax.servlet.ServletResponse;
import java.util.Enumeration;

public class TrimFilter implements Filter {
  private FilterConfig filterConfig = null;
  public void destroy() {
    System.out.println("Filter destroyed");
    this.filterConfig = null;
  }

  public void doFilter(ServletRequest request, ServletResponse response,
    FilterChain chain)
    throws IOException, ServletException {
    System.out.println("Filter");
   Enumeration enum = request.getParameterNames();
    while (enum.hasMoreElements()) {
      String parameterName = (String) enum.nextElement();
      String parameterValue = request.getParameter(parameterName);
      request.setAttribute(parameterName, parameterValue.trim());
    }

    chain.doFilter(request, response);
  }

  public void init(FilterConfig filterConfig) throws ServletException {
    System.out.println("Filter initialized");
    this.filterConfig = filterConfig;
  }
}
```

To illustrate the filter's use, you can write a servlet that does the following:

- Send an HTML form with four input boxes (firstName, lastName, userName, and password) when its doGet method is invoked.
- Display the user input when its doPost method is invoked.

The servlet is called TrimFilteredServlet and is given in Listing 7.9.

Listing 7.9 **TrimFilteredServlet**

```
import javax.servlet.*;
import javax.servlet.http.*;
import java.io.*;
import com.brainysoftware.java.StringUtil;

public class TrimFilteredServlet extends HttpServlet {

  public void doGet(HttpServletRequest request, HttpServletResponse response)
    throws ServletException, IOException {
    response.setContentType("text/html");
    PrintWriter out = response.getWriter();
    out.println("<HTML>");
    out.println("<HEAD>");
    out.println("<TITLE>User Input Form</TITLE>");
    out.println("</HEAD>");
    out.println("<BODY>");
    out.println("<CENTER>");
    out.println("<BR>Please enter your details.");
    out.println("<BR>");
    out.println("<BR><FORM METHOD=POST>");
    out.println("<TABLE>");
    out.println("<TR>");
    out.println("<TD>First Name:</TD>");
    out.println("<TD><INPUT TYPE=TEXT NAME=firstName></TD>");
    out.println("</TR>");
    out.println("<TR>");
    out.println("<TD>Last Name:</TD>");
    out.println("<TD><INPUT TYPE=TEXT NAME=lastName></TD>");
    out.println("</TR>");
    out.println("<TR>");
    out.println("<TD>User Name:</TD>");
    out.println("<TD><INPUT TYPE=TEXT NAME=userName></TD>");
    out.println("</TR>");
    out.println("<TR>");
    out.println("<TD>Password:</TD>");
    out.println("<TD><INPUT TYPE=PASSWORD NAME=password></TD>");
    out.println("</TR>");
    out.println("<TR>");
    out.println("<TD ALIGN=RIGHT COLSPAN=2>");
    out.println("<INPUT TYPE=SUBMIT VALUE=Login></TD>");
```

```
    out.println("</TR>");
    out.println("</TABLE>");
    out.println("</FORM>");
    out.println("</CENTER>");
    out.println("</BODY>");
    out.println("</HTML>");
  }

  public void doPost(HttpServletRequest request, HttpServletResponse
response)
    throws ServletException, IOException {

    String firstName = (String) request.getAttribute("firstName");
    String lastName = (String) request.getAttribute("lastName");
    String userName = (String) request.getAttribute("userName");
    String password = request.getParameter("password");
    response.setContentType("text/html");
    PrintWriter out = response.getWriter();
    out.println("<HTML>");
    out.println("<HEAD>");
    out.println("<TITLE>Displaying Values</TITLE>");
    out.println("</HEAD>");
    out.println("<BODY>");
    out.println("<CENTER>");
    out.println("Here are your details.");
    out.println("<TABLE>");
    out.println("<TR>");
    out.println("<TD>First Name:</TD>");
    out.println("<TD>" + StringUtil(firstName) + "</TD>");
    out.println("</TR>");
    out.println("<TR>");
    out.println("<TD>Last Name:</TD>");
    out.println("<TD>" + StringUtil(lastName) + "</TD>");
    out.println("</TR>");
    out.println("<TR>");
    out.println("<TD>User Name:</TD>");
    out.println("<TD>" + StringUtil(userName) + "</TD>");
    out.println("</TR>");
    out.println("<TR>");
    out.println("<TD>Password:</TD>");
    out.println("<TD>" + StringUtil(password) + "</TD>");
    out.println("</TABLE>");
    out.println("</CENTER>");
    out.println("</BODY>");
    out.println("</HTML>");

  }

}
```

To work properly, your application needs the deployment descriptor in Listing 7.10.

Listing 7.10 **The Deployment Descriptor**

```
<?xml version="1.0" encoding="ISO-8859-1"?>

<!DOCTYPE web-app
  PUBLIC "-//Sun Microsystems, Inc.//DTD Web Application 2.3//EN"
  "http://java.sun.com/dtd/web-app_2_3.dtd">

<web-app>
  <!-- Define servlet-mapped and path-mapped filters -->
  <filter>
    <filter-name>
      Trim Filter
    </filter-name>
    <filter-class>
      TrimFilter
    </filter-class>
  </filter>


  <!-- Define filter mappings for the defined filters -->
  <filter-mapping>
    <filter-name>
      Trim Filter
    </filter-name>
    <servlet-name>
      TrimFilteredServlet
    </servlet-name>
  </filter-mapping>

  <servlet>
    <servlet-name>
      TrimFilteredServlet
    </servlet-name>
    <servlet-class>
      TrimFilteredServlet
    </servlet-class>
  </servlet>
</web-app>
```

When you run the servlet, it will first display something similar to Figure 7.1.

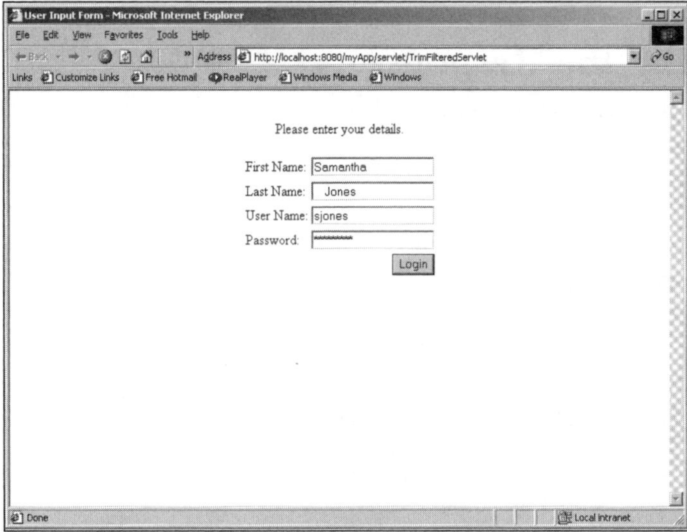

Figure 7.1 The doGet method.

Notice that in this form the user enters a last name with a leading blank space. When the user submits the form, the browser will display the figure similar to Figure 7.2.

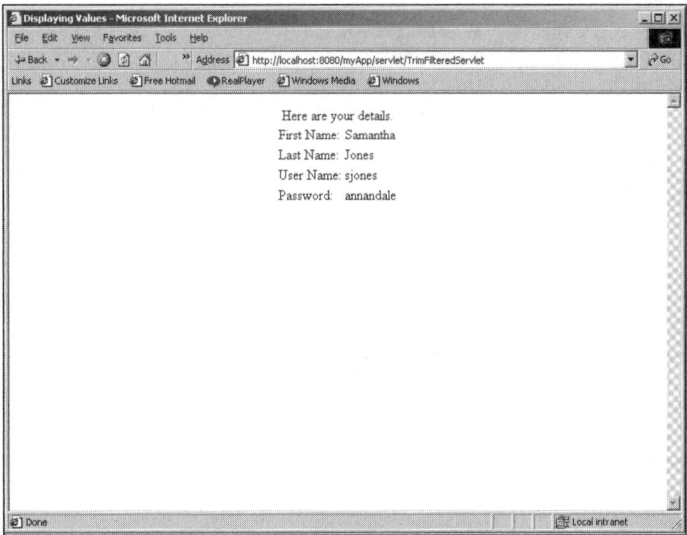

Figure 7.2 The doPost method.

See how the trailing blank spaces have disappeared? This is evidence of the filter at work.

Filtering the Response

You also can filter the response. In this example, you write a filter that appends a header and a footer of every servlet in the application. The filter code is given in Listing 7.11.

Listing 7.11 **The ResponseFilter Class**

```
import java.io.*;
import javax.servlet.Filter;
import javax.servlet.FilterChain;
import javax.servlet.FilterConfig;
import javax.servlet.ServletContext;
import javax.servlet.ServletException;
import javax.servlet.ServletRequest;
import javax.servlet.ServletResponse;
import java.util.Enumeration;

public class ResponseFilter implements Filter {
  private FilterConfig filterConfig = null;
  public void destroy() {
    System.out.println("Filter destroyed");
    this.filterConfig = null;
  }

  public void doFilter(ServletRequest request, ServletResponse response,
    FilterChain chain)
    throws IOException, ServletException {
    System.out.println("doFilter");
    PrintWriter out = response.getWriter();
    // this is added to the beginning of the PrintWriter
    out.println("<HTML>");
    out.println("<BODY>");
    out.println("<CENTER>");
    out.println("Page header");
    out.println("<HR>");



    chain.doFilter(request, response);
    // this is added to the end of the PrintWriter
    out.println("<HR>");
    out.println("Page footer");
    out.println("<CENTER>");
    out.println("</BODY>");
    out.println("</HTML>");
```

```
  }

  public void init(FilterConfig filterConfig) throws ServletException {
    System.out.println("Filter initialized");
    this.filterConfig = filterConfig;
  }
}
```

An example of a servlet that is filtered is given in Listing 7.12.

Listing 7.12 **The ResponseFilteredServlet**

```
import javax.servlet.*;
import javax.servlet.http.*;
import java.io.*;

public class ResponseFilteredServlet extends HttpServlet {

  public void doGet(HttpServletRequest request, HttpServletResponse response)
    throws ServletException, IOException {
    response.setContentType("text/html");
    PrintWriter out = response.getWriter();
    out.println("<BR>Please enter your details.");
    out.println("<BR>");
    out.println("<BR><FORM METHOD=POST>");
    out.println("<TABLE>");
    out.println("<TR>");
    out.println("<TD>First Name:</TD>");
    out.println("<TD><INPUT TYPE=TEXT NAME=firstName></TD>");
    out.println("</TR>");
    out.println("<TR>");
    out.println("<TD>Last Name:</TD>");
    out.println("<TD><INPUT TYPE=TEXT NAME=lastName></TD>");
    out.println("</TR>");
    out.println("<TR>");
    out.println("<TD>User Name:</TD>");
    out.println("<TD><INPUT TYPE=TEXT NAME=userName></TD>");
    out.println("</TR>");
    out.println("<TR>");
    out.println("<TD>Password:</TD>");
    out.println("<TD><INPUT TYPE=PASSWORD NAME=password></TD>");
    out.println("</TR>");
    out.println("<TR>");
    out.println("<TD ALIGN=RIGHT COLSPAN=2>");
    out.println("<INPUT TYPE=SUBMIT VALUE=Login></TD>");
    out.println("</TR>");
    out.println("</TABLE>");
    out.println("</FORM>");
  }

}
```

For the example to work, you need a deployment descriptor, as given in Listing 7.13.

Listing 7.13 **The Deployment Descriptor**

```
<?xml version="1.0" encoding="ISO-8859-1"?>

<!DOCTYPE web-app
  PUBLIC "-//Sun Microsystems, Inc.//DTD Web Application 2.3//EN"
  "http://java.sun.com/dtd/web-app_2_3.dtd">

<web-app>
  <!-- Define servlet-mapped and path-mapped filters -->
  <filter>
    <filter-name>
      Response Filter
    </filter-name>
    <filter-class>
      ResponseFilter
    </filter-class>
  </filter>


  <!-- Define filter mappings for the defined filters -->
  <filter-mapping>
    <filter-name>
      Response Filter
    </filter-name>
    <servlet-name>
      ResponseFilteredServlet
    </servlet-name>
  </filter-mapping>

  <servlet>
    <servlet-name>
      ResponseFilteredServlet
    </servlet-name>
    <servlet-class>
      ResponseFilteredServlet
    </servlet-class>
  </servlet>
</web-app>
```

The result of the filter in Listing 7.13 is shown in Figure 7.3.

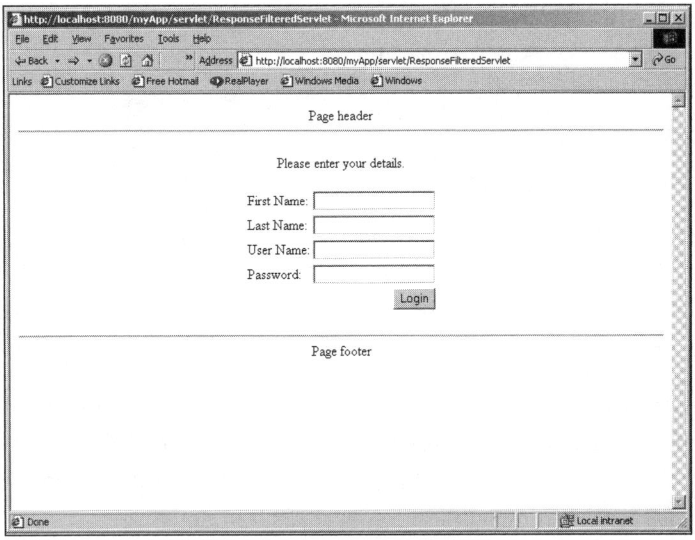

Figure 7.3 Filtering the HttpServletResponse.

When you view the source code for the HTML, it looks like this:

```
<HTML>
<BODY>
<CENTER>
Page header
<HR>
<BR>Please enter your details.
<BR>
<BR><FORM METHOD=POST>
<TABLE>
<TR>
<TD>First Name:</TD>
<TD><INPUT TYPE=TEXT NAME=firstName></TD>
</TR>
<TR>
<TD>Last Name:</TD>
<TD><INPUT TYPE=TEXT NAME=lastName></TD>
</TR>
<TR>
<TD>User Name:</TD>
<TD><INPUT TYPE=TEXT NAME=userName></TD>
</TR>
<TR>
<TD>Password:</TD>
```

```
<TD><INPUT TYPE=PASSWORD NAME=password></TD>
</TR>
<TR>
<TD ALIGN=RIGHT COLSPAN=2>
<INPUT TYPE=SUBMIT VALUE=Login></TD>
</TR>
</TABLE>
</FORM>
<HR>
Page footer
<CENTER>
</BODY>
</HTML>
```

Filter Chain

You can apply more than one filter to a resource. In this example, you create the UpperCaseFilter and use the TrimFilter and a DoublyFilteredServlet. The UpperCaseFilter is given in Listing 7.14, and the DoublyFilteredServlet is given in Listing 7.15.

Listing 7.14 **The UpperCaseFilter**

```
import java.io.*;
import javax.servlet.Filter;
import javax.servlet.FilterChain;
import javax.servlet.FilterConfig;
import javax.servlet.ServletContext;
import javax.servlet.ServletException;
import javax.servlet.ServletRequest;
import javax.servlet.ServletResponse;
import java.util.Enumeration;

public class UpperCaseFilter implements Filter {
  private FilterConfig filterConfig = null;
  public void destroy() {
    System.out.println("Filter destroyed");
    this.filterConfig = null;
  }

  public void doFilter(ServletRequest request, ServletResponse response,
    FilterChain chain)
    throws IOException, ServletException {
    System.out.println("Filter");
    Enumeration enum = request.getAttributeNames();
    while (enum.hasMoreElements()) {
      String attributeName = (String) enum.nextElement();
      String attributeValue = (String) request.getAttribute(attributeName);
      request.setAttribute(attributeName, attributeValue.toUpperCase());
```

```
    }

    chain.doFilter(request, response);
  }

  public void init(FilterConfig filterConfig) throws ServletException {
    System.out.println("Filter initialized");
    this.filterConfig = filterConfig;
  }
}
```

Listing 7.15 **The DoublyFilteredServlet**

```
import javax.servlet.*;
import javax.servlet.http.*;
import java.io.*;
import com.brainysoftware.java.StringUtil;

public class DoublyFilteredServlet extends HttpServlet {

  public void doGet(HttpServletRequest request, HttpServletResponse response)
    throws ServletException, IOException {
    response.setContentType("text/html");
    PrintWriter out = response.getWriter();
    out.println("<HTML>");
    out.println("<HEAD>");
    out.println("<TITLE>User Input Form</TITLE>");
    out.println("</HEAD>");
    out.println("<BODY>");
    out.println("<CENTER>");
    out.println("<BR>Please enter your details.");
    out.println("<BR>");
    out.println("<BR><FORM METHOD=POST>");
    out.println("<TABLE>");
    out.println("<TR>");
    out.println("<TD>First Name:</TD>");
    out.println("<TD><INPUT TYPE=TEXT NAME=firstName></TD>");
    out.println("</TR>");
    out.println("<TR>");
    out.println("<TD>Last Name:</TD>");
    out.println("<TD><INPUT TYPE=TEXT NAME=lastName></TD>");
    out.println("</TR>");
    out.println("<TR>");
    out.println("<TD>User Name:</TD>");
    out.println("<TD><INPUT TYPE=TEXT NAME=userName></TD>");
    out.println("</TR>");
    out.println("<TR>");
    out.println("<TD>Password:</TD>");
    out.println("<TD><INPUT TYPE=PASSWORD NAME=password></TD>");
    out.println("</TR>");
```

continues

Listing 7.15 **Continued**

```
    out.println("<TR>");
    out.println("<TD ALIGN=RIGHT COLSPAN=2>");
    out.println("<INPUT TYPE=SUBMIT VALUE=Login></TD>");
    out.println("</TR>");
    out.println("</TABLE>");
    out.println("</FORM>");
    out.println("</CENTER>");
    out.println("</BODY>");
    out.println("</HTML>");
  }

  public void doPost(HttpServletRequest request, HttpServletResponse
response)
    throws ServletException, IOException {

    String firstName = (String) request.getAttribute("firstName");
    String lastName = (String) request.getAttribute("lastName");
    String userName = (String) request.getAttribute("userName");
    String password = request.getParameter("password");
    response.setContentType("text/html");
    PrintWriter out = response.getWriter();
    out.println("<HTML>");
    out.println("<HEAD>");
    out.println("<TITLE>Displaying Values</TITLE>");
    out.println("</HEAD>");
    out.println("<BODY>");
    out.println("<CENTER>");
    out.println("Here are your details.");
    out.println("<TABLE>");
    out.println("<TR>");
    out.println("<TD>First Name:</TD>");
    out.println("<TD>" + StringUtil.encodeHtmlTag(firstName) + "</TD>");
    out.println("</TR>");
    out.println("<TR>");
    out.println("<TD>Last Name:</TD>");
    out.println("<TD>" + StringUtil.encodeHtmlTag (lastName) + "</TD>");
    out.println("</TR>");
    out.println("<TR>");
    out.println("<TD>User Name:</TD>");
    out.println("<TD>" + StringUtil.encodeHtmlTag(userName) + "</TD>");
    out.println("</TR>");
    out.println("<TR>");
    out.println("<TD>Password:</TD>");
    out.println("<TD>" + StringUtil. encodeHtmlTag(password) + "</TD>");
    out.println("</TABLE>");
    out.println("</CENTER>");
    out.println("</BODY>");
    out.println("</HTML>");

  }

}
```

Note

Notice that the filters in the filter chain modified attributes because you can't modify the parameters in the HTTP request object.

The deployment descriptor is given in Listing 7.16.

Listing 7.16 **The Deployment Descriptor for this Example**

```
<?xml version="1.0" encoding="ISO-8859-1"?>

<!DOCTYPE web-app
  PUBLIC "-//Sun Microsystems, Inc.//DTD Web Application 2.3//EN"
  "http://java.sun.com/dtd/web-app_2_3.dtd">

<web-app>
  <!-- Define servlet-mapped and path-mapped filters -->
  <filter>
    <filter-name>
      Trim Filter
    </filter-name>
    <filter-class>
      TrimFilter
    </filter-class>
  </filter>

  <filter>
    <filter-name>
      UpperCase Filter
    </filter-name>
    <filter-class>
      UpperCaseFilter
    </filter-class>
  </filter>

  <!-- Define filter mappings for the defined filters -->
  <filter-mapping>
    <filter-name>
      Trim Filter
    </filter-name>
    <servlet-name>
      DoublyFilteredServlet
    </servlet-name>
  </filter-mapping>

  <filter-mapping>
    <filter-name>
      UpperCase Filter
    </filter-name>
    <servlet-name>
      DoublyFilteredServlet
```

continues

Listing 7.16 **Continued**

```
      </servlet-name>
    </filter-mapping>

    <servlet>
      <servlet-name>
        DoublyFilteredServlet
      </servlet-name>
      <servlet-class>
        DoublyFilteredServlet
      </servlet-class>
    </servlet>
  </web-app>
```

Finally, Figure 7.4 shows the two filters in action. User input is now trimmed and turned into uppercase characters.

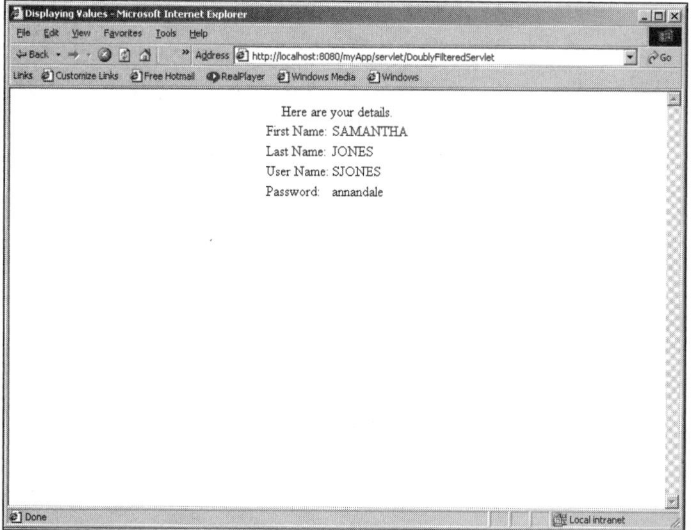

Figure 7.4 The result of the doPost of the DoublyFilteredServlet.

Summary

This chapter introduced you to filters, a new feature in Servlet 2.3 specification that enables you to perform some operations before the HTTP request reaches the servlet. Writing a filter involves in three interfaces: Filter, FilterConfig, and FilterChain. For the filter to work on a certain resource, you need to declare the filter in the deployment descriptor using the <filter> element and map it to the resources it is supposed to filter using the <filter-mapping> element. You can map a filter to a servlet or a URL pattern.

The next chapter will present the second technology for writing Java web application—JavaServer Pages (JSP).

8

JSP Basics

JavaServer Pages (JSP) is another Java technology for developing web applications. JSP was released during the time servlet technology had gained popularity as one of the best web technologies available. JSP is not meant to replace servlets, however. In fact, JSP is an extension of the servlet technology, and it is common practice to use both servlets and JSP pages in the same web applications.

Authoring JSP pages is so easy that you can write JSP applications without much knowledge of the underlying API. If you want to be a really good Java web programmer, however, you need to know both JSP and servlets. Even if you use only JSP pages in your Java web applications, understanding servlets is still very important. As you will see in this chapter and the chapters to come, JSP uses the same techniques as those found in servlet programming. For example, in JSP you work with HTTP requests and HTTP responses, request parameters, request attributes, session management, cookies, URL-rewriting, and so on. This chapter explains the relation between JSP and servlets, introduces the JSP technology, and presents many examples that you can run easily.

Note

If you are not familiar with servlet technology, read this chapter only after reading Chapters 1 to 7, which focus specifically on creating and working with servlets.

What's Wrong with Servlets?

The history of web server-side programming in Java started with servlets. Sun introduced servlets in 1996 as small Java-based applications for adding dynamic content to web applications. Not much later, with the increasing popularity of Java, servlets took off to become one of the most popular technologies for Internet development today.

Servlet programmers know how cumbersome it is to program with servlets, however, especially when you have to send a long HTML page that includes little code. Take the snippet in Listing 8.1 as an example. The code is a fragment from a servlet-based application that displays all parameter names and values in an HTTP request.

Listing 8.1 **Displays All Parameter/Value Pairs in a Request Using a Servlet**

```
import javax.servlet.*;
import javax.servlet.http.*;
import java.io.*;
import java.util.*;

public class MyDearServlet extends HttpServlet {

  //Process the HTTP GET request
  public void doGet(HttpServletRequest request,
    HttpServletResponse response)
    throws ServletException, IOException {

    doPost(request, response);

  }

  //Process the HTTP POST request
  public void doPost(HttpServletRequest request,
    HttpServletResponse response)
    throws ServletException, IOException {

    response.setContentType("text/html");
    PrintWriter out = response.getWriter();
    out.println("<HTML>");
    out.println("<HEAD><TITLE>Using Servlets</TITLE></HEAD>");
```

```
      out.println("<BODY BGCOLOR=#123123>");

      //Get parameter names
      Enumeration parameters = request.getParameterNames();
      String param = null;
      while (parameters.hasMoreElements()) {
        param = (String) parameters.nextElement();
        out.println(param + ":" + request.getParameter(param) +
          "<BR>");
      }
      out.println("</BODY>");
      out.println("</HTML>");
      out.close();

    } //End of doPost method


    /* other parts of the class goes here
      .
      .
      .
    */

  } //End of class
```

Nearly half of the content sent from the doPost method is static HTML. However, each HTML tag must be embedded in a String and sent using the println method of the PrintWriter object. It is a tedious chore. Worse still, the HTML page may be much longer.

Another disadvantage of using servlets is that every single change will require the intervention of the servlet programmer. Even a slight graphical modification, such as changing the value of the <BODY> tag's BGCOLOR attribute from #DADADA to #FFFFFF, will need to be done by the programmer (who in this case will work under the supervision of the more graphic-savvy web designer).

Sun understood this problem and soon developed a solution. The result was JSP technology. According to Sun's web site, "JSP technology is an extension of the servlet technology created to support authoring of HTML and XML pages." Combining fixed or static template data with dynamic content is easier with JSP. Even if you're comfortable writing servlets, you will find in this chapter several compelling reasons to investigate JSP technology as a complement to your existing work.

What needs to be highlighted is that "JSP technology is an extension of the servlet technology." This means that JSP did not replace servlets as the technology for writing server-side Internet/intranet applications. In fact, JSP was built on the servlet foundation and needs the servlet technology to work.

JSP solves drawbacks in the servlet technology by allowing the programmer to intersperse code with static content, for example. If the programmer has to work with an HTML page template written by a web designer, the programmer can simply add code into the HTML page and save it as a .jsp file. If at a later stage the web designer needs to change the HTML body background color, he or she can do it without wasting the charging-by-the-hour programmer's time. He or she can just open the .jsp file and edit it accordingly.

The code in Listing 8.1 can be rewritten in JSP as shown Listing 8.2.

Listing 8.2 **Displays All Parameter/Value Pairs in a Request Using JSP**

```
<%@ page import="java.util.Enumeration" %>
<HTML>
<HEAD><TITLE>Using JSP</TITLE></HEAD>
<BODY BGCOLOR=#DADADA>
<%
  //Get parameter names
  Enumeration parameters = request.getParameterNames();
  String param = null;
  while (parameters.hasMoreElements()) {
    param = (String) parameters.nextElement();
    out.println(param + ":" + request.getParameter(param) +
      "<BR>");
  }
  out.close();
%>
</BODY>
</HTML>
```

You can see that <HTML> tags stay as they are. When you need to add dynamic content, all you need to do is enclose your code in <% ... %> tags.

Again, JSP is not a replacement for servlets. Rather, JSP technology and servlets together provide an attractive solution to web scripting/programming by offering platform independence, enhanced performance, separation of logic from display, ease of administration, extensibility into the enterprise, and most importantly, ease of use.

Running Your First JSP

This section invites you to write a simple JSP page and run it. The emphasis here is not on the architecture or syntax and semantics of a JSP page; instead the section demonstrates how to configure minimally the servlet/JSP container to run JSP. Tomcat 4 is used to run JSP applications. If you have installed and configured Tomcat 4 for your servlet applications, there is no more to do. If you haven't, see Appendix A, "Tomcat 4 Installation and Configuration."

> **Note**
> In the JSP context, Tomcat is often referred to as a "JSP container." Because Tomcat also is used to run servlets, however, it is more common to call it a servlet/JSP container.

After reading this section, you will understand how much JSP simplifies things for servlets. To make your JSP page run, all you need to do is configure your JSP container (Tomcat) and write a JSP page. Configuration is only done once, at the beginning. No compilation is necessary.

Configuring Tomcat to Run a JSP Application

The first thing you need to do before you can run your JSP application is configure Tomcat so that it recognizes your JSP application. To configure Tomcat to run a particular JSP application, follow these steps:

1. Create a directory under %CATALINA_HOME%/webapps called myJSPApp. The directory structure is shown in Figure 8.1.
2. Add a subdirectory named WEB-INF under the myJSPApp directory.
3. Edit server.xml, the server configuration file, so Tomcat knows about this new JSP application. The server.xml file is located in the conf directory under %CATALINA_HOME%. Open the file with your text editor and look for code similar to the following:

```
<Context path="/examples" docBase="examples" debug="0"
                 reloadable="true">
 .
 .
 .
</Context>
```

   Right after the closing tag </Context>, add the following code:

```
<Context path="/myJSPApp" docBase="myJSPApp" debug="0" reloadable="true">
</Context>
```

4. Restart Tomcat.

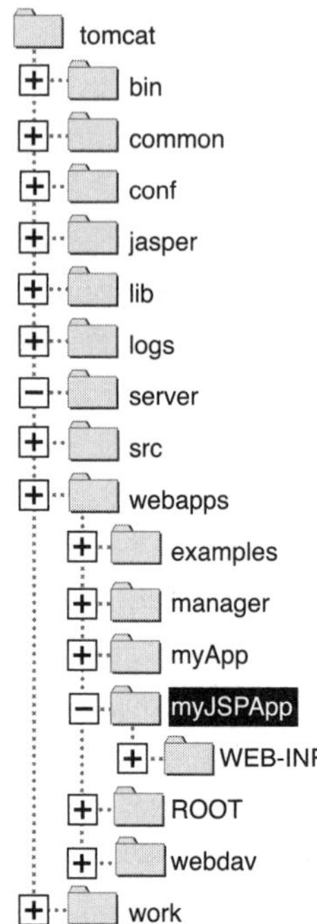

Figure 8.1 The JSP application directory structure for the myJSPApp application.

Now you can write your JSP file and store it under the myJSPApp file. Alternatively, to make it more organized, you can create a subdirectory called jsp under myJSPApp and store your JSP files there. If you do this, you don't need to change the setting in the server.xml file.

Writing a JSP File

A JSP page consists of interwoven HTML tags and Java code. The HTML tags represent the presentation part and the code produces the contents. In its most basic form, a JSP page can include only the HTML part, like the code shown in Listing 8.3.

Listing 8.3 **The Simplest JSP Page**

```
<HTML>
<HEAD>
</HEAD>
<BODY>
JSP is easy.
</BODY>
</HTML>
```

Save this file as SimplePage.jsp in the myJSPApp directory. Your directory structure should resemble Figure 8.1.

Now, start your web browser, and type the following URL:

```
http://localhost:8080/myJSPApp/SimplePage.jsp
```

The browser is shown in Figure 8.2.

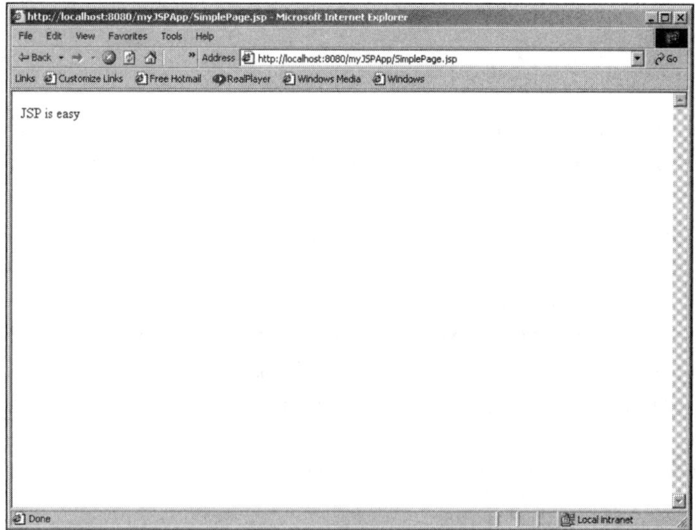

Figure 8.2 Your first JSP page.

Other Examples

Of course, the code in Listing 8.3 is not a really useful page, but it illustrates the point that a JSP page does not need to have code at all. If your page is purely static, like the one in Listing 8.3, you shouldn't put it in a JSP file because JSP files are slower to process than HTML files. You might want to use a JSP file for pure HTML tags, however, if you think the code might include Java code in the future. This saves you the trouble of changing all the links to this page at the later stage.

To write Java code in your JSP file, you embed the code in <% ... %> tags. For example, the code in Listing 8.4 is an example of intertwining Java code and HTML in a JSP file.

Listing 8.4 **Interweaving HTML and Code**

```
<HTML>
<HEAD>
</HEAD>
<BODY>
<%
  out.println("JSP is easy");
%>
</BODY>
</HTML>
```

The code in Listing 8.4 produces the same output as the one in Listing 8.3. Notice, however, the use of the Java code to send the text. If you don't understand what out.println does, bear with me for a moment—it is discussed in detail in the next section. For now, knowing that out.println is used to send a String to the web browser is sufficient.

Notice also that the output of a JSP page is plain text consisting of HTML tags. No code section of the page will be sent to the browser.

Another example is given in Listing 8.5. This snippet displays the string "Welcome. The server time is now" followed by the server time.

Listing 8.5 **Displaying the Server Time**

```
<HTML>
<HEAD>
  <TITLE>Displaying the server time</TITLE>
</HEAD>
<BODY>
Welcome. The server time is now
<%
  java.util.Calendar now = java.util.Calendar.getInstance();
  int hour = now.get(java.util.Calendar.HOUR_OF_DAY);
  int minute = now.get(java.util.Calendar.MINUTE);

  if (hour<10)
    out.println("0" + hour);
  else
    out.println(hour);

  out.println(":");

  if (minute<10)
    out.println("0" + minute);
  else
    out.println(minute);

%>
</BODY>
</HTML>
```

The code in Listing 8.5 displays the time in the hh:mm format. Therefore, if the hour is less than 10, a "0" precedes, which means that nine will be displayed as 09 instead of 9.

How JSP Works

Inside the JSP container is a special servlet called the *page compiler*. The servlet container is configured to forward to this page compiler all HTTP requests with URLs that match the .jsp file extension. This page compiler turns a servlet container into a JSP container. When a .jsp page is first called, the page compiler parses and compiles the .jsp page into a servlet class. If the compilation is successful, the jsp servlet class is loaded into memory. On subsequent calls, the servlet class for that .jsp page is already in memory; however, it could have been updated. Therefore, the page compiler servlet will always compare the timestamp of the jsp servlet with the jsp page. If the .jsp page is more current, recompilation is necessary. With this process, once deployed, JSP pages only go through the time-consuming compilation process once.

You may be thinking that after the deployment, the first user requests for a .jsp page will experience unusually slow response due to the time spent for compiling the .jsp file into a jsp servlet. To avoid this unpleasant situation, a mechanism in JSP allows the .jsp pages to be pre-compiled before any user request for them is received. Alternatively, you deploy your JSP application as a web archive file in the form of a compiled servlet. This technique is discussed in Chapter 16, "Application Deployment."

The JSP Servlet Generated Code

When the JSP is invoked, Tomcat creates two files in the C:\%CATALINA_HOME%\work\localhost\examples\jsp directory. Those two files are SimplePage_jsp.java and SimplePage_jsp.class. When you open the SimplePage_jsp.java file, you will see the following:

```
package org.apache.jsp;

import javax.servlet.*;
import javax.servlet.http.*;
import javax.servlet.jsp.*;
import javax.servlet.jsp.tagext.*;
import org.apache.jasper.runtime.*;


public class SimplePage_jsp extends HttpJspBase {

  static {
```

continues

```
  }

  public SimplePage_jsp( ) {
  }

  private static boolean _jspx_inited = false;

  public final void _jspx_init() throws org.apache.jasper.JasperException {
  }

  public void _jspService(HttpServletRequest request,
    HttpServletResponse  response)
    throws java.io.IOException, ServletException {

    JspFactory _jspxFactory = null;
    PageContext pageContext = null;
    HttpSession session = null;
    ServletContext application = null;
    ServletConfig config = null;
    JspWriter out = null;
    Object page = this;
    String  _value = null;
    try {
      if (_jspx_inited == false) {
        synchronized (this) {
          if (_jspx_inited == false) {
           _jspx_init();
           _jspx_inited = true;
          }
        }
      }
     _jspxFactory = JspFactory.getDefaultFactory();
      response.setContentType("text/html;charset=ISO-8859-1");
      pageContext = jspxFactory.getPageContext(this,
        request, response, "", true, 8192, true);
      application = pageContext.getServletContext();
      config = pageContext.getServletConfig();
      session = pageContext.getSession();
      out = pageContext.getOut();

      // begin
[file="C:\\tomcat4\\bin\\..\\webapps\\examples\\jsp\\SimplePage.jsp";from=(0,
2);to=(2,0)]
      out.println("JSP is easy");
      // end
      // HTML // begin
[file="C:\\tomcat4\\bin\\..\\webapps\\examples\\jsp\\SimplePage.jsp";from=(2,
2);to=(3,0)]
      out.write("\r\n");
      // end
```

```
      }
      catch (Throwable t) {
        if (out != null && out.getBufferSize() != 0)
          out.clearBuffer();
        if (pageContext != null)
          pageContext.handlePageException(t);
      }
      finally {
       if (_jspxFactory != null)
        _jspxFactory.releasePageContext(pageContext);
      }
    }
  }
```

For now, I will defer a full explanation of the preceding code until you learn more about how the interfaces and classes are used to run a JSP page. You can read the section, "The Generated Servlet Revisited," later in this chapter, to learn more about the code listed here.

The JSP API

The JSP technology is based on the JSP API that consists of two packages: javax.servlet.jsp and javax.servlet.jsp.tagext. Both packages are given in detail in Appendix D, "The javax.servlet.jsp Package Reference," and Appendix E, "The javax.servlet.jsp.tagext Package Reference." This chapter will discuss the classes and interfaces of the javax.servlet.jsp package and javax.servlet.jsp.tagext will be discussed in Chapter 11, "Using JSP Custom Tags."

In addition to these two packages, JSP also needs the two servlet packages—javax.servlet and javax.servlet.http. When you study the javax.servlet.jsp package, you will know why we say that JSP is an extension of servlet technology and understand why it is important that a JSP application programmer understands the servlet technology well.

The javax.servlet.jsp package has two interfaces and four classes. The interfaces are as follows:

- JspPage
- HttpJspPage

The four classes are as follows:

- JspEngineInfo
- JspFactory
- JspWriter
- PageContext

In addition, there are also two exception classes: JspException and JspError.

The JspPage Interface

The JspPage is the interface that must be implemented by all JSP servlet classes. This may remind you of the javax.servlet.Servlet interface in Chapter 1, "The Servlet Technology," of course. And, not surprisingly, the JspPage interface does extend the javax.servlet.Servlet interface.

The JSPPage interface has two methods, JspInit and JspDestroy, whose signatures are as follows:

```
public void jspInit()
public void jspDestroy()
```

jspInit, which is similar to the init method in the javax.servlet.Servlet interface, is called when the JspPage object is created and can be used to run some initialization. This method is called only once during the life cycle of the JSP page: the first time the JSP page is invoked.

The jspDestroy method is analogous with the destroy method of the javax.servlet.Servlet interface. This method is called before the JSP servlet object is destroyed. You can use this method to do some clean-up, if you want.

Most of the time, however, JSP authors rarely make full use of these two methods. The following example illustrates how you can implement these two methods in your JSP page:

```
<%!
  public void jspInit() {
    System.out.println("Init");
  }
  public void jspDestroy() {
    System.out.println("Destroy");
  }
%>
<%
  out.println("JSP is easy");
%>
```

Notice that the first line of the code starts with <%!. You will find the explanation of this construct in the Chapter 9, "JSP Syntax."

The HttpJspPage Interface

This interface directly extends the JspPage interface. There is only one method: _jspService. This method is called by the JSP container to generate the content of the JSP page. The _jspService has the following signature:

```
public void _jspService(HttpServletRequest request,
  HttpServletResponse response) throws ServletException, IOException.
```

You can't include this method in a JSP page, such as in the following code:

```
<%!
  public void jspInit() {
    System.out.println("Init");
  }
  public void jspDestroy() {
    System.out.println("Destroy");
  }
  public void _jspService(HttpServletRequest request,
    HttpServletResponse response) throws ServletException, IOException {
    System.out.println("Service");
  }
%>
```

This is because the page content itself represents this method. See the section "The Generated Servlet Revisited."

The JspFactory Class

The JspFactory class is an abstract class that provides methods for obtaining other objects needed for the JSP page processing. The class has the static method getDefaultFactory that returns a JspFactory object. From the JspFactory object, a PageContext and a JspEngineInfo object can be obtained that are useful for the JSP page processing. These objects are obtained using the JspFactory class's getEngineInfo method and the getPageContext method, whose signatures are given here:

```
public abstract JspEngineInfo getEngineInfo()
public abstract PageContext getPageContext (
Servlet requestingServlet, ServletRequest request,
ServletResponse response, String errorPageURL,
boolean needsSession, int buffer, boolean autoFlush)
```

The following code is part of the _jspService method that is generated by the JSP container:

```
JspFactory _jspxFactory = null;
PageContext pageContext = null;
jspxFactory = JspFactory.getDefaultFactory();
.
.
.
pageContext = _jspxFactory.getPageContext(this, request,
  response,  "", true, 8192, true);
```

The JspEngineInfo Class

The JspEngineInfo class is an abstract class that provides information on the JSP container. Only one method, getSpecificationVersion, returns the JSP container's version number. Because this is the only method currently available, this class does not have much use.

You can obtain a JspEngineInfo object using the getEngineInfo method of the JspFactory class.

The PageContext Class

PageContext represents a class that provides methods that are implementation-dependent. The PageContext class itself is abstract, so in the _jspService method of a JSP servlet class, a PageContext object is obtained by calling the getPageContext method of the JspFactory class.

The PageContext class provides methods that are used to create other objects. For example, its getOut method returns a JspWriter object that is used to send strings to the web browser. Other methods that return servlet-related objects include the following:

- getRequest, returns a ServletRequest object
- getResponse, returns a ServletResponse object
- getServletConfig, returns a ServletConfig object
- getServletContext, returns a ServletContext object
- getSession, returns an HttpSession object

The JspWriter Class

The JspWriter class is derived from the java.io.Writer class and represents a Writer that you can use to write to the client browser. Of its many methods, the most important are the print and println methods. Both provide enough overloads that ensure you can write any type of data. The difference between print and println is that println always adds the new line character to the printed data.

Additional methods allow you to manipulate the buffer. For instance, the clear method clears the buffer. It throws an exception if some of the buffer's content has already been flushed. Similar to clear is the clearBuffer method, which clears the buffer but never throws any exception if any of the buffer's contents have been flushed.

The Generated Servlet Revisited

Now that you understand the various interfaces and classes in the javax.servlet.jsp package, analyzing the generated JSP servlet will make more sense.

When you study the generated code, the first thing you'll see is the following:

```
public class SimplePage_jsp extends HttpJspBase {
```

The discussion should start with the questions, "What is HttpJspBase?"and "Why doesn't the JSP servlet class implement the javax.servlet.jsp.JspPage or javax.servlet.jsp.HttpJspPage interface?"

First, remember that the JSP specification defines only standards for writing JSP pages. A JSP page itself will be translated into a java file, which in turn will be compiled into a servlet class. The two processes are implementation dependent and do not affect the way a JSP page author codes. Therefore, a JSP container has the freedom and flexibility to do the page translation in its own way. The JSP servlet-generated code presented in this chapter is taken from Tomcat. You can therefore expect a different Java file to be generated by other JSP containers.

In Tomcat, HttpJspBase is a class whose source can be found under the src\jasper\src\share\org\apache\jasper\runtime directory under the %CATALINA_HOME% directory.

Most importantly, the signature of this class is as follows:

```
public abstract class HttpJspBase extends HttpServlet
  implements HttpJspPage
```

Now you can see that HttpJspBase is an HttpServlet and it does implement the javax.servlet.jsp.HttpJspPage interface. The HttpJspBase is more like a wrapper class so that its derived class does not have to provide implementation for the interface's methods if the JSP page author does not override them. The complete listing of the class follows:

```
/*
 * The Apache Software License, Version 1.1
 *
 * Copyright (c) 1999 The Apache Software Foundation.  All rights
 * reserved.
 *
 * Redistribution and use in source and binary forms, with or without
 * modification, are permitted provided that the following conditions
 * are met:
 *
```

```
 * 1. Redistributions of source code must retain the above copyright
 *    notice, this list of conditions and the following disclaimer.
 *
 * 2. Redistributions in binary form must reproduce the above copyright
 *    notice, this list of conditions and the following disclaimer in
 *    the documentation and/or other materials provided with the
 *    distribution.
 *
 * 3. The end-user documentation included with the redistribution, if
 *    any, must include the following acknowlegement:
 *       "This product includes software developed by the
 *        Apache Software Foundation (http://www.apache.org/)."
 *    Alternately, this acknowlegement may appear in the software itself,
 *    if and wherever such third-party acknowlegements normally appear.
 *
 * 4. The names "The Jakarta Project", "Tomcat", and "Apache Software
 *    Foundation" must not be used to endorse or promote products derived
 *    from this software without prior written permission. For written
 *    permission, please contact apache@apache.org.
 *
 * 5. Products derived from this software may not be called "Apache"
 *    nor may "Apache" appear in their names without prior written
 *    permission of the Apache Group.
 *
 * THIS SOFTWARE IS PROVIDED ``AS IS'' AND ANY EXPRESSED OR IMPLIED
 * WARRANTIES, INCLUDING, BUT NOT LIMITED TO, THE IMPLIED WARRANTIES
 * OF MERCHANTABILITY AND FITNESS FOR A PARTICULAR PURPOSE ARE
 * DISCLAIMED.  IN NO EVENT SHALL THE APACHE SOFTWARE FOUNDATION OR
 * ITS CONTRIBUTORS BE LIABLE FOR ANY DIRECT, INDIRECT, INCIDENTAL,
 * SPECIAL, EXEMPLARY, OR CONSEQUENTIAL DAMAGES (INCLUDING, BUT NOT
 * LIMITED TO, PROCUREMENT OF SUBSTITUTE GOODS OR SERVICES; LOSS OF
 * USE, DATA, OR PROFITS; OR BUSINESS INTERRUPTION) HOWEVER CAUSED AND
 * ON ANY THEORY OF LIABILITY, WHETHER IN CONTRACT, STRICT LIABILITY,
 * OR TORT (INCLUDING NEGLIGENCE OR OTHERWISE) ARISING IN ANY WAY OUT
 * OF THE USE OF THIS SOFTWARE, EVEN IF ADVISED OF THE POSSIBILITY OF
 * SUCH DAMAGE.
 * ====================================================================
 *
 * This software consists of voluntary contributions made by many
 * individuals on behalf of the Apache Software Foundation.  For more
 * information on the Apache Software Foundation, please see
 * <http://www.apache.org/>.
 *
 */
 package org.apache.jasper.runtime;

import java.io.IOException;
import java.io.FileInputStream;
import java.io.InputStreamReader;

import java.net.URL;
```

```
import java.net.MalformedURLException;

import javax.servlet.*;
import javax.servlet.http.*;
import javax.servlet.jsp.*;

import org.apache.jasper.JasperException;
import org.apache.jasper.Constants;

/**
 * This is the subclass of all JSP-generated servlets.
 *
 * @author Anil K. Vijendran
 */
public abstract class HttpJspBase extends HttpServlet
  implements HttpJspPage {

  protected PageContext pageContext;

  protected HttpJspBase() {
  }

  public final void init(ServletConfig config)
    throws ServletException {
    super.init(config);
    jspInit();
  }

  public String getServletInfo() {
    return Constants.getString ("jsp.engine.info");
  }

  public final void destroy() {
    jspDestroy();
  }

  /**
   * Entry point into service.
   */
  public final void service(HttpServletRequest request,
    HttpServletResponse response)
    throws ServletException, IOException {
    _jspService(request, response);
  }

  public void jspInit() {
  }

  public void jspDestroy() {
  }
```

continues

```
    public abstract void _jspService(HttpServletRequest request,
      HttpServletResponse response)
      throws ServletException, IOException;

}
```

Back to the generated JSP servlet class, remember that the JSP page source code is simply the following three lines of code:

```
<%
  out.println("JSP is easy");
%>
```

There are no jspInit and jspDestroy methods in the source code, so there are no implementations for these two methods in the resulting servlet code. The three lines of code, however, translate into the _jspService method. For reading convenience, the method is reprinted here. Notice that, for clarity, the comments have been removed.

```
public void _jspService(HttpServletRequest request,
  HttpServletResponse  response)
  throws java.io.IOException, ServletException {

  JspFactory _jspxFactory = null;
  PageContext pageContext = null;
  HttpSession session = null;
  ServletContext application = null;
  ServletConfig config = null;
  JspWriter out = null;
  Object page = this;
  String  _value = null;
  try {
    if (_jspx_inited == false) {
      synchronized (this) {
        if (_jspx_inited == false) {
         _jspx_init();
         _jspx_inited = true;
        }
      }
    }
   _jspxFactory = JspFactory.getDefaultFactory();
    response.setContentType("text/html;charset=ISO-8859-1");
    pageContext = jspxFactory.getPageContext(this,
      request, response, "", true, 8192, true);
    application = pageContext.getServletContext();
    config = pageContext.getServletConfig();
    session = pageContext.getSession();
    out = pageContext.getOut();

    out.println("JSP is easy");
    out.write("\r\n");
```

```
    }
    catch (Throwable t) {
      if (out != null && out.getBufferSize() != 0)
        out.clearBuffer();
      if (pageContext != null)
        pageContext.handlePageException(t);
    }
    finally {
     if (_jspxFactory != null)
      _jspxFactory.releasePageContext(pageContext);
    }
  }
```

Implicit Objects

Having examined the generated JSP servlet source code, you know that the code contains several object declarations in its _jspService method. Recall this part from the code in the preceding section:

```
public void _jspService(HttpServletRequest request,
  HttpServletResponse  response)
  throws java.io.IOException, ServletException {

  JspFactory _jspxFactory = null;
  PageContext pageContext = null;
  HttpSession session = null;
  ServletContext application = null;
  ServletConfig config = null;
  JspWriter out = null;
  Object page = this;
  String  _value = null;
  try {
      .
      .
      .
   _jspxFactory = JspFactory.getDefaultFactory();
    response.setContentType("text/html;charset=ISO-8859-1");
    pageContext = jspxFactory.getPageContext(this,
      request, response, "", true, 8192, true);
    application = pageContext.getServletContext();
    config = pageContext.getServletConfig();
    session = pageContext.getSession();
    out = pageContext.getOut();
  .
  .
  .
}
```

You see that there are object references, such as pageContext, session, application, config, out, and so on. These object references are created whether they are used from inside the page. They are automatically available for the JSP page author to use! These objects are called *implicit objects* and are summarized in the Table 8.1.

Table 8.1 **JSP Implicit Objects**

Object	Type
request	javax.servlet.http.HttpServletRequest
response	javax.servlet.http.HttpServletResponse
out	javax.servlet.jsp.JspWriter
session	javax.servlet.http.HttpSession
application	javax.servlet.ServletContext
config	javax.servlet.ServletConfig
pageContext	javax.servlet.jsp.PageContext
page	javax.servlet.jsp.HttpJspPage
exception	java.lang.Throwable

By looking at Table 8.1, you now know why you can send a String of text by simply writing:

```
<%
  out.println("JSP is easy.");
%>
```

In the case of the code above, you use the implicit object out that represents a javax.servlet.jsp.JspWriter. All the implicit objects are discussed briefly in the following subsections.

request and response Implicit Objects

In servlets, both objects are passed in by the servlet container to the service method of the javax.servlet.http.HttpServlet class. Remember its signature?

```
protected void service(HttpServletRequest request,
  HttpServletResponse response)
  throws ServletException, IOException
```

Note

If you want to review servlets, you can go back to Chapters 1, "The Servlet Technology," and Chapter 2,"Inside Servlets," for more details.

In a servlet, before you send any output, you are required to call the setContentType of the HttpServletResponse to tell the browser the type of the content, as in the following code:

```
response.setContentType("text/html");
```

In JSP, this is done automatically for you in the generated JSP servlet class, as follows:

```
response.setContentType("text/html;charset=ISO-8859-1");
```

Having an HttpServletRequest and an HttpServletResponse, you can do anything you like as you would in a servlet. For example, the following JSP page retrieves the value of a parameter called firstName and displays it in the browser:

```
<HTML>
<HEAD>
<TITLE>Simple Page</TITLE>
</HEAD>
<BODY>
<%
  String firstName = request.getParameter("firstName");
  out.println("First name: " + firstName);
%>
</BODY>
</HTML>
```

The following example uses the sendRedirect method of the javax.servlet.http.HttpServletResponse to redirect the user to a different URL:

```
<%
response.sendRedirect("http://www.newriders.com");
%>
```

out Implicit Object

out is probably the most frequently used implicit object. You call either its print method or its println method to send text or other data to the client browser. In a servlet, you always need to call the getWriter method of the javax.servlet.http.HttpServletResponse interface to obtain a PrintWriter before you can output anything to the browser, as follows:

```
PrintWriter out = response.getWriter();
```

In JSP, you don't need to do this because you already have an out that represents a javax.servlet.jsp.JspWriter object.

session Implicit Object

The session implicit object represents the HttpSession object that you can retrieve in a servlet by calling the getSession method of the javax.servlet.http.HttpServletRequest interface, as in the following code:

```
request.getSession();
```

The following code is a JSP page that uses a session object to implement a counter:

```
<HTML>
<HEAD>
<TITLE>Counter</TITLE>
</HEAD>
<BODY>
<%
  String counterAttribute = (String) session.getAttribute("counter");
  int count = 0;
  try {
    count = Integer.parseInt(counterAttribute);
  }
  catch (Exception e) {
  }
  count++;
  session.setAttribute("counter", Integer.toString(count));
  out.println("This is the " + count + "th time you visited this page in this
session.");
%>
</BODY>
</HTML>
```

See how session is readily available without efforts from the programmer's side?

> **Warning**
>
> Note that the session object is available only in a JSP page that participates in the session management. To decide whether or not your JSP page should participate in the session management, see the discussion of the session management as discussed in Chapter 5, "Session Management."

application

The application implicit object represents the javax.servlet.ServletContext object. In an HttpServlet, you can retrieve the ServletContext method by using the getServletContext method.

config

The config implicit object represents a javax.servlet.ServletConfig object that in a servlet can be retrieved by using the getServletConfig method.

pageContext

The pageContext implicit object represents the javax.servlet.jsp.PageContext object discussed in the section, "The PageContext Class."

page

The page implicit object represents the javax.servlet.jsp.HttpJspPage interface explained in the section, "The HttpJspPage Interface."

exception

The exception object is available only on pages that have been defined as error pages.

Summary

This chapter is the introduction to the JSP technology. You may be able to author a JSP page without understanding the underlying API. However, mastering the classes and interfaces in the javax.servlet.jsp package and understanding how JSP extends the servlet technology provides you with the knowledge to write more powerful and efficient code.

9

JSP Syntax

In Chapter 8, "JSP Basics," you learned that a JSP page can have Java code and HTML tags. More formally, you can say that a JSP page has elements and template data. The elements, which also are called *JSP tags*, make up the syntax and semantics of JSP. Template data is everything else. Template data includes parts that the JSP container does not understand, such as HTML tags.

There are three types of elements:

- Directive elements
- Scripting elements
- Action elements

To write an effective JSP page, you need to understand all these elements well. Elements have two forms: the XML form and the <% … %> alternative form. The conversion between the XML form and the alternative form is presented at the end of the chapter in the section, "Converting into XML Syntax." Template data remains as it is, normally passed through the client uninterpreted.

This chapter discusses the three types of JSP elements and comments. It also presents examples on how to use these elements. You will also learn how incorporating these elements affects the JSP servlets—servlets that result from the translation of JSP pages.

Directives

Directives are messages to the JSP container containing information on how the JSP container must translate a JSP page into a corresponding servlet. Directives have the following syntax:

```
<%@ directive (attribute="value")* %>
```

The asterisk (*) means that what is enclosed in the brackets can be repeated zero or more times. The syntax can be re-written in a more informal way as follows:

```
<%@ directive attribute1="value1" attribute2="value2" ... %>
```

White spaces after the opening <%@ and before the closing %> are optional, but are recommended to enhance readability.

> **Warning**
> Note that an attribute value must be quoted.

Warning the three types of directives are as follows:

- Page directives
- Include directives
- Tag library directives

The first two directives are discussed in detail in this chapter. Discussion on the tag library directive is deferred until Chapter 11, "Using JSP Custom Tags."

The Page Directive

The Page directive has the following syntax:

```
<%@ page (attribute="value")* %>
```

Or, if you want to use the more informal syntax:

```
<%@ page attribute1="value1" attribute2="value2" ... %>
```

The Page directive supports 11 attributes. These attributes are summarized in Table 9.1.

Table 9.1 **The Page Directive's Attributes**

Attribute	Value Type	Default Value
language	Scripting language name	"java"
info	String	Depends on the JSP container
contentType	MIME type, character set	"text/html;charset=ISO-8859-1"
extends	Class name	None
import	Fully qualified class name or package name	None
buffer	Buffer size or false	8192
autoFlush	Boolean	"true"
session	Boolean	"true"
isThreadSafe	Boolean	"true"
errorPage	URL	None
isErrorPage	Boolean	"false"

An example of the use of the Page directive is as follows:

```
<%@ page buffer="16384" session="false" %>
```

With JSP, you can specify multiple page directives in your JSP page, such as the following:

```
<%@ page buffer="16384" %>
<%@ page session="false" %>
```

Except for the import attribute, however, JSP does not allow you to repeat the same attribute within a page directive or in multiple directives on the same page.

The following is illegal because the info attribute appears more than once in a single page:

```
<%@ page info="Example Page" %>
<%@ page buffer="16384" %>
<%@ page info="Unrestricted Access" %>
```

The following also is illegal because the buffer attribute appears more than once in the same page directive:

```
<%@ page buffer="16384" info="Example Page" buffer="8192" %>
```

The following is legal, however, because the import attribute can appear multiple times:

```
<%@ page import="java.io.*" info="Example Page" %>
<%@ page import="java.util.Enumeration" %>
<%@ page import="com.brainysoftware.web.FileUpload" %>
```

Alternatively, imported libraries can appear in a single import attribute, separated by commas, as shown in the following code:

```
<%@ page import="java.io.*, java.util.Enumeration" %>
```

The following section discusses each attribute in more detail and examines the effect on the generated servlet.

The language Attribute

The language attribute specifies the scripting language used in the JSP page. By default, the value is "java" and all JSP containers must support Java as the scripting language. With Tomcat, this is the only accepted language. Other JSP containers might accept different languages, however.

Specifying this attribute, as in the following code, does not have any effect on the generated servlet:

```
<%@ page language="java" %>
<%
  out.println("JSP is easy");
%>
```

In fact, this attribute is useful only in a JSP container that supports a language other than Java as the scripting language.

The info Attribute

The info attribute allows you to insert any string that later can be retrieved using the getServletInfo method. For example, you can add the following page directive with an info attribute:

```
<%@ page info="Written by Bulbul" %>
```

The JSP container then will create a public method getServletInfo in the resulting servlet. This method returns the value of the info attribute specified in the page. For the previous page directive, the getServletInfo method will be written as follows:

```
public String getServletInfo() {
  return "Written by Bulbul";
}
```

In the same JSP page, you can retrieve the info attribute's value by calling the getServletInfo method. For instance, the following JSP page will return "Written by Bulbul" on the client browser.

```
<%@ page info="Written by Bulbul" %>
<%
  out.println(getServletInfo());
%>
```

The default value for this attribute depends on the JSP container.

The contentType Attribute

The contentType attribute defines the Multipurpose Internet Mail Extension (MIME) type of the HTTP response sent to the client. The default value is "text/html;charset=ISO-8859-1" and this is reflected in _jspService method in the generated servlet. For example, this is the cleaned up version of the servlet that is generated from a JSP page that does not specify the contentType attribute in its page directive; that is, the default value is used:

```
public void _jspService(HttpServletRequest request,
  HttpServletResponse  response)
  throws java.io.IOException, ServletException {
    .
    .
    .
  try {
    .
    .
    .
   _jspxFactory = JspFactory.getDefaultFactory();
    response.setContentType("text/html;charset=ISO-8859-1");
    .
    .
    .
  }
  catch (Throwable t) {
    .
    .
    .
  }
  finally {
    .
    .
    .
  }
}
```

You will want to use this attribute when working with pages that need to send characters in other encoding schemes. For example, the following directive tells the JSP container that the output should be sent using simplified Chinese characters:

```
<%@ page contentType="text/html;charset=GB2312" %>
```

The extends Attribute

The extends attribute defines the parent class that will be inherited by the generated servlet. You should use this attribute with extra care. In most cases, you should not use this attribute at all. In Tomcat, the parent class that will be subclassed by the resulting servlet is HttpJspBase.

The import Attribute

The import attribute is similar to the import keyword in a Java class or interface. The attribute is used to import a class or an interface or all members of a package. You will definitely use this attribute often. Whatever you specify in the import attribute of a page directive will be translated into an import statement in the generated servlet class. By default, Tomcat specifies the following import statements in every generated servlet class. You don't need to import what has been imported by default:

```
import javax.servlet.*;
import javax.servlet.http.*;
import javax.servlet.jsp.*;
import javax.servlet.jsp.tagext.*;
import org.apache.jasper.runtime.*;
```

As an example, consider the following JSP page that imports the java.io package and the java.util.Enumeration interface:

```
<%@ page import="java.io.*" %>
<%@ page import="java.util.Enumeration" %>
```

The two will be added before the default import statements in the generated servlet class, as described in the following code fragment:

```
import java.io.*;
import java.util.Enumeration;
import javax.servlet.*;
import javax.servlet.http.*;
import javax.servlet.jsp.*;
import javax.servlet.jsp.tagext.*;
import org.apache.jasper.runtime.*;
```

The buffer Attribute

By default, a JSP page's content is buffered to increase performance. The default size of the buffer is 8Kb or 8192 characters.

Consider an example that specifies the buffer attribute with a size of 16Kb:

```
<%@ page buffer="16kb" %>
```

This attribute is reflected in the _jspService method in the generated servlet class, as in the following cleaned up code. The buffer size is passed to the getPageContext method of the javax.servlet.jsp.JspFactory class when creating a PageContext object.

```
public void _jspService(HttpServletRequest request,
  HttpServletResponse  response)
  throws java.io.IOException, ServletException {
  .
  .
  .
```

```
    try {
      .
      .
      .
     _jspxFactory = JspFactory.getDefaultFactory();
      response.setContentType("text/html;charset=ISO-8859-1");

      // 8192 in the following line represents the buffer size
      pageContext = jspxFactory.getPageContext(this, request,
        response, "", true, 16384, true);
      .
      .
      .
    }
    catch (Throwable t) {
      .
      .
      .
    }
    finally {
      .
      .
      .
    }
  }
```

With the buffer attribute in a page directive, you can do two things:

- Eliminate the buffer by specifying the value “none”, as in the following code:

  ```
  <%@ page buffer="none" %>
  ```

  If you decide not to use a buffer, the getPageContext method will be invoked passing 0 as the buffer size, as in the following code:

  ```
  pageContext = _jspxFactory.getPageContext(
  this, request, response, "", true, 0, true);
  ```

- Change the size of the buffer by assigning a number to the attribute. The attribute value represents the number in kilobytes. Therefore, “16” means 16Kb alias 16384 characters. You can either write the number only, or the number plus “Kb”. For example, “16” is the same as “16Kb”.

The following example shows two page directives in two different JSP pages. The first cancels the use of the buffer, and the second changes the size of the buffer to 12Kb.

```
<%@ page import="java.io.*" buffer="none" %>
<%@ page import="java.io.*" buffer="12" %>
```

> **Warning**
> Note that the JSP container has the discretion to use a buffer size larger than specified to improve performance.

The autoFlush Attribute

The autoFlush attribute is related to the page buffer. When the value is "true", the JSP container will automatically flush the buffer when the buffer is full. If the value is "false", however, the JSP author needs to flush the buffer manually using the flush method of the JspWriter object, such as the following:

```
out.flush();
```

For example, the following code specifies a false value for the autoFlush attribute:

```
<%@ page autoFlush="false" %>
```

The session Attribute

By default, a JSP page participates in the JSP container's session management. This is indicated by the declaration of a javax.servlet.http.HttpSession object reference and the creation of it through the getSession method of the javax.servlet.jsp.PageContext, as illustrated by the following code:

```
public void _jspService(HttpServletRequest request,
  HttpServletResponse  response)
  throws java.io.IOException, ServletException {

  JspFactory _jspxFactory = null;
  PageContext pageContext = null;
  // declare an HttpSession object reference
  HttpSession session = null;

  try {
    .
    .
    .
  jspxFactory = JspFactory.getDefaultFactory();
  response.setContentType("text/html;charset=ISO-8859-1");
  pageContext = _jspxFactory.getPageContext(
    this, request, response, "", true, 0, true);
  application = pageContext.getServletContext();
  config = pageContext.getServletConfig();
  // create a HttpSession object
  session = pageContext.getSession();
    .
    .
    .
```

```
    }
    catch (Throwable t) {
      .
      .
      .
    }
    finally {
      .
      .
      .
    }
  }
```

Whether your JSP page participates in the session management is determined by the value of the session attribute in a page directive. By default this value is true; that is, the JSP page is part of the session management. I want to make an important point, however: *You should not let your JSP page participate in the session management unnecessarily because this consumes resources.* Because of this, you should always use the session attribute and assign it the value of "false" unless you are specifically needing session management.

When the value of this attribute is "false", no javax.servlet.http.HttpSession object reference is declared and no HttpSession object is created. As a result, the session implicit object is not available in the JSP page.

The following shows an example of the use of the session attribute:

```
<%@ page session="false" %>
```

The isThreadSafe Attribute

As discussed in Chapter 2, "Inside Servlets," you can make a servlet thread-safe by inheriting the javax.servlet.SingleThreadModel. You can control this behavior in the JSP page by using the isThreadSafe attribute, which by default has the value of "true". When the value of this attribute is true, you guarantee that simultaneous access to this page is safe. However, you can assign "false" to this attribute as in the following code:

```
<%@ page isThreadSafe="false" %>
```

By setting the isThreadSafe attribute to false, you are telling the JSP translator that you (the programmer of this page) cannot guarantee that simultaneous accesses to this page will be safe. Therefore, you are asking the JSP translator to make this page thread-safe. This will make the generated servlet implement the javax.servlet.SingleThreadModel interface, as in the following signature of the JSP servlet class:

```
public class SimplePage_jsp extends HttpJspBase
  implements SingleThreadModel
```

In other words, when the value of this attribute is false, the JSP container will serialize multiple requests for this page; that is, the JSP container will wait until the JSP servlet finishes responding to a request before passing another request to it.

The errorPage Attribute

The errorPage attribute specifies the URL of an error page that will be displayed if an uncaught exception occurs in this current JSP page. Referring to the URL of the error page is sometimes tricky. The easiest solution is to store the error page in the same directory as the current JSP page. In this case, you need only to mention the name of the error page, as in the following example:

```
<%@ page errorPage="ErrorPage.jsp" %>
<%
  String name = request.getParameter("otherName");
  // this will throw an exception because the parameter "otherName"
  // does not exist, so name will be null.
  // this will cause the ErrorPage.jsp to be displayed
  name.substring(1, 1);
%>
```

When the page is called, the error page is displayed. An error page must specify the isErrorPage attribute in its page directive and the value of this attribute must be "true".

The following is an errorPage attribute that is assigned an error page in a URL:

```
<%@ page errorPage="/myJspApp/ErrorPage.jsp" %>
```

The isErrorPage Attribute

The isErrorPage attribute can accept the value of "true" or "false", and the default value is "false". It indicates whether the current JSP page is an error page; that is, the page that will be displayed when an uncaught exception occurs in the other JSP page. If the current page is an error page, it has access to the exception implicit object, as explained in Chapter 8.

The include Directive

The include directive is the second type of the JSP directive elements. This directive enables JSP page authors to include the contents of other files in the current JSP page.

The include directive is useful if you have a common source that will be used by more than one JSP page. Instead of repeating the same code in every JSP page, thus creating a maintenance problem, you can place the common code in a separate file and use an include directive from each JSP page.

The included page itself can be static, such as an HTML file, or dynamic, such as another JSP page. If you are including a JSP page, the included JSP page itself can include another file. Therefore, nesting include directives is permitted in JSP.

The syntax for the include directive is as follows:

```
<%@ include file="relativeURL" %>
```

The following is an example of how to include HTML files:

```
<%@ include file="includes/header.html" %>
<%
  out.println("<BODY>");
  // other content;
%>
<%@ include file="includes/footer.html" %>
```

> **Note**
> If the *relativeURL* part begins with a forward slash character (/), it is interpreted as an absolute path on the server. If *relativeURL* does not start with a "/", it is interpreted as relative to the current JSP page.

Now, we'll look at how included files are translated into the JSP servlet file. The following example is a simple JSP page that includes two HTML files: Header.html and Footer.html. Both included files are located under the includes subdirectory, which itself is under the directory that hosts the current JSP file. The JSP page is called SimplePage.jsp and is given in Listing 9.1. The page simply displays the current server time. The Header.html is given in Listing 9.2 and the Footer.html in Listing 9.3. What you are interested in here is the generated servlet code.

Listing 9.1 **A Simple JSP Page that Includes Two Files**

```
<%@ page session="false" %>
<%@ page import="java.util.Calendar" %>
<%@ include file="includes/Header.html" %>
<%
  out.println("Current time: " + Calendar.getInstance().getTime());
%>
<%@ include file="includes/Footer.html" %>
```

Listing 9.2 **The Header.html File**

```
<HTML>
<HEAD>
<TITLE>Welcome</TITLE>
<BODY>
```

Listing 9.3 **The Footer.html File**

```
</BODY>
</HTML>
```

The generated servlet is as follows:

```
package org.apache.jsp;

import java.util.Calendar;
import javax.servlet.*;
import javax.servlet.http.*;
import javax.servlet.jsp.*;
import javax.servlet.jsp.tagext.*;
import org.apache.jasper.runtime.*;


public class SimplePage_jsp extends HttpJspBase {

  static {
  }

  public SimplePage_jsp( ) {
  }

  private static boolean _jspx_inited = false;

  public final void _jspx_init() throws org.apache.jasper.JasperException {
  }

  public void _jspService(HttpServletRequest request,
    HttpServletResponse  response)
    throws java.io.IOException, ServletException {

    JspFactory _jspxFactory = null;
    PageContext pageContext = null;
    ServletContext application = null;
    ServletConfig config = null;
    JspWriter out = null;
    Object page = this;
    String  _value = null;
    try {
      if (_jspx_inited == false) {
        synchronized (this) {
          if (_jspx_inited == false) {
           _jspx_init();
            jspx_inited = true;
          }
        }
      }
     _jspxFactory = JspFactory.getDefaultFactory();
      response.setContentType("text/html;charset=ISO-8859-1");
```

```
      pageContext = _jspxFactory.getPageContext(
        this, request, response, "", false, 8192, true);
      application = pageContext.getServletContext();
      config = pageContext.getServletConfig();
      out = pageContext.getOut();

      // HTML // begin
[file="C:\\tomcat4\\bin\\..\\webapps\\myJSPApp\\SimplePage.jsp";from=(0,27);
to=(1,0)]
      out.write("\r\n");

      // end
      // HTML // begin
[file="C:\\tomcat4\\bin\\..\\webapps\\myJSPApp\\SimplePage.jsp";from=(1,39);
to=(2,0)]
      out.write("\r\n");

      // end
      // HTML
      // begin
[file="C:\\tomcat4\\bin\\..\\webapps\\myJSPApp\\includes\\Header.html";
from=(0,0);to=(4,0)]

       out.write("<HTML>\r\n<HEAD>\r\n<TITLE>Welcome</TITLE>\r\n<BODY>\r\n");

       // end
       // HTML // begin
[file="C:\\tomcat4\\bin\\..\\webapps\\myJSPApp\\SimplePage.jsp";from=(2,42);
to=(3,0)]
       out.write("\r\n");

       // end
       // begin
[file="C:\\tomcat4\\bin\\..\\webapps\\myJSPApp\\SimplePage.jsp";from=(3,2);to
=(5,0)]

       out.println("Current time: " + Calendar.getInstance().getTime());
       // end
       // HTML // begin
[file="C:\\tomcat4\\bin\\..\\webapps\\myJSPApp\\SimplePage.jsp";from=(5,2);to
=(6,0)]
       out.write("\r\n");

       // end
       // HTML // begin
[file="C:\\tomcat4\\bin\\..\\webapps\\myJSPApp\\includes\\Footer.html";
from=(0,0);to=(2,0)]
       out.write("</BODY>\r\n</HTML>\r\n");

       // end
       // HTML
```

continues

Listing 9.3 **Continued**

```
        // begin
[file="C:\\tomcat4\\bin\\..\\webapps\\myJSPApp\\SimplePage.jsp";from=(6,42);
to=(7,0)]
        out.write("\r\n");
        // end

    }
    catch (Throwable t) {
      if (out != null && out.getBufferSize() != 0)
        out.clearBuffer();
      if (pageContext != null) pageContext.handlePageException(t);
    }
    finally {
      if (_jspxFactory != null) _jspxFactory.releasePageContext(pageContext);
    }
  }
}
```

The lines in bold denote the beginning of the included file. Because all the included files are placed inline before being compiled, including files does not have any performance effect on the application.

The taglib Directive

The taglib, or tag library, directive can be used to extend JSP functionality. This is a broad topic and has been given a chapter of its own. (See Chapter 11, "Using JSP Custom Tags," for more information.)

Scripting Elements

Scripting elements allow you to insert Java code in your JSP pages. There are three types of scripting elements:

- Scriptlets
- Declarations
- Expressions

The three elements are discussed in the following sections.

Scriptlets

Throughout the previous chapters and up to this point in this chapter, you have seen scriptlets in the examples. Scriptlets are the code blocks of a JSP page. Scriptlets start with an opening <% tag and end with a closing %> tag.

Note

Directives also start with <% and end with %>. However, in a directive a @ follows the <%.

The following JSP page is an example of using scriptlets. In the JSP page, you try to connect to a database and retrieve all records from a table called Users. Among the fields in the Users table are FirstName, LastName, UserName, and Password. Upon obtaining a ResultSet object, you display all the records in an HTML table. The JSP page is given in Listing 9.4.

Listing 9.4 **Displaying Database Records**

```
<%@ page session="false" %>
<%@ page import="java.sql.*" %>
<%
  try {
    Class.forName("sun.jdbc.odbc.JdbcOdbcDriver");
    System.out.println("JDBC driver loaded");
  }
  catch (ClassNotFoundException e) {
    System.out.println(e.toString());
  }
%>
<HTML>
<HEAD>
<TITLE>Display All Users</TITLE>
</HEAD>
<BODY>
<CENTER>
<BR><H2>Displaying All Users</H2>
<BR>
<BR>
<TABLE>
<TR>
<TH>First Name</TH>
<TH>Last Name</TH>
<TH>User Name</TH>
<TH>Password</TH>
</TR>
<%
  String sql = "SELECT FirstName, LastName, UserName, Password" +
    " FROM Users";
  try {
    Connection con = DriverManager.getConnection("jdbc:odbc:JavaWeb");

    Statement s = con.createStatement();
    ResultSet rs = s.executeQuery(sql);

    while (rs.next()) {
      out.println("<TR>");
```

continues

Listing 9.4 **Continued**

```
        out.println("<TD>" + rs.getString(1) + "</TD>");
        out.println("<TD>" + rs.getString(2) + "</TD>");
        out.println("<TD>" + rs.getString(3) + "</TD>");
        out.println("<TD>" + rs.getString(4) + "</TD>");
        out.println("</TR>");
      }
      rs.close();
      s.close();
      con.close();
    }
    catch (SQLException e) {
    }
    catch (Exception e) {
    }
  %>
  </TABLE>
  </CENTER>
  </BODY>
  </HTML>
```

The result of this JSP page in a browser is given in Figure 9.1.

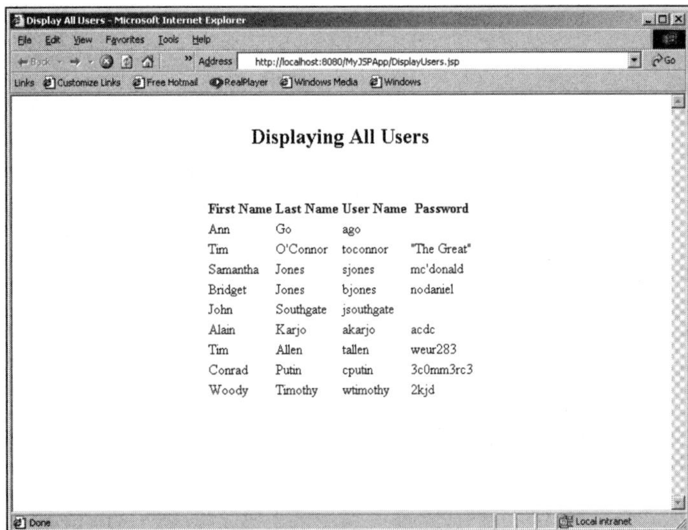

Figure 9.1 Displaying database records in a JSP page.

Note that you don't do any HTML encoding to the data returned by the getString method of the ResultSet because you don't know yet how to write and use a method in a JSP page. If, for example, the data contains something like <BR>, this will ruin the display in the web browser.

When writing scriptlets, it is commonplace to interweave code with HTML tags, for writing convenience. For instance, you can modify the while statement block of the code in Listing 9.4 to the following:

```
while (rs.next()) {
%>
<TR>
<TD><% out.print(rs.getString(1)); %></TD>
<TD><% out.print(rs.getString(2)); %></TD>
<TD><% out.print(rs.getString(3)); %></TD>
<TD><% out.print(rs.getString(4)); %></TD>
</TR>
<%
}
```

This is perfectly legal syntax.

> **Note**
> Switching from scriptlets to HTML tags and vice versa does not incur any performance penalty. The code in Listing 9.4 can therefore be written into Listing 9.5.

Listing 9.5 **JSP Page that Interweaves HTML Tags with Scriptlets**

```
<%@ page session="false" %>
<%@ page import="java.sql.*" %>
<%
  try {
    Class.forName("sun.jdbc.odbc.JdbcOdbcDriver");
    System.out.println("JDBC driver loaded");
  }
  catch (ClassNotFoundException e) {
    System.out.println(e.toString());
  }
%>
<HTML>
<HEAD>
<TITLE>Display All Users</TITLE>
</HEAD>
<BODY>
<CENTER>
<BR><H2>Displaying All Users</H2>
<BR>
<BR>
<TABLE>
<TR>
<TH>First Name</TH>
<TH>Last Name</TH>
<TH>User Name</TH>
<TH>Password</TH>
```

continues

Listing 9.5 **Continued**

```
</TR>
<%
  String sql = "SELECT FirstName, LastName, UserName, Password" +
    " FROM Users";
  try {
    Connection con = DriverManager.getConnection("jdbc:odbc:JavaWeb");

    Statement s = con.createStatement();
    ResultSet rs = s.executeQuery(sql);

    while (rs.next()) {
%>
<TR>
<TD><% out.print(rs.getString(1)); %></TD>
<TD><% out.print(rs.getString(2)); %></TD>
<TD><% out.print(rs.getString(3)); %></TD>
<TD><% out.print(rs.getString(4)); %></TD>
</TR>
<%
    }
    rs.close();
    s.close();
    con.close();
  }
  catch (SQLException e) {
  }
  catch (Exception e) {
  }
%>
</TABLE>
</CENTER>
</BODY>
</HTML>
```

Scriptlets alone are not sufficient to write efficient and effective JSP pages. As mentioned earlier, you can't declare a method with scriptlets. Additionally, in the code in Listings 9.4 and 9.5, the JSP page will try to load the JDBC driver every time the page is requested. This is unnecessary because the page needs to load it only once. How do you run an initialization code as you do in servlets? The answer is explained in the following section: declarations.

Declarations

Declarations allow you to declare methods and variables that can be used from any point in the JSP page. Declarations also provide a way to create initialization and clean-up code by utilizing the jspInit and jspDestroy methods.

A declaration starts with a <%! and ends with a %> and can appear anywhere throughout the page. For example, a method declaration can appear above a page directive that imports a class, even though the class is used in the method.

The code in Listing 9.6 shows the use of declarations to declare a method called getSystemTime and an integer i.

Listing 9.6 **Using Declarations to Declare a Method and a Variable**

```
<%!
  String getSystemTime() {
    return Calendar.getInstance().getTime().toString();
  }
%>
<%@ page import="java.util.Calendar" %>
<%@ page session="false" %>
<%
  out.println("Current Time: " + getSystemTime());
%>
<%! int i; %>
```

The resulting servlet follows. For clarity, some comments have been added to the code.

```
package org.apache.jsp;

import java.util.Calendar;
import javax.servlet.*;
import javax.servlet.http.*;
import javax.servlet.jsp.*;
import javax.servlet.jsp.tagext.*;
import org.apache.jasper.runtime.*;


public class SimplePage_jsp extends HttpJspBase {

  // method declaration
  String getSystemTime() {
    return Calendar.getInstance().getTime().toString();
  }
  // variable declaration
  int i;

  static {
  }
  public SimplePage_jsp( ) {
  }

  private static boolean _jspx_inited = false;
```

continues

Listing 9.6 **Continued**

```
  public final void _jspx_init() throws org.apache.jasper.JasperException {
  }

  public void _jspService(HttpServletRequest request,
    HttpServletResponse  response)
    throws java.io.IOException, ServletException {
    // the content has been removed
    .
    .
    .
  }
}
```

See how the variable and method are added as a class-level variable and method in the servlet class?

Having the capability to declare a method, I will present the example in Listings 9.4 and 9.5 to also apply HTML encoding to the data from the database. The modified code is presented in Listing 9.7.

Listing 9.7 **JSP Page with a Method Declaration**

```
<%!
  String encodeHtmlTag(String tag) {
    if (tag==null)
      return null;
    int length = tag.length();
    StringBuffer encodedTag = new StringBuffer(2 * length);
    for (int i=0; i<length; i++) {
      char c = tag.charAt(i);
      if (c=='<')
        encodedTag.append("&lt;");
      else if (c=='>')
        encodedTag.append("&gt;");
      else if (c=='&')
        encodedTag.append("&amp;");
      else if (c=='"')
        encodedTag.append("&quot;");
        //when trying to output text as tag's value as in
        // values="???".
      else if (c==' ')
        encodedTag.append(" ");
      else
        encodedTag.append(c);

    }
    return encodedTag.toString();
  }
%>
```

```
<%@ page session="false" %>
<%@ page import="java.sql.*" %>
<%
  try {
    Class.forName("sun.jdbc.odbc.JdbcOdbcDriver");
    System.out.println("JDBC driver loaded");
  }
  catch (ClassNotFoundException e) {
    System.out.println(e.toString());
  }
%>
<HTML>
<HEAD>
<TITLE>Display All Users</TITLE>
</HEAD>
<BODY>
<CENTER>
<BR><H2>Displaying All Users</H2>
<BR>
<BR>
<TABLE>
<TR>
<TH>First Name</TH>
<TH>Last Name</TH>
<TH>User Name</TH>
<TH>Password</TH>
</TR>
<%
  String sql = "SELECT FirstName, LastName, UserName, Password" +
    " FROM Users";
  try {
    Connection con = DriverManager.getConnection("jdbc:odbc:JavaWeb");

    Statement s = con.createStatement();
    ResultSet rs = s.executeQuery(sql);

    while (rs.next()) {
%>
<TR>
<TD><% out.print(encodeHtmlTag(rs.getString(1))); %></TD>
<TD><% out.print(encodeHtmlTag(rs.getString(2))); %></TD>
<TD><% out.print(encodeHtmlTag(rs.getString(3))); %></TD>
<TD><% out.print(encodeHtmlTag(rs.getString(4))); %></TD>
</TR>
<%
    }
    rs.close();
    s.close();
    con.close();
  }
  catch (SQLException e) {
```

continues

Listing 9.7 **Continued**

```
  }
  catch (Exception e) {
  }
%>
</TABLE>
</CENTER>
</BODY>
</HTML>
```

Writing Initialization and Clean-up Code

The code in Listings 9.4, 9.5, and 9.7 suffer from unnecessary repetition: The JSP page tries to load the JDBC driver every time the page is called. This is just a small example. In real life, you may have similar cases where you need to do initialization and clean-up; that is, you want a piece of code to be run only when the JSP servlet is first initialized or when it is destroyed.

In Chapter 8, you learned that every servlet generated from a JSP page must directly or indirectly implement the javax.servlet.jsp.JspPage interface. This interface has two methods: jspInit and jspDestroy. The JSP container calls the jspInit the first time the JSP servlet is initialized and calls the jspDestroy when the JSP servlet is about to be removed. These two methods provide a way for initialization and clean-up code. With declarations, you can override these two methods.

You can now modify the code in Listing 9.7 by moving the part that loads the JDBC driver to the jspInit method. The code is given in Listing 9.8.

Listing 9.8 **Utilizing the jspInit Method**

```
<%!
  public void jspInit() {
    try {
      Class.forName("sun.jdbc.odbc.JdbcOdbcDriver");
      System.out.println("JDBC driver loaded");
    }
    catch (ClassNotFoundException e) {
      System.out.println(e.toString());
    }
  }

  String encodeHtmlTag(String tag) {
    if (tag==null)
      return null;
    int length = tag.length();
    StringBuffer encodedTag = new StringBuffer(2 * length);
    for (int i=0; i<length; i++) {
```

```
      char c = tag.charAt(i);
      if (c=='<')
        encodedTag.append("&lt;");
      else if (c=='>')
        encodedTag.append("&gt;");
      else if (c=='&')
        encodedTag.append("&amp;");
      else if (c=='"')
        encodedTag.append("&quot;");
        //when trying to output text as tag's value as in
        // values="???".
      else if (c==' ')
        encodedTag.append(" ");
      else
        encodedTag.append(c);

    }
    return encodedTag.toString();
  }


%>
<%@ page session="false" %>
<%@ page import="java.sql.*" %>
<HTML>
<HEAD>
<TITLE>Display All Users</TITLE>
</HEAD>
<BODY>
<CENTER>
<BR><H2>Displaying All Users</H2>
<BR>
<BR>
<TABLE>
<TR>
<TH>First Name</TH>
<TH>Last Name</TH>
<TH>User Name</TH>
<TH>Password</TH>
</TR>
<%
  String sql = "SELECT FirstName, LastName, UserName, Password" +
    " FROM Users";
  try {
    Connection con = DriverManager.getConnection("jdbc:odbc:JavaWeb");

    Statement s = con.createStatement();
    ResultSet rs = s.executeQuery(sql);

    while (rs.next()) {
%>
```

continues

Listing 9.8 **Continued**

```
<TR>
<TD><% out.print(encodeHtmlTag(rs.getString(1))); %></TD>
<TD><% out.print(encodeHtmlTag(rs.getString(2))); %></TD>
<TD><% out.print(encodeHtmlTag(rs.getString(3))); %></TD>
<TD><% out.print(encodeHtmlTag(rs.getString(4))); %></TD>
</TR>
<%
    }
    rs.close();
    s.close();
    con.close();
  }
  catch (SQLException e) {
  }
  catch (Exception e) {
  }
%>
</TABLE>
</CENTER>
</BODY>
</HTML>
```

The generated servlet is presented here. Note that some parts of the servlet code have been removed for brevity.

```
public class SimplePage_jsp extends HttpJspBase {

  public void jspInit() {
    try {
      Class.forName("sun.jdbc.odbc.JdbcOdbcDriver");
      System.out.println("JDBC driver loaded");
    }
    catch (ClassNotFoundException e) {
      System.out.println(e.toString());
    }
  }

  String encodeHtmlTag(String tag) {
    .
    .
    .
  }

  static {
  }

  public SimplePage_jsp( ) {
  }

  private static boolean _jspx_inited = false;
```

```
    public final void _jspx_init() throws org.apache.jasper.JasperException {
    }

    public void _jspService(HttpServletRequest request,
      HttpServletResponse  response)
      throws java.io.IOException, ServletException {

          .
          .
          .
    }
}
```

Expressions

Expressions are the last type of JSP scripting elements. Expressions get evaluated when the JSP page is requested and their results are converted into a String and fed to the print method of the out implicit object. If the result cannot be converted into a String, an error will be raised at translation time. If this is not detected at translation time, at request-processing time, a ClassCastException will be raised.

An expression starts with a <%= and ends with a %>. You don't add a semicolon at the end of an expression.

An example of an expression is given in Listing 9.9.

Listing 9.9 **Using an Expression**

```
Current Time: <%= java.util.Calendar.getInstance().getTime() %>
```

This expression will be translated into the following statement in the _jspService method of the generated servlet:

```
out.print( java.util.Calendar.getInstance().getTime() );
```

The expression in listing 9.9 is equivalent to the following scriptlet:

```
Current Time: <% out.print(java.util.Calendar.getInstance().getTime()); %>
```

As you can see, an expression is shorter because the return value is automatically fed into the out.print.

As another example, the while block shown in Listing 9.8 can be re-written as follows using expressions:

```
while (rs.next()) {
%>
<TR>
<TD><%= encodeHtmlTag(rs.getString(1)) %></TD>
<TD><%= encodeHtmlTag(rs.getString(2)) %></TD>
```

```
<TD><%= encodeHtmlTag(rs.getString(3)) %></TD>
<TD><%= encodeHtmlTag(rs.getString(4)) %></TD>
</TR>
<%
}
```

Standard Action Elements

Standard action elements basically are tags that can be embedded into a JSP page. At compile time, they also are replaced by Java code that corresponds to the predefined task.

The following is the list of JSP standard action elements:

- jsp:useBean
- jsp:setProperty
- jsp:getProperty
- jsp:param
- jsp:include
- jsp:forward
- jsp:plugin
- jsp:params
- jsp:fallback

The jsp:useBean, jsp:setProperty, and jsp:getProperty elements are related to Bean and are discussed in Chapter 10, "Developing JSP Beans." The jsp:param element is used in the jsp:include, jsp:forward, and jsp:plugin elements to provide information in the name/value format, and therefore will be discussed with the three other elements.

jsp:include

The jsp:include action element is used to incorporate static or dynamic resources into the current page. This action element is similar to the include directive, but jsp:include provides greater flexibility because you can pass information to the included resource.

The syntax for the jsp:include action element has two forms. For the jsp:include element that does not have a parameter name/value pair, the syntax is as follows:

```
<jsp:include page="relativeURL" flush="true"/>
```

If you want to pass information to the included resource, use the second syntax:

```
<jsp:include page="relativeURL" flush="true">
  ( <jsp:param . . . /> )*
</jsp:include>
```

The page attribute represents the URL of the included resource in the local server. The flush attribute indicates whether the buffer is flushed. In JSP 1.2, the value of the flush attribute must be true.

In the second form, the * indicates that there can be zero or more elements in the brackets. This means that you also can use this form even though you are not passing any information to the included resource.

jsp:forward

The jsp:forward action element is used to terminate the execution of the current JSP page and switch control to another resource. You can forward control either to a static resource or a dynamic resource.

The syntax for the jsp:forward action element has two forms. For the jsp:forward element that does not have a parameter name/value pair, the syntax is as follows:

```
<jsp:forward page="relativeURL"/>
```

If you want to pass information to the included resource, use the second syntax:

```
<jsp:forward page="relativeURL">
  ( <jsp:param . . . /> )*
</jsp:include>
```

The page attribute represents the URL of the included resource in the local server.

jsp:plugin

The jsp:plugin action element is used to generate HTML <OBJECT> or <EMBED> tags containing appropriate construct to instruct the browser to download the Java Plugin software, if required, and initiates the execution of a Java applet or a JavaBeans component specified. This is beyond the scope of this book and won't be discussed further.

jsp:params

The jsp:params action element can occur only as part of the <jsp:plugin> action and will not be discussed in this book.

jsp:fallback

The jsp:fallback action element can occur only as part of the <jsp:plugin> action and will not be discussed in this book.

Comments

Commenting is part of good programming practice. You can write two types of comments inside a JSP page:

- Comments that are to be displayed in the resulting HTML page at the client browser
- Comments used in the JSP page itself

For comments that are meant to be displayed in the HTML page, you use the comments tags in HTML. This kind of comment must be sent as normal text in a JSP page. For example, the following code sends an HTML comment to the browser:

```
<%
 out.println("<!-- Here is a comment -->");
%>
```

This is equivalent to the following:

```
<!-- Here is a comment -->
```

For comments in the JSP page itself, you use the <%-- ... --%> tag pair. For example, here is a JSP comment:

```
<%--
  Here is a comment
--%>
```

A JSP comment can contain anything except the closing tag.

For example, this is an illegal comment:

```
<%--
  Here is a comment --%>
--%>
```

Converting into XML Syntax

XML is getting more and more important in the computing world. JSP pages can be represented using XML, and representing a JSP page as an XML document presents the following benefits:

- The content of the JSP page can be validated against a set of descriptions.

- The JSP page can be manipulated using an XML tool.
- The JSP page can be generated from a textual representation by applying an XML transformation.

Except for the standard action elements, the other JSP programming elements have been presented using the alternative syntax throughout this chapter. This section will show you how non-XML syntax can be converted into XML syntax to share the benefits presented earlier.

Directives

The non-XML syntax for a JSP directive takes the following form:

```
<%@ directive (attribute="value")* %>
```

The XML syntax for a directive is as follows:

```
<jsp:directive:directiveName attribute_list />
```

Scripting Elements

A scripting element can be one of the following: declaration, scriptlet, or expression. The XML syntax for each of the three is given in the following sections.

Declarations

The alternative syntax for a declaration is as follows:

```
<%! declaration code %>
```

This is equivalent to the following XML syntax:

```
<jsp:declaration> declaration code </jsp:declaration>
```

Scriptlets

The alternative syntax for a scriptlet is as follows:

```
<% scriptlet code %>
```

This is equivalent to the following XML syntax:

```
<jsp:scriptlet> scriptlet code </jsp:scriptlet>
```

Expressions

The alternative syntax for an expression is as follows:

```
<%= expression %>
```

This is equivalent to the following XML syntax:

```
<jsp:expression> expression </jsp:expression>
```

Template Data

The <jsp:text> XML tag is used to enclose template data in JSP. The syntax is as follows:

```
<jsp:text> text </jsp:text>
```

Summary

This chapter presents the JSP syntax and semantics, the language specification that you need to master writing JSP pages. You have learned the three types of JSP elements: directives, scripting elements, and action elements. You also have learned declarations, scripting elements, and action elements, and have been shown how to use all of them. The last main section of the chapter, "Converting into XML Syntax," presents a discussion on the importance of XML syntax as an alternative for the <% … %> syntax and shows you how to convert the non-XML syntax into XML equivalents.

10 Developing JSP Beans

IN CHAPTER 8, "JSP BASICS," AND CHAPTER 9, "JSP Syntax," you learned how you can write JSP pages by interweaving HTML tags and Java code. Although this makes writing JSP pages easy and straightforward, there are at least two disadvantages to this approach. First, the resulting spaghetti-like page seriously lacks readability. Second, there is no separation of the presentation and business rule implementation. To write a JSP page this way means a JSP author must master both Java and HTML.

Versatility is not something very common in the real world, however. Finding a Java programmer who also is good at HTML page design is as difficult as finding a graphic designer who is proficient in Java. A separation of labor would be nice to have in developing a JSP application; that is, let the graphic designer do the page design and the Java programmer author the code. In JSP, this is possible through the use of JSP components, such as JavaBeans. In this component-centric approach, the Java programmer writes and compiles JavaBeans that incorporate all the functionality needed in an application. While the programmer is doing this, the page designer can work with the page design at the same time. When the JavaBeans are ready, the page designer uses tags similar to HTML to call methods and properties of the beans from the JSP page.

In fact, using beans is a very common practice in JSP application development. This approach is popular because JavaBeans introduces reusability. This is to say, rather than building your own piece of code, you can simply use what other people have written. For example, you can purchase a bean for file upload and start uploading files within 30 seconds.

> **Warning**
>
> Note that when you are designing a JavaBean for your JSP page, reusability and modularity are of utmost importance. Therefore, it is not common to use a bean to send HTML tags to the web browser because this makes the bean customized for that page. If you need to achieve this task, you can use custom tags instead (this is the subject of Chapter 11, "Using JSP Custom Tags.")

In this chapter, you learn how to use JavaBeans in JSP pages. You start with a step-by-step approach to quickly write a bean and call it from a JSP page. After you have the confidence that you can comfortably write your own bean, you will look at how to use beans optimally in your JSP page using the three action elements briefly mentioned in Chapter 9 (jsp:useBean, jsp:getProperty, and jsp:setProperty).

Calling Your Bean from a JSP Page

This section presents a step-by-step tutorial on how to write and deploy a simple bean called CalculatorBean that is part of the com.brainysoftware package. After it is deployed, you then can call the bean from a JSP page. In total, there are six steps you need to follow:

1. Write a bean class whose code is given in Listing 10.1. Save it as CalculatorBean.java.

Listing 10.1 **The CalculatorBean**

```
package com.brainysoftware;
public class CalculatorBean {
  public int doubleIt(int number) {
    return 2 * number;
  }
}
```

   The code has one public class called doubleIt that returns an integer as a result of multiplication of the argument by 2.

2. Compile the bean to obtain a class file called CalculatorBean.class.

3. Copy the bean class file to the classes directory under WEB-INF under your application directory. The deployment must take into account the package name. In this case, you need to create a directory called com under the classes directory. Under com, create a directory named brainysoftware. Copy your CalculatorBean.class file to this brainysoftware directory.

Note

In Chapter 16, "Application Deployment," you will examine other ways of deploying beans in a JSP application.

The directory structure is shown in Figure 10.1.

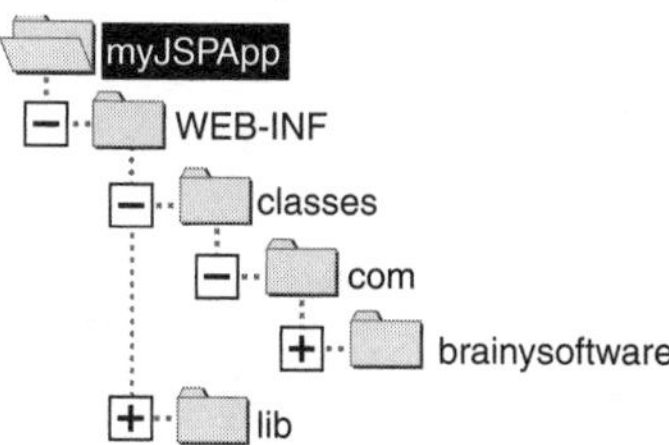

Figure 10.1 The directory structure for your bean class.

4. Create a JSP page that will call the bean you just created. For this example, just use the code in Listing 10.2.

Listing 10.2 **Calling a Bean from Your JSP Page**

```
<jsp:useBean id="theBean" class="com.brainysoftware.CalculatorBean"/>
<HTML>
<HEAD>
</HEAD>
<BODY>
<%
  int i = 4;
  int j = theBean.doubleIt(i);
  out.print("2*4=" + j);
%>
</BODY>
</HTML>
```

5. Restart Tomcat.
6. Open and direct your browser to the URL of the JSP page your wrote in Step 4.

Your browser should display something like Figure 10.2.

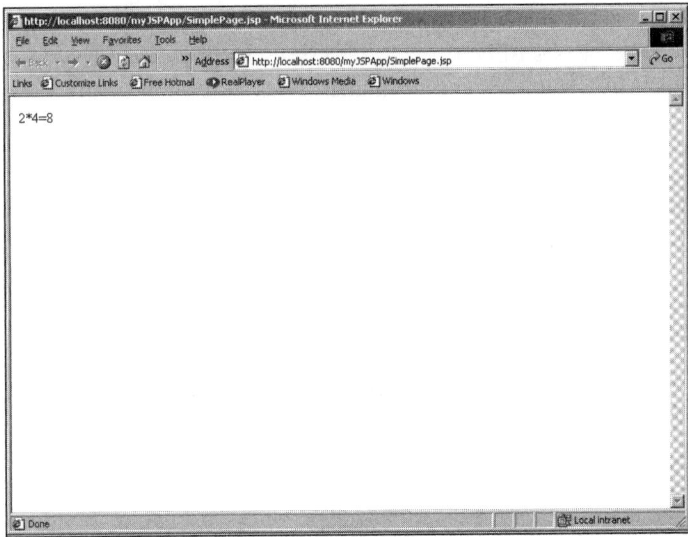

Figure 10.2 Result from calling the bean from a JSP page.

> **Note**
>
> If your JavaBean comes in the form of a .jar file, copy the .jar file into the lib directory under the WEB-INF directory of your application directory to make it available to JSP pages in your application.

Now that you can write your own bean and call it from a JSP page, let's dig deeper into it.

A Brief Theory of JavaBeans

This section presents JavaBeans briefly. You'll find a concise discussion here—it's not meant to be a comprehensive tutorial on the topic. JavaBeans have been discussed in dozens of Java books and other online resources. For example, an excellent resource can be found at Sun's Java web site: `http://java.sun.com/docs/books/tutorial/javabeans/index.html`.

Really, a bean is just a Java class. You don't need to extend any base class or implement any interface. To be a bean, however, a Java class must follow certain rules specified by the JavaBeans specification. In relation to JavaBeans that can be used from a JSP page, these rules are as follows:

- The bean class must have a no-argument constructor. In the bean in Listing 10.1, the class does not have a constructor at all. This still is legal because the Java compiler will automatically create a no-argument constructor for any Java class that does not have a constructor.
- Optionally, a bean can have a public method that can be used to set the value of a property. This method is called a *setter method*. The method does not return any value, and its name starts with "set" followed by the name of the property. A setter method has the following signature:

```
public void setPropertyName (PropertyType value);
```

  For example, the setter method for the property operand must be named setOperand. Note that the spelling for the property name is not exactly the same. A property name starts with a lowercase letter, but the name of the setter uses an uppercase letter after "set"; hence setOperand.
- Optionally, a bean can have a public method that can be called to obtain the value of a property. This method is called a *getter method*, and its return type is the same as the property type. Its name must begin with "get"; followed by the name of the property. A getter method has the following signature:

```
public PropertyType getPropertyName();
```

  As an example, the getter method for the property named operand is getOperand. A property name starts with a lowercase letter, but the name of the getter uses an uppercase letter after "get;" hence getOperand.

Both setter and getter methods are known as *access methods*. In JSP, the jsp:getProperty and jsp:setProperty action elements are used to invoke a getter and a setter method, respectively. You can call these methods the same way you call an ordinary method, however.

Making a Bean Available

Before you can use a bean in your JSP page, you must make the bean available, using the jsp:useBean action element. This element has attributes that you can use to control the bean's behavior. The syntax for the jsp:useBean element has two forms. The first form is used when you don't need to write any initialization code, and the second form is used if you have Java code that needs to be run when the bean initializes. Code initialization is discussed in the next section.

The two forms of the jsp:useBean action element are as follows:

```
<jsp:useBean (attribute="value")+/>
```

and

```
<jsp:useBean (attribute="value")+>
  initialization code
</jsp:useBean>
```

The (attribute="value")$^+$ part of the code means that one or more attributes must be present. The five attributes that can be used in a jsp:useBean action element are as follows:

- id
- class
- type
- scope
- beanName

Either the class attribute or the type attribute must be present.

The five attributes are explained in the following sections.

id

The id attribute defines a unique identifier for the bean. This identifier can be used throughout the page and can be thought of as the object reference for the bean. The value for the id attribute has the same requirements as a valid variable name in the current scripting language.

class

The class attribute specifies the fully qualified name for the JavaBean class. A fully qualified name is not required if the bean's package is imported using the page directive, however.

type

If the type attribute is present in a jsp:useBean element, it specifies the type of the JavaBean class. The type of the bean could be the type of the class itself, the type of its superclass, or an interface the bean class implements. Normally, this attribute isn't often used.

scope

The scope attribute defines the accessibility and the life span of the bean. This attribute can take one of the following values:

- page
- request
- session
- application

The default value of the scope attribute is page.

The scope is a powerful feature that lets you control how long the bean will continue to exist. Each of the attribute values is discussed in the following sections.

page

Using the page attribute value, the bean is available only in the current page after the point where the jsp:useBean action element is used. A new instance of the bean will be instantiated every time the page is requested. The bean will be automatically destroyed after the JSP page loses its scope; namely, when the control moves to another page. If you use the jsp:include or jsp:forward tags, the bean will not be accessible from the included or forwarded page.

request

With the request attribute value, the accessibility of the bean is extended to the forwarded or included page referenced by a jsp:forward or jsp:include action element. The forwarded or included page can use the bean without having a jsp:useBean action element. For example, from inside a forwarded or included page, you can use the jsp:getProperty and jsp:setProperty action elements that reference to the bean instantiated in the original page.

session

A bean with a session scope is placed in the user's session object. The instance of the bean will continue to exist as long as the user's session object exists. In other words, the bean's accessibility extends to other pages.

Because the bean's instance is put in the session object, you cannot use this scope if the page on which the bean is instantiated does not participate in the JSP container's session management. For example, the following code will generate an error:

```
<%@ page session="false" %>
<jsp:useBean id="theBean" scope="session"
  class="com.brainysoftware.CalculatorBean"/>
```

application

A bean with an application scope lives throughout the life of the JSP container itself. It is available from any page in the application.

beanName

The beanName attribute represents a name for the bean that the instantiate method of the java.beans.Beans class expects.

As an example, the following is a jsp:useBean that instantiates the bean called com.newriders.HomeLoanBean:

```
<jsp:useBean id="theBean" class="com.newriders.HomeLoanBean"/>
```

Alternatively, you can import the package com.newriders using a page directive and refer to the class using its name, as follows:

```
<%@ page import="com.newriders" %>
<jsp:useBean id="theBean" class="HomeLoanBean"/>
```

> **Note**
>
> The bean is available in the page after the jsp:useBean action element. It is not available before that point.

The Generated Servlet

The jsp:useBean action element causes the JSP container to generate Java code that loads the bean's class. Let's now examine the generated servlet.

Consider again the JSP page that uses a bean in Listing 10.1:

```
<jsp:useBean id="theBean" scope="page"
  class="com.brainysoftware.CalculatorBean"/>
<%
  int i = 4;
  int j = theBean.doubleIt(i);
  out.println("2*4=" + j);
%>
```

If you open the generated servlet class file, you will see that some code is added to the _jspService method that translates the jsp:useBean action element.

```
public void _jspService(HttpServletRequest request,
  HttpServletResponse  response)
  throws java.io.IOException, ServletException {

  JspFactory _jspxFactory = null;
  PageContext pageContext = null;
  HttpSession session = null;
```

```
ServletContext application = null;
ServletConfig config = null;
JspWriter out = null;
Object page = this;
String  _value = null;

try {
  if (_jspx_inited == false) {
    synchronized (this) {
      if (_jspx_inited == false) {
        jspx_init();
        _jspx_inited = true;
      }
    }
  }
  _jspxFactory = JspFactory.getDefaultFactory();
  response.setContentType("text/html;charset=ISO-8859-1");
  pageContext = _jspxFactory.getPageContext(
    this, request, response, "", true, 8192, true);

  application = pageContext.getServletContext();
  config = pageContext.getServletConfig();
  session = pageContext.getSession();
  out = pageContext.getOut();

  // an object reference to the Bean
  com.brainysoftware.CalculatorBean theBean = null;
  boolean _jspx_specialtheBean  = false;
  synchronized (pageContext) {
    theBean = (com.brainysoftware.CalculatorBean)
      pageContext.getAttribute("theBean",PageContext.PAGE_SCOPE);
    if ( theBean == null ) {
      _jspx_specialtheBean = true;
      try {
        theBean = (com.brainysoftware.CalculatorBean)
          java.beans.Beans.instantiate(this.getClass().getClassLoader(),
            "com.brainysoftware.CalculatorBean");
      }
      catch (Exception exc) {
        throw new ServletException (
          " Cannot create bean of class" +
          "com.brainysoftware.CalculatorBean", exc);
      }
      pageContext.setAttribute("theBean", theBean, PageContext.PAGE_SCOPE);
    }
  }
  if(_jspx_specialtheBean == true) {
  }
  out.write("\r\n");
  int i = 4;
  int j = theBean.doubleIt(i);
  out.println("2*4=" + j);
```

continues

```
    }
    catch (Throwable t) {
      if (out != null && out.getBufferSize() != 0)
        out.clearBuffer();
      if (pageContext != null) pageContext.handlePageException(t);
    }
    finally {
      if (_jspxFactory != null) _jspxFactory.releasePageContext(pageContext);
    }
  }
```

The most important line of code in the generated servlet is the one that instantiates the bean and casts it to the bean's class type:

```
theBean = (com.brainysoftware.CalculatorBean)
  java.beans.Beans.instantiate(this.getClass().getClassLoader(),
    "com.brainysoftware.CalculatorBean");
```

See how the jsp:useBean action element is translated into the instantiate method of java.beans.Beans?

Also note that the generated servlet will be slightly different if you use a different scope for the bean. To be more precise, the getAttribute and setAttribute methods of the PageContext class will be passed a scope according to the scope used for the bean. For instance, if the bean has an application scope, APPLICATION_SCOPE will be used instead of PAGE_SCOPE. If the bean has a session scope, SESSION_SCOPE will be used.

Accessing Properties Using jsp:getProperty and jsp:setProperty

In accessing a property in a bean, you can conveniently use the jsp:getProperty and jsp:setProperty action elements. The jsp:getProperty element is used to obtain the value of an internal variable, and the bean must provide a getter method. The syntax of the jsp:getProperty element is as follows:

```
<jsp:getProperty name="Bean Name" property="propertyName"/>
```

The name attribute must be assigned the name of the bean instance from which the property value will be obtained. The property attribute must be assigned the name of the property.

A jsp:getProperty element returns the property value converted into String. The return value is then automatically fed into an out.print method so it will be displayed in the current JSP page.

The jsp:setProperty action element is used to set the value of a property. Its syntax has four forms:

```
<jsp:setProperty name="Bean Name" property="PropertyName" value="value"/>

<jsp:setProperty name="Bean Name" property="PropertyName"/>

<jsp:setProperty name="Bean Name" property="PropertyName"
param="parameterName"/>

<jsp:setProperty name="Bean Name" property="*"/>
```

In all the forms, the name attribute is assigned the name of the bean instance available in the current JSP page. In this section, however, you learn about and use only the first form. The other three forms will be explained in the next section, "Setting a Property Value from a Request."

In the first form of the syntax, the property attribute is assigned the name of the property whose value is to be set, and the value attribute is assigned the value of the property.

The following example demonstrates the use of the jsp:getProperty and jsp:setProperty action elements.

Consider the bean called CalculatorBean in the com.brainysoftware package in Listing 10.3. It has a private integer called memory. (Note that the variable name starts with a lowercase m.) It also has a getter called getMemory and a setter named setMemory. Note that in both accessor methods, memory is spelled using an uppercase M.

Listing 10.3 **The CalculatorBean with Accessors**

```
package com.brainysoftware;
public class CalculatorBean {
  private int memory;

  public void setMemory(int number) {
    memory = number;
  }

  public int getMemory() {
    return memory;
  }
  public int doubleIt(int number) {
    return 2 * number;
  }
}
```

Using the jsp:setProperty and jsp:getProperty action elements, you can set and obtain the value of memory, as demonstrated in the JSP page in Listing 10.4.

Listing 10.4 **Accessing the Property Using jsp:setProperty and jsp:getProperty**

```
<jsp:useBean id="theBean" class="com.brainysoftware.CalculatorBean"/>
<jsp:setProperty name="theBean" property="memory" value="169"/>
The value of memory is <jsp:getProperty name="theBean" property="memory"/>
```

Calling this page in a web browser, you should be able to see something similar to Figure 10.3.

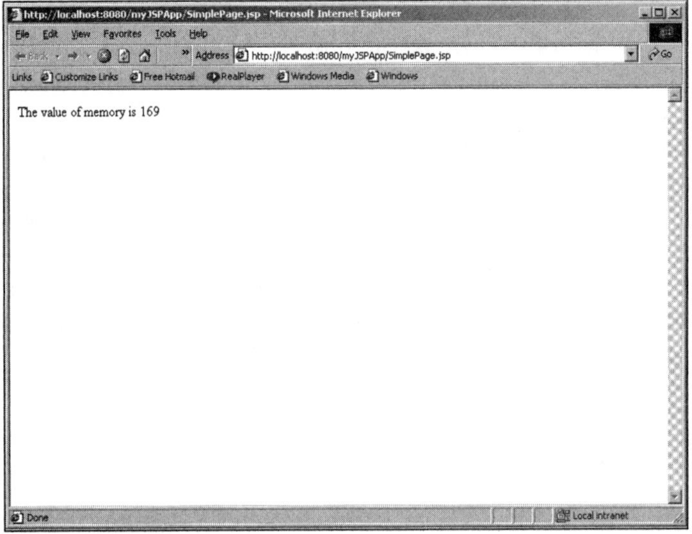

Figure 10.3 Calling the accessor in the bean.

As shown in Figure 10.3, the result of the jsp:getProperty is displayed on the current JSP page.

Note that you also can access the accessor methods in a conventional way, as described in Listing 10.5.

Listing 10.5 **Calling Accessor Methods Like Ordinary Methods**

```
<jsp:useBean id="theBean" class="com.brainysoftware.CalculatorBean"/>
<%
  theBean.setMemory(987);
%>
The value of memory is <%= theBean.getMemory()%>
```

In many cases, it is also common to use an expression as the value of the value attribute. For example, the code in Listing 10.6 feeds a JSP expression to the value attribute in a jsp:setProperty action element.

Listing 10.6 **Feeding a JSP Expression to the Value Attribute**

```
<jsp:useBean id="theBean" class="com.brainysoftware.CalculatorBean"/>
<%
  int i = 2;
%>
<jsp:setProperty name="theBean" property="memory" value="<%= 100 * i %>"/>
The value of memory is <jsp:getProperty name="theBean" property="memory"/>
```

Setting a Property Value from a Request

You can use a more concise way of setting a property value using the jsp:setProperty action element if the value happens to come from the Request object's parameter(s). In fact, there are three forms of syntax, as discussed in the previous section. The three forms are re-written here:

```
<jsp:setProperty name="Bean Name" property="PropertyName"
param="parameterName"/>

<jsp:setProperty name="Bean Name" property="PropertyName"/>

<jsp:setProperty name="Bean Name" property="*"/>
```

The first form allows you to assign a Request object parameter value to a property. The param attribute of the jsp:setProperty action element must be assigned the name of the Request object's parameter name. The following example demonstrates the use of this form. The example has two pages. The first page is a simple HTML with a form containing a Text box into which the user can enter a number. The code for this page is shown in Listing 10.7.

Listing 10.7 **The Page Where the User Can Type a Number**

```
<HTML>
<HEAD>
<TITLE>Passing a value</TITLE>
</HEAD>
<BODY>
<CENTER>
Please type in a number in the box
<BR>
<FORM METHOD=POST ACTION=SimplePage.jsp>
<INPUT TYPE=TEXT NAME=memory>
<INPUT TYPE=SUBMIT>
```

continues

Listing 10.7 **Continued**

```
</FORM>
</CENTER>
</BODY>
</HTML>
```

Note that the TEXT element name is memory and the form is passed to a JSP page called SimplePage.jsp. The SimplePage.jsp is given in Listing 10.8.

Listing 10.8 **The SimplePage.jsp Page**

```
<jsp:useBean id="theBean" class="com.brainysoftware.CalculatorBean"/>
<jsp:setProperty name="theBean" property="memory" param="memory"/>
The value of memory is <jsp:getProperty name="theBean" property="memory"/>
```

If the parameter name is the same as the bean's property name, you can even omit the param attribute:

```
<jsp:setProperty name="theBean" property="memory"/>
```

This is, of course, the third form of the jsp:setProperty syntax.

The last form allows you to assign the values of Request object's parameters to multiple properties in a bean as long as the names of the properties are the same as the parameter names. The second line in Listing 10.8 can be replaced with the following:

```
<jsp:setProperty name="theBean" property="*"/>
```

JavaBeans Code Initialization

The jsp:useBean action element allows you to write code that will be executed after the bean is initialized. For a bean that has a page scope, the initialization code is run every time the JSP page is requested.

Initialization code can be as simple as writing a piece of text, such as the following:

```
<jsp:useBean id="theBean" scope="page"
  class="com.brainysoftware.CalculatorBean">
  Initializing the Bean
</jsp:useBean>
```

Remember that any template data will be translated into an argument to an out.print method. It's not hard to guess that the initialization code will be added to the code block that instantiates the bean. Consider the following _jspService method of the servlet generated from the previous JSP page. The method has been cleaned up for clarity:

```
public void _jspService(HttpServletRequest request,
  HttpServletResponse  response)
  throws java.io.IOException, ServletException {

  JspFactory _jspxFactory = null;
  PageContext pageContext = null;
  HttpSession session = null;
  ServletContext application = null;
  ServletConfig config = null;
  JspWriter out = null;
  Object page = this;
  String  _value = null;
  try {
    .
    .
    .
    com.brainysoftware.CalculatorBean theBean = null;
    .
    .
    .
    synchronized (pageContext) {
      theBean = (com.brainysoftware.CalculatorBean)
        pageContext.getAttribute("theBean",PageContext.PAGE_SCOPE);
      if ( theBean == null ) {
        _jspx_specialtheBean = true;
        try {
          theBean = (com.brainysoftware.CalculatorBean)
            java.beans.Beans.instantiate(this.getClass().getClassLoader(),
            "com.brainysoftware.CalculatorBean");
        }
        catch (Exception exc) {
          throw new ServletException (" Cannot create bean of class "
            +"com.brainysoftware.CalculatorBean", exc);
        }
        pageContext.setAttribute("theBean", theBean, PageContext.PAGE_SCOPE);
      }
    }
    if(_jspx_specialtheBean == true) {
```

continues

```
          // here is the initialization code
          out.write("\r\nInitializing the Bean\r\n");

        }
      }
      catch (Throwable t) {
        .
        .
        .
      }
      finally {
        .
        .
        .
      }
    }
```

At the time of initialization, you even can use the jsp:setProperty action element to set the value of a bean's property, as demonstrated in the code in Listing 10.9.

Listing 10.9 **Using jsp:setProperty in a Bean's Initialization Code**

```
<jsp:useBean id="theBean" class="com.brainysoftware.CalculatorBean">
<jsp:setProperty name="theBean" property="*"/>
</jsp:useBean>
```

The SQLToolBean Example

I will now present an example bean that can be used as a tool to execute an SQL statement in a database server. This code is a modification of the SQLToolServlet presented in Chapter 4, "Accessing Databases with JDBC." Instead of a servlet, you now have a JavaBean.

The example consists of a bean class and two JSP pages. The first JSP page, Login.jsp, is used to obtain the user name and password for the database user authentication. It consists of an HTML form with two TEXT elements—one for the user name and one for the password.

After the form is submitted, the user name and password will be passed as properties to the bean in the second JSP page, SQLTool.jsp. The values of the user name and password will also be preserved in two hidden fields in the form in the SQLTool.jsp page. When the form is submitted, the values of the user name and password are passed back to the server. This way, a user needs to log in only once.

Figures 10.4 through 10.6 show the appearance of this small JSP application.

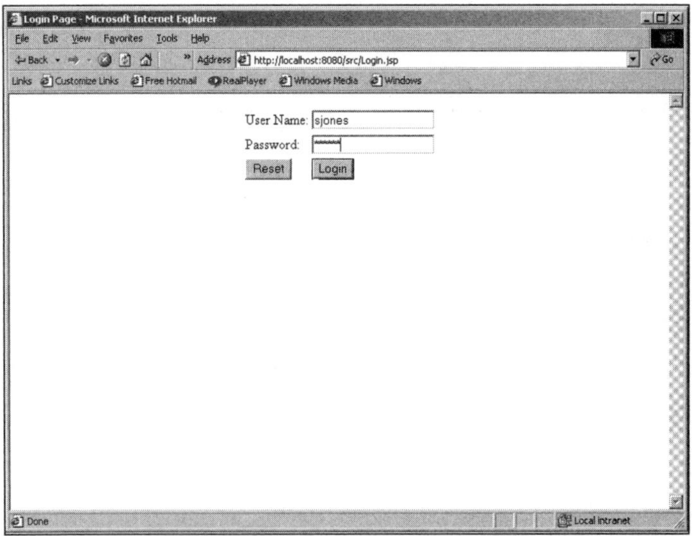

Figure 10.4 The Login.jsp page.

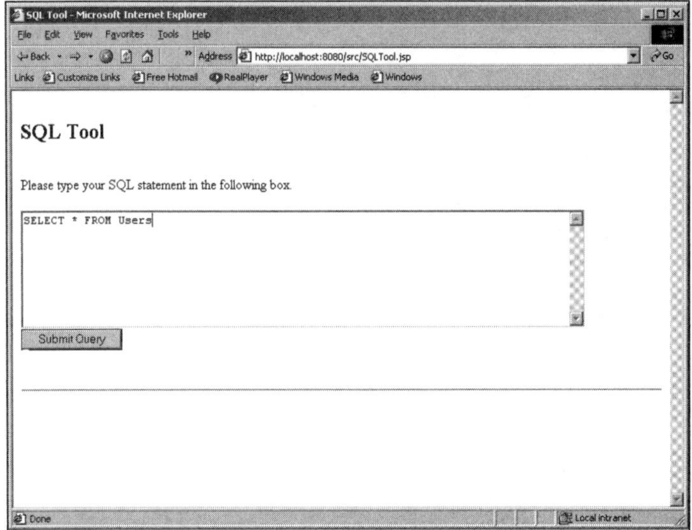

Figure 10.5 The SQLTool.jsp page.

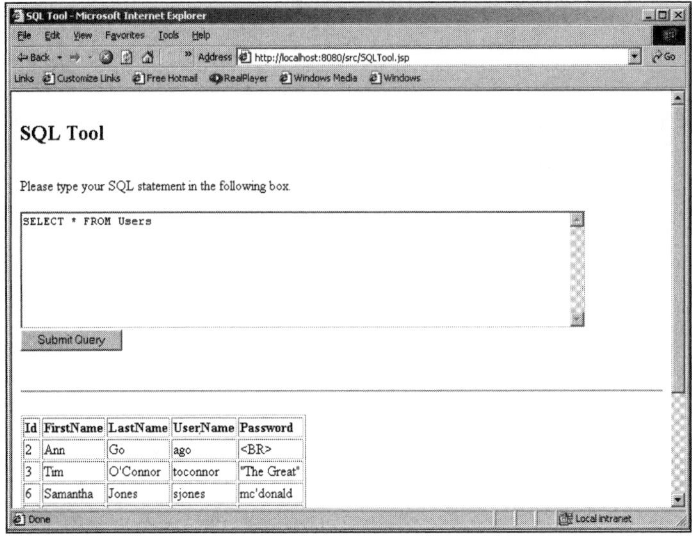

Figure 10.6 The SQLTool.jSP page with some results.

All the business rules can be found in the JavaBean shown in Listing 10.10.

Listing 10.10 **The SQLToolBean**

```
package com.brainysoftware.web;

import java.sql.*;
import com.brainysoftware.java.StringUtil;

public class SQLToolBean {
  private String sql = "";
  private String userName = "";
  private String password = "";
  private String connectionUrl;

  public String getSql() {
    return StringUtil.encodeHtmlTag(sql);
  }

  public void setSql(String sql) {
    if (sql!=null)
      this.sql = sql;
  }

  public void setUserName(String userName) {
    if (userName!=null)
      this.userName = userName;
```

```
  }
  public String getUserName() {
    return StringUtil.encodeHtmlTag(userName);
  }
  public void setPassword(String password) {
    if (password!=null)
      this.password = password;
  }
  public String getPassword() {
    return StringUtil.encodeHtmlTag(password);
  }

  public void setConnectionUrl(String url) {
    connectionUrl = url;
  }
public String getResult() {
    if (sql==null || sql.equals(""))
      return "";
    StringBuffer result = new StringBuffer(1024);
    try {
      Connection con = DriverManager.getConnection(connectionUrl, userName,
password);
      Statement s = con.createStatement();
      if (sql.toUpperCase().startsWith("SELECT")) {
        result.append("<TABLE BORDER=1>");
        ResultSet rs = s.executeQuery(sql);
        ResultSetMetaData rsmd = rs.getMetaData();
        // Write table headings
        int columnCount = rsmd.getColumnCount();
        result.append("<TR>");
        for (int i=1; i<=columnCount; i++) {
          result.append("<TD><B>" + rsmd.getColumnName(i) + "</B></TD>\n");
        }
        result.append("</TR>");
        while (rs.next()) {
          result.append("<TR>");
          for (int i=1; i<=columnCount; i++) {
            result.append("<TD>" + StringUtil.encodeHtmlTag(rs.getString(i)) +
"</TD>" );
          }
          result.append("</TR>");
        }
        rs.close();
        result.append("</TABLE>");
      }
      else {
        int i = s.executeUpdate(sql);
        result.append("Record(s) affected: " + i);
      }
      s.close();
      con.close();
```

continues

Listing 10.10 **Continued**

```
        result.append("</TABLE>");
      }
      catch (SQLException e) {
        result.append("<B>Error</B>");
        result.append("<BR>");
        result.append(e.toString());
      }
      catch (Exception e) {
        result.append("<B>Error</B>");
        result.append("<BR>");
        result.append(e.toString());
      }

      return result.toString();
    }
  }
```

The SQLToolBean has four internal variables: connectionUrl, userName, password, and sql. The first three are used to obtain a Connection object to the database server, whereas sql is the SQL statement to be executed by the server. The userName, password, and sql have a getter and setter method of their own, whereas the connectionUrl only has a setter.

```
public String getSql() {
  return StringUtil.encodeHtmlTag(sql);
}

public void setSql(String sql) {
  if (sql!=null)
    this.sql = sql;
}

public void setUserName(String userName) {
  if (userName!=null)
    this.userName = userName;
}
public String getUserName() {
  return StringUtil.encodeHtmlTag(userName);
}
public void setPassword(String password) {
  if (password!=null)
    this.password = password;
}
public String getPassword() {
  return StringUtil.encodeHtmlTag(password);
}

public void setConnectionUrl(String url) {
  connectionUrl = url;
}
```

The only method the bean has is the getResult method. For an SQL statement, the return value of this method is a String containing an HTML table. For other types of SQL statements, this method returns the number of records affected by the SQL statement.

Used in various places in the SQLToolBean is the encodeHtmlTag method of the com.brainysoftware.java.StringUtil class. This method encodes a String so that characters with special meanings in HTML are converted to their equivalents. This class is included in the jar file in the CD that accompanies this book. However, you also can copy and paste the encodeHtmlTag method so that you don't have to depend on the jar file. This method is given in Listing 10.11.

Listing 10.11 **The encodeHtmlTag Method**

```
public static String encodeHtmlTag(String tag) {
  if (tag==null)
    return null;
  int length = tag.length();
  StringBuffer encodedTag = new StringBuffer(2 * length);
  for (int i=0; i<length; i++) {
    char c = tag.charAt(i);
    if (c=='<')
      encodedTag.append("&lt;");
    else if (c=='>')
      encodedTag.append("&gt;");
    else if (c=='&')
      encodedTag.append("&amp;");
    else if (c=='"')
      encodedTag.append("&quot;");  //when trying to output text as tag's
      // value as in values="???".
    else if (c==' ')
      encodedTag.append(" ");
    else
      encodedTag.append(c);

  }
  return encodedTag.toString();
}
```

As discussed in Chapter 4, you need to load the JDBC driver from which you can get a database connection. The JDBC driver needs to be loaded only once, and the code that loads it is given as the initialization code of the bean.

The login page for this application is shown in Listing 10.12.

Listing 10.12 **The Login.jsp Page**

```
<HTML>
<HEAD>
<TITLE>Login Page</TITLE>
</HEAD>
<BODY>
<CENTER>
<FORM METHOD=POST ACTION=SQLTool.jsp>
<TABLE>
<TR>
  <TD>User Name:</TD>
  <TD><INPUT TYPE=TEXT NAME=userName></TD>
</TR>
<TR>
  <TD>Password:</TD>
  <TD><INPUT TYPE=PASSWORD NAME=password></TD>
</TR>
<TR>
  <TD><INPUT TYPE=RESET></TD>
  <TD><INPUT TYPE=SUBMIT VALUE="Login"></TD>
</TR>
</TABLE>
</FORM>
</CENTER>
</BODY>
</HTML>
```

This is basically a static HTML that can be safely converted into an HTML page to avoid any processing by the JSP container.

When the form in the HTML page is submitted, the request is passed to the SQLTool.jsp page. This page is given in Listing 10.13.

Listing 10.13 **The SQLTool.jsp Page**

```
<jsp:useBean id="theBean" class="com.brainysoftware.web.SQLToolBean">
<%
  try {
    Class.forName("sun.jdbc.odbc.JdbcOdbcDriver");
  }
  catch (Exception e) {
    out.println(e.toString());
  }
%>
</jsp:useBean>
<jsp:setProperty name="theBean" property="userName"/>
<jsp:setProperty name="theBean" property="password"/>
<jsp:setProperty name="theBean" property="connectionUrl"
value="jdbc:odbc:JavaWeb"/>
```

```
<jsp:setProperty name="theBean" property="sql"/>
<HTML>
<HEAD>
<TITLE>SQL Tool</TITLE>
</HEAD>
<BODY>
<BR><H2>SQL Tool</H2>
<BR>Please type your SQL statement in the following box.
<BR>
<BR><FORM METHOD=POST>
<INPUT TYPE=HIDDEN NAME=userName VALUE="<jsp:getProperty name="theBean"
property="userName"/>">
<INPUT TYPE=HIDDEN NAME=password VALUE="<jsp:getProperty name="theBean"
property="password"/>">
<TEXTAREA NAME=sql COLS=80 ROWS=8>
<jsp:getProperty name="theBean" property="sql"/>
</TEXTAREA>
<BR>
<INPUT TYPE=SUBMIT>
</FORM>
<BR>
<HR>
<BR>
<%= theBean.getResult() %>
</BODY>
</HTML>
```

First, this code initializes the SQLToolBean using the jsp:useBean action element. Included as the bean initialization code is the code that loads the JDBC driver:

```
<jsp:useBean id="theBean" class="com.brainysoftware.web.SQLToolBean">
<%
  try {
    Class.forName("sun.jdbc.odbc.JdbcOdbcDriver");
  }
  catch (Exception e) {
    out.println(e.toString());
  }
%>
</jsp:useBean>
```

Next, it sets the properties of the Bean:

```
<jsp:setProperty name="theBean" property="userName"/>
<jsp:setProperty name="theBean" property="password"/>
<jsp:setProperty name="theBean" property="connectionUrl"
  value="jdbc:odbc:JavaWeb"/>
<jsp:setProperty name="theBean" property="sql"/>
```

Note that, except for the connectionUrl property, all property values come from the request object.

The values are written as hidden values and obtained using the jsp:getProperty action elements. Here is the form in the SQLTool.jsp page:

```
<FORM METHOD=POST>
<INPUT TYPE=HIDDEN NAME=userName VALUE="<jsp:getProperty name="theBean"
property="userName"/>">
<INPUT TYPE=HIDDEN NAME=password VALUE="<jsp:getProperty name="theBean"
property="password"/>">
<TEXTAREA NAME=sql COLS=80 ROWS=8>
<jsp:getProperty name="theBean" property="sql"/>
</TEXTAREA>
<BR>
<INPUT TYPE=SUBMIT>
</FORM>
```

When you view the source code of the resulting HTML page, you should be able to see that the user name and password are preserved to be submitted again to the server when the user submits the form:

```
<HTML>
<HEAD>
<TITLE>SQL Tool</TITLE>
</HEAD>
<BODY>
<BR><H2>SQL Tool</H2>
<BR>Please type your SQL statement in the following box.
<BR>
<BR><FORM METHOD=POST>
<INPUT TYPE=HIDDEN NAME=userName VALUE="sjones">
<INPUT TYPE=HIDDEN NAME=password VALUE="dingoblue">
<TEXTAREA NAME=sql COLS=80 ROWS=8>

</TEXTAREA>
<BR>
<INPUT TYPE=SUBMIT>
</FORM>
<BR>
<HR>
<BR>

</BODY>
</HTML>
```

Summary

This chapter presents the component-centric architecture of a JSP page, a preferable approach offering several advantages over JSP pages that mix template data and elements. The advantages are more readability, separation of presentation and business rule implementation, and code reusability.

You have learned how to write your own bean and run it with Tomcat. You now also know the various scopes of a bean and how to set and obtain the value of a bean property using the jsp:setProperty and jsp:getProperty action elements.

11

Using JSP Custom Tags

USING JAVABEANS, YOU CAN SEPARATE the presentation part of a JSP page from the business rule implementation (Java code). However, only three action elements—jsp:useBean, jsp:getProperty, and jsp:setProperty—are available for accessing a bean. As such, in some situations, we have to resort to using code in a JSP page. In other words, oftentimes JavaBeans don't offer complete separation of presentation and business rule implementation.

Take Listing 10.13, from the previous chapter, as an example. Even though the JSP page consists mainly of tags, we still need to write some Java code as initialization code for the bean. This part of Listing 10.13 is reproduced here for reading convenience.

```
<jsp:useBean id="theBean" class="com.brainysoftware.web.SQLToolBean">
<%
  try {
    Class.forName("sun.jdbc.odbc.JdbcOdbcDriver");
  }
  catch (Exception e) {
    out.println(e.toString());
  }
%>
</jsp:useBean>
```

In other parts of Listing 10.13, everything is represented by a tag, except when we need to call the getResult method of the bean, in which case we use a JSP expression—as in the following code fragment.

```
<%= theBean.getResult() %>
```

Also, JavaBeans are designed with reusability in mind, meaning that using a bean to output HTML tags directly is not recommended. Outputting HTML tags from a bean makes the Bean useable only from a certain page, even though there are always exceptions to this rule.

In recognition of the imperfection of JavaBeans as a solution to separation of presentation and business rule implementation, JSP 1.1 defined a new feature: custom tags that can be used to perform *custom actions*.

Custom tags offer some benefits that are not present in JavaBeans. Among others, custom tags have access to all the objects available to JSP pages, and custom tags can be customized using attributes. However, custom tags are not meant to replace JavaBeans completely or make the use of JavaBeans in JSP pages obsolete. JavaBeans have their own fans, too. As you can see, sometimes it is more appropriate to use beans for their reusability, and sometimes it is better to use custom tags. In some circumstances, the choice whether to use JavaBeans or custom tags is not really clear, leaving you with a decision to make based on your experience.

In this chapter, we explore another great feature of JSP: custom tags. It will begin with writing a JSP page that uses custom tags, deploy the small application with Tomcat, and run it in your web browser. After this experience, we start diving deep into the details of the underlying API—the classes and interfaces in the javax.servlet.jsp.tagext package. We then create more examples based on those classes and interfaces.

Writing Your First Custom Tag

This section demonstrates the use of custom tags in a JSP page. As usual, you are encouraged to quickly build a small application, deploy it in Tomcat, and call the page from a web browser. For this example, we build a Java component that sends the following String to the browser: "Hello from the custom tag."

This section also presents the step-by-step approach to building a JSP application that uses custom tags.

Before we start developing the application, Figure 11.1 shows the directory structure of our JSP application called myJSPApp. You need to complete the directory structure if you have not done so in the previous chapters.

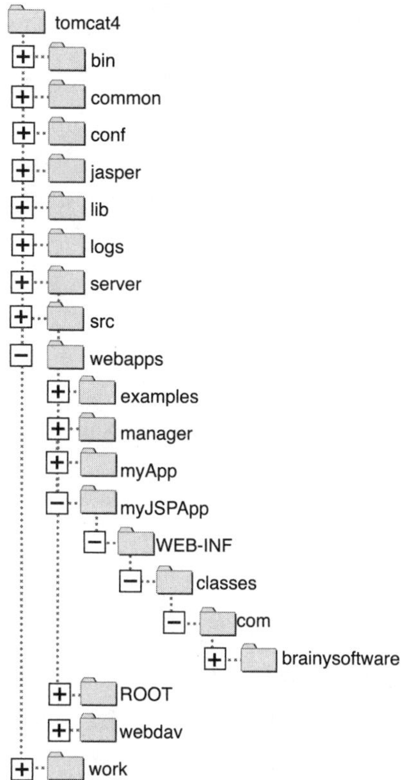

Figure 11.1 The directory structure of the application.

Now, follow the following five easy steps.

1. Create a TLD file named taglib.tld, as shown in Listing 11.1, and save it in the WEB-INF directory.

Listing 11.1 **The TLD File**

```
<?xml version="1.0" encoding="ISO-8859-1" ?>
<!DOCTYPE taglib
  PUBLIC "-//Sun Microsystems, Inc.//DTD JSP Tag Library 1.1//EN"
  "http://java.sun.com/j2ee/dtds/web-jsptaglibrary_1_1.dtd">
<taglib>
  <tlibversion>1.0</tlibversion>
  <shortname></shortname>
  <tag>
    <name>myTag</name>
    <tagclass>com.brainysoftware.MyCustomTag</tagclass>
  </tag>
</taglib>
```

2. Write, compile, and deploy the Java class called MyCustomTag.java given in Listing 11.2. Make sure that the .class file is located in the brainysoftware directory, under WEB-INF/classes/com/ directory.

Listing 11.2 **The MyCustomTag.java**

```
package com.brainysoftware;
import javax.servlet.jsp.*;
import javax.servlet.jsp.tagext.*;

public class MyCustomTag extends TagSupport {

  public int doEndTag() throws JspException {
    JspWriter out = pageContext.getOut();
    try {
      out.println("Hello from the custom tag.");
    }
    catch (Exception e) {
    }
    return super.doEndTag();
  }
}
```

3. Create a JSP file from the code given in Listing 11.3. Call it SimplePage.jsp and save it under the myJSPApp directory.

Listing 11.3 **The SimplePage.jsp Page**

```
<%@ taglib uri="/myTLD" prefix="easy"%>
<easy:myTag/>
```

4. Edit your deployment descriptor (web.xml) file. To use custom tags, you must specify a <taglib> element in your web.xml file. The <taglib> element must appear after the <servlet> and <servlet-mapping> if any. An example of the deployment descriptor is given in Listing 11.4.

Listing 11.4 **The Deployment Descriptor for This Application**

```
<!DOCTYPE web-app
  PUBLIC "-//Sun Microsystems, Inc.//DTD Web Application 2.3//EN"
  "http://java.sun.com/dtd/web-app_2_3.dtd">

<web-app>
  <display-name>template</display-name>
  <taglib>
    <taglib-uri>/myTLD</taglib-uri>
    <taglib-location>/WEB-INF/taglib.tld</taglib-location>
  </taglib>
</web-app>
```

5. Restart Tomcat.

   Open your web browser and type `http://localhost:8080/myJSPApp/SimplePage.jsp` in the Address box. You should see something similar to Figure 11.2.

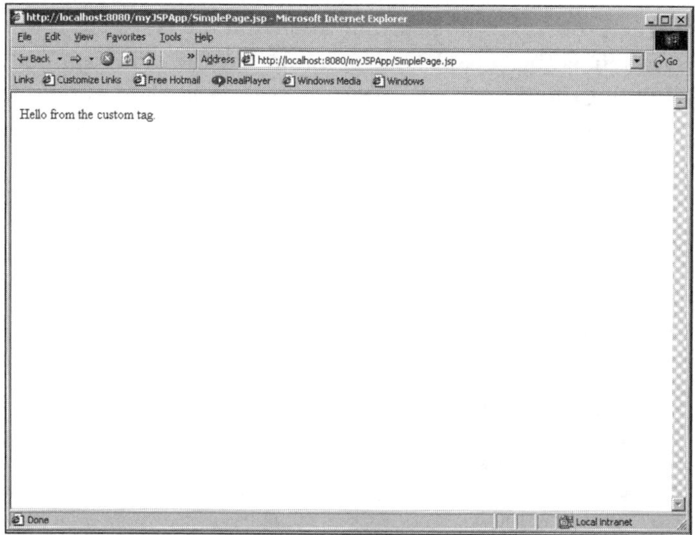

Figure 11.2 A simple JSP page.

Figure 11.3 shows how all the parts work.

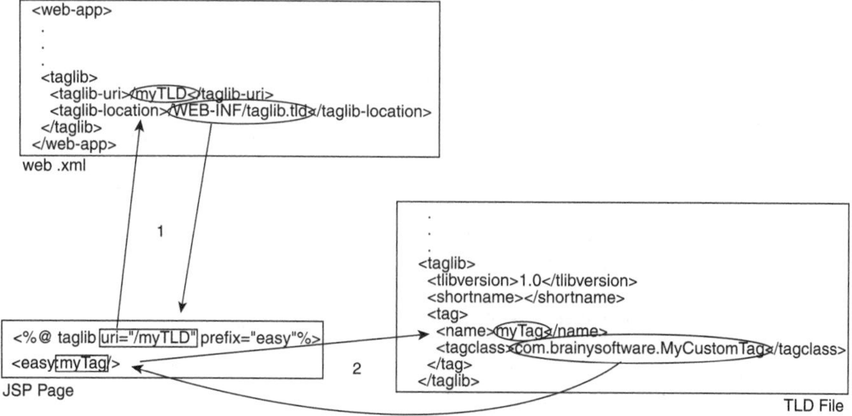

Figure 11.3 The relationship between the deployment descriptor, the JSP page, and the TDL file.

When the user requests the JSP page, the JSP container sees the <taglib> tag. Because of this, the JSP container knows that it is seeing a custom tag. It then:

- Consults the deployment descriptor (web.xml) to find the location of the taglib where the URI is "/myTLD". The deployment descriptor returns the path to the TLD file. The JSP container will remember this path.
- Continues processing the next line and encounters the custom tag myTag, prefixed by "easy". Having found out the name and location of the TLD file, the JSP container reads the TLD file and obtains the fully qualified name of the Java class for the tag myTag. It reads: com.brainysoftware.MyCustomTag.

  The JSP container can then load the class for the tag and start processing it.

The generated servlet is not that complicated, as you see here:

```
package org.apache.jsp;

import javax.servlet.*;
import javax.servlet.http.*;
import javax.servlet.jsp.*;
import javax.servlet.jsp.tagext.*;
import org.apache.jasper.runtime.*;


public class SimplePage_jsp extends HttpJspBase {

  static {
  }

  public SimplePage_jsp( ) {
  }

  private static boolean _jspx_inited = false;

  public final void _jspx_init() throws org.apache.jasper.JasperException {
  }

  public void _jspService(HttpServletRequest request,
    HttpServletResponse  response)
    throws java.io.IOException, ServletException {

    JspFactory _jspxFactory = null;
    PageContext pageContext = null;
    HttpSession session = null;
    ServletContext application = null;
    ServletConfig config = null;
    JspWriter out = null;
```

```
Object page = this;
String  _value = null;
try {
  if (_jspx_inited == false) {
    synchronized (this) {
      if (_jspx_inited == false) {
        _jspx_init();
        _jspx_inited = true;
      }
    }
  }
  _jspxFactory = JspFactory.getDefaultFactory();
  response.setContentType("text/html;charset=ISO-8859-1");
  pageContext = _jspxFactory.getPageContext(this, request,
    response, "", true, 8192, true);
  application = pageContext.getServletContext();
  config = pageContext.getServletConfig();
  session = pageContext.getSession();
  out = pageContext.getOut();
  out.write("\r\n");
  /* ----  easy:myTag ---- */
  com.brainysoftware.MyCustomTag _jspx_th_easy_myTag_0 =
    new com.brainysoftware.MyCustomTag();
  _jspx_th_easy_myTag_0.setPageContext(pageContext);
  _jspx_th_easy_myTag_0.setParent(null);
  try {
    int _jspx_eval_easy_myTag_0 = _jspx_th_easy_myTag_0.doStartTag();
    if (_jspx_eval_easy_myTag_0 == BodyTag.EVAL_BODY_BUFFERED)
      throw new JspTagException("Since tag handler class" +
      " com.brainysoftware.MyCustomTag does not implement BodyTag," +
      " it can't return BodyTag.EVAL_BODY_TAG");
    if (_jspx_eval_easy_myTag_0 != Tag.SKIP_BODY) {
      do {
      }
      while (_jspx_th_easy_myTag_0.doAfterBody() ==
        BodyTag.EVAL_BODY_AGAIN);
    }
    if (_jspx_th_easy_myTag_0.doEndTag() == Tag.SKIP_PAGE)
      return;
    }
    finally {
      _jspx_th_easy_myTag_0.release();
    }
  out.write("\r\n");
}
catch (Throwable t) {
  if (out != null && out.getBufferSize() != 0)
    out.clearBuffer();
  if (pageContext != null)
    pageContext.handlePageException(t);
}
```

```
      finally {
        if (_jspxFactory != null)
          _jspxFactory.releasePageContext(pageContext);
      }
    }
  }
```

Having seen a custom tag in action, you are now ready to dissect componentization using custom tags bit by bit. Let's start with the easiest part—the deployment descriptor.

The Role of the Deployment Descriptor

The preceding example illustrates how the JSP container can find the name and location of the TLD file by looking up the deployment descriptor.

Even though this is a common practice, you can eliminate the role of the deployment descriptor by writing the name and location of the TLD file directly on the JSP page. Therefore, the code in Listing 11.3 can be replaced with the code in Listing 11.5.

Listing 11.5 **An Alternative JSP Page for the Application**

```
<%@ taglib uri="/WEB-INF/taglib.tld" prefix="easy"%>
<easy:myTag/>
```

However, directly referring to the TLD file lacks the flexibility to move and change the name of the TLD file without having to edit all the JSP pages that utilize it.

Therefore, indirect reference of the TLD file involving the deployment descriptor is preferable.

> **Note**
>
> Note that in all examples in this chapter, the taglib tag's URI attribute is assigned to /myTLD. It is assumed you have edited the web.xml file accordingly.

The Tag Library Descriptor

A tag library descriptor (TLD) file is an XML document that defines a tag library and its tags. The first lines of a TLD file are the standard XML header information, as follows:

```
<?xml version="1.0" encoding="ISO-8859-1" ?>
<!DOCTYPE taglib
  PUBLIC "-//Sun Microsystems, Inc.//DTD JSP Tag Library 1.1//EN"
  "http://java.sun.com/j2ee/dtds/web-jsptaglibrary_1_1.dtd">
```

A TLD file contains the <taglib> root element. This element can have the following subelements:

- tlibversion
- jspversion
- shortname
- info
- uri
- tag

Of these six elements, the tag element is the only one that can have attributes. However, the tlibversion, shortname, and tag are required in the TLD file.

The tlibversion element specifies the version number of the tag library in the following format:

```
([0-9])* ("." [0-9])? ("." [0-9])? ("." [0-9])?
```

The asterisk means that the values in the bracket can be repeated zero or more times, and the question mark means that the value in the bracket is optional. The following are some valid values for a tlibversion element: 1.1.1.1, 2, 2.3, 3.3.6, and so on.

The jspversion element specifies the JSP version. The format is the same as the tlibversion element.

```
([0-9])* ("." [0-9])? ("." [0-9])? ("." [0-9])?
```

The shortname element specifies a short name for the tag library. The value for this element must begin with a letter and must not contain blank space.

The info element contains the information used for documentation purposes. Its default value is an empty string.

The uri element specifies the link to an additional source of documentation for the tag library.

The tag element is the most important element in a tag library. You can specify more than one tag element in the same TLD file. Therefore, you only have one TLD file for each JSP application. The tag element is explained in more detail in the following section.

The following is an example of a TLD file:

```
<?xml version="1.0" encoding="ISO-8859-1" ?>
<!DOCTYPE taglib
  PUBLIC "-//Sun Microsystems, Inc.//DTD JSP Tag Library 1.1//EN"
  "http://java.sun.com/j2ee/dtds/web-jsptaglibrary_1_1.dtd">
<taglib>
  <tlibversion>1.0.123.123.234</tlibversion>
  <jspversion>1.2</jspversion>
  <shortname></shortname>
  <info>Example tags</info>
```

```
    <uri></uri>
    <tag>
      <name>myTag</name>
      <tagclass>com.brainysoftware.MyCustomTag</tagclass>
      <attribute>
        <name>number</name>
        <required>true</required>
      </attribute>
      <attribute>
        <name>power</name>
        <required>true</required>
      </attribute>
    </tag>
  </taglib>
```

The tag Element

The tag element specifies a custom tag in the library. This element can have six subelements:

- name
- tagclass
- teiclass
- bodycontent
- info
- attribute

Of these six tag subelements, name and tagclass are mandatory.

The name element specifies an identifier for the tag.

The tagclass element specifies the fully qualified name of the Java class that handles the processing of this tag.

The teiclass element specifies the helper class for this tag, if there is one. tei is short for TagExtraInfo, the name of a class in the javax.servlet.jsp.tagext package. TagExtraInfo is explained in more detail later in this chapter when we discuss the API.

The bodycontent element specifies the type of the body content of the tag, if any. A body content is what appears between the opening and closing tags. This element can have one of the following values: empty, JSP, or tagdependent. The empty value means that there is no body content supported by the tag. Assigning "JSP" as the value of the bodycontent element indicates that the body content values are one or more JSP elements. The last value, tagdependent, indicates that the tag's body is to be interpreted by the tag.

The info element of the tag element contains an informational description.

The attribute element specifies zero or more attributes. The attribute element can have three subelements: name, required, and rtextprvalue. Only name is a required subelement of the attribute.

The name subelement is the identification for the attribute. The required subelement indicates whether the attribute is mandatory and can take a value of true or false, with false as the default value.

The rtexprvalue subelement indicates whether the value for this attribute can be determined at request time. If the value of this subelement is true, you can assign a request time value such as a JSP expression.

The Custom Tag Syntax

To use a custom tag in a JSP page, you first need to use a taglib directive in your page. The taglib directive has the following syntax:

```
<%@ taglib uri="tagLibraryURI" prefix="tagPrefix" %>
```

The uri attribute specifies an absolute or relative URI that uniquely identifies the tag library descriptor associated with this prefix.

The prefix attribute defines a string that will become the prefix to distinguish a custom action.

With a taglig directive, you then can use a custom tag of the following format for a custom tag that does not have a content body:

```
<prefix:tagName/>
```

Or, you can use the following format for a custom tag that has a content body:

```
<prefix:tagName>body</prefix:tagName>
```

You can pass attributes to the tag handler by specifying the attribute(s) in the custom tag, each with the following format:

```
attributeName="attributeValue"
```

The following example is a custom tag whose prefix is m and whose name is myTag. The tag has two attributes: number with a value of 12, and power with a value of 13.

```
<m:myTag number="12" power="13"/>
```

Note

Note that an attribute value must be quoted.

The JSP Custom Tag API

A tag handler is the Java class that is linked to a custom tag and gets invoked every time the JSP container encounters the custom tag. The tag handler is so named because it handles the processing of the tag. To be functional, a tag handler must implement an interface in the javax.servlet.jsp.tagext package or extend one of the classes in the same package.

In JSP 1.2, the javax.servlet.jsp.tagext has four interfaces and twelve classes, four more members than the same package in the JSP 1.1 specification. Some of the members of the javax.servlet.jsp.tagext package are explained here. For a complete reference of this package, see Appendix E, "The javax.servlet.jsp.tagext Package Reference."

The two most important interfaces are Tag and BodyTag. These two interfaces also set the life cycle of a tag handler. Either Tag or BodyTag must be implemented by a tag handler, either directly or indirectly.

The Tag Interface

Tag handlers that implement the Tag interface must provide implementations for all the interface's methods. These methods are as follows:

- doStartTag
- doEndTag
- getParent
- setParent
- setPageContext
- release

You can write a tag handler by simply implementing the Tag interface and providing blank implementations of all its six methods. For example, the code in Listing 11.6 is a tag handler called BasicTagHandler that does not do anything.

Listing 11.6 **A Simple Tag Handler that Does Not Do Anything**

```
package com.brainysoftware;

import javax.servlet.jsp.*;
import javax.servlet.jsp.tagext.*;

public class BasicTagHandler implements Tag {

  public void setParent(Tag t) {
  }
```

```
    public void setPageContext(PageContext p) {
  }

    public void release() {
    }

    public Tag getParent() {
      return null;
    }

    public int doStartTag() {
      return EVAL_BODY_INCLUDE;
    }

    public int doEndTag() {
      return EVAL_PAGE;
    }
  }
```

Note that both doStartTag and doEndTag return an integer. Their return values are one of the four static final integers defined in the Tag interface: SKIP_BODY, EVAL_BODY_INCLUDE, SKIP_PAGE, and EVAL_PAGE. Tag.SKIP_BODY and Tag.EVAL_BODY_INCLUDE are valid return values of the doStartTag method, whereas Tag.SKIP_PAGE and Tag.EVAL_PAGE are valid return values of the doEndTag method.

The Life Cycle of a Tag Handler

The life cycle of a tag handler that implements the Tag interface is controlled by the JSP container by calling the methods in the following order:

1. The JSP container obtains an instance of the tag handler from the pool or creates a new one. It then calls the setPageContext, passing a PageContext object representing the JSP page where the custom tag is found. If you want to access the JSP page, you need to assign this PageContext object to an object reference that has class scope. The setPageContext method has the following signature:

```
public void setPageContext(PageContext pageContext)
```

2. The JSP container then calls the setParent method. This method passes a tag object, which represents the closest tag enclosing the current tag handler. If there is no enclosing tag, a null object reference is passed.

   The signature of the setParent method is as follows:

```
public void setParent(Tag parent)
```

3. The JSP container then sets all the attributes in the custom tag, if any. Attributes are handled like properties in a JavaBean, namely by using the getter and setter methods. For example, if the custom tag has an attribute named temperature, the getter is called getTemperature and the setter is called setTemperature. The JSP container calls all the available setter methods to set attribute values.
4. Next, the JSP container calls the doStartTag, whose signature is as follows:

```
public int doStartTag() throws javax.servlet.jsp.JspException
```

   The doStartTag method can return either Tag.SKIP_BODY and Tag.EVAL_BODY_INCLUDE. If Tag.SKIP_BODY is returned, the JSP container will not process the tag's body contents, if any. If the doStartTag method returns Tag.EVAL_BODY_INCLUDE, the body contents, if any, will be processed normally.
5. Regardless of the return value of the doStartTag method, the JSP container next calls the doEndTag method. This method has the following signature:

```
public int doEndTag() throws javax.servlet.jsp.JspException
```

   The doEndTag method returns either Tag.SKIP_PAGE or Tag.EVAL_PAGE. If Tag.SKIP_PAGE is returned, the JSP container will not process the remaining of the JSP page. If Tag.EVAL_PAGE is returned, the JSP container processes the rest of the JSP page as normal.
6. The release method is the last method that the JSP container calls. This method has the following signature:

```
public void release()
```

   You should write any clean-up code in this method implementation. For example, you might want to close a file that was opened in the other method or destroy a database connection.
7. The JSP container returns the instance of the tag handler to a pool for future use.

A Content Substitution Tag Handler

The following example illustrates a tag handler that provides implementations for the setPageContext and doStartTag methods. The setPageContext assigns the PageContext object passed in by the JSP container to an object reference.

The doStartTag then obtains the JspWriter object through the getOut method of the PageContext and writes something to it. Because the tag handler writes directly to the JspWriter object of the current JSP page, whatever it writes is sent to the web browser. The tag handler is called MyCustomTag and is shown in Listing 11.7.

Listing 11.7 **The Content Substitution Tag Handler**

```
package com.brainysoftware;

import javax.servlet.jsp.*;
import javax.servlet.jsp.tagext.*;

public class MyCustomTag implements Tag {
  PageContext pageContext;

  public void setParent(Tag t) {
  }

  public void setPageContext(PageContext p) {
    pageContext = p;
  }

  public void release() {
  }

  public Tag getParent() {
    return null;
  }
  public int doStartTag() {
    try {
      JspWriter out = pageContext.getOut();
      out.println("Hello from the tag handler.");
    }
    catch(Exception e) {
    }
    return EVAL_BODY_INCLUDE;
  }

  public int doEndTag() throws JspException {
    return EVAL_PAGE;
  }
}
```

To test the tag handler, you need a JSP page as given in Listing 11.8 and a TLD file as given in Listing 11.9.

Listing 11.8 **The JSP Page that Contains a Custom Tag that Uses the Content Substitution Tag Handler**

```
<%@ taglib uri="/myTLD" prefix="easy"%>
<easy:myTag/>
```

Listing 11.9 **The TLD File for This Example**

```
<?xml version="1.0" encoding="ISO-8859-1" ?>
<!DOCTYPE taglib
  PUBLIC "-//Sun Microsystems, Inc.//DTD JSP Tag Library 1.1//EN"
  "http://java.sun.com/j2ee/dtds/web-jsptaglibrary_1_1.dtd">
<taglib>
  <tlibversion>1.0</tlibversion>
  <shortname></shortname>
  <tag>
    <name>myTag</name>
    <tagclass>com.brainysoftware.MyCustomTag</tagclass>
  </tag>
</taglib>
```

An Example: Using Attributes in a custom Tag

The following example presents a tag handler named DoublerTag that doubles an integer and outputs the result to the web browser. It demonstrates the use of an attribute called number. The tag handler has a setter called setNumber that is called by the JSP container to set the attribute value. The code for the tag handler is given in Listing 11.10.

Listing 11.10 **The DoublerTag**

```
package com.brainysoftware;

import javax.servlet.jsp.*;
import javax.servlet.jsp.tagext.*;

public class DoublerTag implements Tag {
  private int number;
  public void setNumber(int number) {
    this.number = number;
  }
  PageContext pageContext;

  public void setParent(Tag t) {
  }

  public void setPageContext(PageContext p) {
    pageContext = p;
```

```
  }

  public void release() {
  }

  public Tag getParent() {
    return null;
  }
  public int doStartTag() {
    try {
      JspWriter out = pageContext.getOut();
      out.println("Double of " + number + " is " + (2 * number));
    }
    catch(Exception e) {
    }
    return EVAL_BODY_INCLUDE;
  }

  public int doEndTag() throws JspException {
    return EVAL_PAGE;
  }
}
```

For the code to run, you need a JSP page, as shown in Listing 11.11, and a TLD file given in Listing 11.12.

Listing 11.11 **The JSP Page that Calls the DoublerTag**

```
<%@ taglib uri="/myTLD" prefix="easy"%>
<easy:myTag number="12"/>
```

Listing 11.12 **The TLD File for the Example**

```
<?xml version="1.0" encoding="ISO-8859-1" ?>
<!DOCTYPE taglib
        PUBLIC "-//Sun Microsystems, Inc.//DTD JSP Tag Library 1.1//EN"
        "http://java.sun.com/j2ee/dtds/web-jsptaglibrary_1_1.dtd">
<taglib>
  <tlibversion>1.0</tlibversion>
  <shortname></shortname>
  <tag>
    <name>myTag</name>
    <tagclass>com.brainysoftware.DoublerTag</tagclass>
    <attribute>
      <name>number</name>
      <required>true</required>
    </attribute>
  </tag>
</taglib>
```

The IterationTag Interface

The IterationTag interface extends the Tag interface by adding a new method called doAfterBody and a static final integer EVAL_BODY_AGAIN. This method is invoked after the doStartTag method and can return either the Tag.SKIP_BODY or IterationTag.EVAL_BODY_AGAIN. If the latter is returned, the doAfterBody is called again. If the return value is Tag.SKIP_BODY, the body will be skipped and the JSP container will call the doEndTag method.

An Example: A PowerTag

The following example demonstrates a tag handler that implements the IterationTag interface and illustrates the use of the doAfterBody method.

The tag handler, called PowerTag, calculates a base number raised to the power of another number. It then writes to the Web browser the following:

```
number^power=result
```

For instance, if you pass 2 for number and 3 for power, the tag handler returns the following String to the browser:

```
2^3=8
```

The code of the tag handler is given in Listing 11.13.

Listing 11.13 **The PowerTag Tag Handler**

```
package com.brainysoftware;

import javax.servlet.jsp.*;
import javax.servlet.jsp.tagext.*;

public class PowerTag implements IterationTag {
  PageContext pageContext;

  private int number;
  private int power;
  private int counter;
  private int result = 1;

  // the setter for number
  public void setNumber(int number) {
    this.number = number;
  }

  // the setter for power
  public void setPower(int power) {
    this.power = power;
```

```
  }

  public void setParent(Tag t) {
  }

  public void setPageContext(PageContext p) {
    pageContext = p;
  }

  public void release() {
  }

  public Tag getParent() {
    return null;
  }

  public int doStartTag() {
    return EVAL_BODY_INCLUDE;
  }

  public int doAfterBody() {
    counter++;
    result *= number;
    if (counter==power)
      return SKIP_BODY;
    else
      return EVAL_BODY_AGAIN;
  }

  public int doEndTag() throws JspException {
    System.out.println("doEndTag");
    try {
      JspWriter out = pageContext.getOut();
      out.println(number + "^" + power + "=" + result);
    }
    catch(Exception e) {
    }
    return EVAL_PAGE;
  }
}
```

To test the code, you need a JSP page, such as the one in Listing 11.14, and a TLD file given in Listing 11.15.

Listing 11.14 **The JSP Page that Calls PowerTag**

```
<%@ taglib uri="/myTLD" prefix="easy"%>
<easy:myTag number="2" power="3"/>
```

Listing 11.15 **The TLD File that Is Used in the Example**

```
<?xml version="1.0" encoding="ISO-8859-1" ?>
<!DOCTYPE taglib
        PUBLIC "-//Sun Microsystems, Inc.//DTD JSP Tag Library 1.1//EN"
        "http://java.sun.com/j2ee/dtds/web-jsptaglibrary_1_1.dtd">
<taglib>
  <tlibversion>1.0</tlibversion>
  <shortname></shortname>
  <tag>
    <name>myTag</name>
    <tagclass>com.brainysoftware.PowerTag</tagclass>
    <attribute>
      <name>number</name>
      <required>true</required>
    </attribute>
    <attribute>
      <name>power</name>
      <required>true</required>
    </attribute>
  </tag>
</taglib>
```

Manipulating Body Contents with BodyTag and BodyContent

A JSP custom tag can have a body content, such as the following tag:

```
<%@ taglib uri="/myTLD" prefix="x"%>
<x:theTag>This is the body content</x:theTag>
```

When you use the Tag and IterationTag interfaces, you cannot manipulate the body content. You don't even have access to it.

If you want to manipulate the body content of the custom tag, you have to use the BodyTag interface and the BodyContent class in the javax.servlet.jsp.tagext package. This section introduces you to these two elements and builds an example of a tag handler that manipulates the body content.

The BodyTag Interface

The BodyTag interface extends the IterationTag interface by adding two methods, doInitBody and setBodyContent, and two static final integers, EVAL_BODY_BUFFERED and EVAL_BODY_TAG. As of JSP 1.2, however, EVAL_BODY_TAG is deprecated.

A tag handler that implements the BodyTag interface has a life cycle similar to the ones implementing the IterationTag interface. The difference is that the doStartTag method of the tag handler implementing BodyTag can return

SKIP_BODY, EVAL_BODY_INCLUDE, or EVAL_BODY_BUFFERED. If the method returns EVAL_BODY_INCLUDE, the body is evaluated as it is in IterationTag. If the method returns EVAL_BODY_BUFFERED, a BodyContent object is created that represents the custom tag's body content. You learn more about the BodyContent class later in this section.

Two extra methods are called by the JSP container in tag handlers implementing the BodyTag interface: setBodyContent and doInitBody. The two methods have the following signatures:

```
public void setBodyContent(BodyContent bodyContent)
public void doInitBody() throws javax.servlet.jsp.JspException
```

The setBodyContent method is called after the doStartTag, followed by the doInitBody method. The setBodyContent will not be invoked, however, if one or both of the following is true:

- The custom tag does not have a body content.
- The custom tag has a body content but the doStartTag method returns SKIP_BODY or EVAL_BODY_INCLUDE.

The doInitBody method can be used to prepare for evaluation of the body. Normally, this method is called by the JSP container after the setBody Content method. This method will not be called, however, if one of the following is true:

- The custom tag does not have a body content.
- The custom tag has a body content, but the doStartTag method returns SKIP_BODY or EVAL_BODY_INCLUDE.

The BodyContent Class

The BodyContent class is an abstract class that extends the javax.servlet.jsp.JspWriter class. The BodyContent class represents the body content of the custom tag, if any. You obtain the body content from the setBodyContent method in the BodyTag interface.

An Example: Manipulating the Body Content

The following example shows a tag handler that manipulates the body content of a JSP custom tag. The tag handler does two things: HTML encode the body content and print the encoded version of the body content to the browser. The tag handler is called EncoderTag and incorporates the htmlEncodeTag method from the com.brainysoftware.java.StringUtil class. The tag handler is given in Listing 11.16.

Listing 11.16 **The EncoderTag**

```
package com.brainysoftware;

import javax.servlet.jsp.*;
import javax.servlet.jsp.tagext.*;

public class EncoderTag implements BodyTag {

  PageContext pageContext;
  BodyContent bodyContent;

  /**
   * Encode an HTML tag so it will be displayed
   * as it is on the browser.
   * Particularly, this method searches the
   * passed in String and replace every occurrence
   * of the following characters:
   * '<' with "&lt;"
   * '>' with "&gt;"
   * '&' with "&amp;"
   * //'"' with "&quot;"
   * ' ' with " "
   */
  private String encodeHtmlTag(String tag) {
    if (tag==null)
      return null;
    int length = tag.length();
    StringBuffer encodedTag = new StringBuffer(2 * length);
    for (int i=0; i<length; i++) {
      char c = tag.charAt(i);
      if (c=='<')
        encodedTag.append("&lt;");
      else if (c=='>')
        encodedTag.append("&gt;");
      else if (c=='&')
        encodedTag.append("&amp;");
      else if (c=='"')
        encodedTag.append("&quot;");
        //when trying to output text as tag's value as in
        // values="???".
      else if (c==' ')
        encodedTag.append(" ");
      else
        encodedTag.append(c);

    }
    return encodedTag.toString();
  }

  public void setParent(Tag t) {
```

```
    }

    public void setPageContext(PageContext p) {
      pageContext = p;
    }

    public void release() {
    }

    public Tag getParent() {
      return null;
    }

    public int doStartTag() {
      return EVAL_BODY_BUFFERED;
    }

    public void setBodyContent(BodyContent bodyContent) {
      this.bodyContent = bodyContent;
    }

    public void doInitBody() {

    }
    public int doAfterBody() {
      String content = bodyContent.getString();
      try{
        JspWriter out = bodyContent.getEnclosingWriter();
        out.print(encodeHtmlTag(content));
      }
      catch(Exception e) {}

      return SKIP_BODY;
    }

    public int doEndTag() throws JspException {
      return EVAL_PAGE;
    }
  }
```

The important methods are the setBodyContent and the doAfterBody. The setBodyContent method passes the BodyContent objects from the JSP container to the bodyContent object reference that has class-scope, as shown here:

```
public void setBodyContent(BodyContent bodyContent) {
  this.bodyContent = bodyContent;
}
```

You cannot manipulate the body content in the setBodyContent method. You must wait until the doInitBody is called. You write the following manipulation code in the doAfterBody method to take care of this:

```
String content = bodyContent.getString();
try{
  JspWriter out = bodyContent.getEnclosingWriter();
  out.print(encodeHtmlTag(content));
}
catch(Exception e) {}

return SKIP_BODY;
```

First, you obtain the String representation of the body content using the getString method of the BodyContent class. Next, to write to the browser, you first need to use the getEnclosingWriter method to obtain the implicit object out of the current JSP page. Finally, to output a String to the browser, you call the print method of JspWriter.

To use the tag handler, you need the JSP page like the one given in Listing 11.17 and a TLD file, as shown in Listing 11.18.

Listing 11.17 **The JSP Page that Uses the EncoderTag Tag Handler**

```
<%@ taglib uri="/myTLD" prefix="easy"%>
<easy:myTag><BR> means change line</easy:myTag>
```

Listing 11.18 **The TLD File for this Example**

```
<?xml version="1.0" encoding="ISO-8859-1" ?>
<!DOCTYPE taglib
        PUBLIC "-//Sun Microsystems, Inc.//DTD JSP Tag Library 1.1//EN"
        "http://java.sun.com/j2ee/dtds/web-jsptaglibrary_1_1.dtd">
<taglib>
  <tlibversion>1.0</tlibversion>
  <shortname></shortname>
  <tag>
    <name>myTag</name>
    <tagclass>com.brainysoftware.EncoderTag</tagclass>
    <bodycontent>tagdependent</bodycontent>
  </tag>
</taglib>
```

The Support Classes

Although the three interfaces—Tag, IterationTag, and BodyTag—provide a great way to write tag handlers, one apparent drawback is inherent to all interfaces: You must provide implementations for all the methods, including those you don't use. This, of course, makes the code look more complex than necessary, and the class takes longer to write and debug.

To solve this problem, the javax.servlet.jsp.tagext package provides support classes that implement those interfaces. These classes are TagSupport and BodyTagSupport. Now, instead of implementing an interface, you can extend one of these classes, as this section explains.

The TagSupport Class

The TagSupport class implements the IterationTag interface. Its signature is as follows:

```
public class TagSupport implements IterationTag, java.io.Serializable
```

The TagSupport class is intended to be used as the base class for tag handlers.

The BodyTagSupport Class

The BodyTagSupport class implements the BodyTag interface and has the following signature:

```
public class BodyTagSupport extends TagSupport implements BodyTag
```

This class is meant to be subclassed by tag handlers that need to implement the BodyTag interface.

To illustrate the usefulness of these support classes, the following example shows a tag handler called CapitalizerTag that converts a body content to its uppercase version and outputs it to the browser. The code is given in Listing 11.19.

Listing 11.19 **The CapitalizerTag**

```
package com.brainysoftware;

import javax.servlet.jsp.*;
import javax.servlet.jsp.tagext.*;

public class CapitalizerTag extends BodyTagSupport {

  public int doAfterBody() {
    String content = bodyContent.getString();
    try{
      JspWriter out = bodyContent.getEnclosingWriter();
      out.print(content.toUpperCase());
    }
    catch(Exception e) {}
    return SKIP_BODY;
  }

}
```

See how simple the tag handler has become? You don't need to provide implementations of methods you don't use.

To complete the example, here is the JSP page that uses the CapitalizerTag tag handler (in Listing 11.20) and the TLD file (Listing 11.21).

Listing 11.20 **The JSP Page that Uses the CapitalizerTag**

```
<%@ taglib uri="/myTLD" prefix="easy"%>
<easy:myTag>See the big picture?</easy:myTag>
```

Listing 11.21 **The TLD File for this Example**

```
<?xml version="1.0" encoding="ISO-8859-1" ?>
<!DOCTYPE taglib
        PUBLIC "-//Sun Microsystems, Inc.//DTD JSP Tag Library 1.1//EN"
        "http://java.sun.com/j2ee/dtds/web-jsptaglibrary_1_1.dtd">
<taglib>
  <tlibversion>1.0</tlibversion>
  <shortname></shortname>
  <tag>
    <name>myTag</name>
    <tagclass>com.brainysoftware.CapitalizerTag</tagclass>
    <bodycontent>tagdependent</bodycontent>
  </tag>
</taglib>
```

Summary

You have seen in this chapter that custom tags are an alternative to JavaBeans that enable you to make JSP pages contain only the presentation part of an application. A JSP custom tag is used to invoke an associated tag handler, a Java class that handles the processing of the tag.

Tag handlers implement the Tag, IterationTag, or BodyTag interface, or they extend one of the two support classes: TagSupport and BodyTagSupport.

12

Programmable File Download

To Internet surfers, downloading files is a day-to-day activity that can be done without effort. Writing a web program that allows only authorized users to download certain files is a totally different story. Normally, the operating system or web container authentication system lets you password protect files so that file download is allowed only if the user enters the correct user name and password. However, at least two problems exist with this approach:

- If you have more than one user, the password must be shared. However, a password is supposed to be private and confidential. The more people who know the password, the less secure it is. Furthermore, if many users know the password, it is not easy to record who downloads a particular file. Also, in some cases, using the operating system or web container authentication system is not as flexible as matching a user's credential against a database table.
- Depending on the type of downloaded file, the browser tries to open it with the correct application—if the browser knows the file type. Sometimes, this is not what you want. You need the browser to display the File Download dialog box, shown in Figure 12.1.

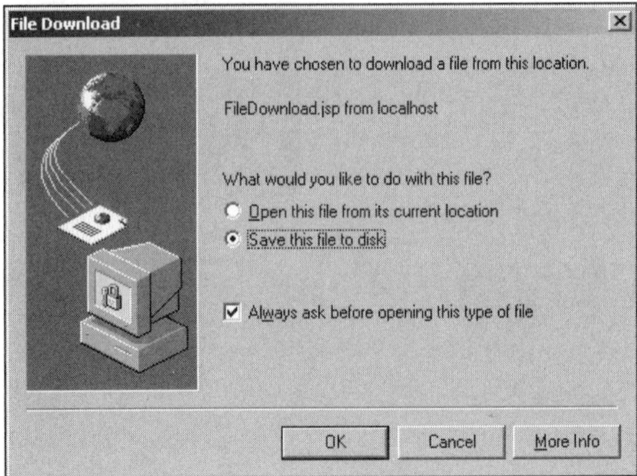

Figure 12.1 The File Download dialog box in Internet Explorer.

This chapter discusses a technique that allows you to programmatically send a file to a browser. I call it *programmable file download*. Using this technique, you have full control over the downloaded file. This chapter offers an example of how to perform programmable file downloads from a JSP page.

Alternatively, you can use the file download bean (com.brainysoftware.web.FileDownload), which can be found in the software/FileDownload directory on the accompanying CD. Just copy the FileDownload.jar file onto the WEB-INF/lib directory of your application directory and restart Tomcat.

> **Warning**
> File Download is commercially available from the Brainysoftware.com web site at `http://www.brainysoftware.com`. Brainysoftware.com grants the first purchaser of this book a license to deploy the File Download bean, but only on one server. This license does not include technical support and is void if the book is re-sold.

Keys to Programmable File Download

Some issues that you need to consider when writing an application that will send a file to a browser are the following:

- Unauthorized users should not be able to download a file by typing its URL. This means, the file should be stored in a directory outside of the virtual directory. For example, if your virtual directory is C:\Tomcat\webapps\MyVir, storing the file in this directory or in a subdirectory under this one makes your file visible by anyone on the Internet.

- Regardless of the type of file, the browser must display a File Download dialog box (like the one shown in Figure 12.1). It should not automatically fire up the application to run the file if the browser recognizes the file extension. (For example, if the downloaded file is a Microsoft Word document, the browser should not load Microsoft Word in the browser.)

Programmable file download has a number of applications, such as document management applications, for securing a file, and so on. A few things that you need to do to create an application for programmable file download are outlined in the following list:

1. Set the response's content type to APPLICATION/OCTET-STREAM. This value is not case sensitive.
2. Add an HTTP response header named Content-Disposition and give it the following value:

```
attachment; filename=theFileName
```

   where *theFileName* is the default name for the file that appears in the File Download dialog box. This is normally the same name as the file, but not necessarily.
3. Do not send any characters other than the actual file content. This could happen without you realizing it. For example, if you need to write some page directives in your file download JSP page, you might write the directives in a normal way, such as the following:

```
<%@ page import="java.io.FileInputStream"%>
<jsp:useBean id="DBBeanId" scope="page" class="docman.DBBean" />
```

Without you realizing it, the carriage return at the end of the first page directive will be sent to the browser. Instead, write those directives like the following:

```
<%@ page import="java.io.FileInputStream"
%><jsp:useBean id="DBBeanId" scope="page" class="docman.DBBean" />
```

This looks unusual, but it is safe.

Writing programmable file download code in JSP requires you to use the setContentType method to set the response content type to APPLICATION/OCTET-STREAM. It also requires that you use the setHeader method to add the required header. Afterward, reading the file one character at a time is easy using a java.io.FileInputStream class. The code in Listing 12.1 allows the user to programmatically download the C:\access.log file in a Windows operating system. If you use a different operating system, change the value of the filename and filepath variables accordingly.

Listing 12.1 **Programmable File Download in JSP**

```
<%
  // fetch the file
  String filename = "access.log";
  String filepath = "C:\\";
  response.setContentType(
    "APPLICATION/OCTET-STREAM");
  response.setHeader("Content-Disposition",
    "attachment; filename=\"" + filename + "\"");

  java.io.FileInputStream fileInputStream =
    new java.io.FileInputStream(filepath + filename);
  int i;
  while ((i=fileInputStream.read()) != -1) {
    out.write(i);
  }
  fileInputStream.close();
  out.close();
%>
```

Using the Brainysoftware.com File Download Bean

An easier way to programmatically download a file is by using the bean found in the software/FileDownload directory on the accompanying CD. The code in Listing 12.2 offers a user authentication prior to sending a file to the browser. Only if the userName and password parameters carry the values “james” and “cook” respectively, will the file be sent.

In the bean, the buffer is cleared prior to sending the file, therefore you can write directives as usual.

Listing 12.2 **Authenticating the User Before Sending a File**

```
<jsp:useBean id="theBean" scope="page"
  class="com.brainysoftware.web.FileDownload" />
<%
  String userName = request.getParameter("userName");
  String password = request.getParameter("password");

  // only allow download if the user supplied the
  // correct user name and passwrd

  if (userName!=null && password !=null &&
    userName.equals("james") &&
    password.equals("cook")) {
```

```
    String filepath = "C:\\TV.bmp";
    theBean.download(response, filepath);
  }
  else
    out.print("Login incorrect");
%>
```

Summary

Programmable file download is an important function that can be useful in a number of applications. This chapter showed you the things you need to do to send a file to the browser, and how to force the browser to display the File Download dialog box. Knowing the key points enables you to write a programmable file download application in any technology. For more application of programmable file download, see Chapter 20, "Web-Based Document Management."

13

File Upload

FILE UPLOAD PLAYS A SIGNIFICANT ROLE—beyond email applications—in Java development. Uploading files to the server is an important function that is offered in more and more types of applications, including web-based document management systems and the likes of "Secure File Transfer via HTTP."

This chapter discusses all you need to know about file upload. But first thing first. Before you jump excitedly into coding, you need to understand the underlying theory: the HTTP request. Understanding the HTTP request is critical because when you process an uploaded file, you work with raw data not obtainable by simply querying the HTTP Request object.

The last section of the chapter talks about the File Upload bean from Brainysoftware.com, included on the accompanying CD. Purchasing this book grants you the right to use it *only* for learning purposes. To use it in deployment, commercial or non-commercial, you must obtain a separate license. For more information on the license agreement, see the terms and conditions of the software that can be found in the software/fileUpload directory of the CD.

Let's now start by examining the HTTP request.

The HTTP Request

Each HTTP request from the web browser or other web client applications consists of three parts. These are as follows:

- The part containing the HTTP request method, the Uniform Resource Identifier (URI), and the protocol and the protocol version
- HTTP request headers
- The entity body

These three parts are explained in the following sections.

The request Method, URI, and Protocol

The first part of an HTTP request consists of the request method, the URI, and the protocol. The HTTP request method indicates the method used in the HTTP request. In HTTP 1.0, the method could be one of the following three methods: GET, HEAD, or POST. In HTTP 1.1, four more methods are added to the initial three: DELETE, PUT, TRACE, and OPTIONS.

Among these seven methods, the two methods that you use most frequently are GET and POST. GET is the default method. You use it, for example, when you type a URL, such as `http://www.brainysoftware.com`, in the Location or Address box of your browser to request a page. The POST method is also common. You normally use this as the value of the <FORM> tag's METHOD attribute. When you upload a file, you *must* use the POST method.

The second subpart of the HTTP request, the URI, specifies an Internet resource. A URI is normally interpreted as relative to the web server's root directory. Thus, it starts with a forward slash (/), as follows:

```
/virtualRoot/pageName
```

For example, in a typical JavaServer pages application, the URI could be the following:

```
/eshop/login.jsp
```

> **Note**
> You can find more information on URI at `http://rfc.net/rfc2396.html`.

The third subpart of the first part is the protocol and the protocol version understood by the requester (the browser). The protocol must be HTTP, and the version could be 1.0 or 1.1. Most web servers nowadays understand both versions 1.0 and 1.1 of HTTP; therefore, this kind of web server can serve HTTP requests in both versions as well. If you are still using an old HTTP 1.0 web server, you could be in trouble if your users use modern browsers that send requests using HTTP 1.1 protocol.

Combining the three subparts, the first part of the HTTP request looks like the following:

```
POST /virtualRoot/pageName HTTP/version
```

For instance, the following is a typical first part of an HTTP request:

```
POST /eshop/login.jsp HTTP/1.1
```

The HTTP Request Headers

The second component of an HTTP request consists of a number of HTTP headers. The four types of HTTP headers are general, entity, request, and response. These headers are summarized in Table 13.1, Table 13.2, and Table 13.3. The response headers are HTTP response-specific and as a result are not relevant to this discussion.

Table 13.1 **HTTP General Headers**

Header	Description
Pragma	The Pragma general header is used to include implementation-specific directives that may apply to any recipient along the request/response chain. In other words, pragmas tell the servers used to send this request to behave in a certain way. The Pragma header may contain multiple values. For example, the following line of code tells all proxy servers that relay this request not to use a cached version of the object, but instead to download the object from the specified location: `Pragma: no-cache`
Date	The Date general header represents the date and time at which the message originated.

Table 13.2 **HTTP Entity Headers**

Header	Description
Allow	The Allow header lists the set of methods supported by the resource identified by the requested URL. This field informs the recipient of valid methods associated with the resource. The Allow header is not permitted in a request using the POST method and thus should be ignored if it is received as part of a POST entity. For instance, the following Allow header specifies that GET and HEAD are allowed methods: `Allow: GET, HEAD`
Content-Encoding	The Content-Encoding header is used to describe the type of encoding used on the entity. When present, its value indicates the decoding mechanism that must be applied to obtain the media type referenced by the Content-Type header. For example, the following header specifies that x-gzip is the decoding mechanism that needs to be applied to obtain the media type referenced by the Content-Type header: `Content-Encoding: x-gzip`
Content-Length	The Content-Length header indicates the size (in decimal number of octets) of the entity body sent to the recipient or, in the case of the HEAD method, the size of the entity body that would have been sent had the request been a GET. Applications should use this field to indicate the size of the entity body to be transferred, regardless of the media type of the entity. A valid Content-Length field value is required on all HTTP/1.0 request messages containing an entity body. Any Content-Length header greater than or equal to 0 is a valid value. For example, the following header specifies that the content length is 123,452 bytes: `Content-Length: 123452`
Content-Type	The Content-Type header indicates the media type of the entity body sent to the recipient or, in the case of the HEAD method, the media type that would have been sent had the request been a GET. For example, the following header specifies that text/html is the media type of the HTTP response's entity body: `Content-Type: text/html`

Expires	The Expires header gives the date and time after which the entity should be considered invalid. This allows information providers to suggest the volatility of the resource or a date after which the information may no longer be accurate. Applications must not cache this entity beyond the date given. The presence of an Expires header does not imply that the original resource will change or cease to exist at, before, or after that time. However, information providers should include an Expires header with that date. For example, the following header specifies that the content should expire at 13:13:13 on August 6, 2002: `Expires: Tue, 6 Aug 2002 13:13:13 GMT`
Last-Modified	The Last-Modified header indicates the date and time at which the sender believes the resource was last modified. The exact semantics of this field are defined in terms of how the recipient should interpret it: If the recipient has a copy of this resource that is older than the date given by the Last-Modified field, that copy should be considered stale. For example, this header specifies that the resource was last updated at 12:12:12 on Aug 6, 2002: `Last-Modified: Tue, 6 Aug 2002 12:12:12 GMT`

Table 13.3 **HTTP Request Headers**

Header	Description
From	The From header specifies who is taking responsibility for the request. This field contains the email address of the user submitting the request. For example, the following header indicates that the user's email is rembrant@labsale.com: `From: rembrant@labsale.com`
Accept	The Accept header contains a semicolon-separated list of MIME representation schemes that are accepted by the client. The server uses this information to determine which data types are safe to send to the client in the HTTP response. Although the Accept field can contain multiple values, the Accept line itself also can be used more than once to specify additional accept types. (This has the same effect as specifying multiple accept types on a single line.) If the Accept field is not used in the request header, the

continues

Table 13.3 **Continued**

	default accept types of text/plain and text/html are assumed. For example, the following header specifies a few MIME schemes accepted by the client:
	`Accept: text/plain;`
	`text/htmlAccept; image/gif;`
	`image/jpeg`

Accept-Encoding	The Accept-Encoding header is similar in syntax to the Accept header; however, it specifies the content-encoding schemes that are acceptable in the response. For instance, the following header indicates that x-compress and x-zip are the content-encoding schemes that the response can accept: `Accept-Encoding: x-compress; x-zip`
Accept-Language	The Accept-Language header also is similar to the Accept header. This header specifies the preferred response language. The following example specifies English as the accepted language: `Accept-Language: en`

User-Agent	The User-Agent header, if present, specifies the name of the client browser. The first word should be the name of the software, followed by a slash and an optional version number. Any other product names that are part of the complete software package also may be included. Each name/version pair should be separated by a space. This field is used mostly for statistical purposes and allows servers to track software usage and protocol violation. For example, the following header specifies that the client is using Internet Explorer 4.01 on Windows 98 operating system:
	`User-Agent: Mozilla/4.0`
	`(compatible; MSIE 4.01; Windows 98)`

Referer	The Referer header specifies the URI that contained the URI in the request header. In HTML, this would be the address of the page that contained the link to the requested object. Like the User-Agent header, this header is not required but is mostly for the server's statistical and tracking purpose. For example, the following header specifies that the current request is sent as the result of the user clicking the link `http://localhost:8080/MyApp/Page1.jsp`. `Referer: http://localhost:8080/MyApp/Page1.jsp`

Authorization	The Authorization header contains authorization information. The first word contained in this header specifies the type of authorization system to be used. Then, separated by a space, it should be followed by authorization information such as a user name, password, and so forth. For example, here is a typical Authorization header:
	`Authorization: user`
	`ken:dragonlancer`

If-Modified-Since	The If-Modified-Since header is used with the GET method to make it conditional. Basically, if the object hasn't changed since the date and time specified by this header, the object is not sent. A local cached copy of the object is used instead. For example, the following is such a header:
	`If-Modified-Since: Thu, 6 Aug 2002`
	`11:12:29 GMT`

The Entity Body

The entity body is the content of the HTTP request itself. The following section illustrates this in the best way—with an example.

HTTP Request Example

The following is an example of an HTTP header:

```
Accept: application/vnd.ms-excel, application/msword, */*
Accept-Language: en-au
Connection: Keep-Alive
Host: localhost
Referer: http://localhost/examples/jsp/num/demo.jsp
User-Agent: Mozilla/4.0 (compatible; MSIE 4.01; Windows 98)
Content-Length: 32
Content-Type: application/x-www-form-urlencoded
Accept-Encoding: gzip, deflate

LastName=truman&FirstName=daniel
```

The preceding HTTP header reveals a lot. The first line tells you that the browser sending this request can accept a number of file formats, including Microsoft Excel and Microsoft Word. This information is followed by the language used (in this case, Australian English), the type of connection (keep-alive), and the name of the host (localhost). The header also tells the server that the request is sent from the demo.jsp, which is located in `http://localhost/examples/jsp/num/` directory. Then in the User-Agent entry, the request shows that the user is using Microsoft Internet Explorer version 4.01, which is compatible with Netscape Navigator 4.0. The user's operating system is also recorded as Windows 98. The meaning of the information can be retrieved from Table 13.1, Table 13.2, and Table 13.3.

Following the header are two pairs of carriage-return line-feed characters. The length of this separator is 4 bytes because each carriage-return line-feed character pair consists of the ASCII character numbers 13 and 10. From the previous HTTP header, you can see that the body consists of the following code:

```
LastName=truman&FirstName=daniel
```

The HTTP header clearly comes from a form with two input elements: one called LastName with the value truman and the other called FirstName with the value daniel.

Note that the length of LastName=truman&FirstName=daniel is 32, as indicated by the Content-Length header.

Now that you have finished dissecting an HTTP request, you are ready to take this information to the coding stage. To program a complete file-upload application, you need to know both the server side and the client side. The next section takes a look at the client side.

Client-Side HTML

Prior to the RFC 1867 standard, eight values were possible for the TYPE attribute of an INPUT element: CHECKBOX, HIDDEN, IMAGE, PASSWORD, RADIO, RESET, SUBMIT, and TEXT. Although these form elements have proven useful in a wide variety of applications in which input from the user needs to be transferred to the server, none of these is useful for sending either a text or binary file. For this reason, the TYPE attribute of an Input element was given another possible value: FILE. In addition, the RFC defines a new MIME media type, multipart/form-data, and specifies the behavior of HTML user agents when interpreting a form with ENCTYPE="multipart/form-data" and/or <INPUT type="file"> tags.

For example, an HTML form author who wants to request one or more files from a user would write this:

```
<FORM ACTION=Jsp1.jsp ENCTYPE="MULTIPART/FORM-DATA" METHOD=POST>
File to Upload: <INPUT NAME=filename TYPE=FILE>
<BR>
<INPUT TYPE=SUBMIT VALUE="Upload">
</FORM>
```

When an INPUT tag of type FILE is encountered, the browser might show a display of previously selected filenames and a Browse button or selection method. Clicking the Browse button would cause the browser to enter into a file-selection mode appropriate for the platform. Window-based browsers might display a file-selection window, for example. In such a file-selection dialog box, the user would have the option of replacing a current selection, adding a new file selection, and so on.

HTTP Request of an Uploaded File

Before you process a file upload, you should first familiarize yourself with the HTTP request of an uploaded file. The following small application is not for processing an uploaded file; however, it demonstrates how to prepare an HTML page to upload a file and write the HTTP request into a file for further study. Viewing the produced file with a text editor reveals the format of the request, which in turn enables you to extract the filename, the file content, and other useful information. This small application consists of an HTML file called main.html, a JSP file called Jsp1.jsp, and a JavaBean called SimpleBean.

The main.html file is the one that the client can use to select a file to upload to the server. Listing 13.1 presents the code for it.

Listing 13.1 **The main.html File**

```
<HTML>
<HEAD>
<TITLE>File Upload</TITLE>
</HEAD>
<BODY>
<FORM ACTION=Jsp1.jsp ENCTYPE="MULTIPART/FORM-DATA" METHOD=POST>
Author: <INPUT TYPE=TEXT Name=Author>
<BR>
Company: <INPUT TYPE=TEXT Name=Company>
<BR>
Select file to upload <INPUT TYPE=FILE Name=Filename>
<BR>
<INPUT TYPE=SUBMIT VALUE="Upload">
</FORM>
</BODY>
</HTML>
```

You can see that the ENCTYPE attribute is used in the <FORM> tag and its value is MULTIPART/FORM-DATA. There are four input elements, including the Submit button. The first two are normal TEXT elements called Author and Company. The third one is an element of type FILE, the input element that is used to select a file.

The ACTION attribute of the form has the value of Jsp1.jsp, meaning that the request (and also the file uploaded) is sent to the Jsp1.jsp file.

The Jsp1.jsp file simply calls a bean called SimpleBean, as presented in Listing 13.2.

Listing 13.2 **The Jsp1.jsp File**

```
<jsp:useBean id="TheBean" scope="page" class="SimpleBean " />
<%
  TheBean.doUpload(request);
%>
```

Listing 13.3 presents the code for the SimpleBean bean.

Listing 13.3 **The SimpleBean Bean**

```
import java.io.*;
import javax.servlet.http.HttpServletRequest;
import javax.servlet.http.HttpServletResponse;
import javax.servlet.ServletInputStream;

public class FileUploadBean {

  public void doUpload(HttpServletRequest request) throws
    IOException {
    PrintWriter pw = new PrintWriter(
      new BufferedWriter(new FileWriter("Demo.out")));
    ServletInputStream in = request.getInputStream();

    int i = in.read();
    while (i != -1) {
      pw.print((char) i);
      i = in.read();
    }
    pw.close();
  }
}
```

The user interface is given by the main.html file and is shown in Figure 13.1. For this example, I enter some input values for the Author and Company input elements and select a file called abisco.html with the following content. I select an HTML file to upload because I would like to show the content of the file. Because an HTML file is basically a text file, the content is easy to display.

The content of the abisco.html file is as follows:

```
<HTML>
<HEAD>
<TITLE>Abisco</TITLE>
</HEAD>
</HTML>
```

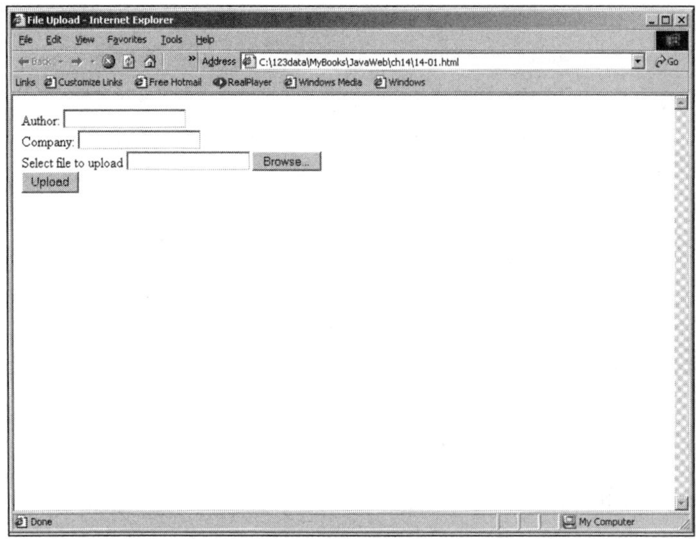

Figure 13.1 **The example's user interface.**

After the form in the main.html file is submitted to the Jsp1.jsp page, the Jsp1.jsp page calls the SimpleBean bean to write everything on the HttpServletRequest object to a file named Demo.out.

When you open the Demo.out file, you will see something similar to the following:

```
-----------------------------7d15340138
Content-Disposition: form-data; name="Author"

A. Christie
-----------------------------7d15340138
Content-Disposition: form-data; name="Company"

Abisco
-----------------------------7d15340138
Content-Disposition: form-data; name="Filename";
filename="C:\123data\abisco.html"
Content-Type: text/html
```

```
<HTML>
<HEAD>
<TITLE>Abisco</TITLE>
</HEAD>
</HTML>
-----------------------------7d15340138--
```

In brief, the entity body of the HTTP request contains all the form input, including the uploaded file. Those input values are separated from each other by a delimiter. Sometimes called a *boundary*, this delimiter consists of a few dozen dash characters followed by a random number. In the previous example, the delimiter is the following line:

```
-----------------------------7d15340138
```

And the same delimiter acts as a separator between two form elements' values. The last delimiter ends the entity body with two more dashes:

```
-----------------------------7d15340138--
```

For an input value that comes from a nonfile element, the delimiter is followed by the following line:

```
Content-Disposition: form-data; name=inputName
```

In the previous line, *inputName* is the name of the form element. For example:

```
Content-Disposition: form-data; name="Author"
```

The line is followed by two sequences of carriage-return line-feed characters and the element value.

For a file, the delimiter is followed by two lines. The first contains the name of the FILE input element and the complete path of the file in the user's computer. From the previous HTTP request, this line is as follows:

```
Content-Disposition: form-data; name="Filename";
filename="C:\123data\abisco.html"
```

This line states that the FILE input element is called Filename and the file path is C:\123data\abisco.html.

The second line contains the content type of the file. Its value depends on the file being uploaded. For this example, the value is text/html:

```
Content-Type: text/html
```

Like the non-File input element, the content starts after two sequences of carriage-return line-feed characters.

Warnning

The value of the file separator will differ according to the client's operating system. The preceding code illustrates the output from a Windows machine. Linux/Unix will have a forward slash (/) as a file separator and Macintosh a colon (:).

Uploading a File

Based on the explanation in the previous sections, you can now write a JSP page to handle file upload. This JSP page is given in Listing 13.4.

Listing 13.4 **File Upload JSP Page**

```
<%@ page import="java.io.*" %>
<%
  // the directory where the uploaded file will be saved.
  String savePath = "C:\\123data\\";

  String filename = "";

  ServletInputStream in = request.getInputStream();

  byte[] line = new byte[128];
  int i = in.readLine(line, 0, 128);
  int boundaryLength = i - 2;
  String boundary = new String(line, 0, boundaryLength);
➥//-2 discards the newline character

  while (i != -1) {
    String newLine = new String(line, 0, i);
    if (newLine.startsWith("Content-Disposition: form-data; name=\"")) {
      String s = new String(line, 0, i-2);
      int pos = s.indexOf("filename=\"");
      if (pos != -1) {
        String filepath = s.substring(pos+10, s.length()-1);
        // Windows browsers include the full path on the client
        // But Linux/Unix and Mac browsers only send the filename
        // test if this is from a Windows browser
        pos = filepath.lastIndexOf("\\");
        if (pos != -1)
          filename = filepath.substring(pos + 1);
        else
          filename = filepath;
      }

      //this is the file content
      i = in.readLine(line, 0, 128);
      i = in.readLine(line, 0, 128);
      // blank line
```

continues

Listing 13.4 **Continued**

```
        i = in.readLine(line, 0, 128);

        ByteArrayOutputStream buffer = new ByteArrayOutputStream();
        newLine = new String(line, 0, i);

        while (i != -1 && !newLine.startsWith(boundary)) {
          // the problem is the last line of the file content
          // contains the new line character.
          // So, we need to check if the current line is
          // the last line.
          buffer.write(line, 0, i);
          i = in.readLine(line, 0, 128);
          newLine = new String(line, 0, i);
        }
        try {
          // save the uploaded file
          RandomAccessFile f = new RandomAccessFile(
            savePath + filename, "rw");
          byte[] bytes = buffer.toByteArray();
          f.write(bytes, 0, bytes.length - 2);
          f.close();
        }
        catch (Exception e) {}
      }
      i = in.readLine(line, 0, 128);

    } // end while
%>
```

The code in Listing 13.4 begins by obtaining a reference to the ServletInputStream object from the HTTP request. The ServletInputStream contains the content of the uploaded file as you see here:

```
ServletInputStream in = request.getInputStream();
```

The beginning of the uploaded file is separated by the boundary and a sequence of carriage-return line-feed characters. Therefore, you can read the content of the HttpServletRequest object line by line. The following line of code defines a byte array called line:

```
byte[] line = new byte[128];
```

You then use the readLine method of ServletInputStream to read the first line of the HttpServletRequest object's content:

```
int i = in.readLine(line, 0, 128);
```

The first line gives the boundary and its length. The boundary and the length of the boundary are important values, as you will see later. The boundary is terminated by a sequence of carriage-return line-feed characters; therefore, the actual length is 2 less than the number of bytes returned by the readLine method:

```
int boundaryLength = i - 2;
```

The boundary is retrieved from the byte array line by discarding the last two carriage-return line-feed characters, as follows:

```
String boundary = new String(line, 0, boundaryLength);
```

Having retrieved the boundary, you then can start extracting the form element value by reading the HttpServletRequest object's content line by line using the while loop, until it reaches the end when the readLine method returns -1. The following code gives an example of this:

```
while (i != -1) {
  String newLine = new String(line, 0, i);
  .
  .
  .
}
```

With browsers on Windows operating systems, the uploaded filename is sent along with the file path. In other operating systems, no file path information is sent.

Now, you can obtain the filename from the read string by using the following code:

```
      String s = new String(line, 0, i-2);
      int pos = s.indexOf("filename=\"");
      if (pos != -1) {
        String filepath = s.substring(pos+10, s.length()-1);
        // Windows browsers include the full path on the client
        // But Linux/Unix and Mac browsers only send the filename
        // test if this is from a Windows browser
        pos = filepath.lastIndexOf("\\");
        if (pos != -1)
          filename = filepath.substring(pos + 1);
        else
          filename = filepath;
      }
```

After you obtain the filename, you will notice two pairs of carriage-return linefeed characters before the beginning of the uploaded file content. Therefore, you call the readLine method twice:

```
i = in.readLine(line, 0, 128);
i = in.readLine(line, 0, 128);
```

Then begins the actual file content. The content of the file is buffered into a ByteArrayOutputStream; thus you instantiate one with the following:

```
ByteArrayOutputStream buffer = new ByteArrayOutputStream();
```

Then, you keep reading the line until you find another boundary, as shown here:

```
newLine = new String(line, 0, i);

while (i != -1 && !newLine.startsWith(boundary)) {
  // the problem is the last line of the file content
  // contains the new line character.
  // So, we need to check if the current line is
  // the last line.
  buffer.write(line, 0, i);
  i = in.readLine(line, 0, 128);
  newLine = new String(line, 0, i);
}
```

The boundary signals the end of the uploaded file. The last step is to save the buffer into a file, as shown in the following code:

```
try {
  // save the uploaded file
  RandomAccessFile f = new RandomAccessFile(
    savePath + filename, "rw");
  byte[] bytes = buffer.toByteArray();
  f.write(bytes, 0, bytes.length - 2);
  f.close();
}
catch (Exception e) {}
```

To use the FileUpload.jsp file in Listing 13.4, you need another page where the upload form is displayed. An example is given in Listing 13.5.

Listing 13.5 **The Form to Select a File to Be Uploaded**

```
<HTML>
<HEAD>
<TITLE>File Upload</TITLE>
</HEAD>
<BODY>
<FORM ACTION=http://localhost:8080/myApp/servlet/FileUpload.jsp
➥ENCTYPE="MULTIPART/FORM-DATA" METHOD=POST>
Select file to upload <INPUT TYPE=FILE Name=Filename>
<BR>
<INPUT TYPE=SUBMIT VALUE="Upload">
</FORM>
</BODY>
</HTML>
```

FileUpload Bean

The code in Listing 13.4 allows you to upload a file and save it in the specified directory on the server. Oftentimes, however, you also want to send other pieces of information along with the file. The File Upload bean, on the accompanying CD, lets you upload a file and an unlimited number of field values. This component takes the form of a class called com.brainysoftware.web.FileUpload and can be found in the software/FileUpload/ directory of the CD.

The following is the list of methods in the FileUploadBean class:

```
public String getFilepath()
```

This method returns the file path where the uploaded file is saved.

```
public String getFilename()
```

Returns the name of the uploaded file.

```
public String getContentType()
```

Returns the value of the content type of the uploaded file.

```
public String getFieldValue(String fieldName)
```

Returns the value of the HTML form element whose name is specified by fieldName.

```
public void setSavePath(String savePath)
```

Specifies the name of the directory where the uploaded file should be saved on the server.

```
public void doUpload(HttpServletRequest request) throws IOException
```

The most important method in the FileUploadBean class, this method extracts the field names and values from the HTML form and processes and saves the uploaded file.

Using the File Upload Bean

To use the file, copy the BrainySoftwareFileUpload.jar file in the software/FileUpload directory on the accompanying CD to the WEB-INF/lib directory under your application directory and restart Tomcat.

The following listings provide an HTML file and a JSP file that illustrate the use of the bean. The HTML file contains a form with a few elements. The HTML file is given in Listing 13.6, and the JSP file is given in Listing 13.7.

Listing 13.6 **The HTML File to Upload a File**

```
<HTML>
<HEAD>
<TITLE>File Upload</TITLE>
</HEAD>
<BODY>
<FORM ACTION=Jsp1.jsp ENCTYPE="MULTIPART/FORM-DATA" METHOD=POST>
Author: <INPUT TYPE=TEXT Name=Author>
<BR>
Company: <INPUT TYPE=TEXT Name=Company>
<BR>
Comment: <TEXTAREA NAME=Comment></TEXTAREA>
<BR>
Select file to upload <INPUT TYPE=FILE Name=Filename>
<BR>
Description: <INPUT TYPE=TEXT Name=Description>
<BR>
<INPUT TYPE=SUBMIT VALUE="Upload">
</FORM>
</BODY>
</HTML>
```

When the user submits the form, the HTTP request will be handed to Jsp1.jsp, which uses the FileUpload bean to process the request. The Jsp1.jsp is given in Listing 13.7.

Listing 13.7 **The Jsp1.jsp File**

```
<jsp:useBean id="theBean" scope="page"
➥class="com.brainysoftware.web.FileUploadBean" />
<%
  //in Windows
  theBean.setSavePath("C:\\123data\\");

  //in Linux/Unix, you might have something like
  //theBean.setSavePath("/home/budi/");

  theBean.doUpload(request);
  theBean.save();
  out.println("Filename:" + theBean.getFilename());
  out.println("<BR>Content Type:" + theBean.getContentType());
  out.println("<BR>Author:" + theBean.getFieldValue("Author"));
  out.println("<BR>Company:" + theBean.getFieldValue("Company"));
  out.println("<BR>Comment:" + theBean.getFieldValue("Comment"));
%>
```

Multiple File Upload

Multiple file upload is possible using the Pro version of the Brainysoftware.com File Upload bean (`http://www.brainysoftware.com`)

Summary

File upload is an important function that is used in many different applications. Such applications include the web-based email (for uploading attachments), document management, and FTP by HTTP.

In this chapter, you learned how to upload a file by first presenting the HTTP request header. You also learned how to process an uploaded file on the server and use the Upload bean from BrainySoftware.com.

14

Security Configuration

IN THE PREVIOUS CHAPTERS, YOU LEARNED how to implement a Login page using both servlets and JSP to restrict access to a certain resource. The common practice is to write code that takes a user's name and password and matches them against those stored in a database.

Although this practice is great, there is another approach to securing your application that does not require you to write a single line of code. Instead, you configure the deployment descriptor of the web application you want to secure.

This chapter discusses the security configuration in the deployment descriptor and introduces you to various methods of authentications. This chapter also shows you how to use the security-constraint and login-config elements to configure security for your applications.

Imposing Security Constraints

By configuring the deployment descriptor, you can restrict access to some resources in an application in many different ways. For example, you can require the user to log in to view one resource, but not another resource. You also can restrict access to a resource if the request is sent using a particular HTTP method. For instance, you can mandate that a resource is viewable as long as the user requests it using the POST method.

Normally, if access to a resource is restricted, you will require the user to log in—that is, enter a user name and password. If the user provides the correct user name and password, access to the page is given. Of course, you can restrict a resource without even allowing the user to enter credentials. If you intend to make a resource unreachable, however, why put it there in the first place?

You can display a Login page automatically. In this case, the browser will display its own Login dialog box. Alternatively, you can use your own Login dialog box if you want.

When imposing security constraints, you need to choose what resources to protect by drafting a URL pattern. If the HTTP request's URL matches that pattern, access to the resource is restricted; that is, the user will be required to log in. For instance, if the URL pattern you give is /servlet/FirstServlet, the web container will restrict any request whose URL contains that pattern, such as `http://domain/myApp/servlet/FirstServlet`. You can use the wild card * in a URL pattern to represent any set of characters. For instance, the URL pattern /servlet/* will restrict access to any URL that contains "/servlet/", such as `http://domain/myApp/servlet/Testing` or `http://domain/myApp/servlet/Filter`.

After you determine what resource(s) to protect, you also need to consider who can have access to that resource. Programmatically, as in the examples in previous chapters, you can hard-code a set of user names and passwords or match a user name and password against a table in a database. With the deployment descriptor, however, the concept is slightly different. In addition to user names and passwords, you need to be familiar with principals and roles. These items are explained in the next section.

Principals and Roles

The concept of the principal is simple. You can think of principals as users. Basically, a *principal* is an entity. It could be an individual, a corporate, or another type of entity. "Principal" and "user" are used interchangeably to refer to an identity.

A *role* is an abstract grouping of users. It refers more to a position rather than an individual. You can think of a role as a group. As such, a user can fill one or more roles.

How do you specify the list of users and roles? Tomcat includes a file called tomcat-users.xml in the conf directory under %CATALINA_HOME%. By default, it declares three users, as follows:

```
<tomcat-users>
  <user name="tomcat" password="tomcat" roles="tomcat" />
  <user name="role1"  password="tomcat" roles="role1"  />
  <user name="both"   password="tomcat" roles="tomcat,role1" />
</tomcat-users>
```

The file says the following about the users:

- The first user is called "tomcat". It can fill the "tomcat" role.
- The second user has the name of "role1" and can fill the "role1" role.
- The third one is "both" and can play both "tomcat" and "role1" roles.

This is probably not a good example to explain users and roles, so let's use the following example:

```
<tomcat-users>
  <user name="Joe" password="pwd" roles="marketingManager" />
  <user name="Peter" password="0192" roles="HRManager" />
  <user name="MrDirector" password="humblepine"
    roles="marketingManager,HRManager" />
</tomcat-users>
```

This example also works with three users; their user names are Joe, Peter, and MrDirector. Joe is the Marketing Manager in the organization; therefore, he can fill the marketingManager role. Peter is the HR Manager and he fills the HRManager role. MrDirector is the Director of the company. He is the highest in the organization rank. He can play both marketingManager and HRManager roles.

Each restricted resource is associated with a role that can have access to it. A servlet that displays the salary list, for example, is likely to be associated with the HRManager role. In this case, Peter can use his user name and password to access it. Joe has a valid user name and password as well. Joe is not in the position to access the salary list, however. If he ever tries to log in and access the servlet by using his user name and password, he will be refused access.

On the other hand, MrDirector can play both roles. If one day Peter is not in because he is ill (or having another job interview), MrDirector can use his user name and password to access the servlet that displays the salary list.

You can add as many users as you want to the tomcat-users.xml file.

Using the Security-Constraint Element

As previously mentioned, you can restrict access to a resource without entering a single line of code by configuring the deployment descriptor. You can use several elements to assist in doing this. The elements most frequently used are security-constraint and login-config.

You use the security-constraint element to restrict access to one or more resources. The security-constraint element can appear multiple times in a deployment descriptor.

> **Note**
> You can find out more about the elements that can be used in the deployment descriptor in Chapter 16, "Application Deployment."

The security-constraint element can contain the following elements:

- **display-name**. An optional element that contains a descriptive name to be displayed by an XML manipulation tool.
- **web-resource-collection**. This element identifies a subset of resources to which access needs to be restricted. In the web-resource-collection, you can define the URL pattern(s) and the HTTP method. If no HTTP method is present, the security constraint applies to all methods.
- **auth-constraint**. This element specifies the user roles that should have access to this resource collection. If no auth-constraint element is specified, the security constraint applies to all roles.
- **user-data-constraint**. This element is used to indicate how the data that is sent to the client and web container (and vice versa) must be protected.

The web-resource-collection element can have the following required and optional subelements:

- **web-resource-name**. A name identifying a resource. This is a required element.
- **description**. An optional element containing a description of the resource collection.
- **url-pattern**. An optional element specifying a URL pattern to which the restriction must be applied. There could be zero or more url-pattern elements in a web-resource-collection element.
- **http-method**. An optional element specifying the restricted method. There could be zero or more http-method elements in a web-resource-collection element.

The auth-constraint element can have the following subelements:

- **description.** An optional element describing the auth-constraint element.
- **role-name.** The roles that have access to the restricted resource. This element is required.

The user-data-constraint element can contain the following elements:

- **description.** An optional element describing the user-data-constraint element.
- **transport-guarantee.** This element must have one of the following values: NONE, INTEGRAL, or CONFIDENTIAL. NONE means that the application does not require any transport guarantees. INTEGRAL means that the data between the server and the client should be sent in such a way that it can't be changed in transit. CONFIDENTIAL means that the data transmitted must be encrypted. In most cases, SSL is used for either INTEGRAL or CONFIDENTIAL. This element is required.

Let's start with an example of a deployment descriptor, given in Listing 14.1.

Listing 14.1 **The Deployment Descriptor**

```
<?xml version="1.0" encoding="ISO-8859-1"?>

<!DOCTYPE web-app
  PUBLIC "-//Sun Microsystems, Inc.//DTD Web Application 2.3//EN"
  "http://java.sun.com/j2ee/dtds/web-app_2_3.dtd">

<web-app>

  <security-constraint>

    <web-resource-collection>
      <web-resource-name>
        Restricted Area
      </web-resource-name>
      <url-pattern>/servlet/*</url-pattern>
    </web-resource-collection>
    <auth-constraint>
      <role-name>manager</role-name>
    </auth-constraint>

  </security-constraint>

</web-app>
```

Having a deployment descriptor, such as the one in Listing 14.1, causes the web container to block any request that matches the URL pattern that does not come from a user in the manager role. The auth-constraint element inside the security-constraint element says that the resource can be accessed only by users in the manager role. Figure 14.1 shows the result when a non-manager tries to access the resource.

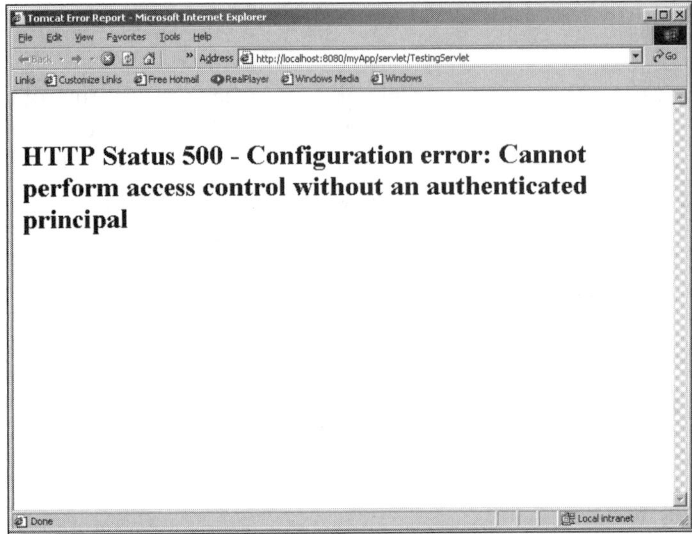

Figure 14.1 Unauthorized user trying to access a restricted area.

Using the login-config Element

The preceding section discussed the security-constraint element. Now, let's have a look at the second element for security configuration—login-config.

Firstly, let's add another user to the tomcat-users.xml file. This user has a user name of "GM", a password of "lontong", and a role of "manager". The tomcat-users.xml file is given in Listing 14.2.

Listing 14.2 **Adding a New User to the tomcat-users.xml File**

```
<tomcat-users>
  <user name="GM" password="lontong" roles="manager" />
  <user name="tomcat" password="tomcat" roles="tomcat" />
  <user name="role1"  password="tomcat" roles="role1"  />
  <user name="both"   password="tomcat" roles="tomcat,role1" />
</tomcat-users>
```

How does a user access a resource using a specified role? Each user needs to log in using the user name and password assigned to the role.

How do you allow them to log in? By using the login-config element.

> **Note**
> When you ask a user to enter credentials (user name and password), you are *authenticating* the user. See the sidebar later in this section for more about authentication methods.

The login-config element can contain the following optional elements:

- **auth-method**. This element contains the authentication methods and can have one of the following values: BASIC, DIGEST, FORM, or CLIENT-CERT. The following sidebar, "Authentication Methods," explains more about these methods.
- **realm-name**. This is the descriptive name that will be displayed in the standard Login dialog box if BASIC is specified as the value of the auth-method element.
- **form-login-config**. This element specifies the Login and error pages that will be used if the value of the auth-method element is FORM. This is explained in more detail in the following section.

Authentication Methods

When you are securing a Java-based web application, you can choose from the following four authentication methods:

- Basic authentication
- Form-based authentication
- Digest authentication
- Secure Socket Layer (SSL) and client certificate authentication

Using the Basic authentication, when a user tries to access a restricted resource, the web container asks the browser to display a standard Login dialog box containing two boxes: one for entering a user name, and one for the password. If the user enters the correct user name and password, the server displays the requested resource. Otherwise, the Login dialog box is redisplayed, asking the user to try again. The server will let the user try to log in three times, after which an error message is sent. The drawback of this method is that the user name and password are transmitted to the server using the base64 encoding, which is a very weak encryption scheme.

Form-based authentication is similar to Basic authentication; however, instead of sending an instruction to the browser to display a standard Login page, the server uses a custom Login page that must be prepared by the developer. This authentication method will also display a custom Error page written by the developer on a failed attempt to login.

continues

> The authentication methods take care only of displaying the login form. Without SSL, the password is sent as plain text and is insecure. With SSL, the password is sent encrypted.
>
> Even though both basic authentication and form-based authentication send the login information in almost plain text, you can use SSL to encrypt the data.
>
> Digest authentication works like Basic authentication; however, the login information is not transmitted. Instead, the hash of the passwords are sent. This protects the information from malicious sniffers.
>
> Basic and digest authentication methods are specified in RFC2617, which you can find at `ftp://ftp.isi.edu/in-notes/rfc2617.txt`.
>
> When the transmitted data is sensitive, you need to use SSL to encrypt it. For more information about SSL, see `http://home.netscape.com/eng/ssl3/3-SPEC.HTM`.

As an example of requiring the user to log in, consider the deployment descriptor in Listing 14.3.

Listing 14.3 **Deployment Descriptor that Requires the User to Log In**

```
<?xml version="1.0" encoding="ISO-8859-1"?>

<!DOCTYPE web-app
  PUBLIC "-//Sun Microsystems, Inc.//DTD Web Application 2.3//EN"
  "http://java.sun.com/j2ee/dtds/web-app_2_3.dtd">

<web-app>
  <security-constraint>
    <web-resource-collection>
      <web-resource-name>
        Restricted Area
      </web-resource-name>
      <url-pattern>/servlet/*</url-pattern>
    </web-resource-collection>
    <auth-constraint>
      <role-name>manager</role-name>
    </auth-constraint>
  </security-constraint>

  <login-config>
    <auth-method>BASIC</auth-method>
    <realm-name>User Basic Authentication</realm-name>
  </login-config>
</web-app>
```

See how you use the login-config element? The authentication method used is BASIC. Now every time a user accesses a resource using a URL matching the pattern, the web browser will display a dialog box as shown in Figure 14.2.

Figure 14.2 The Login dialog box.

The user can then type the user name and password for the manager role. The user name must be "GM" and the password is "lontong".

If the user does not login successfully, the dialog box reappears. If the user fails to login three times, the browser will display Figure 14.3:

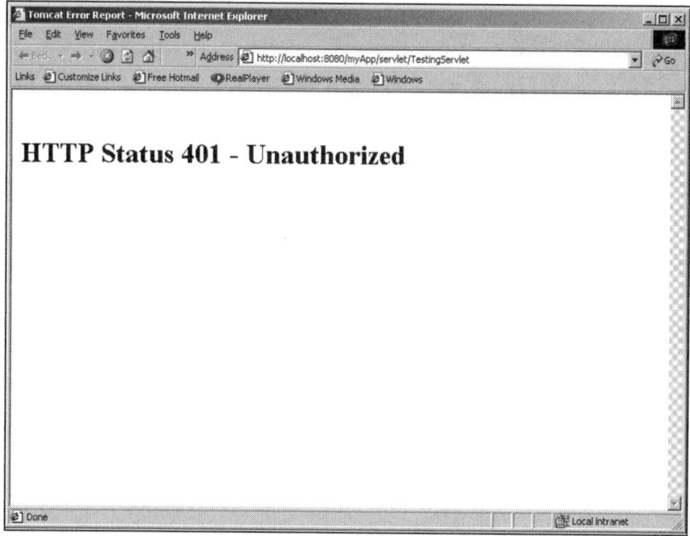

Figure 14.3 HTTP Status 401.

If the login is successful, the resource is displayed and an authentication token is sent in the response. After the user logs in successfully, requests for another resource matching the pattern will not require login because the user already has the authentication token.

If the user logs in correctly using the user name and password of another role, the browser will display a different page, as you see in Figure 14.4. For example, the user might type "tomcat" as the user name and "tomcat" as the password (using the role tomcat in the tomcat-users.xml file).

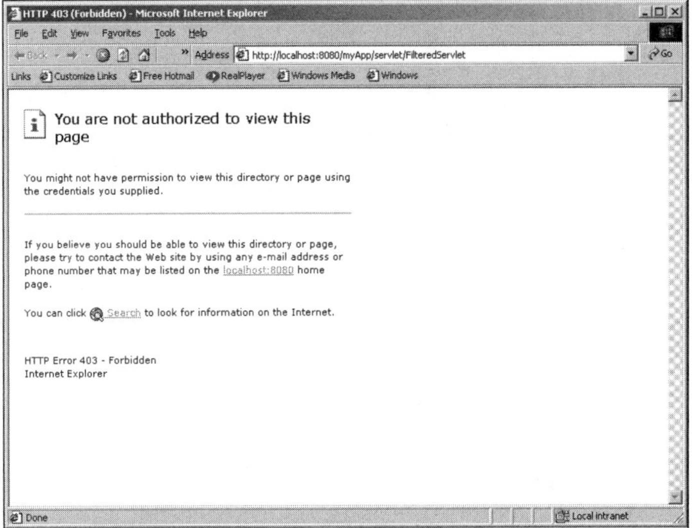

Figure 14.4 Using the wrong role.

Allowing Multiple Roles

You can specify more than one role to have access to a resource. For example, Listing 14.4 gives the deployment descriptor that allows two roles to access a certain resource.

Listing 14.4 **Allowing Multiple Roles to Access a Resource**

```
<?xml version="1.0" encoding="ISO-8859-1"?>

<!DOCTYPE web-app
  PUBLIC "-//Sun Microsystems, Inc.//DTD Web Application 2.3//EN"
  "http://java.sun.com/j2ee/dtds/web-app_2_3.dtd">
```

```
<web-app>
  <security-constraint>
    <web-resource-collection>
      <web-resource-name>
        Restricted Area
      </web-resource-name>
      <url-pattern>/servlet/*</url-pattern>
    </web-resource-collection>
    <auth-constraint>
      <role-name>manager</role-name>
      <role-name>tomcat</role-name>
    </auth-constraint>
  </security-constraint>

  <login-config>
    <auth-method>BASIC</auth-method>
    <realm-name>User Basic Authentication</realm-name>
  </login-config>
</web-app>
```

You also need the tomcat-users.xml file in Listing 14.5.

Listing 14.5 **The tomcat-users.xml File for the Example**

```
<tomcat-users>
  <user name="GM" password="lontong" roles="manager" />
  <user name="tomcat" password="tomcat" roles="tomcat" />
  <user name="role1"  password="tomcat" roles="role1"  />
  <user name="both"   password="tomcat" roles="tomcat,role1" />
</tomcat-users>
```

Now you can use both the manager role and the tomcat role to access the single resource. Note that the tomcat role appears both in the second and fourth user elements. This means that you also can use the user name "both" and password "tomcat" to access the resource.

Form-Based Authentication

The auth-method element in the login-config element allows you to specify FORM as its value. Assigning FORM as the value of auth-method means that you don't want to use the browser's standard Login page. Instead, you are telling the web container that you want to use your own custom page. This is called *form-based authentication*.

You need to prepare two pages if you decide to use form-based authentication: a Login page and an Error page. The Login page, which can be a static file or a dynamic resource, is a page that is displayed when a user tries to access a restricted resource. Basically, the Login page can be as simple or as complex as you like. The requirements are that the Login page needs to contain an HTML form with the following requisites:

- The method of the form must be POST.
- The value of the ACTION attribute must be "j_security_check".
- The form must have two input elements called j_username and j_password. Into these elements the user enters the user name and password.

In addition, you need an Error page that can also be a static page or a dynamic resource. This page is displayed when the user does not log in successfully. Note that the web container will display the Error page on the first failed attempt to login.

The following is an example of form-based authentication. The deployment descriptor is given in Listing 14.6.

Listing 14.6 **The Deployment Descriptor for Form-Based Authentication**

```
<?xml version="1.0" encoding="ISO-8859-1"?>

<!DOCTYPE web-app
  PUBLIC "-//Sun Microsystems, Inc.//DTD Web Application 2.3//EN"
  "http://java.sun.com/j2ee/dtds/web-app_2_3.dtd">

<web-app>
  <security-constraint>
    <web-resource-collection>
      <web-resource-name>
        Restricted Area
      </web-resource-name>
      <url-pattern>/servlet/*</url-pattern>
    </web-resource-collection>
    <auth-constraint>
      <role-name>manager</role-name>
      <role-name>tomcat</role-name>
    </auth-constraint>
  </security-constraint>

  <login-config>
    <auth-method>FORM</auth-method>
    <form-login-config>
      <form-login-page>/Login.html</form-login-page>
```

```
      <form-error-page>/Error.html</form-error-page>
    </form-login-config>
  </login-config>
</web-app>
```

The form-login-config element specifies the URL of the Login page and the Error page. The deployment descriptor mandates that the Login page is called Login.html and is to be found under the application directory. The descriptor also tells the web container that the Error page for this form-based authentication is named Error.html and is also found under the application directory.

Listings 14.7 and 14.8 list the Login page and the Error page, respectively.

Listing 14.7 **Login.html**

```
<HTML>
<HEAD>
<TITLE>Login Page</TITLE>
</HEAD>
<BODY>
<CENTER>
<H2>Please enter your user name and password</H2>
<FORM ACTION="j_security_check" METHOD="POST">
<TABLE>
<TR>
  <TD>User name:</TD>
  <TD><INPUT TYPE=TEXT NAME="j_username"></TD>
</TR>
<TR>
  <TD>Password:</TD>
  <TD><INPUT TYPE=PASSWORD NAME="j_password"></TD>
</TR>
<TR>
  <TD><INPUT TYPE=RESET></TD>
  <TD><INPUT TYPE=SUBMIT VALUE="Login"></TD>
</TR>
</TABLE>
</FORM>
</BODY>
</HTML>
```

Listing 14.8 **Error.html**

```
<HTML>
<HEAD>
<TITLE>Error Page</TITLE>
</HEAD>
```

continues

Listing 14.8 **Continued**

```
<BODY>
Login failed. Click <A HREF="Login.html">here</A> to try again.
</BODY>
</HTML>
```

When a user tries to access the resource whose URL matches the pattern specified in the deployment descriptor, the browser displays the Login page shown in Figure 14.5.

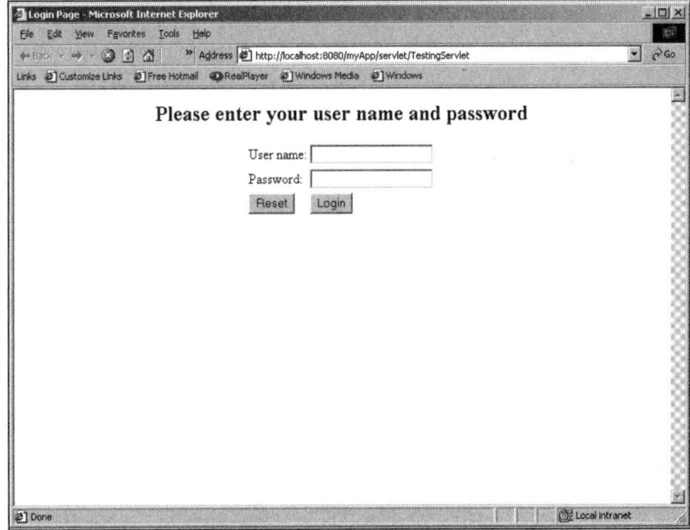

Figure 14.5 Login page.

If the login fails, the Error page is displayed, as shown in Figure 14.6.

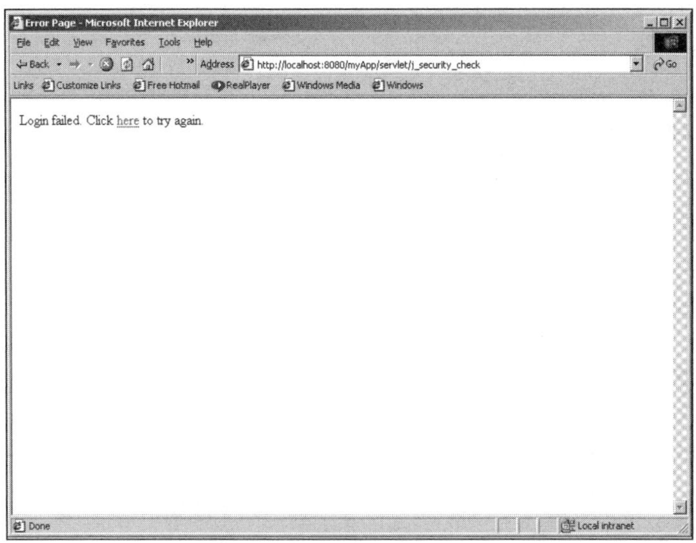

Figure 14.6 Error page.

A successful login will display the requested page.

Digest Authentication

Using digest authentication does not require you to change too much in the deployment descriptor. The main difference between Basic and form-based authentication and digest authentication is that you don't specify a realm if the authentication method used is DIGEST.

The following example demonstrates the use of digest authentication. The deployment descriptor is given in Listing 14.9.

Listing 14.9 **The Deployment Descriptor that Uses the Digest Authentication Method**

```
<?xml version="1.0" encoding="ISO-8859-1"?>

<!DOCTYPE web-app
  PUBLIC "-//Sun Microsystems, Inc.//DTD Web Application 2.3//EN"
  "http://java.sun.com/j2ee/dtds/web-app_2_3.dtd">

<web-app>
  <security-constraint>
    <web-resource-collection>
      <web-resource-name>
```

```
          Restricted Area
        </web-resource-name>
        <url-pattern>/servlet/*</url-pattern>
      </web-resource-collection>
      <auth-constraint>
        <role-name>manager</role-name>
        <role-name>tomcat</role-name>
      </auth-constraint>
    </security-constraint>

    <login-config>
      <auth-method>DIGEST</auth-method>
    </login-config>
  </web-app>
```

When the user tries to access the restricted resource, a dialog box, such as the one shown in Figure 14.7, is displayed.

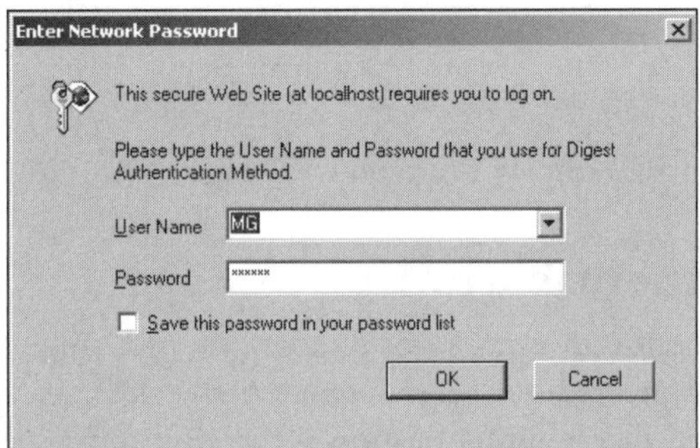

Figure 14.7 Digest Authentication Method dialog box.

Note that this dialog box is very similar to the one used in the Basic authentication method.

Methods Related to Security

Even though configuring the deployment descriptor and specifying roles in the tomcat-users.xml file means that you don't need to do any programming in your code, sometimes some coding is inevitable. For example, you might want to record all users that log in. The javax.servlet.http.HttpServletRequest interface provides a few methods that enable you to have access to portions of the user's login information. These methods are getAuthType, isUserInRole, getPrincipal, and getRemoteUser. The methods are explained here:

```
public String getAuthType()
```

This method returns the name of the authentication scheme used to protect the servlet. The return value is one of the following values: BASIC_AUTH, FORM_AUTH, CLIENT_CERT_AUTH, and DIGEST_AUTH. It returns null if the request was not authenticated.

```
public boolean isUserInRole(String role)
```

This method indicates whether the authenticated user is included in the specified logical "role". If the user has not been authenticated, the method returns false.

```
public java.security.Principal getUserPrincipal()
```

This method returns a java.security.Principal object containing the name of the current authenticated user. If the user has not been authenticated, the method returns null.

```
public String getRemoteUser()
```

Returns the login of the user making this request, if the user has been authenticated, or null if the user has not been authenticated. Whether the user name is sent with each subsequent request depends on the browser and type of authentication.

For example, the JSP code in Listing 14.10 demonstrates the use of the different methods.

Listing 14.10 **Using HttpServletRequest Methods to Obtain the User Name Login Information**

```
<%
  out.println("Auth Type:" + request.getAuthType());
  out.println("<BR>User Principal:" + request.getUserPrincipal());
  out.println("<BR>Remote User:" + request.getRemoteUser());
  if (request.isUserInRole("tomcat"))
    out.println("<BR>User in role");
  else
    out.println("<BR>User not in role");
%>
```

If you run this code, you should see something similar to Figure 14.8.

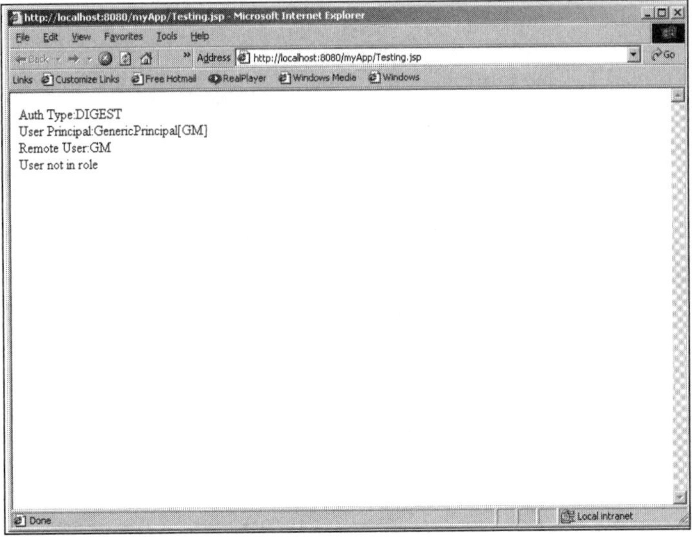

Figure 14.8 Finding out who the user is.

Restricting Certain Methods

The previous examples restrict access to a resource regardless of the HTTP method used to request the resource. You also can selectively choose HTTP methods that you need to restrict. For example, you may want to restrict access to a request that is submitted using the GET method, but yet allows access if the user is using the POST method.

The deployment descriptor in Listing 14.11 restricts the GET method. If the page is requested using the GET method, the user needs to log in. If the page is requested using the other methods, such as POST, no authentication is required.

Listing 14.11 **Restricting a Certain Method**

```
<?xml version="1.0" encoding="ISO-8859-1"?>

<!DOCTYPE web-app
  PUBLIC "-//Sun Microsystems, Inc.//DTD Web Application 2.3//EN"
  "http://java.sun.com/j2ee/dtds/web-app_2_3.dtd">

<web-app>
```

```
  <security-constraint>
    <web-resource-collection>
      <web-resource-name>
        Restricted Area
      </web-resource-name>
      <url-pattern>/*</url-pattern>
       <http-method>GET</http-method>
    </web-resource-collection>
    <auth-constraint>
      <role-name>manager</role-name>
      <role-name>tomcat</role-name>
    </auth-constraint>
  </security-constraint>

  <login-config>
    <auth-method>DIGEST</auth-method>
  </login-config>
</web-app>
```

Summary

In this chapter, you have learned how to configure your deployment descriptor so that the web container restricts access to some or all of the resources. The configuration means that you need only to modify your deployment descriptor file—no programming is necessary.

If you need to access the user login's information, you can use the following methods of the javax.servlet.http.HttpServletRequest interface: getRemoteUser, getPrincipal, getAuthType, and isUserInRole.

15 Caching

YOU NORMALLY STORE DATA IN A RELATIONAL DATABASE. Connecting to the database, however, is one of the most resource-consumptive operations that you commonly perform in a web application. Therefore, if you can reduce the number of times your application needs to access the database, your application will generally be faster and more scalable. Many people avoid databases entirely by storing their data in text files or XML files, but this solution is not suitable for every application. In addition, if you have an existing database-based application, using XML will require a change to your data structure and eventually to your application architecture.

This chapter presents two solutions to the database-access problem: caching data in a text file and caching data in memory.

The first solution writes frequently accessed, but hardly changed data, into text files. Hard disk space is very cheap today and having an easily read copy of data will not hurt at all. When your application needs the data from the database, instead of hitting the database server, the application can just include a text file. Unless the database server caches the data in its memory, embedding a text file is an operation that is probably a thousand times faster than opening a connection to a database.

When you include a text file, you can use a server-side include feature of the web server, which is normally achieved by using a .shtml or .shtm file. This technique is, of course, much faster than processing a similar JSP file because with JSP files, you need at least one extra step—the process hand-over from the web server to the JSP container.

This technique presents its own problem, however: maintenance. When the data in the database changes, its copy in the text file must also change.

The second technique, caching data in memory, is even faster. Because a server normally has limited amount of RAM, however, you normally cache only selected data in memory.

This chapter shows you how to use these two techniques to improve your application performance.

Caching Data into a Text File

What sort of data can be cached into a text file? Almost anything—as long as the data meets the following criteria:

- Frequently accessed
- Not sensitive data, such as user names and passwords
- Does not change very often

A large amount of data should qualify. These data items could include the product categories in an online shop, the details of each product, the items in an online auction, and so on.

Consider the example of an online shop. The product categories are seldom changed—maybe not even once a year. These product categories, however, are accessed from the database every time a user visits your online shop because you need to list all categories in the Search In select box. (I'm assuming that your site has search capability because all proper online shops allow the user to search for a specific product.) How many times has your application accessed the database for exactly the same piece of data?

The code in Listing 15.1 is a typical HTML code fragment used for a search feature in a computer book online bookstore.

Listing 15.1 **HTML Code for a Search Feature in an Online Bookstore**

```
<FORM METHOD=POST ACTION=Search.jsp>
Keyword: <INPUT TYPE=TEXT Name=Keyword><BR>Search In:
<SELECT Name=Category>
<OPTION VALUE=1>Programming</OPTION>
<OPTION VALUE=2>Operating System</OPTION>
<OPTION VALUE=3>Database</OPTION>
<OPTION VALUE=4>Certification</OPTION>
```

```
</SELECT>
<INPUT TYPE=SUBMIT VALUE=Search>
</FORM>
```

When viewed in a web browser, the code in Listing 15.1. will look similar to Figure 15.1.

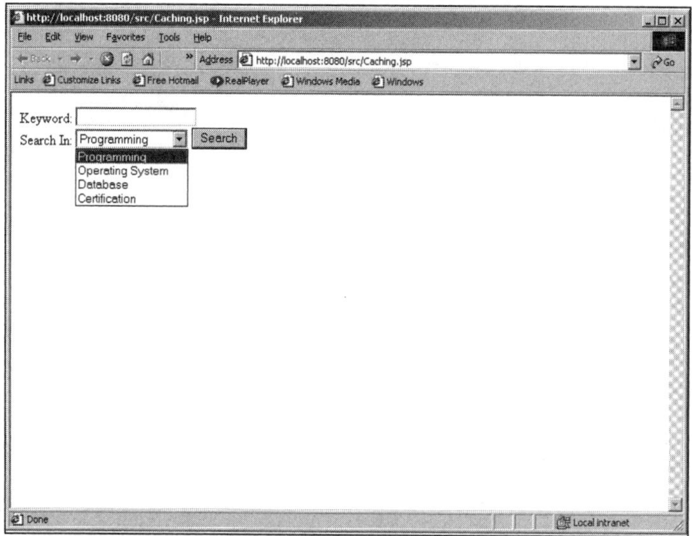

Figure 15.1 The search feature in an online store.

Using JSP, on the server side, you would have the code presented in Listing 15.2.

Listing 15.2 **Extracting Categories Without Caching**

```
<%@ page import="java.sql.*" %>
<%!
  public void jspInit() {
    try {
      Class.forName("sun.jdbc.odbc.JdbcOdbcDriver");
    }
    catch (ClassNotFoundException e) {
    }
  }
%>
<FORM METHOD=POST ACTION=Search.jsp>
Keyword: <INPUT TYPE=TEXT Name=Keyword><BR>
Search In: <SELECT Name=Category>
<%
  //Open the Categories table
  try {
    String sql = "SELECT * FROM Categories";
```

continues

Listing 15.2 **Continued**

```
      Connection con =
DriverManager.getConnection("jdbc:odbc:JavaWeb");
      Statement s = con.createStatement();
      ResultSet rs = s.executeQuery(sql);
     while (rs.next()) {
        out.print("<OPTION VALUE=");
        out.print(rs.getString(1));
        out.print(">");
        out.print(rs.getString(2));
        out.print("</OPTION>\n");
      }
      s.close();
      con.close();
    }
    catch (SQLException e) {
      out.println(e.toString());
    }
    catch (Exception e) {
      out.println(e.toString());
    }
%>
</SELECT>
<INPUT TYPE=SUBMIT VALUE=Search>
</FORM>
```

Now if you put the categories in a text file called Categories.txt that contains the text in Listing 15.3, you don't need to access the database to display the categories in the Search In select box.

Listing 15.3 **The Categories.txt File**

```
<OPTION VALUE=1>Programming</OPTION>
<OPTION VALUE=2>Operating System</OPTION>
<OPTION VALUE=3>Database</OPTION>
<OPTION VALUE=4>Certification</OPTION>
```

The JSP code is much simpler, as you see in Listing 15.4.

Listing 15.4 **The JSP Code when a Text File Is Used**

```
<FORM METHOD=POST ACTION=Search.jsp>
Keyword: <INPUT TYPE=TEXT Name=Keyword><BR>
Search In: <SELECT Name=Category>

<%@ include file="Categories.txt" %>

</SELECT>
<INPUT TYPE=SUBMIT VALUE=Search>
</FORM>
```

Better still, you might not need a JSP page at all. You can use an .shtml extension for that page if your web server supports it. This capability, however, relies on the web server itself and you should consult the documentation that comes with your web server to find out more.

In the case of caching product details into text files, a reasonable approach is to copy the details of each product to a text file and name the text file using the product's ID. What if you have one thousand or one million products? The quantity does not matter here because if your clients have a million products to sell, it is very likely they can afford to buy a high-speed hard disk.

The drawback of this technique is that there appears to be an inevitable maintenance problem. The data items cached into text files are seldom changed, but they do change. When they change, you need to have a way of updating the copy in the text file. Additionally, when a cached item is deleted, you must also remove its copy in the text file.

The solution to this maintenance problem is to modify your administration pages so that when something changes on the database, the copy in the text file also changes. For example, if you cache the product category into a file, whenever you add a new product category to the database, the categories.txt file must be updated.

The code in Listing 15.5 shows an example of the Category Admin page, which changes the copy of the product categories in the text file. At first, the page looks similar the one shown in Figure 15.2.

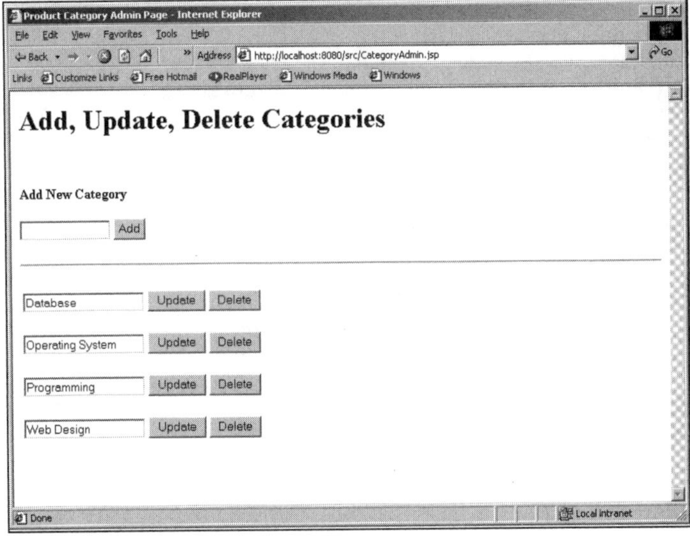

Figure 15.2 The administration page to add, update, and delete categories.

Listing 15.5 **The Categories Admin Page**

```
<%@ page import="java.sql.*" %>
<%@ page import="java.io.*" %>
<%!
  public void jspInit() {
    try {
      Class.forName("sun.jdbc.odbc.JdbcOdbcDriver");
    }
    catch (ClassNotFoundException e) {
    }
  }
%>
<HTML>
<HEAD>
<TITLE>Product Category Admin Page</TITLE>
</HEAD>

<BODY>
<H1>Add, Update, Delete Categories</H1>
<BR><BR>
<B>Add New Category</B>
<BR>
<FORM METHOD=POST>
<INPUT TYPE=HIDDEN NAME=action VALUE=add>
<INPUT TYPE=TEXT NAME=category SIZE=14>
<INPUT TYPE=SUBMIT VALUE=Add>
</FORM>
<HR>
<BR>
<%
  String id = request.getParameter("id");
  String category = request.getParameter("category");
  String action = request.getParameter("action");
  String sql;
  StringBuffer categories = new StringBuffer(2048);
  //Open the Categories table
  try {
    Connection con =
DriverManager.getConnection("jdbc:odbc:JavaWeb");
    Statement s = con.createStatement();
    ResultSet rs;
    if (action!=null && action.equals("add")) {
      sql = "SELECT CategoryName FROM Categories WHERE
CategoryName='" +
➥category + "'";
      ➥rs = s.executeQuery(sql);
      if (!rs.next()) {
        sql = "INSERT INTO Categories (CategoryName) VALUES ('" +
➥category + "')";
        s.executeUpdate(sql);
```

```
      }
      else
        out.println(category + " is already in the database");
    }
    else if (action!=null && action.equals("delete")) {
      sql = "DELETE FROM Categories WHERE CategoryID=" + id;
      s.executeUpdate(sql);
    }
    else if (action!=null && action.equals("update")) {
      sql = "UPDATE Categories SET CategoryName='" + category + "'" +
        " WHERE CategoryId=" + id;
      s.executeUpdate(sql);
    }

    sql = "SELECT CategoryID, CategoryName FROM Categories ORDER BY
➥CategoryName ASC";
    rs = s.executeQuery(sql);

    // Now list all categories plus the DELETE and UPDATE buttons
    out.println("<TABLE>");
    while (rs.next()) {
      id = rs.getString(1);
      category = rs.getString(2);
%>

<TR>
<TD>
<FORM METHOD=POST>
<INPUT TYPE=HIDDEN NAME=id VALUE="<%=id%>">
<INPUT TYPE=HIDDEN NAME=action VALUE="update">
<INPUT TYPE=TEXT NAME=category VALUE="<%=category%>">
<INPUT TYPE=SUBMIT VALUE=Update>
</FORM>
</TD>
<TD>
<FORM METHOD=POST>
<INPUT TYPE=HIDDEN NAME=id VALUE="<%=id%>">
<INPUT TYPE=HIDDEN NAME=action VALUE="delete">
<INPUT TYPE=SUBMIT VALUE=Delete>
</FORM>
</TD>
</TR>
<%
      categories.append("<OPTION VALUE=").append(id).append(">");
      categories.append(category).append("</OPTION>\n");
    }

    out.println("</TABLE>");
    s.close();
    con.close();
```

continues

Listing 15.5 **Continued**

```
      //Create a text file called Categories.txt in the specified
➥folder
      String path = "C:\\123data\\";
      FileWriter fw = new FileWriter(path + "categories.txt");
      fw.write(categories.toString());
      fw.close();
    }
    catch (SQLException e) {
      out.println(e.toString());
    }
    catch (Exception e) {
      out.println(e.toString());
    }
%>
</BODY>
</HTML>
```

In the code in Listing 15.5, categories.txt is updated every time the administrator adds, deletes, or updates a category, which solves the maintenance problem of caching data in a text file.

> **Note**
> The path variable should be assigned the actual location of the category.txt file.

Caching in Memory

Caching selected data in memory is preferable if you know which data is requested most often. This data is dumped into memory at the initialization time of a servlet and is only done once. Subsequent requests for the cached data will result in faster responses.

The code in Listing 15.6 demonstrates caching product details from the Products table in memory. All products marked as "hot" products are retrieved from the database at initialization time and stored in a java.util.HashMap object.

Listing 15.6 **Caching Data in Memory**

```
<%@ page import="java.sql.*" %>
<%@ page import="java.util.HashMap" %>
<%!
  HashMap products = new HashMap(50);
```

```
  public void jspInit() {
    try {
      Class.forName("sun.jdbc.odbc.JdbcOdbcDriver");
      Connection con =
DriverManager.getConnection("jdbc:odbc:JavaWeb");
      Statement s = con.createStatement();
      String sql = "SELECT ProductId, ProductName, Description,
➥Price" +
        " FROM Products" +
        " WHERE Hot=True";
      ResultSet rs = s.executeQuery(sql);
      while (rs.next()) {
        Product product = new Product();
        String productId = rs.getString("ProductId");
        product.productId = productId;
        product.productName = rs.getString("ProductName");
        product.description = rs.getString("Description");
        product.price = rs.getFloat("Price");
        products.put(productId, product);
      }
      con.close();
    }
    catch (ClassNotFoundException e) {
    }
    catch (Exception e) {
    }
  }

  class Product {
    String productId;
    String productName;
    String description;
    float price;
  }
%>
<%
  long t1 = System.currentTimeMillis();
%>
<HTML>
<HEAD>
<TITLE>Product Details</TITLE>
</HEAD>
<BODY>
<%
  String productId = request.getParameter("id");
  //productId="2";
  if (productId==null) {
    out.println("The request did not carry a product identifier");
    return;
  }
  String productName = null;
```

continues

Listing 15.6 **Continued**

```
  String description = null;
  float price = 0;

  Product product = (Product) products.get(productId);
  if (product!=null) {
    productName = product.productName;
    description = product.description;
    price = product.price;
  }
  else {
    // not found in the cache, grab from the database
    try {
      Connection con =
DriverManager.getConnection("jdbc:odbc:JavaWeb");
      Statement s = con.createStatement();
      String sql = "SELECT ProductName, Description, Price" +
        " FROM Products" +
        " WHERE ProductId=" + productId;
      ResultSet rs = s.executeQuery(sql);
      if (rs.next()) {
        productName = rs.getString("ProductName");
        description = rs.getString("Description");
        price = rs.getFloat("Price");
      }
      rs.close();

      s.close();
      con.close();
    }
    catch (SQLException e) {
      out.println(e.toString());
    }
    catch (Exception e) {
      out.println(e.toString());
    }
  }
%>
<BR>Product Id: <%=productId%>
<BR>Product Name: <%=productName%>
<BR>Description: <%=description%>
<BR>Price: <%=price%>
<BR>
<%
  long t2 = System.currentTimeMillis();
  out.println("Processing time: " + (t2 - t1));
%>
</BODY>
</HTML>
```

Each product that needs to be cached is represented by the Product class, whose definition is as follows:

```
class Product {
  String productId;
  String productName;
  String description;
  float price;
}
```

The initialization code is written in the jspInit method of the JSP page. This code is executed only once when the JSP servlet is loaded into memory.

The jspInit( ) method first loads the JDBC driver, opens a connection object, and retrieves all products marked as "hot" products from the Products table, as you see here

```
public void jspInit() {
  try {
    Class.forName("sun.jdbc.odbc.JdbcOdbcDriver");
    Connection con = DriverManager.getConnection("jdbc:odbc:JavaWeb");
    Statement s = con.createStatement();
    String sql = "SELECT ProductId, ProductName, Description, Price" +
      " FROM Products" +
      " WHERE Hot=True";
    ResultSet rs = s.executeQuery(sql);
    .
    .
    .
    con.close();
  }
  catch (ClassNotFoundException e) {
  }
  catch (Exception e) {
  }
}
```

After you get the ResultSet object from the Statement's executeQuery method, you instantiate a Product object, assign values to each field in the Product object, and add the Product object into the HashMap object, as follows:

```
    while (rs.next()) {
      Product product = new Product();
      String productId = rs.getString("ProductId");
      product.productId = productId;
      product.productName = rs.getString("ProductName");
      product.description = rs.getString("Description");
      product.price = rs.getFloat("Price");
      products.put(productId, product);
    }
```

The product identifier is used as the key for each product added to the HashMap.

When a product is requested, the JSP page first checks to see whether it is available in the HashMap. If it is, the product is obtained from the HastMap, as you see here:

```
Product product = (Product) products.get(productId);
if (product!=null) {
  productName = product.productName;
  description = product.description;
  price = product.price;
}
```

If the requested product is not available, you have to connect to the database and retrieve the product from the Products table, like this:

```
  // not found in the cache, grab from the database
  try {
    Connection con = DriverManager.getConnection("jdbc:odbc:JavaWeb");
    Statement s = con.createStatement();
    String sql = "SELECT ProductName, Description, Price" +
      " FROM Products" +
      " WHERE ProductId=" + productId;
    ResultSet rs = s.executeQuery(sql);
    if (rs.next()) {
      productName = rs.getString("ProductName");
      description = rs.getString("Description");
      price = rs.getFloat("Price");
    }
    rs.close();

    s.close();
    con.close();
  }
  catch (SQLException e) {
    out.println(e.toString());
  }
  catch (Exception e) {
    out.println(e.toString());
  }
}
```

The JSP page is displayed in Figure 15.3.

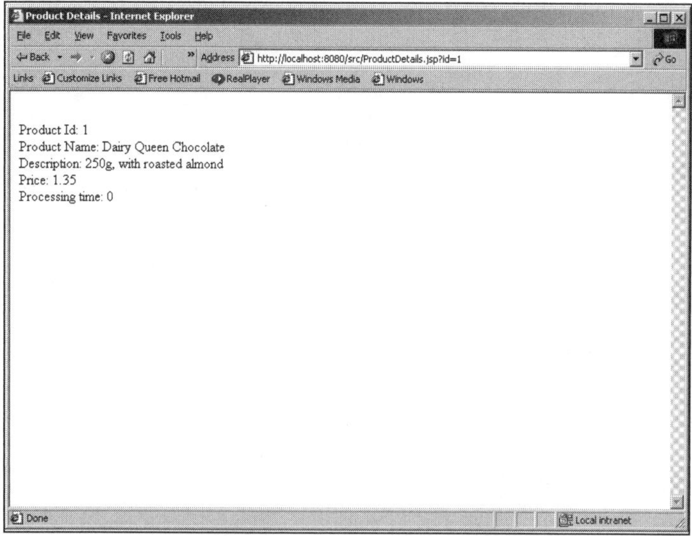

Figure 15.3 Caching data in memory.

The JSP page also defines two variables—t1 and t2—to help measure the time taken to process the JSP page. t1 is written at the beginning of the page, and t2 is written toward the end of the page.

You want to know the result, don't you?

Good news. It works!

My example shows a significant improvement. For a request for a cached product, t2 - t1 equals 0. This, of course, only means that the processing time is too fast to measure.

For requests for products not in the cache, t2 - t1 results in between 110 and 250 milliseconds.

Conclusion: Caching data in memory really speeds up response time.

Summary

Data caching is a popular technique used on busy web sites. Caching improves scalability of the web application because it reduces the number of times database-related resource-consumptive operations are performed. This chapter demonstrated how you can cache data in text files as well as in memory.

16 Application Deployment

THIS CHAPTER DISCUSSES THE PROCESS OF deploying your servlet and JSP application. To understand how to properly display your web application, you first need to understand the directory structure of an application. For that reason, this chapter starts with a review of the directory structure. The next topic, which is the primary focus of the chapter, covers the deployment descriptor where you can configure each application. Finally, this chapter helps you learn how to create an alias for your servlet and your JSP page and then map them to a new URL. By creating an alias, you can call your application using a shorter or more preferable URL.

Application Directory Structure

When you first install Tomcat, several directories are created under the directory in which you install Tomcat. Figure 16.1 shows an example.

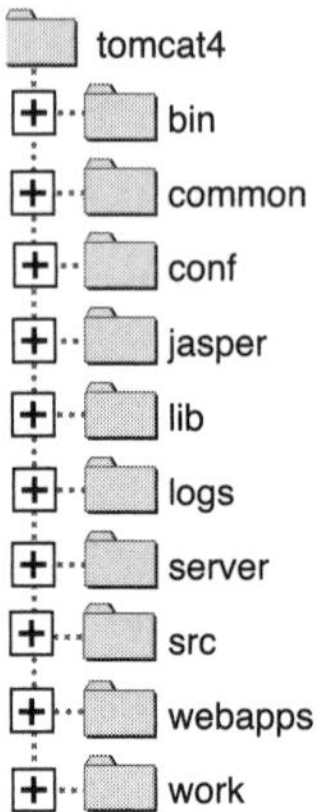

Figure 16.1 Tomcat's directory structure.

In this case, Tomcat is installed in a directory called tomcat4. This directory is also known as %CATALINA_HOME%. See Appendix A, "Tomcat Installation and Configuration," to find information on the function of each subdirectory.

In this chapter, you are interested in one of the subdirectories that Tomcat installation creates: *webapps*. The webapps directory is the parent directory of every web application that will be run under this Tomcat installation. When you first install Tomcat, a number of sample applications are also created. One such application is the examples application. Figure 16.2 illustrates a webapps directory that includes a number of applications.

Let's look at the application myWebApp, which represents a typical web application. This myWebApp directory is called the *application directory*.

Right under an application directory is a directory called WEB-INF, which has special significance in a web application. Figure 16.2 shows two other directories under the myWebApp directory: images and jsp. These two directories are optional. The jsp directory is where you store all your JSP pages. You could place them directly under the application directories if you choose; however, organizing all your JSP pages in separate directories is a good practice. The image directory is used to store all the image files. Again, this image directory does not play a significant role except to make your application more organized.

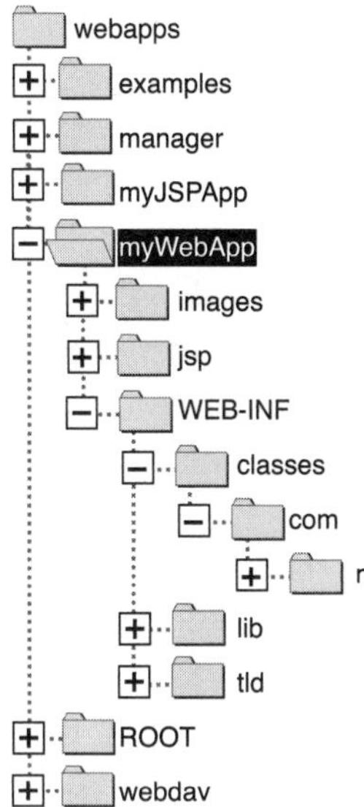

Figure 16.2 The myWebApp application.

If your web application uses some static files, such as HTML files, you put them under the application directory as well. Alternatively, again for the sake of being organized, you can create a subdirectory under the application directory to group similar files. In a real-world application, having a directory called html for all your HTML files is not uncommon.

As mentioned, the WEB-INF directory has a special meaning. This directory is not visible from a client web browser, and everything you put under it is also hidden from the client. First, the WEB-INF is where you put your deployment descriptor (web.xml file). Including this deployment descriptor is optional, but you can do a lot of things with it, as you'll see in the following section, "Deployment Descriptor."

If you use any servlet, you must have a directory called classes under WEB-INF. Servlets that don't belong to a package must be copied to the classes directory. For servlets with a package, you must create a valid directory structure that reflects the Java package. In Figure 16.2, you saw a directory structure under class for servlets that belong to the com.newriders package.

The lib directory under WEB-INF is useful if you use a library files, such as .jar files. Library files copied here will be available to all resources in the application. If you have a library that needs to be available to more than one application, you can put it under the lib directory under %CATALINA_HOME%.

If you use custom tag libraries for your JSP pages, the TLD file(s) must also go under WEB-INF or in a subdirectory beneath it. In Figure 16.2, a directory called tld is created to hold all TLD files. JavaBeans and custom tag component class files are stored in the classes directory under WEB-INF.

Deployment Descriptor

A deployment descriptor is an XML document that contains information describing a specific servlet or JSP application. Some of the elements in a deployment descriptor are related to servlets, and some are related to JSP applications.

A typical deployment descriptor starts with the following header:

```
<?xml version="1.0" encoding="ISO-8859-1"?>
```

This header specifies the version of XML and the encoding used. The header is followed by the following DOCTYPE declaration:

```
<!DOCTYPE web-app
  PUBLIC "-//Sun Microsystems, Inc.//DTD Web Application 2.3//EN"
  "http://java.sun.com/dtd/web-app_2_3.dtd">
```

This code specifies the document type definition (DTD) against which you can check the validity of the XML document. The previous <!DOCTYPE> element has several attributes that tell us a lot about the DTD.

The following list describes the information you can learn from the <!DOCTYPE> element:

- web-app defines the root element of this document (deployment descriptor, not DTD file).
- PUBLIC means that the DTD file is intended for public use.
- "-//Sun Microsystems, Inc.//DTD Web Application 2.3//EN" means that the DTD is maintained by Sun Microsystems, Inc. This information also tells us that the type of the document it describes is DTD Web Application 2.3, and the DTD is written in English.
- The URL `"http://java.sun.com/dtd/web-app_2_3.dtd">` represents the location of the DTD file.

> **Warning**
>
> Note that the DTD file location shown in the preceding list is a new address: The DTD file location used to be `http://java.sun.com/j2ee/dtds/web-app_2_3.dtd`.

The root element of a deployment descriptor is web-app. This element can have up to 23 kinds of subelements, all of which are optional. Some subelements can appear only once, and others can appear more than once. Additionally, some of these subelements can have subelements.

> **Note**
>
> For those of you who are not XML experts, here are some notes that can be useful in understanding the following discussion about DTDs:
>
> x+ : one or more occurrences of x.
>
> x* : zero or more occurrences of x.
>
> x? : optional x.
>
> x, y : x followed by y.
>
> x | y : x or y
>
> PCDATA = parsed character data. Parsed character data is text that does not contain markup, but rather simple character data.

According to the DTD file, the syntax of the web-app element's subelements is briefly described as follows:

```
<!ELEMENT web-app (icon?, display-name?, description?, distributable?,
➥context-param*, filter*, filter-mapping*, listener*, servlet*,
➥servlet-mapping*, session-config?,mime-mapping*, welcome-file-list?,
➥error-page*, taglib*, resource-env-ref*, resource-ref*,
➥security-constraint*, login-config?, security-role*,env-entry*,
➥ejb-ref*, ejb-local-ref*)>
```

The question mark (?) character indicates that a subelement is optional and can appear only once. The asterisks (*) are used to specify subelements that can appear more than once in the deployment descriptor. The description of the subelements indicates that all subelements are optional.

Following this web-app element declaration comes the declarations of each subelement. This chapter discusses each element based on its functionality.

> **Note**
>
> Subelements must appear in the order specified previously. For example, if the web-app element in a deployment descriptor has both servlet and servlet-mapping subelements, the servlet subelement must appear before the servlet-mapping subelement.

A deployment descriptor generally looks like the following:

```
<?xml version="1.0" encoding="ISO-8859-1"?>

<!DOCTYPE web-app
  PUBLIC "-//Sun Microsystems, Inc.//DTD Web Application 2.3//EN"
  "http://java.sun.com/j2ee/dtds/web-app_2.3.dtd">

<web-app>
  <element-1>
    <subelement-1>value of subelement-1 of element-1</subelement-1>
    <subelement-2>value of subelement-2 of element-1</subelement-2>
    .
    .
    .
  </element-1>
  <element-2>
    <subelement-1>value of subelement-1 of element-2</subelement-1>
    <subelement-2>value of subelement-2 of element-2</subelement-2>
    .
    .
    .
  </element-2>

  .
  .
  .

  <element-n>
    <subelement-1>value of subelement-1 of element-n</subelement-1>
    <subelement-2>value of subelement-2 of element-n</subelement-2>
    .
    .
    .
  </element-n>
</web-app>
```

The following example shows the deployment descriptor of a servlet application:

```
<?xml version="1.0" encoding="ISO-8859-1"?>

<!DOCTYPE web-app
  PUBLIC "-//Sun Microsystems, Inc.//DTD Web Application 2.3//EN"
  "http://java.sun.com/j2ee/dtds/web-app_2.3.dtd">

<web-app>
  <servlet>
    <servlet-name>HttpRequestDemo</servlet-name>
    <servlet-class>HttpRequestDemoServlet</servlet-class>
  </servlet>
  <servlet>
```

```
    <servlet-name>Primitive</servlet-name>
    <servlet-class>PrimitiveServlet</servlet-class>
  </servlet>
  <servlet>
    <servlet-name>ConfigDemo</servlet-name>
    <servlet-class>ConfigDemoServlet</servlet-class>
    <init-param>
      <param-name>adminEmail</param-name>
      <param-value>admin@brainysoftware.com</param-value>
    </init-param>
    <init-param>
      <param-name>adminContactNumber</param-name>
      <param-value>0414371237</param-value>
    </init-param>
  </servlet>
</web-app>
```

Note

A deployment descriptor, like other XML documents, can also contain comments. A comment in XML is anything between the <!-- tag and the --> tag.

The subelements are explained in the following sections. An example is given for each subelement.

icon

The icon element contains an optional small-icon subelement and an optional large-icon subelement. Its element description is as follows:

```
<!ELEMENT icon (small-icon?, large-icon?)>
<!ELEMENT small-icon (#PCDATA)>
<!ELEMENT large-icon (#PCDATA)>
```

The icon element is used to specify the filenames for a small (16 × 16) and or a large (32 × 32) icon in either GIF or JPEG format. The filename is a path relative to the root of the web application archive (WAR).

The icon can be used by an XML tool if you happen to use a tool to edit your deployment descriptor. The web container does not use this element.

For example, the following is a deployment descriptor that uses an icon element. The icon element has both a small icon and a large icon:

```
<?xml version="1.0" encoding="ISO-8859-1"?>

<!DOCTYPE web-app
  PUBLIC "-//Sun Microsystems, Inc.//DTD Web Application 2.3//EN"
  "http://java.sun.com/dtd/web-app_2_3.dtd">

<web-app>
  <icon>
```

```
      <small-icon>/CompanyLogo.jpg</small-icon>
      <large-icon>/CompanyBigLogo.jpg</large-icon>
    </icon>
</web-app>
```

display-name

The display-name element contains a name to be displayed by an XML tool if you use a tool to edit your deployment descriptor. The element descriptor for display-name is as follows:<!ELEMENT display-name (#PCDATA)>
The following example is a deployment descriptor that has both icon and display-name elements:

```
<?xml version="1.0" encoding="ISO-8859-1"?>

<!DOCTYPE web-app
  PUBLIC "-//Sun Microsystems, Inc.//DTD Web Application 2.3//EN"
  "http://java.sun.com/dtd/web-app_2_3.dtd">

<web-app>
   <icon>
     <small-icon>/CompanyLogo.jpg</small-icon>
     <large-icon>/CompanyBigLogo.jpg</large-icon>
   </icon>
   <display-name>Superposition Marketing</display-name>
</web-app>
```

description

You use the description element to provide information about the deployment descriptor. The value of the description element can be used by an XML tool.

The description element has the following element descriptor:

```
<!ELEMENT description (#PCDATA)>
```

The following is an example of a deployment descriptor that uses a description element:

```
<?xml version="1.0" encoding="ISO-8859-1"?>

<!DOCTYPE web-app
  PUBLIC "-//Sun Microsystems, Inc.//DTD Web Application 2.3//EN"
  "http://java.sun.com/dtd/web-app_2_3.dtd">

<web-app>
  <display-name>Superposition Marketing</display-name>
  <description>This application tracks statistical changes</description>
</web-app>
```

distributable

If present in a deployment descriptor, the distributable element indicates that the application is written to be deployed into a distributed web container. The syntax for this element is as follows:

```
<!ELEMENT distributable EMPTY>
```

For example, the following is a deployment descriptor that contains a distributable element:

```
<?xml version="1.0" encoding="ISO-8859-1"?>

<!DOCTYPE web-app
  PUBLIC "-//Sun Microsystems, Inc.//DTD Web Application 2.3//EN"
  "http://java.sun.com/dtd/web-app_2_3.dtd">

<web-app>
  <display-name>Superposition Marketing</display-name>
  <distributable/>
</web-app>
```

context-param

The context-param element contains a pair of parameter names and values used as the application's servlet context initialization parameter. The parameter name must be unique throughout the web application. The syntax for the context-param element and its subelements is as follows:

```
<!ELEMENT context-param (param-name, param-value, description?)>
<!ELEMENT param-name (#PCDATA)>
<!ELEMENT param-value (#PCDATA)>
<!ELEMENT description (#PCDATA)>
```

The param-name subelement contains the parameter name, and the param-value subelement contains the parameter value. Optionally, a description subelement also can be present to describe the parameter.

The following is a valid deployment descriptor with a few context-param elements:

```
<?xml version="1.0" encoding="ISO-8859-1"?>

<!DOCTYPE web-app
  PUBLIC "-//Sun Microsystems, Inc.//DTD Web Application 2.3//EN"
  "http://java.sun.com/dtd/web-app_2_3.dtd">

<web-app>
  <context-param>
    <param-name>adminName</param-name>
    <param-value>Tommy Matena</param-value>
  </context-param>
  <context-param>
```

```
      <param-name>initValue</param-name>
      <param-value>8060</param-value>
      <description>the port number used</description>
    </context-param>
  </web-app>
```

filter

This element specifies a filter in the web application. The filter is mapped either to a servlet or a URL pattern using the filter-mapping element described in the next section. The filter element and the filter-mapping element that does the mapping for this filter must have the same name. Filters are discussed in Chapter 7, "Servlet Filtering."

The element descriptor for filter is as follows:

```
<!ELEMENT filter (icon?, filter-name, display-name?, description?,
filter-class, init-param*)>
<!ELEMENT filter-name (#PCDATA)>
<!ELEMENT filter-class (#PCDATA)>
```

The icon, display-name, and description elements are the same as the previous sections. The init-param has the same element descriptor as context-param.

The filter-name element defines the name of the filter. The filter name must be unique within the application. The filter-class element specifies the fully qualified name for the filter class.

The following is a valid deployment descriptor for a web application that uses two filters: UpperCaseFilter and Double Filter:

```
<?xml version="1.0" encoding="ISO-8859-1"?>

<!DOCTYPE web-app
  PUBLIC "-//Sun Microsystems, Inc.//DTD Web Application 2.3//EN"
  "http://java.sun.com/dtd/web-app_2_3.dtd">

<web-app>
  <filter>
    <filter-name>
      UpperCase Filter
    </filter-name>
    <filter-class>
      UpperCaseFilter
    </filter-class>
  </filter>
  <filter>
    <filter-name>
      Double Filter
    </filter-name>
    <filter-class>
      DoubleFilter
    </filter-class>
```

```
    <init-param>
      <param-name>frequency</param-name>
      <param-value>1909</param-value>
    </init-param>
  </filter>
</web-app>
```

filter-mapping

The filter-mapping element declares the filter mappings in the web application. A filter can be mapped either to a servlet or a URL pattern. Mapping a filter to a servlet causes the filter to work on the servlet. Mapping a filter to a URL pattern makes filtering occur to any resource whose URL matches the URL pattern. Filtering is performed in the same order as the appearance of filter-mapping elements in the deployment descriptor.

The element descriptor for filter-mapping is as follows:

```
<!ELEMENT filter-mapping (filter-name, (url-pattern | servlet-name))>
<!ELEMENT filter-name (#PCDATA)>
<!ELEMENT url-pattern (#PCDATA)>
<!ELEMENT servlet-name (#PCDATA)>
```

The filter-name value must match one of the filter names declared in the filter elements.

The following is a deployment descriptor that contains two filter-mapping elements:

```
<?xml version="1.0" encoding="ISO-8859-1"?>

<!DOCTYPE web-app
  PUBLIC "-//Sun Microsystems, Inc.//DTD Web Application 2.3//EN"
  "http://java.sun.com/dtd/web-app_2_3.dtd">

<web-app>
  <!-- Define servlet-mapped and path-mapped filters -->
  <filter>
    <filter-name>
      Basic Filter
    </filter-name>
    <filter-class>
      BasicFilter
    </filter-class>
  </filter>
  <filter>
    <filter-name>
      Advanced Filter
    </filter-name>
    <filter-class>
      AdvancedFilter
    </filter-class>
  </filter>
```

```
  <!-- Define filter mappings for the defined filters -->
  <filter-mapping>
    <filter-name>
      Basic Filter
    </filter-name>
    <servlet-name>
      FilteredServlet
    </servlet-name>
  </filter-mapping>
  <filter-mapping>
    <filter-name>
      Advanced Filter
    </filter-name>
    <url-pattern>
      /*
    </url-pattern>
  </filter-mapping>
</web-app>
```

listener

The listener element is used to register a listener class that you include in a web application. The listener element has the following element descriptor:

```
<!ELEMENT listener (listener-class)>
<!ELEMENT listener-class (#PCDATA)>
```

The following is a valid deployment descriptor containing a listener element:

```
<?xml version="1.0" encoding="ISO-8859-1"?>

<!DOCTYPE web-app
  PUBLIC "-//Sun Microsystems, Inc.//DTD Web Application 2.3//EN"
  "http://java.sun.com/dtd/web-app_2_3.dtd">

<web-app>
  <listener>
    <listener-class>
      AppLifeCycleEvent
    </listener-class>
  </listener>
</web-app>
```

servlet

The servlet element is used to declare a servlet. It has the following element descriptor:

```
<!ELEMENT servlet (icon?, servlet-name, display-name?, description?,
(servlet-class|jsp-file), init-param*, load-on-startup?, run-as?,
security-role-ref*)>
<!ELEMENT servlet-name (#PCDATA)>
<!ELEMENT servlet-class (#PCDATA)>
```

```
<!ELEMENT jsp-file (#PCDATA)>
<!ELEMENT init-param (param-name, param-value, description?)>
<!ELEMENT load-on-startup (#PCDATA)>
<!ELEMENT run-as (description?, role-name)>
<!ELEMENT role-name (#PCDATA)>
```

The icon, display-name, and description elements are described in the previous sections. The init-param element descriptor is the same as context-param.

A servlet element must contain a servlet-name element and a servlet-class element, or a servlet-name element and a jsp-file element. The servlet-name element defines the name for that servlet and must be unique thoroughout the application.

The servlet-class element specifies the fully qualified class name of the servlet.

The jsp-file element specifies the full path to a JSP file within the application. The full path must begin with a /.

You use the init-param subelement to pass an initial parameter name and value to the servlet.

The load-on-startup element is used to load the servlet automatically into memory when the web container starts up. Loading a servlet means instantiating the servlet and calling its init method. You use this element to avoid delay in the response for the first request to the servlet, caused by the servlet loading to memory. If this element is present and a jsp-file element is specified, the JSP file is precompiled into a servlet and the resulting servlet is loaded.

The content of a load-on-startup value is either empty or an integer number. The value indicates the order of loading into memory by the web container. For example, if there are two servlet elements and both contain load-on-startup subelements, the servlet with a lower number in the load-on-startup subelement is loaded first. If the value of the load-on-startup is empty or a negative number, it is up to the web container to decide when to load the servlet. If two servlets have the same value for their load-on-startup subelements, the web container is free to choose which servlet to load first.

If a run-as element is defined, it overrides the security identity used to call an Enterprise Java Bean by that servlet in this web application. The role-name is one of the security roles defined for the current web application.

The security-role-ref element defines a mapping between the name of the role called from a servlet using isUserInRole(String name) and the name of a security role defined for the web application. The security-role-ref element is described as follows:

```
<!ELEMENT security-role-ref (description?, role-name, role-link)>
<!ELEMENT description (#PCDATA)>
<!ELEMENT role-name (#PCDATA)>
<!ELEMENT role-link (#PCDATA)>
```

The role-link element is used to link a security role reference to a defined security role. The role-link element must contain the name of one of the security roles defined in the security-role elements.

For example, to map the security role reference "MG" to the security role with role-name "manager," the syntax would be as follows:

```
<security-role-ref>
  <role-name>MG</role-name>
  <role-link>manager</manager>
</security-role-ref>
```

In this case, if the servlet called by a user belonging to the "manager" security role made the API call isUserInRole("MG"), the result would be true. The role-name "*" is not permitted because it has a special meaning for authorization constraints.

The following is a deployment descriptor containing several servlet elements:

```
<?xml version="1.0" encoding="ISO-8859-1"?>

<!DOCTYPE web-app
  PUBLIC "-//Sun Microsystems, Inc.//DTD Web Application 2.3//EN"
  "http://java.sun.com/dtd/web-app_2_3.dtd">

<web-app>
  <servlet>
    <servlet-name>
      First
    </servlet-name>
    <servlet-class>
      FirstServlet
    </servlet-class>
    <load-on-startup>
      1
    </load-on-startup>
  </servlet>
  <servlet>
    <servlet-name>
      JDBCServlet
    </servlet-name>
    <servlet-class>
      com.newriders.db.JDBCServlet
    </servlet-class>
    <load-on-startup>
      2
    </load-on-startup>
  </servlet>
</web-app>
```

servlet-mapping

The servlet-mapping element maps a URL pattern to a servlet. The element descriptor for servlet-mapping is as follows:

```
<!ELEMENT servlet-mapping (servlet-name, url-pattern)>
<!ELEMENT servlet-name (#PCDATA)>
<!ELEMENT url-pattern (#PCDATA)>
```

The following is a deployment descriptor that maps a servlet with a URL pattern. For more details, see the section "Servlet Alias and Mapping," later in this chapter.

```
<?xml version="1.0" encoding="ISO-8859-1"?>

<!DOCTYPE web-app
  PUBLIC "-//Sun Microsystems, Inc.//DTD Web Application 2.3//EN"
  "http://java.sun.com/dtd/web-app_2_3.dtd">

<web-app>
  <servlet>
    <servlet-name>AnAlias</servlet-name>
    <servlet-class>com.newriders.OtherServlet</servlet-class>
  </servlet>
  <!-- servlet mapping -->
  <servlet-mapping>
    <servlet-name>AnAlias</servlet-name>
    <url-pattern>/newURL</url-pattern>
  </servlet-mapping>
</web-app>
```

session-config

The session-config element defines the parameters for the javax.servlet.http.HttpSession objects in the web application. The element descriptor is as follows:

```
<!ELEMENT session-config (session-timeout?)>
<!ELEMENT session-timeout (#PCDATA)>
```

The session-timeout element specifies the default session timeout interval in minutes. This value must be an integer. If the value of the session-timeout element is zero or a negative number, the session will never time out.

The following is a deployment descriptor that makes the default HttpSession object invalid 10 minutes after the last access from the user:

```
<?xml version="1.0" encoding="ISO-8859-1"?>

<!DOCTYPE web-app
  PUBLIC "-//Sun Microsystems, Inc.//DTD Web Application 2.3//EN"
  "http://java.sun.com/dtd/web-app_2_3.dtd">
```

```
<web-app>
  <session-config>
    <session-timeout>
      10
    </session-timeout>
  </session-config>
</web-app>
```

mime-mapping

The mime-mapping element maps a mime type to an extension. Its element decriptor is as follows:

```
<!ELEMENT mime-mapping (extension, mime-type)>
<!ELEMENT extension (#PCDATA)>
<!ELEMENT mime-type (#PCDATA)>
```

The extension element describes the extension, and mime-type is the MIME type. For example, the following deployment descriptor maps the extension "txt" to "text/plain":

```
<?xml version="1.0" encoding="ISO-8859-1"?>

<!DOCTYPE web-app
    PUBLIC "-//Sun Microsystems, Inc.//DTD Web Application 2.3//EN"
    "http://java.sun.com/dtd/web-app_2_3.dtd">

<web-app>
  <mime-mapping>
    <extension>
      txt
    </extension>
    <mime-type>
      text/plain
    </mime-type>
  </mime-mapping>
</web-app>
```

welcome-file-list

The welcome-file-list element specifies the default file that is displayed when the URL entered by the user in the browser does not contain a servlet name or a JSP page. For example, assume the user types in something like the following:

```
http://www.yourdomain.com/appName/
```

If no welcome-file-list element is specified in the deployment descriptor for a web application, the user sees a permission error message or the list of files and directories in the application directory.

The welcome-file-list is described as follows:

```
<!ELEMENT welcome-file-list (welcome-file+)>
<!ELEMENT welcome-file (#PCDATA)>
```

The welcome-file subelement contains the default filename. A welcome-file-list element can contain one or more welcome-file subelements. If the file specified in the first welcome-file element cannot be found, the web container will try to display the second one, and so on.

The following is a deployment descriptor that contains a welcome-file-list element. The element contains two welcome-file elements. The first welcome-file specifies a file in the application directory called index.html; the second defines the welcome.html file under the src directory, which is under the application directory:

```
<?xml version="1.0" encoding="ISO-8859-1"?>

<!DOCTYPE web-app
  PUBLIC "-//Sun Microsystems, Inc.//DTD Web Application 2.3//EN"
  "http://java.sun.com/dtd/web-app_2_3.dtd">

<web-app>
  <welcome-file-list>
    <welcome-file>
      index.html
    </welcome-file>
    <welcome-file>
      src/welcome.html
    </welcome-file>
  </welcome-file-list>
</web-app>
```

If the index.html file is not found in the application directory when a user types a URL that does not contain a servlet name or a JSP page or other resource, the welcome.html file in the src directory will be displayed.

error-page

The error-page element maps an error code or an exception type to a resource path in the web application, so that if a particular HTTP error or a specified Java exception occurs, the resource will be displayed instead. Its element descriptor is as follows:

```
<!ELEMENT error-page ((error-code | exception-type), location)>
<!ELEMENT error-code (#PCDATA)>
<!ELEMENT exception-type (#PCDATA)>
<!ELEMENT location (#PCDATA)>
```

The error-code element contains an HTTP error code, exception type is the fully qualified name of a Java exception type, and location is the path to the resource in the web application relative to the application directory. The value of location must start with a /.

For example, the following deployment descriptor causes the web container to display the error.html page in the application directory every time the HTTP 404 error code occurs:

```
<?xml version="1.0" encoding="ISO-8859-1"?>

<!DOCTYPE web-app
  PUBLIC "-//Sun Microsystems, Inc.//DTD Web Application 2.3//EN"
  "http://java.sun.com/dtd/web-app_2_3.dtd">

<web-app>
  <error-page>
    <error-code>
      404
    </error-code>
    <location>
      /error.html
    </location>
  </error-page>
</web-app>
```

taglib

The taglib element describes a JSP custom tag library. The taglib element is described as follows:

```
<!ELEMENT taglib (taglib-uri, taglib-location)>
<!ELEMENT taglib-uri (#PCDATA)>
<!ELEMENT taglib-location (#PCDATA)>
```

The taglib-uri element is the URI of the tag library used in the web application. The value for taglib-uri is relative to the location of the deployment descriptor.

The taglib-location contains the location where the TLD file for the tag library can be found.

The following is a deployment descriptor that contains taglib elements:

```
<?xml version="1.0" encoding="ISO-8859-1" ?>
<!DOCTYPE taglib
  PUBLIC "-//Sun Microsystems, Inc.//DTD Web Application 2.3//EN"
  "http://java.sun.com/dtd/web-app_2_3.dtd">
<web-app>
  <taglib>
    <taglib-uri>
      http://java.apache.org/tomcat/examples-taglib
    </taglib-uri>
    <taglib-location>
```

```
      /WEB-INF/jsp/example-taglib.tld
    </taglib-location>
  </taglib>
</web-app>
```

resource-env-ref

You use the resource-env-ref element to specify a declaration of a servlet's reference to an administered object associated with a resource in the servlet's environment. The element descriptor of resource-env-ref is as follows:

```
<!ELEMENT resource-env-ref (description?, resource-env-ref-name,
resource-env-ref-type)>
<!ELEMENT resource-env-ref-name (#PCDATA)>
<!ELEMENT resource-env-ref-type (#PCDATA)>
```

The resource-env-ref-name is the name of a resource environment reference whose value is the entry name of the environment used in servlet code. The name is a Java Naming and Directory Interface (JNDI) name relative to the java:comp/env context and must be unique throughout the web application.

resource-env-ref-type defines the type of a resource environment reference. Its value must be the fully qualified name of a Java class or interface.

As an example, the following deployment descriptor contains a resource-env-ref element:

```
<?xml version="1.0" encoding="ISO-8859-1"?>

<!DOCTYPE web-app
  PUBLIC "-//Sun Microsystems, Inc.//DTD Web Application 2.3//EN"
  "http://java.sun.com/dtd/web-app_2_3.dtd">

<web-app>
  <resource-env-ref>
    <resource-env-ref-name>jms/XQueue</resource-env-ref-name>
    <resource-env-ref-type>javax.jms.Queue</resource-env-ref-type>
  </resource-env-ref>
</web-app>
```

resource-ref

The resource-ref element specifies a declaration of a servlet's reference to an external resource. Its element descriptor is as follows:

```
<!ELEMENT resource-ref (description?, res-ref-name, res-type, res-auth,
➥res-sharing-scope?)>
<!ELEMENT description (#PCDATA)>
<!ELEMENT res-ref-name (#PCDATA)>
<!ELEMENT res-type (#PCDATA)>
<!ELEMENT res-auth (#PCDATA)>
<!ELEMENT res-sharing-scope (#PCDATA)>
```

The subelements of resource-ref are described as follows:

- res-ref-name is the name of the resource factory reference name. The name is a JNDI name relative to the java:comp/env context. The name must be unique throughout the web application.
- res-auth indicates whether the servlet code signs on programmatically to the resource manager or whether the Container will sign on to the resource manager on the servlet's behalf. The value of this element must be either Application or Container.
- res-sharing-scope indicates whether connections obtained through the given resource manager connection factory reference can be shared. The value of this element must be either Shareable (default) or Unshareable.

The following is a deployment descriptor that contains a resource-ref element:

```
<?xml version="1.0" encoding="ISO-8859-1"?>

<!DOCTYPE web-app
  PUBLIC "-//Sun Microsystems, Inc.//DTD Web Application 2.3//EN"
  "http://java.sun.com/dtd/web-app_2_3.dtd">

<web-app>
  <resource-ref>
    <description>JDBC Data Source</description>
    <res-ref-name>db/JDBCDatabase</res-ref-name>
    <res-type>javax.sql.DataSource</res-type>
    <res-auth>Application</res-auth>
    <res-sharing-scope>Unshareable</res-sharing-scope>
  </resource-ref>
</web-app>
```

security-constraint

The security-constraint in the deployment descriptor allows you to restrict access to certain resources without programming. To use this element, you should understand some security terms discussed in Chapter 14, "Security Configuration."

The security-constraint element is described as follows:

```
<!ELEMENT security-constraint (display-name?, web-resource-collection+,
auth-constraint?, user-data-constraint?)>
<!ELEMENT display-name (#PCDATA)>
<!ELEMENT web-resource-collection (web-resource-name, description?,
url-pattern*, http-method*)>
<!ELEMENT auth-constraint (description?, role-name*)>
<!ELEMENT user-data-constraint (description?, transport-guarantee)>
```

The web-resource-collection element identifies a subset of resources to which access needs to be restricted. In the web-resource-collection, you can define the URL pattern(s) and the HTTP method. If no HTTP method is present, the security constraint applies to all methods.

The auth-constraint element specifies the user roles that should have access to this resource collection. If no auth-constraint element is specified, the security constraint applies to all roles.

The user-data-constraint element is used to indicate how data transmitted between the client and web container must be protected.

The description of the web-resource-collection element is shown as follows:

```
<!ELEMENT web-resource-collection (web-resource-name, description?,
url-pattern*, http-method*)>
<!ELEMENT web-resource-name (#PCDATA)>
<!ELEMENT description (#PCDATA)>
<!ELEMENT url-pattern (#PCDATA)>
<!ELEMENT http-method (#PCDATA)>
```

The web-resource-name is a name associated with the protected resource.

The http-method element can be assigned one of the HTTP methods, such as GET and POST.

The description of the auth-constraint element is shown here:

```
<!ELEMENT auth-constraint (description?, role-name*)>
<!ELEMENT description (#PCDATA)>
<!ELEMENT role-name (#PCDATA)>
```

The role-name element contains the name of a security role.

The description of the user-data-constraint element is given here:

```
<!ELEMENT user-data-constraint (description?, transport-guarantee)>
<!ELEMENT description (#PCDATA)>
<!ELEMENT transport-guarantee (#PCDATA)>
```

The transport-guarantee element must have one of the following values: NONE, INTEGRAL, or CONFIDENTIAL. NONE means that the application does not require transport guarantees. INTEGRAL means that the data between the server and the client should be sent in such a way that it can't be changed in transit. CONFIDENTIAL means that the data transmitted must be encrypted. In most cases, Secure Sockets Layer (SSL) is used for either INTEGRAL or CONFIDENTIAL.

The following is a deployment descriptor that restricts access to any resource with a URL matching the pattern /servlet/*. Only a user in a manager role will be allowed access. The login-config element will require a user to log in and the Basic authentication method is used. The user must then enter the user name and password of the manager role to successfully log in:

```
<?xml version="1.0" encoding="ISO-8859-1"?>

<!DOCTYPE web-app
  PUBLIC "-//Sun Microsystems, Inc.//DTD Web Application 2.3//EN"
  "http://java.sun.com/dtd/web-app_2_3.dtd">

<web-app>
  <security-constraint>
    <web-resource-collection>
      <web-resource-name>
        Restricted Area
      </web-resource-name>
      <url-pattern>/servlet/*</url-pattern>
  </web-resource-collection>
    <auth-constraint>
      <role-name>manager</role-name>
    </auth-constraint>
  </security-constraint>

  <login-config>
    <auth-method>BASIC</auth-method>
    <realm-name>User Basic Authentication</realm-name>
  </login-config>
</web-app>
```

login-config

The login-config element is used to specify the authentication method used, the realm name, and the attributes needed by the form login mechanism. Its element descriptor is as follows:

```
<!ELEMENT login-config (auth-method?, realm-name?, form-login-config?)>
<!ELEMENT auth-method (#PCDATA)>
<!ELEMENT realm-name (#PCDATA)>
<!ELEMENT form-login-config (form-login-page, form-error-page)>
```

The auth-method specifies the authentication method. Its value is one of the following: BASIC, DIGEST, FORM, or CLIENT-CERT.

The realm name element specifies the realm name to use in HTTP Basic authorization.

The form-login-config element specifies the login and error pages that should be used in form-based login. If form-based authentication is not used, these elements are ignored.

The form-login-config element is further elaborated as follows:

```
<!ELEMENT form-login-config (form-login-page, form-error-page)>
<!ELEMENT form-login-page (#PCDATA)>
<!ELEMENT form-error-page (#PCDATA)>
```

The form-login-page element specifies a path to a resource that displays a Login page. The path must start with a / and is relative to the application directory.

The form-error-page element specifies a path to a resource that displays an error page when user login fails. The path must begin with a / and is relative to the application directory.

security-role

The security-role element specifies the declaration of a security role used in the security-constraints. It is described as follows:

```
<!ELEMENT security-role (description?, role-name)>
<!ELEMENT description (#PCDATA)>
<!ELEMENT role-name (#PCDATA)>
```

The following deployment descriptor illustrates the use of the security-role element:

```
<?xml version="1.0" encoding="ISO-8859-1"?>

<!DOCTYPE web-app
  PUBLIC "-//Sun Microsystems, Inc.//DTD Web Application 2.3//EN"
  "http://java.sun.com/dtd/web-app_2_3.dtd">

  <security-role>
    <role-name>manager</role-name>
  </security-role>
</web-app>
```

env-entry

The env-entry element specifies an application environment entry. This element is described using the following descriptor:

```
<!ELEMENT env-entry (description?, env-entry-name, env-entry-value?,
env-entry-type)>
<!ELEMENT description (#PCDATA)>
<!ELEMENT env-entry-name (#PCDATA)>
<!ELEMENT env-entry-value (#PCDATA)>
<!ELEMENT env-entry-type (#PCDATA)>
```

The env-entry-name element contains the name of a web application's environment entry. The name is a JNDI name relative to the java:comp/env context. The name must be unique throughout the application.

The env-entry-value element contains the value of a web application's environment entry. The value must be a String that is valid for the constructor of the specified type that takes a single String parameter—or for java.lang.Character, a single character.

The env-entry-type element contains the fully qualified Java type of the environment entry value that is expected by the web application's code. This element must have one of the following values:

```
java.lang.Boolean
java.lang.Byte
java.lang.Character
java.lang.String
java.lang.Short
java.lang.Integer
java.lang.Long
java.lang.Float
java.lang.Double
```

The ejb-ref element specifies a reference to an Enterprise JavaBean's home. Its descriptor is as follows:

```
<!ELEMENT ejb-ref (description?, ejb-ref-name, ejb-ref-type, home,
remote, ejb-link?)>
<!ELEMENT description (#PCDATA)>
<!ELEMENT ejb-ref-name (#PCDATA)>
<!ELEMENT ejb-ref-type (#PCDATA)>
<!ELEMENT home (#PCDATA)>
<!ELEMENT remote (#PCDATA)>
<!ELEMENT ejb-link (#PCDATA)>
```

The ejb-ref-name element contains the name of an EJB reference. The EJB reference is an entry in the servlet's environment and is relative to the java:comp/env context. The name must be unique within the web application. Its name is recommended to begin with "ejb/".

The ejb-ref-type element contains the expected type of the referenced enterprise bean. The value of the ejb-ref-type element must be either Entity or Session.

The home element contains the fully qualified name of the enterprise bean's home interface.

The remote element contains the fully qualified name of the enterprise bean's remote interface.

The ejb-link element is used in the ejb-ref or ejb-local-ref elements to specify that an EJB reference is linked to another enterprise bean.

The value of the ejb-link element must be the ejb-name of an enterprise bean in the same J2EE application unit.

The name in the ejb-link element may be composed of a path name specifying the ejb-jar containing the referenced enterprise bean. The ejb-name of the target bean has been appended and separated from the path name by using #. The path name is relative to the WAR containing the web application that is referencing the enterprise bean. This allows multiple enterprise beans with the same ejb-name to be identified uniquely.

The ejb-local-ref element is used for the declaration of a reference to an enterprise bean's local home. It is described as follows:

```
<!ELEMENT ejb-local-ref (description?, ejb-ref-name, ejb-ref-type,
➥local-home, local, ejb-link?)>
<!ELEMENT description (#PCDATA)>
<!ELEMENT ejb-ref-name (#PCDATA)>
<!ELEMENT ejb-ref-type (#PCDATA)>
<!ELEMENT local-home (#PCDATA)>
<!ELEMENT local (#PCDATA)>
<!ELEMENT ejb-link (#PCDATA)>
```

The local element contains the fully qualified name of the enterprise bean's local interface.

The local-home element contains the fully qualified name of the enterprise bean's local home interface.

Servlet Alias and Mapping

With Tomcat, you actually don't need a deployment descriptor for a servlet. Consider the following directory structure given in Figure 16.3. This is the structure for a web application called myApp.

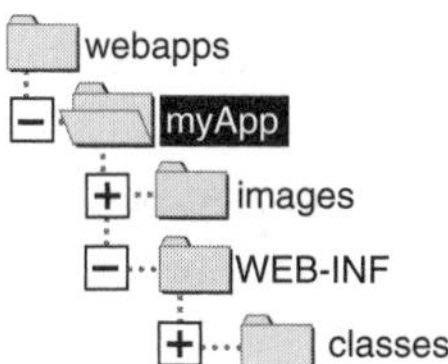

Figure 16.3 The directory structure for myApp.

As long as you put your servlet class file under the classes directory under myApp, your servlet should be accessible from the following URL: `http://domain/myApp/servlet/ServletClassName`.

For instance, if your servlet is called TestingServlet and your domain name is `www.blahblahblah.com`, the URL to the servlet is the following:

```
http://www.blahblahblah.com/myApp/servlet/TestingServlet
```

> **Note**
> Note that the servlet is accessed through the default port 8080. Appendix A provides information on how to make your servlet work on a non-default port.

The previous URL assumes that the servlet is not contained in a package. If the servlet is part of a package, you must store your class file under a directory structure that reflects the Java package. For example, the following servlet called OtherServlet is part of the package com.newriders.

First, you need the directory structure given in Figure 16.4. The OtherServlet class file must be stored in the newriders directory.

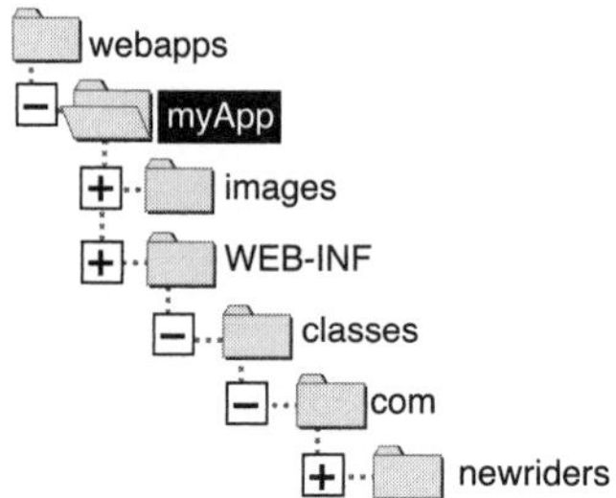

Figure 16.4 The directory structure for a servlet in a package.

The servlet then can be accessed using the following URL:

```
http://domain/myApp/servlet/com.newriders.OtherServlet
```

You can see that the package name is reflected in the URL; however, the deployment descriptor allows you to call your servlet by another name. This simply means you can make your servlet available with a non-standard URL.

For example, the deployment descriptor in Listing 16.1 creates an alias called AnAlias for com.newriders.OtherServlet.

Listing 16.1 **The Deployment Descriptor that Provides an Alias**

```
<?xml version="1.0" encoding="ISO-8859-1"?>

<!DOCTYPE web-app
    PUBLIC "-//Sun Microsystems, Inc.//DTD Web Application 2.3//EN"
    "http://java.sun.com/dtd/web-app_2_3.dtd">

<web-app>
  <servlet>
    <servlet-name>AnAlias</servlet-name>
    <servlet-class>com.newriders.OtherServlet</servlet-class>
  </servlet>
</web-app>
```

In the deployment descriptor, first you define a name (AnAlias) for the servlet com.newriders.OtherServlet. Then your servlet is available from both of the following URLs:

```
http://domain/myApp/servlet/com.newriders.OtherServlet
http://domain/myApp/servlet/AnAlias
```

In the preceding example, the URL still must contain the word "servlet," even though you can choose your own name. With servlet-mapping, you can remove the word "servlet" from the URL. The next example shows you how to create a different URL for the previous servlet (com.newriders.OtherServlet) using the deployment descriptor in Listing 16.2.

Listing 16.2 **The Deployment Descriptor that Provides Mapping**

```
<?xml version="1.0" encoding="ISO-8859-1"?>

<!DOCTYPE web-app
    PUBLIC "-//Sun Microsystems, Inc.//DTD Web Application 2.3//EN"
    "http://java.sun.com/dtd/web-app_2_3.dtd">

<web-app>
  <servlet>
    <servlet-name>AnAlias</servlet-name>
    <servlet-class>com.newriders.OtherServlet</servlet-class>
  </servlet>
  <!-- mapping -->
  <servlet-mapping>
    <servlet-name>AnAlias</servlet-name>
    <url-pattern>/newURL</url-pattern>
  </servlet-mapping>
</web-app>
```

Now, you can access your servlet using the following three URLs:

```
http://localhost:8080/myApp/servlet/com.newriders.OtherServlet
http://localhost:8080/myApp/servlet/AnAlias
http://localhost:8080/myApp/newURL
```

Note that the word "servlet" disappears in the third URL.

The URL pattern can go beyond a simple word. For example, to give the impression that the class file is in a subdirectory, consider the deployment descriptor in Listing 16.3.

Listing 16.3 **The Deployment Descriptor that Uses a More Complex Map**

```
<?xml version="1.0" encoding="ISO-8859-1"?>

<!DOCTYPE web-app
    PUBLIC "-//Sun Microsystems, Inc.//DTD Web Application 2.3//EN"
    "http://java.sun.com/dtd/web-app_2_3.dtd">

<web-app>
  <servlet>
    <servlet-name>AnAlias</servlet-name>
    <servlet-class>com.newriders.OtherServlet</servlet-class>
  </servlet>
  <!-- mapping -->
  <servlet-mapping>
    <servlet-name>AnAlias</servlet-name>
    <url-pattern>/newURL/level-1/level-2</url-pattern>
  </servlet-mapping>
</web-app>
```

Now you can use the following URL to access your servlet:

```
http://domain/myApp/newURL/level-1/level-2
```

Note also that you can use the wild-card character * to indicate that you accept anything. For example, the URL pattern /whatever/* will make your servlet accessible with any URL that ends with /whatever/, such as:

```
http://domain/myApp/whatever/noname
http://domain/myApp/whatever/favorite
```

JSP Alias and Mapping

With a JSP application, you have a similar directory structure as that of a servlet application. Consider a JSP application named myJSPApp. This application has the directory structure given in Figure 16.5.

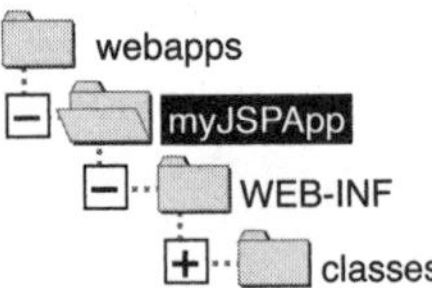

Figure 16.5 The directory structure for a JSP application called myJSPApp.

You store your JSP files in the myJSPApp directory and additional class files under the WEB-INF/classes directory. The JSP page then is callable using the following URL:

```
http://domain/appName/pageName
```

This means that if your domain and domain name is www.blahblahblah.com, your application name is myJSPApp, and the page is called SimplePage.jsp, once you register your application in the server.xml file (see Appendix A), the URL to access the page is as follows:

```
http://www.blahblahblah.com/myJSPApp/SimplePage.jsp
```

If you don't have a JavaBean and tag library, you don't even need the WEB-INF file. If you are happy with the URL to access your JSP page, you don't need a deployment descriptor, either.

Using a deployment descriptor, however, you can configure your application. Among other things, you can create an alias so that you can access your JSP page with another name.

For example, the following is a deployment descriptor that provides an alias for a JSP page called SimplePage.jsp:

```
<?xml version="1.0" encoding="ISO-8859-1"?>

<!DOCTYPE web-app
  PUBLIC "-//Sun Microsystems, Inc.//DTD Web Application 2.3//EN"
  "http://java.sun.com/dtd/web-app_2_3.dtd">

<web-app>
  <servlet>
    <servlet-name>
      AnAlias
    </servlet-name>
    <jsp-file>
      /SimplePage.jsp
    </jsp-file>
    <load-on-startup>1</load-on-startup>
  </servlet>
</web-app>
```

Note

Having a web application that consists of both servlets and JSP pages as well as other resources is very common. In this case, servlet classes and JSP pages can be stored in their own directories without affecting each other.

Packaging and Deploying a Web Application

You can deploy an application with the directory structure explained in the previous section. There is a more elegant way for deploying your application, however; you can first package your application into a web archive (WAR) file. A web archive file has a .war extension.

Basically, a WAR file is a .jar file you create using the jar program. Into a WAR file, you package every file in an application. The name of the WAR file normally is the same as the application name; however, you can use any name you like.

After you have a WAR file, you deploy it under the webapps directory. You then can access your application just as you would an unpackaged application. The name used for your packaged application is the .war filename. For example, if you package an application called myApp into a WAR file called dontcare.war, when deployed, the application name is dontcare, not myApp. This is the result because when you archive your application, the application name is not included in the WAR file.

Summary

This chapter explained to you how you can configure and deploy your web application. The chapter started by introducing the directory structure of a typical application and then moved to an explanation of the deployment descriptor.

After the application is ready for deployment, you can deploy it by retaining the files and directory structure of your application. Alternatively, you can package the application into a WAR file and deploy the whole application using a single file.

17

Architecting Java Web Applications

NOW THAT YOU KNOW THE TECHNIQUES, tips, and tricks for working with servlets and JSP, it is time to look at the architectural designs of a Java web application. Two models are commonly used and this chapter explains them and shows why JSP does not make servlets obsolete. In fact, in complex applications, JSP pages and servlets go hand in hand.

The terms for the two architectural designs first appeared in the early drafts of the JSP specifications: *Model 1* and *Model 2*. These two terms are not mentioned in the more current JSP specification documents. However, the designs are still widely in use today. The models are explained in the next two sections. Similar applications are given in both Model 1 and Model 2 to illustrate the models' differences.

> **Note**
> A project based on Model 2 application is presented in Chapter 18, "Developing E-Commerce Applications."

Model 1 Architecture

In Model 1 architecture, the application is page-centric. The client browser navigates through a series of JSP pages in which any JSP page can employ a JavaBean that performs business operations. However, the highlight of this architecture is that each JSP page processes its own input. Applications implementing this architecture normally have a series of JSP pages where the user is expected to proceed from the first page to the next. If needed, a servlet or an HTML page can be substituted for the JSP page in the series.

The Model 1 architecture is depicted in Figure 17.1.

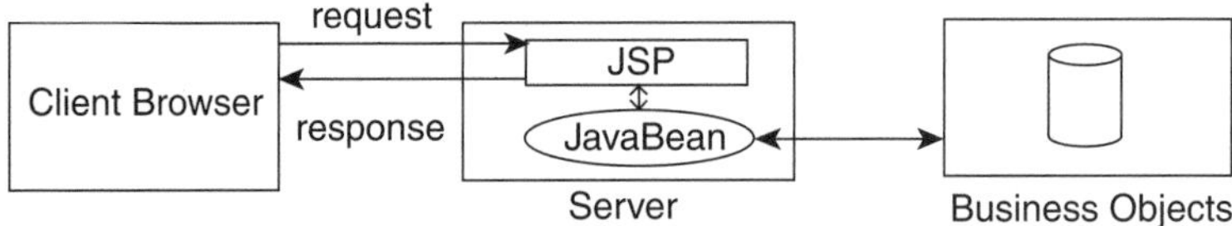

Figure 17.1 Model 1 architecture.

Example of Model 1 Architecture: A Login Application

The following example is a Login application that uses the Model 1 architecture. It consists of three JSP pages and a JavaBean. As the name implies, this application is for users to log in. The sequence of this series of JSP applications starts from the Login.jsp page that is given in Listing 17.1

Listing 17.1 **Login.jsp**

```
<%@ page session="false" %>
<HTML>
<HEAD>
<TITLE>Login</TITLE>
</HEAD>
<BODY>
<FORM METHOD="POST" ACTION="ProcessLogin.jsp">
<%
  if (request.getParameter("error")!=null) {
%>
Login failed. Please try again
<BR><HR>
<%
```

```
  }
%>
<TABLE>
<TR>
  <TD>User Name</TD>
  <TD><INPUT TYPE=TEXT NAME="userName"></TD>
</TR>
<TR>
  <TD>Password</TD>
  <TD><INPUT TYPE=PASSWORD NAME="password"></TD>
</TR>
<TR>
  <TD COLSPAN="2"><INPUT TYPE=SUBMIT VALUE="Login"></TD>
</TR>
</TABLE>
</FORM>
</BODY>
</HTML>
```

The Login.jsp page is nothing more than an HTML page with a form. The only code present is the scriplet after the <FORM> tag that checks to see if the request object contains a parameter called "error". If so, a message is displayed.

```
<%
  if (request.getParameter("error")!=null) {
%>
Login failed. Please try again
<BR><HR>
<%
  }
%>
```

The form in the Login page is submitted to the second JSP page—ProcessLogin.jsp, which is illustrated in Listing 17.2.

Listing 17.2 **ProcessLogin.jsp**

```
<%@ page session="false" %>
<jsp:useBean id="loginBean" scope="page" class="model1.LoginBean" />
<%
  if (loginBean.login(request.getParameter("userName"),
    request.getParameter("password")))
    request.getRequestDispatcher("Welcome.jsp").forward(request, response);
  else
    //we have to use sendRedirect because we want to send the ?error part
    //to the Login.jsp page.
    //with RequestDispatcher.forward(), the URL will still be
    //the current URL
    response.sendRedirect("Login.jsp?error=yes");
%>
```

This page employs a JavaBean called model1.LoginBean. The ProcessLogin.jsp page calls the login method of the bean, passing the userName parameter and the password parameter of the request object. The login method returns true if the user is an authorized user. It returns false otherwise.

In a successful login the ProcessLogin.jsp page displays the Welcome page.

```
if (loginBean.login(request.getParameter("userName"),
    request.getParameter("password")))
    request.getRequestDispatcher("Welcome.jsp").forward(request, response);
  .
  .
  .
```

Note that rather than using the sendRedirect method of the javax.servlet.http.HttpServletResponse interface, use a request dispatcher obtained from the getRequestDispatcher method of the request object. Then, the RequestDispatcher object's forward method transfers processing to the Welcome.jsp page. The forward method is faster than the sendRedirect method because there is no round trip to the client, such as with the sendRedirect method.

If the login failed, however, the user is sent back to the Login.jsp page.

```
response.sendRedirect("Login.jsp?error=yes");
```

In this example, the sendRedirect method of the javax.servlet.http.HttpServletResponse interface is used because we need to send the "error" parameter in the URL. Alternatively, the attribute in the request object can be used as shown in the example in the section "Model 2 Architecture," later in this chapter.

The Welcome.jsp page is given in Listing 17.3.

Listing 17.3 **Welcome.jsp**

```
<%@ page session="false" %>
<HTML>
<HEAD>
<TITLE>Welcome</TITLE>
</HEAD>
<BODY>
Welcome. You have successfully logged in.
</BODY>
</HTML>
```

The JavaBean used in the ProcessLogin.jsp page is given in Listing 17.4.

Listing 17.4 **LoginBean.java**

```
package model1;

public class LoginBean {
  public boolean login(String userName, String password) {
    if (userName==null || password==null ||
      !(userName.equals("aibo") && password.equals("kitada")))
      return false;
    else
      return true;
  }
}
```

In the login method in the JavaBean, a successful login occurs if the userName equals "aibo" and the password is the same as "kitada". The login method is purposely very simple. In a real-life application, these two values are normally matched against a database table.

To test the application, complete the following steps:

1. Use the myJSPApp application.
2. Copy all the .jsp pages in the myJSPApp directory under webapps.
3. Compile the LoginBean.java and copy the .class file into the WEB-INF/classes/model1/ directory.
4. Restart Tomcat and load the Login page using the following URL: `http://localhost:8080/myJSPApp/Login.jsp`.

This application is illustrated in Figures 17.2 to 17.4.

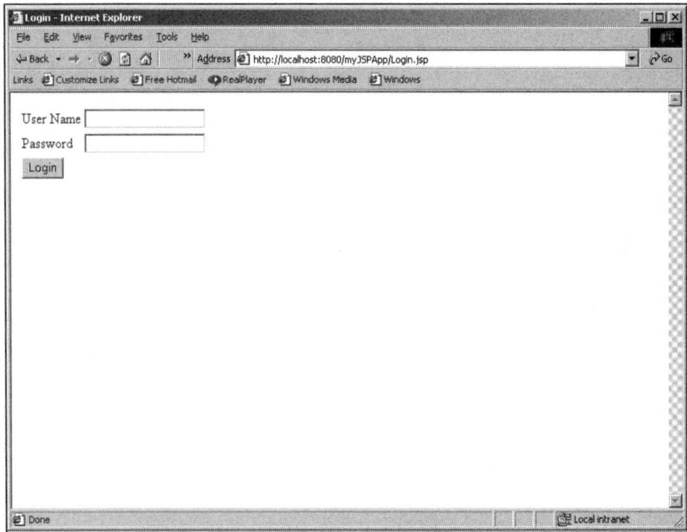

Figure 17.2 The Login page.

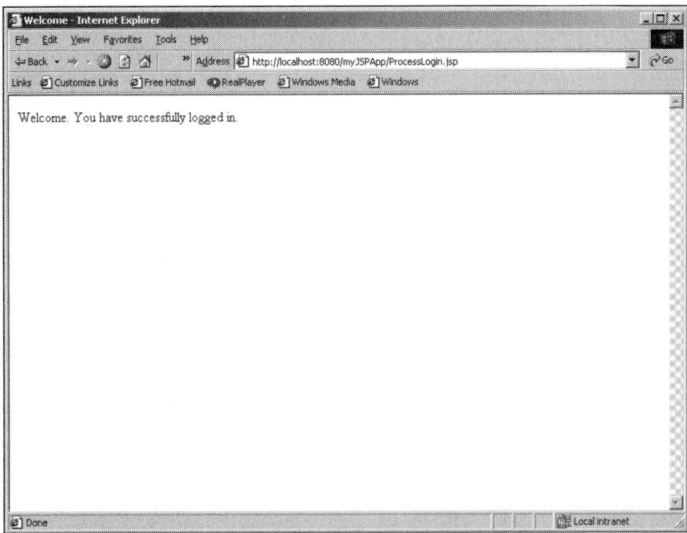

Figure 17.3 The Welcome page.

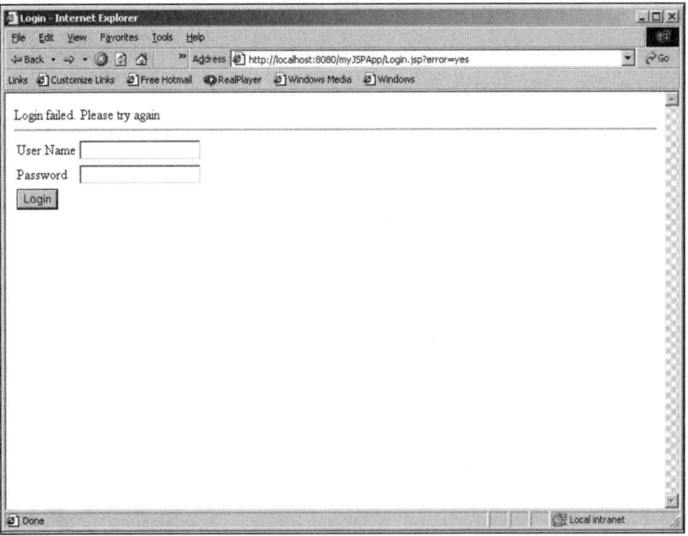

Figure 17.4 The Login page after a failed login.

The Advantages and Disadvantages of Model 1 Architecture

The advantage of this model is its ease of development. This architectural design, therefore, is suitable for small projects, or when you want to quickly finish something.

Two disadvantages of this model are as follows:

- It is hard to achieve division of labor between the page designer and the web developer because normally the web developer needs to be involved in the development of the page and the business objects.
- Model 1 architecture is hard to maintain and it is not flexible. This is especially true for large projects.

Due to the drawbacks of this architectural design, Model 2 architecture was introduced.

Model 2 Architecture

The Model 2 architecture is basically a Model-View-Controller (MVC) architecture that separates content generation and content presentation. A Model 2 architecture is indicated by the presence of a controller servlet between the client browser and the JSP pages (or the servlets that present the content). The controller servlet dispatches HTTP requests to the corresponding presentation JSP pages—based on the request URL, input parameters, and application state. In this model, presentation parts (JSP pages or servlets) are isolated from each other.

Model 2 applications are more flexible and easier to maintain, and to extend, because views do not reference each other directly. The Model 2 controller servlet provides a single point of control for security and logging, and often encapsulates incoming data into a form usable by the back-end MVC model.

> **Warning**
>
> Unless you are sure that your small application will remain small, always elect Model 2 as the architectural design of your application. It is true that Model 2 architecture adds some complexity to the application. However, an MVC application framework can greatly simplify the implementation of a Model 2 application.

Figure 17.5 depicts the Model 2 architecture.

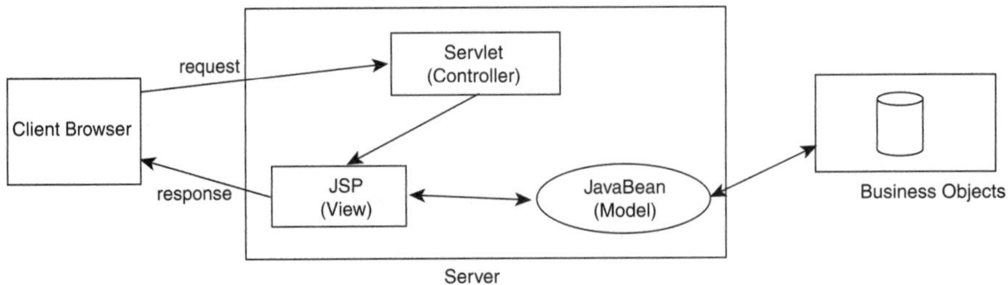

Figure 17.5 Model 2 architecture.

Example of Model 2 Application

To illustrate the use of Model 2 architecture, the following example is the rewrite of the previous Login application described in the section "Model 1 Architecture."

At the center is the controller servlet, which is the single entry point of the application. The servlet is named Model2Servlet and is given in Listing 17.5.

Listing 17.5 **The Model2Servlet**

```
import javax.servlet.*;

public class Model2Servlet extends GenericServlet {

  public void service(ServletRequest request, ServletResponse response)
    throws ServletException, java.io.IOException {

    String userName = request.getParameter("userName");
    String password = request.getParameter("password");

    if (userName==null) {
      RequestDispatcher rd = request.getRequestDispatcher("/Login.jsp");
      rd.forward(request, response);
    }
    else {
      if (password!=null && userName.equals("aibo")
        && password.equals("kitada")) {
        // login successful
        RequestDispatcher rd = request.getRequestDispatcher("/Welcome.jsp");
        rd.forward(request, response);
      }
      else {
        // login failed
```

```
            request.setAttribute("error", "yes");
            RequestDispatcher rd = request.getRequestDispatcher("/Login.jsp");
            rd.forward(request, response);
        }
      }
    }
  }
```

The application is very simple because there are only two JSP pages for presentation: the Login page and the Welcome page. The Login page is used for the user to log in, and the Welcome page is displayed after a successful login. Therefore, the servlet dispatches the request either to the Login page or to the Welcome page.

However, how does the servlet know what JSP page to dispatch to? The answer lies in the logic inside the service method of the servlet.

The service method checks for a parameter called userName in the ServletRequest object. Absence of this parameter results in the servlet dispatching the request to the Login page.

```
if (userName==null) {
  RequestDispatcher rd = request.getRequestDispatcher("/Login.jsp");
  rd.forward(request, response);
}
```

Therefore, the first time the user requests a page from the application, the Login page displays because there is no userName parameter in the request.

If the userName parameter is present, the controller servlet knows that the user is trying to log in. The servlet then checks to see if the username is "aibo" and the password is "kitada". If so, the servlet dispatches the request to the Welcome.jsp page.

```
if (password!=null && userName.equals("aibo") &&
  password.equals("kitada")) {
  // login successful
  RequestDispatcher rd = request.getRequestDispatcher("/Welcome.jsp");
  rd.forward(request, response);
}
```

Otherwise, it returns the user to the Login page after setting an attribute called error in the ServletRequest object. The presence of this attribute makes the Login.jsp page display an error message.

The Login.jsp and Welcome.jsp are given in Listings 17.6 and 17.7 respectively.

Listing 17.6 **Login Page**

```
<%@ page session="false" %>
<HTML>
<HEAD>
<TITLE>Login</TITLE>
</HEAD>
<BODY>
<FORM METHOD="POST">
<%
  if (request.getAttribute("error")!=null) {
%>
Login failed. Please try again
<BR><HR>
<%
  }
%>
<TABLE>
<TR>
  <TD>User Name</TD>
  <TD><INPUT TYPE=TEXT NAME="userName"></TD>
</TR>
<TR>
  <TD>Password</TD>
  <TD><INPUT TYPE=PASSWORD NAME="password"></TD>
</TR>
<TR>
  <TD COLSPAN="2"><INPUT TYPE=SUBMIT VALUE="Login"></TD>
</TR>
</TABLE>
</FORM>
</BODY>
</HTML>
```

Listing 17.7 **Welcome Page**

```
<%@ page session="false" %>
<HTML>
<HEAD>
<TITLE>Welcome</TITLE>
</HEAD>
<BODY>
Welcome. You have successfully logged in.
</BODY>
</HTML>
```

To test this application, complete the following steps:

1. Copy Login.jsp and Welcome.jsp to the myJSPApp directory.
2. Compile the servlet and copy the .class file into the WEB-INF/classes directory.
3. Restart Tomcat and type the following in the browser:

   ```
   http://localhost:8080/myJSPApp/servlet/Model2Servlet
   ```

Summary

This chapter briefly explains the two models of Java web application design: Model 1 and Model 2. Model 1 architecture provides rapid development for small projects, and is suitable for small projects that will remain small or for building prototypes. Model 2 is the recommended architecture for any medium-sized to large projects. Model 2 is harder to build, but it provides more maintainability and extensibility.

Chapter 18 presents an e-commerce application that is built based on Model 2 architectural design.

18

Developing E-Commerce Applications

In Chapter 17, "Architecting Java Web Applications," you learned that there are two design models you can adopt to build Java web applications with servlets and JSP. The first model, simply called Model 1, is a page-centric model in which an application consists of a series of JSP pages. In this model, a JSP page calls another JSP page. Developing applications based on this model is very easy; however, for complex applications, this model presents maintenance nightmares. Therefore, this model is suitable only for small applications that will never grow in complexity.

The second model, Model 2, is a Model-View-Controller (MVC) architecture that separates content generation and content presentation. A Model 2 architecture is indicated by the presence of a controller servlet between the client browser and the JSP pages or servlet content that presents the content. The controller servlet dispatches HTTP requests to the corresponding presentation JSP pages based on the request URL, input parameters, and application state. In this model, presentation parts (JSP pages or servlets) are isolated from each other.

Model 2 applications are more flexible and easier to maintain and extend because views do not reference each other directly. The Model 2 controller servlet provides a single point of control for security and logging, and often encapsulates incoming data into a form usable by the back-end MVC model.

Model 2 architecture is recommended for complex applications. Building an application using this model is not as simple as using Model 1; however, this model offers many advantages over the first model. In this chapter, you see how this model is used in an e-commerce application that implements an online store.

The project is called Burnaby (named after the city east of Vancouver, British Columbia), and it is an online store that sells foods in many different categories. Here you can find chocolate, biscuits, milk, cheese, and other things you normally might find in a superstore. The project's sole purpose is to demonstrate how Model 2 applications can be designed and developed. For brevity and clarity, little or no error handling has been included and no optimization is used. The graphic design also is kept simple. A Microsoft Access database accompanies this project and is ready to use if you happen to be using Windows. Otherwise, you can build your own database based on the database structure given in the section, "The Database Structure," with any favorite database server, as long as there is a JDBC driver for that database server.

Project Specification

If you have shopped online or browsed an electronic store such as Amazon.com, you will easily understand the specification for this project.

Loosely defined, the application you will be building is an online store users can visit and do the following things:

- Search for certain products based on product names or descriptions
- Browse the list of products by category
- View a product's details
- Place a product in the shopping cart
- View and edit the shopping cart
- Check out and place an order

The Database Structure

For simplicity, a Microsoft Access database is used as the example in this chapter. For deployment, however, you are encouraged to port it in a more scalable and powerful database. The Access database file is located in the \db directory under the application's WEB-INF directory. You use four tables for this project: Categories, Products, Orders, and OrderDetails. The structure of each table is given next.

The Categories Table

The Categories table is used to store product categories. It is a simple table whose design is given in Table 18.1.

Table 18.1 **The Structure of the Categories Table**

Column Name	Data Type
CategoryId	AutoNumber
Category	Text

The Products Table

The Products table is used to store the details of every product sold. Its structure is presented in Table 18.2. Note that the table uses a CategoryId column to categorize the products.

Table 18.2 **The Structure of the Products Table**

Column Name	Data Type
ProductId	AutoNumber
CategoryId	Number
Name	Text
Description	Text
Price	Number

The Orders Table

The Orders table holds order information, including the delivery address, the credit card details, and the contact name. A unique identifier is used for each order, which is used to link to all shopping items in the OrderDetails table.

The structure of the Orders table is given in Table 18.3.

Table 18.3 **The Structure of the Orders Table**

Column Name	Data Type
OrderId	Number
ContactName	Text
DeliveryAddress	Text
CCName	Text
CCNumber	Text
CCExpiryDate	Text

The OrderDetails Table

The OrderDetails table is used to store all shopping items for each order. Its structure is given in Table 18.4.

Table 18.4 **The Structure of the OrderDetails Table**

Column Name	Data Type
Id	AutoNumber
OrderId	Number
ProductId	Number
Quantity	Number
Price	Number

Page Design

For consistency in the look and feel of the application, every JSP page uses the same design. There is a header on top of each page and a menu on the left. Every page has the following structure:

```
<HTML>
<BODY>
<TABLE>
<TR>
  <!-- header -->
</TR>
<TR>
  <TD VALIGN="TOP">
    <!-- menu -->
  </TD>
  <TD VALIGN="TOP">
   <!-- page content-->
</TD>
</TR>
</TABLE>
</BODY>
</HTML>
```

Preparation

Before you start coding, you need to do these steps in preparation:

1. Copy the directory Burnaby and its content from the software/burnaby directory on the CD to %CATALINA_HOME%/webapps/. The directory structure of the application is shown in Figure 18.1.

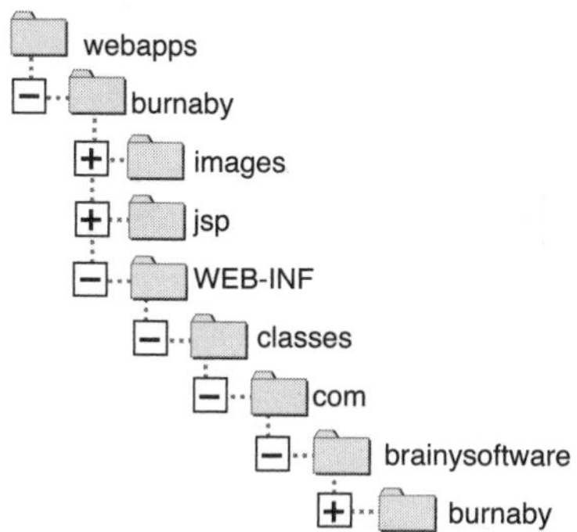

Figure 18.1 The application directory structure.

2. Create a DSN name called Burnaby for the Microsoft Access database. Or, if you are using a different database, make sure that the JDBC driver for the database can be found and loaded by the JVM.
3. Edit the server.xml file, which is the server configuration file located in the conf directory under %CATALINA_HOME%. Open the file with your text editor and look for something like the following:

```
<Context path="/examples" docBase="examples" debug="0"
                 reloadable="true">
 .
 .
 .
</Context>
```

Right after the closing tag </Context>, add this line:

```
<Context path="/burnaby" docBase="burnaby" debug="0" reloadable="true">
</Context>
```

Application Design

The application consists of a controller servlet that receives all the requests and forwards each request to one of the JSP pages. The architecture is shown in Figure 18.2.

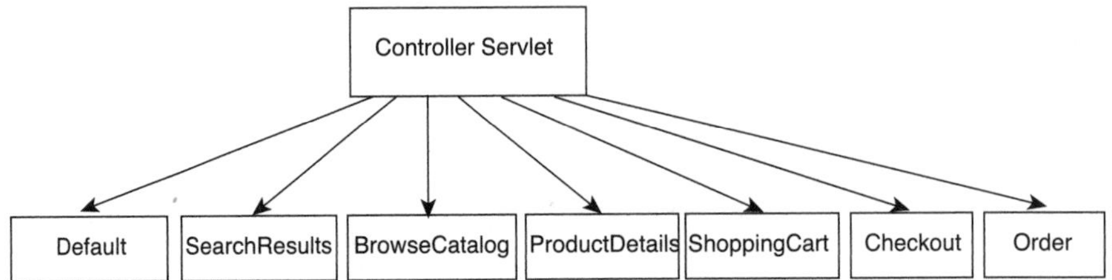

Figure 18.2 The application architecture.

Figures 18.3 to 18.8 show the user interface of the Burnaby project.

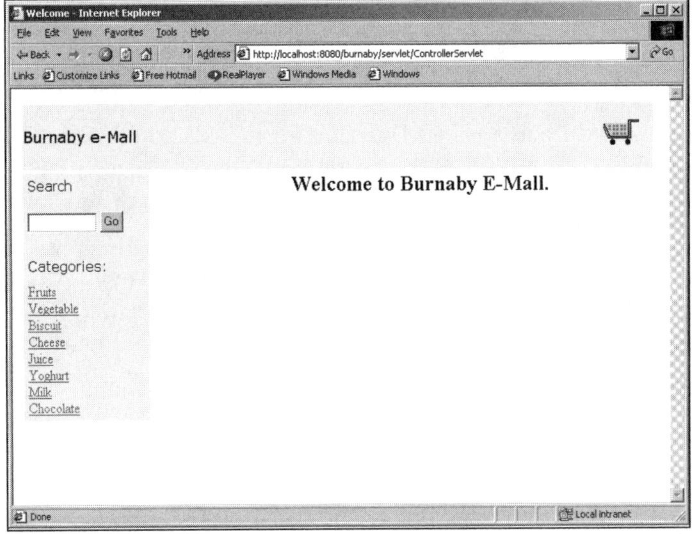

Figure 18.3 The Default page.

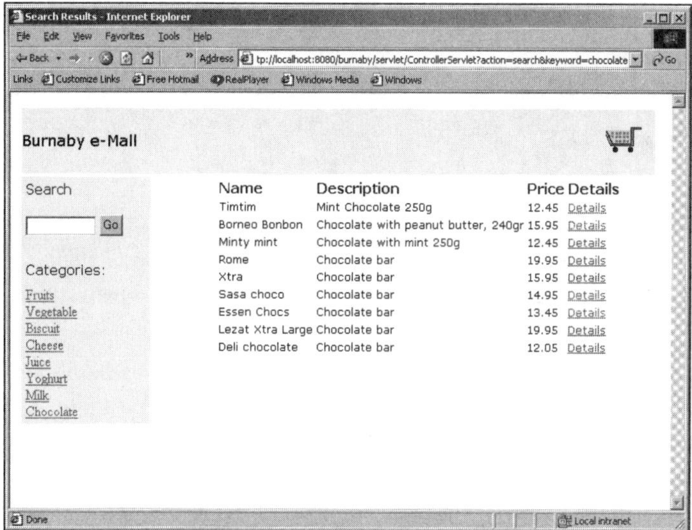

Figure 18.4 The SearchResults page.

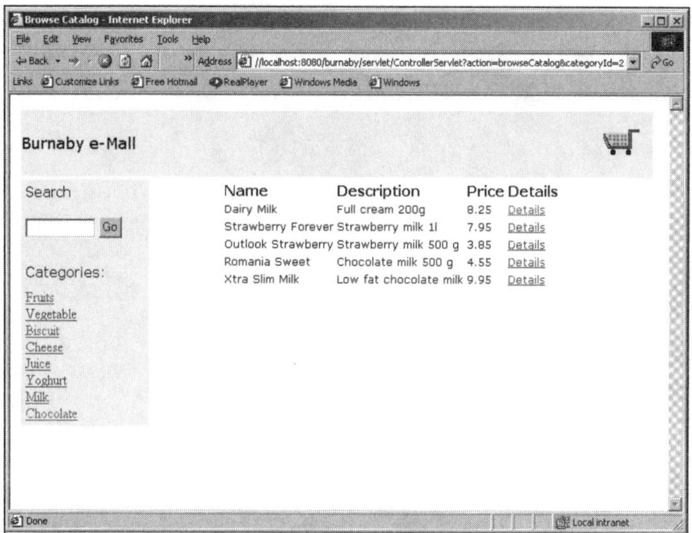

Figure 18.5 The BrowseCatalog page.

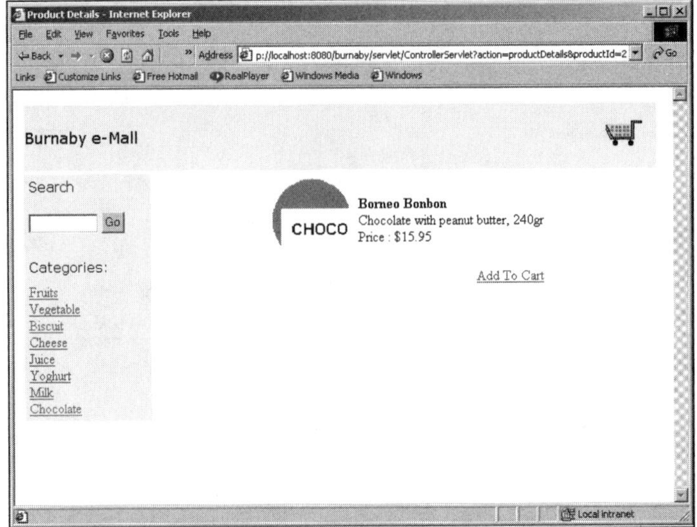

Figure 18.6 The ProductDetails page.

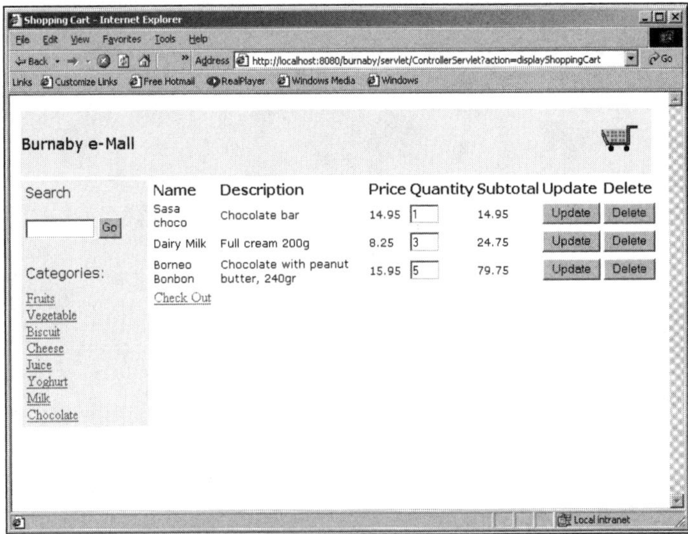

Figure 18.7 The Shopping Cart page.

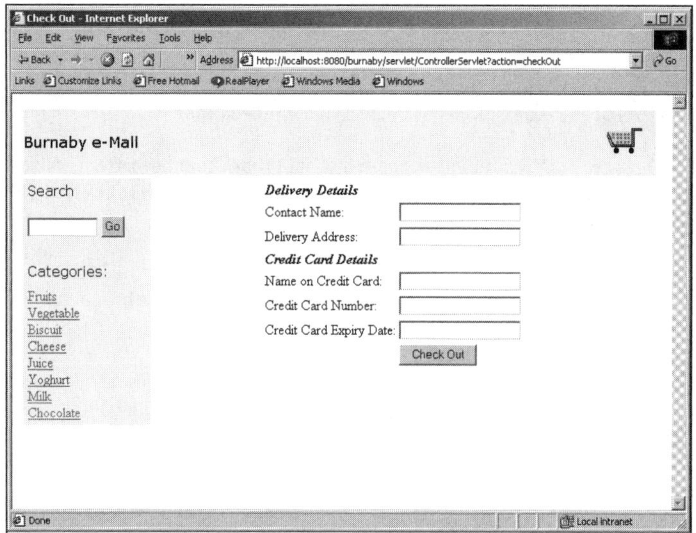

Figure 18.8 The Checkout page.

Building the Project

The following section discusses the files that make up the application, starting with the deployment descriptor and continuing with the controller servlet. The section then discusses each of the JSP pages and other classes in detail.

The Deployment Descriptor

One of the files included in the Burnaby directory is the deployment descriptor (web.xml). This file can be found in the WEB-INF directory. In this web.xml file, you specify several initial parameters that will become global variables in the servlet/JSP pages. These global variables are loaded into the ServletContext object when the servlet is initialized. The deployment descriptor is given in Listing 18.1.

Listing 18.1 **Web.xml File**

```
<?xml version="1.0" encoding="ISO-8859-1"?>
<!DOCTYPE web-app
  PUBLIC "-//Sun Microsystems, Inc.//DTD Web Application 2.3//EN"
  "http://java.sun.com/dtd/web-app_2_3.dtd">

<web-app>
  <!-- Define the controller servlet -->
```

continues

Listing 18.1 **Continued**

```
  <servlet>
    <servlet-name>ControllerServlet</servlet-name>
    <servlet-class>ControllerServlet</servlet-class>

    <!-- Define initial parameters that will be loaded into
       the ServletContext object in the controller servlet -->
    <init-param>
      <param-name>base</param-name>
      <param-value>
➥http://localhost:8080/burnaby/servlet/ControllerServlet</param-value>
    </init-param>
    <init-param>
      <param-name>jdbcDriver</param-name>
      <param-value>sun.jdbc.odbc.JdbcOdbcDriver</param-value>
    </init-param>
    <init-param>
      <param-name>imageUrl</param-name>
      <param-value>http://localhost:8080/burnaby/images/</param-value>
    </init-param>
    <init-param>
      <param-name>dbUrl</param-name>
      <param-value>jdbc:odbc:Burnaby</param-value>
    </init-param>
    <init-param>
      <param-name>dbUserName</param-name>
      <param-value></param-value>
    </init-param>
    <init-param>
      <param-name>dbPassword</param-name>
      <param-value></param-value>
    </init-param>
  </servlet>
</web-app>
```

The following list describes each initial parameter:

- **base**. The URL of the controller servlet that will be used in the HREF attribute of a hyperlink or the ACTION attribute of an HTML form in the JSP pages. For example, base will have the following value if you are using Tomcat on the local machine on port 8080:

  ```
  http://localhost:8080/burnaby/servlet/ControllerServlet
  ```

  When deploying the application, replace "localhost:8080" with your domain name.
- **jdbcDriver**. The JDBC driver used to access the database.
- **imageUrl**. The URL where images are located.

- **dbUrl.** The database URL used when opening a java.sql.Connection object.
- **dbUserName.** The username used when opening a java.sql.Connection object.
- **dbPassword.** The password used when opening a java.sql.Connection object.

The Controller Servlet

The controller servlet is contained in the ControllerServlet.java file in the burnaby/src directory and is given in Listing 18.2.

Listing 18.2 **ControllerServlet**

```
import java.sql.*;
import javax.servlet.*;
import javax.servlet.http.*;
import java.io.*;
import java.util.*;
import com.brainysoftware.burnaby.DbBean;

public class ControllerServlet extends HttpServlet {

  /**Initialize global variables*/
  public void init(ServletConfig config) throws ServletException {

    System.out.println("initializing controller servlet.");

    ServletContext context = config.getServletContext();
    context.setAttribute("base", config.getInitParameter("base"));
    context.setAttribute("imageUrl", config.getInitParameter("imageUrl"));

    // instantiating the DbBean
    DbBean dbBean = new DbBean();
    // initialize the DbBean's fields
    dbBean.setDbUrl(config.getInitParameter("dbUrl"));
    dbBean.setDbUserName(config.getInitParameter("dbUserName"));
    dbBean.setDbPassword(config.getInitParameter("dbPassword"));

    // put the bean in the servlet context
    // the bean will be accessed from JSP pages
    context.setAttribute("dbBean", dbBean);

    try {
      // loading the database JDBC driver
      Class.forName(config.getInitParameter("jdbcDriver"));
    }
```

continues

Listing 18.2 **Continued**

```
    catch (ClassNotFoundException e) {
      System.out.println(e.toString());
    }
    super.init(config);
  }


  /**Process the HTTP Get request*/
  public void doGet(HttpServletRequest request, HttpServletResponse
➥response) throws ServletException, IOException {
    doPost(request, response);
  }

  /**Process the HTTP Post request*/
  public void doPost(HttpServletRequest request, HttpServletResponse
➥response) throws ServletException, IOException {

    String base = "/jsp/";
    String url = base + "Default.jsp";
    String action = request.getParameter("action");

    if (action!=null) {
      if (action.equals("search"))
        url = base + "SearchResults.jsp";
      else if (action.equals("browseCatalog"))
        url = base + "BrowseCatalog.jsp";
      else if (action.equals("productDetails"))
        url = base + "ProductDetails.jsp";
      else if (action.equals("productDetails"))
        url = base + "ProductDetails.jsp";
      else if (action.equals("addShoppingItem") ||
        action.equals("updateShoppingItem") ||
        action.equals("deleteShoppingItem") ||
        action.equals("displayShoppingCart"))
        url = base + "ShoppingCart.jsp";
      else if (action.equals("checkOut"))
        url = base + "CheckOut.jsp";
      else if (action.equals("order"))
        url = base + "Order.jsp";
    }
    RequestDispatcher requestDispatcher =
➥getServletContext().getRequestDispatcher(url);
    requestDispatcher.forward(request, response);

  }
}
```

As you can see from Listing 18.2, the two important methods are init and doPost. The init method does the following things:

- Reads initial parameters from the deployment descriptor and initializes global variables for the whole application, as follows:

```
ServletContext context = config.getServletContext();
context.setAttribute("base", config.getInitParameter("base"));
context.setAttribute("imageUrl", config.getInitParameter("imageUrl"));
```

- Instantiates the DbBean JavaBean and puts it in the servlet context object:

```
// instantiating the DbBean
    DbBean dbBean = new DbBean();
    // initialize the DbBean's fields
    dbBean.setDbUrl(config.getInitParameter("dbUrl"));
    dbBean.setDbUserName(config.getInitParameter("dbUserName"));
    dbBean.setDbPassword(config.getInitParameter("dbPassword"));

    // put the bean in the servlet context
    // the bean will be accessed from JSP pages
    context.setAttribute("dbBean", dbBean);
```

  This bean can be accessed from the JSP pages using the following useBean tag.

```
<jsp:useBean id="dbBean" scope="application"
class="com.brainysoftware.burnaby.DbBean"/>
```

- Loads the JDBC driver for the database, as follows:

```
try {
      // loading the database JDBC driver
      Class.forName(config.getInitParameter("jdbcDriver"));
    }
    catch (ClassNotFoundException e) {
      System.out.println(e.toString());
    }
```

The doPost method controls the application by forwarding requests to corresponding JSP pages based on the value of the action parameter. Requests are forwarded to JSP pages using the forward method of the RequestDispatcher object, as follows:

```
RequestDispatcher requestDispatcher =
  getServletContext().getRequestDispatcher(url);
requestDispatcher.forward(request, response);
```

Supporting Classes

Two supporting classes are used for this project. The first one is the Product class that represents a product in the shopping application. The second one, the ShoppingItem class, represents a shopping item. Both classes are similar except that the Product class does not have a quantity field.

The Product class and the ShoppingItem class are given in Listings 18.3 and 18.4, respectively.

Listing 18.3 **Product.java**

```
package com.brainysoftware.burnaby;

public class Product {
  public int id;
  public String name;
  public String description;
  public double price;
}
```

Listing 18.4 **ShoppingItem.java**

```
package com.brainysoftware.burnaby;

public class ShoppingItem {
  public int productId;
  public String name;
  public String description;
  public double price;
  public int quantity;
}
```

Included Files

Every JSP page has the same design—the header and the menu on the left of the page. The header is represented by the Header.jsp file, and the menu by the Menu.jsp file. These files are given in Listings 18.5 and 18.6, respectively.

Listing 18.5 **Header.jsp**

```
<%
  String base = (String) application.getAttribute("base");
  String imageUrl = (String) application.getAttribute("imageUrl");
%>
```

```
<TABLE WIDTH="740" CELLPADDING="0"
  HEIGHT="75" CELLSPACING="0" BORDER="0">
<TR>
  <TD ALIGN="left" BGCOLOR="F6F6F6">
    <FONT FACE="Verdana" SIZE="4">Burnaby e-Mall</FONT>
  </TD>
  <TD ALIGN="RIGHT" BGCOLOR="F6F6F6">
    <A HREF="<%=base%>?action=displayShoppingCart"><IMG
      BORDER="0" SRC="<%=(imageUrl + "cart.gif")%>"></A>
       
  </TD>
</TR>
</TABLE>
```

The first four lines of the code obtain the base and imageUrl attributes from the ServletContext object, which in a JSP page is represented by the application implicit, as you see here:

```
<%
  String base = (String) application.getAttribute("base");
  String imageUrl = (String) application.getAttribute("imageUrl");
%>
```

The base and imageUrl variables are used to compose the link to the shopping cart, as follows:

```
<A HREF="<%=base%>?action=displayShoppingCart"><IMG
  BORDER="0" SRC="<%=(imageUrl + "cart.gif")%>"></A>
```

Listing 18.6 **Menu.jsp**

```
<%@ page import="java.util.*" %>
<jsp:useBean id="dbBean" scope="application"
➥class="com.brainysoftware.burnaby.DbBean"/>
<%
  String base = (String) application.getAttribute("base");
%>
<TABLE CELLSPACING="0" CELLPADDING="5" WIDTH="150" BORDER="0">
<TR>
  <TD BGCOLOR="F6F6F6">
    <FONT FACE="Verdana">Search</FONT>
    <FORM>
    <INPUT TYPE="HIDDEN" NAME="action" VALUE="search">
    <INPUT TYPE="TEXT" NAME="keyword" SIZE="10">
    <INPUT type="SUBMIT" VALUE="Go">
    </FORM>
  </TD>
</TR>
<TR>
  <TD BGCOLOR="F6F6F6"><FONT FACE="Verdana">Categories:</FONT></TD>
```

continues

Listing 18.6 **Continued**

```
</TR>
<TR VALIGN="TOP">
  <TD BGCOLOR="F6F6F6">
<%
  Hashtable categories = dbBean.getCategories();
  Enumeration categoryIds = categories.keys();
  while (categoryIds.hasMoreElements()) {
    Object categoryId = categoryIds.nextElement();
    out.println("<A HREF=" + base + "?action=browseCatalog&categoryId=" +
      categoryId.toString() + ">" +
      categories.get(categoryId) +
      "</A><BR>");
  }
%>
  </TD>
</TR>
</TABLE>
```

The Menu.jsp page includes a form that allows the user to search for certain products. The form also retrieves all records from the Categories table and displays them as clickable links to the BrowseCatalog page. Retrieving the categories is done through a bean whose class is com.brainysoftware.burnaby.DbBean. This bean has an application scope shown here:

```
<jsp:useBean id="dbBean" scope="application"
  class="com.brainysoftware.burnaby.DbBean"/>
```

The Default Page

The main page of this application is the Default.jsp page. Any request that does not carry an action parameter or any request whose "action" parameter's value is invalid will be forwarded to this page. This page simply displays a welcome message that is given in Listing 18.7.

Listing 18.7 **Default.jsp**

```
<HTML>
<HEAD>
<TITLE>Welcome</TITLE>
</HEAD>
<BODY>
<TABLE>
<TR>
  <TD COLSPAN=2><jsp:include page="Header.jsp" flush="true"/></TD>
```

```
</TR>
<TR>
  <TD><jsp:include page="Menu.jsp" flush="true"/></TD>
  <TD VALIGN="TOP">

    <H2>Welcome to Burnaby E-Mall.</H2>

  </TD>
</TR>
</TABLE>
</BODY>
</HTML>
```

The SearchResults Page

The Menu.jsp page contains a search form and a number of hyperlinks to enable catalog browsing. When submitted, the search form will be forwarded to the SearchResults.jsp page, presented in Listing 18.8.

Listing 18.8 **SearchResults.jsp**

```
<%@ page import="com.brainysoftware.burnaby.Product" %>
<%@ page import="java.sql.*" %>
<%@ page import="java.util.*" %>
<jsp:useBean id="dbBean" scope="application"
  class="com.brainysoftware.burnaby.DbBean"/>
<%
  String base = (String) application.getAttribute("base");
%>
  <HTML>
<HEAD>
<TITLE>Search Results</TITLE>
</HEAD>
<BODY>
<TABLE>
<TR>
  <TD COLSPAN=2><jsp:include page="Header.jsp" flush="true"/></TD>
</TR>
<TR>
  <TD><jsp:include page="Menu.jsp" flush="true"/></TD>
  <TD VALIGN="TOP">
<%
  String keyword = request.getParameter("keyword");
  if (keyword!=null && !keyword.trim().equals("")) {
%>
    <TABLE>
    <TR>
      <TD><FONT FACE="Verdana" SIZE="3"><B>Name</B></FONT></TD>
```

continues

Listing 18.8 **Continued**

```
        <TD><FONT FACE="Verdana" SIZE="3"><B>Description</B></FONT></TD>
        <TD><FONT FACE="Verdana" SIZE="3"><B>Price</B></FONT></TD>
        <TD><FONT FACE="Verdana" SIZE="3"><B>Details</B></FONT></TD>
      </TR>
<%
      ArrayList products = dbBean.getSearchResults(keyword);
      Iterator iterator = products.iterator();
      while (iterator.hasNext()) {
        Product product = (Product) iterator.next();
%>
      <TR>
        <TD><FONT FACE="Verdana" SIZE="2"><%=product.name%></FONT></TD>
        <TD><FONT FACE="Verdana" SIZE="2"><%=product.description%></FONT></TD>
        <TD><FONT FACE="Verdana" SIZE="2"><%=product.price%></FONT></TD>
        <TD><A
HREF="<%=base%>?action=productDetails&productId=<%=product.id%>">
          <FONT FACE="Verdana" SIZE="2">Details</FONT></A></TD>
      </TR>
<%
      }
    }
    else
      out.println("Please enter a search keyword.");


%>
    </TD>
  </TR>
  </TABLE>
  </BODY>
  </HTML>
```

Note that the search keyword is contained in the "keyword" parameter.

The BrowseCatalog Page

When the user clicks one of the category hyperlinks on the menu, all products in that category are displayed by the BrowseCatalog.jsp page. This JSP page is similar to the SearchResults.jsp page, except that it accepts a "categoryId" parameter instead of "keyword."

The BrowseCatalog.jsp page is given in Listing 18.9.

Listing 18.9 **BrowseCatalog.jsp**

```
<%@ page import="com.brainysoftware.burnaby.Product" %>
<%@ page import="java.sql.*" %>
<%@ page import="java.util.*" %>
<jsp:useBean id="dbBean" scope="application"
```

```
➥class="com.brainysoftware.burnaby.DbBean"/>
<%
  String base = (String) application.getAttribute("base");
%>
<HTML>
<HEAD>
<TITLE>Browse Catalog</TITLE>
</HEAD>
<BODY>
<TABLE>
<TR>
  <TD COLSPAN=2><jsp:include page="Header.jsp" flush="true"/></TD>
</TR>
<TR>
  <TD><jsp:include page="Menu.jsp" flush="true"/></TD>
  <TD VALIGN="TOP">
<%
  String categoryId = request.getParameter("categoryId");
  if (categoryId!=null && !categoryId.trim().equals("")) {
%>
    <TABLE>
    <TR>
      <TD><FONT FACE="Verdana" SIZE="3"><B>Name</B></FONT></TD>
      <TD><FONT FACE="Verdana" SIZE="3"><B>Description</B></FONT></TD>
      <TD><FONT FACE="Verdana" SIZE="3"><B>Price</B></FONT></TD>
      <TD><FONT FACE="Verdana" SIZE="3"><B>Details</B></FONT></TD>
    </TR>
<%
    ArrayList products = dbBean.getProductsInCategory(categoryId);
    Iterator iterator = products.iterator();
    while (iterator.hasNext()) {
      Product product = (Product) iterator.next();
%>
    <TR>
      <TD><FONT FACE="Verdana" SIZE="2"><%=product.name%></FONT></TD>
      <TD><FONT FACE="Verdana" SIZE="2"><%=product.description%></FONT></TD>
      <TD><FONT FACE="Verdana" SIZE="2"><%=product.price%></FONT></TD>
      <TD><A
HREF="<%=base%>?action=productDetails&productId=<%=product.id%>">
        <FONT FACE="Verdana" SIZE="2">Details</FONT></A></TD>
    </TR>
<%
    }
  }
  else
    out.println("Invalid category.");
%>
  </TD>
</TR>
</TABLE>
</BODY>
</HTML>
```

The ProductDetails Page

From the SearchResults page or the BrowseCatalog page, the user can click the Details hyperlink to display a product's details. A product's details are processed by the ProductDetails.jsp page, and from this page, the user can click the Add to Cart link to add the product to the shopping cart. The ProductDetails.jsp page is given in Listing 18.10.

Listing 18.10 **ProductDetails.jsp**

```
<%@ page import="com.brainysoftware.burnaby.Product" %>
<%@ page import="java.sql.*" %>
<%@ page import="java.util.*" %>
<jsp:useBean id="dbBean" scope="application"
class="com.brainysoftware.burnaby.DbBean"/>
<%
  String base = (String) application.getAttribute("base");
  String imageUrl = (String) application.getAttribute("imageUrl");
%>
<HTML>
<HEAD>
<TITLE>Product Details</TITLE>
</HEAD>
<BODY>
<TABLE>
<TR>
  <TD COLSPAN=2><jsp:include page="Header.jsp" flush="true"/></TD>
</TR>
<TR>
  <TD><jsp:include page="Menu.jsp" flush="true"/></TD>
  <TD VALIGN="TOP">
<%
  try {
    int productId = Integer.parseInt(request.getParameter("productId"));
    Product product = dbBean.getProductDetails(productId);
    if (product!=null) {
%>
<TABLE>
<TR>
  <TD><IMG BORDER="0" WIDTH="100" SRC="<%=(imageUrl +
➥product.id)%>.gif"></TD>
  <TD><B><%=product.name%></B><BR>
      <%=product.description%><BR>
      Price : $<%=product.price%></TD>
</TR>
<TR>
  <TD COLSPAN="2" ALIGN="RIGHT">
    <A HREF="<%=base%>?action=addShoppingItem&productId=<%=product.id%>">
      Add To Cart</A>
  </TD>
```

```
</TR>
</TABLE>
<%
    }
  }
  catch (Exception e) {
    out.println("Error: Invalid product identifier.");
  }
%>
  </TD>
</TR>
</TABLE>
</BODY>
</HTML>
```

The ShoppingCart.jsp Page

The shopping cart in this application is session based. Each shopping item is represented by the ShoppingItem class and stored in a Hashtable object called shoppingCart. This Hashtable object is stored in the Session object of each particular user.

The ShoppingCart.jsp is given in Listing 18.11.

Listing 18.11 **ShoppingCart.jsp**

```
<%@ page import="com.brainysoftware.burnaby.Product" %>
<%@ page import="com.brainysoftware.burnaby.ShoppingItem" %>
<%@ page import="java.sql.*" %>
<%@ page import="java.util.*" %>
<jsp:useBean id="dbBean" scope="application"
➥class="com.brainysoftware.burnaby.DbBean"/>
<%
  String base = (String) application.getAttribute("base");
  Hashtable shoppingCart = (Hashtable) session.getAttribute("shoppingCart");
  if (shoppingCart==null)
    shoppingCart = new Hashtable(10);

  String action = request.getParameter("action");
  if (action!=null && action.equals("addShoppingItem")) {
    try {
      int productId = Integer.parseInt(request.getParameter("productId"));
      Product product = dbBean.getProductDetails(productId);
      if (product!=null) {
        ShoppingItem item = new ShoppingItem();
        item.productId = productId;
        item.quantity = 1;
        item.price = product.price;
```

continues

Listing 18.11 **Continued**

```
        item.name = product.name;
        item.description = product.description;

        shoppingCart.remove(Integer.toString(productId));
        shoppingCart.put(Integer.toString(productId), item);
        session.setAttribute("shoppingCart", shoppingCart);
      }
    }
    catch (Exception e) {
      out.println("Error adding the selected product to the shopping cart");
    }
  }

  if (action!=null && action.equals("updateShoppingItem")) {
    try {
      int productId = Integer.parseInt(request.getParameter("productId"));
      int quantity = Integer.parseInt(request.getParameter("quantity"));
      ShoppingItem item = (ShoppingItem)
➥shoppingCart.get(Integer.toString(productId));
      if (item!=null) {
        item.quantity = quantity;
      }
    }
    catch (Exception e) {
      out.println("Error updating shopping cart");
    }
  }

  if (action!=null && action.equals("deleteShoppingItem")) {
    try {
      int productId = Integer.parseInt(request.getParameter("productId"));
      shoppingCart.remove(Integer.toString(productId));
    }
    catch (Exception e) {
      out.println("Error deleting the selected item from the shopping cart");
    }
  }

%>
<HTML>
<HEAD>
<TITLE>Shopping Cart</TITLE>
</HEAD>
<BODY>
<TABLE>
<TR>
  <TD COLSPAN=2><jsp:include page="Header.jsp" flush="true"/></TD>
</TR>
<TR>
  <TD><jsp:include page="Menu.jsp" flush="true"/></TD>
```

```
  <TD VALIGN="TOP">
<%
%>
    <TABLE>
    <TR>
      <TD><FONT FACE="Verdana" SIZE="3"><B>Name</B></FONT></TD>
      <TD><FONT FACE="Verdana" SIZE="3"><B>Description</B></FONT></TD>
      <TD><FONT FACE="Verdana" SIZE="3"><B>Price</B></FONT></TD>
      <TD><FONT FACE="Verdana" SIZE="3"><B>Quantity</B></FONT></TD>
      <TD><FONT FACE="Verdana" SIZE="3"><B>Subtotal</B></FONT></TD>
      <TD><FONT FACE="Verdana" SIZE="3"><B>Update</B></FONT></TD>
      <TD><FONT FACE="Verdana" SIZE="3"><B>Delete</B></FONT></TD>
    </TR>
<%

    Enumeration enum = shoppingCart.elements();
    while (enum.hasMoreElements()) {
      ShoppingItem item = (ShoppingItem) enum.nextElement();
%>
    <TR>
      <TD><FONT FACE="Verdana" SIZE="2"><%=item.name%></FONT></TD>
      <TD><FONT FACE="Verdana" SIZE="2"><%=item.description%></FONT></TD>
      <TD><FONT FACE="Verdana" SIZE="2"><%=item.price%></FONT></TD>
      <FORM>
      <INPUT TYPE="HIDDEN" NAME="action" VALUE="updateShoppingItem">
      <INPUT TYPE="HIDDEN" NAME="productId" VALUE="<%=item.productId%>">
      <TD><INPUT TYPE="TEXT" Size="2" NAME="quantity"
➥VALUE="<%=item.quantity%>"></TD>
      <TD><FONT FACE="Verdana"
➥SIZE="2"><%=item.quantity*item.price%></FONT></TD>
      <TD><INPUT TYPE="SUBMIT" VALUE="Update"></TD>
      </FORM>
      <FORM>
      <INPUT TYPE="HIDDEN" NAME="action" VALUE="deleteShoppingItem">
      <INPUT TYPE="HIDDEN" NAME="productId" VALUE="<%=item.productId%>">
      <TD><INPUT TYPE="SUBMIT" VALUE="Delete"></TD>
      </FORM>
    </TR>
<%
    }
%>
    <TR>
      <TD COLSPAN="7"><A HREF="<%=base%>?action=checkOut">Check Out</A></TD>
    </TR>
    </TABLE>
  </TD>
</TR>
</TABLE>
</BODY>
</HTML>
```

The CheckOut Page

When users are finished shopping, they need to check out. This is done by confirming the purchase and filling in an HTML form in the CheckOut.jsp page. The Checkout page is given in Listing 18.12 and is basically a very simple HTML form on which users fill in the delivery and credit card details.

Listing 18.12 **CheckOut.jsp**

```
<%
  String base = (String) application.getAttribute("base");
%>
<HTML>
<HEAD>
<TITLE>Check Out</TITLE>
</HEAD>
<BODY>
<TABLE>
<TR>
  <TD COLSPAN=2><jsp:include page="Header.jsp" flush="true"/></TD>
</TR>
<TR>
  <TD><jsp:include page="Menu.jsp" flush="true"/></TD>
  <TD VALIGN="TOP">
    <FORM>
    <INPUT TYPE="HIDDEN" NAME="action" VALUE="order">
    <TABLE>
    <TR>
      <TD COLSPAN="2"><I><B>Delivery Details</B></I></TD>
    </TR>
    <TR>
      <TD>Contact Name:</TD>
      <TD><INPUT TYPE="TEXT" NAME="contactName"></TD>
    </TR>
    <TR>
      <TD>Delivery Address:</TD>
      <TD><INPUT TYPE="TEXT" NAME="deliveryAddress"</TD>
    </TR>
    <TR>
      <TD COLSPAN="2"><I><B>Credit Card Details</B></I></TD>
    </TR>
    <TR>
      <TD>Name on Credit Card:</TD>
      <TD><INPUT TYPE="TEXT" NAME="ccName"</TD>
    </TR>
    <TR>
      <TD>Credit Card Number:</TD>
      <TD><INPUT TYPE="TEXT" NAME="ccNumber"></TD>
    </TR>
    <TR>
```

```
    <TD>Credit Card Expiry Date:</TD>
    <TD><INPUT TYPE="TEXT" NAME="ccExpiryDate"</TD>
  </TR>
  <TR>
    <TD> </TD>
    <TD><INPUT TYPE="SUBMIT" VALUE="Check Out"></TD>
  </TR>
  </TABLE>
  </FORM>
 </TD>
</TR>
</TABLE>
</BODY>
</HTML>
```

The Order Page

When the user submits the form on the CheckOut page, the request will go to the Order page. This page inserts a record into the Orders table and inserts each shopping item into the OrderDetails table. The Order.jsp page is presented in Listing 18.3.

Listing 18.13 **Order.jsp**

```
<%@ page import="com.brainysoftware.burnaby.Product" %>
<%@ page import="java.sql.*" %>
<%@ page import="java.util.*" %>
<jsp:useBean id="dbBean" scope="application"
class="com.brainysoftware.burnaby.DbBean"/>
<HTML>
<HEAD>
<TITLE>Order</TITLE>
</HEAD>
<BODY>
<TABLE>
<TR>
  <TD COLSPAN=2><jsp:include page="Header.jsp" flush="true"/></TD>
</TR>
<TR>
  <TD><jsp:include page="Menu.jsp" flush="true"/></TD>
  <TD VALIGN="TOP">
<%
  if (dbBean.insertOrder(request.getParameter("contactName"),
    request.getParameter("deliveryAddress"),
    request.getParameter("ccName"),
    request.getParameter("ccNumber"),
    request.getParameter("ccExpiryDate"),
    (Hashtable) session.getAttribute("shoppingCart"))) {
```

continues

Listing 18.13 **Continued**

```
    session.invalidate();
    out.println("Thank you for your purchase");
  }
  else
    out.println("Error");
%>
  </TD>
</TR>
</TABLE>
</BODY>
</HTML>
```

The DbBean JavaBean

All the JSP pages are kept as presentation pages wherever possible and use a JavaBean called DbBean. This bean is given in Listing 18.14 and contains all the methods used by the JSP pages.

Listing 18.14 **DbBean.java**

```
package com.brainysoftware.burnaby;

import java.util.Hashtable;
import java.util.ArrayList;
import java.util.Enumeration;
import java.sql.*;

public class DbBean {
  public String dbUrl = "";
  public String dbUserName = "";
  public String dbPassword = "";

  public void setDbUrl(String url) {
    dbUrl = url;
  }
  public void setDbUserName(String userName) {
    dbUserName = userName;
  }
  public void setDbPassword(String password) {
    dbPassword = password;
  }

  public Hashtable getCategories() {
    Hashtable categories = new Hashtable();
    try {
      Connection connection = DriverManager.getConnection(dbUrl,
```

```
➥dbUserName, dbPassword);
      Statement s = connection.createStatement();
      String sql = "SELECT CategoryId, Category FROM Categories" +
        " ";
      ResultSet rs = s.executeQuery(sql);
      while (rs.next()) {
        categories.put(rs.getString(1), rs.getString(2) );
      }
      rs.close();
      s.close();
      connection.close();
    }
    catch (SQLException e) {}
    return categories;
  }

  public ArrayList getSearchResults(String keyword) {
    ArrayList products = new ArrayList();
    try {
      Connection connection = DriverManager.getConnection(dbUrl, dbUserName,
➥dbPassword);
      Statement s = connection.createStatement();
      String sql = "SELECT ProductId, Name, Description,
➥Price FROM Products" +
        " WHERE Name LIKE '%" + keyword.trim() + "%'" +
        " OR Description LIKE '%" + keyword.trim() + "%'";
      ResultSet rs = s.executeQuery(sql);
      while (rs.next()) {
        Product product = new Product();
        product.id = rs.getInt(1);
        product.name = rs.getString(2);
        product.description = rs.getString(3);
        product.price = rs.getDouble(4);
        products.add(product);
      }
      rs.close();
      s.close();
      connection.close();
    }
    catch (SQLException e) {}
    return products;
  }

  public ArrayList getProductsInCategory(String categoryId) {
    ArrayList products = new ArrayList();
    try {
      Connection connection = DriverManager.getConnection(dbUrl,
➥dbUserName, dbPassword);
      Statement s = connection.createStatement();
      String sql = "SELECT ProductId, Name, Description,
➥Price FROM Products" +
```

continues

Listing 18.14 **Continued**

```
        " WHERE CategoryId=" + categoryId;
      ResultSet rs = s.executeQuery(sql);
      while (rs.next()) {
        Product product = new Product();
        product.id = rs.getInt(1);
        product.name = rs.getString(2);
        product.description = rs.getString(3);
        product.price = rs.getDouble(4);
        products.add(product);
      }
      rs.close();
      s.close();
      connection.close();
    }
    catch (SQLException e) {}
    return products;
  }

  public Product getProductDetails(int productId) {
    Product product = null;
    try {
      Connection connection = DriverManager.getConnection(dbUrl,
➥dbUserName, dbPassword);
      Statement s = connection.createStatement();
      String sql = "SELECT ProductId, Name, Description,
➥Price FROM Products" +
        " WHERE ProductId=" + Integer.toString(productId);
      ResultSet rs = s.executeQuery(sql);
      if (rs.next()) {
        product = new Product();
        product.id = rs.getInt(1);
        product.name = rs.getString(2);
        product.description = rs.getString(3);
        product.price = rs.getDouble(4);
      }
      rs.close();
      s.close();
      connection.close();
    }
    catch (SQLException e) {}
    return product;
  }

  public boolean insertOrder(String contactName, String deliveryAddress,
    String ccName, String ccNumber, String ccExpiryDate,
➥Hashtable shoppingCart) {
    boolean returnValue = false;
    long orderId = System.currentTimeMillis();
    Connection connection = null;
```

```
    try {
      connection = DriverManager.getConnection(dbUrl, dbUserName,
➥dbPassword);
      connection.setAutoCommit(false);
      Statement s = connection.createStatement();
      String sql = "INSERT INTO Orders" +
        " (OrderId, ContactName, DeliveryAddress,
➥CCName, CCNumber, CCExpiryDate)" +
        " VALUES" +
        " (" + orderId + ",'" + contactName + "','" + deliveryAddress + "'," +
        "'" + ccName + "','" + ccNumber + "','" + ccExpiryDate + "')";
      s.executeUpdate(sql);
      // now insert items into OrderDetails table
      Enumeration enum = shoppingCart.elements();
      while (enum.hasMoreElements()) {
        ShoppingItem item = (ShoppingItem) enum.nextElement();
        sql = "INSERT INTO OrderDetails (OrderId, ProductId,
➥Quantity, Price)" +
        " VALUES (" + orderId + "," + item.productId + "," +
        item.quantity + "," + item.price + ")";
        s.executeUpdate(sql);
      }

      s.close();
      connection.commit();
      connection.close();
      returnValue = true;
    }
    catch (SQLException e) {
      try {
        connection.rollback();
        connection.close();
      }
      catch (SQLException se) {}
    }
    return returnValue;
  }
}
```

Summary

In this chapter, you saw the development process of the Burnaby project, which is an online store. Its sole purpose was to demonstrate how Model 2 applications can be designed and developed.

In the next chapter, "XML-Based E-Books," you take a look at another web project.

19 XML-Based E-Books

BECAUSE THE INTERNET IS GETTING MORE POPULAR every day, more content is available online. Some content is simple HTML, but some is structured to resemble books. The latter includes online manuals, electronic books, and more.

An electronic book, also called an *e-book*, is not much different from a printed book in that it has a table of contents and a number of chapters. Because an electronic book is online, however, the publisher can take advantage of many features that are not available in printed books. For example, you can make an electronic book easy to navigate by displaying the table of contents all the time. When readers want to change chapters, they can do it straight away by clicking the link to that chapter.

The format you choose for an electronic book is an important decision. The most popular format makes the electronic content viewable in a web browser window. In this type of project, the table of contents is displayed in an HTML frame on the left, as shown in Figure 19.1. The frame on the right displays in HTML format the content of the selected chapter or chapter heading.

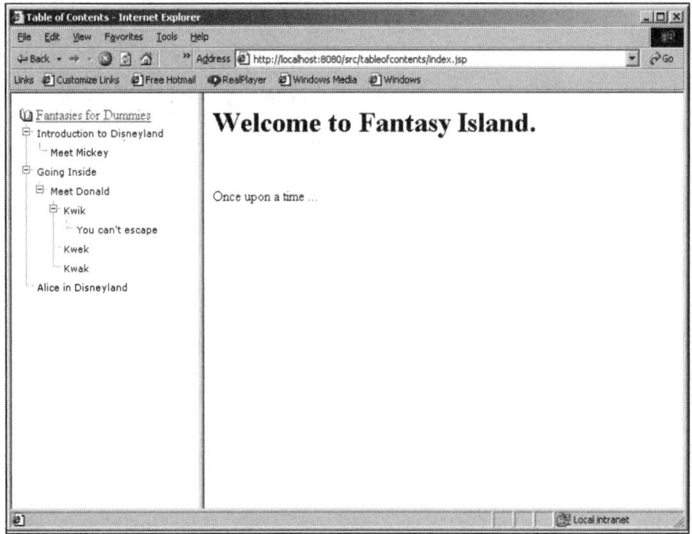

Figure 19.1 The visual representation of the book structure.

Compared to a paper book, an e-book gives you advantages beyond being easier to navigate. First, you can make your e-book available to an unlimited number of people by putting it on the Internet. Second, you can update your electronic book at almost any time. No printing cost is incurred when you issue the next edition of your book. The main disadvantage is that your readers need an Internet connection every time they want to read the book. Because access to the Internet is becoming more commonplace, however, this disadvantage is arguable. Also debatable is whether it is more convenient to read a non-electronic book.

This chapter discusses the many aspects of publishing an electronic book. Of utmost importance is the table of contents, which gets the first priority in this discussion. Then you see how to implement an easy-to-navigate browser-independent electronic book. The two parts to this project are the client side and the server side. Finally, you explore a project implemented using JavaServer pages. The same project can be implemented using any Internet technology, however, after you understand the concept.

The Table of Contents

The first issue in the electronic book system is to decide how you are going to store the book's table of contents; that is, the structure of chapters and headings. A book can have any number of chapters, and each chapter can have any number of headings. These headings, in turn, can have subheadings with sub-subheadings, and so on. In other words, a book's table of content, can be viewed as a tree of chapters/headings. It is hierarchical.

Having said that, you need a format in which you can easily work with hierarchical data. XML is probably the first and best choice available today. XML is widely accepted, and editing is easy because XML is essentially plain text. By storing your book structure in an XML document, you need only to edit the XML document when the book structure changes.

For example, the table of contents of the online book shown in Figure 19.1 is given in Listing 19.1.

Listing 19.1 **A Book's Table of Contents in XML**

```
<?xml version="1.0" encoding="ISO-8859-1"?>
<book title="Fantasies for Dummies" url="bookTitle.html">
  <chapter title="Introduction to Disneyland" url="ch1.html">
    <heading1 title="Meet Mickey" url="mickey.html">
    </heading1>
  </chapter>
  <chapter title="Going Inside" url="ch2.html">
    <heading1 title="Meet Donald" url="donald.html">
      <heading2 title="Kwik" url="kwik.html">
        <heading3 title="You can't escape" url="noEscape.html" />
      </heading2>
      <heading2 title="Kwek" url="kwek.html">
      </heading2>
      <heading2 title="Kwak" url="kwak.html" />
    </heading1>
  </chapter>
  <chapter title="Alice in Disneyland" url="Ch3.html" />
</book>
```

As you can see, the table of contents has the <book> tag as the root. Because of the difficulty in naming the multiple elements, this example calls the section under chapters "heading." Therefore, instead of subchapter, you call it heading1. Instead of sub-subchapter, you have heading2. A heading2 can have a subheading called heading3, heading3 can have a subheading called heading4, and so on.

Translating XML into the Object Tree

Having a very structured book content in an XML format is one thing; making it viewable by your reader is another. To make sure that your book can be used on as many browsers as possible, you should use JavaScript to make it browser-independent.

Note

Chapter 26, "Working with Object Trees," gives you the background to understand how to implement an object tree in JavaScript.

Because changing the appearance of the JavaScript object tree involves clearing and writing to a document object, working with frames is much easier. The frameset, which is the main document that the user requests, contains all the JavaScript code and two frames. The left frame displays the structure of the book. The right frame displays the selected HTML page.

As mentioned in Chapter 26, a JavaScript object tree is a hierarchical structure with objects and parent-child relationships between objects. Each object is a separate entity made from a JavaScript array. To create this object tree, you need two custom JavaScript functions: createObject and append. You use the createObject function to create an object in the object tree and the append function to create a relationship between two objects.

An object in the tree represents the book, a chapter, or a heading. Note that by heading I mean any heading: heading1, heading2, ... or heading*n*. Each object has a unique identifier that is used to search for this object, a title to display, and a URL to the HTML content that is the object's content. In addition to these three elements, an object also has a state: whether it is open or closed. An open object displays all its children, if any. A closed object that has children displays a plus sign (+) at its node. To open this object, you click this node (plus sign). An open object has a minus sign (–) at its node. To close this object, you click the minus sign. In more technical terms, opening and closing an object is also called expanding or collapsing the object.

To create an object, you call the createObject function, passing a unique identifier, a title, and the URL to the content. This function is given in Listing 19.2.

Listing 19.2 **The createObject Function**

```
function createObject(id, title, url) {
  var element = new Array();
  element[0] = id;
  element[1] = title;
  element[2] = url;
  element[3] = 0;
  return element;
}
```

For example, to create the object that represents the book, you write the following line:

```
var e1 = createObject(1, "Fantasies for Dummies",  "bookTitle.html");
```

This code creates an object with identifier 1, title "Fantasies for Dummies," and "bookTitle.html" as the URL. Remember that an object in JavaScript is merely an array. The identifier is stored as the first array element, the title as the second, the URL as the third. The fourth element (element[3]) stores the object state. 0 indicates that the object is closed. 1 indicates the object is open. By default, an object is created closed.

To create a relationship between two objects, you use the append function, as shown in Listing 19.3. The function accepts two arguments: the object to be the parent in the relationship and the object that is intended to be the child in the relationship.

Listing 19.3 **The append Function**

```
function append(parent, child) {
  parent[parent.length] = child;
}
```

To create the XML document in Listing 19.1, you need to call the createObject and append functions repeatedly to make the whole object tree. The code part is given in Listing 19.4.

Listing 19.4 **Creating a JavaScript Object Tree Based on the Structure in Listing 19.1**

```
var e1 = createObject(1, "Fantasies for Dummies",  "bookTitle.html");
var e2 = createObject(2, "Introduction to Disneyland", "ch1.html");
append(e1 , e2);
var e3 = createObject(3, "Meet Mickey", "mickey.html");
append(e2 , e3);
var e4 = createObject(4, "Going Inside", "ch2.html");
append(e1 , e4);
var e5 = createObject(5, "Meet Donald", "donald.html");
append(e4 , e5);
var e6 = createObject(6, "Kwik", "kwik.html");
append(e5 , e6);
var e7 = createObject(7, "You can't escape", "noEscape.html");
append(e6 , e7);
var e8 = createObject(8, "Kwek", "kwek.html");
append(e5 , e8);
var e9 = createObject(9, "Kwak", "kwak.html");
append(e5 , e9);
var e10 = createObject(10, "Alice in Disneyland", "Ch3.html");
append(e1 , e10);
```

Note that each object is given a unique identifier.

The challenge in creating a JavaScript object tree based on an XML document is resolving how to translate the XML document in Listing 19.1 into JavaScript code in Listing 19.4. When the table of contents changes, the XML document also changes. This change must be reflected by the JavaScript objects and relationships between objects in Listing 19.4. This is the reason you need the server-side processing to read the XML file every time the electronic book is requested: You need to ensure that the table of contents the user sees is current.

The Project

In this implementation, the complete project consists of two files: index.jsp and TocBean.java. You also need HTML files for the contents, of course; but those static files are outside this discussion.

In addition to these two files, you need two other dummy files called toc.html and content.html, because a frameset must have physical pages to fill the frames.

The index.jsp file is the main file that contains the JavaScript functions for creating and manipulating the object tree. Its code is given in Listing 19.5.

Listing 19.5 **The index.jsp File**

```
<jsp:useBean id="TocBeanId" scope="page" class="TocBean" />
<HTML>
<HEAD>
<TITLE>Table of Contents</TITLE>
<SCRIPT LANGUAGE="JavaScript">
<!--  Hiding Script

var selectedElementId = 1;
var root;

function createObject(id, title, url) {
  var element = new Array();
  element[0] = id;
  element[1] = title;
  element[2] = url;
  element[3] = 0;
  return element;
}

function append(parent, child) {
  parent[parent.length] = child;
}
```

```
function redrawTree() {
  var doc = top.treeFrame.window.document;
  doc.clear();
  doc.write("<HTML><HEAD><STYLE TYPE=\"text/css\">\n" +
    ".normal:link { text-decoration:none; color:black;
➥font-family:verdana; font-size: 8pt; }\n" +
    ".selected:link { text-decoration:none; color:red;
➥font-family:verdana; font-size: 9pt; }\n" +
    "</STYLE></HEAD>");

  doc.write("<BODY BGCOLOR='#ffffff'>");
  redrawNode(root, doc, 0, 1, "");
  doc.write("</BODY></HTML>");
  doc.close();
}

function closeBook() {
  root[3] = 0;
  redrawTree();
}

function openBook() {
  root[3] = 1;
  redrawTree();
}

function redrawNode(
  foldersNode, doc, level, lastNode, leftSide) {
  var j=0;
  var i=0;
  var id = foldersNode[0];
  var title = foldersNode[1];
  var url = foldersNode[2];
  var hasSubNode = (foldersNode.length>4);
  var expanded = foldersNode[3];


  doc.write("<TABLE BORDER=0 CELLSPACING=0" +
    " CELLPADDING=0>");
  doc.write("<TR><TD VALIGN=middle NOWRAP>");
  doc.write(leftSide);

  if (id==1) { // this is the book
    if (root[3]==0)
      doc.write("<A HREF='javascript:top.openBook()'>
➥<IMG SRC=images/ClosedBook.gif BORDER=0></A>");
    else
      doc.write("<A HREF='javascript:top.closeBook()'>
➥<IMG SRC=images/OpenBook.gif BORDER=0></A>");
  }
```

continues

Listing 19.5 **Continued**

```
  var nodeLink =
    "<A HREF='javascript:top.clickNode(" + id + ")'>";

  if (level>0)
    if (lastNode) { //the last folder in array
      if (hasSubNode) {
        if (expanded)
          doc.write(nodeLink +
"<IMG SRC='images/LastNodeMinus.gif'" +
" BORDER=0 WIDTH=16 HEIGHT=22>" + "</A>");
        else
          doc.write(nodeLink +
"<IMG SRC='images/LastNodePlus.gif'" +
" BORDER=0 WIDTH=16 HEIGHT=22>" + "</A>");
      }
      else
        doc.write("<IMG SRC='images/LastNode.gif'" +
          " WIDTH=16 HEIGHT=22>");

      leftSide += "<IMG SRC='images/blank.gif'" +
        " WIDTH=16 HEIGHT=22>";
    }
    else { //not last folder
      if (hasSubNode) {
        if (expanded)
          doc.write(nodeLink +
"<IMG SRC='images/NodeMinus.gif'" +
" BORDER=0 WIDTH=16 HEIGHT=22>" + "</A>");
        else
          doc.write(nodeLink +
            "<IMG SRC='images/NodePlus.gif'" +
            " BORDER=0 WIDTH=16 HEIGHT=22></A>");
      }
      else
        doc.write("<IMG SRC='images/Node.gif'" +
          " WIDTH=16 HEIGHT=22>");
      leftSide += "<IMG SRC='images/VertLine.gif'" +
        " WIDTH=16 HEIGHT=22>";
    }

    doc.write("<TD> ");


    if (id == selectedElementId)
      doc.write("<A CLASS=selected");
    else
      doc.write("<A CLASS=normal");
```

```
  doc.write(" HREF='javascript:top.clickElement("
    + id + ", \"" + url + "\")'>" + title + "</A>");

  doc.write("</TABLE>")

  if (hasSubNode && expanded) {
    level++;
    for (i=4; i<foldersNode.length;i++)
      if (i==foldersNode.length-1)
      redrawNode(
          foldersNode[i], doc, level, 1, leftSide);
      else
        redrawNode(
          foldersNode[i], doc, level, 0, leftSide);
  }
}

function clickElement(id, url) {
  selectedElementId = id;
  redrawTree();
  parent.frames[1].location = url;
}

function toggleNode(foldersNode, folderId) {
  if (foldersNode[0]==folderId)
    foldersNode[3] = 1 - foldersNode[3];
  else if (foldersNode[3])
    for (var i=4; i< foldersNode.length; i++)
      toggleNode(foldersNode[i], folderId);
}


function clickNode(folderId) {
  toggleNode(root, folderId);
  redrawTree();
}

function initialize() {
  root = e1;
  redrawTree();
}
<%
  TocBeanId.getToc("toc.xml");
  out.println(TocBeanId.getString());
%>

// end hiding script  -->
</SCRIPT>
</HEAD>

<FRAMESET onLoad="initialize()" cols="225,*">
```

continues

Listing 19.5 **Continued**

```
  <FRAME SRC="toc.html" NAME="treeFrame">
  <FRAME SRC="content.html" NAME="objectFrame">
  <NOFRAMES>
  <BODY>
    Unfortunately, your browser cannot render frames.
    Please upgrade your browser.
  </BODY>
  </NOFRAMES>
</FRAMESET>
</HTML>>
```

The rendered HTML file is given as follows:

```
<HTML>
<HEAD>
<TITLE>Table of Contents</TITLE>
<SCRIPT LANGUAGE="JavaScript">
<!--  Hiding Script

var selectedElementId = 1;
var root;

function createElement(id, title, url) {
  var element = new Array();
  element[0] = id;
  element[1] = title;
  element[2] = url;
  element[3] = 0;
  return element;
}

function append(parent, child) {
  parent[parent.length] = child;
}

function redrawTree() {
  var doc = top.treeFrame.window.document;
  doc.clear();
  doc.write("<HTML><HEAD><STYLE TYPE=\"text/css\">\n" +
    ".normal:link { text-decoration:none; color:black;
➥font-family:verdana; font-size: 8pt; }\n" +
    ".selected:link { text-decoration:none; color:red;
➥font-family:verdana; font-size: 9pt; }\n" +
    "</STYLE></HEAD>");

  doc.write("<BODY BGCOLOR='#ffffff'>");
  redrawNode(root, doc, 0, 1, "");
  doc.write("</BODY></HTML>");
  doc.close();
}
```

```
function closeBook() {
  root[3] = 0;
  redrawTree();
}

function openBook() {
  root[3] = 1;
  redrawTree();
}

function redrawNode(
  foldersNode, doc, level, lastNode, leftSide) {
  var j=0;
  var i=0;
  var id = foldersNode[0];
  var title = foldersNode[1];
  var url = foldersNode[2];
  var hasSubNode = (foldersNode.length>4);
  var expanded = foldersNode[3];


  doc.write("<TABLE BORDER=0 CELLSPACING=0" +
    " CELLPADDING=0>");
  doc.write("<TR><TD VALIGN=middle NOWRAP>");
  doc.write(leftSide);

  if (id==1) { // this is the book
    if (root[3]==0)
      doc.write("<A HREF='javascript:top.openBook()'>
➥<IMG SRC=images/ClosedBook.gif BORDER=0></A>");
    else
      doc.write("<A HREF='javascript:top.closeBook()'>
➥<IMG SRC=images/OpenBook.gif BORDER=0></A>");
  }

  var nodeLink =
    "<A HREF='javascript:top.clickNode(" + id + ")'>";

  if (level>0)
    if (lastNode) { //the last folder in array
      if (hasSubNode) {
        if (expanded)
          doc.write(nodeLink +
"<IMG SRC='images/LastNodeMinus.gif'" +
" BORDER=0 WIDTH=16 HEIGHT=22>" + "</A>");
        else
          doc.write(nodeLink +
"<IMG SRC='images/LastNodePlus.gif'" +
" BORDER=0 WIDTH=16 HEIGHT=22>" + "</A>");
      }
```

continues

Listing 19.5 **Continued**

```
      else
        doc.write("<IMG SRC='images/LastNode.gif'" +
          " WIDTH=16 HEIGHT=22>");

      leftSide += "<IMG SRC='images/blank.gif'" +
        " WIDTH=16 HEIGHT=22>";
    }
    else { //not last folder
      if (hasSubNode) {
        if (expanded)
          doc.write(nodeLink +
"<IMG SRC='images/NodeMinus.gif'" +
" BORDER=0 WIDTH=16 HEIGHT=22>" + "</A>");
        else
          doc.write(nodeLink +
"<IMG SRC='images/NodePlus.gif'" +
" BORDER=0 WIDTH=16 HEIGHT=22>" + "</A>");
      }
      else
        doc.write("<IMG SRC='images/Node.gif'" +
          " WIDTH=16 HEIGHT=22>");
      leftSide += "<IMG SRC='images/VertLine.gif'" +
        " WIDTH=16 HEIGHT=22>";
    }

    doc.write("<TD> ");


    if (id == selectedElementId)
      doc.write("<A CLASS=selected");
    else
      doc.write("<A CLASS=normal");


  doc.write(" HREF='javascript:top.clickElement("
    + id + ", \"" + url + "\")'>" + title + "</A>");

  doc.write("</TABLE>")

  if (hasSubNode && expanded) {
    level++;
    for (i=4; i<foldersNode.length;i++)
      if (i==foldersNode.length-1)
      redrawNode(
          foldersNode[i], doc, level, 1, leftSide);
      else
        redrawNode(
          foldersNode[i], doc, level, 0, leftSide);
  }
```

```
}

function clickElement(id, url) {
  selectedElementId = id;
  redrawTree();
  parent.frames[1].location = url;
}

function toggleNode(foldersNode, folderId) {
  if (foldersNode[0]==folderId)
    foldersNode[3] = 1 - foldersNode[3];
  else if (foldersNode[3])
    for (var i=4; i< foldersNode.length; i++)
      toggleNode(foldersNode[i], folderId);
}


function clickNode(folderId) {
  toggleNode(root, folderId);
  redrawTree();
}



function initialize() {
  root = e1;
  redrawTree();
}

var e1 = createElement(1, "Fantasies for Dummies",  "bookTitle.html");
var e2 = createElement(2, "Introduction to Disneyland", "ch1.html");
append(e1 , e2);
var e3 = createElement(3, "Meet Mickey", "mickey.html");
append(e2 , e3);
var e4 = createElement(4, "Going Inside", "ch2.html");
append(e1 , e4);
var e5 = createElement(5, "Meet Donald", "donald.html");
append(e4 , e5);
var e6 = createElement(6, "Kwik", "kwik.html");
append(e5 , e6);
var e7 = createElement(7, "You can't escape", "noEscape.html");
append(e6 , e7);
var e8 = createElement(8, "Kwek", "kwek.html");
append(e5 , e8);
var e9 = createElement(9, "Kwak", "kwak.html");
append(e5 , e9);
var e10 = createElement(10, "Alice in Disneyland", "Ch3.html");
append(e1 , e10);

// end hiding script  -->
</script>
```

continues

Listing 19.5 **Continued**

```
</HEAD>
<FRAMESET onLoad="initialize()" cols="225,*"> <FRAME SRC="toc.html"
➥NAME="treeFrame"> <FRAME SRC="content.html" NAME="objectFrame">

<NOFRAMES>
<BODY>Unfortunately, your browser cannot render frames.
    Please upgrade your browser.
</BODY>
</NOFRAMES>

</FRAMESET>
</HTML>
```

As you can see from the bottom part of Listing 19.5, the index.jsp file hosts two frames: toc.html and content.html. The first frame is named treeFrame and the second frame objectFrame, as follows:

```
<FRAMESET onLoad="initialize()" cols="225,*">
  <FRAME SRC="toc.html" NAME="treeFrame">
  <FRAME SRC="content.html" NAME="objectFrame">
  <NOFRAMES>
  <BODY>
    Unfortunately, your browser cannot render frames.
    Please upgrade your browser.
  </BODY>
  </NOFRAMES>
</FRAMESET>
```

The treeFrame frame is where you display the structure of you book. The objectFrame frame, on the other hand, displays the content of the selected page. For example, if the user clicks the first chapter title, the content of Chapter 1 is displayed (refer to Figure 19.1)

The index.jsp file also contains the following JavaScript functions:

createObject. As given in Listing 19.3, this function creates an array object with four elements. Each element has a unique identifier.

append. Creates a parent-child relationship between two objects.

redrawTree. This function is responsible for clearing the treeFrame document and writing new content to it when the user interacts with the object tree. From the frameset (index.jsp), the document of the treeFrame frame is referred to as treeFrame.window.document. Because this function will be invoked from the treeFrame page, however, the document is referred to as the following:

```
var doc = top.treeFrame.window.document;
```

Therefore, the variable doc here refers to the document object of the treeFrame frame.

The redrawTree function first clears the document and writes some static HTML to doc, as follows:

```
doc.clear();
doc.write("<HTML><HEAD><STYLE TYPE=\"text/css\">\n" +
  ".normal:link { text-decoration:none; color:black; " +
  "font-family:verdana; font-size: 8pt; }\n" +
  ".selected:link { text-decoration:none; color:red; " +
  "font-family:verdana; font-size: 9pt; }\n" +
  "</STYLE></HEAD>");
doc.write("<BODY BGCOLOR='#ffffff'>");
```

Then it calls the redrawNode function, passing the variable root and doc:

```
redrawNode(root, doc, 0, 1, "");
```

Then it outputs the closing </BODY> and </HTML> tags to doc:

```
doc.write("</BODY></HTML>");
```

Finally, it closes the document:

```
doc.close();
```

redrawNode. This is a recursive function that actually redraws the book structure.

closeBook. Changes the root object to the collapsed state, as follows:

```
function closeBook() {
  root[3] = 0;
  redrawTree();
}
```

openBook. Changes the root object to the expanded state, as you see here:

```
function openBook() {
  root[3] = 1;
  redrawTree();
}
```

clickElement. The clickElement function is invoked when the user clicks an element in the object tree. It accepts two arguments: id and url. When the user clicks an element, the element with its identifier id becomes the selected element.

The selected element is drawn with a different color, which means that because the tree has a new selected element, the tree must be redrawn using the following:

```
redrawTree();
```

The last thing this function does is change the content of the second frame using frames[1].location = url. However, because the clickElement function is invoked from the treeFrame frame, the correct code is as follows:

```
parent.frames[1].location = url;
```

Note that url is the second argument passed to the function.

clickNode. This function is invoked when the user clicks a node. This function calls the toggleNode function and the redrawTree function:

```
toggleNode(root, folderId);
redrawTree();
```

toggleNode. Toggles the clicked node from the expanded state to the collapsed state and vice versa. To do this, the function must first search for the node with the correct identifier. When it is found, the function changes the fourth array element of the object from 0 to 1 or 1 to 0, as you see here:

```
if (foldersNode[0]==folderId)
  foldersNode[3] = 1 - foldersNode[3];
```

If the current node is not the clicked node, the function continues searching by recursively calling itself:

```
else if (foldersNode[3])
  for (var i=4; i< foldersNode.length; i++)
    toggleNode(foldersNode[i], folderId);
```

The index.jsp also contains the following code that uses the TocBean.java bean:

```
<%
  TocBeanId.getToc("toc.xml");
  out.println(TocBeanId.getString());
%>
```

These two lines uses the JavaBean that translates the table of contents in XML (as shown in Listing 19.1) into the JavaScript object tree (as shown in Listing 19.4).

TocBean.java

As previously mentioned, you need server-side code to translate the XML document containing the table of contents into the JavaScript code like the one in Listing 19.4. The TocBean.java bean is the one responsible for it. The code is given in Listing 19.6.

First, you need a Java XML parser. Here I use the one from Sun, downloadable from `http://java.sun.com/xml/index.html`. If you choose to use another parser from another vendor, however, you should still be able to use the code without any modification other than the import statement in Listing 19.6.

Listing 19.6 **The TocBean.java File**

```
import java.io.*;
import org.w3c.dom.*;
import javax.xml.parsers.*;
import com.sun.xml.tree.*;

public class TocBean {

  DocumentBuilderFactory factory;
  Document document;
  StringBuffer output = new StringBuffer(2048);
  int objectId = 1;

  public String getString() {
    return output.toString();
  }

  public void getToc(String tocFilename) {
    factory = DocumentBuilderFactory.newInstance();
    try {
      DocumentBuilder builder = factory.newDocumentBuilder();
      document = builder.parse( new File(tocFilename) );
      Node rootNode = document.getFirstChild();
      NamedNodeMap nnm = rootNode.getAttributes();
      if (nnm!= null) {
        Node title = nnm.getNamedItem("title" );
        Node url = nnm.getNamedItem("url");
        // output the first element of the following form
        // var e1 = createObject(1, "book title", "book url.html");
        output.append("var e1 = createObject(1, \"" +
          title.getNodeValue() + "\",  \"" +
          url.getNodeValue() + "\");\n");
      }
      getChildNode(rootNode, output);
    }
    catch (Exception e) {
      e.toString();
    }
  }

  void getChildNode(Node parentNode, StringBuffer s) {
    try {
      int currentObjectId = objectId;
      Node childNode = parentNode.getFirstChild();
```

continues

Listing 19.6 **Continued**

```
        // get chapters' & headings' titles and URLs
        while (childNode != null) {
          String nodeName = childNode.getNodeName();
          if (nodeName!= null && (nodeName.equals("chapter") ||
            nodeName.startsWith("heading")) ) {

            objectId++;
            NamedNodeMap nnm = childNode.getAttributes();
            if (nnm!= null) {
              Node title = nnm.getNamedItem("title" );
              Node url = nnm.getNamedItem("url");
              s.append("var e" + objectId + " =
                createObject(" + objectId + ", " +
                (title==null? "null" : "\"" + title.getNodeValue() +
                "\"") + ", " +
                (url==null? "null" : "\"" + url.getNodeValue() +
                "\"") + ");\n");
              s.append("append(e" + currentObjectId + " , " +
                "e" + objectId + ");\n");
            }
            if (childNode.hasChildNodes())
              getChildNode(childNode, s);
          }
          childNode = childNode.getNextSibling();
        } // end while
      }
      catch (Exception e) {
        System.out.println("Error:" + e.toString() );
      }
    }

} // end class
```

Basically, the JavaBean reads the XML file passed to it in the getToc() method and composes a string in the StringBuffer called output. You then can read this output using the getString method and send it to the web browser.

The getToc and getChildNode methods are explained in the following sections.

getToc()

The getToc method accepts one argument: the filename of the XML document containing the book's table of contents. The method retrieves the root object (the <book> tag) as the first object with identifier 1 and appends this information to the output StringBuffer. Using the XML document in Listing 19.1, the output should be the following:

```
var e1 = createObject(1, "Fantasies for Dummies",  "bookTitle.html");
```

The method then calls the getChildNode method to process the rest of the tags. Note that objectId is used to register the object identifier.

getChildNode()

This method reads a tag whose name starts with "chapter" or "heading." The tag found is appended to the output StringBuffer.

Pre-Render the Table of Contents

Every time someone reads your electronic book, the XML document containing the table of contents must be parsed into the HTML/JavaScript equivalent of the hierarchical structure. This takes more time than simply sending a static page to the browser. Because the table of contents most likely does not change every day, you can pre-render the table of contents for a busy site so that it is available as a static page. For this purpose, you can use the output caching technique explained in Chapter 15, "Caching."

Summary

In this chapter, you learned how to create an electronic book application whose table of content is based on an XML document. When the structure changes, you need to update only the XML document.

20

Web-Based Document Management

HOW DO YOU SECURE A FILE ON the web so that only authorized people can access it? Some people simply put the file in one of the virtual host's subdirectories and provide no link to it, so that only those who know the full path can download it. This method is of course, only as secure as the full path to the document, and you probably would not secure your corporate confidential documents this way.

What people normally do is to utilize the web server and operating system authentication method so that every time someone tries to download a file, that person needs to type in the correct user name and password. This is a good approach, but it is too simple in many circumstances. One problem with this solution is that you need to tell the password to everyone you want to be able to download the file. This approach is like sharing the same NT or UNIX user name and password with everyone in the corporation—it doesn't work. People don't share passwords for the same reasons they don't share secrets. In addition to the privacy and security issues, this approach is less than suitable when you want more functionality, such as document versioning and full activity records, without relying on the web server log files.

Another solution is to store the files in a database and allow access to them only after authenticating the user. Putting Binary Large Object Blocks (BLOBs) in the database is excruciatingly slow and resource-hungry, however. The better solution is to store those files in a directory outside the virtual host (virtual directory) so they are not visible from the Internet/intranet when the user types a URL. To download a file, the user has to direct the browser to a special page and type the user name and password. Upon successful authentication, the web server fetches the file and sends it to the browser.

This chapter introduces the concept of document management, an important topic not often discussed in beginner or advanced Java or web programming books. The discussion presented in this chapter is based on *docman*, the commercial web-based document management project from Brainysoftware.com. Not all of its features are included in here, though, because of space limitations. The complete project may take a book of its own.

The basic concepts of this project are revealed in this chapter. By understanding these concepts, you easily can extend the functionality according to your needs. The four key features discussed in this chapter are these:

- Database structure of the project.
- Programmable file download.
- File upload.
- The client-side tool that makes navigating through the document as easy as using Windows Explorer. In fact, the user interface will look very familiar to any Windows user.

> **Note**
> Programmable file download and file upload are discussed in Chapter 12, "Programmable File Download," and Chapter 13, "File Upload" and will not be repeated here. If you would like to understand this project fully, you should first read those two chapters. Also important to understanding how the navigation tool works is Chapter 26, "Working with Object Trees."

The Docman Project

In brief, docman is a Windows Explorer on the web. This Internet application is implemented using Java Server Pages technology to present a web-based hierarchical file system similar to those in a non-web environment. There are two types of objects: files and folders/directories. A *file* is any document you store in the file system. A *folder* or *directory* is a container that can store any number of files and any number of other folders. If Folder B is located under

Folder A, Folder B is said to be a subfolder of Folder A. Folder A is referred to as the parent folder of Folder B and any file Folder A contains. The topmost folder in the hierarchy is called *root.* It is the first folder that users see when they browse the system. As you would expect, root does not have a parent folder.

Docman supports any number of users. Users each have their own permission set. This means you can allow users to view files in one directory but not in the other. This is naturally useful in an organization with different departments. For example, the marketing people can see the documents belonging to the marketing department but not IT-related files. Those working in the IT department, on the other hand, have access to these IT-related documents, but not to the HR's remuneration archive. Users can browse the system from root down the hierarchy as long as they have the permission.

Figure 20.1 shows the user interface of docman. Notice the familiar object tree on the left side.

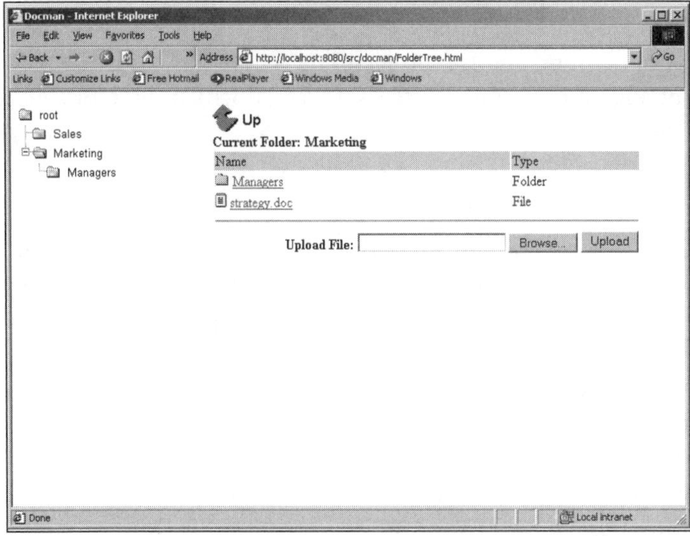

Figure 20.1 The docman project's user interface.

System Requirements

The docman project relies on the two JavaBeans included on the accompanying CD:

- The BrainySoftware.com File Download bean for programmable file download
- The BrainySoftware.com File Upload bean version 2.0 for uploading files

Using these two beans will save you writing hundreds of lines of Java code and make your code look neater.

Before you start, you need to copy the .jar files in the software/FileDownloadBean and software/FileUploadBean directories into your WEB-INF/lib directory of your application directory and restart Tomcat. Please also look at the license agreement of the two beans. If you choose to write your own beans, Chapters 12 and 13 should give you sufficient information to do so.

The following section discusses the database structure and all the JSP pages and bean comprising the project. The whole project is ready for deployment and can be found in the software/docman directory on the accompanying CD.

The Database Structure

In this implementation, file or folder information is stored in a relational database. However, all files are stored in one single folder outside the virtual root or virtual directory, regardless of their position in the hierarchy. This may sound strange at first but will seem logical after you read the next section.

The way in which files are stored doesn't matter as long as they are not directly accessible to users who type a URL in the web browser and the information on the file system structure remains intact. In this implementation, each object (file or folder) has the following properties:

- **Id.** A unique object identifier
- **Parent Id.** The identifier of the parent folder.
- **Type.** The object type, whether it is a folder or a file. A folder has a type of 0 and a file of 1.
- **Name.** The name of the object. In other words, either a filename or a folder name.

Of special interest is the record that has an object Id of 1 and is called root. root is the first object in the system and has a parent Id of 0, which means it does not have a parent.

Object-related information is stored in a table called Objects. As you can see, the object Id and the parent Id of each object gives you enough information to know the hierarchical structure of all folders and files

The structure of the Objects table in the Access database is given in Table 20.1.

Table 20.1 **The Structure of the Objects Table**

Field Name	Data Type
ID	Number
ParentID	Number
Type	Number
Name	Text

Note

You also can use your favorite database server to create these tables. One thing to note, though; your database server must support subqueries because they are used in the SQL statements used to access the database. Most popular database servers, such as Microsoft SQL Server, Oracle, Sybase, and IBM's DB2, support subqueries.

This implementation also uses two other tables: Users and Permissions. The Users table stores information about users, and the Permissions table stores information about which users have permission to various files or folders. The structures of these two tables in an Access database are given in Table 20.2 and Table 20.3.

Table 20.2 **The Structure of the Users Table**

Field Name	Data Type
ID	Number
UserName	Text
Password	Text

Table 20.3 **The Structure of the Permissions Table**

Field Name	Data Type
UserId	Number
ObjectId	Number

The Permissions table is very important in the docman project. If a user has permission to an object, this information must be present in the Permissions table. Therefore, if user A, whose user ID is 7, has permission to access a folder whose object ID is 133, there must be a record in the Permissions table with UserID 7 and ObjectID 133.

Now that you understand the database structure, let's work on an example: the directory structure of a fictitious company called Door Never Closed Pty, Ltd. The file and folder collection in this example is small for the sake of simplicity, but the hierarchy should reflect that of a real system. The hierarchy of all the folders and files is shown in Figure 20.2.

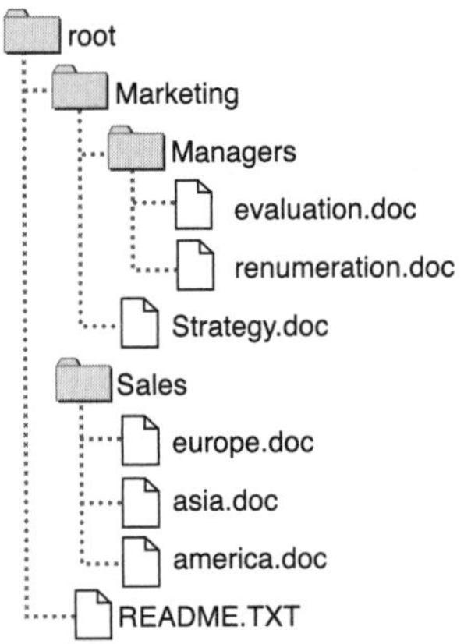

Figure 20.2 The directory structure of the file system.

Under root, you see two directories: Marketing and Sales. There is also a README.TXT for everyone new to read. (This file contains instructions from the system administrator on how to use the system). The people in the Marketing department store their folders and files in the Marketing folder. Access to this folder is limited to the Marketing people only. The Sales folder is for the Sales department, and only the employees working in the Sales department can access it.

The content of the Objects table looks like Table 20.4.

Table 20.4 **The Data in the Objects Table**

ID	ParentID	Type	Name
1	0	0	root
2	1	0	Marketing
3	2	1	Strategy.doc
4	1	1	README.TXT
5	1	0	Sales
6	2	0	Managers
7	6	1	evaluation.doc
8	6	1	remuneration.doc
9	5	1	europe.doc
10	5	1	asia.doc
11	5	1	america.doc

Note

The ID is assigned to an object at the time of the file upload, which means that there is no guarantee that files in a folder will have consecutive object IDs. This doesn't matter, however, because object IDs and other metadata are invisible to the user. All users see is a hierarchical file system.

Note also that files are stored in one single directory using their object Ids. This means that the Strategy.doc file is stored as 3. Because all files are given unique numbers as names, you can have two or more files with the same filename. When a file is sent as an attachment, the system will translate the object ID into the original filename.

Again, for simplicity, this example includes only two users: one with the login name boni, and the other with the login name bulbul. The content of the Users table looks like that shown in Table 20.5.

Table 20.5 **The Data in the Users Table**

ID	UserName	Password
1	boni	secret
2	bulbul	brownhair

Now comes the tricky part—the permission set. Boni is the marketing manager. She definitely has access to the Marketing department's files but has nothing to do with the Sales department. Bulbul, on the other hand, is the National Sales Director of Door Never Closed Pty, Ltd. He has access to all

Sales department's files, but Marketing is not his territory. The README.TXT is for everyone, so both Boni and Bulbul have access to it. This description is reflected in the Permissions table shown in Table 20.6.

Table 20.6 **The Permissions Table**

ObjectID	UserID
1	1
1	2
2	1
3	1
4	1
4	2
5	2
6	1
7	1
8	1
9	2
10	2
11	2

The Code

After the database is in place, the coding part comes easy. In fact, with a complete system like this, you need only three files and one bean for database and object manipulation. The three files are as follows:

- **Login.html.** A simple HTML file for users to type in their user name and password.
- **DisplayObjects.jsp.** A jsp file that displays all objects in a particular folder. This file also contains the form to upload a file into a folder.
- **DownloadObject.jsp.** A jsp file that fetches a file and sends it to the browser as an attachment.

The DBBean Bean

The DBBean bean does most of the work. You use it to connect to the database, get all objects in a particular folder, and get a filename for download. Of particular importance are the two connect methods. The first method is the one that receives three parameters: url, userName, and password. The url is your JDBC URL, whereas userName and password are the connection details that you need to get access to the database. You use only one user name and one password for getting a database connection. This user name and password pair is used by the system only and is referred to in the bean as dbUserName and dbPassword. All application end users know nothing about this. Don't confuse them with the user name and password that belong to a user. The latter are used to get access to a particular object in the database tables.

The second connect method accepts no parameter. You use this when you want to use the default values in the bean or you have passed those three arguments in previous statements (you set the url, dbUserName, and dbPassword using the setDbUrl, setDbUserName, and setDbPassword methods, respectively). There is another database-related method: setJDBCDriverName. You call this method if your driver name is that other than "sun.jdbc.odbc.JdbcOdbcDriver".

This example uses the JDBC-ODBC driver to access a Microsoft Access database on a Windows system. You must create a Data Source Name (DSN) called docman for the application to work. The choice of database is your decision. You need only to make sure that you use the correct JDBC driver. Because of the SQL statements used, as stated earlier, your database must support sub-queries.

The following is the code for the connect methods:

```
try {
  Class.forName( JDBCDriverName );
  connection = DriverManager.getConnection(url,
    userName, password);
}
catch (Exception e) {}
```

> **Note**
>
> The code for the connect methods could be different, depending on your database JDBC driver. Refer to your JDBC driver documentation for details.

The DBBean also has a static final String called DATA_PATH that contains the physical path to a special directory that will host all the uploaded files. You can change the value of this string to any directory you want to use. For security purposes, however, make sure the directory is outside your application directory.

The other methods used in the bean are listed in the following sections.

verifyUser(String userName, String password)

Use this method to verify that the user is authorized. This method checks the Users table for the UserName *userName* and Password *password*. The method returns true if it can find the user name and password in the table; otherwise, it returns false (not an authorized user). The SQL statement used is this:

```
SELECT ID FROM Users
WHERE UserName=userName AND Password = password
```

getDataPath()

This method returns the physical directory on the server where you store all the files. You use this method when downloading or uploading a file. The data path must be set to a directory outside the virtual host.

getFolderName(String id, String userName, String password)

You call this method in the DisplayObjects.jsp to get the folder name of the current folder. You need this information because you need to display the folder name to make users aware of their position in the hierarchy tree. You might think that you could easily get the folder name and parent ID by using the following SQL statement:

```
SELECT Name, ParentID FROM Objects WHERE ID=id
```

However, you want to make sure that only users with sufficient permission can get information about specific folders. Therefore, you use the following more complex SQL statement instead:

```
SELECT O.Name, O.ParentID
FROM Objects O, Permissions P, Users U
WHERE O.ID = id
AND O.ID = P.ObjectID
AND P.UserID = U.ID
AND U.UserName = userName
AND U.Password = password
```

getParentId()

This method returns the object ID of the parent folder for the current folder. The SQL statement that retrieves a ParentID only if the user has permission to view the parent object is as follows:

```
SELECT O.ParentID
FROM Objects O, Users U, Permissions P
WHERE O.ID=objectID
AND O.ParentID = P.ObjectID
```

```
AND P.UserID = U.ID
AND U.UserName = userName
AND U.Password = password
```

getChildObjects(String parentId, String userName, String password)

This method returns an ArrayList containing all child objects in the current folder. You will need the ID, Type, and Name of each object. These three fields are joined together into a string and each field is separated by a comma. Again, instead of using the following SQL statement:

```
SELECT ID, Type, Name
FROM Objects
WHERE ParentID = id
```

Use the more "secure" SQL statement:

```
SELECT ID, Type, Name
FROM Objects
WHERE ParentID =
  (SELECT ObjectID FROM Permissions
  WHERE ObjectID = id
  AND UserID =
    (SELECT ID FROM Users
    WHERE UserName = userName
    AND Password = password
    )
  )
ORDER BY Type ASC
```

The ORDER BY clause is there to guarantee that all folders (Type=0) will appear first.

getFilename(String objectId, String userName, String password)

This method is used to get the filename of the file object the user requests to download. The following SQL statement is used to guarantee that only users who have permission to access this file can download it:

```
SELECT Name
FROM Objects
WHERE ID =
  (SELECT ObjectID FROM Permissions
  WHERE ObjectID = objectId
   AND UserID =
    (SELECT ID FROM Users
    WHERE UserName = userName
    AND Password = password
    )
  )
```

getCookie(javax.servlet.http.HttpServletRequest request, String cookie)

This method returns the value of a cookie if the cookie is found in the HTTP request; otherwise, it returns null. Finding a cookie is done by looping the Cookie array of the HTTP request, comparing the cookie sought and the name of each cookie in the array, as follows:

```
Cookie cookies[] = request.getCookies();
if (cookies!=null)
  for (int i=0; i<cookies.length; ++i)
    if (cookies[i].getName().equals(cookie))
      return cookies[i].getValue();
```

> **Note**
> The complete code for the DBBean method is given later in this chapter in Listing 20.2. Some methods not described here will also be explained later.

hasUploadPermission(String id, String userName, String password)

This method is called when the user tries to upload a file. It returns true if the user can upload a file into a directory whose identifier is specified as the id argument.

synchronized public int getLastObjectId()

This method returns the last object identifier in the Objects table. The output of this method plus one is the identifier for the next object to be uploaded.

insertObject(String parentId, String objectId, String filename)

This method inserts a row into the Tables object and is called when uploading a file.

insertPermissions(String parentId, String objectId)

This method inserts a row in the Permissions table for a given object and the user who uploads the file.

The complete code of the DBBean class is given in Listing 20.1.

Listing 20.1 **The DBBean**

```
package docman;
import java.sql.*;
import java.util.ArrayList;
import java.io.FileOutputStream;
import java.io.File;
import javax.servlet.ServletInputStream;
```

```
import javax.servlet.http.HttpServletRequest;
import javax.servlet.http.Cookie;

public class DBBean {

  public static final String DATA_PATH =
    "C:\\123Data\\JavaProjects\\docman\\Data\\";

  public String getDataPath() {
    return DATA_PATH;
  }

  // database connection
  private Connection connection=null;
  // JDBC URL, change the string value below
  // appropriately
  String dbUrl = "jdbc:odbc:docman";
  // user name for database access
  String dbUserName = "";
  // password for database access
  String dbPassword = "";
  // JDBC driver name, the value depends
  // on the driver you are using
  String JDBCDriverName =
    "sun.jdbc.odbc.JdbcOdbcDriver";

  public void setUrl(String dbUrl) {
    // this method allows the JDBC URL to be changed
    // if the different one from the default
    // is needed
    this.dbUrl = dbUrl;
  }

  public void setDbUserName(String dbUserName) {
    // this method allows the database
    // user name to be changed
    this.dbUserName = dbUserName;
  }

  public void setDbPassword(String dbPassword) {
    // this method allows the database
    // password to be changed
    this.dbPassword = dbPassword;
  }

  public void setJDBCDriverName
    (String JDBCDriverName) {
    // this method allows the database
    // JDBC driver to be changed
    this.JDBCDriverName = JDBCDriverName;
  }
```

continues

Listing 20.1 **Continued**

```
public void connect() {
  // try to connect to the database
  // using url, username, and password
  // previously set
  connect(dbUrl, dbUserName, dbPassword);
}

public void connect
  (String url, String userName, String password) {
  // try to connect to the database
  // using url, username, and password
  // passed as parameters
  try {
    Class.forName( JDBCDriverName);
    connection = DriverManager.getConnection(url,
      userName, password);
  }
  catch (Exception e) {}
}

public ArrayList getChildObjects(String id,
  String userName, String password) {
  // the return value;
  ArrayList records = new ArrayList();

  try {
    if (connection==null)
      connect();

    String sql = "SELECT ID, Type, Name" +
      " FROM Objects" +
      " WHERE ParentID=" +
        " (SELECT ObjectID FROM Permissions" +
        " WHERE ObjectID=" + id +
        " AND UserID=" +
          " (SELECT ID FROM Users" +
          " WHERE UserName='" + userName + "'" +
          " AND Password='" + password + "'))" +
      " ORDER BY Type ASC";

    Statement s = connection.createStatement();
    ResultSet r = s.executeQuery( sql );
    while(r.next()) {
      records.add(r.getString("ID") + "," +
        r.getString("Type") + "," +
        r.getString("Name"));
    }
    s.close(); // Also closes ResultSet
  }
  catch(Exception e) {
    e.printStackTrace();
```

```
  }
  return records;
}

public String getCookie(
  HttpServletRequest request, String cookie) {
  // returns the cookie value if the cookie
  // is found in request; otherwise returns null
  Cookie cookies[] = request.getCookies();
  if (cookies!=null)
    for (int i=0; i<cookies.length; ++i)
      if (cookies[i].getName().equals(cookie))
        return cookies[i].getValue();
  return null;
}


public String getParentId(String objectId,
  String userName, String password) {
  String parentId = null;
  String sql = "SELECT O.ParentID" +
    " FROM Objects O, Users U, Permissions P" +
    " WHERE O.ID=" + objectId +
    " AND O.ParentID = P.ObjectID" +
    " AND P.UserID = U.ID" +
    " AND U.UserName='" + userName + "'" +
    " AND U.Password='" + password + "'";
  try {
    if (connection==null)
      connect();
    Statement s = connection.createStatement();
    // SQL code:
    ResultSet r = s.executeQuery( sql );
    while(r.next()) {
      parentId = r.getString("ParentID");
    }
    s.close(); // Also closes ResultSet
  }
  catch(Exception e) { }
  return parentId;
}

public boolean verifyUser(String userName,
  String password) {
  String sql = "SELECT ID FROM Users" +
    " WHERE UserName='" + userName + "'" +
    " AND Password='" + password + "'";
  boolean retval = false;
  try {
    if (connection==null)
      connect();
```

continues

Listing 20.1 **Continued**

```
      Statement s = connection.createStatement();
      ResultSet r = s.executeQuery( sql );
      if (r.next()) {
        retval = true;
      }
      s.close(); // Also closes ResultSet
    }
    catch(Exception e) {
      return false;
    }
    return retval;
  }

  public String getFolderName(String id,
    String userName, String password) {
    String folderName = null;
    String sql = "SELECT O.Name, O.ParentID" +
      " FROM Objects O, Permissions P, Users U" +
      " WHERE O.ID=" + id +
      " AND O.ID = P.ObjectID" +
      " AND P.UserID = U.ID" +
      " AND U.UserName='" + userName + "'" +
      " AND U.Password = '" + password + "'";
    try {
      if (connection==null)
        connect();
      Statement s = connection.createStatement();
      ResultSet r = s.executeQuery( sql );
      while(r.next()) {
        folderName = r.getString("Name");
      }
      s.close(); // Also closes ResultSet
    }
    catch(Exception e) { }
    return folderName;
  }

  public String getFilename(String objectId,
    String userName, String password) {
    String filename = null;
    String sql = "SELECT Name" +
      " FROM Objects" +
      " WHERE ID=" +
        " (SELECT ObjectID FROM Permissions" +
        " WHERE ObjectID=" + objectId +
        " AND UserID=" +
          " (SELECT ID FROM Users" +
          " WHERE UserName='" + userName + "'" +
          " AND Password='" + password + "'))";
    try {
      if (connection==null)
```

```
        connect();

      java.sql.Statement s =
        connection.createStatement();
      java.sql.ResultSet r = s.executeQuery( sql );
      if (r.next())
        filename = r.getString("Name");
      s.close(); // Also closes ResultSet
    }
    catch (Exception e) {}
    return filename;
  }

  public boolean hasUploadPermission(String id,
    String userName, String password) {

    boolean retval = false;
    try {
      if (connection==null)
        connect();

      String sql = "SELECT ObjectID FROM Permissions" +
        " WHERE ObjectID=" + id +
        " AND UserID=" +
          " (SELECT ID FROM Users" +
          " WHERE UserName='" + userName + "'" +
          " AND Password='" + password + "')";

      Statement s = connection.createStatement();
      ResultSet r = s.executeQuery( sql );
      while(r.next()) {
        retval = true;
      }
      s.close(); // Also closes ResultSet
    }
    catch(Exception e) {
      e.printStackTrace();
    }
    return retval;
  }

  synchronized public int getLastObjectId() {
    int retval = 0;
    try {
      if (connection==null)
        connect();

      String sql = "SELECT MAX(ID) AS LastID FROM Objects";
      Statement s = connection.createStatement();
      ResultSet r = s.executeQuery( sql );
      while (r.next())
```

continues

Listing 20.1 **Continued**

```
        retval = Integer.parseInt(r.getString("LastID"));

      s.close(); // Also closes ResultSet
    }
    catch(Exception e) {}
    return retval;
  }

  public void insertObject(String parentId,
    String objectId, String filename) {

    try {
      if (connection==null)
        connect();
      // insert record into the Objects table
      String sql = "INSERT INTO Objects" +
        " (ID, ParentID, Type, Name)" +
        " VALUES" +
        " (" + objectId +
        "," + parentId +
        ",1," +
        "'" + filename + "')";
      Statement s = connection.createStatement();
      ResultSet r = s.executeQuery( sql );
      s.close();
    }
    catch(Exception e) {}
  }

  public void insertPermissions(String parentId,
    String objectId) {
    try {
      if (connection==null)
        connect();

      // insert records to the Permissions table
      String sql = "INSERT INTO Permissions" +
        " (ObjectID, UserID)" +
        " SELECT " + objectId + ", UserID" +
        " FROM Permissions" +
        " WHERE ObjectID=" + parentId;
      Statement s = connection.createStatement();
      ResultSet r = s.executeQuery( sql );
      s.close();
    }
    catch(Exception e) {}
  }
}
```

The Pages

The project has three JSP pages, each of which is described in the following sections.

Login.html

Login.html, the first page in the application, is a simple HTML file with a form whose ACTION attribute is set to "DisplayObjects.jsp". The HTML code is given in Listing 20.2 and the page is shown in Figure 20.3.

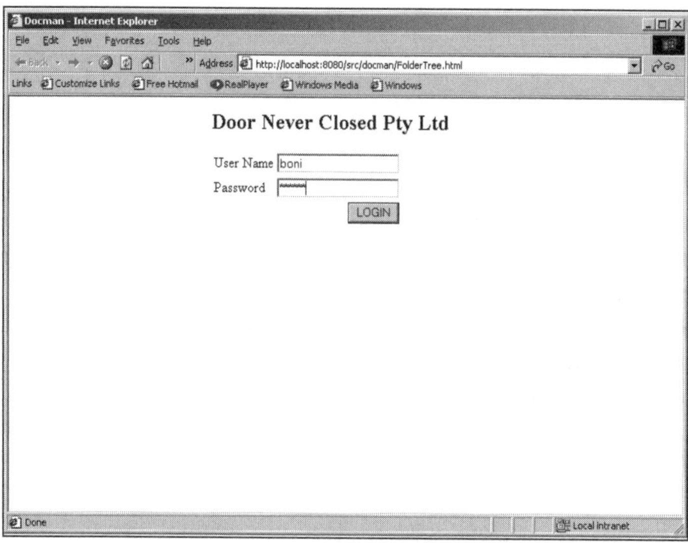

Figure 20.3 The Login page.

Listing 20.2 **Login.html**

```
<HTML>
<HEAD>
<TITLE>Login Page</TITLE>
</HEAD>

<BODY>
<H2>Door Never Closed Pty Ltd</H2>
<FORM METHOD="POST" ACTION="DisplayObjects.jsp">
<TABLE BORDER="0">
<TR>
  <TD>User Name</TD>
  <TD><INPUT TYPE="TEXT" NAME="userName"></TD>
</TR>
```

continues

Listing 20.2 **Continued**

```
<TR>
  <TD>Password</TD>
  <TD><INPUT TYPE="PASSWORD" NAME="password"></TD>
</TR>
<TR>
  <TD COLSPAN="2" ALIGN="RIGHT">
    <INPUT TYPE="SUBMIT" VALUE="LOGIN">
  </TD>
</TR>
</TABLE>
</FORM>
</BODY>
</HTML>
```

DisplayObjects.jsp

After the user types the user name and password and presses the Submit button in Login.html, the HTTP request is processed by the DisplayObjects.jsp page. The page first checks the validation of the user name and password. If the user name and password are not valid, the user is redirected back to the Login page. If the entries are valid, the page tries to display the objects.

Cookies are used so that the user needs to log in only once. After a successful login happens, the user name and password are sent to the browser as cookies. These cookies will be sent back to the server on the next HTTP request. The cookies live until the user closes the browser.

The code for DisplayObjects.jsp is given in Listing 20.3.

Listing 20.3 **The DisplayObjects.jsp**

```
<%@ page import="java.util.ArrayList" %>
<%@ page import="java.util.StringTokenizer" %>
<jsp:useBean id="DBBeanId" scope="page"
  class="docman.DBBean" />
<%
  // check HTTP request for userName and password
  // for request from the Login page
  String userName = request.getParameter("userName");
  String password = request.getParameter("password");

  if (userName==null || password==null) {
    // either userName or password is not found,
    // the request is not from the Login page,
    // check cookies
    userName =
```

```
        DBBeanId.getCookie(request, "userName");
      password =
        DBBeanId.getCookie(request, "password");
    }

    if (userName==null || password==null) {
      // userName and password still not found
      // this must be an illegal attempt to bypass
      // the Login page
      response.sendRedirect("Login.html");
    }

    // now userName and password are found,
    // verify if it is an authorized user
    if (!DBBeanId.verifyUser(userName, password))
      response.sendRedirect("Login.html");
    else {
      //authorized user, create cookies here
      Cookie cookieUserName =
        new Cookie("userName", userName);
      Cookie cookiePassword =
        new Cookie("password", password);
      response.addCookie(cookieUserName);
      response.addCookie(cookiePassword);
    }
%>
<HTML>
<HEAD>
<TITLE>DisplayObjects</TITLE>
</HEAD>
<BODY>
<%
  // string containing javascript script
  // built on the fly.
  String js="";
  // -------------------------------------

  String parentId = null;
  // the current folder id
  String id = request.getParameter("id");
  boolean atRoot = false;

  if (id==null)
    id = "1";  // 1 is the root
  if (id.equals("1"))
    atRoot = true;

  if (!atRoot) {
    // display the link to go up one level.
    // this link calls this same page,
    // passing the parent id
```

continues

Listing 20.3 **Continued**

```
    parentId = DBBeanId.getParentId(id, userName,
      password);
    out.println("<A HREF=\"DisplayObjects.jsp?id="
      + parentId + "\">"
      + "<IMG SRC=\"images/Up.gif\" "
      + "BORDER=\"0\"></A><BR>");
  }

  String currentFolderName =
    DBBeanId.getFolderName(id, userName, password);
  if (currentFolderName==null)
    out.println("<B>You don't have permission to"
      + " view this folder.</B>");
  else {
    out.println("<B>Current Folder: "
      + currentFolderName + "</B>");
%>

<TABLE WIDTH=600>
<TR BGCOLOR=#D6D6D6>
  <TD WIDTH=100>Name</TD>
  <TD >Type</TD>
</TR>
<%
    ArrayList records = DBBeanId.getChildObjects(
      id, userName, password);

    for (int i=0; i<records.size(); i++) {
      String row = (String) records.get(i);
      StringTokenizer st =
        new StringTokenizer(row, ",");
      String objectId = (String) st.nextElement();
      String type = (String) st.nextElement();
      String name = (String) st.nextElement();
      String imagePath;
      String objectLink;
      String objectType;

      if (type.equals("0")) {  //folder
        imagePath =
"<IMG SRC=\"images/folder.gif\" BORDER=\"0\">";
        objectLink =
          "<A HREF=\"DisplayObjects.jsp?id=" +
          objectId + "\">";
        objectType = "Folder";

        // ---- this is for part 2 -----------------
        //create javascript string for subfolders
        js+="parent.appendFolder(parent.folderTree,"
```

```
          + id + ",parent.createFolder("
          + objectId + ",'" + name + "'));\n";
        // -----------------------.

      }
      else { //file
        imagePath =
"<IMG SRC=\"images/file.gif\" BORDER=\"0\">";
        objectLink =
          "<A HREF=\"DownloadObject.jsp?id=" +
          objectId + "\">";
        objectType = "File";
      }

      out.println("<TR>\n");
      out.println("  <TD>" + objectLink + imagePath
        + "</A> " + objectLink + name
        + "</A></TD>\n");
      out.println("  <TD>" + objectType +
        "</TD>\n");
      out.println("</TR>\n");
    }
%>
<TR>
  <TD COLSPAN=2><HR></TD>
</TR>
<TR>
  <TD COLSPAN=2 ALIGN=RIGHT>
    <FORM METHOD=POST ENCTYPE=MULTIPART/FORM-DATA
      ACTION=UploadObject.jsp>
    <INPUT TYPE=HIDDEN NAME=parentId VALUE="<%=id%>">
    <B>Upload File:</B>
    <INPUT TYPE=FILE NAME=filename SIZE=25>
    <INPUT TYPE=SUBMIT VALUE=Upload>
    </FORM>
  </TD>
</TR>

</TABLE>

<SCRIPT LANGUAGE="JavaScript">
parent.deleteSubfolder(parent.folderTree, <%=id%>);
<%=js%>
parent.openFolderId=<%=id%>;
parent.redrawTree();
</SCRIPT>

<%
  }
%>
</BODY>
</HTML>
```

The DisplayObjects.jsp page is a recursive page that gets called from the link in its own body. It will first try to find the request parameters "userName" and "password".

```
String userName = request.getParameter("userName");
String password = request.getParameter("password");
```

This assumes that the request is from the Login page. The DisplayObjects.jsp page can also be called from within itself, however. If this is the case, the request parameters "userName" and "password" aren't used, but there must be cookies by the same names, which means the code needs to check for the cookies in the HTTP request:

```
if (userName==null || password==null) {
  // either userName or password is not found,
  // the request is not from the Login page,
  // check cookies
  userName =
    DBBeanId.getCookie(request, "userName");
  password =
    DBBeanId.getCookie(request, "password");
}
```

If the cookies are not found, the HTTP request could be coming from someone who is trying to bypass the Login page, or it could be that the browser is not supporting cookies. In either case, the user is redirected to the Login page.

If user name and password entries are found, either as request parameters or as cookies, you can't assume that the request is coming from an authorized user. You still need to verify the user name and password against the database each time this page is requested. If verification fails, the page sends the user back to the Login page. If it is successful, the code creates the "userName" and "password" cookies so that future requests from the user in the session will be successful. This is done in the following snippet:

```
if (!DBBeanId.verifyUser(userName, password))
  response.sendRedirect("Login.html");
else {
  //authorized user, create cookies here
  Cookie cookieUserName =
    new Cookie("userName", userName);
  Cookie cookiePassword =
    new Cookie("password", password);
  response.addCookie(cookieUserName);
  response.addCookie(cookiePassword);
}
```

Every HTTP request for this page should bring with it the folder ID of the folder whose child objects are to be displayed. An exception to this is when the user first logs in. In this case, folder ID 1 (root) is implied and the atRoot flag is set. The code is given here:

```
String id = request.getParameter("id");
boolean atRoot = false;

if (id==null)
  id = "1";  // 1 is the root

if (id.equals("1"))
  atRoot = true;
```

If the current folder is not the root, the folder must have a parent folder. The following code creates the link that the user can click to go back to the parent folder:

```
if (!atRoot) {
  // display the link to go up one level.
  // this link calls this same page,
  // passing the parent id
  parentId = DBBeanId.getParentId(id, userName,
    password);
  out.println("<A HREF=\"DisplayObjects.jsp?id="
    + parentId + "\">"
    + "<IMG SRC=\"images/Up.gif\" "
    + "BORDER=\"0\"></A><BR>");
}
```

Note that this code uses the getParentID method of the DBBean to get the parent ID of the current folder. This parent ID will then be fed as the value for the ID parameter of the DisplayObjects.jsp page. This shows the recursive nature of this page.

To give users indication of their position in the hierarchy, you display the folder name here. Notice that if an unauthorized user tries to bypass the Login page, the getFolderName method will return null:

```
String currentFolderName =
  DBBeanId.getFolderName(id, userName, password);
if (currentFolderName==null)
  out.println("<B>You don't have permission to"
    + " view this folder.</B>");
else {
  out.println("<B>Current Folder: "
    + currentFolderName + "</B>");
```

Now comes the main method that actually retrieves all the child objects of the current folder. The getChildObjects method of the DBBean returns an ArrayList. Again, only authorized users can view this:

```
ArrayList records =
  DBBeanId.getChildObjects(id, userName, password);
```

Each item in the records ArrayList is a String containing the Object ID, Type, and Name of the child object separated by commas. Therefore, you need a StringTokenizer to get each field. The following code loops through the records ArrayList and gets the values of Object ID, Type, and Name of each object:

```
for (int i=0; i<records.size(); i++) {
  String row = (String) records.get(i);
  StringTokenizer st =
    new StringTokenizer(row, ",");
  String objectId = (String) st.nextElement();
  String type = (String) st.nextElement();
  String name = (String) st.nextElement();
  String imagePath;
  String objectLink;
  String objectType;
  .
  .
  .
}
```

If you want to give users a descriptive visual interface, use different icons to represent files and folders. To be precise, for each folder, use the Folder.gif image, and for each file, use the File.gif image. The other difference is the destination links of each type. When the user clicks on a folder, the application will display all the child objects of that folder that the user has permission to view. This will call the DisplayObjects.jsp. When the user clicks on a file, however, the application will send the file as an attachment to the browser if the user has permission to view that file. This is depicted in the following code:

```
if (type.equals("0")) {  //folder
  imagePath =
"<IMG SRC=\"images/folder.gif\" BORDER=\"0\">";
  objectLink =
    "<A HREF=\"DisplayObjects.jsp?id=" +
    objectId + "\">";
  objectType = "Folder";
}
else { //file
  imagePath =
"<IMG SRC=\"images/file.gif\" BORDER=\"0\">";
  objectLink =
    "<A HREF=\"DownloadObject.jsp?id=" +
    objectId + "\">";
  objectType = "File";
}
```

And finally display the child objects.

```
out.println("<TR>\n");
out.println("  <TD>" + objectLink + imagePath +
  "</A> " + objectLink + name +
  "</A></TD>\n");
out.println("  <TD>" + objectType + "</TD>\n");
out.println("</TR>\n");
```

Figure 20.4 shows this page in action.

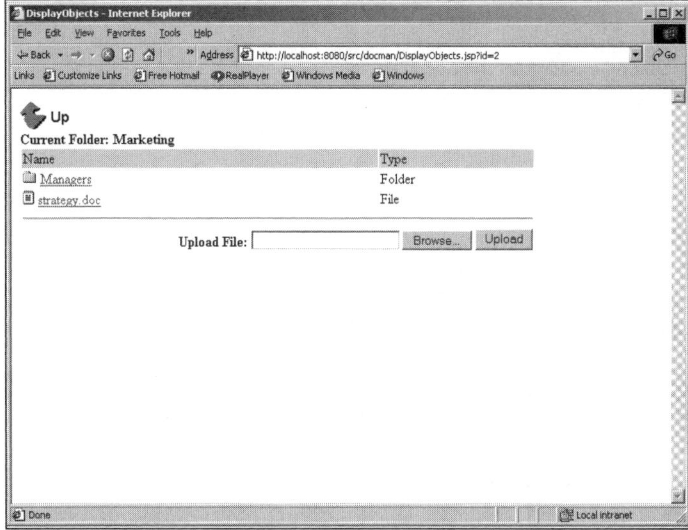

Figure 20.4 The DisplayObjects.jsp page.

The DisplayObjects.jsp page displays the list of objects in a directory and a form the user can use to upload a file to the directory.

DownloadObject.jsp

The DownloadObject.jsp page is given in Listing 20.4.

Listing 20.4 **The DownloadObject.jsp Code**

```
<jsp:useBean id="dbBean" scope="page" class="docman.DBBean" />
<jsp:useBean id="downloadBean" scope="page"
class="com.brainysoftware.web.FileDownloadBean" />
<%
  String objectId = request.getParameter("id");
  String userName = dbBean.getCookie(request, "userName");
  String password = dbBean.getCookie(request, "password");

  if (userName==null || password==null)
    response.sendRedirect("Login.html");

  // 'userName' and 'password' cookies are found
  // now let's see if user has access to the file
  String filename = dbBean.getFilename(objectId, userName, password);
  if (filename==null)
```

continues

Listing 20.4 **Continued**

```
      response.sendRedirect("Login.html");
    else {
      downloadBean.forceFilename(filename);
      downloadBean.download(response, dbBean.getDataPath() + objectId);
    }
  %>
```

First, this page checks whether the Request object carries the user name and password cookies:

```
String objectId = request.getParameter("id");
String userName = dbBean.getCookie(request, "userName");
String password = dbBean.getCookie(request, "password");
```

If the user is an authorized user, the user name and password are passed to the getFilename method along with the object identifier of the object to be downloaded. The getFilename() returns the filename if the user has the permission to download the file. Otherwise, it returns null, as follows:

```
String filename = dbBean.getFilename(objectId, userName, password);
if (filename==null)
  response.sendRedirect("Login.html");
else {
    .
    .
    .
}
```

You then obtain the data file path where all files are saved.

After you know the user is authorized to download the requested file, downloading the file is easy using the File Download bean. In fact, you need only two lines of code:

```
downloadBean.forceFilename(filename);
downloadBean.download(response, dbBean.getDataPath() + objectId);
```

The forceFilename( ) method is called to pass the filename that should appear in the Download dialog box of the browser. If you don't call this method, the Download dialog box will display the object identifier of the file.

File Upload

File upload is an important feature of a web-based document management system. File upload allows the user to add a file to a selected folder. File upload is discussed fully in Chapter 13. You will be using the File Upload bean for this project.

The HTML code for the form used to upload a file is included in the DisplayObjects.jsp file, whose full listing was given in Listing 20.2. This is the fragment you need:

```
<FORM METHOD=POST ENCTYPE=MULTIPART/FORM-DATA
  ACTION=UploadObject.jsp>
  <INPUT TYPE=HIDDEN NAME=parentId VALUE="<%=id%>">
  <B>Upload File:</B>
  <INPUT TYPE=FILE NAME=filename SIZE=25>
  <INPUT TYPE=SUBMIT VALUE=Upload>
</FORM>
```

When this form is submitted, the content will go to the UploadObject.jsp page, whose listing is given in Listing 20.5.

Listing 20.5 **The UploadObject.jsp**

```
<%@ page import="java.io.FileOutputStream" %>
<jsp:useBean id="dbBean" scope="page" class="docman.DBBean" />
<jsp:useBean id="uploadBean" scope="page"
class="com.brainysoftware.web.FileUploadBean" />
<%
  String userName =
    dbBean.getCookie(request, "userName");
  String password =
    dbBean.getCookie(request, "password");

  if (userName==null || password==null)
    response.sendRedirect("Login.html");
  else {

    uploadBean.setSavePath(dbBean.getDataPath());
    uploadBean.doUpload(request);
    String uploadedFilename = uploadBean.getFilename();
    String objectId = Integer.toString(dbBean.getLastObjectId() + 1);
    String parentId = uploadBean.getFieldValue("parentId");
    if (dbBean.hasUploadPermission(parentId, userName, password)) {
      uploadBean.forceFilename(objectId);
      uploadBean.save();
      dbBean.insertObject(parentId, objectId, uploadedFilename);
      dbBean.insertPermissions(parentId, objectId);
    }
    response.sendRedirect("DisplayObjects.jsp?id="
      + parentId);
  }
%>
```

As usual, this code checks whether the user is authorized by using the first lines of the code:

```
String userName =
  dbBean.getCookie(request, "userName");
String password =
  dbBean.getCookie(request, "password");

if (userName==null || password==null)
  response.sendRedirect("Login.html");
```

Start the uploading process by first setting the directory in which the uploaded file will be saved. You do this by passing the value of the static final DATA_PATH string in the DBBean, obtainable from the getDataPath() method, as follows:

```
uploadBean.setSavePath(dbBean.getDataPath());
```

Next, you call the doUpload( ) method of the FileUpload Bean, as follows:

```
uploadBean.doUpload(request);
```

The file is not stored by its original filename, but rather by using the object identifier. The original filename is included in the new row inserted into the Objects table, however. You can obtain the original name of the uploaded file by using the getFilename( ) method of the FileUpload bean:

```
String uploadedFilename = uploadBean.getFilename();
```

The object identifier for the new file is the next number in the Objects table, as the following line shows:

```
String objectId = Integer.toString(dbBean.getLastObjectId() + 1);
```

You also need the parent directory of the file. The parent identifier is included in the file upload form and sent to the server, which means that it is one of the fields accompanying the uploaded file. You can obtain this field value by calling the getFieldValue( ) method of the FileUpload Bean, as follows:

```
String parentId = uploadBean.getFieldValue("parentId");
```

As the last attempt to prevent a security breach, you need to use the hasUploadPermission method to check whether the user has the permission to upload a file into the specified directory:

```
if (dbBean.hasUploadPermission(parentId, userName, password)) {
```

If the user is authorized, you force the uploaded file to take the name of the object identifier and call the save( )method to save it:

```
uploadBean.forceFilename(objectId);
uploadBean.save();
```

Next, you need to store the meta data of the uploaded file so that it can be retrieved, as follows:

```
dbBean.insertObject(parentId, objectId, uploadedFilename);
dbBean.insertPermissions(parentId, objectId);
```

Finally, you redirect the user back to the DisplayObjects.jsp page with the following code:

```
response.sendRedirect("DisplayObjects.jsp?id=" + parentId);
```

Folder Tree

The folder tree is a docman feature that provides easier navigation. You can implement the folder tree using an applet or JavaScript. With an applet, you have Java at your disposal, which makes complex programming tasks achievable. However, this also means that the user pays a price for downloading a few kilobytes of this applet. What's more, you have communication problems between the applet and the HTML/JavaScript code. These two factors made JavaScript more appealing in this project.

Even though JavaScript is not as powerful as Java, a folder tree implementation is very straightforward in JavaScript. The result has been tested successfully using the two major browsers—Microsoft Internet Explorer and Netscape Navigator—but the code also works in a JavaScript-enabled browser. The folder tree is explained in length later in this chapter.

Each folder has a few attributes, such as the id and the name, but more importantly, a folder can have from zero to an unlimited number of child folders. Each child folder in turn can have any number of its own child folders and this hierarchy can go on to an unlimited number of levels. The first folder in the hierarchy, the root, is at level 0 of the tree. Its child folders will be at level 1, and so on.

The JavaScript script for manipulating the folder tree can be found in the FolderTree.html file, which is given in Listing 20.6. This file hosts two frames. The left frame is the folder tree and the right frame is for the pages discussed earlier in this first chapter; that is, the Login page and the DisplayObjects.jsp.

Listing 20.6 **The FolderTree.html**

```
<HTML>
<HEAD>
<TITLE>Docman</TITLE>
<SCRIPT LANGUAGE="JavaScript">
<!--  Hiding Script

// the open folder, by default it's the root
```

continues

Listing 20.6 **Continued**

```
var openFolderId = 1;
var folderTree = 0;

function createFolder(id, name) {
  var folder;
  folder = new Array;
  folder[0] = id;
  folder[1] = name;
  // folder[2] indicates whether the folder is
  // expanded/collapsed
  // folder[2]=1 means expanded, 0 collapsed
  folder[2] = 1;
  return folder;
}

function appendFolder(
  foldersNode, parentId, childFolder) {
  // appends a folder as a subfolder of another
  // folder
  // first, find the parent folder by comparing
  // the parentId with foldersNode[0]
  if (foldersNode[0]==parentId)
    foldersNode[foldersNode.length] = childFolder;
  else if (foldersNode.length>3)
    for (var i=3; i< foldersNode.length; i++)
      appendFolder(
        foldersNode[i], parentId, childFolder);
}

function redrawTree() {
  var doc = top.treeFrame.window.document;
  doc.clear();
  doc.write("<BODY BGCOLOR='#ffffff'>");
  redrawNode(folderTree, doc, 0, 1, "");
  doc.close();
}

function redrawNode(
  foldersNode, doc, level, lastNode, leftSide) {
  if (foldersNode=="0")
    return;
  var j=0;
  var i=0;
  var folderId = foldersNode[0];
  var folderName = foldersNode[1];
  var hasSubNode = (foldersNode.length>3);
  var expanded = foldersNode[2];

  doc.write("<TABLE BORDER=0 CELLSPACING=0" +
```

```
    " CELLPADDING=0>");
  doc.write("<TR><TD VALIGN=middle NOWRAP>");
  doc.write(leftSide);
  var nodeLink =
    "<A HREF='javascript:top.clickNode("
      + folderId + ")'>";

  if (level>0)
    if (lastNode) { //the last folder in array
      if (hasSubNode) {
        if (expanded)
          doc.write(nodeLink +
"<IMG SRC='images/LastNodeMinus.gif'" +
" BORDER=0 WIDTH=16 HEIGHT=22>" + "</A>");
        else
          doc.write(nodeLink +
"<IMG SRC='images/LastNodePlus.gif'" +
" BORDER=0 WIDTH=16 HEIGHT=22>" + "</A>");
      }
      else
        doc.write("<IMG SRC='images/LastNode.gif'" +
          " WIDTH=16 HEIGHT=22>");

      leftSide += "<IMG SRC='images/blank.gif'" +
        " WIDTH=16 HEIGHT=22>";
    }
    else { //not last folder
      if (hasSubNode) {
        if (expanded)
          doc.write(nodeLink +
"<IMG SRC='images/NodeMinus.gif'" +
" BORDER=0 WIDTH=16 HEIGHT=22>" + "</A>");
        else
          doc.write(nodeLink +
"<IMG SRC='images/NodePlus.gif'" +
" BORDER=0 WIDTH=16 HEIGHT=22>" + "</A>");
      }
      else
        doc.write("<IMG SRC='images/Node.gif'" +
          " WIDTH=16 HEIGHT=22>");
      leftSide += "<IMG SRC='images/vertline.gif'" +
        " WIDTH=16 HEIGHT=22>";
    }

  doc.write("<A HREF='javascript:top.clickFolder("
    + folderId + ")'><IMG SRC=images/");


  if (folderId == openFolderId)
    doc.write("openfolder.gif WIDTH=24 HEIGHT=22"
      + " BORDER=0></A>");
```

continues

Listing 20.6 **Continued**

```
  else
    doc.write("closedfolder.gif WIDTH=24 HEIGHT=22"
      + " BORDER=0></A>");
  doc.write("<TD VALIGN=middle ALIGN=left NOWRAP>");
  doc.write("<FONT SIZE=-1 FACE='Arial, Helvetica'>"
    + folderName +"</FONT>");
  doc.write("</TABLE>")

  if (hasSubNode && expanded) {
    level++;
    for (i=3; i<foldersNode.length;i++)
      if (i==foldersNode.length-1)
      redrawNode(
          foldersNode[i], doc, level, 1, leftSide);
      else
        redrawNode(
          foldersNode[i], doc, level, 0, leftSide);
  }
}


function toggleNode(foldersNode, folderId) {
  if (foldersNode[0]==folderId)
    foldersNode[2] = 1 - foldersNode[2];
  else if (foldersNode[2])
    for (var i=3; i< foldersNode.length; i++)
      toggleNode(foldersNode[i], folderId);
}


function clickNode(folderId) {
  toggleNode(folderTree, folderId);
  redrawTree();
}

function clickFolder(folderId) {
  if (openFolderId != folderId) {
    openFolderId = folderId;
    redrawTree();
    objectFrame.location="DisplayObjects.jsp?id=" +
      folderId;
  }
}

function deleteSubfolder(foldersNode, parentId) {
//delete all subfolders in parent folder
  if (foldersNode[0]==parentId) {
    for (var i=foldersNode.length-1; i>=3; i—) {
      foldersNode[i] = "0";
```

```
      }
    }
    else if (foldersNode.length>3)
      for (var i=foldersNode.length-1; i>=3; i--)
        deleteSubfolder(foldersNode[i], parentId);
  }

  function initialize() {
    folderTree = createFolder(1, "root");
  }

  // end hiding script  -->
  </SCRIPT>
  </HEAD>

  <FRAMESET onLoad="initialize()" FRAMEBORDER="0"
    FRAMESPACING="0" BORDER="0" cols="225,*">
    <FRAME SRC="Tree.html" NAME="treeFrame">
    <FRAME SRC="Login.html" NAME="objectFrame">
    <NOFRAMES>
    <BODY>
      Please upgrade your browser to
      one that understands frames.
    </BODY>
    </NOFRAMES>
  </FRAMESET>
  </HTML>
```

Note that in the following snippet, the code for the frames, you use for the first frame a file called Tree.html. This file is blank and basically not used—it is here only because Netscape browsers will complain if you don't have an SRC attribute for every FRAME tag:

```
<FRAMESET onLoad="initialize()" FRAMEBORDER="0"
  FRAMESPACING="0" BORDER="0" cols="225,*">
  <FRAME SRC="Tree.html" NAME="treeFrame">
  <FRAME SRC="Login.html" NAME="objectFrame">
  <NOFRAMES>
  <BODY>
    Please upgrade your browser to
    one that understands frames.
  </BODY>
  </NOFRAMES>
</FRAMESET>
```

If Tree.html is blank and not used at all, how do you get the HTML code to paint the folder tree? As you will see later, the code is generated on the fly by the JavaScript functions on FolderTree.html. This code is updated continually as the user navigates the folder structure. When the user clicks one of the folders in the tree, that folder opens and the left frame receives instruction to request the DisplayObjects.jsp file passing the clicked folder id. This effectively displays in the right frame all child objects of the clicked folder. Upon displaying the child objects, the DisplayObjects.jsp file writes JavaScript code that sends an instruction to the FolderTree.html file to update the previously clicked folder with all child folders it contains. This gives the clicked folder the opportunity to refresh its content if it has been clicked previously.

Before you start dissecting the FolderTree.html file, notice the number of supporting .gif files used in building the folder tree (see Figure 20.5).

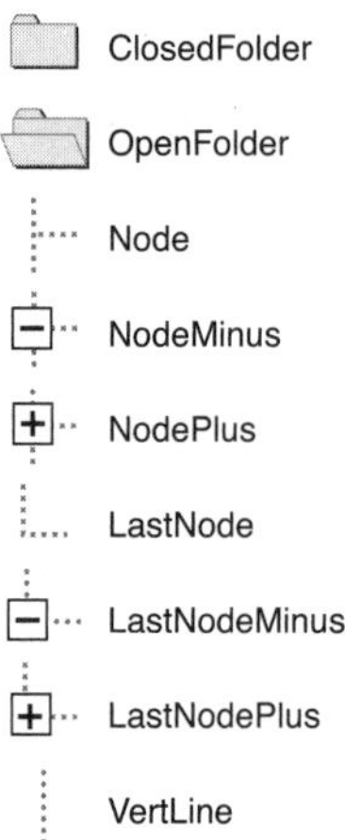

Figure 20.5 The supporting .gif files for the folder tree.

For example, a node is simply a vertical dotted line with a shorter horizontal line in the middle, represented in the figure by the Node.gif image file. If the folder connected by the node has one or more child folders, however, the node is represented by the NodeMinus.gif or NodePlus.gif image files. The NodeMinus.gif file is used for expanded nodes and the NodePlus.gif file for collapsed nodes. Also, for the last child folder, these three image files will be used instead: LastNode.gif, LastNodeMinus.gif, and LastNodePlus.gif.

The first function to notice in Listing 20.6 is the createFolder function. Used to create an array that represents a folder, createFolder receives two arguments: the folder id and the folder name. The id is the unique object id stored in the Objects table. The root, for instance, is the first folder with id equal to 1. The array has three mandatory elements: the id, the name, and the state that describes whether the node is expanded or collapsed, if it has child folder(s):

```
var folder;
folder = new Array;
folder[0] = id;
folder[1] = name;
folder[2] = 1;
return folder;
```

When it is first created, a folder array has only three elements. The folder in its original state has no child folder. To know whether a folder has child folders or how many child folders a folder has, you can measure the length property of the array. The number of child folders is the value of the length property minus three.

In a folder tree, a folder never stands alone. Every folder except the root has a parent folder, and every folder can potentially have one child folder or more. Every folder can be appended as a child folder of another folder. This is why the appendFolder function is very important here. It receives three arguments: *foldersNode*, *parentId*, and *childFolder*. The *parentId* argument is the id of the folder to be the parent of childFolder. The *foldersNode* argument is the variable that makes possible a recursive process to find the parent folder. When the appendFolder is called, you pass the root as *foldersNode*. When the function calls itself recursively, however, a child folder is passed as *foldersNode*, as shown here:

```
if (foldersNode[0]==parentId)
  foldersNode[foldersNode.length] = childFolder;
```

As you can see, if *foldersNode* is the folder in question, an array element is implicitly created by assigning the child folder to the next element after the last element in the array. If it is not the folder you want, the function recursively calls itself, passing each subfolder as the first argument:

```
else if (foldersNode.length>3)
  for (var i=3; i< foldersNode.length; i++)
    appendFolder(
      foldersNode[i], parentId, childFolder);
```

If a folder has at least one child folder, its node is displayed as a vertical line with a small box containing a minus (–) or a plus (+) sign. The minus sign is used when the node is expanded; that is, the child folder is displayed in the folder tree. The plus sign, on the other hand, indicates that the node is collapsed, meaning that the folder has one or more child folders that are not shown in the folder tree. As in Windows Explorer, you can click these nodes to change the state from expanded to collapsed and vice versa.

To enable a node to change its state, you put the Node image in a link that will trigger the clickNode function when clicked. For example, the following image, which represents an expanded node, is put inside such a link:

```
<A HREF='javascript:top.clickNode(folderId)'>
<IMG SRC='images/NodeMinus.gif'>
</A>
```

The clickNode function calls the toggleNode function and the redrawTree function. The toggleNode function searches the folder tree for a folder with the id equal to the *folderId* argument. When it finds a match, the function changes the value of the third element of the folder array, as follows:

```
if (foldersNode[0]==folderId)
  foldersNode[2] = 1 - foldersNode[2];
else if (foldersNode[2])
  for (var i=3; i< foldersNode.length; i++)
    toggleNode(foldersNode[i], folderId);
```

Note that the toggleNode function uses the same algorithm as the appendFolder function to browse through the folder tree for the sought folder. The redrawTree function redraws the whole folder tree. This function is discussed in detail in the next section.

Similar to a node, a user's click on a folder triggers the clickFolder function, which in turn sends a message to the other frame to request for the DisplayObjects.jsp with the correct id parameter value. In order for each folder to be clicked, the image representing the folder must be embedded in an <A> tag, as the following shows:

```
<A HREF='javascript:top.clickFolder(folderId)'>
<IMG SRC=images/openfolder.gif>
</A>
```

The clickFolder function will do three things if the folder clicked is not the currently open folder:

- Set the *openFolder* variable to *folderId* argument
- Call the redrawTree function
- Send a message to the frame on the right to request for the DisplayObjects.jsp with the appropriate *id* parameter value using the following line of code. This in effect will display the correct child objects of the folder clicked.

```
objectFrame.location="DisplayObjects.jsp?id=" +
  folderId;
```

For every action the user takes, such as collapse a node or open a folder, the left frame has to be cleared and the folder tree repainted to reflect the change. This task is done by calling the redrawTree function. In a nutshell, the function clears the left frame's document object, calls the redrawNode function to repaint the folder tree, and closes the document object:

```
var doc = top.treeFrame.window.document;
doc.clear();
doc.write("<BODY BGCOLOR='#ffffff'>");
redrawNode(folderTree, doc, 0, 1, "");
doc.close();
```

The redrawNode function is a recursive function that draws all the nodes, folders, and vertical lines between two nodes. To align all the objects in the folder tree, a table with no border and cellspacing and cellpadding both set to 0 is used. The redrawNode accepts these five arguments:

- *foldersNode*. Which is a folder array.
- *doc*. The document object to write the HTML code to.
- *level*. The position of the folder in hierarchy relative to the root. For example, the root has a level of 0, the child folders of the root have a level of 1, and so on.
- *lastNode*. A flag to indicate whether *foldersNode* is the last child folder of its parent folder. This does not have an "y" important effect except for selecting the .gif file for the node.
- *leftSide*. A string of HTML code that draws one or more Blank.gif and VertLine.gif files to the left of a folder that has a level greater than 0. This HTML code is necessary because folders other than the root are aligned a few pixels to the right of their parent folder.

The important thing to note is that you call the redrawNode function by passing the *foldersNode* variable as the first parameter. This variable represents the first folder in the tree, which is the root. Subsequent recursive calls to this function, however, will pass each folder in the hierarchy. In addition, *foldersNode* set as "0" means that the folder has been deleted and therefore will not be drawn, as follows:

```
if (foldersNode=="0")
  return;
```

For each node, get the properties of the folder array by using the following code:

```
var folderId = foldersNode[0];
var folderName = foldersNode[1];
var hasSubNode = (foldersNode.length>3);
var expanded = foldersNode[2];
```

hasSubNode will be true if *foldersNode* has more than three elements, which indicates the folder has child folder(s).

If you look carefully at Figure 20.1, you will notice that no two folders have the same vertical position. You can imagine the folder tree as a table with many rows in which every row is occupied by only one single folder. In fact, every row is represented by an HTML table to align the images easily, as you see here:

```
doc.write("<TABLE BORDER=0 CELLSPACING=0" +
  " CELLPADDING=0>");
doc.write("<TR><TD VALIGN=middle NOWRAP>");
doc.write(leftSide);
var nodeLink =
  "<A HREF='javascript:top.clickNode("
    + folderId + ")'>";
```

The rest of the code of the redrawNode function draws the nodes, folders, and vertical lines for each folder in the tree. For folders whose level is greater than 0, a number of Blank.gif files will be drawn to the left of the node, as follows:

```
if (level>0)
  if (lastNode) { //the last folder in array
    if (hasSubNode) {
      if (expanded)
        doc.write(nodeLink +
"<IMG SRC='images/LastNodeMinus.gif'" +
" BORDER=0 WIDTH=16 HEIGHT=22>" + "</A>");
      else
        doc.write(nodeLink +
"<IMG SRC='images/LastNodePlus.gif'" +
" BORDER=0 WIDTH=16 HEIGHT=22>" + "</A>");
    }
    else
      doc.write("<IMG SRC='images/LastNode.gif'" +
        " WIDTH=16 HEIGHT=22>");

    leftSide += "<IMG SRC='images/blank.gif'" +
      " WIDTH=16 HEIGHT=22>";
  }
  else { //not last folder
    if (hasSubNode) {
      if (expanded)
        doc.write(nodeLink +
"<IMG SRC='images/NodeMinus.gif'" +
" BORDER=0 WIDTH=16 HEIGHT=22>" + "</A>");
      else
        doc.write(nodeLink +
"<IMG SRC='images/NodePlus.gif'" +
" BORDER=0 WIDTH=16 HEIGHT=22>" + "</A>");
    }
    else
      doc.write("<IMG SRC='images/Node.gif'" +
        " WIDTH=16 HEIGHT=22>");
    leftSide += "<IMG SRC='images/vertline.gif'" +
      " WIDTH=16 HEIGHT=22>";
  }
```

```
doc.write("<A HREF='javascript:top.clickFolder("
  + folderId + ")'><IMG SRC=images/");


if (folderId == openFolderId)
  doc.write("openfolder.gif WIDTH=24 HEIGHT=22"
    + " BORDER=0></A>");
else
  doc.write("closedfolder.gif WIDTH=24 HEIGHT=22"
    + " BORDER=0></A>");
doc.write("<TD VALIGN=middle ALIGN=left NOWRAP>");
doc.write("<FONT SIZE=-1 FACE='Arial, Helvetica'>"
  + folderName +"</FONT>");
doc.write("</TABLE>")
```

At the end of the code, the function will call itself to draw the child folder(s) if the folder is expanded, incrementing level by one:

```
  if (hasSubNode && expanded) {
    level++;
    for (i=3; i<foldersNode.length;i++)
      if (i==foldersNode.length-1)
     redrawNode(
          foldersNode[i], doc, level, 1, leftSide);
      else
        redrawNode(
          foldersNode[i], doc, level, 0, leftSide);
  }
}
```

The last function in the folder tree system is the deleteSubfolder function. Because of the difficulty of deleting an array element, a folder will be considered deleted when set to "0". The deleteSubfolder function accepts two arguments: *foldersNode* and *parentId*. The latter argument is the id of the folder to be "deleted," and the first argument is used to find the correct folder to delete. You pass the root when you call this function. If the folder id is the same as *parentId*, the folder will be marked as "0".

```
if (foldersNode[0]==parentId) {
  for (var i=foldersNode.length-1; i>=3; i--) {
    foldersNode[i] = "0";
  }
}
```

If the folder is not the intended folder, the function will call itself, passing each child folder as the first argument, as follows:

```
else if (foldersNode.length>3)
  for (var i=foldersNode.length-1; i>=3; i--)
    deleteSubfolder(foldersNode[i], parentId);
```

The deleteSubfolder function would not be needed if not for this fact: The user can navigate the folder tree, opening a folder, and collapsing or expanding a node; however, the folder tree also must reflect in the right frame (the DisplayObjects.jsp page) the user's navigation. When the user clicks a child folder in the current folder, the child folder will be the open folder, and this must be reflected in the folder tree. When the user goes one level up by clicking the Up image, the folder tree must change the open folder. When the user opens another folder, the folder tree must display all the child folders of that folder. Because a child folder can be deleted or a new child folder can be appended by other users, you need to refresh the open folder. You do this from the DisplayObjects.jsp by calling the appendFolder functions on the frame's parent for every child folder:

```
for (int i=0; i<records.size(); i++) {
  .
  .
  .

  js+="parent.appendFolder(parent.folderTree,"
    + id + ",parent.createFolder("
    + objectId + ",'" + name + "'));\n";
  .
  .
  .
}
```

Before you append new child folders, however, you must delete the previous child folders appended the first time the folder is opened. The following is the code to do that:

```
parent.deleteSubfolder(parent.folderTree, <%=id%>);
```

Otherwise, the child folders will be displayed twice.

Further Enhancement

As stated at the beginning of the project, not all features of this project are discussed here because of space limitation. For example, this example provides no way for the user to add or delete a file or folder. Additionally, you can't edit the permission for each user, and I haven't introduced the concept of groups.

You may also want to include more information for each object, such as file size, date creation, multiple-level permissions, and so on. For multiple-level permissions, you could have permissions to view, to edit, and to view/edit. Another important feature not covered here is document versioning and the logging of user activity.

You can add countless features to make this project better. The features you choose to implement depend on your needs; and implementing them will be left as an exercise for you to explore.

Summary

Web-based document management is a broad topic, and creating a complete system takes many different features. This chapter presented the concept of web-based document management and gave you the basic features.

II

Client-Side Programming with JavaScript

21
JavaScript Basics

THE LAST 20 CHAPTERS HAVE DEMONSTRATED server-side programming using servlets and JSP pages. In this type of programming, the server takes all the workload. Because a popular web site can attract a large number of hits per hour, scalability is important. Otherwise, your web site can get knocked out several times a week by the sheer number of visitors it receives. You can make your site more scalable a number of different ways, one of which is to reduce your server's workload by moving some of the processing to the client side—namely, in the web browser.

To understand this point, consider the case in which you have an HTML registration form that contains some fields that must be filled in by users. With only server-side processing, you will have to check whether the user has entered all mandatory values. Even if one mandatory field is not filled in, your code will have to send an error message. The error message can be sent within a different HTML page or in the same registration page. If you choose the first approach, the user can then use the Back button in the web browser to go back to the previous page. If you decide to embed the error message in the same registration form, you have to resend the form and make sure that the previously entered values also are sent back to the user, which keeps users from having to type the same values a second time.

Either method you choose, however, creates an extra round trip to the server that could be avoided. Not only could this cause your user frustration if the connection is very slow, but it also creates an unnecessary workload for the web server. What's more, input validation doesn't end here. You still need to check whether the user has entered a correct value for all inputs—such as numeric values for a numeric type of data, and so forth. If one of the input fields is incorrect, you have to do the same thing to ask the user to make some correction. Lastly, you also need to truncate all leading and trailing spaces that might be present in a field value.

Wouldn't it be nice if all input values were sent to the server only if they were all valid and their leading and trailing spaces, if any, had been truncated? You can do this with JavaScript client-side processing. Why JavaScript? The reason is simple: JavaScript is understood by the two dominant browsers at present—Microsoft Internet Explorer and Netscape Navigator. For an Internet developer, an understanding of JavaScript is as important as an understanding of HTML.

The JavaScript lessons in this chapter and the chapters to come do not cover all features of this scripting language; instead, they are intended to provide a basic foundation. JavaScript is a serious subject that requires a book of its own to be covered thoroughly. By studying the lessons in these chapters, however, you will be prepared to tackle most of the client-side programming problems in web application development.

This chapter is offered as a crash course on JavaScript and is for those readers who have little or no understanding of JavaScript. Those who are already JavaScript gurus can skip this chapter entirely and move on to the next.

Introduction to JavaScript

Originally, JavaScript was called *LiveScript*. Contrary to what some people believe, JavaScript has nothing to do with Java. The name selection for JavaScript was more for marketing purposes. JavaScript was created by Netscape, and Java is a product of Sun Microsystems. Although JavaScript is a complete and mature language of its own, when we talk about JavaScript in this book, we are referring to the JavaScript as implemented in web browsers.

Another important fact to remember is that JavaScript is implemented somewhat differently in Internet Explorer and Navigator. Microsoft has even developed its own version of JavaScript called JScript. This book uses the portion of JavaScript that is implemented both browsers, in particular by versions 3.0 and later.

That being said, it is true that some aspects of JavaScript are similar to those in Java. These aspects are contrasted in the sections that follow.

Case-Sensitivity

As a starter, JavaScript is case-sensitive. Therefore, myVar is different from MyVar or myvar. Names for event handlers, such as onclick, must be written in lowercase letters in JavaScript, even though it can be written as onClick or OnClick in HTML because HTML is not case-sensitive. Confusion often arises regarding case-sensitivity because JavaScript is not implemented exactly the same in the two major browsers. Netscape browsers regard case-sensitivity as sacred, whereas Internet Explorer takes it half-heartedly. For example, the objects, methods, and properties added to the language in IE are case-insensitive while built-in objects, such as Math and Date, are case-sensitive in IE.

For this reason, you should apply strict case-sensitivity in your code to maintain compatibility between the two browsers. The reason for some case-insensitivity in IE is that IE allows the same client-side objects to be used by VBScript, a scripting language that is not case-sensitive. Microsoft therefore reckons that their client-side objects must not be case-sensitive either. Because of Microsoft's requirement for VBScript, it's not likely that the client-side objects will become case-sensitive in a future version of IE. This means that you can't take advantage of Navigator's case-sensitivity to create different variables with the same spelling but different capitalizations.

Terminating a Line of Code

Unlike in Java, the semicolon that terminates a line of code in JavaScript is optional. For instance, it is perfectly legal to write these two lines without semicolons:

```
str = "Cockroaches can live up to one year. ";
a = 123;
```

But if you put more than one statement in one single line, the semicolons are required, as follows:

```
str = "Cockroaches can live up to one year. "; a = 123;
```

For clarity, always use a semicolon.

Comments

JavaScript comments are exactly like Java comments: Use the // for commenting one single line and the /* .. */ pair for comments that are one line long or longer. Consider this example:

```
// divide by two
b = 489 / 2;
/* Now check which one of the two
   is larger
*/
```

Strings

Strings can be enclosed within single or double quotation marks. For example, both of the following lines are legal in JavaScript:

```
s1 = "Silk was discovered in about 3000 BC.";
s2 = 'Silk was first discovered in China.';
```

Further, double-quote characters may be contained within strings delimited by single-quote characters, and single-quote characters may be contained within a string delimited by double quotes. For example, these are valid statements:

```
s1 = "His name is Tim O'Connor.";
s2 = 'He is known as Tim "The Great".';
```

If you like to stick to one string programming style, you can use a preceding backslash character (\) before the single quote or the double quote. The two preceding strings can be rewritten as follows:

```
s1 = 'His name is Tim O\'Connor.';
s2 = "He is known as Tim \"The Great\".";
```

Like in Java, you use the plus (+) sign to concatenate strings. For instance,

```
s1 = 'His name is Tim O\'Connor.';
s2 = "He is known as Tim \"The Great\".";
s3 = s1 + ' ' + s2;
// s3 now contains: His name is Tim O'Connor. He is known as Time "The
Great".
```

Typedness

Java is strongly typed, whereas JavaScript is loosely typed. JavaScript variables can hold values of any data type; however, you use functions to convert one data type to another, as you see later in this chapter.

Variable Declarations

You can use a variable without first declaring it. Good programming practice, however, suggests that you always declare your variables. You can declare a variable using the var keyword, followed by the variable name, as in the following:

```
var myVar;
```

You also can initialize a variable at the same time you declare it. For example:

```
var s1 = "users";
```

You also can initialize a variable when the first occurrence of the variable is in a statement:

```
for (var i = 0; i < 100; i++)
```

The if Statements

The if statement in JavaScript is the same as the if statement in Java. It has the following syntax:

```
if (expression) {
     statement-1
    statement-2
   .
   .
   .
   statement-m
   }
   [else {
   statement-n
   statement-o
  .
  .
  .
  statement-z
  }]
```

The while Loop

As in Java, the while loop has the following syntax:

```
while (expression) {
  statement-1
  statement-2
  .
  .
  .
  statement-m
}
```

The for loop

Again, identical to Java, the for loop in JavaScript has the following syntax:

```
for (initialize ; test ; increment) {
  statement-1
  statement-2
  .
  .
  .
  statement-m
}
```

The with keyword

JavaScript uses the with keyword, which is not available in Java. The syntax is shown here:

```
with (object) {
  statement-1
  statement-2
  .
  .
  .
  statement-m
}
```

So, instead of writing this code:

```
x = Math.sin(a);
y = Math.cos(a);
```

you can write the following:

```
with(Math) {
  x = sin(a);
  y = cos(a);
}
```

Boolean Expressions

A boolean expression can be evaluated using the == and != operators, just like in Java. For example, consider this code:

```
if (a==b)
  str = 'The two numbers are equal.';
else {
  a = b + 12;
  str = 'The two numbers are not equal.';
}
```

Logical and Bitwise Operators

As in Java, you use the double ampersand (&&) as the logical AND, and the double pipe characters (||) as the logical OR. You use a single ampersand (&) as the bitwise AND, and a single pipe character (|) as the bitwise OR.

Functions

A function uses the following syntax:

```
function functionName(arg-1, arg-2, ... arg-n) {
  statement-1;
  statement-2;
  .
  .
  .
  statement-m;
}
```

The following example defines the factorial function that computes factorials:

```
function factorial(n) {
  if (n <=1)
    return 1;
  else
    return n * factorial(n-1);
}
```

Knowing the answer to the following question is important when you are learning a new programming language: How do arguments get passed in a function? By value or reference? In JavaScript, whether an argument is passed by value or by reference depends on the type of the argument. The basic rule says that primitive types are manipulated by value and reference types by reference. Examples of primitive types include numbers and booleans. They are primitive because they consist of nothing more than a small fixed number of bytes; bytes that are easily manipulated at the low (primitive) levels of the JavaScript interpreter. On the other hand, objects and arrays are reference types. These data types can contain arbitrary numbers of properties or elements. Because objects and arrays can become very large, it doesn't make sense to manipulate these types by value, because doing so could involve the inefficient copying and comparing of large amount of memory. There is an anomaly in string data type, though. Strings are passed by reference, but when you compare a string in your function, it is the value that is being compared, not the reference.

The String Object and the string Data Type

The String object is widely used in JavaScript. Among other properties, String has the length property that returns the number of characters in a string:

```
var str, a;
str = "Let's use JavaScript";
a = str.length; // a has a value of 20 after this line is executed
```

String also has the following methods that should be familiar to any Java programmer: charAt, toUpperCase, substring, and so on. The list of members of the String object can be found in the last section of this chapter.

JavaScript Keywords

The following is the list of keywords in JavaScript:

break

continue

delete

else

false

for

function

if

in

new

null

return

this

true

typeof

var

void

while

with

Reserved Words

The following is the list of the reserved words in JavaScript:

abstract
boolean
byte
case
catch
char
class
const
default
do
double
extends
final
finally
float
goto
implements
import
instanceof
int
interface
long
native
package
private
protected
public
short
static
super

switch

synchronized

throw

throws

transient

try

Illegal Identifiers

The following are identifiers that are used by the JavaScript language itself and should not be used in your JavaScript code:

alert

Anchor

Area

Array

assign

blur

Boolean

Button

Checkbox

clearTimeout

close

closed

confirm

Date

defaultStatus

Document

document

Element

escape

eval

FileUpload

focus

Form
Frame
frames
Function
getClass
hidden
History
history
Image
isNaN
java
JavaArray
JavaClass
JavaObject
JavaPackage
length
Link
Location
location
Math
MimeType
name
navigate
Navigator
navigator
netscape
Number
Object
onblur
onerror
onfocus
onload

onunload
open
opener
Option
Packages
parent
parseFloat
parseInt
password
Plugin
prompt
prototype
Radio
ref
Reset
scroll
Select
self
setTimeout
status
String
Submit
sun
taint
Text
Textarea
top
toString
unescape
untaint
valueOf
Window
window

Adding JavaScript Code to HTML

To the server, JavaScript code is merely text, just like HTML. To the web browser, however, this text has special meaning that can be interpreted differently. To tell the web browser that a piece of text is actually JavaScript code, you enclose it between the <script> and </script> tags, as in the following example:

```
<script language="JavaScript" type="text/javascript">

  // your scripts go here

</script>
```

Actually, unless you want your HTML page to pass the validation by a W3 HTML validating machine, you don't need the type attribute in the script tag. The Language attribute is necessary because there is more than one scripting language that can be embedded between the <script> and </script> tags. By specifying in the <Script> tag which language is used to write a script, the browser can decide whether it should try to interpret it. If the script is written in a language the web browser doesn't understand, the script should then be skipped.

You can write your JavaScript code anywhere in the HTML page. You can write your JavaScript script between the <head> and </head> tags, like this:

```
<html>
<head>
<script language="JavaScript" type="text/javascript">

  // your scripts go here

</script>
</head>
<body>

Here if your HTML body

</body>
</html>
```

Alternatively, you can present it in the body section, as these two examples show:

```
<html>
<head>
</head>
<body>
<script language="JavaScript" type="text/javascript">
```

```
    // your scripts go here

  </script>

  Here if your HTML body

  </body>
  </html>
```

or

```
<html>
<head>
</head>
<body>

Here if your HTML body

<script language="JavaScript" type="text/javascript">

  // your scripts go here

</script>
</body>
</html>
```

The <script> and </script> tags can appear more than once in different sections, if necessary.

Like other HTML tags, the JavaScript code is executed whenever the web browser sees it. This means that if you put your JavaScript code in the Head section, it will be executed even before the HTML tags in the Body section are parsed. If the processing time is too long, however, the user might see the delay and might find it annoying.

As an example, this HTML page contains JavaScript that writes "Hello" inside the page body:

```
<html>
<head>
  <title>Some JavaScript</title>
</head>
<body>
<script Language="JavaScript">
  document.write("Hello.");
</script>
</body>
</html>
```

This is the same as writing the following:

```
<html>
<head>
  <title>Some JavaScript</title>
</head>
```

```
<body>
Hello.
</body>
</html>
```

Note

In JavaScript, functions can appear anywhere throughout the HTML page. When you call a function, however, you have to make sure that the function has existed when it is being called. (When I say 'has existed' I mean the web browser has passed the point where the function is defined in the HTML page.)

JavaScript Object Model

Programming JavaScript basically revolves around the JavaScript object model. Figure 21.1 shows a subset of the object model.

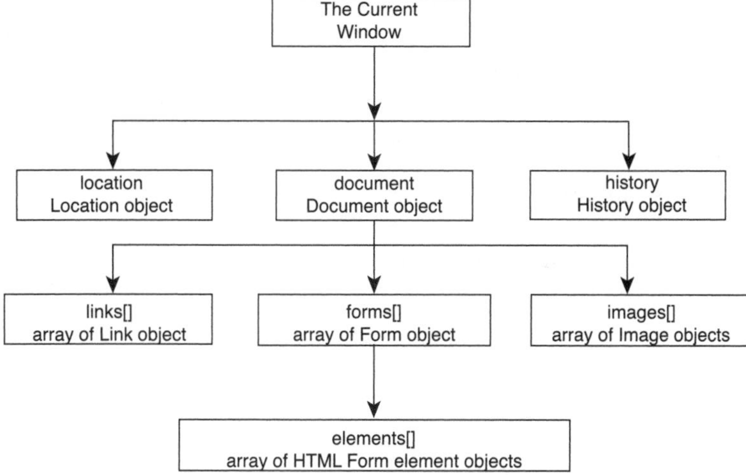

Figure 21.1 The subset of JavaScript's object model.

The Window object is the central object that represents the web browser window. It has a number of child objects: the Location object, the Document object, the History object, and others that are not shown in Figure 21.1. Each Window object contains a document property that refers to the Document object associated with the window. The convention in JavaScript is that the Window object is referenced by default. This means that to use one of its child objects or properties, you just mention the child object, the property, or the method in your code. To refer to an object in the lower hierarchy, you use a period to separate it from its parent object. For example, to refer to the first HTML element in the second form in the HTML page, you use this code:

```
document.forms[1].elements[0]
```

The Window object also has a number of methods, such as alert( ), confirm( ), and prompt( ).You can use the Window object's method without mentioning the Window object in your code, as in the following:

```
alert('Please enter a value in the "Phone" box.');
```

This is the same as writing:

```
window.alert('Please enter a value in the "Phone" box.');
```

The Window object is discussed in further detail at the end of this chapter.

Event Handler

JavaScript adds interactivity to the static HTML by allowing you to write event-driven code. An HTML element can then be connected to a function that gets called automatically when something happens to the HTML element. For example, you can connect a button to a function that gets invoked when the user clicks the button by using the following code:

```
<Input type=button Name=Send onClick="handler">
```

Table 21.1 lists supported JavaScript event handlers.

Table 21.1 **JavaScript Event Handlers**

Object	Event Handlers
Area	onClick, onMouseOut, onMouseOver
Button	onBlur, onClick, onFocus
Checkbox	onBlur, onClick, onFocus
FileUpload	onBlur, onChange, onFocus
Form	onReset, onSubmit
Frame	onLoad, onUnload
Image	onAbort, onError, onLoad
Link	onClick, onMouseOut, onMouseOver
Radio	onBlur, onClick, onFocus
Reset	onBlur, onClick, onFocus
Select	onBlur, onChange, onFocus
Submit	onBlur, onClick, onFocus
Text	onBlur, onChange, onFocus
Textarea	onBlur, onChange, onFocus
Window	onBlur, onError, onFocus, onLoad, onUnload

Unfortunately, some incompatibilities exist between browsers running in UNIX and those running in Windows. Netscape Navigator for Windows, for instance, doesn't recognize the Click event for an Area element. With Netscape Navigator for UNIX, some form elements—such as Area, button, checkbox, radio, reset, select, and submit—recognize only the Click event but not the Blur and Focus events.

Another type of event is not triggered by user interaction: The Timer event gets triggered when specified periods of time have elapsed. As you might expect, this can be useful for animation.

Window and String Objects

This last section provides a short reference of the two most widely used objects in JavaScript: the Window object and the String object.

Window Object

The Window object represents a browser window or frame. This is the root of the JavaScript object hierarchy.

Properties

The following is the list of properties of the Window object.

closed A read-only Boolean that specifies whether a window has been closed.

defaultStatus A read/write string that specifies the default message to appear in the status line.

document A reference to the Document object contained in the window.

frames[ ] An array of frames contained by this window.

history A reference to the History object for this window.

java A reference to the JavaPackage object that is the top of the package name hierarchy for the core Java packages that comprise the Java language.

length A read-only value that evaluates to the number of elements in the frames[ ] array.

location A reference to the Location object for this window.

Math A reference to an object holding various mathematical functions and constants.

name A string that contains the name of the window. The name is optionally specified when the window is created with the open( ) method.

navigator A reference to the Navigator object that applies to this and all other windows.

netscape A reference to the JavaPackage object which is the top of the Java package name hierarchy for the netscape Java packages from Netscape.

opener A read/write property that refers to the Window object that called open( ) to create this window.

packages A reference to a JavaPackage object that represents the top of the Java package name hierarchy.

parent A reference to the parent window or frame of the current window. This is useful only when the current window is a frame rather than a top-level window.

self A reference to the window itself. A synonym of window.

status A read/write string that specifies the current contents of the status line.

sun A reference to the JavaPackage object which is the top of the Java package name hierarchy for the sun Java packages from Sun Microsystems.

top A reference to the top-level window that contains the current window. This is useful only when the current window is a frame rather than a top-level window.

window A reference to the window itself. A synonym of self.

Methods

The following are the methods of the Window object.

alert( ) Displays a simple message in a dialog box.

blur( ) Takes keyboard focus from the top-level browser window; this sends the window to the background on most platforms.

clearTimeout( ) Cancels a pending timeout operation.

close( ) Closes a window.

confirm( ) Asks a yes or no question using a dialog box.

focus( ) Gives the top-level browser window keyboard focus; this brings the window to the front on most platforms.

open( ) Creates and opens a new window.

prompt( ) Asks for simple string input with a dialog box.

scroll( ) Scrolls the document displayed in the window.

setTimeout( ) Executes code after a specified amount of time elapses.

The String Object

The String object provides the length property, which returns the number of characters in the string, and the following methods:

anchor( ) Returns a copy of the string in an <A Name=> environment.

big( ) Returns a copy of the string in a <BIG> environment.

blink( ) Returns a copy of the string in a <BLINK> environment.

bold( ) Returns a copy of the string in a <B> environment.

charAt( ) Extracts the character at a given position from a string.

fixed( ) Returns a copy of the string in a <TT> environment.

fontcolor( ) Returns a copy of the string in a <FONT COLOR=> environment.

fontsize( ) Returns a copy of the string in a <FONT SIZE=> environment.

indexOf( ) Searches the string for a character or substring.

italics( ) Returns a copy of the string in an <I> environment.

lastIndexOf( ) Searches the string backward for a character or substring.

link( ) Returns a copy of the string in an <A HREF=> environment.

small( ) Returns a copy of the string in a <SMALL> environment.

split( ) Converts a string to an array of strings using a specified delimiter character.

strike( ) Returns a copy of the string in a <STRIKE> environment.

sub( ) Returns a copy of the string in a <SUB> environment.

substring( ) Extracts a substring of a string.

sup( ) Returns a copy of the string in a <SUP> environment.

toLowerCase( ) Returns a copy of the string with all characters converted to lowercase.

toUpperCase( ) Returns a copy of the string with all characters converted to uppercase.

Summary

This chapter presented a crash course on JavaScript for those of you not familiar with the language. This chapter is not a complete reference on this language; but by reading and mastering the examples shown here, you should be able to write client-side programs to be executed in the web browser.

22

Client-Side Programming Basics

CLIENT-SIDE PROGRAMMING OFFERS BENEFITS that not only contribute to the level of scalability of your web application, but also can make a big difference in user satisfaction. When writing code for the client side, however, you are faced with a different challenge from server-side programming. Your code will be run by many different browsers from different vendors with different power and capabilities. As such, cross-browser code is the biggest issue and making your code executable in all browsers is the biggest challenge.

In this chapter, you learn the sort of problems that you will encounter when programming for the client side, problems that you should be aware of even before you write your first line of code. There are, of course, codes that can help you solve the problems.

This chapter starts with some techniques for a very basic function: tips on how to check whether your JavaScript code can run in the user browser. This chapter then continues with a discussion of how various versions of browsers and various versions of JavaScript affect the way you should write your code.

Checking Whether JavaScript Is Enabled

JavaScript enables you to go beyond HTML. Before you start coding JavaScript, however, bear in mind that some people in some parts of this planet still use what can be categorized as direct descendants of the browser "origin of species," those which are too primitive to understand JavaScript. Living in an era where everything is Internet-ready, you may find that hard to believe.

Even if you can guarantee that all the users who come to visit your web site have at least the fourth generation of web browsers, you don't have the discretion to turn the JavaScript features on or off. Some of your users probably have the feature switched off without realizing it. Additionally, a large number of Internet surfers don't know what JavaScript is, let alone know how to turn this capability on. This means that when you are programming JavaScript for your web pages, it is important to make sure that JavaScript is supported *and* turned on. You cannot assume that everyone can see the JavaScript magic you send to the browser.

You can use a number of techniques for checking whether the user browser supports and/or is supporting JavaScript. These techniques are given in the following sections.

Checking with Redirection

Using redirection is the easiest way to determine whether JavaScript is enabled. This technique is the simplest of all. You use this script on the first page of your web site that requires JavaScript processing. The script presumes that JavaScript is not supported or not enabled, so users will get a message asking them to change the browser or turn on the JavaScript feature. Users who have JavaScript enabled will be redirected to the actual main page before they can see the message. They then can continue surfing happily.

Listing 22.1 shows such a page. You redirect the user to another page using the window object's location property of the Netscape Navigator's document object model.

Listing 22.1 **Redirection Using the Location Property**

```
<HTML>
<HEAD>
<TITLE>Checking whether JavaScript is on</TITLE>
<SCRIPT LANGUAGE="JavaScript">
location="ActualMainPage.html"
</SCRIPT>
</HEAD>
<BODY>
```

```
This web site requires that you use a JavaScript enabled
browser. Unfortunately, your browsers are either too old
to understand JavaScript or the feature is turned off.
Please click <A HREF="Message.html">here</A> for more information.
</BODY>
</HTML>
```

Users who don't have JavaScript enabled will see the message; hopefully, they will not be too disheartened to come back to your site.

This technique can be used with Netscape Navigator versions 2 and higher, and Internet Explorer version 3 and higher.

Checking JavaScript with a Form

The previous tip works well, but sometimes only one specific page in your entire web application needs the browser's JavaScript power—such as when the user needs to submit a form. At that point, you should not disrupt the users' enjoyment by forcing them to enable their JavaScript feature. For example, suppose that in your membership web application you use JavaScript only to validate input in the member-only pages. In this case, your users can still visit the promotional non-JavaScript pages that try to attract them to join. Only if they become members will they be required to enable the JavaScript feature. You then can do the testing when your users are ready to submit a form—perhaps the Login form—before they enter the member-only area.

Listing 22.2 shows a form that checks whether JavaScript is on. The HTML page includes a HIDDEN element called JavaScriptEnabled whose initial value is 0. When the form is submitted, you can check the value of JavaScriptEnabled on the server side. If the value is 0, it means JavaScript is not supported or not enabled in the user's browser. You can either warn the user by sending a "Message" page or just keep quiet and take an extra processing step. At least you know that JavaScript is not enabled for this user. If you use JavaScript for input validation in this way, you are prepared to validate user input on the server for people who are using non-scriptable browsers.

On the other hand, if the server receives the value of 1 for the JavaScriptEnabled element, the JavaScript on the browser is doing its job.

Listing 22.2 **Using a Form to Detect Whether JavaScript Is On**

```
<HTML>
<HEAD>
<TITLE>Checking JavaScript using a form</TITLE>
</HEAD>
```

continues

Listing 22.2 **Continued**

```
<BODY>
<FORM NAME =LoginForm METHOD=POST ACTION=Register.jsp
➥onSubmit="document.LoginForm.JavaScriptEnabled.value=1">
<INPUT TYPE=HIDDEN NAME=JavaScriptEnabled VALUE=0>
<INPUT TYPE=TEXT NAME=UserName><BR>
<INPUT TYPE=PASSWORD NAME=Password><BR>
<INPUT TYPE=RESET> <INPUT TYPE=SUBMIT VALUE=Login>
</FORM>
</BODY>
</HTML>
```

Warning

Note that you should not rely on JavaScript working and assume that the browser will send valid input if JavaScript is on. A clever user can have JavaScript turned off and yet give the server the impression that it is on. For example, the form in Listing 22.3 can trick the server into thinking that JavaScript is on, when it actually is not.

Listing 22.3 **Trying to Fool the Server that Checks Whether JavaScript Is On**

```
<HTML>
<HEAD>
<TITLE>Let the server think JavaScript is on </TITLE>
</HEAD>
<BODY>
<FORM NAME =LoginForm METHOD=POST ACTION=Register.jsp>
<INPUT TYPE=HIDDEN NAME=JavaScriptEnabled VALUE=1>
<INPUT TYPE=TEXT NAME=UserName><BR>
<INPUT TYPE=PASSWORD NAME=Password><BR>
<INPUT TYPE=RESET> <INPUT TYPE=SUBMIT VALUE=Login>
</FORM>
</BODY>
</HTML>
```

If input validation is critical in your application, always do both the client-side and server-side validations. The client-side validation using JavaScript is still useful for reducing server's workload.

This technique works in Netscape Navigator version 2.0 and higher, and Internet Explorer version 3.0 and higher.

Checking Whether JavaScript Is On in JavaScript-Capable Browsers

Unlike the previous two techniques that assume no knowledge of whether the browser supports JavaScript, the following technique is used to determine whether JavaScript is turned on in a browser that supports JavaScript. It works like this: All JavaScript-capable browsers will ignore the <SCRIPT> ... </SCRIPT> tags if JavaScript is turned off. When JavaScript is off, however, these browsers will interpret the <NOSCRIPT> ... </NOSCRIPT> tags. Using these tags, you can tell users to turn on their JavaScript feature in the browser.

An HTML page that uses this trick is given in Listing 22.4.

Listing 22.4 **Code for Checking for JavaScript in JavaScript-Capable Browsers**

```
<HTML>
<HEAD>
<TITLE>Checking if JavaScript is on in a JavaScript-capable browser</TITLE>
</HEAD>
<BODY>
<SCRIPT LANGUAGE="JavaScript">
  //your JavaScript code here
</SCRIPT>
<NOSCRIPT>
Your browser understands JavaScript. However, the feature
is turned off. Please turn it on to enjoy the full
capability of this page.
</NOSCRIPT>
</BODY>
</HTML>
```

This technique can be used with Netscape Navigator version 2 and higher, and Internet Explorer version 3 and higher.

Handling JavaScript-Unaware Browsers

Even though they are rare, some very old browsers that don't support JavaScript are still used. If you cannot guarantee that all your users will be using browsers that understand JavaScript, you need to understand what will happen to the rendering process of the script in those browsers. At least the script will be displayed as it is, potentially confusing your users because they see text that does not make sense. The worst effect could be disastrous: Your JavaScript could mess up the whole content of the page.

You can handle this situation by enclosing the script lines between HTML comment symbols; that is, between the <!-- and --> tags. Most scriptable browsers completely ignore the content between those tags. See Listing 22.5 for an example of a page that hides JavaScript code from JavaScript-unaware browsers.

Listing 22.5 **Hiding JavaScript Code from JavaScript-Unaware Browsers**

```
<HTML>
<HEAD>
<TITLE>Page that hides JavaScript from primitive browsers</TITLE>
<SCRIPT LANGUAGE="JavaScript">
<!--
   your JavaScript code here

// -->
</SCRIPT>
</HEAD>
</HTML>
```

The two forward slashes at the end of the construction are for JavaScript-aware browsers. They tell the JavaScript interpreter to skip the line entirely; otherwise JavaScript would try to interpret the ending HTML comment tag (-->).

You can use this technique with Netscape Navigator version 2 and higher, and Internet Explorer version 3 and higher.

Handling Different Versions of JavaScript

JavaScript came to this world as version 1.0, embedded in Netscape Navigator 2. When Navigator 3 was released, it brought with it a more mature version of JavaScript: version 1.1. JavaScript included in Navigator 4 is version 1.2. With Microsoft browsers, JavaScript's versioning story is much different. Internet Explorer 3 understands the level of JavaScript in Navigator 2; however, Internet Explorer 4 understands JavaScript 1.2.

Naturally each newer version of JavaScript includes features that were not available in the previous versions. If you must use JavaScript 1.2 language but cannot guarantee that your users will not be using Navigator 2 and 3 and Internet Explorer 3 browsers, you need to include JavaScript versions that will be understood by the older browsers.

Listing 22.6 outlines the handling of multiple versions of JavaScript. For this to work, you must lay out the <SCRIPT> tags in ascending order of version. The last function that the browser knows how to interpret is the one that gets executed.

Listing 22.6 **A Page that Handles Different Versions of JavaScript**

```
<HTML>
<HEAD>
<TITLE>Handling different versions of JavaScript</TITLE>
<SCRIPT LANGUAGE="JavaScript">
<!--
  // statements for JavaScript 1.0 browsers
</SCRIPT>

<SCRIPT LANGUAGE="JavaScript1.1">
<!--
  // statements for JavaScript 1.1 browsers
</SCRIPT>

<SCRIPT LANGUAGE="JavaScript1.2">
<!--
  // statements for JavaScript 1.2 browsers
</SCRIPT>
</HEAD>
</HTML>
```

You can use this technique with Netscape Navigator version 2 and higher, and Internet Explorer version 3 and higher.

Including a JavaScript File

When you write JavaScript code to be executed in the client side, oftentimes you have a bunch of JavaScript functions that will be used in many pages. Pasting all functions into all pages that will use them creates a maintenance horror. The solution is to save the functions in a separate file (preferably a .js file) and include it in the SRC attribute of the <SCRIPT> tag. Listing 22.7 shows a page that uses the SRC attribute of the <SCRIPT> tag to include a JavaScript source file.

Listing 22.7 **Including a JavaScript Source File**

```
<HTML>
<HEAD>
<TITLE>Including a JavaScript source file</TITLE>
<SCRIPT LANGUAGE='JavaScript' SRC="MyFunctions.js">
</HEAD>
<BODY>
<SCRIPT LANGUAGE='JavaScript'>
  // you can call the JavaScript function in MyFunctions.js file here
</SCRIPT>
</BODY>
</HTML>
```

Note that the included file does not begin with a <SCRIPT> tag and does not end with a </SCRIPT> tag. Also, the included file does not have to end with a .js extension.

You can use this technique with Netscape Navigator version 2 and higher, and Internet Explorer version 3 and higher.

Checking the Operating System

You may be wondering whether there is any circumstance that requires you to check the operating systems your web site visitors are using. After all, it's their business to stick to any "ideology" in choosing an operating system. And, as long as their browser supports some version of JavaScript, you can sit happily coding. I can tell you about a few scenarios, however, that are more than hypothetical situations. One such scenario occurs when your web site provides device drivers for various operating systems ranging from Windows to Mac to UNIX to Linux. You want your site visitors (who clearly are visiting to download a device driver) to be given the link to the version of the operating system of the computers they are using. The technique to check the operating system is given in Listing 22.8.

Listing 22.8 **Checking the User Operating System**

```
<HTML>
<HEAD>
<SCRIPT LANGUAGE="JavaScript">
<!--
function getOperatingSystem(){
  var os;
  var v = navigator.appVersion.toUpperCase();
  if (1+v.indexOf('WIN95') || 1+v.indexOf('WINDOWS 95')
    || 1+v.indexOf('WIN32'))
    os = 'Win95';
```

```
  else if (1+v.indexOf('WIN98')
    || 1+v.indexOf('WINDOWS 98'))
    os = 'Win98';
  else if (1+v.indexOf('WINNT')
    ||  1+v.indexOf('WINDOWS NT'))
    os = 'WinNT'; //WinNT or Win2K
  else if (1+v.indexOf('WINDOWS 3.1'))
    os = 'Win3.1';
  else if (1+v.indexOf('WINDOWS 3'))
    os = 'Win3';
  else if (1+v.indexOf('WIN16'))
    os = 'Win16';  // might be 3.x or NT.
  else if((1+v.indexOf('MAC')) &&
    (1+v.indexOf('PPC') || 1+v.indexOf('POWERPC')))
    os = 'Macintosh ppc';
  else if (1+v.indexOf('MAC'))
    os = 'Mac68K';
  else if (1+v.indexOf('SUNOS'))
    os = 'Sun';
  else if (1+v.indexOf('LINUX'))
    os = 'Linux';
  else if (1+v.indexOf('IRIX'))
    os = 'Irix'
  else if (1+v.indexOf('HP-UX'))
    os = 'HP-UX';
  else if (1+v.indexOf('OSF'))
    os = 'OSF';
  else if (1+v.indexOf('AIX'))
    os = 'AIX';
  else if (1+v.indexOf('OS/2'))
    os = 'OS/2';
  else if (1+v.indexOf('WEBTV'))
    os = 'WebTv';
  document.forms[0].OS.value=os;
}
//-->
</SCRIPT>
</HEAD>
<BODY>
Welcome to Brainy Software. We are happy to provide you
with the version of device driver that works with
your operating system.
Please click the button below to start downloading.
<BR>
<FORM METHOD=POST ACTION="Download.jsp"
  onSubmit='getOperatingSystem()'>
<INPUT TYPE=HIDDEN NAME=OS>
<INPUT TYPE=SUBMIT VALUE="Download">
</FORM>
</BODY>
</HTML>
```

Upon submit, the OS hidden input element will have the value according to the user's operating system. Another way to determine the operating system in use is to check the HTTP header's USER AGENT string value on the server; however, processing it in the client side reduces the server work.

You can use this technique with Netscape Navigator version 2 and higher, and Internet Explorer version 3 and higher.

Checking the Browser Generation

Knowing which generation of browser the user is running enables you to cater to various JavaScript versions by sending the appropriate function that works for that browser.

You can use the appVersion property of the navigator object for this purpose. The value returned by this property is as follows:

```
version number [language] (operating system information)
```

For example, in the Netscape Navigator 4.02 browser for Windows 95, a typical returned value of this property is 4.02 – (Win95; I; Nav). In Internet Explorer 3.01 for Windows 95 it is 2.0 (compatible; MSIE 3.01; Windows 95). The latter browser actually emulates Navigator 2. Therefore, version 3 of IE has the application version of 2. Note also that the language part is optional.

The getBrowserGeneration JavaScript function in Listing 22.9 can be used to obtain the browser generation information.

Listing 22.9 **Obtaining the Browser Generation Information**

```
<SCRIPT LANGUAGE="JavaScript">
<function getBrowserGeneration() {
  return navigator.appVersion.charAt(0);
}
</SCRIPT>
```

This technique can be used with Netscape Navigator version 2 and higher, and Internet Explorer 3 and higher.

Checking the Browser Type

Many times when you are programming JavaScript, especially when you are touching the area of dynamic HTML (DHTML), you need to check whether IE or Netscape is being used because the browsers have different standards for DHTML. The two JavaScript functions in Listing 22.10 do the trick. The isNetscapeBrowser function returns true if the user is using a Netscape browser. The isMicrosoftBrowser function returns true if the user is using a Microsoft browser.

Listing 22.10 **Checking the Browser Type**

```
<SCRIPT LANGUAGE="JavaScript">
function isNetscapeBrowser() {
  return (navigator.appName=="Netscape");
}

function isMicrosoftBrowser() {
  return (navigator.userAgent.indexOf("MSIE")!=-1);
}
</SCRIPT>
```

This technique works with Netscape Navigator version 2 and higher, and Internet Explorer version 3 and higher.

Checking the Browser Language

If you happen to be the webmaster for an international corporation, you probably need to maintain several versions of the company web site in different languages. In Netscape Navigator 4 and higher, you can query the language property of the navigator object to find out the language version of the browser. Such a property does not exist in Internet Explorer, however.

For example, if the browser language is German, the value of navigator.language is de. Table 22.1 lists the language code and its language.

Table 22.1 **The Language Code for navigator.language for Several Languages**

Language Code	Language
da	Danish
de	German
en	English
es	Spanish
fr	French
it	Italian
ja	Japanese
ko	Korean
nl	Dutch
pt	Brazilian Portuguese
sv	Swedish

If you cannot guarantee that all your users will use a Netscape browser of version 4 and higher, you need to check this on the server side.

This technique works only with Netscape Navigator 4 and higher versions.

Handling Dynamic Variable-Names

At some stage of your JavaScript programming career, you might find a situation in which you need to use a variable whose name is not fixed. Can JavaScript handle variable variable-names? Yes—when the variable name may be dynamic, the eval function is certainly useful.

The code in Listing 22.11 presents an example that uses a variable whose name must change.

Listing 22.11 **Handling a Variable variable-name**

```
<SCRIPT LANGUAGE="JavaScript">
var n0 = "train";
var n1 = "abc4";
var n2 = 2;

for (var i=0; i<3; i++) {
  alert(eval("n" + i));
}
</SCRIPT>
```

Without the eval function, the code in Listing 22.11 would have to be written in a less efficient way, as given in Listing 22.12.

Listing 22.12 **Rewriting the Code in Listing 22.11 Without the eval Function**

```
<SCRIPT LANGUAGE="JavaScript">
var n0 = "train";
var n1 = "abc4";
var n2 = 2;

alert(n0);
alert(n1);
alert(n2);
</SCRIPT>
```

This technique works with Netscape Navigator version 2 and higher, and Internet Explorer version 3 and higher.

Summary

In this chapter, you have seen several techniques that can help you with your client-side coding. You now know how to check to make sure the user browser supports JavaScript and the JavaScript feature is turned on, and you understand how to include a collection of JavaScript functions in a file. Additionally, you discovered how important the fourth generation of the browser is and saw how to use the eval function to handle variables whose names can change throughout the page.

These techniques may seem simple, but they constitute the most important technique collection you should know if you want to consider yourself a serious web developer.

23 Redirection

REDIRECTING THE USER TO A DIFFERENT page is a useful technique frequently used in web programming. For example, you might want to create a splash screen effect—displaying the company logo for a few seconds and then redirect the user to the main page. Or, you might want to send cookies to the browser by writing the cookies in the HTTP response, plus the bit that tells the browser to fetch another page—effectively creating the cookies in one go. The two examples mentioned redirect the user without user interaction. In other situations, you might want the redirection to happen after the user performs an action.

This chapter presents several techniques for page redirection, including a discussion of anticipating a failed redirection (which can happen for a number of reasons). Failed redirection, in fact, should be the first thing you take into account when using a redirection technique.

Anticipating Failed Redirection

When automatic redirection should take place without user intervention, be sure to provide users with a link to click in case the redirection fails. Redirection could fail, for example, if the browser does not support JavaScript or it supports JavaScript, but the feature is turned off. When the redirection is to create a cookie on the browser, it could also fail if the browser does not accept cookies.

For every redirection attempt, always take precaution by sending a link that the user can manually click in case the redirection fails. For example, Listing 23.1 is a page that provides such a link.

Listing 23.1 **A Page that Anticipates a Failed Redirection**

```
<HTML>
<HEAD>
<TITLE>Anticipating failed redirection</TITLE>
<SCRIPT LANGUAGE="JavaScript">
  // code for redirection here
</SCRIPT>
</HEAD>
<BODY>
Click <A HREF="RedirectionURL">here</A>
if you do not get redirected automatically.
</BODY>
</HTML>
```

Using the Refresh Meta Tag

The easiest way to redirect a page that has been displayed for a period of time is to use the meta tag. The meta tag for redirection takes the following form:

```
<META HTTP-EQUIV="Refresh" CONTENT="x;URL=http://anotherURL">
```

where *x* is the number of seconds the browser will wait before redirection occurs.

For example, the script in Listing 23.2 redirects the browser to `http://www.newriders.com` after 5 seconds.

Listing 23.2 **Redirection with the Meta Tag**

```
<HTML>
<HEAD>
<TITLE>Using the meta tag to redirect the user</TITLE>
<META HTTP-EQUIV="Refresh" CONTENT="5;URL=http://www.newriders.com">
</HEAD>
<BODY>
This will be redirected to another page.
Click <A HREF="http://www.newriders.com">here</A> if you do not
 get redirected automatically.
</BODY>
</HTML>
```

If you set *x* to 0, the redirection will happen without delay.

Using a non-zero value for *x*, you can create a splash screen that is displayed for *x* seconds before the browser gets redirected to another page. Listing 23.3 gives the code for a splash screen that gets displayed for 3 seconds before the user is redirected to somewhere else.

Listing 23.3 **A Splash Screen**

```
<HTML>
<HEAD>
<TITLE>Using the meta tag to redirect the user</TITLE>
<META HTTP-EQUIV="Refresh" CONTENT="3;URL=http://anotherPage">
</HEAD>
<BODY>
Welcome to Brainy Software
<IMG SRC="logo.jpg">
</BODY>
</HTML>
```

This technique works in Netscape Navigator 3 and higher and Internet Explorer 4 and higher.

Using the location Object

An alternative way to redirect the user to another page is to use the location object in JavaScript. The syntax is simple, as follows:

```
<SCRIPT LANGUAGE="JavaScript">
location=newURL
</SCRIPT>
```

where *newURL* is the new URL to which the browser will be redirected. Listing 23.4 gives an example of redirection using the location object.

Listing 23.4 **Redirection Using the location Object**

```
<HTML>
<HEAD>
<TITLE>Redirection using the location object </TITLE>
<SCRIPT LANGUAGE="JavaScript">
location='http://www.newriders.com';
</SCRIPT>
</HEAD>
<BODY>
This will be redirected to another page.
Click <A HREF="http://www.newriders.com">here</A> if you do not
 get redirected automatically.
</BODY>
</HTML>
```

To redirect the user after a few seconds (for example, to create a splash screen) use the setTimeout method with the location object. The syntax is as follows:

```
setTimeout("location='anotherURL'", y);
```

where *y* is the number of milliseconds before the user is redirected to *anotherURL*. Listing 23.5 redirects the user to `www.newriders.com` after two seconds.

Listing 23.5 **A Splash Screen Using the location Object**

```
<HTML>
<HEAD>
<TITLE>A splash screen using the location object </TITLE>
<SCRIPT LANGUAGE="JavaScript">
  setTimeout("location='http://www.newriders.com'", 2000);
</SCRIPT>
</HEAD>
<BODY>
Greeting
<IMG SRC="logo.gif">
</BODY>
</HTML>
```

This technique works with Netscape Navigator 2 and higher and Internet Explorer 3 and higher.

Going Back to the Previous Page

Sometimes you might want to provide a link for the user to go back to the previous page. For example, you might have an entry form and a page that displays an error message if one of the user inputs is invalid. From the Error page, you can provide a link that can be clicked to go back to the entry form.

The history object has two methods that can be used to go back to the previous page: the back method and the go method. The syntax for using the history object to go back to the previous page is as follows:

```
history.back()
```

or

```
history.go(-1)
```

For example, the code in Listing 23.6 provides a link for the user to go back to the previous page.

Listing 23.6 **Going Back to the Previous Page**

```
<HTML>
<HEAD>
<TITLE>Going back to the previous page</TITLE>
</HEAD>
<BODY>
The password you typed in is not long enough.
  Please <A HREF="javascript:history.back()">go back</A> to correct it.
</BODY>
</HTML>
```

Using the history object's go method, you can pass any negative number to go back *n* pages before the current page. The code in Listing 23.7 serves as an example of a page that has a link to bring the user 3 pages back.

Listing 23.7 Going *n* Pages Back

```
<HTML>
<HEAD>
<TITLE>Going n pages back </TITLE>
</HEAD>
<BODY>
Click <A HREF="javascript:history.go(-3)">here</A>
to go back the the beginning of the entry form go back.
</BODY>
</HTML>
```

This technique works with Netscape Navigator 2 and higher and Internet Explorer 3 and higher.

Moving Forward

You may have guessed that you can use the history object's go method to move forward. Yes, you can. The secret is to pass a positive number as the argument of the go method. The code in Listing 23.8 provides a page with a link to move forward.

Listing 23.8 **Moving Forward**

```
<HTML>
<HEAD>
<TITLE>Moving forward</TITLE>
</HEAD>
<BODY>
Click <A HREF="javascript:history.go(1)">here</A>
to move forward.
</BODY>
</HTML>
```

Note that you don't need to use the plus sign (+) in front of the number for the parameter to the go method.

This technique works with Netscape Navigator 2 and higher and Internet Explorer 3 and higher.

Navigation with a SELECT Element

From the current page, you might want to let the user choose a new destination, such as the product they want to review or the branch office of your corporate they are interested in. You can use a SELECT element for this purpose. For example, the code in Listing 23.9 uses a SELECT element to list one of the regional offices. The user can click an option to get redirected to the URL linked to that option.

Listing 23.9 **Selecting a New Destination**

```
<HTML>
<HEAD>
<TITLE>Navigating to a new world</TITLE>
</HEAD>
<BODY>
Please select one of our regional offices
<BR>
```

```
<FORM>
<SELECT onChange="location=this.options[this.selectedIndex].value">
<OPTION>Select a destination</OPTION>
<OPTION VALUE="asia.html">Asia</OPTION>
<OPTION VALUE="europe.html">Europe</OPTION>
<OPTION VALUE="northAmerica.html">North America</OPTION>
<OPTION VALUE="australasia.html">Australasia</OPTION>
</SELECT>
</FORM>
</BODY>
</HTML>
```

The code in Listing 23.9 uses the onChange event to change the value of the location object. The syntax is as follows.

```
location="newURL"
```

where *newURL* is an option value of the following form:

```
this.options[this.selectedIndex].value
```

The this keyword refers to the current object, which is the SELECT element. options is an array of options. In Listing 23.9 options has four elements: asia.html, europe.html, northAmerica.html, and australasia.html. To select a value, you just need to pass an index to the brackets […]. Thus, the following will return the first element in the options array:

```
this.options[0].value
```

In the case of the code in Listing 23.9, it will return asia.html.

Finally, this.selectedIndex returns the index number of the option clicked by the user. Therefore, if the user clicks Australasia from the SELECT element, this.options[this.selectedIndex].value will be translated into australasia.html.

This technique works with Netscape Navigator 2 and higher and Internet Explorer 3 and higher.

Summary

In this chapter you have learned several tips for both automatic and manual redirection. Automatic redirection redirects the user to another URL or another page without the user intervention, whereas manual redirection redirects the user when the user does something, such as clicking a button or a hyperlink.

You have also learned how to anticipate failed automatic redirection by providing a link the user can click to manually go to another page. This anticipation tip should be used whenever you use automatic redirection. The automatic redirection can be used to display a splash screen or to send cookies to the browser.

For manual redirection, you normally use the go or back methods of the history object.

24

Client-Side Input Validation

When you apply client-side validation, you ensure that the values of form elements are valid before the form is submitted. From the server's perspective, this means reduced workload because it does not have to return the user to the form to correct a value. For users, this means a much faster response because they get an instant warning when a form entry is not correct.

When you use client-side validation, be aware that some users have their JavaScript capability turned off, and some clever people can bypass your client-side validation entirely. Normally you need to perform server-side input validation to check for those conditions. Using client-side input validation still makes the overall system more scalable, however, because in most cases server-side validation needs only to perform a last check for input validity.

On the client side, there are two types of input validation: at the form level and at the field- or form- element level. With form-level validation, you perform a check on every form element just before the form is submitted. You do this by writing an event handler for the form's onSubmit event, as follows:

```
<FORM METHOD=POST ACTION=buy.jsp onSubmit='validate()'>
```

In the preceding code, validate( ) is a JavaScript function that does the input validation.

With form-level validation, you perform the validation right after a user finishes entering a value for that form element. If the element is a TEXT box, which is the case for most forms, you can write a handler for the onBlur or onChange event of that TEXT element. The onChange event is triggered whenever a user makes a change to the text in a TEXT element and then either tabs or clicks out of the element. The onBlur event is triggered when the focus moves from the TEXT element to another object, such as when the user clicks another element.

For example, the following line of code checks the value of the ProductQuantity TEXT element every time its value changes:

```
<INPUT TYPE=TEXT Name=ProductQuantity
  onChange='isNumeric(document.forms[0].ProductQuantity.value)'>
```

In the preceding code, isNumeric is a custom function that accepts a string parameter and checks whether the string parameter is a valid numeric value.

This chapter begins with helpful JavaScript functions that you can copy and paste to any of your forms. You even can bundle everything in a .js file if you use these functions often enough.

> **Note**
> All the techniques in this chapter can be used with Netscape Navigator version 2.0 and later, Internet Explorer version 3.0 and higher.

The isEmpty Function

The isEmpty function tests whether the string parameter passed to it is a null or a zero-length string. It returns true if the string parameter is a null or a blank string; otherwise, it returns false. The isEmpty function is shown in Listing 24.1.

Listing 24.1 **The isEmpty Function**

```
<SCRIPT LANGUAGE="JavaScript">
function isEmpty(str) {
  if (str==null || str=="")
    return true;
  return false;
}
</SCRIPT>
```

The most common application of this function is making sure a user does not leave a TEXT element blank. Listing 24.2 demonstrates the use of isEmpty. The code is for a form with two input elements: UserName and Password. When the user submits the form, the function validate uses the isEmpty function to check the two elements. The form submission will be cancelled if either one of the two boxes is empty.

Listing 24.2 **Using the isEmpty Function**

```
<HTML>
<HEAD>
<TITLE>Using the isEmpty Function</TITLE>
<SCRIPT LANGUAGE="JavaScript">
function isEmpty(str) {
  if (str==null || str=="")
    return true;
  return false;
}

function validate(userName, password) {
  if (isEmpty(userName)) {
    alert('User name must have a value');
    return false;
  }
  if (isEmpty(password)) {
    alert('Password must have a value');
    return false;
  }
  return true;
}
</SCRIPT>
</HEAD>
<BODY>
<FORM ACTION=Login.jsp METHOD=POST
  OnSubmit="return validate(this.UserName.value,
    this.Password.value);">
User Name: <INPUT TYPE=TEXT NAME=UserName>
<BR>
Password: <INPUT TYPE=PASSWORD NAME=Password>
<BR>
<INPUT TYPE=SUBMIT VALUE="Login">
</FORM>
</BODY>
</HTML>
```

The trim Function

When validating user input, you want to make sure that the user does not accidentally (or deliberately) type leading or trailing spaces that have to be removed on the server. The code in Listing 24.3 provides a function that trims the leading and trailing spaces.

Listing 24.3 **The trim Function**

```
<SCRIPT LANGUAGE="JavaScript">
function trim(str) {
  while (str.charAt(str.length - 1)==" ")
    str = str.substring(0, str.length - 1);
  while (str.charAt(0)==" ")
    str = str.substring(1, str.length);
  return str;
}
</SCRIPT>
```

The trim function accepts one parameter—str, which is the string that needs to be trimmed. The brains of this function are the two while loops. The first while loop continuously checks the last character of the string and truncates the last character if it is a white space, as you see in the following:

```
while (str.charAt(str.length - 1)==" ")
    str = str.substring(0, str.length - 1);
```

The second while loop checks the first character in the string, removes the first character if it is a space, and shifts the rest of the string one character to the left, as follows:

```
while (str.charAt(0)==" ")
    str = str.substring(1, str.length);
```

The function then returns the trimmed string:

```
return str;
```

You might wonder if you need to check against null being passed to the function. The answer is no, as long as the trim function is used to check the value of a form element. The value of a form element will never be null even if a user does not type anything in it. If a TEXT element is left untouched by the user, it has the value of a blank string.

If you are going to pass a variable to the trim function, you need to modify it to check for null. Otherwise, it will generate an error and cause the JavaScript execution to stop. The code in Listing 24.3 is the modified trim function that can safely handle a string variable. The code in Listing 24.3 is safe only for processing form elements.

Listing 24.4 **Another Version of the trim Function that Can Handle a String Variable Safely**

```
<SCRIPT LANGUAGE="JavaScript">
function trim(str) {
  if (str!=null) {
    while (str.charAt(str.length - 1)==" ")
      str = str.substring(0, str.length - 1);
    while (str.charAt(0)==" ")
      str = str.substring(1, str.length);
  }
  return str;
}
</SCRIPT>
```

Note that the trim function in Listing 24.4 first checks whether the parameter is null. This is not done by the trim function in Listing 24.3 because a form element is never null.

The trimAll Function

The trim function works with the form's TEXT input element, but it does not work for elements that can accept carriage return characters, such as a TEXTAREA. The trimAll in Listing 24.5 extends the trim function to trim any leading or trailing blank space, carriage return character, new line character, or tab character.

Listing 24.5 **The trimAll Function**

```
function trimAll(str) {
  if (str!=null) {
    while (str.length > 0 &&
      "\n\r\t ".indexOf(str.charAt(str.length - 1)) != -1)
      str = str.substring(0, str.length - 1);
    while (str.length > 0 &&
      "\n\r\t ".indexOf(str.charAt(0)) != -1)
      str = str.substring(1, str.length);
  }
  return str;
}
```

The first while loop first makes sure that the string str is not empty. It then creates a string "\n\r\t " and uses the indexOf function to check whether the last character of str matches any of the characters in the string "\n\r\t ". If there is a match, indexOf returns the matching character position in "\n\r\t ";

otherwise, it returns -1. Note that in JavaScript \n represents a new line character, \r represents a carriage return, and \t is a tab character.

The second while loop does the same thing with the first character in str.

The isPositiveInteger Function

The isPositiveInteger function returns true only if all the characters that compose the string argument passed to it are numeric characters—that is, 0 to 9 inclusive. The function loops through the string argument from the first character to the last. It compares each character with a pattern and stops and returns false if it finds a character that does not match any composing character of the pattern.

Listing 24.6 presents the isPositiveInteger function. If you are using the function in a form, you also should trim the string you want to check before feeding it to the isPositiveInteger function.

Listing 24.6 **The isPositiveInteger Function**

```
<SCRIPT LANGUAGE="JavaScript">
function isPositiveInteger(str) {
  var pattern = "0123456789"
  var i = 0;
  do {
    var pos = 0;
    for (var j=0; j<pattern.length; j++)
      if (str.charAt(i)==pattern.charAt(j)) {
        pos = 1;
        break;
      }
    i++;
  } while (pos==1 && i<str.length)
  if (pos==0)
    return false;
  return true;
}
</SCRIPT>
```

In addition to validating a positive numeric value, you can use the isPositiveInteger function to check a ZIP code.

You can easily modify the isPositiveInteger to create similar functions by changing the value of the variable pattern. Examples include the isValidPhoneNumber and isMoney functions, which are described in the following sections.

The isValidPhoneNumber Function

The isValidPhoneNumber function is derived from the isPositiveInteger function and works in a similar manner. The only difference between the two functions is the value of the pattern string. Listing 24.7 illustrates the isValidPhoneNumber function.

Listing 24.7 **The isValidPhoneNumber Function**

```
<SCRIPT LANGUAGE="JavaScript">
function isValidPhoneNumber(str) {
  var pattern = "0123456789( )-"
  var i = 0;
  do {
    var pos = 0;
    for (var j=0; j<pattern.length; j++)
      if (str.charAt(i)==pattern.charAt(j)) {
pos = 1;
      break;
      }
    i++;
  } while (pos==1 && i<str.length)
  if (pos==0)
    return false;
  return true;
}
</SCRIPT>
```

Note

Note that the isValidPhoneNumber function only validates that the string is comprised of valid characters. It does not verify the validity of the phone number itself.

The preceding isValidPhoneNumber function checks only the string input based on a pattern. It does not, for example, check that the "("character appears before ")". First, the validity of phone numbers depends on the country. Secondly, checking phone number validity requires you to draw certain rules that need to apply. The more complex the rule is, the harder it is to create a validating function. The isValidPhoneNumber given here therefore provides only for a basic validating function. You should extend this function based on your need.

Note that you can perform string checking more easily using regular expressions. For example, the following function checks whether the string input has the format of (xx)yy, where both xx and yy are any number of numeric characters and both the "(" and ")" characters are optional. Therefore, using the following function, (999)5565656 is valid, but (ab)8989898 is not:

```
function isValidPhoneNumber(str) {
  var re = new RegExp(/^\(?\d*\)?\d*$/);
  if (re.test(str))
    return true;
  else
    return false;
}
```

The problem with regular expressions is that browsers prior to version 4.0 of Internet Explorer and Netscape Navigator do not recognize them. Additionally, compatibility between the two types of browser is not guaranteed. For instance, the preceding function returns true in IE 5.5 for str equals (121)888. In Navigator 4.7, however, the same function with the same input returns false.

The isMoney Function

The isMoney function, which derives from the isPositiveInteger function, checks the string parameter passed to it. The function returns true if the string parameter is a valid monetary unit; otherwise, it returns false.

An example of the isMoney function is presented in Listing 24.8.

Listing 24.8 **The isMoney Function**

```
<SCRIPT LANGUAGE="JavaScript">
function isMoney(str) {
  var pattern = "0123456789,."
  var i = 0;
  do {
    var pos = 0;
    for (var j=0; j<pattern.length; j++)
      if (str.charAt(i)==pattern.charAt(j)) {
pos = 1;
        break;
      }
    i++;
  } while (pos==1 && i<str.length)
  if (pos==0)
    return false;

  // now make sure that the decimal point, if any,
  // only appears one and at the (str.length-3)
  // position, so that the valid format is xxx.yy
  // the following statement also returns
  // false if there are 2 or more decimal points
```

```
 pos = str.indexOf(".");
  if (pos!=-1 && pos!=str.length-3)
    return false

  // now check that if comma exists, the
  // format must be xxx,xxx,xxx,...,xxx
  if (pos==-1)
    pos = str.length;


  while (str.lastIndexOf(",", pos-1) != -1) {
    if (str.lastIndexOf(",", pos-1) != pos-4)
      return false;
    else
      pos -= 4;
  }
  return true;
}
</SCRIPT>
```

One thing to remember when you validate a monetary unit string is that even though a comma can be in the string, you must remove the comma when you pass the value if you don't want to have to remove it on the server. The removeComma function in Listing 24.9 can do the job.

Listing 24.9 **The removeComma Function**

```
<SCRIPT LANGUAGE="JavaScript">
function removeComma(str) {
  var result = "";
  for (var i=0; i<str.length; i++)
    if (str.charAt(i)!=",")
      result += str.charAt(i);
  return result;
}
```

The removeComma function checks the whole string for the comma character and recomposes result from str. The variable result is free of commas.

The isUSDate and isOZDate Functions

Another important data type that needs attention is the date. The various date formats always add complexity to your code, either on the client or the server side. When you ask a user to enter a date on the client side, it's a good idea to have three SELECT boxes with valid options: one for the day, one for the month, and one for the year. This way, the date entered will always be valid because the user can't enter any value beyond those given in the SELECT boxes.

If your design does not permit you to use the previous technique and you can have only one text box for the day, the month, and the year, the isUSDate and isOZDate functions can help. OZ stands for aussie or Australia, one of the countries whose valid date is dd/mm/yyyy. Both functions assume that a valid date must be 10 characters long and have two backslash characters as separators. As a result, if the day or the month of the date is only one character long, it must be padded with a zero character. For example, May 5, 2002 must be written as 05/05/2002.

The difference between the two functions lies in the order of the day and the month. The isUSDate function accepts a date as valid if the format is mm/dd/yyyy. The isOZDate function, on the other hand, accepts a date as valid date in the dd/mm/yyyy format.

A function to check the validity of a date is always made more complex by the fact that a normal year has 365 days, while a leap year has 366 days. Keep in mind that a leap year is one that meets the following mathematical criteria:

- It is evenly divisible by 400.
- If it is not evenly divisible by 400, it is evenly divisible by 4 but not evenly divisible by 100.

Therefore, the year 2000 is a leap year because it is divisible by 400, but 1900 is not a leap year because it is divisible by 100. Other examples of leap years are 1980, 1984, and 1988, because they are divisible by 4 but not divisible by 100. Listing 24.10 presents the isUSDate function, and Listing 24.11 presents the isOZDate function.

Listing 24.10 **The isUSDate Function**

```
<SCRIPT LANGUAGE="JavaScript">
function isUSDate(str) {
  if (str.length!=10 || str.charAt(2)!="/" || str.charAt(5)!="/" ||
    !isPositiveInteger(str.substring(0,2) +
    str.substring(3,5) + str.substring(6,10)))
    return false;
  var d = str.substring(3,5) - 0;
  var m = str.substring(0,2) - 0;
  var y = str.substring(6,10) - 0;
  if (d==0 || m==0 || y==0)
    return false;

  if (m>12) return false;
  if (m==1 || m==3 || m==5 || m==7 || m==8 || m==10 || m==12)
    var dmax = 31;
  else
    if (m==4 || m==6 || m==9 || m==11) dmax = 30;
```

```
      else
        if ((y%400==0) || (y%4==0 && y%100!=0)) dmax = 29;
        else dmax = 28;
  if (d>dmax) return false;
  return true;
}
</SCRIPT>
```

Listing 24.11 **The isOZDate Function**

```
<SCRIPT LANGUAGE="JavaScript">
function isOZDate(str) {
  if (str.length!=10 || str.charAt(2)!="/" || str.charAt(5)!="/" ||
    !isPositiveInteger(str.substring(0,2) +
    str.substring(3,5) + str.substring(6,10)))
    return false;
  var d = str.substring(0,2) - 0;
  var m = str.substring(3,5) - 0;
  var y = str.substring(6,10) - 0;
  if (d==0 || m==0 || y==0)
    return false;

  if (m>12) return false;
  if (m==1 || m==3 || m==5 || m==7 || m==8 || m==10 || m==12)
    var dmax = 31;
  else
    if (m==4 || m==6 || m==9 || m==11) dmax = 30;
    else
      if ((y%400==0) || (y%4==0 && y%100!=0)) dmax = 29;
      else dmax = 28;
  if (d>dmax) return false;
  return true;
}
</SCRIPT>
```

The isUSDate function first checks whether the variable str is 10 characters long and whether the third and fifth characters are forward slashes (/). The function also checks that the rest of the characters are integers 0 to 9 inclusive, as you see here:

```
if (str.length!=10 || str.charAt(2)!="/" || str.charAt(5)!="/" ||
  !isPositiveInteger(str.substring(0,2) +
  str.substring(3,5) + str.substring(6,10)))
```

Note that the isUSDate function uses the isPositiveInteger function in Listing 24.6 to check whether all characters except the third and fifth characters are numbers. When you use the isUSDate function, you also must copy the isPositiveInteger function.

The function then extracts the day, month, and year components from str and stores them in variables d, m, and y, respectively:

```
var d = str.substring(3,5) - 0;
var m = str.substring(0,2) - 0;
var y = str.substring(6,10) - 0;
```

The result of the substring operations for d, m, and y have 0 subtracted from them, forcing them to convert to numbers. Alternatively, you can use the parseInt function to convert a string into an integer.

The function then uses the following line to check that the value of the month does not exceed 12:

```
if (m>12) return false;
```

The number of days in January, March, May, July, August, October, and December is 31, so the maximum value for d is 31, as you see in the following:

```
if (m==1 || m==3 || m==5 || m==7 || m==8 || m==10 || m==12)
    var dmax = 31;
```

For April, June, September, and November, however, the maximum number of days is 30:

```
if (m==4 || m==6 || m==9 || m==11) dmax = 30;
```

The month of February is most difficult. In a leap year, the number of days is 29, but in non-leap years, the number of days is 28. The code for this is as follows:

```
if ((y%400==0) || (y%4==0 && y%100!=0)) dmax = 29;
  else dmax = 28;
```

The isOZDate function works similarly, except that the day and month are reversed.

Converting Date Formats

If you happen to use different date formats on the client and server sides, you need to convert your dates upon submitting the form to avoid the need for processing on the server. For example, if you want to publish your web site in the United Kingdom, but the data will go directly to a server in the United States, you need to validate the dates using the isOZDate function and convert them to a U.S. format upon form submittal. If you are never sure where the client is located, however, use the three select boxes to force the date to have a specific format; that is, either dd/mm/yyyy or mm/dd/yyyy.

Again, two functions are provided here. The convertToUSDate function converts an already valid date in dd/mm/yyyy format to the mm/dd/yyyy format. The convertToOZDate function does the reverse.

You'll find the convertToUSDate function in Listing 24.12 and the convertToOZDate function in Listing 24.13.

Listing 24.12 **The convertToUSDate Function**

```
<SCRIPT LANGUAGE="JavaScript">
function convertToUSDate(str) {
  // maybe you should validate that this IsOZDate first?
  return (str.substring(3,5) + "/" + str.substring(0,2) + "/"
➥+ str.substring(6,10));
}
</SCRIPT>
```

Listing 24.13 **The convertToOZDate Function**

```
<SCRIPT LANGUAGE="JavaScript">
function convertToOZDate(str) {
  // validate that this isUSDate first?
  return (str.substring(3,5) + "/" + str.substring(0,2) + "/" +
str.substring(6,10));
}
</SCRIPT>
```

Data Type Conversion: String to Numeric

To understand the importance of data type conversion in JavaScript, consider the code in Listing 24.14.

Listing 24.14 **A Logic Error Resulting from Not Understanding the Importance of Data Conversion**

```
<HTML>
<HEAD>
<TITLE>A logic error</TITLE>
<SCRIPT LANGUAGE="JavaScript">
function getTotalCost() {

  var freight = 2;
  var totalCost =  freight + document.forms[0].price.value;
  alert(totalCost); //result: 2300
}
```

continues

Listing 24.14 **Continued**

```
</SCRIPT>
</HEAD>
<BODY>
<FORM>
<INPUT TYPE=HIDDEN NAME=price VALUE="300">
<INPUT TYPE=BUTTON VALUE="Get Total Cost"
➥onClick="javascript:getTotalCost()">
</FORM>
</BODY>
</HTML>
```

You might think the result of the getTotalCost function would be 302 (from 300 + 2); however, the result is 2300. What happened? Whatever is entered into a TEXT element is considered a string, even though all the typed characters are digits 0 to 9. When you perform the + operation with freight with a value of 2, a string concatenation is performed rather than a mathematical addition operation. To correct the problem, you need to explicitly or implicitly convert the string to a numeric type.

Most JavaScript textbooks teach developers to use the parseInt and parseFloat functions. The difference between an integer and a floating-point number in JavaScript is that integers are always whole numbers, with no decimal point or numbers to the right of a decimal. In contrast, a floating-point number can have fractional value to the right of the decimal. JavaScript math operations don't differentiate between integers and floating-point numbers, however.

Consider the result of the parseInt function:

```
parseInt("98");     //result = 98
parseInt("98.87");  //result = 98
```

The parseFloat function returns an integer if it can; otherwise, it returns a floating-point number:

```
parseFloat("98");    //result = 98
parseFloat("98.87");  //result = 98.87
```

To get the expected result, put the string in the bracket and add – 0 (minus 0) to force the string to change to numeric.

Applying string-to-numeric data conversion, the getTotalCost function in Listing 24.14 is rewritten in Listing 24.15.

Listing 24.15 **The Correct getTotalCost Function**

```
<SCRIPT LANGUAGE="JavaScript">
function getTotalCost() {
  var freight = 2;
  var totalCost =  freight + (document.forms[0].price.value - 0);
  alert(totalCost); //result: 302
}
</SCRIPT>
```

Note that the use of the minus sign (–) to force a string to convert to a number can be used as the alternative to the parseInt or parseFloat function. This approach makes your function less readable, however.

Data Type Conversion: Numeric to String

You'll sometimes need to convert a number into a string. For example, after doing a mathematical calculation, you want to pass the result to a format function that performs different operations for a number argument and a string argument. If you want the string operation to take place, you must convert your number into a string prior to passing it to the format function. This is done by concatenating the number with a blank string. The code in Listing 24.16 presents an example of number-to-string conversion.

Listing 24.16 Number to String Conversion

```
<SCRIPT LANGUAGE="JavaScript">
function toString(n) {
  return "" + n;
}
/* note
"" + 98;  //result = "98"
("" + 98).length;  //result = 2
*/
</SCRIPT>
```

Using the Validation Functions

This section does not provide a tip, but rather offers an example of how to use the validation functions in a form. Listing 24.17 is an HTML page with a form containing three input elements: Company, ProductID, and ProductQuantity. As you may have guessed, this form enables customers to order products. The Company, ProductID, and ProductQuantity boxes must not be left empty. In addition, ProductQuantity can contain only a number. Note that the HTML page includes a <SCRIPT> section with three functions: trim, isPositiveInteger, and validateForm. The validateForm function is assigned as the handler for the form's onSubmit event. It is called just before the form is submitted. The validateForm function will return true only if the three boxes have valid values. If the validateForm function returns false, the form is not submitted. If one of the three form elements has an invalid value, an alert box is issued and the focus shifts to the box whose value is invalid.

Listing 24.17 **A Client-Side Input Validation Example**

```
<HTML>
<HEAD>
<TITLE>Form Validation</TITLE>

<SCRIPT LANGUAGE="JavaScript">
function trim(str) {
  while (str.charAt(str.length - 1)==" ")
    str = str.substring(0, str.length - 1);
  while (str.charAt(0)==" ")
    str = str.substring(1, str.length);
  return str;
}

function isPositiveInteger(str) {
  var pattern = "0123456789"
  var i = 0;
  do {
    var pos = 0;
    for (var j=0; j<pattern.length; j++)
      if (str.charAt(i)==pattern.charAt(j)) {
pos = 1;
        break;
      }
    i++;
  } while (pos==1 && i<str.length)
  if (pos==0)
    return false;
  return true;
}

function validateForm(theForm) {
  if (trim(theForm.Company.value)=='') {
    alert('Please enter a value in the "Company" box');
```

```
    theForm.Company.focus();
    return false;
  }
  if (trim(theForm.ProductID.value)=='') {
    alert('Please enter a value in the "ProductID" box');
    theForm.ProductID.focus();
    return false;
  }
  if (trim(theForm.ProductQuantity.value)=='') {
    alert('Please enter a value in the "Product Quantity" box');
    theForm.ProductQuantity.focus();
    return false;
  }
  if (!isPositiveInteger(trim(theForm.ProductQuantity.value))) {
    alert('Please enter a number only in the "Product Quantity" box');
    theForm.ProductQuantity.focus();
    return false;
  }
  return true;
}
</SCRIPT>
</HEAD>

<BODY>
<FORM METHOD=POST ACTION=buy.jsp onSubmit='return validateForm(this)'>
<TABLE>
<TR>
  <TD>Company:</TD>
  <TD><INPUT TYPE=TEXT NAME=Company></TD>
</TR>
<TR>
  <TD>Product ID:</TD>
  <TD><INPUT TYPE=TEXT NAME=ProductID></TD>
</TR>
<TR>
  <TD>Product Quantity:</TD>
  <TD><INPUT TYPE=TEXT NAME=ProductQuantity></TD>
</TR>
<TR>
  <TD COLSPAN=2 ALIGN=RIGHT><INPUT TYPE=SUBMIT></TD>
</TR>
</TABLE>
</FORM>
</BODY>
</HTML>
```

Figure 24.1 shows the form and the alert box that appear when a value is not valid.

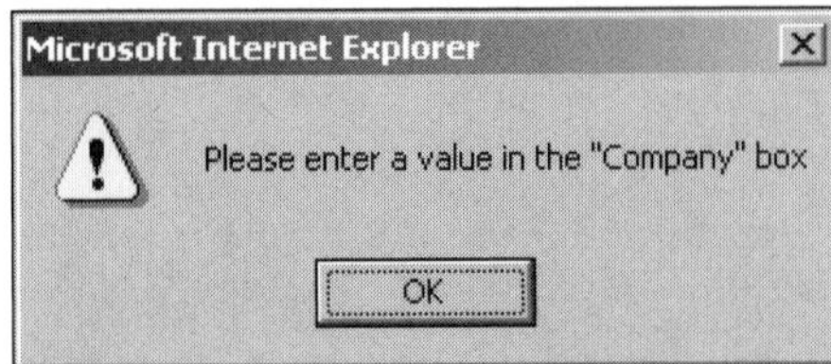

Figure 24.1 Checking the validity of user input at the client side.

Summary

Client-side input validation is important for reducing server workload and responding quickly to clients. In this chapter, you learned some tips that are useful for checking the validity of client input, including checking strings, numbers, and dates. You also learned data type conversion techniques.

25

Working with Client-Side Cookies

CHAPTER 5, "SESSION MANAGEMENT," EXAMINED the use of cookies for session management. In this chapter, we look at cookies in more detail, especially in regards to manipulating cookies at the client side (for example, in a browser).

To recap, a cookie is a small piece of information that is stored by the web browser in a client's machine or kept in the machine's memory. This information is sent to the server each time the client requests a page from where the information originated. Cookies are normally used to retain state or information in the stateless HTTP protocol.

Some users, however, prefer not to accept cookies because they don't want anything from the server written to their computer. Users can configure their web browsers not to receive cookies. The major browsers do not handle cookies exactly the same. Netscape Navigator allows the user to choose to only accept cookies that get sent back to the originating server. Internet Explorer distinguishes between cookies that only stay in memory (per-session cookies) and cookies that live after the browser is closed (stored in the computer).

What does this mean to you as a web developer? It means it is critical for you to test the user's browser for acceptance of cookies before allowing the user to enter a cookies-rich area of your web site.

This chapter presents tips for working with cookies, including how to create, delete, and edit a cookie—both on the server side and the client side.

Creating Cookies with a <META> Tag

You can create and read cookies on both the server side and the client side. On the client side, JavaScript is used. When you need to create cookies on the server side, you need Java in servlets or JSP pages, to write the cookie on the HTTP response. However, cookies can also be created using a <META> tag.

Creating cookies with a <META> tag is very easy. One advantage of using the <META> tag is that you can use an HTML page to create your cookies. This is in contrast with the technique described in Chapter 5, where you learned how to create cookies by instantiating the javax.servlet.http.Cookie class.

Another advantage of using the <META> tag is that it still works even if JavaScript is turned off in the user's browser. The drawback is that some old browsers might not understand <META> tags. However, some web servers translate the <META> tag directly into the HTTP header so that the browser does not have to translate it by itself. That said, the <META> tag is the best way to create a cookie.

Listing 25.1 and Listing 25.2 present examples of using the <META> tag to create a cookie in the user's web browser. The code in Listing 25.1 uses an expiration date so that the cookie survives the user closing the browser, and it is saved to disk (until it expires). The code in Listing 25.2 creates a cookie that is only valid for the current session and is erased upon the user closing the web browser.

Listing 25.1 **Creating a Cookie that Is Valid Until a Certain Date**

```
<HTML>
<HEAD>
<TITLE>Creating a cookie that is valid until a certain date</TITLE>
➥<META HTTP-EQUIV="Set-Cookie" CONTENT="userId=678;expires=Wednesday,
➥26-Dec-01 16:00:00 GMT; path=/">
</HEAD>
<BODY>
Unless you set your browser to not accept cookies, a cookie called
➥userId with a value of 678 has been created for you.
</BODY>
</HTML>
```

Listing 25.2 **Creating a Cookie that Is Only Valid Until the Browser Is Closed**

```
<HTML>
<HEAD>
<TITLE>Creating a cookie that is valid for this session only</TITLE>
➥<META HTTP-EQUIV="Set-Cookie" CONTENT="ProductID=2x3;">
</HEAD>
<BODY>
Unless you set your browser not to accept cookies, this page creates a
➥cookie called ProductID with a value of "2x3". The cookie won't be
➥written to your hard drive. It lives until the browser is closed.
</BODY>
</HTML>
```

Creating Cookies with document.cookie

On the client side, JavaScript is used to create cookies. There are several ways to do this. The easiest way is to use document.cookie. The following is the syntax for creating a cookie this way:

```
document.cookie = "cookieName=cookieValue
  [; expires=timeInGMTString]
  [; path=pathName]
  [; domain=domainName]
  [; secure]"
```

The code in Listing 25.3 creates a cookie called Quantity with a value of 7 that lives as long as the browser is open.

Listing 25.3 **Creating a Cookie with document.cookie**

```
<HTML>
<HEAD>
<TITLE>Creating a cookie with document.cookie</TITLE>
<SCRIPT LANGUAGE="JavaScript">
document.cookie="Quantity=7";
</SCRIPT>
</HEAD>
<BODY>
This page creates a cookie on the client side.
Make sure that your browser is set to accept cookies.
</BODY>
</HTML>
```

Creating Cookies with the setCookie Function

The preceding technique creates cookies when a user loads the page. However, sometimes you want to interactively create cookies on the client side. For example, you'll want to create a cookie when your user chooses to buy something in your online store web application. The setCookie function in Listing 25.4 is handy for creating a cookie on the browser. It has six arguments, but only the name and value arguments need to be present. For any optional argument that's not present, a default value is assigned to that argument.

> **Note**
>
> The setCookie function in Listing 25.4 and the getCookie function in Listing 25.8 can be found on the Internet. I am not sure who the cool guy was who wrote these functions the first time.

Listing 25.4 **The setCookie Function**

```
<SCRIPT LANGUAGE="JavaScript">
function setCookie(name, value, expires, path, domain, secure) {
  document.cookie = name + "=" + escape(value) +
    ((expires) ? "; expires=" + expires.toGMTString() : "") +
    ((path) ? "; path=" + path : "") +
    ((domain) ? "; domain=" + domain : "") +
    ((secure) ? "; secure" : "");
}
</SCRIPT>
```

The code in Listing 25.5 is an HTML file that uses the setCookie function to create a cookie if the user wants to. The HTML page has a form with a button and a TEXT element called UserID. When the user clicks the button, a cookie called UserID is created. The value of the cookie is the value typed into the UserID TEXT element.

Listing 25.5 **Using the setCookie Function**

```
<HTML>
<HEAD>
<TITLE>Using the setCookie function</TITLE>
<SCRIPT LANGUAGE="JavaScript">
function setCookie(name, value, expires, path, domain, secure) {
  document.cookie = name + "=" + escape(value) +
    ((expires) ? "; expires=" + expires.toGMTString() : "") +
    ((path) ? "; path=" + path : "") +
    ((domain) ? "; domain=" + domain : "") +
    ((secure) ? "; secure" : "");
```

```
}
</SCRIPT>
</HEAD>
<BODY>
Type your user id, and then click the button below.
A cookie will be created for you.
<BR>
<FORM>
User ID: <INPUT TYPE=TEXT NAME=UserID>
<BR>
<INPUT TYPE=BUTTON VALUE="Create Cookie"
onClick='setCookie("UserID", document.forms[0].UserID.value);'>
</FORM>
</BODY>
</HTML>
```

In Listing 25.5, the cookie exists until the user closes the browser. If you want to set the expiration date so that the cookie can last longer than the current browser session, you need to pass a date as the argument expires. However, as a result of a bug in some browsers, you need to use the fixDate to "repair" your date before it is passed to the setCookie function. The fixDate function is presented in Listing 25.6.

Listing 25.6 **The fixDate Function**

```
<SCRIPT LANGUAGE="JavaScript">
// date - any instance of the Date object
// hand all instances of the Date object to this function for "repairs"
function fixDate(date) {
  var base = new Date(0);
  var skew = base.getTime();
  if (skew > 0) date.setTime(date.getTime() - skew);
}
</SCRIPT>
```

The example in Listing 25.7 sets a cookie called authorizationLevel with the value of 2 and an expiration date of one year after it is set. Notice how the date is repaired before being passed to the function.

Listing 25.7 **An Example that Creates a Cookie with an Expiration Date**

```
<HTML>
<HEAD>
<TITLE>Using the setCookie function</TITLE>
<SCRIPT LANGUAGE="JavaScript">
```

continues

Listing 25.7 **Continued**

```
function setCookie(name, value, expires, path, domain, secure) {
  document.cookie = name + "=" + escape(value) +
    ((expires) ? "; expires=" + expires.toGMTString() : "") +
    ((path) ? "; path=" + path : "") +
    ((domain) ? "; domain=" + domain : "") +
    ((secure) ? "; secure" : "");
}

function fixDate(date) {
  var base = new Date(0);
  var skew = base.getTime();
  if (skew > 0) date.setTime(date.getTime() - skew);
}

var expiryDate = new Date();
fixDate(expiryDate);
expiryDate.setTime(expiryDate.getTime() + 365 * 24 * 60 * 60 * 1000);
setCookie("authorizationLevel", 2, expiryDate);

</SCRIPT>
</HEAD>
<BODY>
A cookie which is valid for a year has been created for this page.
</BODY>
</HTML>
```

Reading Cookies on the Browser

The function getCookie provided in Listing 25.8 has one argument: name. This argument is the name of the cookie whose value you want to retrieve.

Listing 25.8 **The getCookie Function**

```
<SCRIPT LANGUAGE="JavaScript">
function getCookie(name) {
  var cName = name + "=";
  var dc = document.cookie;
  if (dc.length>0) {
    begin = dc.indexOf(cName);
    if (begin != -1) {
      begin += cName.length;
      end = dc.indexOf(";", begin);
      if (end == -1) end = dc.length;
        return unescape(dc.substring(begin,end));
    }
  }
  return null;
}
</SCRIPT>
```

An example is given in Listing 25.9. The HTML page contains buttons that the user can click to write and read cookies.

Listing 25.9 **Writing and Reading Cookies**

```
<HTML>
<HEAD>
<TITLE>Writing and Reading Cookies</TITLE>
<SCRIPT LANGUAGE="JavaScript">

function setCookie(name, value, expires, path, domain, secure) {
  document.cookie = name + "=" + escape(value) +
    ((expires) ? "; expires=" + expires.toGMTString() : "") +
    ((path) ? "; path=" + path : "") +
    ((domain) ? "; domain=" + domain : "") +
    ((secure) ? "; secure" : "");
}

function getCookie(name) {
  var cName = name + "=";
  var dc = document.cookie;
  if (dc.length>0) {
    begin = dc.indexOf(cName);
    if (begin != -1) {
      begin += cName.length;
      end = dc.indexOf(";", begin);
      if (end == -1) end = dc.length;
        return unescape(dc.substring(begin,end));
    }
  }
  return null;
}

</SCRIPT>
</HEAD>
<BODY>
Type in your user id, and then click the Create Cookie button.
A cookie will be created for you.
<BR>
<FORM>
User ID: <INPUT TYPE=TEXT NAME=UserID>
<BR>
<INPUT TYPE=BUTTON VALUE="Create Cookie"
onClick='setCookie("UserID", document.forms[0].UserID.value)'>
<BR>
Click the Read Cookie button to display the cookie.
<INPUT TYPE=BUTTON VALUE="Read Cookie"
onClick='alert(getCookie("UserID"))'>
</FORM>
</BODY>
</HTML>
```

Deleting a Cookie on the Browser

You don't really delete a cookie, you just make it expire by setting the expiration date to the first second of the year 1970, as in the deleteCookie function in Listing 25.10. Note that the function uses the getCookie function from Listing 25.8, so you need to paste the getCookie function in your page as well.

Listing 25.10 **Deleting a Cookie**

```
<SCRIPT LANGUAGE="JavaScript">
function deleteCookie (name, path, domain) {
  if (getCookie(name)) {
    document.cookie = name + "=" +
    ((path==null) ? "" : "; path=" + path) +
    ((domain==null) ? "" : "; domain=" + domain) +
    "; expires=Thu, 01-Jan-70 00:00:01 GMT";
  }
}

function getCookie(name) {
  var cName = name + "=";
  var dc = document.cookie;
  if (dc.length>0) {
    begin = dc.indexOf(cName);
    if (begin != -1) {
      begin += cName.length;
      end = dc.indexOf(";", begin);
      if (end == -1) end = dc.length;
        return unescape(dc.substring(begin,end));
    }
  }
  return null;
}
</SCRIPT>
```

The deleteCookie function in Listing 25.10 first uses the getCookie function to check if the cookie you want to delete is already created. If the getCookie function returns false, the cookie you want to delete does not exist. The function then exits gracefully. If the cookie does exist, its expiration date is set to the first second in January 1970, which makes it expire straight away.

Checking If the Browser Can Accept Cookies Using JavaScript

This section outlines the simplest way of testing a browser's acceptance of cookies. Using JavaScript, the page simply creates a cookie called "test" with the value "OK". It then tries to read back the cookie immediately after the cookie is created. Failure to find the cookie means that the browser does not accept cookies.

Listing 25.11 presents an example of an HTML page that uses this technique.

Listing 25.11 **Checking If the Browser Can Accept Cookies Using JavaScript**

```
<HTML>
<HEAD>
<SCRIPT LANGUAGE="JavaScript">
document.cookie="test=OK";

function getCookie(name) {
  var cName = name + "=";
  var dc = document.cookie;
  if (dc.length>0) {
    begin = dc.indexOf(cName);
    if (begin != -1) {
      begin += cName.length;
      end = dc.indexOf(";", begin);
      if (end == -1) end = dc.length;
        return unescape(dc.substring(begin,end));
    }
  }
  return null;
}

if (getCookie('test')==null)
  alert("Please change your browser to accept cookies.");
else
  alert("Browser accepts cookies");

</SCRIPT>
</HEAD>

<BODY>
The page content
</BODY>
</HTML>
```

Checking If the Browser Accepts Cookies Without JavaScript

The drawback of the preceding section is that you must first make sure the browser understands JavaScript. The preceding section will not work if the JavaScript is turned off.

Another way to check if the browser is willing to accept cookies is by creating a cookie on one page and then immediately redirecting the user to a second page. In the second page you can then try to read the cookies. The code in Listing 25.12 uses the <META> tag to create a cookie called "test" and then redirects the browser to a second page called checkCookie.jsp (in Listing 25.13).

Listing 25.12 **Checking Browser Cookie Acceptance with Redirection**

```
<HTML>
<HEAD>
<META HTTP-EQUIV="Set-Cookie" CONTENT="test=ok;">
<META HTTP-EQUIV="Refresh" CONTENT="0;URL=checkCookie.jsp">
</HEAD>
</HTML>
```

In the second page, implemented using ASP in this example, you try to read the same cookie using the code in Listing 25.13.

Listing 25.13 **Reading the Cookies in the Browser Cookie Acceptance Test**

```
<%
  If Request.Cookies("test") <> "" Then
    Response.Write "Cookies accepted."
  Else
    Response.Write "Cookies not accepted."
  End If
%>
```

Even though the code in this example only sends a message to the user telling him or her whether or not his or her browser accepts cookies, you can modify it to suit your needs. For instance, you can transfer the user to a warning page if the cookies are not accepted.

Summary

Cookies are very useful in various applications. In this chapter, you learned techniques useful for manipulating cookies, both on the server side and on the client side. However, bear in mind that a user can turn off cookies in his or her browser. Make sure you perform the cookie acceptance test every time you write code that uses cookies in your applications.

26

Working with Object Trees

THIS CHAPTER COVERS WORKING WITH OBJECTS in a hierarchy using JavaScript. There are various applications for this. For example, you can have a folder tree like the one in Windows Explorer. In that application, you can navigate through a file directory system and open a directory by clicking a folder icon, as you saw in the document management application in Chapter 20, "Web-Based Document Management." Other examples are an XML-based online help system and a table of contents for an online book, as described in Chapter 19, "XML-Based E-Books."

When you work with objects in JavaScript, the array object is basically your only choice. This chapter reviews the array object in JavaScript and then explains all the operations you need to work with an object tree: create an object, append a child object to the root, search an object in the object tree, append an object to another object, and delete an object.

The chapter concludes with an example of a folder tree. You'll find other applications of this tree in upcoming chapters.

The Array Object

The Array object is the only data structure in JavaScript available for storing and manipulating ordered collections of data that work in all scriptable browsers. Unlike arrays in Java, a JavaScript array can be used to store different types of data as its elements. Also, as you'll see later in this section, you can create an array with or without specifying the number of elements. If you create an array without specifying the number of elements, the array behaves like a Vector object in Java, where you can add elements arbitrarily.

The array object has one drawback: Deleting an element in an array is very difficult.

You also can use the new Object( ) constructor to create an object, but this works only in Navigator version 3 and later and in Internet Explorer version 4 and later.

Creating an Array

Creating an array is as easy as assigning a variable with Array( ) using the new keyword:

```
var myArray = new Array();
```

Don't worry about specifying the number of elements, because a JavaScript array is perfectly dynamic. You can add elements at any time after the array is created. If you must presize your array for any reason, however, you can use the following statement:

```
var myArray = new Array(20);
```

The array element count starts from 0. If you specify an array with 20 elements as in the preceding statement, the array has an element index from 0 to 19.

An array also has the length property. The length property adjusts itself when you add an element with an index greater than the array size. For example, in the code in Listing 26.1 you first define an array with 20 elements and then add the twenty-first element to the array. The length property adjusts accordingly.

Listing 26.1 **Creating Arrays**

```
<SCRIPT LANGUAGE="JavaScript">
var myArray = new Array(20);
myArray[20] = "new element.";
// myArray.length value is 21
</SCRIPT>
```

Populating an Array

You populate an array by assigning values to its elements. For example, the code in Listing 26.2 creates an array called myArray and populates its first and second elements. In this case, the first element is a number and the second element is a string. Unlike in some other languages where an array must contain elements of the same data type, it is perfectly legal in JavaScript to populate an array with various types of elements.

Listing 26.2 **Populating an Array**

```
<SCRIPT LANGUAGE="JavaScript">
// define an array variable and create an Array object
var myArray = new Array();
// populate the first and second elements
myArray[0] = 1;
myArray[1] = "the name";
</SCRIPT>
```

You even can assign an array as an element of another array, as demonstrated in the code in Listing 26.3.

Listing 26.3 **Assigning an Array as an Element of Another Array**

```
<SCRIPT LANGUAGE="JavaScript">
// define an array variable and create an Array object
var anArray = new Array();
var anotherArray = new Array();
anArray[0] = 1;
// assinging another array as an element of anArray
anArray[1] = anotherArray;
</SCRIPT>
```

Knowing how to create and populate an array is the foundation for working with an object hierarchy in JavaScript.

The delete Operator

Not until Navigator 4.0 did JavaScript include the delete operator for deleting an array element. As you will soon see, however, using the delete operator is not an ideal way of deleting an element because it does not decrease the length property of the array.

Listing 26.4 lists the code that uses the delete operator to delete the third element of an array. Notice that the third element's value changes.

Listing 26.4 **Deleting an Array Element**

```
<HTML>
<SCRIPT LANGUAGE="JavaScript">
var myArray = new Array();
myArray[0] = "first element.";
myArray[1] = "second element.";
myArray[2] = "third element.";
document.write(myArray.length + "<BR>");
document.write(myArray[2] + "<BR>");
delete myArray[2];
document.write(myArray.length + "<BR>");
document.write(myArray[2] + "<BR>");
</SCRIPT>
</HTML>
```

The code in Listing 26.4 writes the length property of myArray and the third element of it before and after the third element is deleted using the delete operator. If you run the code in Internet Explorer 4.0 and 5.0 and Netscape Navigator 4.0, you will see the following result:

```
3
third element.
3
undefined
```

Note

Note that the length property does not change after you delete the third element.

If you run the code in Netscape Navigator 3.0, you'll receive the following result:

```
3
third element.
3
null
```

The code in Listing 26.5 deletes an array element and reassigns a new value to the deleted element.

Listing 26.5 **Deleting an Array Element and Reassigning a New Value**

```
<HTML>
<SCRIPT LANGUAGE="JavaScript">
var myArray = new Array();
myArray[0] = "first element.";
myArray[1] = "second element.";
myArray[2] = "third element.";
```

```
document.write(myArray.length + "<BR>");
document.write(myArray[1] + "<BR>");
delete myArray[1];
document.write(myArray.length + "<BR>");
document.write(myArray[1] + "<BR>");
myArray[1] = "new element.";
document.write(myArray.length + "<BR>");
document.write(myArray[1] + "<BR>");
document.write(myArray.length + "<BR>");
document.write(myArray[2] + "<BR>");
</SCRIPT>
</HTML>
```

If you run the code in Listing 26.5 in Internet Explorer 4.0 and 5.0 and Netscape Navigator 4.0, you'll receive the following result:

```
3
second element.
3
undefined
3
new element.
3
third element.
```

Obviously, the delete operator does not really remove the element from memory. Because of this, you sometimes need to devise another way to delete an array element.

Truly Deleting an Array Element

By now, you are probably as disappointed with the delete operator as I was. However, my experiment reveals that you actually can decrease the length property of an array, which effectively deletes the last element. Consider the code in Listing 26.6.

Listing 26.6 **Truly Deleting an Array Element**

```
<HTML>
<SCRIPT LANGUAGE="JavaScript">

var myArray = new Array();
myArray[0] = "first element.";
myArray[1] = "second element.";
myArray[2] = "third element.";

myArray.length--;
```

continues

Listing 26.6 **Continued**

```
document.write("Array length : " + myArray.length + "<BR>");

for (var i=0; i<myArray.length; i++)
  document.write("element " + i + " : " + myArray[i] + "<BR>");

document.write("element " + 3 + " : " + myArray[2] + "<BR>");

</SCRIPT>
</HTML>
```

The code in Listing 26.6 produces the following result:

```
Array length : 2
element 0 : first element.
element 1 : second element.
element 3 : undefined
```

The result of the code in Listing 26.6 shows that after you decrement the length property, the last element is really gone. Listing 26.7 presents a cross-browser function to delete the *n*th element of an array.

Listing 26.7 **The deleteElement Function**

```
function deleteElement(array, n) {
  //delete the nth element of array
  var length = array.length;
  if (n >= length || n<0)
    return;

  for (var i=n; i<length-1; i++)
    array[i] = array[i+1];
  array.length--;
}
```

In Listing 26.7, *n* is assumed to be a numeric value. Consider the example in Listing 26.8, which uses the deleteElement function.

Listing 26.8 **Using the deleteElement Function**

```
<HTML>
<SCRIPT LANGUAGE="JavaScript">

function deleteElement(array, n) {
  //delete the nth element of array
  var length = array.length;
  if (n >= length || n<0)
    return;
```

```
    for (var i=n; i<length-1; i++)
      array[i] = array[i+1];
    array.length--;
  }

  var myArray = new Array();
  myArray[0] = "first element.";
  myArray[1] = "second element.";
  myArray[2] = "third element.";
  myArray[3] = "4th";

  document.write("length : " + myArray.length + "<BR>");
  for (var i=0; i<myArray.length; i++)
    document.write("element " + i + " : " + myArray[i] + "<BR>");

  deleteElement(myArray, 1);
  document.write("length : " + myArray.length + "<BR>");
  for (var i=0; i<myArray.length; i++)
    document.write("element " + i + " : " + myArray[i] + "<BR>");

  </SCRIPT>
  </HTML>
```

The code in Listing 26.8 creates and populates an array called myArray and displays the value of the length property. It then loops through the myArray Array object to display the values of its elements:

```
for (var i=0; i<myArray.length; i++)
  document.write("element " + i + " : " + myArray[i] + "<BR>");
```

The code then deletes the second element of myArray and redisplays the length property and the contents. The result is as follows:

```
length : 4
element 0 : first element.
element 1 : second element.
element 2 : third element.
element 3 : 4th
length : 3
element 0 : first element.
element 1 : third element.
element 2 : 4th
```

Creating an Object

Making an array behave like an object is another technique that comes in handy. The createObject function in Listing 26.9 is a function that will return an object (which is technically an Array object, of course).

Listing 26.9 **The createObject Function to Create an Object**

```
<SCRIPT LANGUAGE="JavaScript">
function createObject() {
  var anArray = new Array();
  return anArray;
}
</SCRIPT>
```

Alternatively, you can write a function that creates an object with predefined properties. For example, the createDog function in Listing 26.10 creates a dog object with a name and fur color.

Listing 26.10 **A Function that Creates an Object with Predefined Properties**

```
<SCRIPT LANGUAGE="JavaScript">
function createDog(name, color) {
  var dog = new Array();
  dog[0] = name;
  dog[1] = color;
  return dog;
}
</SCRIPT>
```

A Hierarchy of Objects

Now that you have a function to create objects, you can have a hierarchy of objects. Having a hierarchy of objects means establishing parent-child relationships among your objects. Consider, for example, the Windows operating system's directory system, which has a drive called the C drive. The C drive has a folder under it called Program Files. The Program Files folder is the child object of the C drive. The C drive is the parent of the Program Files folder. The Program Files folder in turn can have its own child objects.

In a hierarchy like the Windows directory system, there is always an object that does not have a parent. In the directory system, it is the C drive. In many contexts, it is simply called the *root*. The root plays an important role because it is the entry point of the hierarchy. Every single operation involves the root. For example, if you create a family tree of dogs and you want to search for a particular dog, the search starts from the root.

Appending a Child Object to Another Object

To create an object tree, you must have at least two objects and you must create a parent-child relationship between them. Suppose, for example, that a Dog object has a name, a color, and zero or more child Dog object(s). You can use an array to represent the Dog object. The first and second elements are reserved for the name and color, and then the third element and all following elements are used for each child Dog object. Therefore, a Dog object has at least two elements: its name and color. A Dog object with no child object will have only two elements. A Dog object with one child object has three elements: name, color, and a reference to another Dog object. If the Dog object has two child objects, it then has a fourth element for yet another Dog object.

The important thing here is creating a Dog object and establishing a relationship between a parent and a child Dog object. You saw in the previous section the function used to create an object, and now you need another function to append an object as a child object to another object. Just call this function append. Listing 26.11 presents the append function.

Listing 26.11 **The append Function**

```
<SCRIPT LANGUAGE="JavaScript">
function append(parent, child) {
  parent[parent.length] = child;
}
</SCRIPT>
```

The append function accepts two arguments: the object that will be the parent and the object that will be the child in the relationship. Because an array is completely dynamic, you easily can create a new element for the child object. The length property returns the number of elements, but the element index starts with 0. Therefore, the length property returns the index that is the next element in the array.

For example, the code in Listing 26.12 creates two Dog objects called doggy and puppy and then creates a parent-child relationship between them.

Listing 26.12 **Creating a Parent Object and a Child Object**

```
<SCRIPT LANGUAGE="JavaScript">

function createDog(name, color) {
  var dog = new Array();
  dog[0] = name;
  dog[1] = color;
  return dog;
```

continues

Listing 26.12 **Continued**

```
}
function append(parent, child) {
  parent[parent.length] = child;
}

var doggy = createDog("boli", "black");
var puppy = createDog("boni", "white");
append(doggy, puppy);

</SCRIPT>
```

If you are curious about the parent-child relationship between the two objects, paste this at the end of the code:

```
for (var i = 0; i<doggy.length; i++) {
  alert(doggy[i] );
}
```

When you run the code in a web browser, three alert windows appear. The first alert window displays "boli," the second displays "black," and the third displays "boni, white."

Navigating the Tree

Assume that you are creating the family tree of Bo, the famous family dog. To simplify things, also assume that a dog only has one parent in the tree. Bo had two puppies: Boli and Boy. Although Boy stayed a bachelor for the rest of his life, Boli later had two other puppies: Boni and Bulbul. Boni later had Spotty and Mary.

The dog family tree is illustrated as follows:

```
Bo  -- Boli    -- Bulbul
               -- Boni    -- Spotty
                          -- Mary
    -- Boy
```

To create this tree, you first need to create individual dogs. Then, you need to build the tree structure by appending a child dog to its parent object. Listing 26.13 presents the code to build Bo's family tree.

Listing 26.13 **Creating a Dog Family Tree**

```
<HTML>
<SCRIPT LANGUAGE="JavaScript">
function createDog(name, color) {
  var dog = new Array();
  dog[0] = name;
  dog[1] = color;
```

```
  return dog;
}
function append(parent, child) {
  parent[parent.length] = child;
}
var bo = createDog("bo", "brown");
var boli = createDog("boli", "black and white");
var boy = createDog("boy", "brown");
var bulbul = createDog("bulbul", "brown");
var boni = createDog("boni", "black and white");
var spotty = createDog("spotty", "black and white");
var mary = createDog("boni", "black and white");
append(bo, boli);
append(bo, boy);
append(boli, bulbul);
append(boli, boni);
append(boni, spotty);
append(boni, mary);
</SCRIPT>
</HTML>
```

Now you can navigate the tree by printing each dog's name. To navigate, you need to learn about the generation of each dog. The generation starts from 1. Bo is the root, so she is the first generation in the tree. Navigating the tree basically means you start from the root, which is the only object in the first generation. If the root has descendants (obviously it does—hence the tree), the descendants are the second generation. You then loop through each member of the second generation and find the descendants. The descendants of the second generation are the third generation.

Listing 26.14 shows how to navigate an object tree using a recursive function.

Listing 26.14 **Navigating an Object Tree**

```
<HTML>
<SCRIPT LANGUAGE="JavaScript">
function navigate(dog, generation) {
  var name = dog[0];
  document.write(name + "<BR>");
  generation++;
  for (var j=2; j<dog.length; j++ )  // has descendants
    navigate(dog[j], generation);
}

navigate(bo, 1);
</SCRIPT>
</HTML>
```

When you run the code in Listing 26.14 in a web browser, the result is as follows:

```
bo
boli
bulbul
boni
spotty
mary
boy
```

Searching for an Object in the Object Tree

In the preceding section, you learned how to navigate an object tree. Navigation works from the root toward the objects in the next generations. The same principle is used when you search for a particular object in the tree. You begin the search from the root and continue until you find a match. Sometimes, when you find a match, you can return the object without continuing the navigation until the last object.

For example, the code in Listing 26.15 builds an object tree like the previous one and then searches for a dog called "Bulbul." When that dog is found, the name and the color of the dog are displayed and the function raises the flag found. This flag, when true, stops the search.

Listing 26.15 **Searching for an Object in an Object Tree**

```
<HTML>
<HEAD>
<TITLE>Searching for Bulbul</TITLE>
</HEAD>
<BODY>
<SCRIPT LANGUAGE="JavaScript">

function createDog(name, color) {
  var dog = new Array();
  dog[0] = name;
  dog[1] = color;
  return dog;
}

function append(parent, child) {
  parent[parent.length] = child;
}

var bo = createDog("bo", "brown");
var boli = createDog("boli", "black and white");
var boy = createDog("boy", "brown");
```

```
var bulbul = createDog("bulbul", "brown");
var boni = createDog("boni", "black and white");
var spotty = createDog("spotty", "black and white");
var mary = createDog("mary", "black and white");
append(bo, boli);
append(bo, boy);
append(boli, bulbul);
append(boli, boni);
append(boni, spotty);
append(boni, mary);

var found = false;
function search(dog, generation, name) {
  if (name == dog[0]) {
    found = true;
    alert("name:" + dog[0] + "\ncolor:" + dog[1]);
  }
  else if (!found) {
    generation++;
    for (var j=2; j<dog.length; j++ )    // has descendants
      if (!found)
        search(dog[j], generation, name);
  }
}

search(bo, 1, "bulbul");

</SCRIPT>
</BODY>
</HTML>
```

Note that the search function is called by passing the root (bo), the generation (1), and the name of the search criteria ("bulbul").

Displaying an Object Tree

Displaying an object tree is an important task. You can modify the code in Listing 26.15 to create a new function that displays an object tree. Listing 26.16 presents this modified code.

Note that the code in Listing 26.16, as well as some other code listings, use the blank.gif image located under the images subdirectory of the directory hosting the HTML file. This file is a normal transparent .gif image. The blank.gif file is included on the CD that accompanies this book, in the images directory.

Listing 26.16 **Displaying an Object Tree**

```
<HTML>
<HEAD>
<TITLE>Displaying an object tree</TITLE>
</HEAD>
<BODY>
<SCRIPT LANGUAGE="JavaScript">

function createDog(name, color) {
  var dog = new Array();
  dog[0] = name;
  dog[1] = color;
  return dog;
}

function append(parent, child) {
  parent[parent.length] = child;
}

var bo = createDog("bo", "brown");
var boli = createDog("boli", "black and white");
var boy = createDog("boy", "brown");
var bulbul = createDog("bulbul", "brown");
var boni = createDog("boni", "black and white");
var spotty = createDog("spotty", "black and white");
var mary = createDog("mary", "black and white");
append(bo, boli);
append(bo, boy);
append(boli, bulbul);
append(boli, boni);
append(boni, spotty);
append(boni, mary);


function navigate(dog, generation) {
  var name = dog[0];
  for (var i=1; i<generation; i++)
    document.write("<IMG BORDER=1 SRC=images/blank.gif>");
  document.write(name + "<BR>");
  generation++;
  for (var j=2; j<dog.length; j++ )   // has descendants
    navigate(dog[j], generation);
}

navigate(bo, 1);

</SCRIPT>
</BODY>
</html>
```

The result displayed in a web browser is shown in Figure 26.1.

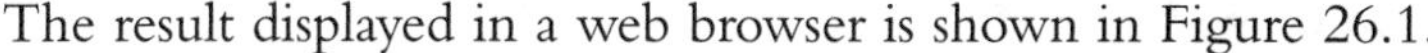

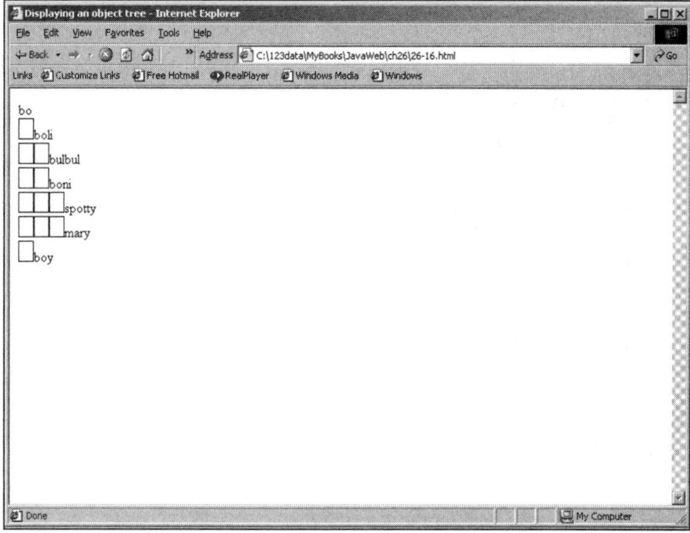

Figure 26.1 Displaying an object tree.

Deleting a Child Object

Listing 26.17 presents the code for deleting an object in an object tree using the deleteElement function. You need to use the deleteElement function with caution, however. For example, in the dog family tree, the array indexes 0 and 1 are reserved for the name and fur color. If you delete the array index 0 or 1, your tree will lose its structure. Using the deleteElement wisely, however, can result in a safe object deletion, as demonstrated in the code in Listing 26.17. The code in Listing 26.17 deletes Boni's third element (Spotty) from the tree.

Listing 26.17 **Deleting a Child Object**

```
<HTML>
<HEAD>
<TITLE>Deleting a child object</TITLE>
</HEAD>
<BODY>
<SCRIPT LANGUAGE="JavaScript">

function createDog(name, color) {
  var dog = new Array();
  dog[0] = name;
  dog[1] = color;
```

continues

Listing 26.17 **Continued**

```
  return dog;
}

function append(parent, child) {
  parent[parent.length] = child;
}

var bo = createDog("bo", "brown");
var boli = createDog("boli", "black and white");
var boy = createDog("boy", "brown");
var bulbul = createDog("bulbul", "brown");
var boni = createDog("boni", "black and white");
var spotty = createDog("spotty", "black and white");
var mary = createDog("mary", "black and white");
append(bo, boli);
append(bo, boy);
append(boli, bulbul);
append(boli, boni);
append(boni, spotty);
append(boni, mary);

function deleteElement(array, n) {
  //delete the nth element of array
  var length = array.length;
  if (n >= length || n<0)
    return;

  for (var i=n; i<length-1; i++)
    array[i] = array[i+1];
  array.length--;
}

function navigate(dog, generation) {
  var name = dog[0];
  for (var i=1; i<generation; i++)
    document.write("<IMG BORDER=1 SRC=images/blank.gif>");
  document.write(name + "<BR>");
  generation++;
  for (var j=2; j<dog.length; j++ )   // has descendants
    navigate(dog[j], generation);
}

navigate(bo, 1);
deleteElement(boni, 2);
navigate(bo, 1);


</SCRIPT>
</BODY>
</HTML>
```

The result of the code in Listing 26.17 is shown in Figure 26.2.

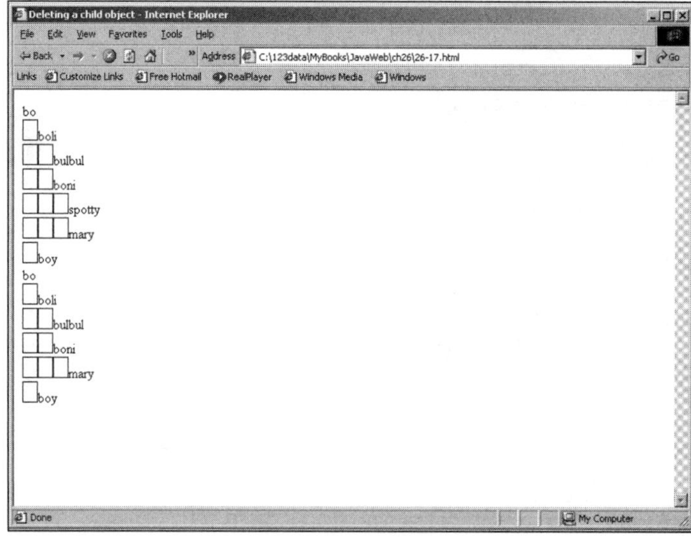

Figure 26.2 The object tree before and after the deletion.

Notice that Spotty is missing from the second tree.

Event Handling in an Object Tree

You can add an event handler to the tree so that your application can respond when the user clicks the mouse or rolls the mouse over an object. For example, the code in Listing 26.18 adds a function called handler that responds when a user clicks an object. The response is a simple alert window displaying the name of the dog.

Listing 26.18 **Adding Event Handling to an Object Tree**

```
<HTML>
<HEAD>
<TITLE>Event handling in an object tree</TITLE>
</HEAD>
<BODY>
<SCRIPT LANGUAGE="JavaScript">

function createDog(name, color) {
  var dog = new Array();
  dog[0] = name;
  dog[1] = color;
```

continues

Listing 26.18 **Continued**

```
  return dog;
}

function append(parent, child) {
  parent[parent.length] = child;
}

var bo = createDog("bo", "brown");
var boli = createDog("boli", "black and white");
var boy = createDog("boy", "brown");
var bulbul = createDog("bulbul", "brown");
var boni = createDog("boni", "black and white");
var spotty = createDog("spotty", "black and white");
var mary = createDog("mary", "black and white");
append(bo, boli);
append(bo, boy);
append(boli, bulbul);
append(boli, boni);
append(boni, spotty);
append(boni, mary);

function handler(name) {
  alert(name);
}

function navigate(dog, generation) {
  var name = dog[0];
  for (var i=1; i<generation; i++)
    document.write("<IMG BORDER=1 SRC=images/blank.gif>");
  document.write("<A HREF=\"javascript:handler('" + name + "')\">" +
    name + "</A><BR>");
  generation++;
  for (var j=2; j<dog.length; j++ )   // has descendants
    navigate(dog[j], generation);
}

navigate(bo, 1);

</SCRIPT>
</BODY>
</HTML>
```

Now, instead of plain text, each object is represented by a hyperlink that can respond to the user's click, as shown in Figure 26.3.

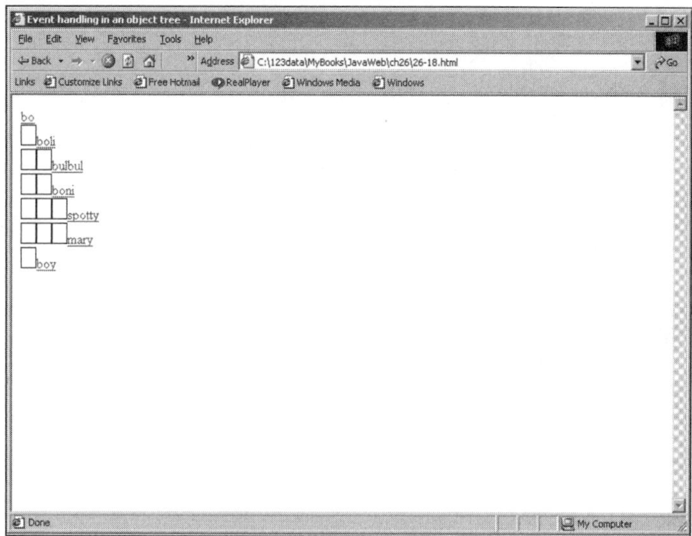

Figure 26.3 Demonstration of event handling in an object tree.

Sometimes you'll want to change the look of the object tree when responding to the user event. For example, in a folder tree, you probably want to display an open folder icon to indicate the folder clicked by the user. This poses a problem, however, because the tree must be redrawn. The trick is to store your JavaScript code in another page.

The example in Listing 26.19 uses a frame to store the JavaScript code and draws the object tree in a different document.

Listing 26.19 **Using a Frame**

```
<HTML>
<SCRIPT LANGUAGE="JavaScript">

function createDog(name, color) {
  var dog = new Array();
  dog[0] = name;
  dog[1] = color;
  return dog;
}

function append(parent, child) {
  parent[parent.length] = child;
}

var bo = createDog("bo", "brown");
var boli = createDog("boli", "black and white");
```

continues

Listing 26.19 **Continued**

```
var boy = createDog("boy", "brown");
var bulbul = createDog("bulbul", "brown");
var boni = createDog("boni", "black and white");
var spotty = createDog("spotty", "black and white");
var mary = createDog("mary", "black and white");
append(bo, boli);
append(bo, boy);
append(boli, bulbul);
append(boli, boni);
append(boni, spotty);
append(boni, mary);

var dogClicked="";
function handler(name) {
  dogClicked = name;
  var doc = frames[0].document;
  doc.clear();
  redraw(bo, 1, doc);
  doc.close();
}

function redraw(dog, generation, doc) {
  var name = dog[0];
  for (var i=1; i<generation; i++)
    doc.write("<IMG BORDER=1 SRC=images/blank.gif>");
  doc.write("<A HREF=\"javascript:parent.handler('" +
    name + "')\">");
  if (name==dogClicked)
    doc.write("<I><B>" + name + "</B></I>");
  else
    doc.write(name);
  doc.write("</A><BR>");
  generation++;
  for (var j=2; j<dog.length; j++ )   // has descendants
    redraw(dog[j], generation, doc);
}


</SCRIPT>

<FRAMESET onLoad="redraw(bo, 1, frames[0].document); frames[0].document.close()"
ROWS="100%, *">
<FRAME NAME=frame1 SRC=frame1.html>
<FRAME NAME=frame2 SRC=frame2.html>
</FRAMESET>

</HTML>
```

> **Note**
>
> Netscape browsers will complain if frame1.html or frame2.html is blank. To make them happy, write a blank string.

Note that you need to close the document at the frameset's onLoad event; otherwise Internet Explorer will behave unexpectedly—for example, it might refuse to clear the document.

An object tree that can change its appearance is shown in Figure 26.4. In this example, "boni" is printed in italic because it is the selected dog.

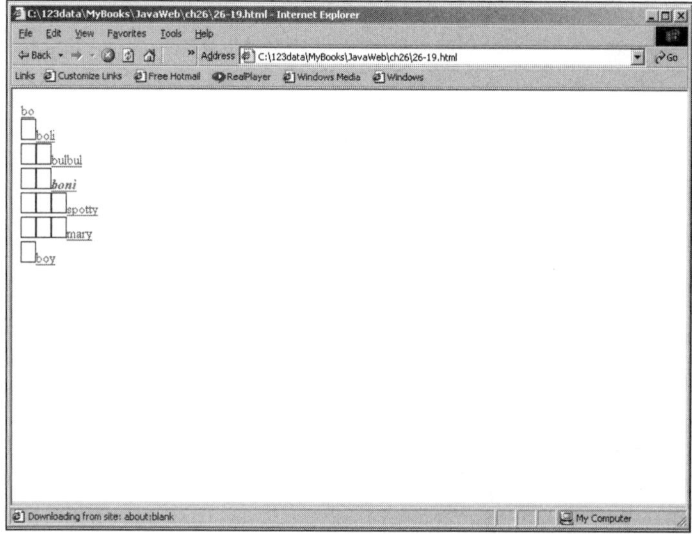

Figure 26.4 An object tree that can change its appearance.

Summary

The Array object is one of the few data structures available when you need to work with objects in JavaScript. Thanks to the flexibility of the Array object, you can assign an array as an element of another array, which enables you to create a linked list or an object tree.

As you have seen in this chapter, object trees have many applications. Equipped with functions to create objects, append an object to another object, and delete an object, you can manipulate an object tree easily. This chapter also presented other functions for navigating, displaying, and searching—all of which you need when using an object tree.

27 Controlling Applets

JAVA APPLETS ARE POWERFUL, AND WITH them you can do many things—create animations, communicate with the server, write a simple text editor, display news headlines, and other interesting things that can humor any sedentary worker. Using applets, you can do almost everything you can do with Java.

Applets are widely accepted, too; they are workable in both Netscape and Microsoft browsers. You may be aware that you can do similar things with ActiveX components; however, ActiveX components only feel at home in Microsoft browsers. You will need a plug-in if you want to play ActiveX toys with Netscape Navigator.

What a shame that Microsoft decided not to support Java applets in its new operating system, Windows XP. The user can download the plug-in separately, however.

This chapter does not discuss how to write applets. Indeed, that is beyond the scope of this book. However, this chapter does discuss a different aspect of working with applets: how you can control applets from an HTML page using JavaScript. You might want to run an applet's methods, read its properties, or pass a value to it for further processing. For example, imagine that you have a password-protected chat applet. In this applet, a user logs in on an HTML page before being able to download the applet itself on the next web page. This is because you don't want unauthorized people to be able to download the applet. The problem may sound simple, but it requires the following steps:

1. Display the Login page, where the user can type in the user name and password.
2. Capture the user name and password and pass it back in the second page as cookies.
3. Display the second page.
4. Check whether the browser has finished downloading the applet.
5. If the browser has finished downloading the applet, pass the cookies (the user name and password) to the applet. If the browser hasn't finished downloading the applet, go back to Step 4.

In addition, before you even let the server send a Java applet to the browser, you must make sure that the browser understands Java and that the feature is enabled.

This chapter demonstrates how to achieve these tasks and much more. Also, this chapter provides a discussion on how to write applets that can communicate with the document object model of an HTML page.

Is Java Enabled?

Even though modern browsers leave their factories with Java support turned on, users can easily switch this feature off for a number of reasons. If you use applets in any of your pages, you need to make sure that this feature is on. You can do this easily with the navigator object's javaEnabled method. A function, isJavaEnabled, is written using this method to check whether your applet can be run in the page. Using this function, you can warn the user if the browser has Java capability switched off. Listing 27.1 presents the isJavaEnabled function.

Listing 27.1 **The isJavaEnabled Function**

```
<SCRIPT LANGUAGE="JavaScript">
function isJavaEnabled() {
  return ( navigator.javaEnabled() );
}
</SCRIPT>
```

Is the Applet Ready?

When you communicate with a Java applet using JavaScript, you need to make sure that the browser has finished downloading the applet and the applet has initialized itself. If the JavaScript function or statement tries to access an applet that is not ready, an error will occur. The isAppletReady function in Listing 27.2 can prevent user confusion and save the web developer embarrassment.

Listing 27.2 **The isAppletReady Function**

```
<SCRIPT LANGUAGE="JavaScript">
function isAppletReady(applet) {
  return applet.isActive();
}
</SCRIPT>
```

The isAppletReady function accepts a parameter: the applet that needs to be checked for readiness. An applet object has the isActive property, whose value should be true if the applet is ready to be accessed.

In an HTML page, an applet is like any other object. For example, suppose that there is a collection of applets represented by applets in the document object model. To refer to the first applet in the document, you can use document.applets[0]. The *n*th applet in the document is document.applets[n-1].

The code in Listing 27.3 shows an HTML page with an applet. In addition, it has a form with a button that the user can click to check whether the first applet in the document is ready.

Listing 27.3 **Code to Check Whether an Applet Is Ready**

```
<HTML>
<HEAD>
<TITLE>Checking if an applet is ready</TITLE>
<SCRIPT LANGUAGE="JavaScript">
function isAppletReady(applet) {
  return applet.isActive();
}
</SCRIPT>
</HEAD>
<BODY>
<APPLET
  CODEBASE = "."
  CODE     = "MyApplet.class"
  NAME     = "TestApplet"
  WIDTH    = 200
  HEIGHT   = 50
  HSPACE   = 0
```

continues

Listing 27.3 **Continued**

```
  VSPACE   = 0
  ALIGN    = middle
>
</APPLET>
Click the button below to check if the applet is ready.
<BR>
<FORM>
<INPUT TYPE=button VALUE="Check if the applet is ready"
  onClick="if (!isAppletReady(document.applets[0])) alert('not ready');" >
</FORM>
</BODY>
</HTML>
```

Resizing an Applet

A browser treats an applet like other document objects. As a result, you can refer to an applet by its name or by its order of appearance in the document. For example, the JavaScript code in Listing 27.4 changes the height of the first applet on the page to 90 pixels and its width to 60 pixels.

Listing 27.4 **Resizing an Applet**

```
<SCRIPT LANGUAGE="JavaScript">
document.applets[0].height = 90;
document.applets[0].width = 60;
</SCRIPT>
```

Calling an Applet's Method

You can call any method in an applet from JavaScript code as long as the applet's method is public. Suppose that, for example, you have an applet with one method called myMethod that returns an int and accepts an int argument, as shown in Listing 27.5.

Listing 27.5 **An Applet Whose public Method Will Be Called from JavaScript Script**

```
import java.applet.*;

public class MyApplet extends Applet {
```

```
  public int myMethod(int a) {
    return (5 + a);
  }

}
```

If you know how to refer to the applet object in the HTML document, you can call the applet's public method as if it is a method of any other JavaScript object. The code in Listing 27.6 shows an example of how to use the myMethod method of the applet in Listing 27.5.

Listing 27.6 **Calling an Applet's public Method**

```
<HTML>
<HEAD>
<TITLE>Call an applet's method</TITLE>
<SCRIPT>

function add() {
  var result = document.applets[0].myMethod("3");
  alert("The sum is " + result);
}

</SCRIPT>
</HEAD>
<BODY>
Click the following button to run the applet's method.
<BR>
<FORM>
<INPUT TYPE=BUTTON onClick='add();'
  VALUE="Run Applet's Method ">
</FORM>

<APPLET
  CODEBASE = "."
  CODE     = "MyApplet.class"
  NAME     = "TestApplet"
  WIDTH    = 200
  HEIGHT   = 50
  HSPACE   = 0
  VSPACE   = 0
  ALIGN    = middle
>
</APPLET>
</BODY>
</HTML>
```

Getting an Applet's Property

You cannot read an applet's property directly, even though the property is public. To read an applet's property, you need to create a public method in the applet that simply returns the property. You then call this method from your JavaScript code to indirectly read the property.

The HTML file in Listing 27.7 shows a JavaScript function, getSecretValue, which in turn calls the getAppletSecretValue method in the first applet in the document. The getAppletSecretValue method in the applet must be written to return the applet property you want to read from JavaScript code.

Listing 27.7 **Reading an Applet's Property**

```
<HTML>
<HEAD>
<TITLE>Read an applet's property</TITLE>
<SCRIPT LANGUAGE="JavaScript">

function getSecretValue() {
  var secret = document.applets[0].getAppletSecretValue();
  alert("The secret is " + secret);
}

</SCRIPT>
</HEAD>

<BODY>
Click <A HREF="javascript:getSecretValue()">
here</A> to display the secret value.
<BR>
<APPLET
  CODEBASE = "."
  CODE     = "MyApplet.class"
  NAME     = "TestApplet"
  WIDTH    = 200
  HEIGHT   = 50
  HSPACE   = 0
  VSPACE   = 0
  ALIGN    = middle
>
</APPLET>
</BODY>
</HTML>
```

The MyApplet applet code could look like the code in Listing 27.8.

Listing 27.8 **Writing a public Method that Returns a Property**

```
import java.applet.*;

public class MyApplet extends Applet {

  private String secretValue = ":-)";
  public String getAppletSecretValue() {
    return secretValue;
  }

}
```

Setting an Applet Property

As in the preceding code, you have to write to an applet property indirectly by writing a public method in the applet that does the job. In the Java applet, create a public method that accepts an argument. This argument is the value you need to assign to the property.

Listing 27.9 **Writing an Applet's Property**

```
<HTML>
<HEAD>
<TITLE>Write to an applet's property</TITLE>
<SCRIPT>

function setSecretValue(str) {
  document.applets[0].setSecretValue(str);
}

</SCRIPT>
</HEAD>
<BODY>
<FORM>
Type your message in the following box as the applet's property value.
 <INPUT TYPE=TEXT NAME=Secret>
 <INPUT TYPE=BUTTON onClick='setSecretValue(this.form.Secret.value);'
  VALUE="Set Property">
</FORM>
<BR>
<APPLET
  CODEBASE = "."
  CODE     = "MyApplet.class"
  NAME     = "TestApplet"
```

continues

Listing 27.9 **Continued**

```
    WIDTH    = 200
    HEIGHT   = 50
    HSPACE   = 0
    VSPACE   = 0
    ALIGN    = middle
    MAYSCRIPT
>
</APPLET>
</BODY>
</HTML>
```

Listing 27.10 shows an applet with a public method to write a property.

Listing 27.10 **Writing a public Method that Writes to an Applet's Property**

```
import java.applet.*;

public class MyApplet extends Applet {

  private String secretValue = "";
  public void setSecretValue(String str) {
    secretValue = str;
  }

}
```

Using Java Classes Directly

Java on an HTML page without an applet? You may think it's not possible, but it actually is. This technique works only in Netscape browsers, however. For example, the code in Listing 27.11 uses the java.awt.Toolkit class' methods to display the monitor width and height.

Listing 27.11 **Using Java Classes Directly**

```
<HTML>
<HEAD>
<TITLE>Accessing Java directly from JavaScript</TITLE>
<SCRIPT LANGUAGE="JavaScript">
 alert("Screen Dimension\n" +
   "  width:" +
   java.awt.Toolkit.getDefaultToolkit().getScreenSize().width +
   " height:" +
```

```
    java.awt.Toolkit.getDefaultToolkit().getScreenSize().height);
  </SCRIPT>
</HEAD>
</HTML>
```

Applet-to-JavaScript Communication

You can perform applet-to-JavaScript communication to access the document object model or to call a JavaScript function on an HTML page. Internet Explorer version 4.0 and later and Netscape Navigator version 3.0 and later enable this through the Java wrapper class netscape.javascript.JSObject. In Navigator 3.0, the JSObject class comes in the file named java_30 or java_301; in Navigator 4.0, the file is called java40.jar. In Internet Explorer 4.0, the file is in the H3rfb7jn.zip file.

Due to security reasons, JSObject support is not enabled by default. To enable JSObject support, a new attribute called MAYSCRIPT needs to be present in the APPLET tag, as follows:

```
<APPLET CODE="MyApplet.class" CODEBASE="." WIDTH="200"
➥HEIGHT="100" MAYSCRIPT>
```

JSObject will be disabled if MAYSCRIPT is absent.

Each JSObject encapsulates an entity in the document object model in the JavaScript world. The JSObject's methods are listed in Table 27.1.

Table 27.1 **JSObject's Methods**

Method	Description
public Object call(String methodName, Object args[ ])	Invokes JavaScript function. Pass null if the function does not have an argument; otherwise pass an Object array. Equivalent "`this.methodName(args[0], args[1], ...`)" in JavaScript.
public Object eval(String s)	Evaluates a JavaScript expression. The expression is a string of JavaScript source code that will be evaluated in the context given by the keyword "this".
public Object getMember (String name)	Retrieves a named member of a JavaScript object. Equivalent to "`this.name`" in JavaScript.
public Object getSlot (int index)	Retrieves an indexed member of a JavaScript object. Equivalent to "`this[index]`" in JavaScript.

continues

Table 27.1 **Continued**

public static JSObject getWindow(Applet applet)	Returns a `JSObject` for the window containing the given applet. This method is available only on the client.
public void removeMember(String name)	Removes a named member of a JavaScript object.
public void setMember (String name, Object value)	Sets a named member of a JavaScript object. Equivalent to "`this.name = value`" in JavaScript.
public void setSlot (int index, Object value)	Sets an indexed member of a JavaScript object. Equivalent to "`this[index] = value`" in JavaScript.
public String toString( )	Converts a `JSObject` to a `String`.

To compile Java code to take advantage of JSObject, you must have the package `netscape.javascript` in the CLASSPATH. Currently, Java Plug-in 1.2.2, which is downloadable from Sun's web site, ships `netscape.javascript` in a JAR file called JAWS.JAR. To compile an applet that uses JSObject, add JAWS.JAR in the CLASSPATH before compilation. If you are using modern Java tools, such as JBuilder 4.0 or 5.0, this package has been included.

Notice that although JSObject is supported in Java Plug-in 1.2.2, it is not supported in AppletViewer in the Java 2.0 platform, Standard Edition version 1.2.2. As a result, applets using JSObject may not run in AppletViewer, or they may result in exceptions. To test your applet that accesses the document object model of an HTML page, open the HTML page that hosts the <APPLET> tag in a browser.

For browser compatibility, use only the getWindow( ), call( ), eval( ), setMember( ), and getMember( ) methods. The implementation of getSlot( ), setSlot( ), removeMember( ), and toString( ) is browser-dependent, so the result of the execution may vary depending on the version and platform of the browser.

Any development using JSObject starts with the static method, as follows:

```
public static JSObject getWindow(Applet a)
```

This method returns a JSObject, which represents the Window object in the JavaScript script for the window containing the given applet. Because this method takes only java.awt.Applet as a parameter, JSObject can be accessed from an applet, but not from a bean unless the bean is also an applet.

> **Note**
> In Internet Explorer, Java Plug-in provides full support of JSObject in Internet Explorer 3.0/4.0 by accessing the document object model through COM.
>
> In Netscape Navigator, Java Plug-in provides limited support of JSObject in Navigator 3.0/4.0 by accessing the document object model through Netscape's Plug-in API.

Currently, in Navigator 3.0 the following JavaScript objects can be accessed through JSObject:

- Anchor
- Document
- Element
- Form
- Frame
- History
- Image
- Link
- Location
- Navigator
- Option
- URL
- Window

In Netscape Navigator 4.0, all the JavaScript objects mentioned previously are supported. In addition, Navigator supports the following:

- Layer
- UIBar

All have JavaScript objects not mentioned are not supported, and accessing them through JSObject will result in Java exceptions being thrown.

Notice that even though different browsers may support the same JavaScript object, the methods and properties the JavaScript object supports may be different.

Accessing the Document Object Model from an Applet

As mentioned previously, you can use the JSObject object to access the document object model. For example, the code in Listing 27.12 is an applet called MyApplet that reads the value of the firstName TEXT element into a String object reference called str. The applet then writes str to the loginName TEXT element in the same form.

Listing 27.12 **Applet that Accesses the Document Object Model**

```
import java.applet.*;
import netscape.javascript.*;

public class MyApplet extends Applet {

  public void init() {
    JSObject window = JSObject.getWindow(this);
    JSObject doc = (JSObject) window.getMember("document");
    JSObject form = (JSObject) doc.getMember("form1");
    JSObject firstName = (JSObject) form.getMember("firstName");
    String str = (String) firstName.getMember("value");
    JSObject loginName = (JSObject) form.getMember("loginName");
    loginName.setMember("value", str);
  }

}
```

The HTML page in Listing 27.13 hosts the applet in Listing 27.12 to demonstrate how the applet can access an HTML document.

Listing 27.13 **The HTML Page that Hosts the Applet that Accesses the Document Object Model**

```
<HTML>
<HEAD>
<TITLE>Accessing the document object model</TITLE>
</HEAD>

<BODY>
<FORM NAME=form1 ACTION=BLAH.ASP METHOD=POST>
<BR>firstName: <INPUT TYPE=TEXT NAME=firstName VALUE=Laylian>
<BR>loginName: <INPUT TYPE=TEXT NAME=loginName>
<BR><INPUT TYPE=SUBMIT>
</FORM>

<BR>The applet will copy the value of firstName to loginName.
<BR>
<APPLET
```

```
    CODEBASE = "."
    CODE     = "MyApplet.class"
    NAME     = "TestApplet"
    WIDTH    = 40
    HEIGHT   = 30
    HSPACE   = 0
    VSPACE   = 0
    ALIGN    = middle
    MAYSCRIPT
>
</APPLET>
</BODY>
</HTML>
```

Invoking JavaScript Functions from an Applet

After your applet has access to the document object model, it can do anything that can be done from JavaScript. This includes invoking a JavaScript function. The code in Listing 27.14 shows an applet that invokes the noArg and twoArgs JavaScript functions, as well as the alert method.

Listing 27.14 **An Applet that Invokes JavaScript Functions**

```
import java.applet.*;
import netscape.javascript.*;

public class MyApplet extends Applet {

  public void init() {
    JSObject window = JSObject.getWindow(this);
    // invoking a custom function called noArg
    // that accepts no argument.
    window.call("noArg", null);

    // invoking the alert method, passing one
    // argument obj1;
    Object[] obj1 = new Object[1];
    obj1[0] = "Hello from MyApplet!!!";
    window.call("alert", obj1);

    // invoking the custom function twoArgs
    // with two arguments.
    Object[] obj2 = new Object[2];
    obj2[0] = "one ";
    obj2[1] = "2";
    window.call("twoArgs", obj2);
  }

}
```

The applet in Listing 27.14 can be used in the HTML page in Listing 27.15.

Listing 27.15 **HTML Page that Hosts an Applet that Invokes JavaScript Functions**

```
<HTML>
<HEAD>
<TITLE>Invoke a JavaScript function from an applet</TITLE>
<SCRIPT LANGUAGE="JavaScript">
function noArg() {
  alert("You have successfully invoked a no argument " +
    "JavaScript function from an Applet.");
}

function twoArgs(arg1, arg2) {
  alert(arg1 + arg2);
}
</SCRIPT>
</HEAD>
<BODY>
```

The following applet invokes the alert method and the two custom functions noArg and twoArgs:

```
<APPLET
  CODEBASE = "."
  CODE     = "MyApplet.class"
  NAME     = "TestApplet"
  WIDTH    = 400
  HEIGHT   = 300
  HSPACE   = 0
  VSPACE   = 0
  ALIGN    = middle
  MAYSCRIPT
>
</APPLET>
</BODY>
</HTML>
```

Evaluating a JavaScript Statement from an Applet

This technique demonstrates how to evaluate a JavaScript statement from an applet. An example that shows how this happens is presented in Listing 27.16 and Listing 27.17. The code in Listing 27.16 shows an applet that evaluates a JavaScript function. The code in Listing 27.17 is an HTML page that uses such an applet. The applet in Listing 27.16 uses the eval method to write to the loginName and password HIDDEN elements and then to invoke the alert method.

Listing 27.16 **The Applet that Uses the JavaScript eval Method to Evaluate a JavaScript Statement**

```
import java.applet.*;
import netscape.javascript.*;

public class MyApplet extends Applet {

  public void init() {
    JSObject window = JSObject.getWindow(this);
    String loginName = "boni";
    String password = "secret";
    window.eval("document.forms[0].loginName.value='" + loginName + "'");
    window.eval("document.forms[0].password.value='" + password + "'");
    window.eval("alert('Secret login name and password copied.')");

  }

}
```

Listing 27.17 **The HTML Page that Hosts the Applet that Evaluates JavaScript Statements**

```
<HTML>
<HEAD>
<TITLE>Invoke a JavaScript statement</TITLE>
</HEAD>
<BODY>
<FORM ACTION=Login.jsp METHOD=POST>
<INPUT TYPE=HIDDEN NAME=loginName>
<INPUT TYPE=HIDDEN NAME=password>
<INPUT TYPE=SUBMIT VALUE="Click to Login">
</FORM>
The following applet will copy the secret login name and
password to the HIDDEN elements.
<APPLET
  CODEBASE = "."
  CODE     = "MyApplet.class"
  NAME     = "TestApplet"
  WIDTH    = 400
  HEIGHT   = 300
  HSPACE   = 0
  VSPACE   = 0
  ALIGN    = middle
  MAYSCRIPT
>
</APPLET>
</BODY>
</HTML>
```

Setting the Applet Parameter

The PARAM VALUE of the <APPLET> tag can't be changed at run time—it can only be changed during layout time. Working only on Netscape browsers, the code in Listing 27.18 uses JavaScript "entities" to set calculated VALUES that could come from a JavaScript variable, a JavaScript function, or a JavaScript expression.

Listing 27.18 **Setting Applet Parameters in Netscape Browsers**

```
<HTML>
<HEAD>
<SCRIPT LANGUAGE="JavaScript">
var greeting = "Hello World";

function sayHello () {
  return "Hello again";
}
</SCRIPT>
</HEAD>

<BODY>
<APPLET CODE="MyApplet.class" HEIGHT=100 WIDTH=400>
<PARAM NAME="jsVariable" VALUE="&{greeting};">
<PARAM NAME="jsFunction" VALUE="&{sayHello()};">
<PARAM NAME="jsExpression"
  VALUE="&{'This is an expression'.toUpperCase()};">
</APPLET>
</BODY>
</HTML>
```

For Microsoft browsers, use the document.write() method to customize the APPLET PARAM during layout time.

Applet-to-Applet Communication Through JavaScript

Now that you know how to call a JavaScript function from inside an applet and invoke an applet's method from JavaScript, applet-to-applet communication is at your disposal. If you need to run a method on the second applet from the first method, for example, you can create an intermediary JavaScript function that invokes the method on the second applet and then calls the JavaScript function from the first applet.

Figure 27.1 illustrates how an applet can send a message to another applet. The first applet has a text box and a button, and the second applet has only one text box. A user can type a string in the text box of the first applet. When the user clicks the button on the first applet, the string typed will also be displayed in the second applet's text box.

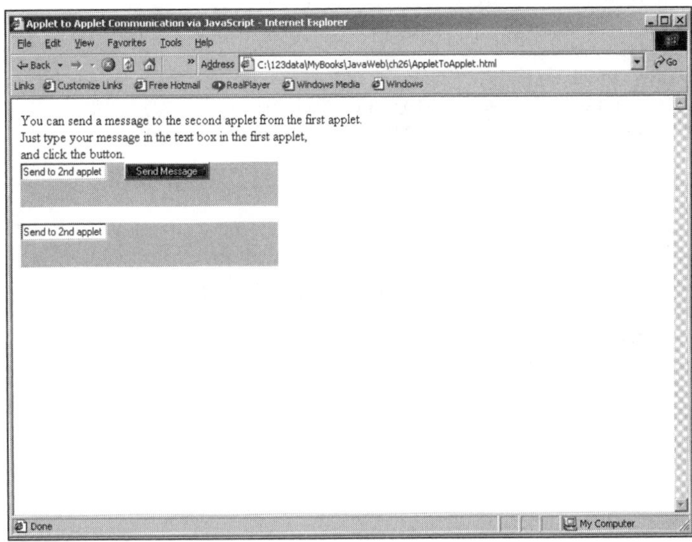

Figure 27.1 Applet-to-applet communication.

Listing 27.19 and Listing 27.20 present the code for both applets. Listing 27.21 shows the HTML page that hosts both applets.

Listing 27.19 **The First Applet in Applet-to-Applet Communication**

```
import java.applet.*;
import java.awt.*;
import java.awt.event.*;
import netscape.javascript.*;

public class MyApplet extends Applet implements ActionListener {
  TextField textField1 = new TextField();
  Button button1 = new Button("Send Message");
  TextField textField2 = new TextField();
  JSObject window;

  public void init() {
    this.setLayout(null);
    add(textField1, null);
```

continues

Listing 27.19 **Continued**

```
    textField1.setSize(100, 20);
    add(button1, null);
    button1.setBounds(120, 0, 100, 20);
    button1.setForeground(new Color(255, 255, 255));
    button1.setBackground(new Color(0, 0, 0));
    button1.addActionListener(this);
    window = JSObject.getWindow(this);
  }

  public void actionPerformed(ActionEvent ae) {
    window.eval("sendMessage('" + textField1.getText() + "')");
  }
}
```

Listing 27.20 **The Second Applet in Applet-to-Applet Communication**

```
import java.applet.*;
import java.awt.TextField;

public class SecondApplet extends Applet {
  TextField textField1 = new TextField();

  public void init() {
    this.setLayout(null);
    add(textField1, null);
    textField1.setSize(100, 20);
  }

  public void setMessage(String message) {
    textField1.setText(message);
  }
}
```

Listing 27.21 **The HTML Page Where the Applet-to-Applet Communication Happens**

```
<HTML>
<HEAD>
<TITLE>Applet-to-applet communication through JavaScript</TITLE>
<SCRIPT LANGUAGE="JavaScript">
function sendMessage(message) {
  document.applets[1].setMessage(message);

}
```

```
</SCRIPT>
</HEAD>
<BODY>

You can send a message to the second applet from the first applet.
<BR>Just type your message in the text box in the first applet,
<BR>and click the button.
<BR>
<APPLET
  CODEBASE = "."
  CODE     = "MyApplet.class"
  NAME     = "TestApplet"
  WIDTH    = 300
  HEIGHT   = 50
  HSPACE   = 0
  VSPACE   = 0
  ALIGN    = middle
  MAYSCRIPT
>
</APPLET>
<BR><BR>
<APPLET
  CODEBASE = "."
  CODE     = "SecondApplet.class"
  NAME     = "SecondApplet"
  WIDTH    = 300
  HEIGHT   = 50
  HSPACE   = 0
  VSPACE   = 0
  ALIGN    = middle
>
</APPLET>
</BODY>
</HTML>
```

Direct Applet-to-Applet Communication

Rather than having JavaScript functions in applet-to-applet communication, you can have a direct applet-to-applet communication that bypasses the JavaScript part entirely.

The following examples show direct communication between two applets. The first applet sends a message to the second applet in the same HTML page. Listing 27.22 and Listing 27.23 show the code for the first applet and second applet, respectively. Listing 27.24 presents the HTML page that hosts the two applets.

Listing 27.22 **The First Applet in Direct Applet-to-Applet Communication**

```
import java.applet.*;
import java.awt.*;
import java.awt.event.*;
import netscape.javascript.*;

public class MyApplet extends Applet implements ActionListener {
  TextField textField1 = new TextField();
  Button button1 = new Button("Send Message");
  TextField textField2 = new TextField();
  JSObject window;

  public void init() {
    this.setLayout(null);
    add(textField1, null);
    textField1.setSize(100, 20);
    add(button1, null);
    button1.setBounds(120, 0, 100, 20);
    button1.setForeground(new Color(255, 255, 255));
    button1.setBackground(new Color(0, 0, 0));
    button1.addActionListener(this);
    window = JSObject.getWindow(this);
  }

  public void actionPerformed(ActionEvent ae) {
    window.eval("document.applets[1].setMessage('"
➥+ textField1.getText() + "')");
  }
}
```

Listing 27.23 **The Second Applet in Direct Applet-to-Applet Communication**

```
import java.applet.*;
import java.awt.TextField;

public class SecondApplet extends Applet {
  TextField textField1 = new TextField();

  public void init() {
    this.setLayout(null);
    add(textField1, null);
    textField1.setSize(100, 20);
  }
```

```
  public void setMessage(String message) {
    textField1.setText(message);
  }
}
```

Listing 27.24 **The HTML File for Direct Applet-to-Applet Communication**

```
<HTML>
<HEAD>
<TITLE>Direct applet-to-applet communication</TITLE>
</HEAD>
<BODY>

You can send a message to the second applet from the first applet.
<BR>Just type your message in the text box in the first applet,
<BR>and click the button.
<BR>
<APPLET
  CODEBASE = "."
  CODE     = "MyApplet.class"
  NAME     = "TestApplet"
  WIDTH    = 300
  HEIGHT   = 50
  HSPACE   = 0
  VSPACE   = 0
  ALIGN    = middle
  MAYSCRIPT
>
</APPLET>
<BR><BR>
<APPLET
  CODEBASE = "."
  CODE     = "SecondApplet.class"
  NAME     = "SecondApplet"
  WIDTH    = 300
  HEIGHT   = 50
  HSPACE   = 0
  VSPACE   = 0
  ALIGN    = middle
>
</APPLET>
</BODY>
</HTML>
```

Summary

Applets are useful objects that can do many things beyond HTML and JavaScript. For this reason, understanding how to work with applets in the document object model context is very helpful.

This chapter presented techniques to help you work with applets. You learned how to check whether Java is enabled in a browser, set and get a property from an applet, and send messages to an applet from JavaScript. Additionally, you discovered how to achieve applet-to-applet communication.

Developing Scalable Applications with EJB

28

Enterprise JavaBeans

IN PREVIOUS CHAPTERS, YOU LEARNED HOW to develop and deploy servlet and JSP applications. Both servlet and JSP are good technologies in use today that are continuing to get more and more popular.

From this chapter on, you will learn how to develop and deploy Enterprise JavaBeans (EJB) applications. For the most part, for simple web applications you should probably stick with servlets/JSP and avoid EJB altogether. If robustness and scalability are an issue, however, you should consider developing an EJB application. As this chapter shows, there are many benefits that make EJB appealing.

The EJB technology depends on other Java technologies to function properly. First, it uses Java Remote Method Invocation (RMI) as the communication protocol between two enterprise beans and between an enterprise bean and its client. If you are a seasoned Java programmer, you should know how RMI is used in Java-distributed computing to invoke remote methods on a remote machine.

Another technology used in EJB is Remote Method Invocation over Internet Inter-ORB Protocol (RMI-IIOP), where ORB stands for *Object Request Broker*. RMI-IIOP is a more portable version of RMI that can use the IIOP from the Object Management Group (OMG). RMI-IIOP is especially used in communications between an enterprise bean and a client.

Lastly, EJB uses Java Naming and Directory Interface (JNDI) as the naming service that binds a name with an enterprise bean.

> **Note**
> To understand EJB completely, an understanding of these supporting technologies is mandatory.

This chapter serves as the introduction to EJB. The discussion starts by defining EJB and presenting some of EJB's benefits, most of which are not available in servlets/JSP. The chapter then discusses the architecture and the distinct roles in the EJB application and deployment life cycle, and provides a sample application and some technical insights by presenting a review of the javax.ejb package. Lastly, the chapter presents two client applications to test the sample application.

The phrases *Enterprise JavaBean* or *enterprise bean* in this chapter and the chapters to come are interchangeable. Don't confuse them with beans that are used in a JSP application, which is a totally different thing. The word *bean* in all cases in this chapter refers to an enterprise bean.

What Is an Enterprise JavaBean?

In a nutshell, an enterprise JavaBean is a server-side component. Just like any other component, an enterprise bean encapsulates business logic. Enterprise beans must conform to the EJB specifications, however, and they are deployed and can run only in an EJB container, identical to the way servlets run inside a servlet container.

A servlet container provides services for servlets, such as session management and security. Likewise, an EJB container provides system-level services for EJB applications. In fact, as you will soon find out, it's the EJB container that makes EJB so great. Despite the similarity of names, EJB has little to do with JavaBeans.

Benefits of EJB

EJB applications are much more complex and more difficult to build and administer than servlets/JSP applications. For someone new to EJB, the learning curve also is steeper. If this is the case, why is EJB so popular and why do so many organizations want to invest in it? The answer is simple—after you know the nuts and bolts of EJB, writing an application is an easy task, and, more importantly, you can enjoy some benefits provided for you by the EJB container.

The following is the list of some of the benefits of EJB:

- EJB applications are easy to develop because the application developer can concentrate on the business logic. At the same time, the developer uses the services provided by the EJB container, such as transactions and connection pooling. Again, the hardest part is the learning process.
- EJBs are components. Chances are good that there are EJB vendors who sell components that encapsulate the functionality that you need. By purchasing a third-party's EJBs, you can avoid needing to develop your own beans, which means your application development is more rapid. The EJB specification makes sure that beans developed by others can be used in your application.
- There is a clear separation of labor in the development, deployment, and administration of an EJB application. This makes the development and deployment process even faster. The roles are discussed in detail in the section, "The Six EJB Roles."
- The EJB container manages transactions, state management details, multithreading, connection pooling, and other low-level APIs without you, the developer, having to understand them.
- The EJB container provides security for the applications.
- The EJB architecture is compatible with other Java APIs.

EJB Application Architecture

The EJB application architecture (shown in Figure 28.1) extends the web application architecture by adding another tier.

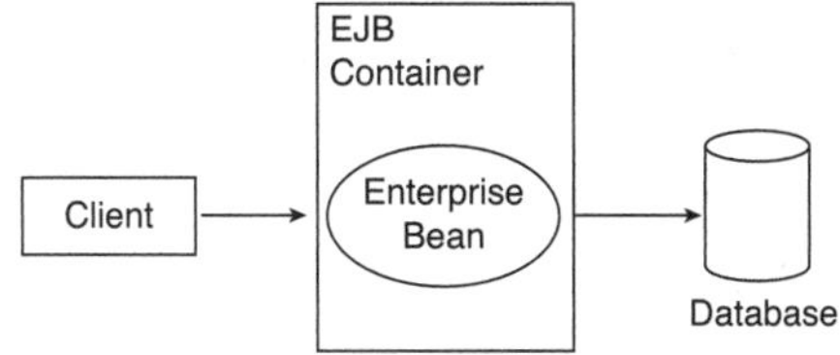

Figure 28.1 The EJB application architecture.

Clients of an enterprise bean can be a traditional Java application, an applet, a JSP page or servlet, another EJB bean, or others.

Note that a client never invokes a bean's methods directly. Communication between clients and beans is done through the EJB container. Compare this with a web application in which a client web browser has to go through the web container to use a servlet or a JSP page.

When a client is a servlet or a JSP page, the structure of an EJB application looks like that shown in Figure 28.2.

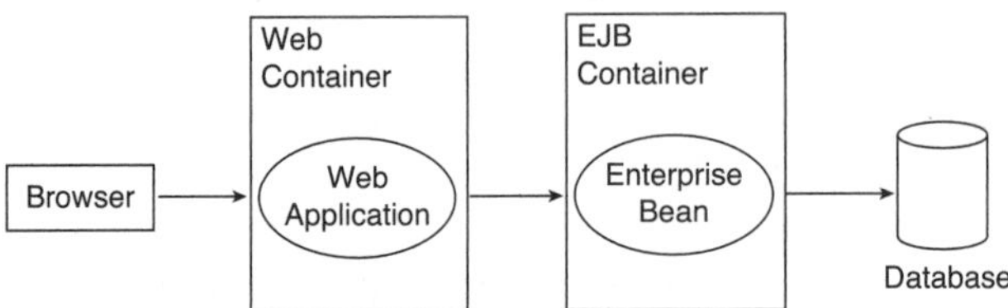

Figure 28.2 An EJB application with a servlet as the client.

The Six EJB Roles

The six distinct roles in the EJB application development and deployment life cycle are as follows:

- Bean developer
- Application assembler
- Deployer
- System administrator
- EJB server provider
- EJB container provider

Each role can be performed by a different individual or organization. Often, however, an individual plays more than one role in a given time. For example, normally there is no clear separation between an EJB server and an EJB container; that is, they normally come in one package from a vendor.

All the six roles are explained in the following sections.

Bean Developer

The bean developer is the programmer who develops enterprise beans. To be a successful bean developer, you need to understand the business logic of the application.

Application Assembler

An EJB application typically consists of more than one enterprise bean. For larger applications, several bean developers may be employed to build the beans. The application assembler is the person responsible for assembling all the beans written by the bean developer(s). The application assembler also writes the deployment descriptor. The examples in this book also require you to be an application assembler.

Deployer

The deployer is the one in charge of deploying the EJB application in a particular EJB container or containers, if there is more than one EJB container used. This person takes the enterprise bean(s) and deployment descriptor from the application assembler as the input. This person must be an expert of the EJB container used. You also are introduced to this role during the development and deployment of the sample EJB application presented in this book.

System Administrator

After the EJB application is deployed successfully, the application still must be maintained on a day-to-day basis—or perhaps *minute-to-minute* is more accurate. It is the system administrator's role to make sure that the application runs 24 hours a day without interruption. If a server crashes, the administrator makes sure that it is restarted immediately.

Also, the system administrator is responsible for managing security. For example, it's the system administrator's job to create a new account for a new user or a group of users. In a large organization, this role is a full-time job.

EJB Container Provider

The EJB container provider is a vendor that has the resources to write an EJB container and to make sure that the software conforms to the EJB specification. The developer of the EJB container also should provide various tools for the system administrator for easily administering the EJB applications deployed. For example, there should be a tool that the system administrator can use to add a user easily. This book is not concerned with this role.

EJB Server Provider

The EJB server provider provides an EJB server which in turn hosts the EJB container. Currently, the EJB architecture does not clearly state the separation of this role from the EJB container provider role. Most EJB containers come packaged in an EJB server. This book does assume that you will write an EJB server.

Types of Enterprise Beans

You use three types of enterprise beans: session, entity, and message-driven. A session bean is a component that performs a certain task for the client. An entity bean represents an entity in the database or other persistent storage. Message-driven beans are a new addition to EJB 2.0. They serve as a listener for the Java Message Service API that enables asynchronous message processing. All these beans are discussed in the next few chapters.

Writing Your First Enterprise Bean

As usual, I will present a sample application as a proof of concept. All the samples in this book run in a JBoss application server; therefore, they require that you install JBoss. If you haven't already installed JBoss, you can use Appendix F, "JBoss Installation and Configuration," as a step-by-step guide.

After finishing the sample application, you need to create a client application to call your bean. You need to know some theory to write a client application. This theory is given in the section, "Writing Client Applications."

Developing and deploying an EJB application requires the following steps:

1. Writing the bean.
2. Writing the deployment descriptor.
3. Creating a deployment file.
4. Deploying the bean.
5. Writing the client application to test the bean.

The following example builds an EJB application consisting of only one enterprise bean that can perform additions of two integers. After successfully compiling the bean, you will write the deployment descriptor and deploy the bean. Lastly, you will create a servlet that serves as the client of our EJB application.

Writing and Compiling the Adder Bean

You have three Java files to write, all of which are part of the com.brainysoftware.ejb package. So the first thing you need to do is to create the appropriate directory structure. Figure 28.3 displays the directory structure of an EJB application.

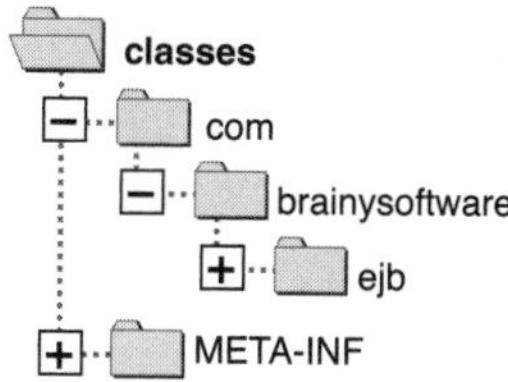

Figure 28.3 The directory structure of an EJB application.

The three Java files you need to create in the com/brainysoftware/ejb directory are AdderHome.java, Adder.java, and AdderBean.java. AdderHome and Adder are the home and remote interfaces of the enterprise bean. Both are explained in the section, "EJB Explained," later in this chapter. Listings 28.1 through 28.3 provide the code for each of these files.

Listing 28.1 **The AdderHome Interface**

```
package com.brainysoftware.ejb;

import java.rmi.RemoteException;
import javax.ejb.CreateException;
import javax.ejb.EJBHome;

public interface AdderHome extends EJBHome {
  Adder create() throws RemoteException, CreateException;
}
```

Listing 28.2 **The Adder Interface**

```
package com.brainysoftware.ejb;

import javax.ejb.EJBObject;
import java.rmi.RemoteException;

public interface Adder extends EJBObject {
  public int add(int a, int b) throws RemoteException;
```

Listing 28.3 **The AdderBean Class**

```
package com.brainysoftware.ejb;

import java.rmi.RemoteException;
import javax.ejb.SessionBean;
import javax.ejb.SessionContext;

public class AdderBean implements SessionBean {

  public int add(int a, int b) {
    System.out.println("from AdderBean");
    return (a + b);
  }

  public void ejbCreate() {
  }

  public void ejbRemove() {
  }

  public void ejbActivate() {
  }

  public void ejbPassivate() {
  }

  public void setSessionContext(SessionContext sc) {
  }
}
```

Writing the Deployment Descriptor

An EJB application must have a deployment descriptor that describes each enterprise bean in that application. The deployment descriptor file is called ejb.xml. For the sample application, the deployment descriptor is given in Listing 28.4.

Listing 28.4 **The Deployment Descriptor**

```
<?xml version="1.0" encoding="UTF-8"?>

<ejb-jar>
  <description>Your first EJB application </description>
  <display-name>Adder Application</display-name>
  <enterprise-beans>
    <session>
      <ejb-name>Adder</ejb-name>
```

```
      <home>com.brainysoftware.ejb.AdderHome</home>
      <remote>com.brainysoftware.ejb.Adder</remote>
      <ejb-class>com.brainysoftware.ejb.AdderBean</ejb-class>
      <session-type>Stateless</session-type>
      <transaction-type>Bean</transaction-type>
    </session>
  </enterprise-beans>
</ejb-jar>
```

Creating a Deployment File

After you finish developing your enterprise bean, you need to package all the class files into one .jar file. The class files are given in the directory structure displayed in Figure 28.3. The ejb directory contains three files: Adder.class, AdderHome.class, and AdderBean.class. The META-INF directory contains one file: the ejb-jar.xml file, the deployment descriptor.

Follow these steps to create the deployment file:

1. Change directory to the parent directory of both com and META-INF.
2. Assuming jar.exe is already in the path, type the following:

```
jar cfv adder.jar com/brainysoftware/ejb/* META-INF/ejb-jar.xml
```

3. This creates a jar file called adder.jar.

Deployment

Copy the adder.jar file into the deployment directory under JBoss home. Restart JBoss. JBoss should spit out some messages. In the lines of messages, look for the following:

```
...
[Auto deploy] Starting
[Auto deploy] Auto deploy of file:/C:/jboss/deploy/adder.jar
...
[J2EE Deployer] Create application adder.jar
[J2EE Deployer] Installing EJB package: adder.jar
[J2EE Deployer] Starting module adder.jar
...
[J2EE Deployer] J2EE application: file:/C:/jboss/deploy/adder.jar is
deployed.
...
```

That's it. Your EJB application has been successfully deployed.

To test your enterprise bean, however, you need a client application. You learn how to write a client application later in the section, "Writing Client Applications." Before you write one, however, you need to see how EJB works.

EJB Explained

As you have seen from the preceding section, an enterprise bean does not consist of a one class. In fact, there are always two interfaces that accompany a bean class. These two interfaces are called the *home interface* and the *remote interface*. They are there to enable communications between a client and an enterprise bean. The enterprise bean contains the implementation of the business rules. Of course, an enterprise bean can have other classes as well. The two interfaces and one implementation class serve as the minimum.

The home interface and the remote interface are crucial because they are the "door" to an enterprise bean for a client application.

The EJB specification states that an enterprise bean and its supporting components are written by implementing or extending members of the javax.ejb package.

The Home Interface

The home interface performs life cycle operations: creating, finding, and removing the enterprise bean. A home interface must extend the EJBHome interface in the javax.ejb package. The javax.ejb.EJBHome interface is given as follows:

```
package javax.ejb;

public interface EJBHome extends java.rmi.Remote {

  EJBMetaData getEJBMetaData()
    throws java.rmi.RemoteException;

  HomeHandle getHomeHandle()
    throws java.rmi.RemoteException;

  void remove(Handle handle)
    throws java.rmi.RemoteException, javax.ejb.RemoveException;

  void remove(Object primaryKey)
    throws java.rmi.RemoteException, javax.ejb.RemoveException;
}
```

See how the EJBHome interface is derived from the java.rmi.Remote interface? This is the first sign you've seen in this chapter that EJB is dependent on RMI.

The java.rmi.Remote interface itself is used to identify interfaces whose methods may be invoked from a non-local virtual machine. Any remote object must implement this interface either directly or indirectly.

A home interface can define methods to create, find, and remove the enterprise bean. The create and find methods are added to the home interface definition; the remove methods are inherited from the javax.ejb.EJBHome interface. For instance, the home interface of the Adder EJB (the AdderHome interface), given in Listing 28.1, defines a no-argument create method in its body, using the following code:

```
import java.rmi.RemoteException;
import javax.ejb.CreateException;
import javax.ejb.EJBHome;

public interface AdderHome extends EJBHome {

  Adder create() throws RemoteException, CreateException;

}
```

A home interface can define multiple overloads of the create and find methods. The create and find methods also can throw additional exceptions, if required. The name for a find method always start with "find".

Both the create and find methods are optional. Not all beans need them. For example, a session bean might define one or more create methods but an entity bean might not. This will become clear when you learn about session and entity beans in Chapters 29 and 30.

> **Note**
> An instance of a home interface is sometimes called a home object.

The Remote Interface

The remote interface duplicates all the business methods that are to be available to a client. This happens, again, because the client cannot access the bean directly.

A remote interface must extend the EJBObject interface in the javax.ejb package. The javax.ejb.EJBObject is defined as follows:

```
package javax.ejb;
public interface EJBObject extends java.rmi.Remote {
  public abstract EJBHome getEJBHome()
    throws java.rmi.RemoteException;
  public abstract Object getPrimaryKey()
    throws java.rmi.RemoteException;

  public abstract void remove()
    throws java.rmi.RemoteException, javax.ejb.RemoveException
```

```
    public abstract Handle getHandle()
      throws java.rmi.RemoteException;

    public abstract boolean isIdentical(EJBObject obj)
      throws java.rmi.RemoteException;
}
```

Like the javax.ejb.EJBHome interface, this interface extends the java.rmi.Remote interface.

In the Adder bean example, the remote interface is called Adder and is given in Listing 28.2. As you can see, it clones the add method found in the bean implementation in Listing 28.3 by using the following code:

```
import javax.ejb.EJBObject;
import java.rmi.RemoteException;

public interface Adder extends EJBObject {
  public int add(int a, int b) throws RemoteException;
}
```

Note

An instance of a remote interface is often called the *EJB object*.

The Enterprise Bean Class

This class provides the implementations of the life cycle methods in the home interface as well as the business logic defined in the remote interface.

An enterprise bean class is either a session bean, an entity bean, or a message-driven bean. In other words, a session bean implements the javax.ejb.SessionBean interface and an entity bean implements the javax.ejb.EntityBean interface. Therefore, an enterprise bean class also must provide the implementation of the EJB container callback methods defined in either the javax.ejb.SessionBean interface or the javax.ejb.EntityBean interface.

The life cycle create and find methods in the home interface correspond to the ejbCreate, ejbPostCreate, and ejbFind methods in the bean class. You learn more about the enterprise bean class in Chapters 18 and 19.

The Deployment Descriptor

An EJB application needs a deployment descriptor that specifies meta information for the EJB container. The deployment descriptor is an XML file called ejb.xml and must be located in the META-INF directory under the application directory.

The following is some is some of the information specified by the deployment descriptor:

- The enterprise bean name
- The type of the bean
- The fully qualified name of the home interface
- The fully qualified name of the remote interface

The deployment descriptor can define more than one bean.

Writing Client Applications

An enterprise bean is a server-side component that sits idle on the server waiting for a call from clients. Writing an EJB client can sometimes be a tricky business. Without a client, however, you can't test your enterprise beans. Understanding how the client gets access and calls your bean is therefore an important part of the EJB application.

An EJB client does not invoke methods in the enterprise bean class directly. In fact, a client can see only the home and remote interfaces of the bean, as shown in Figure 28.4.

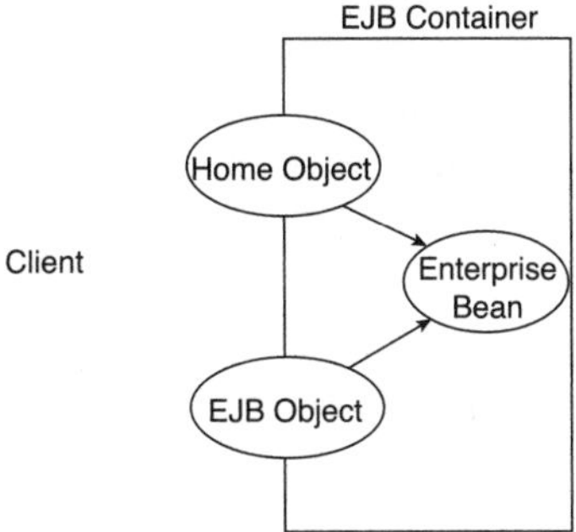

Figure 28.4 A client can see only the home and remote interfaces of an EJB.

Client applications access the enterprise bean through the Java Naming and Directory Interface (JNDI). Therefore, understanding JNDI is very helpful in writing effective and efficient client applications. A brief summary of JNDI is given next that will enable you to write client applications to access enterprise beans.

In this example, you write two types of client applications. The first is a Java application consisting of one simple class called BeanClient. The second client application is a JSP page that demonstrates how to use an enterprise bean from a servlet or a JSP page.

The first client is important because it demonstrates the basic functionality that must exist for the client to call an enterprise bean. The second client is also crucial because, as a web developer, you will need to access an EJB application from inside a servlet or a JSP page.

Let's now take a brief look at JNDI.

Java Naming and Directory Interface (JNDI)

Access to an enterprise bean is done through JNDI. Therefore, it is crucial to understand this API. If you already have good knowledge of JNDI, you can skip this section.

JNDI comes as part of JDK 1.3 and later. If you are currently using JDK 1.2, you need to download JNDI and install it separately. JNDI provides two services: a naming service and a directory service.

A naming service is a very important feature in computing because it finds an object associated with a given name. An example of a popular naming service is the Internet Domain Name System (DNS) that maps domain names (such as `newriders.com`) with IP addresses. In the context of EJB, a naming service finds an enterprise bean for you if you know the name given to the bean.

If a client application wants to call an enterprise bean, it simply needs to supply the name of the bean. JNDI will find the bean for the client. As such, it is not surprising why a naming service plays an important role in EJB.

A directory service is an extension of a naming service. A directory service associates names with objects and also allows those objects to have attributes that describe the objects. These attributes enable you to search for an object without knowing its name. An example of a directory service is the Lightweight Directory Access Protocol (LDAP). Directory services are not used to access enterprise beans—therefore, they are outside the scope of this book.

The JNDI is divided into five packages. These are as follows:

- javax.naming
- javax.naming.directory
- javax.naming.event
- javax.naming.ldap
- javax.naming.spi

Knowing the javax.naming package is sufficient for accessing an enterprise bean. In writing a client application that uses the service of an enterprise bean, you need to understand well two important members of the javax.naming package: the Context interface and the InitialContext class.

The javax.naming.Context Interface

The Context interface represents a naming context consisting of a set of name-to-object association. This association in JNDI terms is called *binding*. The Context interface is important because it contains methods for examining and modifying the name-to-object bindings.

The most frequently used method in the Context interface is probably the lookup method. This method returns a reference to an object, given the name of the object. There are two overloads of this method. The signatures of both overloads are as follows:

```
public Object lookup(javax.naming.Name name)
➥throws javax.naming.NamingException
public Object lookup(String name) throws javax.naming.NamingException
```

You use the lookup method to obtain a reference to an enterprise bean's home object. The second overload of the lookup method is very straightforward. You simply pass the string representation of the bean's name and you get a reference to the bean's home object.

The lookup method throws a javax.naming.NamingException object if the name resolution fails.

The javax.naming.InitialContext Class

Naming operations are relative to a context. The InitialContext class implements the Context interface and provides the starting context for name resolutions.

For a context, you need to define a number of properties for the environment of the context. For example, a naming resolution may be restricted to authorized users only. In this case, you need to supply a user's credentials as properties. You normally create a java.util.Properties object and use its put method to add key/value pairs representing any necessary property names and values.

In accessing an enterprise bean, you need to supply two properties. The first is the environment property java.naming.factory.initial. The value of this property is the fully qualified class name that will be used to create the initial context.

The second property is java.naming.provider.url. This is an environment property whose value specifies configuration information for the service provider to use.

Both property names are conveniently contained in two static fields in the Context interface. They are Context.INITIAL_CONTEXT_FACTORY and Context.PROVIDER_URL, respectively.

For the purpose of accessing an enterprise bean, you need to add these two properties to a java.util.Properties method using its put method, as you see in the following code:

```
import java.util.Properties;

// Create a java.util.Properties object
Properties properties = new Properties();

// Add two properties: "java.naming.factory.initial" and
// "java.naming.provider.url"
properties.put(Context.INITIAL_CONTEXT_FACTORY,
  "org.jnp.interfaces.NamingContextFactory");
properties.put(Context.PROVIDER_URL, "localhost:1099");
```

Because these properties are needed when creating an initial context, the Properties object is passed to the InitialContext class's constructor, as follows:

```
javax.naming.InitialContext jndiContext =
  new javax.naming.InitialContext(properties);
```

To sum up, obtaining a reference to an enterprise bean involves the following steps:

1. Creating a java.util.Properties object.
2. Adding necessary properties to the java.util.Properties object for constructing the initial context.
3. Constructing an javax.naming.InitialContext object.
4. Using the javax.naming.Context interface's lookup method to get a reference to the bean's home object, passing the name of the bean.

The summary can be rewritten in the following code:

```
import java.util.Properties;
import javax.naming.*;

Properties properties = new Properties();
properties.put(Context.INITIAL_CONTEXT_FACTORY,
  "org.jnp.interfaces.NamingContextFactory");
properties.put(Context.PROVIDER_URL, "localhost:1099");

try {
  InitialContext jndiContext = new InitialContext(properties);
  // get the reference to the home interface
  Object ref  = jndiContext.lookup("Adder");
}
catch (NamingException e) {
}
```

Creating a Bean's Instance

Using JNDI, you managed to obtain a reference to the bean's home object. The next step is to create an instance of the bean on the server. This is done using the home interface's create method.

The reference you got to the bean's home object, however, is an RMI object of type java.lang.Object. To call the create method of the home object, you first need to downcast the object reference into the type of the home interface. For example, in the Adder bean example, the code for the downcasting looks like this:

```
AdderHome home = (AdderHome) ref;
```

In this example, ref is the reference obtained from the JNDI initial context's name lookup.

To conform with RMI-IIOP, you must use another method for the previous downcasting. Typically, you use the static narrow method of the javax.rmi.PortableRemoteObject class. This method is used to ensure that an object of a remote or abstract interface type can be cast to a desired type. The signature of this method is as follows:

```
public static Object narrow(Object narrowFrom, Class narrowTo)
  throws ClassCastException
```

Here, narrowFrom is the object to check and the narrowTo is the desired type. If narrowFrom cannot be cast to narrowTo, a ClassCastException object is thrown. If narrowFrom can be cast to narrowTo, the method returns an object of type Object that can be cast to the desired type. Your code then becomes the following:

```
AdderHome home = (AdderHome)
  PortableRemoteObject.narrow (ref, AdderHome.class);
```

Having a home object, you then can call the create method of the home interface to create the bean, as follows:

```
Adder adder = home.create();
```

You are then free to call any exposed methods of the bean. For the Adder bean example, you can call its add method, as follows:

```
int I = adder.add(2, 5);
```

Now let's see how to create client applications based on what you've learned so far.

A Java Client Application

The following is a class called BeanClient that calls the Adder session bean you have previously created. The code is very simple and is given in Listing 28.5.

Listing 28.5 **The Client Application Class**

```
import javax.naming.*;
import javax.rmi.PortableRemoteObject;
import java.util.Properties;
import com.brainysoftware.ejb.Adder;
import com.brainysoftware.ejb.AdderHome;

public class BeanClient {

  public static void main(String[] args) {
    // preparing properties for constructing an InitialContext object
    Properties properties = new Properties();
    properties.put(Context.INITIAL_CONTEXT_FACTORY,
➥"org.jnp.interfaces.NamingContextFactory");
    properties.put(Context.PROVIDER_URL, "localhost:1099");

    try {
      // Get an initial context
      InitialContext jndiContext = new InitialContext(properties);
      System.out.println("Got context");

      // Get a reference to the Bean
      Object ref  = jndiContext.lookup("Adder");
      System.out.println("Got reference");

      // Get a reference from this to the Bean's Home interface
      AdderHome home = (AdderHome)
        PortableRemoteObject.narrow (ref, AdderHome.class);

      // Create an Adder object from the Home interface
      Adder adder = home.create();
      System.out.println ("2 + 5 = " + adder.add(2, 5));
    }
    catch(Exception e) {
      System.out.println(e.toString());
    }
  }
}
```

It is assumed that the client application will run on the same computer as the EJB container. If you run it from a different computer, you need to replace "localhost:1099" with the URL of the naming service on the server.

If you are using JBoss, when you run the client class, you need to include the following files in the classpath:

- client/ejb.jar
- client/jboss-client.jar
- client/jnp-client.jar

The lib and client directories are located under JBoss home.

Calling the Bean from a JSP Page

Calling an enterprise bean from a servlet is basically the same as calling it from another client. Copying all the necessary library files into lib directory under Tomcat is important, however. The following files are needed from the JBoss's home directory:

- client/ejb.jar
- client/jboss-client.jar
- client/jnp-client.jar

Finally, copy the Adder.jar to the lib directory under CATALINA_HOME. Alternatively, deploy the class files under WEB-INF/classes/com/brainysoftware/ejb/ directory under the application directory. We need the Adder.class and AdderHome.class.

The code for the JSP page is given in Listing 28.6.

Listing 28.6 **Calling an Enterprise Bean from a JSP Page**

```
<%@ page import="javax.naming.*"%>
<%@ page import="javax.rmi.PortableRemoteObject"%>
<%@ page import="java.util.Properties"%>
<%@ page import="com.brainysoftware.ejb.Adder"%>
<%@ page import="com.brainysoftware.ejb.AdderHome"%>
<%
  // preparing a Properties object for constructing
  // an initial context
  Properties properties = new Properties();
  properties.put(Context.INITIAL_CONTEXT_FACTORY,
    "org.jnp.interfaces.NamingContextFactory");
  properties.put(Context.PROVIDER_URL, "localhost:1099");

  try {
    // Get an initial context
    InitialContext jndiContext = new InitialContext(properties);
    System.out.println("Got context");
```

continues

Listing 28.6 **Continued**

```
    // Get a reference to the Bean
    Object ref  = jndiContext.lookup("Adder");
    System.out.println("Got reference");

    // Get a reference from this to the Bean's Home interface
    AdderHome home = (AdderHome)
      PortableRemoteObject.narrow (ref, AdderHome.class);

    // Create an Adder object from the Home interface
    Adder adder = home.create();
    out.println ("2 + 5 = " + adder.add(2, 5));
  }
  catch(Exception e) {
    System.out.println(e.toString());
  }
%>
```

Summary

This chapter introduced you to the EJB technology, the benefits of using EJBs, the architecture, and the six distinct roles in an EJB application development and deployment life cycle. You also have learned how to write and deploy your own EJB application, review the javax.ejb package, and write two client applications. For the uninitiated, this chapter also provided a brief introduction to JNDI, which is used by the client to access an enterprise bean.

29 The Session Bean

THIS CHAPTER PRESENTS THE FIRST TYPE OF enterprise bean, called the session bean, by first explaining what a session bean is and then discussing two types of session beans: stateful and stateless. After a discussion of the API, you develop the Tassie project, a simple EJB (Enterprise JavaBeans) application that demonstrates the use of session beans and shows how to write a client application that uses the bean.

What Is a Session Bean?

A session bean is an enterprise bean that implements business logic for its clients. For example, a session bean can perform calculations (as you saw in the example in Chapter 28, "Enterprise JavaBeans"), process orders, encrypt and decrypt data, connect to a database, search data in a database, and so on.

In an EJB application in which the client is a web application, the business logic can reside in the web application itself—either in servlets or JSP pages. Using session beans as components that encapsulate the business logic makes the components reusable by other types of clients and enables them to enjoy benefits offered by the Enterprise JavaBean container, as discussed in Chapter 28.

Session beans are so called because they live as long as the client's session using them. A session bean is created when a client requires its service. When the client finishes with the bean and disconnects, the session bean may be destroyed by the EJB container.

Because object creation is an expensive operation, a session bean may not really be destroyed in the EJB container after the bean services a client. Instead, the container may place the bean in a pool to be quickly made available to another client that requests it later. This is not a concern of the client application developer, however; the EJB container manages the life cycle of a session bean.

Warning

Similar to other enterprise beans, a session bean's method is not instantiated or called directly by the client. A client communicates with the session bean through the session's bean home and remote interfaces.

Session beans are not persisted into a permanent storage, such as a disk or a database. When the server crashes, session beans disappear with all other data in temporary storage.

Stateful and Stateless Session Beans

You will work with two types of session beans: stateful and stateless. An instance of a stateful session bean is associated with a single client. The EJB container always uses the same stateful session bean instance to service a given client. The stateful session bean retains data related to the client that is retrieved from the database or information entered by the client. An instance of a stateful session bean is said to hold the *conversational state* of the client. A client session ends when the client specifies that it no longer needs the stateful session bean or after a certain period of time lapses since the last method invocation by the client. A stateful session bean is analogous to the javax.servlet.http.HttpSession object in a servlet/JSP application.

In contrast, a stateless session object is not client specific. This type of bean does not hold a conversational state of the client. The EJB container may delegate a method invocation by a client to any stateless session bean available in the pool.

Passivation and Activation of Stateful Session Beans

As previously mentioned, the EJB container maintains a pool of stateless and stateful session beans. This is because object creation is expensive and the pool makes a session bean reusable.

Although the EJB container can easily place a stateless session bean in a pool and take it back when the bean is needed, pooling a stateful session bean is not that simple. This is so because a stateful session bean retains the client-specific data.

Suppose that a stateful session bean is servicing a client, and it takes a while for the client to come back. If the EJB container does not have many clients at that time, the stateful session bean can wait until the client comes back. On a busy day, however, the EJB container may have more clients than the number of stateful session beans. The stateful session bean sitting idle waiting for its client to come back may have to be called to service another client. But, what about the conversational state of the previous client it is holding? You can't just discard the conversational state because the client may come back. At the same time, sitting idle waiting is a waste of resources in the EJB container.

The EJB container solves this problem by introducing two processes called *passivation* and *activation*. In passivation, the conversational state of a stateful session bean sitting idle waiting for its client to come back is transferred to secondary storage, such as hard disk space.

Activation is the reverse of passivation. The activation process loads into a stateful session bean the conversational state of a previous client coming back to continue its session. Note that the EJB container does not have to use the same instance of the stateful session bean that serviced the client previously. As long as the conversational state of the client can be loaded intact, any bean instance can take the job. The previous stateful session bean instance is probably busy servicing another client, anyway.

A Stateful Session Bean's Session

The EJB container assigns a unique identifier for each stateful session bean object at the creation of the bean. Unlike a session in a servlet/JSP application, however, session identifiers in an EJB application are not exposed to the client. The client has no way to obtain a session identifier. A client can determine whether two session bean object references refer to the same instance by using the isIdentical method of the javax.ejb.EJBObject interface. The signature of this method is as follows:

```
public boolean isIdentical(javax.ejb.EJBObject object)
  throws java.rmi.RemoteException
```

Writing a Session Bean

In Chapter 28, you learned how to write a stateless session bean, deploy it, and call it from two client applications. Earlier, you might not have understood the technicalities going on in that application; now, however, you will learn more about the process.

To review briefly, you need to write at least three classes for a session bean to function:

- The home interface
- The remote interface
- The session bean class

An instance of the home interface is called a *home object,* and an instance of the remote interface is known as a *remote object.*

The reason you need a home interface and a remote interface for *each* session bean is that the client does not create the bean directly, nor does a client invoke a session bean's method directly.

A home object is required for the client to create an instance of the session bean. When an EJB client application creates an instance of a session bean by invoking one of the home object's create methods, it refers to the procedure in which the EJB container allocates an instance of the requested session bean for the client. Whether the EJB container really creates a new instance of the session bean or simply takes one from the pool is not the client application's problem.

A remote object is returned when an EJB client application invokes the create method of the home object. The remote object is needed because it is the remote representation of the session bean. Remember that the client application does not have direct access to the session bean. Once you get the remote object, you can call any method exposed by the session bean. Therefore, a remote interface must clone all the methods in the session bean that are supposed to be available to an EJB client.

The client view of a session bean deployed in an EJB container is depicted in Figure 29.1.

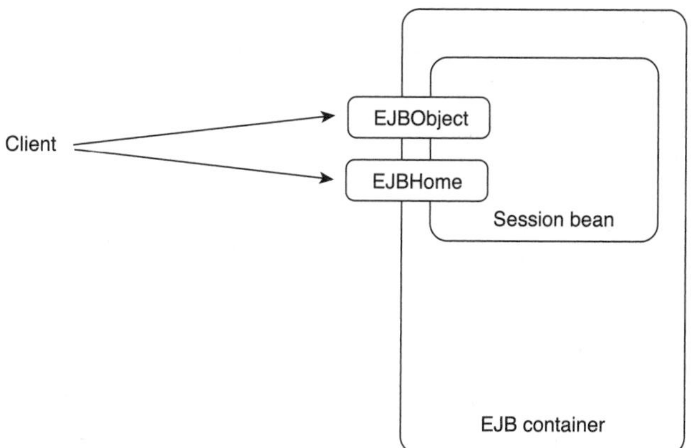

Figure 29.1 Client view of a session bean.

The javax.ejb.SessionBean Interface

A session bean must extend the javax.ejb.SessionBean interface. This interface extends the javax.ejb.EnterpriseBean interface and provides four methods that are invoked by the EJB container. The four methods are as follows:

- **ejbActivate.** The EJB container invokes this method when the session bean instance is retrieved from the pool to service a client whose conversational state has been stored in secondary storage in the previous passivation process. You should write code in this method that re-acquires resources that have been released in the previous passivation. The signature of this method is as follows:

```
public void ejbActivate() throws javax.ejb.EJBException,
➥java.rmi.RemoteException;
```

- **ejbPassivate.** The EJB container invokes this method when the session bean instance is about to be passivated. You should provide implementation code that releases resources such as a database connection. This method has the following signature:

```
public void ejbPassivate() throws javax.ejb.EJBException,
➥java.rmi.RemoteException;
```

- **ejbRemove.** This method is invoked when a client calls a remove method or when the EJB container decides to ends the session object after it times out. The signature of this method is as follows:

```
public void ejbRemove() throws javax.ejb.EJBException,
➥java.rmi.RemoteException;
```

- **setSessionContext.** The EJB container invokes this method after the instance has been created, passing a javax.ejb.SessionContext object. If you need to use the SessionContext object at a later stage, you should assign it to the bean's class-level object variable. The signature of this method is as follows:

```
public void setSessionContext(SessionContext context) throws
➥javax.ejb.EJBException, java.rmi.RemoteException;
```

An Example of a Session Bean

A session bean looks like the code in Listing 29.1. Because it implements the javax.ejb.SessionBean interface, you need to provide implementation for all the methods in that interface, plus the methods that implement the business logic.

Listing 29.1 **A Session Bean Called MySessionBean**

```
import java.rmi.RemoteException;
import javax.ejb.SessionBean;
import javax.ejb.SessionContext;

public class MySessionBean implements SessionBean {

  public void ejbCreate() {
  }

  public void ejbRemove() {
  }

  public void ejbActivate() {
  }

  public void ejbPassivate() {
  }

  public void setSessionContext(SessionContext sc) {
  }

  // implementation methods here
}
```

The javax.ejb.SessionContext Interface and the javax.ejb.EJBContext Interface

As mentioned in the previous section, the EJB container passes a javax.ejb.SessionContext object to the setSessionContext method of the javax.ejb.SessionBean interface. The SessionContext interface extends the javax.ejb.EJBContext interface that provides useful methods to obtain information about the caller client application, the bean home object, the environment, and so on.

The definition of the javax.ejb.EJBContext interface is as follows:

```
public interface javax.ejb.EJBObject
  extends java.rmi.Remote {

  public javax.ejb.EJBHome getEJBHome()
    throws java.rmi.RemoteException;

  public java.lang.Object getPrimaryKey()
    throws java.rmi.RemoteException;

  public void remove()
    throws java.rmi.RemoteException, javax.ejb.RemoveException;

  public javax.ejb.Handle getHandle()
    throws java.rmi.RemoteException;

  public boolean isIdentical(javax.ejb.EJBObject object)
    throws java.rmi.RemoteException;

}
```

The definition of the javax.ejb.SessionContext interface is as follows:

```
public interface javax.ejb.SessionContext
  extends javax.ejb.EJBContext {

  public javax.ejb.EJBLocalObject getEJBLocalObject()
    throws IllegalStateException;

  public javax.ejb.EJBObject getEJBObject()
    throws IllegalStateException;

}
```

Using a Stateful Session Bean from a Servlet/JSP Page

A non-web client of a stateful session bean should not have a problem retaining the reference to the bean for the life of the session. A web client is a different case because HTTP is a stateless protocol, making it difficult to maintain the session. One convenient way of retaining a session in an EJB application from a servlet/JSP page is to use the javax.servlet.http.HttpSession object. You can retain the session to a stateful session bean by following these two rules:

1. The first time you obtain a reference to a stateful session bean, store it as an attribute in the javax.servlet.http.HttpSession object, as you see here:

```
HttpSession session = request.getSession(true);
session.setAttribute("cart", cartBean);
```

   This code obtains an HttpSession object from the request object and then adds the cartBean object to the session object's attribute.

> **Note**
> If you are writing the code in a JSP page, you don't need the first line of the code shown in the previous example because session is an implicit object in JSP.

2. The next time you need to access the session bean object, you obtain the object reference from the HttpSession object, as follows:

```
HttpSession session = request.getSession(true);
Cart cartBean = (Cart) session.getAttribute("cart");
```

The sample application shows you how to use these code fragments.

Deployment Descriptor

Each EJB application must have a deployment descriptor, which is an XML document named ejb-jar.xml. The descriptor's root element is <ejb-jar>, and it contains a node called <enterprise-beans>. Each session bean is then registered under this element and called a <session> element. Therefore, one <session> element is created for each session bean.

> **Note**
> The DTD for EJB 2.0 applications' deployment descriptor can be found at `http://java.sun.com/dtd/ejb-jar_2_0.dtd`.

The <session> element has the following syntax:

```
<! ELEMENT session (description?, display-name?, small-icon?, large-icon?,
➥ejb-name, home?, remote?, local-home?, local?, ejb-class, session-type,
➥transaction-type, env-entry*, ejb-ref*, ejb-local-ref*, security-role-
➥ref*, security-identity?, resource-ref*, resource-env-ref*)>
```

In this element, ? indicates an optional subelement and * indicates that the preceding subelement can be repeated zero or more times. The subelements are explained in the following list:

- **description.** The description of the bean.
- **display-name.** The short name to be displayed by tools used to edit this deployment descriptor.

- **small-icon.** The name of a small (16 × 16) icon image in .gif or .jpg format. The filename is a relative path within the ejb-jar file.
- **large-icon.** The name of a large (32 × 32) icon image in .gif or .jpg format. The filename is a relative path within the ejb-jar file.
- **ejb-name.** The name identifying the session bean. The name must be unique throughout the ejb-jar file.
- **home.** The fully qualified name for the home interface.
- **remote.** The fully qualified name for the remote interface.
- **local-home.** The fully qualified name for the local home interface.
- **local.** The fully qualified name for the bean's local interface.
- **ejb-class.** The fully qualified name for the bean class.
- **session-type.** The type of the session bean. Its value is either Stateless or Stateful.
- **transaction-type.** The type of transaction. Its value is either Bean or Container.
- **env-entry.** The name of the bean's environment entry.
- **ejb-ref.** The declaration of a reference to a bean's home.
- **ejb-local-ref.** The declaration of a reference to a bean's local home.
- **security-role-ref.** The declaration of a security role reference in the bean's code.
- **security-identity.** Whether the caller's security identity is to be used for the execution of the methods of the bean or a specific run-as identity is to be used.
- **resource-ref.** The declaration of the bean's reference to an external resource.
- **resource-env-ref.** The declaration of a bean's reference to an administered object associated with a resource in the bean's environment.

An example of a deployment descriptor follows:

```
<?xml version="1.0" encoding="UTF-8"?>

<ejb-jar>
  <description>The Search Bean for Tassie Online Bookstore</description>
  <display-name>Search Bean</display-name>
  <enterprise-beans>
    <session>
      <ejb-name>Search</ejb-name>
      <home>com.brainysoftware.tassie.ejb.SearchHome</home>
      <remote>com.brainysoftware.tassie.ejb.Search</remote>
      <ejb-class>com.brainysoftware.tassie.ejb.SearchBean</ejb-class>
```

```
      <session-type>Stateless</session-type>
      <transaction-type>Bean</transaction-type>
    </session>
  </enterprise-beans>
</ejb-jar>
```

The Tassie Online Bookstore Example

The following application is called the Tassie Online Bookstore. The example is an incomplete e-commerce application whose sole purpose is to illustrate the use of session beans in an EJB application accessed by a web application. Because this is an application that serves only as a learning tool, the code used here does not provide the efficiency or whole functionality of a true e-commerce application.

This sample application uses four servlets as its user interface. The four servlets represent the four pages of user interface: the Search page, the Book Details page, the Add To Cart page, and the Check Shopping Cart page. The diagram explaining the relationships among those pages is given in Figure 29.2.

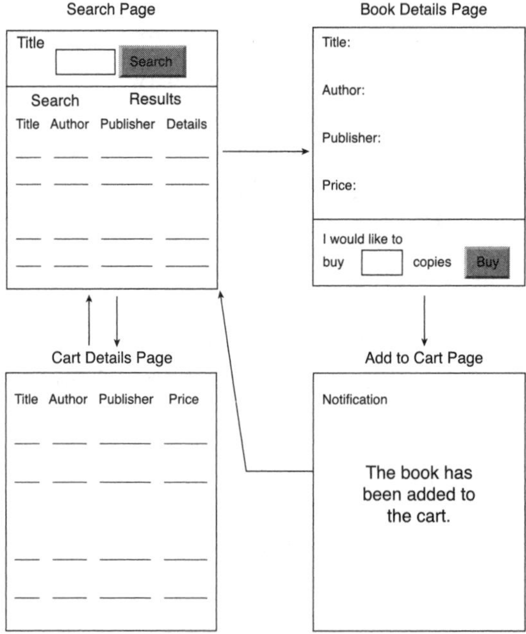

Figure 29.2 The four pages of the Tassie Online Bookstore application.

The project's functionality is listed here:

- A web user can search for a book based on its title by entering a keyword in the Search page. All books whose title contains the keyword are then listed in an HTML table. Each book's, title, author, and publisher is displayed. In addition, there is a fourth item called *details* that displays more details of a selected book.

  The Search page is shown in Figures 29.3 and 29.4. Figure 29.3 shows the initial appearance of the page—what the users see when they request the page.

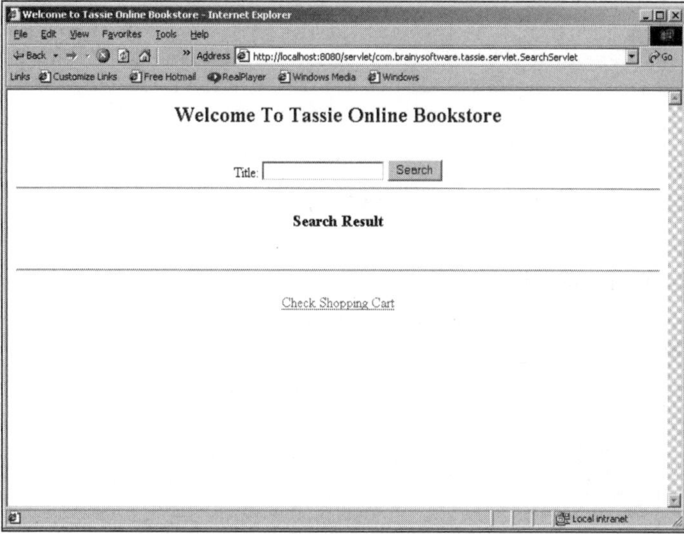

Figure 29.3 The initial Search page.

Figure 29.4 shows the same Search page after a user performs a search by entering the word "computer" as the search string. Note that each title includes a link to the Book Details page.

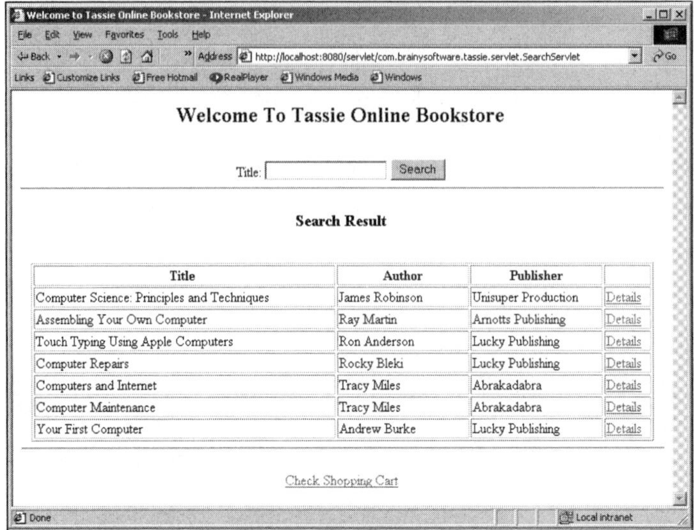

Figure 29.4 The Search page with search results.

- The user can click the details hyperlink of a book to go to the Book Details page. In this page, the user can enter the number of copies of the title to be purchased. Afterwards, the user clicks the Buy button. The Book Details page is shown in Figure 29.5.

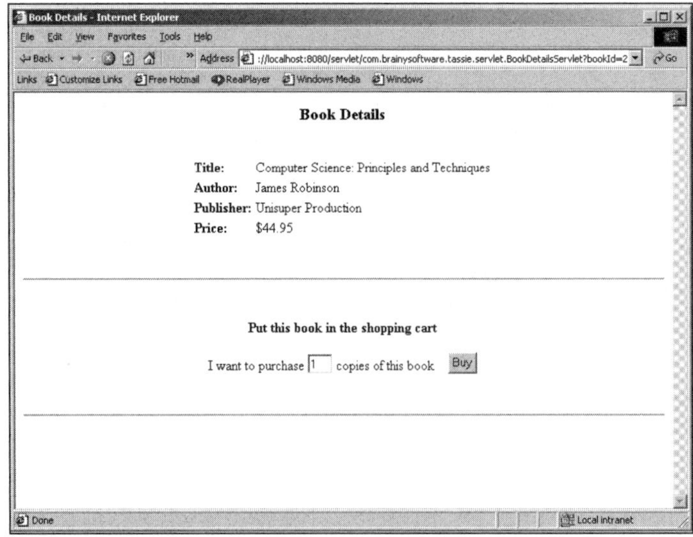

Figure 29.5 The Book Details page.

- After the user clicks the Buy button in the Book Details page, the application notifies the user that the book has been placed in the shopping cart. This is shown in Figure 29.6.

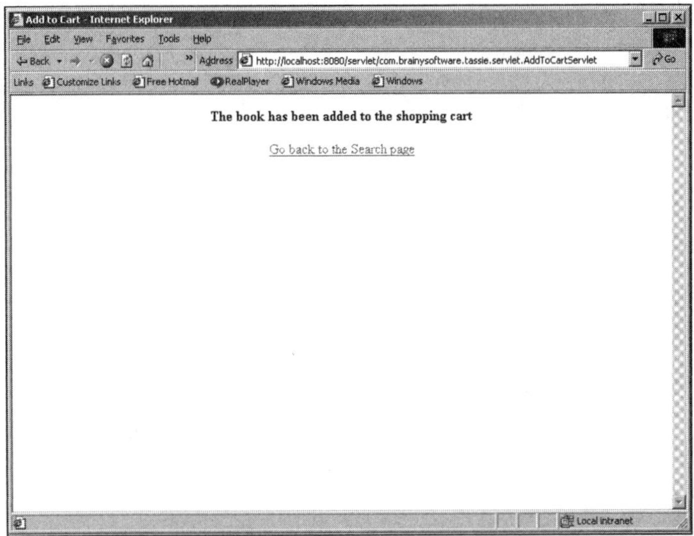

Figure 29.6 The Add To Cart page.

- Clicking the link in the Add To Cart page brings the user to the Search page again where the user can continue searching for other books. The other option is to check the shopping cart by clicking the link at the bottom of the Search page. This brings the user to the Shopping Cart Details page, whose screenshot is given in Figure 29.7.

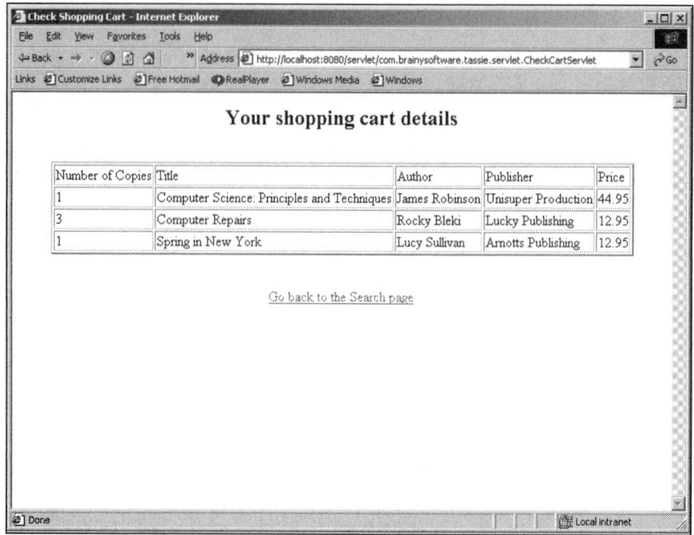

Figure 29.7 The ShoppingCartDetails page.

The Database

The database for this example is very simple, consisting of only a table called Books. This table has the following fields:

- **Id.** A unique identifier for each book.
- **Title.** The title of the book.
- **Author.** The book's author.
- **Publisher.** The company that published the book.
- **Price.** The retail price for each book.

The database structure has been made as easy as possible. Notice that there is no field to list the ISBN numbers of the books. Additionally, you do not need to enter a book category. In a real-world e-commerce application, you would want to normalize the tables, which is something you don't do here.

The sample database is given in a Microsoft Access format and can be found in the CD that accompanies this book. You access the database through the JDBC-ODBC bridge. You must first create a Data Source Name (DSN) for this database named TassieDB.

The Enterprise Beans

The sample application consists of two stateless session beans and one stateful session bean, each of which is discussed in the following sections.

The Search Stateless Session Bean

The first session bean, called Search, finds all the books whose titles match the search keyword. The home interface for this session bean is given in Listing 29.2 and its remote interface is given in Listing 29.3.

Listing 29.2 **The Home Interface of the Search Session Bean**

```
package com.brainysoftware.tassie.ejb;

import java.rmi.RemoteException;
import javax.ejb.CreateException;
import javax.ejb.EJBHome;

public interface SearchHome extends EJBHome {
  Search create() throws RemoteException, CreateException;
}
```

Listing 29.3 **The Remote Interface of the Search Session Bean**

```
package com.brainysoftware.tassie.ejb;

import javax.ejb.EJBObject;
import java.rmi.RemoteException;
import java.util.ArrayList;

public interface Search extends EJBObject {
  public ArrayList search(String keyword) throws RemoteException;
}
```

From the remote interface, you know that there is only one method exposed to the client: search. This method accepts a String representing the search keyword and returns an ArrayList containing all the books that match the search string. Each book in the ArrayList is represented in an array of String.

The bean class is given in Listing 29.4.

Listing 29.4 **The Search Bean Class**

```
package com.brainysoftware.tassie.ejb;

import java.rmi.RemoteException;
import javax.ejb.SessionBean;
import javax.ejb.SessionContext;
import java.sql.*;
import java.util.ArrayList;

public class SearchBean implements SessionBean {


  private Connection getConnection() {
    Connection connection = null;
    try {
      Class.forName("sun.jdbc.odbc.JdbcOdbcDriver");
      connection = DriverManager.getConnection("jdbc:odbc:TassieDB");
    }
    catch (Exception e) {
    }
    return connection;
  }

  public ArrayList search(String keyword) {
    ArrayList retval = new ArrayList(50);
    try {
      Statement statement = getConnection().createStatement();
      String sql = "SELECT Id, Title, Author, Publisher" +
        " FROM Books" +
        " WHERE Title LIKE '%" + keyword + "%'";

      ResultSet rs = statement.executeQuery(sql);
      while (rs.next()) {
        String[] row = new String[4];
        row[0] = rs.getString("Id");
        row[1] = rs.getString("Title");
        row[2] = rs.getString("Author");
        row[3] = rs.getString("Publisher");
        retval.add(row);
      }
      rs.close();
      statement.close();
    }
    catch (Exception e) {
    }
    return retval;
  }

  public void ejbCreate() {
  }
```

```
  public void ejbRemove() {
  }

  public void ejbActivate() {
  }

  public void ejbPassivate() {
  }

  public void setSessionContext(SessionContext sc) {
  }
}
```

The BookDetails Stateless Session Bean

The second session bean is also stateless and is called BookDetails. Its function is to return the details of a book given a book id. This bean is called from a servlet as well as from another bean, representing a remote client and a local client. In this example, you see the difference in the code for a remote client and a local client.

The home interface for the bean is given in Listing 29.5 and its remote interface is given in Listing 29.6.

Listing 29.5 **The Home Interface of the BookDetails Bean**

```
package com.brainysoftware.tassie.ejb;

import java.rmi.RemoteException;
import javax.ejb.CreateException;
import javax.ejb.EJBHome;

public interface BookDetailsHome extends EJBHome {
  BookDetails create() throws RemoteException, CreateException;
}
```

Listing 29.6 **The Remote Interface of the BookDetails Bean**

```
package com.brainysoftware.tassie.ejb;

import javax.ejb.EJBObject;
import java.rmi.RemoteException;
import java.util.ArrayList;

public interface BookDetails extends EJBObject {
  public String[] getBookDetails(String bookId) throws RemoteException;
}
```

Again, only one method is exposed to its client: the getBookDetails method. This method accepts a String representing the book identifier and returns an array of String containing the book id, the title, the author, the publisher, and the price. Listing 29.7 lists the BookDetails bean class implementation.

Listing 29.7 **The BookDetailsBean Class**

```
package com.brainysoftware.tassie.ejb;

import java.rmi.RemoteException;
import javax.ejb.SessionBean;
import javax.ejb.SessionContext;
import java.sql.*;
import java.util.ArrayList;

public class BookDetailsBean implements SessionBean {


  private Connection getConnection() {
    Connection connection = null;
    try {
      Class.forName("sun.jdbc.odbc.JdbcOdbcDriver");
      connection = DriverManager.getConnection("jdbc:odbc:TassieDB");
    }
    catch (Exception e) {
    }
    return connection;
  }

  public String[] getBookDetails(String bookId) {
    String[] row = null;
    try {
      Statement statement = getConnection().createStatement();
      String sql = "SELECT Id, Title, Author, Publisher, Price" +
        " FROM Books" +
        " WHERE Id=" + bookId;

      ResultSet rs = statement.executeQuery(sql);
      if (rs.next()) {
        row = new String[5];
        row[0] = rs.getString("Id");
        row[1] = rs.getString("Title");
        row[2] = rs.getString("Author");
        row[3] = rs.getString("Publisher");
        row[4] = rs.getString("Price");
```

```
      }
      rs.close();
      statement.close();
    }
    catch (Exception e) {
    }
    return row;
  }

  public void ejbCreate() {
  }

  public void ejbRemove() {
  }

  public void ejbActivate() {
  }

  public void ejbPassivate() {
  }

  public void setSessionContext(SessionContext sc) {
  }
}
```

The Cart Stateful Session Bean

The Cart session bean is a stateful one that enables you to maintain a shopping cart for each user. You can add an item to the Cart bean and you can retrieve the bean to check what's inside.

The home interface and remote interface for this bean are given in Listings 29.8 and Listing 29.9, respectively.

Listing 29.8 **The Home Interface for the Cart Bean**

```
package com.brainysoftware.tassie.ejb;

import java.rmi.RemoteException;
import javax.ejb.CreateException;
import javax.ejb.EJBHome;

public interface CartHome extends EJBHome {
  Cart create() throws RemoteException, CreateException;
}
```

Listing 29.9 **The Remote Interface for the Cart Bean**

```
package com.brainysoftware.tassie.ejb;

import javax.ejb.EJBObject;
import java.rmi.RemoteException;
import java.util.ArrayList;

public interface Cart extends EJBObject {
  public ArrayList getCart() throws RemoteException;
  public void addToCart(String bookId, String quantity) throws
RemoteException;
}
```

The addToCart method accepts two arguments: bookId selected by the user and the number of copies the user would like to purchase. The addToCart method returns no value.

The second method, getCart, returns the shopping cart in the form of an ArrayList. Note that you don't pass a user identifier or other tokens to the method to obtain the current shopping cart because the conversational state for each user is retained by this stateful bean.

The bean class is given in Listing 29.10.

Listing 29.10 **The Bean Class for the Cart Bean**

```
package com.brainysoftware.tassie.ejb;

import java.rmi.RemoteException;
import javax.ejb.SessionBean;
import javax.ejb.SessionContext;
import java.sql.*;
import java.util.*;
import javax.naming.*;

public class CartBean implements SessionBean {
private ArrayList cart = new ArrayList();
public void addToCart(String bookId, String quantity) {
    String[] row = new String[6];
    row[0] = bookId;
    row[1] = quantity;

    try {
      InitialContext jndiContext = new InitialContext();
      Object ref = jndiContext.lookup("BookDetails");
      System.out.println("Got ref to BookDetails");
      // don't need to use javax.rmi.PortableRemoteObject
      // because this is a local client
      BookDetailsHome home = (BookDetailsHome) ref;
      System.out.println("Got home to BookDetails");
```

```
        BookDetails bookDetails = home.create();
        System.out.println("Got BookDetails");
        String[] details = bookDetails.getBookDetails(bookId);
        row[2] = details[1];
        row[3] = details[2];
        row[4] = details[3];
        row[5] = details[4];
      }
      catch (Exception e) {
        System.out.println(e.toString());
      }
      cart.add(row);

    }

    public ArrayList getCart() {
      return cart;
    }

    public void ejbCreate() {
    }

    public void ejbRemove() {
    }

    public void ejbActivate() {
    }

    public void ejbPassivate() {
    }

    public void setSessionContext(SessionContext sc) {
    }
  }
```

The EJB Application Deployment Descriptor

The three beans described earlier need a deployment descriptor as given in Listing 29.11.

Listing 29.11 **The Deployment Descriptor for the EJB Application**

```
<?xml version="1.0" encoding="UTF-8"?>

<ejb-jar>
  <description>The Search Bean for Tassie Online Bookstore</description>
  <display-name>Search Bean</display-name>
  <enterprise-beans>
```

continues

Listing 29.11 **Continued**

```
    <session>
      <ejb-name>Search</ejb-name>
      <home>com.brainysoftware.tassie.ejb.SearchHome</home>
      <remote>com.brainysoftware.tassie.ejb.Search</remote>
      <ejb-class>com.brainysoftware.tassie.ejb.SearchBean</ejb-class>
      <session-type>Stateless</session-type>
      <transaction-type>Bean</transaction-type>
    </session>

    <session>
      <ejb-name>BookDetails</ejb-name>
      <home>com.brainysoftware.tassie.ejb.BookDetailsHome</home>
      <remote>com.brainysoftware.tassie.ejb.BookDetails</remote>
      <ejb-class>com.brainysoftware.tassie.ejb.BookDetailsBean</ejb-class>
      <session-type>Stateless</session-type>
      <transaction-type>Bean</transaction-type>
    </session>

    <session>
      <ejb-name>Cart</ejb-name>
      <home>com.brainysoftware.tassie.ejb.CartHome</home>
      <remote>com.brainysoftware.tassie.ejb.Cart</remote>
      <ejb-class>com.brainysoftware.tassie.ejb.CartBean</ejb-class>
      <session-type>Stateful</session-type>
      <transaction-type>Bean</transaction-type>
    </session>
  </enterprise-beans>
</ejb-jar>
```

Note that the client web application has a separate deployment application.

Creating the Deployment File

After you have compiled all the three session beans and placed the deployment descriptor in the META-INF directory, you are ready to generate a deployment file for the EJB application.

Assuming that the jar.exe program has been available from any directory in the computer, type the following to create a jar file called tassie.jar.

```
jar cfv tassie.jar com/brainysoftware/tassie/ejb/* META-INF/ejb-jar.xml
```

Deploying in JBoss

Deployment in JBoss cannot be easier. JBoss supports what is called *hot deploy*. This means that to deploy an EJB application, you just need to copy the jar file into its deploy directory. You don't even need to restart JBoss if it's already running.

The Servlets

Together, the four servlets—SearchServlet, BookDetailsServlet, AddToCartServlet, and CheckCartServlet—represent a client application that uses the session beans in the Tassie Online Bookstore application. Each of the servlets is explained in this section.

The SearchServlet Servlet

The SearchServlet displays the Search page. The Search page is the main page as well as the first page the user will see. The page can be partitioned into three parts:

- The search form
- The search result table
- The Check Shopping Cart link

The code for the SearchServlet servlet is given in Listing 29.12.

Listing 29.12 **The SearchServlet Servlet**

```
package com.brainysoftware.tassie.servlet;

import javax.servlet.*;
import javax.servlet.http.*;
import java.io.*;
import java.util.*;
import javax.naming.*;
import javax.rmi.PortableRemoteObject;
import com.brainysoftware.tassie.ejb.Search;
import com.brainysoftware.tassie.ejb.SearchHome;

public class SearchServlet extends HttpServlet {

  private String keyword;

  /**Process the HTTP Get request*/
  public void doGet(HttpServletRequest request, HttpServletResponse response)
    throws ServletException, IOException {
    displayPage(request, response);
  }

  /**Process the HTTP Post request*/
  public void doPost(HttpServletRequest request, HttpServletResponse
response)
    throws ServletException, IOException {
    keyword = request.getParameter("keyword");
    displayPage(request, response);
  }
```

continues

Listing 29.12 **Continued**

```
  private void displayPage(HttpServletRequest request,
➥HttpServletResponse response)
    throws ServletException, IOException {
    /* In addition to the header and footer,
       There are 4 parts in this page:
       1. The Welcome Title
       2. Search form
       3. The search result table
       4. The link to the Check Shopping Cart page
    */
    response.setContentType("text/html");
    PrintWriter out = response.getWriter();

    // header
    out.println("<HTML>");
    out.println("<HEAD>");
    out.println("<TITLE>Welcome to Tassie Online Bookstore</TITLE>");
    out.println("</HEAD>");
    out.println("<BODY>");
    out.println("<CENTER>");

    // Welcome Title
    out.println("<H2>Welcome To Tassie Online Bookstore</H2>");

    // Search form
    out.println("<BR>");
    out.println("<FORM METHOD=POST>");
    out.println("Title: <INPUT TYPE=TEXT NAME=keyword>");
    out.println("<INPUT TYPE=SUBMIT VALUE=Search");
    out.println("</FORM>");
    out.println("<HR>");

    // Search result
    out.println("<BR>");
    out.println("<H3>Search Result</H3>");
    out.println("<BR>");
    displaySearchResult(out);
    out.println("<HR>");

    // Link to the Check Shopping Cart link
    out.println("<BR>");
    out.println("<A HREF=com.brainysoftware.tassie.servlet.CheckCartServlet>
➥Check Shopping Cart</A>");

    // footer
    out.println("</CENTER>");
    out.println("</BODY>");
    out.println("</HTML>");
```

```
    // Displaying the Search form

  }

  /**Clean up resources*/
  private void displaySearchResult(PrintWriter out) {
    if (keyword!=null && !keyword.trim().equals("")) {
      // keyword okay; display the result here.

      Properties properties = new Properties();
      properties.put(Context.INITIAL_CONTEXT_FACTORY,
➥"org.jnp.interfaces.NamingContextFactory");
      properties.put(Context.PROVIDER_URL, "localhost:1099");
      try {
        // Get a naming context
        InitialContext jndiContext = new InitialContext(properties);

        // Get a reference to the Bean
        Object ref  = jndiContext.lookup("Search");

        // Get a reference from this to the Bean's Home interface
        SearchHome home = (SearchHome)
          PortableRemoteObject.narrow (ref, SearchHome.class);

        // Create an Adder object from the Home interface
        Search searchBean = home.create();
        ArrayList arrayList = searchBean.search(keyword);
        int rowCount = arrayList.size();
        out.println("<TABLE BORDER=1>");
        out.println("<TR>");
        out.println("<TH WIDTH=350>Title</TH>");
        out.println("<TH WIDTH=150>Author</TH>");
        out.println("<TH WIDTH=150>Publisher</TH>");
        out.println("<TH WIDTH=50> </TH>");
        out.println("</TR>");

        for (int i=0; i<rowCount; i++) {
          String[] s = (String[]) arrayList.get(i);
          out.println("<TR>");
          out.println("<TD>" + s[1] + "</TD>");
          out.println("<TD>" + s[2] + "</TD>");
          out.println("<TD>" + s[3] + "</TD>");
          out.println("<TD>
➥HREF=com.brainysoftware.tassie.servlet.BookDetailsServlet?bookId=" +
            s[0] + ">Details</A></TD>");
          out.println("</TR>");
        }
        out.println("</TABLE>");

      }
```

continues

Listing 29.12 **Continued**

```
      catch(Exception e) {
        System.out.println(e.toString());
      }

    }
  }
}
```

The BookDetailsServlet Servlet

The BookDetailsServlet servlet is the second servlet in the client application. Its code is given in Listing 29.13.

Listing 29.13 **The BookDetailsServlet Servlet**

```
package com.brainysoftware.tassie.servlet;

import javax.servlet.*;
import javax.servlet.http.*;
import java.io.*;
import java.util.*;
import javax.naming.*;
import javax.rmi.PortableRemoteObject;
import com.brainysoftware.tassie.ejb.BookDetails;
import com.brainysoftware.tassie.ejb.BookDetailsHome;

public class BookDetailsServlet extends HttpServlet {

  /**Process the HTTP Get request*/
  public void doGet(HttpServletRequest request,
➥HttpServletResponse response) throws ServletException, IOException {
    String bookId = request.getParameter("bookId");
    response.setContentType("text/html");
    PrintWriter out = response.getWriter();
    out.println("<HTML>");
    out.println("<HEAD>");
    out.println("<TITLE>Book Details</TITLE>");
    out.println("</HEAD>");
    out.println("<BODY>");
    out.println("<CENTER>");

    Properties properties = new Properties();
    properties.put(Context.
➥INITIAL_CONTEXT_FACTORY, "org.jnp.interfaces.NamingContextFactory");
    properties.put(Context.PROVIDER_URL, "localhost:1099");
    try {
      // Get a naming context
      InitialContext jndiContext = new InitialContext(properties);
```

```
      // Get a reference to the Bean
      Object ref  = jndiContext.lookup("BookDetails");

      // Get a reference from this to the Bean's Home interface
      BookDetailsHome home = (BookDetailsHome)
        PortableRemoteObject.narrow (ref, BookDetailsHome.class);

      // Create an Adder object from the Home interface
      BookDetails bookDetailsBean = home.create();
      String[] row = bookDetailsBean.getBookDetails(bookId);
      out.println("<H3>Book Details</H3>");
      out.println("<BR>");
      out.println("<TABLE BORDER=0>");
      out.println("<TR>");
      out.println("<TD><B>Title:</B></TD>");
      out.println("<TD>" + row[1] + "</TD>");
      out.println("</TR>");
      out.println("<TR>");
      out.println("<TD><B>Author:</B></TD>");
      out.println("<TD>" + row[2] + "</TD>");
      out.println("</TR>");
      out.println("<TR>");
      out.println("<TD><B>Publisher:</B></TD>");
      out.println("<TD>" + row[3] + "</TD>");
      out.println("</TR>");
      out.println("<TR>");
      out.println("<TD><B>Price:</B></TD>");
      out.println("<TD>$" + row[4] + "</TD>");
      out.println("</TR>");
      out.println("</TABLE>");
      out.println("<BR>");
      out.println("<BR>");
      out.println("<HR>");
      out.println("<BR>");
      out.println("<BR>");
      out.println("<B>Put this book in the shopping cart</B>");
      out.println("<BR>");
      out.println("<FORM
➥METHOD=POST ACTION=com.brainysoftware.tassie.servlet.AddToCartServlet>");
      out.println("<INPUT TYPE=HIDDEN Name=bookId VALUE=" + row[0] + ">");
      out.println("I want to purchase ");
      out.println("<INPUT TYPE=TEXT SIZE=1
➥Name=quantity VALUE=1> copies of this book");
      out.println("  ");
      out.println("<INPUT TYPE=SUBMIT VALUE=Buy>");
      out.println("</FORM>");
      out.println("<BR>");
      out.println("<HR>");

    }
```

continues

Listing 29.13 **Continued**

```
    catch(Exception e) {
      System.out.println(e.toString());
    }
    out.println("</CENTER>");
    out.println("</BODY>");
    out.println("</HTML>");
  }
}
```

The AddToCartServlet Servlet

The AddToCartServlet servlet is invoked after the user clicks the Buy button in the BookDetails servlet. Its code is given in Listing 29.14.

Listing 29.14 **The AddToCartServlet Servlet**

```
package com.brainysoftware.tassie.servlet;

import javax.servlet.*;
import javax.servlet.http.*;
import java.io.*;
import java.util.*;
import javax.naming.*;
import javax.rmi.PortableRemoteObject;
import com.brainysoftware.tassie.ejb.Cart;
import com.brainysoftware.tassie.ejb.CartHome;


public class AddToCartServlet extends HttpServlet {
  /**Process the HTTP Post request*/
  public void doPost(HttpServletRequest request,
➥HttpServletResponse response) throws ServletException, IOException {
    response.setContentType("text/html");
    PrintWriter out = response.getWriter();

    // header
    out.println("<HTML>");
    out.println("<HEAD>");
    out.println("<TITLE>Add to Cart</TITLE>");
    out.println("</HEAD>");
    out.println("<BODY>");
    out.println("<CENTER>");
    String bookId = request.getParameter("bookId");
    String quantity = request.getParameter("quantity");
```

```
    if (bookId!=null && quantity!=null &&
      !bookId.trim().equals("") && !quantity.trim().equals("")) {
      try {
        HttpSession session = request.getSession(true);
        Cart cartBean = (Cart) session.getAttribute("cart");
        if (cartBean==null) { // new session
          Properties properties = new Properties();
          properties.put(Context.INITIAL_CONTEXT_FACTORY,
➥"org.jnp.interfaces.NamingContextFactory");
          properties.put(Context.PROVIDER_URL, "localhost:1099");
          // Get a naming context
          InitialContext jndiContext = new InitialContext(properties);

          // Get a reference to the bean
          Object ref  = jndiContext.lookup("Cart");

          // Get a reference from this to the bean's home interface
          CartHome home = (CartHome)
          PortableRemoteObject.narrow (ref, CartHome.class);

          // Create an Adder object from the home interface
          cartBean = home.create();
        }
        cartBean.addToCart(bookId, quantity);
        session.setAttribute("cart", cartBean);
        out.println("<B>The book has been added to the shopping cart</B>");

      }
      catch(Exception e) {
        out.println(e.toString());
      }
    }
    out.println("<BR>");
    out.println("<BR>");
    out.println("<A HREF=com.brainysoftware.tassie.servlet.SearchServlet>" +
      "Go back to the Search page</A>");
    out.println("</CENTER>");
    out.println("</BODY>");
    out.println("</HTML>");
  }
}
```

The CheckCartServlet Servlet

When the user clicks the Check Shopping Cart link in the Search page, the CheckCartServlet servlet is invoked. This servlet grabs the cart for the user and displays its contents. The code for the CheckCartServlet servlet is given in Listing 29.15.

Listing 29.15 **The CheckCartServlet Servlet**

```
package com.brainysoftware.tassie.servlet;

import javax.servlet.*;
import javax.servlet.http.*;
import java.io.*;
import java.util.*;
//import javax.naming.*;
//import javax.rmi.PortableRemoteObject;
import com.brainysoftware.tassie.ejb.Cart;
//import com.brainysoftware.tassie.ejb.CartHome;

public class CheckCartServlet extends HttpServlet {
  /**Process the HTTP Get request*/
  public void doGet(HttpServletRequest request,
➥HttpServletResponse response) throws ServletException, IOException {
    response.setContentType("text/html");
    PrintWriter out = response.getWriter();

    // header
    out.println("<HTML>");
    out.println("<HEAD>");
    out.println("<TITLE>Check Shopping Cart</TITLE>");
    out.println("</HEAD>");
    out.println("<BODY>");
    out.println("<CENTER>");
    out.println("<H2>Your shopping cart details</H2>");
    out.println("<BR>");
    out.println("<TABLE BORDER=2>");
    out.println("<TR>");
    out.println("<TH>Number of Copies</TH>");
    out.println("<TH>Title</TH>");
    out.println("<TH>Author</TH>");
    out.println("<TH>Publisher</TH>");
    out.println("<TH>Price</TH>");
    out.println("</TR>");
    HttpSession session = request.getSession(false);

    if (session!=null) {
      try {
        Cart cartBean = (Cart) session.getAttribute("cart");
        ArrayList arrayList = cartBean.getCart();
        int count = arrayList.size();
        for (int i=0; i<count; i++) {
          out.println("</TR>");
          String[] row = (String[]) arrayList.get(i);
          out.println("<TD>" + row[1] + "</TD>");
          out.println("<TD>" + row[2] + "</TD>");
          out.println("<TD>" + row[3] + "</TD>");
          out.println("<TD>" + row[4] + "</TD>");
```

```
            out.println("<TD>" + row[5] + "</TD>");
            out.println("</TR>");
          }
        }
        catch(Exception e) {
          System.out.println(e.toString());
        }
      }
      out.println("</TABLE>");
      out.println("<BR>");
      out.println("<BR>");
      out.println("<A HREF=com.brainysoftware.tassie.servlet.SearchServlet>" +
        "Go back to the Search page</A>");
      out.println("</CENTER>");
      out.println("</BODY>");
      out.println("</HTML>");
    }
  }
```

Deploying the Client Application

To deploy the client application, you need to compile the four servlets above and create a deployment descriptor for it. Chapter 16, "Application Deployment," explains all that you need to do to deploy a web application.

Summary

This chapter introduced you to the session bean. There are two types of session beans: stateful and stateless. This chapter also presented how to write a session bean and a deployment descriptor for an EJB application.

An example describing an EJB application accessed from a web application was given in the Tassie Online Bookstore example. This application showed how you can access stateless and stateful session beans and maintain sessions using the javax.servlet.http.HttpSession objects.

30

Entity Beans

CHAPTER 28, "ENTERPRISE JAVABEANS," DISCUSSED THE ENTERPRISE JAVABEANS (EJB) in general and Chapter 29, "The Session Bean, explained the session bean and presented a fragment of an e-commerce web application that uses both stateful and stateless session beans. You should now be familiar with how EJB works and know how to write, package, and deploy session beans.

Session beans, however, are only a third of the story. There are two more types of EJB: entity beans and message-driven beans. This chapter explains the entity bean and shows you how to write entity beans for your applications. Chapter 33 explains how to work with message-driven beans.

What Is an Entity Bean?

An entity bean is a data component that persists the data permanently to a secondary storage such as a database. Like another Java class, an entity bean has fields and methods. It uses fields to store data and methods to perform operations on the fields.

In an EJB application, an entity bean is a view to a record of a database table. Instead of manipulating data in a database directly as you would in non-EJB applications, you manipulate an entity bean that represents a piece of data.

The EJB container then takes care of the synchronization and other tasks in maintaining the data. An entity bean lives as long as the data it represents; therefore, an entity bean could last for weeks, months, or even years. For example, if an entity bean represents a bank account, chances are that it lives as long as the bank account resides in the bank's back-end database. Because a bank account normally is opened and retained for years by the bank, the entity bean representing it also lives for years.

Why do you need an object, such as an entity bean, to store data in the first place? Why don't you access the database directly and manipulate the data in it? Or, why not just write session beans to access the data like you did in Chapter 29? The answer to these questions is twofold. First, managing data as objects is easier. Second, the EJB container provides services that make it much easier to deal with data represented by entity beans.

Having learned about session beans in the previous chapter, you might be wondering how entity beans and session beans are different. Why is a different type of enterprise bean needed? Put simply, a session bean models a business *process*, and an entity bean represents business *data*. The EJB container knows how to synchronize the data in an entity bean with the underlying data in the database that the entity bean represents. In addition, an entity bean survives server crash.

Two types of entity beans exist: entity beans with bean-managed persistence (BMP) and entity beans with container-managed persistence (CMP). Both are discussed later in this chapter, after a general overview of an entity bean.

Just like a session bean, an entity bean must be accompanied by several files you write in addition to the entity bean. Those files are as follows:

- The remote interface
- The home interface
- The primary key class
- The entity bean
- The deployment descriptor

The following sections discuss each of these files. The deployment descriptor is explained in the sections that discuss each type of the entity bean: "Writing a BMP Entity Bean," and "Writing a CMP Entity Bean."

The Remote Interface

The remote interface of an entity bean enables a client to access the instance of an entity bean. An entity bean's remote interface must extend the javax.ejb.EJBObject interface. In the remote interface, the entity bean developer defines methods that can be called by the bean's client. For example, the remote interface of an entity bean that represents a product might have two methods called getPrice and getCategory, as in the following snippet:

```
public interface Product extends javax.ejb.EJBObject {
  double getPrice(int productId) throws java.rmi.RemoteException;
  int getCategory(int productId) throws java.rmi.RemoteException;
}
```

The getPrice method returns the price of the product and the getCategory method returns the identifier of the category the product falls into. The client can use the remote interface to do the following:

- Obtain the home interface for the entity object
- Remove the entity object
- Obtain the entity object's primary key
- Obtain the entity object's handle

Note
An entity object refers to an instance of an entity bean.

The Home Interface

An entity bean's client obtains the home object—that is, an instance of the home interface—from an entity bean's remote object. The client uses the home object to do the following:

- Create an entity object
- Remove an entity object
- Find an entity object
- Obtain the javax.ejb.EJBMetaData interface for an entity bean

The home interface enables the client to do these tasks by providing create, finder, and remove methods. These methods are discussed in the following sections.

Create Methods

A home interface can have zero or more create methods. The home interface can have more than one create method to allow various ways of creating an entity object. For example, following is the create method of the home interface of an entity bean called Product. It allows the user to create a Product entity bean by passing the product identifier, the product name, the description, and the price:

```
public interface ProductHome extends javax.ejb.EJBHome {

  public Product create(int productId, String productName,
    String description, double price)
    throws java.rmi.RemoteException, javax.ejb.CreateException;
  .
  .
  .
}
```

> **Note**
> A create method can throw a java.rmi.RemoteException and a javax.ejb.CreateException.

Finder Methods

Because an entity bean represents a piece of data, one of the most frequently used operations is finding an entity bean. You find an entity bean by using one of the finder methods. In contrast, a session bean does not have a finder method.

A home interface must define a findByPrimaryKey method to enable the client to find an entity object by passing a primary key. In addition, a home interface can have other finder methods. For example, a Product entity bean's home interface might also define the findByName or findByPrice methods to allow the user to find an entity object by passing its name or its price. Although a findByPrimaryKey method always returns either zero or one entity bean that meets the criteria, other finder methods may return multiple values.

For finder methods that may return multiple values, the return value types for these methods are either java.util.Collection or java.util.Enumeration.

As an example, the following home interface for an entity bean called Product defines three finder methods:

```
public interface ProductHome extends javax.ejb.EJBHome {

  public Product findByPrimaryKey(String productId)
    throws java.rmi.RemoteException, javax.ejb.FinderException;

  public Enumeration findByProductName(String productName)
    throws java.rmi.RemoteException, javax.ejb.FinderException;

  public Collection findAll()
```

```
      throws java.rmi.RemoteException, javax.ejb.FinderException;

    .
    .
    .
  }
```

Remove Methods

A remove method is used to remove an entity object. The home interface of an entity bean is derived from the javax.ejb.EJBHome interface, which defines two remove methods. The signatures of the two remove methods are given as follows:

```
void remove(javax.ejb.Handle handle)
  throws java.rmi.RemoteException, javax.ejb.RemoveException;
void remove(Object primaryKey)
  throws java.rmi.RemoteException, javax.ejb.RemoveException;
```

The Primary Key Class

Similar to a database table, which can have a primary key for uniquely identifying each row on the table, an entity bean also has a primary key. The type of the primary key class of an entity bean must be one of those types in RMI-IIOP.

The Entity Bean

An entity bean class must implement the javax.ejb.EntityBean interface. This interface defines methods that determine the life cycle of the bean as well as other callback methods that are called by the EJB container. This section looks at this interface in detail and then elaborates some important functionality of an entity bean. At the end of the section, you also look at the javax.ejb.EntityContext interface.

The javax.ejb.EntityBean Interface

This interface extends the javax.ejb.EnterpriseBean interface and provides callback methods that are invoked by the EJB container. The methods of the EntityBean interface are as follows:

- **ejbActivate.** The EJB container invokes this method when the entity bean instance is retrieved from the pool to become associated with a specific entity object. The signature of this method is as follows:

```
public void ejbActivate() throws
➥javax.ejb.EJBException, java.rmi.RemoteException;
```

- **ejbPassivate.** The EJB container invokes this method when the entity bean instance's association with its entity object is about to be broken. This method has the following signature:

```
public void ejbPassivate() throws
➥javax.ejb.EJBException, java.rmi.RemoteException;
```

- **ejbLoad.** This method is invoked by the EJB container to synchronize the entity bean's state by loading its state from the underlying data. The ejbLoad method has the following signature:

```
public void ejbLoad() throws javax.ejb.EJBException,
java.rmi.RemoteException;
```

- **ejbStore.** This method is invoked by the EJB container to synchronize an entity bean's state with the underlying data. This method is used to store the state back to the underlying data. The signature of this method is as follows:

```
public void ejbStore() throws javax.ejb.EJBException,
➥java.rmi.RemoteException;
```

- **ejbRemove.** This method is invoked by the EJB container before the EJB container removes the entity object. This method is invoked when a client calls a remove method on the entity bean's home interface or remote interface. The signature of this method is as follows:

```
public void ejbRemove() throws javax.ejb.EJBException,
➥java.rmi.RemoteException;
```

- **setEntityContext.** The EJB container invokes this method after the instance has been created, setting the associated entity context. The signature of this method is as follows:

```
public void setEntityContext(EntityContext context) throws
➥javax.ejb.EJBException, java.rmi.RemoteException;
```

- **unsetEntityContext.** The EJB container invokes this method before removing the instance of the entity bean. This method unsets the associated entity context. The signature of this method is as follows:

```
public void unsetEntityContext() throws javax.ejb.EJBException,
➥java.rmi.RemoteException;
```

Note

The EJB container maintains the synchronization between data in an entity bean's fields and the underlying database using two methods in the javax.ejb.EntityBean interface: ejbLoad and ejbStore.

Thanks to the synchronization during the ejbLoad and ejbStore method invocations, if the data with which an entity bean is associated is changed directly in its underlying database, the entity bean's state will also reflect the changes. The data in the underlying database might be changed by another system that manipulates the data directly.

Activation and Passivation

Like a stateful session bean, an entity bean also can undergo the activation and passivation processes. These processes are more involved in an entity bean than they are in a stateful session bean, however. With a stateful session bean, activation includes the acquisition of the previous state and resources for a given client, and passivation requires the bean to release resources it is holding and save the conversation state of a client to a secondary storage.

In an entity bean, passivation includes releasing resources as well as pushing back the data it is holding to the underlying database prior to the passivation process. To save the entity bean's state, the EJB container calls the bean's ejbStore method *before* passivation. Activation in an entity bean, on the other hand, includes acquisition of resources as well as grabbing data from the underlying database. To load data from the underlying database, the EJB container invokes the ejbLoad method of the entity bean *after* activation.

Create Methods

Every create method in the home interface must have a corresponding create method in the entity bean class. This corresponding method has the same arguments as the create method in the home interface; however, the names of the create methods in the entity bean are prefixed with ejb. This means that in an entity bean class, you have zero or more ejbCreate methods, and in the home interface, you have the same number of corresponding create methods.

The ejbCreate methods, however, return a value of the primary key class type. Additionally, an ejbCreate method must be public and must not be declared final or static.

For example, an entity bean named Product has the following ejbCreate method:

```
public class ProductBean implements javax.ejb.EntityBean {

  public String productId;
  public String productName;
  public String description;
  public double price;

  public String ejbCreate(int productId, String productName,
    String description, double price)
    throws java.rmi.RemoteException, javax.ejb.CreateException {
    this.productId = Integer.toString( productId);
    this.productName = productName;
    this.description = description;
    this.price = price;
    return Integer.toString(productId);
  }
  .
  .
  .
}
```

Finder Methods

The entity bean class must have a corresponding finder method of all finder methods in the home interface. Just like the create methods, a finder method in the entity bean class is prefixed with ejb and has the same list of arguments as the corresponding finder method in the home interface.

For example, an entity bean class might contain two finder methods: ejbFindByPrimaryKey and ejbFindByName, as you see here:

```
public ProductPK ejbFindByPrimaryKey(ProductPK primaryKey)
  throws RemoteException, FinderException {
  .
  .
  .
}

public Enumeration ejbFindByName(String name)
  throws RemoteException, FinderException {
  .
  .
  .
}
```

In the example, the return type of the ejbFindByPrimaryKey method is ProductPK, which is the primary key class. The primary key class is explained later in this chapter.

Remove Methods

An entity bean class also can define a remove method. Like the create and finder methods, the remove method name is prefixed with ejb. For example, the following is the remove method of a Product entity bean:

```
public void ejbRemove()
  throws java.rmi.RemoteException, javax.ejb.RemoveException {
    .
    .
    .
}
```

> **Note**
>
> An entity bean is a view to a piece of data in a database. Therefore, invoking the ejbCreate and the ejbRemove methods has different effects on an entity bean than they would on a session bean. When the EJB container calls the ejbCreate method of an entity bean, it creates some data in the underlying database that corresponds to the entity bean instance in memory. When the EJB container invokes the ejbRemove method of an entity bean, the EJB container also deletes the data associated with the entity bean from the underlying database.

Other Methods

The entity bean provides implementations for methods declared in the remote interface. The methods in the entity bean class must have the same return type and argument list as the corresponding method in the remote interface. These methods must be public methods and cannot be static or final. For example, consider the following remote interface:

```
public interface Product extends javax.ejb.EJBObject {
  double getPrice(int productId) throws java.rmi.RemoteException;
  int getCategory(int productId) throws java.rmi.RemoteException;
}
```

This entity bean has the following methods:

```
public class ProductBean implements javax.ejb.EntityBean {
  double getPrice(int productId)
    throws java.rmi.RemoteException {
      .
      .
      .
  }

  int getCategory(int productId)
    throws java.rmi.RemoteException {
      .
      .
      .
```

```
        }
        .
        .
        .
    }
```

The javax.ejb.EntityContext Interface

The EntityContext interface is derived from the javax.ejb.EJBContext interface. It defines two methods: getEJBObject and getPrimaryKey. The getEJBObject method returns a reference to the enterprise object associated with this instance of the entity bean.

The signature of this method is as follows:

```
javax.ejb.EJBObject getEJBObject()
  throws IllegalStateException
```

The getPrimaryKey method returns the primary key of the entity object. This method has the following signature:

```
Object getPrimaryKey()
  throws IllegalStateException
```

Two Types of Entity Beans

By now, you should be aware that the whole point of having an entity bean is that it persists data. Depending on how its data is persisted, an entity bean can be one of these two types:

- An entity bean with bean-managed persistence (BMP)
- An entity bean with container-managed persistence (CMP)

An entity bean with BMP takes care of the process of persisting data itself. The bean programmer can use SQL commands to achieve this.

Data persistence in an entity bean with CMP, however, is taken care of by the EJB container. You give instructions to the EJB container on how to do this in the deployment descriptor of the EJB application. For the programmer, entity beans with CMP require fewer lines of code to program. Entity beans with CMP also are easier to program because there is no more error-prone data access code.

The difference between these two types of entity beans will become clear after the following two sections.

Writing a BMP Entity Bean

A BMP entity bean manages its own persistence. At the very basic level, the bean developer must provide in the entity bean class a method to connect to the underlying database. Alternatively, if a similar method has been made available in another EJB, the entity bean programmer must write a method that returns a java.sql.Connection object obtained from the other bean.

The database connection task is somewhat eased in an entity bean, however. The EJB container loads the database JDBC driver for you. This means that you don't need to use the Class.forName() method to load the driver yourself. You simply tell the EJB container how it can find the JDBC driver. The way in which you do this is application server-specific. In this section, you learn to do this in JBoss.

The following example demonstrates how you can write a BMP entity bean called Product that has the underlying data in a database's Products table. To try this example, you need to have a database and the JDBC driver for that database. This example is developed using a mysql database and uses a freely downloadable JDBC driver.

Here is the list of things you need to do before you can try the source code:

1. Create a Products table containing four columns (ProductId, ProductName, Description, and Price) with the following SQL statement in your database:

```
CREATE TABLE Products
( ProductId int,
  ProductName VarChar(50),
  Description VarChar(100),
  Price double
)
```

2. Get a JDBC driver for your database. If you are using mysql, you can find a JDBC driver for mysql in the software/mmmysql directory of the CD. The file is called mm.mysql-2.0.8-bin.jar.

   Alternatively, if you want a more recent version, you can visit `http://sourceforge.net/project/showfiles.php?group_id=15923&release_id=63046`.

   At the time of this writing, the latest version is 2.0.8 and it is packaged in a file named mm.mysql-2.0.8-you-must-unjar-me.jar.

   That's right—the .jar file must first be unjarred using the following command, assuming that you have jar.exe in your path:

```
jar -xf mm.mysql-2.0.8-you-must-unjar-me.jar
```

This command produces a subdirectory called mm.mysql-2.0.8 under which there is another .jar file named mm.mysql-2.0.8-bin.jar.

3. Configure JDBC Driver in JBoss by following these two steps:

   a. Copy the JDBC driver (the mm.mysql-2.0.8-bin.jar file, if you are using mysql with the included driver in the CD) into the JBOSSDist/lib/ext directory.

   b. Open the jboss.jcml file under JBossDist/conf/default directory and find the following lines:

```
<mbean code="org.jboss.jdbc.JdbcProvider"
  name="DefaultDomain:service=JdbcProvider">
  <attribute name="Drivers">
    org.hsqldb.jdbcDriver
  </attribute>
</mbean>
```

   Next add "org.gjt.mm.mysql.Driver" (or your other driver if you are not using mysql with the mm JDBC driver) as follows:

```
<mbean code="org.jboss.jdbc.JdbcProvider"
  name="DefaultDomain:service=JdbcProvider">
  <attribute name="Drivers">
    org.hsqldb.jdbcDriver,org.gjt.mm.mysql.Driver
  </attribute>
</mbean>
```

4. Prepare the directory structure in your project. The classes you are going to write here are part of the com.brainysoftware.ejb package; therefore, you need to have a directory named com under your working directory, a directory named brainysoftware under the com directory, and a directory called ejb under the brainysoftware directory. You also need to have a directory called META-INF under your working directory for your deployment descriptor. The directory structure is shown in Figure 30.1.

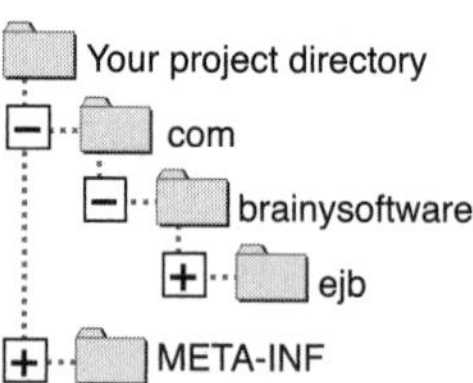

Figure 30.1 The directory structure for your application.

Note
All the .class files must be placed under the com/brainysoftware/ejb directory.

The Remote Interface

The first class to explore is the remote interface for the Product entity bean with BMP. The class file is called Product.java and is given in Listing 30.1.

Listing 30.1 **The Remote Interface (Product.java)**

```
package com.brainysoftware.ejb;

import javax.ejb.EJBObject;
import java.rmi.RemoteException;

/* this is the remote interface for Product */
public interface Product extends EJBObject {
  public int getProductId() throws RemoteException;
  public double getPrice() throws RemoteException;
  public String getProductName() throws RemoteException;
  public String getDescription() throws RemoteException;
}
```

The remote interface defines four business methods: getProductId, getPrice, getProductName, and getDescription.

The Home Interface

The home interface is given in Listing 30.2. The home interface defines a create method that accepts four arguments and two finder methods. The findByPrimaryKey method accepts a primary key object (see the following code) and returns a remote object. The findByName method accepts a product name and returns an Enumeration containing all the products whose product names match the argument.

Listing 30.2 **The Home Interface (ProductHome.java)**

```
package com.brainysoftware.ejb;

import java.rmi.RemoteException;
import javax.ejb.FinderException;
import javax.ejb.CreateException;
import javax.ejb.EJBHome;
import java.util.Enumeration;
```

continues

Listing 30.2 **Continued**

```
public interface ProductHome extends EJBHome {

  public Product create(int productId, String productName,
    String description, double price)
    throws RemoteException, CreateException;

  public Product findByPrimaryKey(ProductPK key)
    throws RemoteException, FinderException;

  public Enumeration findByName(String name)
    throws RemoteException, FinderException;
}
```

The Primary Key Class

An entity bean has a primary key. The primary key class for the Product entity bean is com.brainysoftware.ejb.ProductPK. The code for the primary key class is given in Listing 30.3. Note that it has a public field called productId.

Listing 30.3 **ProductPK.java**

```
package com.brainysoftware.ejb;

import java.io.Serializable;

public class ProductPK implements Serializable {


  public String productId;

  public ProductPK(String productId) {
    this.productId = productId;
  }
  public ProductPK() {
  }

 public boolean equals(Object o) {
    return true;
  }

  public int hashCode() {
    return 0;
  }
}
```

Note

Note that the equals and hashCode methods do not have real implementations here.

The Entity Bean

The entity bean class is the most important class that contains implementations for callback methods and business methods. It is given in Listing 30.4.

Listing 30.4 **Entity Bean Class (ProductBean.java)**

```
package com.brainysoftware.ejb;

import java.sql.*;
import java.util.Properties;
import java.util.Enumeration;
import java.util.Vector;
import java.rmi.RemoteException;
import javax.ejb.EntityBean;
import javax.ejb.EntityContext;
import javax.ejb.CreateException;
import javax.ejb.FinderException;
import javax.ejb.ObjectNotFoundException;
import javax.naming.InitialContext;
import javax.naming.Context;
import javax.naming.NamingException;

public class ProductBean implements EntityBean {

  EntityContext context;
  int productId;
  String productName;
  String description;
  double price;

  public int getProductId() {
    System.out.println("getProductId");
    return productId;
  }

  public String getProductName() {
    System.out.println("getProductName");
    return productName;
  }

  public String getDescription() {
    System.out.println("getDescription");
    return description;
  }
```

continues

Listing 30.4 **Continued**

```
public double getPrice() {
  System.out.println("getPrice");
  return price;
}

public ProductPK ejbCreate(int productId, String productName,
  String description, double price)
  throws RemoteException, CreateException {
  System.out.println("ejbCreate");
  this.productId = productId;
  this.productName = productName;
  this.description = description;
  this.price = price;
  Connection con = null;
  PreparedStatement ps = null;
  try {
    String sql = "INSERT INTO Products" +
      " (ProductId, ProductName, Description, Price)" +
      " VALUES" +
      " (?, ?, ?, ?)";
    con = getConnection();
    ps = con.prepareStatement(sql);
    ps.setInt(1, productId);
    ps.setString(2, productName);
    ps.setString(3, description);
    ps.setDouble(4, price);
    ps.executeUpdate();
  }
  catch (SQLException e) {
    System.out.println(e.toString());
  }
  finally {
    try {
      if (ps!=null)
        ps.close();
      if (con!=null)
        con.close();
    }
    catch (SQLException e) {
    }
  }
  return new ProductPK(Integer.toString(productId));
}


public void ejbPostCreate(int productId, String productName,
  String description, double price)
  throws RemoteException, CreateException {
  System.out.println("ejbPostCreate");
```

```
}

public ProductPK ejbFindByPrimaryKey(ProductPK primaryKey)
  throws RemoteException, FinderException {
  System.out.println("ejbFindByPrimaryKey");
  Connection con = null;
  PreparedStatement ps = null;
  ResultSet rs = null;
  try {
    String sql = "SELECT ProductName" +
      " FROM Products" +
      " WHERE ProductId=?";
    int productId = Integer.parseInt(primaryKey.productId);
    con = getConnection();
    ps = con.prepareStatement(sql);
    ps.setInt(1, productId);
    rs = ps.executeQuery();
    if (rs.next()) {
      rs.close();
      ps.close();
      con.close();
      return primaryKey;
    }
  }
  catch (SQLException e) {
    System.out.println(e.toString());
  }
  finally {
    try {
      if (rs!=null)
        rs.close();
      if (ps!=null)
        ps.close();
      if (con!=null)
        con.close();
    }
    catch (SQLException e) {
    }
  }
  throw new ObjectNotFoundException();

}

public Enumeration ejbFindByName(String name)
  throws RemoteException, FinderException {
  System.out.println("ejbFindByName");
  Vector products = new Vector();
  Connection con = null;
  PreparedStatement ps = null;
  ResultSet rs = null;
```

continues

Listing 30.4 **Continued**

```
    try {
      String sql = "SELECT ProductId " +
        " FROM Products" +
        " WHERE ProductName=?";
      con = getConnection();
      ps = con.prepareStatement(sql);
      ps.setString(1, name);
      rs = ps.executeQuery();
      while (rs.next()) {
        int productId = rs.getInt(1);
        products.addElement(new ProductPK(Integer.toString(productId)));
      }
    }
    catch (SQLException e) {
      System.out.println(e.toString());
    }
    finally {
      try {
        if (rs!=null)
          rs.close();
        if (ps!=null)
          ps.close();
        if (con!=null)
          con.close();
      }
      catch (SQLException e) {
      }
    }
    return products.elements();
  }

  public void ejbRemove() throws RemoteException {
    System.out.println("ejbRemove");
    Connection con = null;
    PreparedStatement ps = null;
    try {
      String sql = "DELETE FROM Products" +
        " WHERE ProductId=?";
      ProductPK key = (ProductPK) context.getPrimaryKey();
      int productId = Integer.parseInt(key.productId);
      con = getConnection();
      ps = con.prepareStatement(sql);
      ps.setInt(1, productId);
      ps.executeUpdate();
    }
    catch (SQLException e) {
      System.out.println(e.toString());
    }
    finally {
```

```
        try {
          if (ps!=null)
            ps.close();
          if (con!=null)
            con.close();
        }
        catch (SQLException e) {
        }
      }
    }

    public void ejbActivate() {
      System.out.println("ejbActivate");
    }

    public void ejbPassivate() {
      System.out.println("ejbPassivate");
    }

    public void ejbLoad() {
      System.out.println("ejbLoad");
      Connection con = null;
      PreparedStatement ps = null;
      ResultSet rs = null;
      try {
        String sql = "SELECT ProductName, Description, Price" +
          " FROM Products" +
          " WHERE ProductId=?";
        con = getConnection();
        ps = con.prepareStatement(sql);
        ps.setInt(1, this.productId);
        rs = ps.executeQuery();
        if (rs.next()) {
          this.productName = rs.getString(1);
          this.description = rs.getString(2);
          this.price = rs.getDouble(3);
        }
      }
      catch (SQLException e) {
        System.out.println(e.toString());
      }
      finally {
        try {
          if (rs!=null)
            rs.close();
          if (ps!=null)
            ps.close();
          if (con!=null)
            con.close();
        }
        catch (SQLException e) {
```

continues

Listing 30.4 **Continued**

```
      }
    }
  }
  public void ejbStore() {
    System.out.println("ejbStore");
    Connection con = null;
    PreparedStatement ps = null;
    try {
      String sql = "UPDATE Products" +
        " SET ProductName=?, Description=?, Price=?" +
        " WHERE ProductId=?";
      ProductPK key = (ProductPK) context.getPrimaryKey();
      int productId = Integer.parseInt(key.productId);
      con = getConnection();
      ps = con.prepareStatement(sql);
      ps.setString(1, this.productName);
      ps.setString(2, this.description);
      ps.setDouble(3, this.price);
      ps.setInt(4, productId);
      ps.executeUpdate();
    }
    catch (SQLException e) {
      System.out.println(e.toString());
    }
    finally {
      try {
        if (ps!=null)
          ps.close();
        if (con!=null)
          con.close();
      }
      catch (SQLException e) {
      }
    }


  }
  public void setEntityContext(EntityContext context) {
    System.out.println("setEntityContext");
    this.context = context;

  }

  public void unsetEntityContext() {
    System.out.println("unsetEntityContext");
    context = null;
  }

  public Connection getConnection() {
```

```
      String dbUrl = null;
      String userName = null;
      String password = null;
      Context initialContext;
      Context environment;
      Connection connection = null;

      try {
        initialContext = new InitialContext();
        environment = (Context) initialContext.lookup("java:comp/env");
        dbUrl = (String) environment.lookup("dbUrl");
        userName = (String) environment.lookup("dbUserName");
        password = (String) environment.lookup("dbPassword");
      }
      catch (NamingException e) {
        System.out.println(e.toString());
      }
      try {
        connection = DriverManager.getConnection(dbUrl, userName, password);
      }
      catch (SQLException e) {
        System.out.println(e.toString());
      }
      return connection;
    }
  }
```

First and foremost, the entity bean class has four fields to store the data: productId, productName, description, and price. Additionally, it has the implementations of the four business methods declared in the remote interface: getProductId, getProductName, getDescription, and getPrice, as you see here:

```
public int getProductId() {
  System.out.println("getProductId");
  return productId;
}

public String getProductName() {
  System.out.println("getProductName");
  return productName;
}

public String getDescription() {
  System.out.println("getDescription");
  return description;
}
public double getPrice() {
  System.out.println("getPrice");
  return price;
}
```

An important method that will be used by several other methods in the entity bean class is the getConnection method, which returns a valid java.sql.Connection object.

As usual, to connect to a database, you need to pass the database URL, the user name, and the password to the getConnection method of the java.sql.DriverManager class. You can hard-code this information in the entity bean class; however, this is not a wise tack. The user credentials change quite often, and hardcoding this information in the entity bean means that you have to recompile and redeploy the bean every time it changes. A better way is to store this information in the deployment descriptor and obtain the values using JNDI, as given in the getConnection method in the entity bean. You see how to store this information in the deployment descriptor later. For now, just assume that the deployment descriptor contains the database URL, the user name, and the password to connect to the database.

In the getConnection method in the entity bean, you first define three String object references and two javax.naming.Context object references called initialContext and environment:

```
String dbUrl = null;
String userName = null;
String password = null;
Context initialContext;
Context environment;
```

The initialContext variable is used to reference the InitialContext object obtained from the following constructor:

```
initialContext = new InitialContext();
```

You then can look up the bean's environment by passing the string "java:comp/env" to the lookup method of the initial context, as follows:

```
environment = (Context) initialContext.lookup("java:comp/env");
```

Then, you can use the environment object to look up the database URL, the user name, and the password:

```
dbUrl = (String) environment.lookup("dbUrl");
userName = (String) environment.lookup("dbUserName");
password = (String) environment.lookup("dbPassword");
```

After you have those values, you can pass them to the getConnection method of the java.sql.DriverManager object to obtain a Connection object, as you see here:

```
connection = DriverManager.getConnection(dbUrl, userName, password);
```

For each create method, the entity bean implements one ejbCreate method and one ejbPostCreate method.

The ejbCreate method accepts the same set of arguments as defined in the create method in the home interface and returns the primary key object of the bean. Its signature is given as follows:

```
public ProductPK ejbCreate(int productId, String productName,
  String description, double price)
  throws RemoteException, CreateException {
```

The ejbCreate method does two things. First, it populates the internal fields with the argument values passed to it:

```
  this.productId = productId;
  this.productName = productName;
  this.description = description;
  this.price = price;
```

Next, the method inserts a record into the underlying database. The code for inserting a new record is as follows. The Connection object is obtained by calling the getConnection method.

```
Connection con = null;
PreparedStatement ps = null;
try {
  String sql = "INSERT INTO Products" +
    " (ProductId, ProductName, Description, Price)" +
    " VALUES" +
    " (?, ?, ?, ?)";
  con = getConnection();
  ps = con.prepareStatement(sql);
  ps.setInt(1, productId);
  ps.setString(2, productName);
  ps.setString(3, description);
  ps.setDouble(4, price);
  ps.executeUpdate();
}
catch (SQLException e) {
  System.out.println(e.toString());
}
finally {
  try {
    if (ps!=null)
      ps.close();
    if (con!=null)
      con.close();
  }
  catch (SQLException e) {
  }
}
```

Finally, the method returns a new ProductPK object, as follows:

```
return new ProductPK(Integer.toString(productId));
```

The ejbPostCreate method does not return a value and does not do anything except print its name to the console:

```
public void ejbPostCreate(int productId, String productName,
  String description, double price)
  throws RemoteException, CreateException {
  System.out.println("ejbPostCreate");
}
```

The entity bean class has two finder methods: findByPrimaryKey and findByName. The findByPrimaryKey method accepts a primary key object and checks whether the database contains a record having that primary key. If a corresponding record is found, the same primary key is returned; otherwise, the findByPrimaryKey method throws a javax.ejb.ObjectNotFoundException.

The ejbFindByPrimaryKey method starts by composing the SQL statement used to select a record having the specified product identifier:

```
String sql = "SELECT ProductName" +
  " FROM Products" +
  " WHERE ProductId=?";
```

The product identifier is obtained from the primary key object, as you see here:

```
int productId = Integer.parseInt(primaryKey.productId);
```

Then the ejbFindByPrimaryKey method obtains a Connection object, creates a PreparedStatement object, and calls the PreparedStatement object's executeQuery method:

```
con = getConnection();
ps = con.prepareStatement(sql);
ps.setInt(1, productId);
rs = ps.executeQuery();
```

The executeQuery method returns a ResultSet object. The ResultSet object's next() method returns true if there is a next record; otherwise, it returns false. If the next() method returns true, the ejbFindByPrimaryKey method returns the primary key object, as follows:

```
if (rs.next()) {
  rs.close();
  ps.close();
  con.close();
  return primaryKey;
}
```

Otherwise, the method throws an ObjectNotFoundException:

```
throw new ObjectNotFoundException();
```

The other finder method is named ejbFindByName and returns an Enumeration object containing all matching products. A Vector object called products is first instantiated, with the following line:

```
Vector products = new Vector();
```

The ejbFindByName method then opens a connection to grab all products having the specified name:

```
try {
  String sql = "SELECT ProductId " +
    " FROM Products" +
    " WHERE ProductName=?";
  con = getConnection();
  ps = con.prepareStatement(sql);
  ps.setString(1, name);
  rs = ps.executeQuery();
```

The resulting ResultSet contains all the matching products. Using a while loop, the method then adds each record to the Vector.

```
  while (rs.next()) {
    int productId = rs.getInt(1);
    products.addElement(new ProductPK(Integer.toString(productId)));
  }
}
```

Then it returns the Enumeration of the Vector:

```
return products.elements();
```

The entity bean also provides an implementation of the ejbRemove method. When the ejbRemove method is invoked, it deletes the corresponding record from the database, as you see here:

```
PreparedStatement ps = null;
try {
  String sql = "DELETE FROM Products" +
    " WHERE ProductId=?";
  ProductPK key = (ProductPK) context.getPrimaryKey();
  int productId = Integer.parseInt(key.productId);
  con = getConnection();
  ps = con.prepareStatement(sql);
  ps.setInt(1, productId);
  ps.executeUpdate();
}
catch (SQLException e) {
  System.out.println(e.toString());
}
```

For synchronization between the data in the entity bean and the data in the underlying database, you also need to provide the implementations of the ejbStore and ejbLoad methods.

The ejbLoad method copies the data from the underlying database to the fields of the entity bean, as follows:

```
String sql = "SELECT ProductName, Description, Price" +
  " FROM Products" +
  " WHERE ProductId=?";
con = getConnection();
ps = con.prepareStatement(sql);
ps.setInt(1, this.productId);
rs = ps.executeQuery();
if (rs.next()) {
  this.productName = rs.getString(1);
  this.description = rs.getString(2);
  this.price = rs.getDouble(3);
}
```

The ejbStore method does the reverse. It copies the values of the internal fields to the underlying database:

```
String sql = "UPDATE Products" +
  " SET ProductName=?, Description=?, Price=?" +
  " WHERE ProductId=?";

ProductPK key = (ProductPK) context.getPrimaryKey();
int productId = Integer.parseInt(key.productId);
con = getConnection();
ps = con.prepareStatement(sql);
ps.setString(1, this.productName);
ps.setString(2, this.description);
ps.setDouble(3, this.price);
ps.setInt(4, productId);
ps.executeUpdate();
```

Deployment Descriptor

Every EJB application must be accompanied by a deployment descriptor that should be saved into the META-INF directory of the project, in a file named ejb-jar.xml. The deployment descriptor for the Product entity bean is given in Listing 30.5.

Listing 30.5 **The Deployment Descriptor (ejb-jar.xml)**

```
<?xml version="1.0" encoding="UTF-8"?>

<ejb-jar>
  <description>Your first EJB application </description>
  <display-name>Products Application</display-name>
```

```
    <enterprise-beans>
      <entity>
        <ejb-name>BMPProduct</ejb-name>
        <home>com.brainysoftware.ejb.ProductHome</home>
        <remote>com.brainysoftware.ejb.Product</remote>
        <ejb-class>com.brainysoftware.ejb.ProductBean</ejb-class>
        <persistence-type>Bean</persistence-type>
        <prim-key-class>com.brainysoftware.ejb.ProductPK</prim-key-class>
        <reentrant>false</reentrant>
        <env-entry>
          <env-entry-name>dbUrl</env-entry-name>
          <env-entry-type>java.lang.String</env-entry-type>
          <env-entry-value>jdbc:mysql://localhost/MyDB</env-entry-value>
        </env-entry>
        <env-entry>
          <env-entry-name>dbUserName</env-entry-name>
          <env-entry-type>java.lang.String</env-entry-type>
          <env-entry-value>yena</env-entry-value>
        </env-entry>
        <env-entry>
          <env-entry-name>dbPassword</env-entry-name>
          <env-entry-type>java.lang.String</env-entry-type>
          <env-entry-value>lang0128934</env-entry-value>
        </env-entry>
      </entity>
    </enterprise-beans>
  </ejb-jar>
```

Like the deployment descriptor accompanying the session beans in Chapters 28 and 29, you need to specify the fully qualified names for the remote interface, the home interface, and the entity bean. In addition, for an entity bean, you also need to tell the EJB container what type of persistence your entity bean is using. In this case, the <persistence-type> element has the value of "Bean".

There are also three <env-entry> elements, each specifying an environment variable. The three values are obtained by the getConenction method in the entity bean class to connect to the underlying database.

Packaging Your Entity Bean

Now you are ready to package your entity bean. Do the following:

1. Compile all the .java class and place the .class files in the com/brainysoftware/ejb/ directory under your project directory.
2. Change the directory to your project directory.
3. Type the following command:

```
jar cfv product.jar com/brainysoftware/ejb/Product*.* META-INF/ejb-jar.xml
```

This command will create a jar file called product.jar in the project directory. Copy this file into the deploy directory of JBoss. If JBoss is not running, start JBoss. If JBoss is already running, you don't need to do anything. JBoss's hot deploy feature will automatically try to deploy any package file saved into the deploy directory.

Client Application

Having a deployed entity bean, you now can write a client application to test your bean. The client application is given in Listing 30.6. Make sure that your database server is running.

Listing 30.6 **The Client Application**

```
import javax.naming.*;
import javax.rmi.PortableRemoteObject;
import java.util.Properties;
import java.util.Enumeration;
import com.brainysoftware.ejb.Product;
import com.brainysoftware.ejb.ProductHome;

public class BeanClient {

  public static void main(String[] args) {
    // preparing properties for constructing an InitialContext object
    Properties properties = new Properties();
    properties.put(Context.INITIAL_CONTEXT_FACTORY,
➥"org.jnp.interfaces.NamingContextFactory");
    properties.put(Context.PROVIDER_URL, "localhost:1099");


    try {
      // Get an initial context
      InitialContext jndiContext = new InitialContext(properties);
      System.out.println("Got context");

      // Get a reference to the Bean
      Object ref  = jndiContext.lookup("BMPProduct");
      System.out.println("Got reference");

      // Get a reference from this to the Bean's Home interface
      ProductHome home = (ProductHome)
        PortableRemoteObject.narrow (ref, ProductHome.class);

      // Create an Interest object from the Home interface
      home.create(11, "Franklin Spring Water", "400ml", 2.25);
      home.create(12, "Franklin Spring Water", "600ml", 3.25);
      home.create(13, "Choco Bar", "Chocolate Bar 200g", 2.95);
```

```
      home.create(14, "Timtim Biscuit", "Biscuit w. mint flavor, 300g",
➥9.25);
      Product product = home.create(15, "Supermie", "Instant Noodle", 1.05);
      product.remove();

      Enumeration enum = home.findByName("Franklin Spring Water");
      while (enum.hasMoreElements()) {
        product = (Product) enum.nextElement();
        System.out.println("Id: " + product.getProductId());
        System.out.println("Product Name: " + product.getProductName());
        System.out.println("Description: " + product.getDescription());
        System.out.println("Price: " + product.getPrice());
      }

    }
    catch(Exception e) {
      System.out.println(e.toString());
    }
  }
}
```

This client application is very similar to the client application used to access the session beans in Chapters 28 and 29. The application inserts five records by calling the create method of the home object and removes the last one. It then also calls the findByName method and iterates the details of each product that has the specified name. Check your database's Products table to make sure that these records are inserted correctly.

Writing a CMP Entity Bean

Although a BMP entity bean is a great object for representing your data, a CMP entity bean is even easier to write. In BMP entity beans, you write your own method implementations for the create and finder methods, as well as for the ejbStore and ejbLoad methods. Additionally, you need to have a method that returns a java.sql.Connection object for your methods to connect to the underlying database.

A CMP entity bean relies on the EJB container to do this database-related task. You don't need to write a getConnection method, you don't need to connect to the database in your create and remove methods, and you don't need to provide implementation in your ejbStore and ejbLoad methods. In fact, you don't need to write a single SQL statement!

You don't even have to write the implementation of a finder method declared in the remote interface. Everything—well, almost everything—is taken care of by the EJB container. As such, an entity bean with CMP is much easier to write and maintain. There is one drawback, however. You need to do more configuration in the deployment descriptor and in the configuration file specific to the application server you are using.

Also note that how your data is persisted depends entirely on the EJB container. The container might use the default built-in database, or it might use files to persist your entity bean's data. You should be able to elect how this is done by configuring some settings in the application server.

In JBoss, for example, if you don't specify anything, the open source EJB container will create a table for you in the default database. You also can use your own database server, however, and you should consult the JBoss documentation if you choose to do so.

JBoss provides the following three finder methods:

- findByPrimaryKey
- findAll
- findBy<field>(<field-type> value)

You see how these finder methods can be used in the client class that accompanies this entity bean application.

In addition, you also can define a custom finder method. Again, you should consult the JBoss documentation.

The following example presents a CMP entity bean that is very similar to the BMP Product entity bean. This similarity is intentional to show the difference between the two types of entity beans. All class files are prefixed with CMP, and the primary key class type is java.lang.String.

The Remote Interface

The remote interface of the CMPProduct bean is similar to that of the BMP Product bean given in Listing 30.1 The code for the remote interface is given in Listing 30.7.

Listing 30.7 **The Remote Interface (CMPProduct.java)**

```
package com.brainysoftware.ejb;

import javax.ejb.EJBObject;
import java.rmi.RemoteException;

/* this is the remote interface for Product */
public interface CMPProduct extends EJBObject {
  public String getProductId() throws RemoteException;
```

```
    public double getPrice() throws RemoteException;
    public String getProductName() throws RemoteException;
    public String getDescription() throws RemoteException;
  }
```

The Home Interface

The home interface defines one create method and three finder methods. The home interface is given in Listing 30.8.

Listing 30.8 **The Home Interface (CMPProductHome.java)**

```
package com.brainysoftware.ejb;

import java.rmi.RemoteException;
import javax.ejb.FinderException;
import javax.ejb.CreateException;
import javax.ejb.EJBHome;
import java.util.Collection;
import java.util.Enumeration;

public interface CMPProductHome extends EJBHome {

  public CMPProduct create(int productId, String productName,
    String description, double price)
    throws RemoteException, CreateException;

  public CMPProduct findByPrimaryKey(String productId)
    throws RemoteException, FinderException;

  public Enumeration findByProductName(String productName)
    throws RemoteException, FinderException;

  public Collection findAll()
    throws RemoteException, FinderException;
}
```

The Entity Bean Class

Compared to the entity bean class of the BMP entity bean, the entity bean class for the CMPProduct is much simpler and shorter. Notice that it does not have implementation to connect to an underlying database. The entity bean class is given in Listing 30.9.

Listing 30.9 **The Entity Bean Class (CMPProductBean.java)**

```
package com.brainysoftware.ejb;

import java.sql.*;
import java.util.Properties;
import java.util.Enumeration;
import java.util.Vector;
import java.rmi.RemoteException;
import javax.ejb.EntityBean;
import javax.ejb.EntityContext;
import javax.ejb.CreateException;
import javax.ejb.FinderException;
import javax.ejb.ObjectNotFoundException;
import javax.naming.InitialContext;
import javax.naming.Context;
import javax.naming.NamingException;

public class CMPProductBean implements EntityBean {

  EntityContext context;

  public String productId;
  public String productName;
  public String description;
  public double price;

  public String getProductId() {
    System.out.println("getProductId");
    return productId;
  }

  public String getProductName() {
    System.out.println("getProductName");
    return productName;
  }

  public String getDescription() {
    System.out.println("getDescription");
    return description;
  }
  public double getPrice() {
    System.out.println("getPrice");
    return price;
  }

  public String ejbCreate(int productId, String productName,
```

```
    String description, double price)
    throws RemoteException, CreateException {
    System.out.println("ejbCreate");
    this.productId = Integer.toString( productId);
    this.productName = productName;
    this.description = description;
    this.price = price;
    return Integer.toString(productId);
  }

  public void ejbPostCreate(int productId, String productName,
    String description, double price)
    throws RemoteException, CreateException {
    System.out.println("ejbPostCreate");
  }

  public void ejbRemove() throws RemoteException {
    System.out.println("ejbRemove");
  }

  public void ejbActivate() {
    System.out.println("ejbActivate");
  }

  public void ejbPassivate() {
    System.out.println("ejbPassivate");
  }

  public void ejbLoad() {
    System.out.println("ejbLoad");
  }
  public void ejbStore() {
    System.out.println("ejbStore");
  }
  public void setEntityContext(EntityContext context) {
    System.out.println("setEntityContext");
    this.context = context;

  }

  public void unsetEntityContext() {
    System.out.println("unsetEntityContext");
    context = null;
  }
}
```

The entity bean class has the familiar four business methods: getProductId, getProductName, getDescription, and getPrice. The only method with substantial content is the ejbCreate method. This method populates the class fields with the arguments passed to the ejbCreate method. However, there is no code to connect the database as in the ejbCreate method in the BMP entity bean, as you see here:

```
String description, double price)
  throws RemoteException, CreateException {
System.out.println("ejbCreate");
this.productId = Integer.toString( productId);
this.productName = productName;
this.description = description;
this.price = price;
return Integer.toString(productId);
```

The Deployment Descriptor

The deployment descriptor is given in Listing 30.10.

Listing 30.10 **The Deployment Descriptor (ejb-jar.xml)**

```
<?xml version="1.0"?>
<!DOCTYPE ejb-jar PUBLIC "-//Sun Microsystems, Inc.//DTD Enterprise
➥JavaBeans 2.0//EN"
"http://java.sun.com/dtd/ejb-jar_2_0.dtd">
<ejb-jar>
  <enterprise-beans>
    <entity>
      <ejb-name>CMPProduct</ejb-name>
      <home>com.brainysoftware.ejb.CMPProductHome</home>
      <remote>com.brainysoftware.ejb.CMPProduct</remote>
      <ejb-class>com.brainysoftware.ejb.CMPProductBean</ejb-class>
      <persistence-type>Container</persistence-type>
      <prim-key-class>java.lang.String</prim-key-class>
      <reentrant>False</reentrant>
      <cmp-field><field-name>productId</field-name></cmp-field>
      <cmp-field><field-name>productName</field-name></cmp-field>
      <cmp-field><field-name>description</field-name></cmp-field>
      <cmp-field><field-name>price</field-name></cmp-field>
      <primkey-field>productId</primkey-field>
    </entity>
  </enterprise-beans>
</ejb-jar>
```

The deployment descriptor is very similar to the one for the BMP entity bean. This deployment descriptor, however, has <cmp-field> elements for all fields that need to be persisted. In this example, those fields are productId, productName, description, and price. The <primkey-field> element also specifies the primary key field.

Note

The value for the <persistence-type> element is Container, not Bean as it is in a BMP entity bean.

Packaging Your CMP Entity Bean

Now you are ready to package your entity bean. Follow these steps:.

1. Compile all the .java files and place the .class files in the com/brainysoftware/ejb/ directory under your project directory.
2. Change the directory to your project directory.
3. Type the following command:

```
jar cfv cmpproduct.jar com/brainysoftware/ejb/CMPProduct*.*
➥META-INF/ejb-jar.xml
```

This command creates a .jar file called cmpproduct.jar in the project directory. Copy this file into the deploy directory of JBoss. If JBoss is not running, start it. If JBoss is already running, you don't need to do anything. JBoss's hot deploy feature automatically tries to deploy any package file saved into the deploy directory.

The Client Application

The client application for the CMP entity bean is given in Listing 30.11. Note that this is similar to the client application in Listing 30.6.

Listing 30.11 **The Client Application**

```
import javax.naming.*;
import javax.rmi.PortableRemoteObject;
import java.util.Properties;
import java.util.Enumeration;
import com.brainysoftware.ejb.CMPProduct;
import com.brainysoftware.ejb.CMPProductHome;
import java.util.Collection;
import java.util.Iterator;

public class BeanClient {
```

continues

Listing 30.11 **Continued**

```
  public static void main(String[] args) {
    // preparing properties for constructing an InitialContext object
    Properties properties = new Properties();
    properties.put(Context.INITIAL_CONTEXT_FACTORY,
"org.jnp.interfaces.NamingContextFactory");
    properties.put(Context.PROVIDER_URL, "localhost:1099");

    try {
      // Get an initial context
      InitialContext jndiContext = new InitialContext(properties);
      System.out.println("Got context");

      // Get a reference to the Bean
      Object ref  = jndiContext.lookup("CMPProduct");
      System.out.println("Got reference");

      // Get a reference from this to the Bean's Home interface
      CMPProductHome home = (CMPProductHome)
➥PortableRemoteObject.narrow(ref, CMPProductHome.class);

      // Create an Interest object from the Home interface
      home.create(61, "Franklin Spring Water", "400ml", 2.25);
      home.create(62, "Franklin Spring Water", "600ml", 3.25);
      home.create(63, "Choco Bar", "Chocolate Bar 200g", 2.95);
      home.create(64, "Timtim Biscuit", "Biscuit w. mint flavor, 300g",
➥9.25);
      CMPProduct product = home.create(65, "Supermie",
➥"Instant Noodle", 1.05);
      product.remove();

      Collection allProducts = home.findAll();
      Iterator iterator = allProducts.iterator();
      while (iterator.hasNext()) {
        product = (CMPProduct) iterator.next();
        System.out.println("Id: " + product.getProductId());
        System.out.println("Product Name: " + product.getProductName());
        System.out.println("Description: " + product.getDescription());
        System.out.println("Price: " + product.getPrice());
      }

      product = home.findByPrimaryKey("53");
      System.out.println("Displaying product with id=63");
      System.out.println("Product Name: " + product.getProductName());
      System.out.println("Description: " + product.getDescription());
      System.out.println("Price: " + product.getPrice());

      Enumeration enum = home.findByProductName("Franklin Spring Water");
      while (enum.hasMoreElements()) {
        product = (CMPProduct) enum.nextElement();
```

```
        System.out.println("Product Id: " + product.getProductId());
        System.out.println("Description: " + product.getDescription());
        System.out.println("Price: " + product.getPrice());
      }


    }
    catch(Exception e) {
      System.out.println(e.toString());
    }
  }
}
```

Summary

In this chapter, you were introduced to the second type of EJB: entity beans. Two types of entity beans are used: bean-managed persistence (BMP) and container-managed persistence (CMP).

Entity beans with BMP provide more flexibility for handling and storing the data in the underlying database. For BMP entity beans, you need to provide information on how to load the JDBC driver for the underlying database.

Entity beans with CMP are very easy to write because the EJB container takes care of how the data is persisted. You don't even have to write a single SQL statement for your entity bean.

31
EJB Query Language

You learned in Chapter 30, "Entity Beans," that there are two types of entity beans: bean-managed persistence (BMP) and container-managed persistence (CMP). The examples in that chapter show how entity beans with CMP can reduce the number of code lines you need. When you use entity beans with CMP, you don't have to worry about how the entity bean's data is persisted. The container takes care of this for you.

Although automatic persistence by the container is a good feature of the CMP entity beans, BMP entity beans are sometimes preferable because they are more flexible in defining complex finder methods. With BMP entity beans, you can write a complex SQL statement for your finder method and have it select any set of records you want.

This flexibility is not present in the CMP entity bean because you don't implement your own finder methods. Instead, you depend on the EJB container's built-in finder methods. In JBoss, you have three: findByPrimaryKey, findAll, and findBy<*field*>.

To get around this limitation in CMP entity beans, EJB 2.0 specifies the Enterprise JavaBeans Query Language (EJB QL), a language similar to Structured Query Language (SQL) that bean developers can use to select data for finder methods of CMP entity beans. For performance optimization, the EJB QL can be compiled to a target language of the database or other persistent store, just as you can create a stored procedure that encapsulates your SQL statement to speed up the execution of your SQL statement.

EJB QL queries can be used in two different ways:

- For selecting entity objects as defined in finder methods in the home interface
- For selecting entity objects or other values derived from an entity bean's abstract schema type

The EJB QL statements for your finder or select methods are specified in the deployment descriptor, under the <query> element. For instance, the following deployment descriptor specifies a finder method named findByDescription, which accepts one parameter of type java.lang.String:

```
<?xml version="1.0"?>
<!DOCTYPE ejb-jar PUBLIC "-//Sun Microsystems, Inc.//DTD Enterprise
➥JavaBeans 2.0//EN"
"http://java.sun.com/dtd/ejb-jar_2_0.dtd">
<ejb-jar>
  <enterprise-beans>
    <entity>
      .
      .
      .
      <query>
        <query-method>
          <method-name>findByDescription</method-name>
          <method-params>
            <method-param>java.lang.String</method-param>
          </method-params>
        </query-method>
        <ejb-ql>
          <![CDATA[SELECT OBJECT(product) FROM CMPProduct
➥AS product WHERE Description=?1]]>
        </ejb-ql>
      </query>

    </entity>
  </enterprise-beans>
</ejb-jar>
```

The name of the find method is specified in the <method-name> element and the parameters are specified in the <method-param> elements. The EJB-QL statement itself is given in the <ejb-ql> element.

This chapter focuses on EJB QL and shows how it can benefit you as a CMP-entity bean developer. The next section starts by presenting the syntax of the EJB QL.

EJB QL Syntax

Understanding the syntax of the EJB QL is key to creating an efficient finder method. This section describes the most important parts of this query language.

An EJB QL query must take the following form:

```
select_clause from_clause [where_clause]
```

In this query, the where_clause is optional. Each clause is explained in the subsections that follow.

The SELECT Clause

The SELECT clause specifies the output of the EJB QL query. It can contain one of the following:

- A single range variable ranging over the abstract schema type of an entity bean
- A single valued path expression

The SELECT clause in a finder method contains either a single range variable ranging over the abstract schema type of the entity bean for which the finder method is defined, or a cmr-field indicated by a single valued path expression that evaluates to the abstract schema type of the entity bean for which the finder method is defined.

In contrast, the SELECT clause of the query for a select method can return the abstract schema types of other entity beans or the values of cmp-fields.

The syntax of the SELECT clause is as follows:

```
SELECT [DISTINCT] {single_valued_path_expression |
➥OBJECT(identification_variable)}
```

When the DISTINCT keyword is present in a SELECT clause, duplicate values are eliminated from the EJB QL query result.

When the DISTINCT keyword is not present in a SELECT clause, but the query is specified for a method whose result type is java.util.Set, all duplicate values also are eliminated from the query result.

As an example, here is a simple EJB QL statement that will find all distinct products:

```
SELECT DISTINCT OBJECT(p)
FROM Product AS p
```

The FROM Clause

The FROM clause defines the domain of the query by declaring identification variables. The domain of the query can be constrained by path expressions. The FROM clause can contain multiple identification variables separated by a comma. It has the following syntax:

```
FROM identification_variable_declaration
➥[,identification_variable_declaration]*
```

In this clause, the asterisk denotes that the value in the bracket it follows can be repeated zero or more times. Further, the identification_variable_declaration is defined as follows:

```
identification_variable_declaration::= collection_member_declaration |
➥range_variable_declaration

collection_member_declaration::= IN (collection_valued_path_expression)
➥[AS] identifier

range_variable_declaration::= abstract_schema_name [AS] identifier
```

An identifier is a case-insensitive sequence of characters of any length. The first character of an identifier must be a valid Java identifier start character, and all other characters must be legal Java identifier part characters. In addition, an identifier must not be one of the following: SELECT, FROM, WHERE, DISTINCT, OBJECT, NULL, TRUE, FALSE, NOT, AND, OR, BETWEEN, LIKE, IN, AS, UNKNOWN, EMPTY, MEMBER, OF, and IS.

An identification variable acts as an identifier in the FROM clause. It is declared using the special operators IN—and optionally, AS. An identification variable is also case-insensitive and must not be a reserved identifier. In addition, it must not have the same name as an abstract-schema-name or ejb-name.

An identification variable declaration is either a range variable declaration or a collection member declaration. If an identification variable declaration is a range variable declaration, it ranges over the abstract schema type of an entity bean. The syntax for declaring an identification variable as a range variable is similar to that of SQL; optionally, it uses the AS operator.

In the case where an identification variable declaration is a collection member declaration, the identification variable declared by the collection member declaration ranges over values of a collection obtained by navigation using a path expression. An identification variable of a collection member declaration is declared using the IN operator.

A path expression is an identification variable that is followed by the navigation operator (.) and a cmp-field or cmr-field.

The following is the syntax for single valued path expressions:

```
single_valued_path::= {single_valued_navigation | identification
➥variable}.cmp_field | single_valued_navigation

single_valued_navigation::=
➥identification_variable.[single_valued_cmr_field.]* single_valued_cmr_field
```

The following is the syntax for collection valued path expressions:

```
collection_valued_path_expression::= identification_variable.
➥[single_valued_cmr_field.]*collection_valued_cmr_field
```

single_valued_cmr_ field is designated by a cmr-field in a one-to-one or many-to-one relationship. The type of the expression is the abstract schema type of the related entity bean. The type of *collection_valued_cmr_ field* is a collection of values of the abstract schema type of the related entity bean.

Consider the following EJB QL statement that incorporates a FROM clause to find all orders for products with category 'book':

```
SELECT DISTINCT OBJECT(o)
FROM Order o, IN(o.lineItems) l
WHERE l.product.category = 'book'
```

The WHERE Clause

The WHERE clause of an EJB QL query determines the selection of data. It has the following syntax:

```
WHERE conditional_expression
```

A conditional expression can contain the following elements:

- Literal
- Identification variable
- Path expression
- Input parameters
- Conditional expression composition
- Operators and operator precedence
- Between expressions
- In expressions
- Like expressions
- Null comparison expressions
- Empty collection comparison expressions
- Collection member expressions
- Functional expressions

Each of these is explained in the following subsections.

Literal

A literal can be a string literal, an exact numeric literal, an approximate numeric literal, or a boolean literal. A string literal appears inside a pair of single quotation marks, such as 'java'. If a string literal contains a single quote character, the character must be escaped using another single quote character. Thus, a string literal containing O'Connor is represented as 'O''Connor'.

An exact numeric literal is a numeric value without a decimal point in the range specified by the Java long. Examples include 123, +80, and -99.

An approximate numeric literal is a numeric value in the range specified by the Java float and is represented in scientific notation or a numeric value with a decimal point. Examples include 9E2, -9E2, +6.6, and -98.98.

A boolean literal is either TRUE or FALSE.

Identification Variable

An identification variable is defined in the earlier section, "The FROM Clause." Any identification that appears in the WHERE clause must be declared in the FROM clause.

Path Expression

Path expression also is defined in the section, "The FROM Clause." It is illegal to use a *collection_valued_path_expression* within a WHERE clause as part of a conditional expression, except in an *empty_collection_comparison_expression* or *collection_member_expression*.

Input Parameters

Input parameters obey the following rules:

- An input parameter is designated by the question mark (?) prefix followed by an integer, such as ?1.
- Input parameters are numbered starting from 1.
- The number of distinct input parameters in an EJB QL query must not be greater than the number of input parameters for the finder or select method.
- Input parameters must appear only in conditional expressions involving single valued path expressions.
- An input parameter evaluates to the type of the corresponding parameter defined in the signature of the finder or select method associated with the query.

- If the input parameter to the finder or select method corresponds to an EJBObject or EJBLocalObject, the container maps the input parameter to the appropriate abstract schema type value.

The following EJB QL statement is an example of a query that uses an input parameter. The statement finds all products that are cheaper than the value passed as the parameter:

```
SELECT DISTINCT OBJECT(o)
FROM Product o
WHERE o.price < ?1
```

Conditional Expression Composition

A conditional expression contains other conditional expressions, comparison operations, logical operations, and path expressions that evaluate to boolean values and boolean literals.

Conditional expressions have the following syntax::

```
conditional_expression::= conditional_term | conditional_expression OR
conditional_term

conditional_term::= conditional_factor | conditional_term AND
conditional_factor

conditional_factor::= [NOT] conditional_test

conditional_primary::= simple_cond_expression | conditional_expression

simple_cond_expression::= comparison_expression | between_expression |
like_expression | in_expression | null_comparison_expression |
empty_collection_comparison_expression | collection_member_expression
```

Operators and Operator Precedence

In a WHERE clause, operators can be one of the following. These operators are ordered in decreasing precedence:

- Navigation operator (.)
- Arithmetic operators: unary, multiplication and division (*,/), addition and subtraction (+,–)
- Comparison operators: =, >, >=, <, <=, <>
- Logical operators: NOT, AND, OR

Between Expressions

The following is the syntax for the use of the comparison operator [NOT] BETWEEN in a conditional expression:

```
arithmetic_expression [NOT] BETWEEN arithmetic-expr AND arithmetic-expr
```

In Expressions

The following is the syntax for the use of the comparison operator [NOT] IN in a conditional expression:

```
single_valued_path_expression [NOT] IN (string-literal [, string-literal]* )
```

Like Expressions

The following is the syntax for the use of the comparison operator [NOT] LIKE in a conditional expression:

```
single_valued_path_expression [NOT] LIKE pattern-value
➥[ESCAPE escape-characater]
```

Null Comparison Expressions

The following is the syntax for the use of the comparison operator IS NULL in a conditional expression:

```
single_valued_path_expression IS [NOT] NULL
```

Empty Collection Comparison Expressions

The following is the syntax for the use of the comparison operator IS EMPTY in an *empty_collection_comparison_expression*:

```
collection_valued_path_expression IS [NOT] EMPTY
```

Collection Member Expressions

The following is the syntax for the use of the comparison operator MEMBER OF in a *collection_member_expression*:

```
single_valued_path_expression [NOT] MEMBER [OF]
collection_valued_path_expression
```

Functional Expressions

The following are built-in functions in EJB QL:

- String functions:

  CONCAT(String, String) returns a String

  SUBSTRING(String, start, length) returns a String

  LOCATE(String, String [, start]) returns an int

  LENGTH(String) returns an int

- Arithmetic functions:

  ABS(number) returns an int, a float or a double

  SQRT(double) returns a double

EJB QL BNF

The BNF notation of an EJB QL is given as follows:

```
EJB QL ::= select_clause from_clause [where_clause]
from_clause ::=FROM identification_variable_declaration
[, identification_variable_declaration]*
identification_variable_declaration ::= collection_member_declaration |
range_variable_declaration
collection_member_declaration ::=IN (collection_valued_path_expression)
➥[AS ] identifier
range_variable_declaration ::= abstract_schema_name [AS ] identifier
single_valued_path_expression ::=
{single_valued_navigation | identification_variable}.cmp_field |
single_valued_navigation
single_valued_navigation ::=
identification_variable.[single_valued_cmr_field.]* single_valued_cmr_field
collection_valued_path_expression ::=
identification_variable.[single_valued_cmr_field.]*collection_valued_cmr_fiel
d
select_clause ::=SELECT [DISTINCT ] {single_valued_path_expression |
OBJECT (identification_variable)}
where_clause ::=WHERE conditional_expression
conditional_expression ::= conditional_term |
➥conditional_expressionOR conditional_term
conditional_term ::= conditional_factor |
➥conditional_termAND conditional_factor
conditional_factor ::= [NOT ] conditional_test
conditional_test :: = conditional_primary
conditional_primary ::= simple_cond_expression | (conditional_expression)
simple_cond_expression ::= comparison_expression |
➥between_expression | like_expression |
in_expression | null_comparison_expression |
empty_collection_comparison_expression |
```

```
collection_member_expression
between_expression ::=
arithmetic_expression [NOT ] BETWEEN
arithmetic_expressionAND arithmetic_expression
in_expression ::=
single_valued_path_expression [NOT ] IN (string_literal [, string_literal]*
)
like_expression ::=
single_valued_path_expression [NOT ]LIKE pattern_value
➥[ESCAPE escape-character]
null_comparison_expression ::= single_valued_path_expressionIS [NOT ] NULL
empty_collection_comparison_expression ::=
collection_valued_path_expressionIS [NOT] EMPTY
collection_member_expression ::=
single_valued_path_expression [NOT ] MEMBER [OF ]
collection_valued_path_expression
comparison_expression ::=
string_value { =|<>} string_expression |
boolean_value { =|<>} boolean_expression} |
datetime_value { = | <> | > | < } datetime_expression |
entity_bean_value { = | <> } entity_bean_expression |
arithmetic_value comparison_operator single_value_designator
arithmetic_value ::= single_valued_path_expression
➥| functions_returning_numerics
single_value_designator ::= scalar_expression
comparison_operator ::=
= | > | >= | < | <= | <>
scalar_expression ::= arithmetic_expression
arithmetic_expression ::= arithmetic_term | arithmetic_expression
➥{ + | - } arithmetic_term
arithmetic_term ::= arithmetic_factor | arithmetic_term
➥{ * | / } arithmetic_factor
arithmetic_factor ::= { + |- } arithmetic_primary
arithmetic_primary ::= single_valued_path_expression |
➥literal | (arithmetic_expression) |
input_parameter | functions_returning_numerics
string_value ::= single_valued_path_expression | functions_returning_strings
string_expression ::= string_primary | input_expression
string_primary ::= single_valued_path_expression | literal
➥| (string_expression) |
functions_returning_strings
datetime_value ::= single_valued_path_expression
datetime_expression ::= datetime_value | input_parameter
boolean_value ::= single_valued_path_expression
boolean_expression ::= single_valued_path_expression | literal
➥| input_parameter
entity_bean_value ::= single_valued_path_expression | identification_variable
entity_bean_expression ::= entity_bean_value | input_parameter
functions_returning_strings ::=CONCAT (string_expression, string_expression) |
SUBSTRING (string_expression, arithmetic_expression, arithmetic_expression)
functions_returning_numerics::=
```

```
LENGTH (string_expression) |
LOCATE (string_expression, string_expression[, arithmetic_expression]) |
ABS (arithmetic_expression) |
SQRT (arithmetic_expression)
```

Note that the following applies:

- { ... } indicates grouping
- [...] indicates optional constructs
- Keyword is printed in boldface

Summary

EJB 2.0 specifies the Enterprise JavaBeans Query Language (EJB QL), a language similar to Structured Query Language (SQL) that bean developers can use to select data for finder methods of CMP entity beans.

EJB QL queries can be used to select entity objects as defined in finder methods in the home interface and to select entity objects or other values derived from an entity bean's abstract schema type.

32

Java Message Service

In Chapters 29 and 30, you learned about the first two types of Enterprise JavaBeans (EJB)—session beans and entity beans. The last type, which you have yet to see, is the message-driven bean, which is a new addition to the EJB 2.0 specification. To understand message-driven beans, you first need a solid background in the Java Message Service (JMS), which is the topic of this chapter. The message-driven bean itself is discussed in Chapter 33, "Message-Driven Beans." If you've already been working with JMS, feel free to skip this chapter.

This chapter starts by introducing you to messaging and the JMS API. This chapter then develops several examples that use JMS to send and receive messages.

Introduction to Messaging

A messaging service is a service that provides communication between applications or between software components. Any application or software component that uses a messaging service is called a *messaging client*. In a typical messaging service, a messaging client can send and receive messages.

A chat application is a good analogy for illustrating a messaging service. Normally, the chat server provides two methods of communication for its users. These are as follows:

- A user can send a chat message that is broadcast to all other chat users
- A user can send a private message to another user that is not visible to other chat users

As you learn later in this chapter, JMS also provides these two similar services.

A messaging service is more sophisticated than a chat application, however. In a chat application, in order to exchange messages, the sender and the receiver(s) must be connected at the same time. In a messaging service, the sender can send a message without the receiver having to be connected at the same moment. The sender sends a message to a destination, and then the receiver collects it from there.

JMS also decoupled its clients. The sender does not need to know anything about the receiver, and vice versa.

The JMS API

Sun joined forces with some partner companies to design the JMS API to enable Java applications to create, send, receive, and read messages, as well as communicate with other messaging implementations. The original version of JMS was released in August 1998, and it was used mainly to allow Java applications to access existing messaging-oriented middleware (MOM) systems, such as IBM's MQSeries. Currently, the most recent version of the JMS API is 1.0.2, which is downloadable from `http://java.sun.com/products/jms/docs.html`.

Java applications that use JMS are called *JMS clients*, and the messaging system that handles the routing and delivery of messages is called the *JMS provider*. A JMS client that sends a message is called a *producer*, and a JMS client that receives a message is called a *consumer*. A single JMS client can be both a producer and a consumer. A JMS application consists of many JMS clients and one or more JMS providers.

The following two nice features are inherent with JMS:

- **asynchronous:** A JMS client does not have to request messages to receive them. The JMS provider delivers messages to the client as the messages arrive.
- **reliable:** A JMS system can ensure that a message is delivered only once.

JMS is normally preferred to a tightly coupled messaging system in the following conditions:

- The clients need to be de-coupled from each other
- Message exchange can occur even though not all clients are up and running at the same time
- The business model requires components to send messages to one another and continue to operate without receiving an immediate response

The JMS API Messaging Domains

Messaging domains are models for messaging. The JMS API provides the following two messaging domains: publish/subscribe and point-to-point.

Publish/Subscribe (pub/sub)

In this model, a client sends a message to a topic and the message is received by any interesting clients that subscribes to that topic. This is a one-to-many model where the sender is also called the *publisher* and the receiver(s) is called the *subscriber(s)*. The act of sending a message is also called *publish*. Topics send the messages straight to all subscribers and don't keep the messages. A client can consume messages only after the client subscribes to a topic, and the subscriber must continue to be active to consume published messages. This restriction is somewhat relaxed in JMS, however, by enabling a client to create durable subscriptions in which the client can receive messages sent while the client is not active.

Compare the pub/sub model with a radio station that broadcasts news all the time. The news can be received by any radio that is tuned to the radio station's frequency and modulation. To receive a particular piece of news, a radio must be turned on at the time the news item is broadcast.

Point-to-Point (PTP)

In this model, a client sends a message that is received only by one client. The sender sends a message to a queue and the receiver extracts this message from the queue at any convenient time the receiver connects to the system. A queue retains all messages it receives until the messages are consumed or until the messages expire.

The PTP model is similar to the U.S. Postal Service in which the addressee has a P.O. Box at a particular post office. The sender sends a letter and the addressee will pick it up in the post office. The letter can be received by only one recipient.

The JMS Object Model

The most important objects in the JMS object model are represented by the following interfaces in the javax.jms package:

- ConnectionFactory
- Destination
- Connection
- Session
- MessageProducer
- MessageConsumer
- Message

These objects are discussed in the following sections.

ConnectionFactory

A ConnectionFactory object is used to create a connection with a JMS provider. This object supports concurrent use and contains connection configuration parameters that have been defined by an administrator.

In the javax.jms package, the ConnectionFactory object is modeled by the ConnectionFactory interface, whose signature is as follows:

```
public interface ConnectionFactory
```

The ConnectionFactory interface does not define any method and has two direct subinterfaces: TopicConnectionFactory and QueueConnectionFactory. The QueueConnectionFactory interface is used to create a connection with a point-to-point JMS provider, and the TopicConnectionFactory interface is used to create a connection with a pub/sub JMS provider.

You usually perform a JNDI lookup of the connection factory in a JMS client program. For example, to get a connection to a point-to-point JMS provider, you would use the following code:

```
Context context = new InitialContext();
QueueConnectionFactory queueConnectionFactory =
  (QueueConnectionFactory) context.lookup("QueueConnectionFactory");
```

And, to get a connection to a pub/sub JMS provider, you use the following code:

```
Context context = new InitialContext();
TopicConnectionFactory topicConnectionFactory =
  (TopicConnectionFactory) context.lookup("TopicConnectionFactory");
```

You then can use the QueueConnectionFactory interface's createQueueConnection method to obtain a QueueConnection object or the TopicConnectionFactory interface's createTopicConnection method to obtain a TopicConnection object.

A connection factory is a JMS administered object.

Note

A JMS administered object is an object that contains configuration information created by an administrator to be used by JMS clients.

Destination

A Destination object encapsulates a provider-specific address. A Destination object supports concurrent use and in the javax.jms package is represented by the Destination interface whose signature is as follows:

```
public interface Destination
```

The Destination interface does not have any method.

In the pub/sub domain, a destination is a topic. In the PTP domain, a destination is a queue. To accommodate this, the Destination interface has two direct subinterfaces: Topic and Queue.

Like the ConnectionFactory object, you get a Destination object by performing a JNDI lookup. Depending on the domain you use, you will need either a Topic object or a Queue object. Here is the code to obtain a Queue in the PTP domain:

```
Context context = new InitialContext();
QueueConnectionFactory queueConnectionFactory =
  (QueueConnectionFactory) context.lookup("QueueConnectionFactory");
Queue queue = (Queue) context.lookup(queueName);
```

And, here is how you obtain a Topic object in the pub/sub domain:

```
Context context = new InitialContext();
TopicConnectionFactory topicConnectionFactory =
  (TopicConnectionFactory) context.lookup("TopicConnectionFactory");
Topic topic = (Topic) context.lookup(topicName);
```

> **Note**
> A Destination object is a JMS-administered object.

Connections

A Connection object represents a JMS client's active connection to a JMS provider. Typically, it is a TCP/IP socket between a JMS client and a JMS provider. Connection objects support concurrent use and are represented by the javax.jms.Connection interface. This Connection interface has the following signature:

```
public interface Connection
```

A Connection object is a relatively heavyweight object because creating a Connection object involves setting up authentication and communication.

In JMS, there are two types of connection: QueueConnection and TopicConnection. A QueueConnection object is used to obtain a connection to a PTP domain, and a TopicConnection is used to obtain a connection to a pub/sub domain. These two types of connections are represented by objects that implement the QueueConnection interface and the TopicConnection interface, respectively. Both QueueConnection and TopicConnection are direct subinterfaces of the Connection interface and have a method to create the corresponding Session object suitable for its domain.

When first created, a connection is in stopped mode, meaning that no messages are being delivered. You usually leave the connection in stopped mode until setup is complete. The client can then call the connection object's start method.

In a PTP domain, you obtain a QueueConnection object by calling the createQueueConnection method of the QueueConnectionFactory object, as shown in the following code:

```
QueueConnection queueConnection =
  queueConnectionFactory.createQueueConnection();
```

In a pub/sub domain, you obtain a TopicConnection object by calling the createTopicConnection method of the TopicConnectionFactory object, as demonstrated in the following code:

```
TopicConnection topicConnection =
topicConnectionFactory.createTopicConnection();
```

Once you get a connection object, you can call the start method of the Connection interface to enable your JMS application to consume messages. Do not forget to release resources by closing a connection when it's no longer in use. You close a connection by calling the close method of the Connection interface.

Session

A Session object is a single-threaded context for producing and consuming messages. A Session object is represented by the Session interface, which uses the following signature:

```
public interface Session extends java.lang.Runnable
```

The Session interface has two direct subinterfaces: TopicSession and QueueSession. These represent a session in a pub/sub domain and in a PTP domain, respectively.

To create a TopicSession object, you call the createTopicSession method of the TopicConnection interface. To construct a QueueSession object, you use the CreateQueueSession method of the QueueConnection interface. The signatures of these methods are as follows:

```
public TopicSession createTopicSession(boolean transacted, int
acknowledgeMode) throws JMSException

public QueueSession createQueueSession(boolean transacted, int
acknowledgeMode) throws JMSException
```

The createTopicSession and the createQueueSession methods have the following common parameters:

- **transacted.** This parameter indicates whether the session is transacted.
- **acknowledgeMode.** This parameter indicates whether the consumer or the client will acknowledge messages it receives. Its value can be one of the three fields of the Session interface.
- **AUTO_ACKNOWLEDGE.** The session automatically acknowledges a client's receipt of a message either when the session has successfully returned from a call to receive or when the message listener the session has called to process the message successfully returns.
- **CLIENT_ACKNOWLEDGE.** The client acknowledges a consumed message by calling the message's acknowledge method.
- **DUPS_OK_ACKNOWLEDGE.** This acknowledgment mode instructs the session to lazily acknowledge the delivery of messages.

The acknowledgeMode parameter is ignored if the session is transacted.

The following code creates an untransacted TopicSession object with AUTO_ACKNOWLEDGE acknowledge mode:

```
TopicSession topicSession =
topicConnection.createTopicSession(false, Session.AUTO_ACKNOWLEDGE);
```

And the following code constructs an untransacted QueueSession object with

CLIENT_ACKNOWLEDGE acknowledge mode:

```
QueueSession queusSession = queueConnection.createQueueSession
➥(false, Session.CLIENT_ACKNOWLEDGE);
```

MessageProducer

A MessageProducer object is used by a JMS client to send messages to a destination. In javax.jms package, this object is represented by the MessageProducer interface, which has the following signature:

```
public interface MessageProducer
```

The MessageProducer interface has two direct subinterfaces:

- **QueueSender.** You use this interface in the PTP domain.
- **TopicPublisher.** You use this interface in the pub/sub domain.

A MessageProducer object is created by passing a Destination object to its message-producer method of the corresponding session object. For example, you create a QueueSender object by calling the createSender method of the QueueSession interface, passing a Queue. Here is a code snippet that creates a QueueSender object:

```
Context context = new InitialContext();
QueueConnectionFactory queueConnectionFactory = (QueueConnectionFactory)
  context.lookup("QueueConnectionFactory");
Queue queue = (Queue) context.lookup(queueName);

QueueConnection queueConnection =
   queueConnectionFactory.createQueueConnection();
QueueSession queueSession =  queueConnection.createQueueSession(false,
  Session.AUTO_ACKNOWLEDGE);
QueueSender queueSender = queueSession.createSender(queue);
```

As another example of creating a MessageProducer object, the following code creates a TopicPublisher object:

```
Context context = new InitialContext();
TopicConnectionFactory topicConnectionFactory = (TopicConnectionFactory)
  context.lookup("TopicConnectionFactory");
Topic topic = (Topic) context.lookup(topicName);

TopicConnection topicConnection =
   topicConnectionFactory.createTopicConnection();
TopicSession topicSession =  topicConnection.createTopicSession(false,
  Session.AUTO_ACKNOWLEDGE);
TopicPublisher topicPublisher = topicSession.createPublisher(topic);
```

MessageConsumer

A MessageConsumer object is used by a JMS client to receive message from a destination. In javax.jms package, this object is represented by the MessageConsumer interface, which has the following signature:

```
public interface MessageConsumer
```

The MessageConsumer interface has two direct subinterfaces:

- **QueueReceiver.** You use this interface in the PTP domain.
- **TopicSubscriber.** You use this interface in the pub/sub domain.

A MessageConsumer object is created by passing a Destination object to its message-consumer method of the corresponding session object. For example, you create a QueueReceiver object by calling the createReceiver method of the QueueSession interface, passing a Queue, as you see in the following code:

```
Context context = new InitialContext();
QueueConnectionFactory queueConnectionFactory = (QueueConnectionFactory)
  context.lookup("QueueConnectionFactory");
Queue queue = (Queue) context.lookup(queueName);

QueueConnection queueConnection =
   queueConnectionFactory.createQueueConnection();
QueueSession queueSession =  queueConnection.createQueueSession(false,
  Session.AUTO_ACKNOWLEDGE);
QueueReceiver queueReceiver = queueSession.createReceiver(queue);
```

To create a TopicSubscriber object, you call the createSubscriber method of the TopicSession interface, passing a Topic. The following code demonstrates how you can create a TopicSubscriber object:

```
Context context = new InitialContext();
TopicConnectionFactory topicConnectionFactory = (TopicConnectionFactory)
  context.lookup("TopicConnectionFactory");
Topic topic = (Topic) context.lookup(topicName);

TopicConnection topicConnection =
   topicConnectionFactory.createTopicConnection();
TopicSession topicSession =  topicConnection.createTopicSession(false,
  Session.AUTO_ACKNOWLEDGE);
TopicSubscriber topicSubscriber = topicSession.createSubscriber(topic);
```

Message

There are many types of messages in JMS:

- **TextMessage.** A message containing a string.
- **MapMessage.** A message containing name/value pairs. Each name is a String object and each value is a Java primitive type.

- **BytesMessage.** A message containing a stream of uninterpreted bytes.
- **StreamMessage.** A message containing a stream of Java primitive values.
- **ObjectMessage.** A message containing a serializable object.

All these messages are represented by interfaces that are derived from the javax.jms.Message interface. The Message interface defines the message header and the acknowledge method for all messages.

JMS messages are composed of the following parts:

- **Header.** All messages support the same set of header fields. Header fields contain values used by both clients and providers to identify and route messages.
- **Properties.** Each message contains a built-in facility for supporting application-defined property values. Properties provide an efficient mechanism for supporting application-defined message filtering.
- **Body.** The JMS API defines several types of message body, which determines the type of message—as mentioned previously.

To send a message, you first must create a Message object by calling one of the create message methods of the Session interface. You can create any type of message by invoking one of the following methods of the Session interface: createBytesMessage, createMapMessage, createObjectMessage, createStreamMessage, and createTextMessage. For example, the following code creates a TextMessage object from a QueueSession object, sets the text in it, and sends it to a queue:

```
TextMessage message = queueSession.createTextMessage();
message.setText("This is a TextMessage");
queueSender.send(message);
```

To receive a message, you use the receive method of the MessageConsumer interface, as illustrated in the following code snippet:

```
Message message = queueReceiver.receive();
```

If necessary, you can use instanceof to query the type of message returned, as you see here:

```
if (message instanceof ObjectMessage) {
  ObjectMessage objectMessage = (ObjectMessage) message;
}
```

Writing JMS Clients

Based on what you learned in the previous sections, you can now write two JMS client applications. The first application, given in Listing 32.1, provides the code to send a message to a queue called MyQueue. The code in Listing 32.2 receives the message and displays it on the Console. You should run the first client application before running the second.

Listing 32.1 **Message Sender JMS Client Application**

```
package com.brainysoftware.ejb;

import javax.jms.*;
import javax.naming.*;

public class MessageSender {

  public static void main(String[] args) {
    QueueConnection queueConnection = null;

    try {
      Context context = new InitialContext();
      QueueConnectionFactory queueConnectionFactory =
        (QueueConnectionFactory) context.lookup("QueueConnectionFactory");
      String queueName = "MyQueue";
      Queue queue = (Queue) context.lookup(queueName);
      queueConnection =
      queueConnectionFactory.createQueueConnection();
      QueueSession queueSession =
        queueConnection.createQueueSession(false, Session.AUTO_ACKNOWLEDGE);
      QueueSender queueSender = queueSession.createSender(queue);
      TextMessage message = queueSession.createTextMessage();
      message.setText("This is a TextMessage");
      queueSender.send(message);
      System.out.println("Message sent.");
    }
    catch (NamingException e) {
      System.out.println("Naming Exception");
    }
    catch (JMSException e) {
      System.out.println("JMS Exception");
    }
    finally {
      if (queueConnection != null) {
        try {
          queueConnection.close();
        }
        catch (JMSException e) {}
      }
    }
  }
}
```

The code in Listing 32.1 starts by performing a JNDI lookup to obtain a QueueConnectionFactory, as you see here:

```
Context context = new InitialContext();
QueueConnectionFactory queueConnectionFactory =
  (QueueConnectionFactory) context.lookup("QueueConnectionFactory");
```

Having a QueueConnectionFactory object, you then can obtain a Queue object by performing another JNDI lookup, as follows:

```
String queueName = "MyQueue";
Queue queue = (Queue) context.lookup(queueName);
```

From the QueueConnectionFactory object, you then use the createQueueConnection method to create a QueueConnection object:

```
queueConnection =
queueConnectionFactory.createQueueConnection();
```

The QueueConnection object created in the previous line enables you to create a QueueSession object. You do this by invoking the createQueueSession method, as shown here:

```
QueueSession queueSession =
  queueConnection.createQueueSession(false, Session.AUTO_ACKNOWLEDGE);
```

Once you have the QueueSession object, you create a QueueSender object by calling the createSender method of the QueueSession object, passing the Queue object you obtain from the JNDI lookup:

```
QueueSender queueSender = queueSession.createSender(queue);
```

Now, you are ready to send a message. The code in Listing 32.2 composes a TextMessage object called message from the createTextMessage method of the QueueSession object, sets its text, and calls the send method of the QueueSender object to send the message, using this code:

```
TextMessage message = queueSession.createTextMessage();
message.setText("This is a TextMessage");
queueSender.send(message);
```

Listing 32.2 **Message Receiver JMS Client Application**

```
package com.brainysoftware.ejb;

import javax.jms.*;
import javax.naming.*;
public class MessageReceiver {
  public static void main(String[] args) {
    QueueConnection queueConnection = null;
    try {
      Context context = new InitialContext();
      QueueConnectionFactory queueConnectionFactory =
        (QueueConnectionFactory) context.lookup("QueueConnectionFactory");
```

```
        String queueName = "MyQueue";
        Queue queue = (Queue) context.lookup(queueName);
        queueConnection =
          queueConnectionFactory.createQueueConnection();
        QueueSession queueSession = queueConnection.createQueueSession
➥(false, Session.AUTO_ACKNOWLEDGE);
        QueueReceiver queueReceiver = queueSession.createReceiver(queue);
        queueConnection.start();
        Message message = queueReceiver.receive(1);
        if (message != null) {
          if (message instanceof TextMessage) {
            TextMessage textMessage = (TextMessage) message;
            System.out.println(textMessage.getText());
          }
        }
      }
      catch (NamingException e) {
        System.out.println("Naming Exception");
      }
      catch (JMSException e) {
        System.out.println("JMS Exception");
      }
      finally {
        if (queueConnection != null) {
          try {
            queueConnection.close();
          }
          catch (JMSException e) {}
        }
      }
    }
  }
```

The code in Listing 32.2 is used to receive a message from the JMS provider. Like the code in Listing 32.1, you first perform two JNDI lookups, first to obtain a QueueConnectionFactory object, and then to obtain a Queue object. The following is the code to do that:

```
Context context = new InitialContext();
      QueueConnectionFactory queueConnectionFactory =
        (QueueConnectionFactory) context.lookup("QueueConnectionFactory");
      String queueName = "MyQueue";
      Queue queue = (Queue) context.lookup(queueName);
```

Using the QueueConnectionFactory object from the first JNDI lookup, you call its createQueueConnection method to create a QueueConnection object:

```
queueConnection =
  queueConnectionFactory.createQueueConnection();
```

Using the resulting QueueConnection object, you obtain a QueueSession object by invoking the createQueueSession method of the QueueConnection object, as follows:

```
QueueSession queueSession = queueConnection.createQueueSession
➥(false, Session.AUTO_ACKNOWLEDGE);
```

To receive a message from a queue, you need a QueueReceiver object. This is constructed from the createReceiver method of the QueueSession object, passing the Queue object obtained from the second JNDI lookup, as you see here:

```
QueueReceiver queueReceiver = queueSession.createReceiver(queue);
```

With the QueueReceiver object, you can call its receive method to obtain a message with the following code:

```
Message message = queueReceiver.receive(1);
```

Next, you make sure that the message is not null and that the message is a TextMessage object. If it is, display the text of the TextMessage object by calling its getText method, as shown here:

```
if (message != null) {
  if (message instanceof TextMessage) {
    TextMessage textMessage = (TextMessage) message;
    System.out.println(textMessage.getText());
  }
}
```

Summary

In this chapter, you have learned the basics of JMS, including the JMS architecture and object model. You also saw how two client applications were developed. You are now ready to move to the next chapter to write your first message-driven beans.

33

Message-Driven Beans

In Chapter 32, "Java Message Service," you learned about the messaging service and the Java Message Service (JMS). This provides the basic knowledge for working with the third type of Enterprise JavaBeans (EJB): message-driven beans (MDB). Message-driven beans are a new type of bean added to the EJB 2.0 specification. The MDB model is designed to enable an enterprise bean to be asynchronously invoked to handle the processing of incoming JMS messages. With the other two types of beans, you can send and receive messages only synchronously, not asynchronously.

This chapter begins with a definition of message-driven beans and gives you a close look at the object model. It then continues with an example of a message-driven bean and provides instruction on how to deploy it in JBoss.

> **Note**
> If you have not previously worked with JMS, you should read Chapter 32 before you read this chapter.

What Is a Message-Driven Bean?

To the client (and in relation to the messaging service), a message-driven bean is an asynchronous message consumer. Looking at its behavior, however, a message-driven bean is similar to the stateless session bean in that a message-driven bean has no conversational state. A message-driven bean is created and controlled by the EJB container. Unlike session beans and entity beans, however, message-driven beans do not have a home or remote interface. Client applications access a message-driven bean through JMS by sending messages to the JMS destination.

The Application Programming Interface

A message-driven bean class must be a public class and must implement the following two interfaces:

- javax.ejb.MessageDrivenBean
- javax.jms.MessageListener

In addition to the two interfaces, you need to know about the MessageDrivenContext interface that is provided by the EJB container for the message-driven bean instance. The following subsections discuss the javax.ejb.MessageDrivenBean interface and the javax.MessageDrivenContext interface. Because the javax.jms.MessageListener is discussed in Chapter 32, it is not repeated here.

The javax.ejb.MessageDrivenBean Interface

The javax.ejb.MessageDrivenBean has the following signature:

```
public interface MessageDrivenBean extends EnterpriseBean
```

It defines two methods: setMessageDrivenContext and ejbRemove. The signatures of both methods are as follows:

```
public void setMessageDrivenContext(MessageDrivenContext context)
➥throws EJBException

public void ejbRemove() throws EJBException
```

The setMessageDrivenContext sets the associated message-driven context, and the ejbRemove method is invoked by the EJB container before the container ends the life of the message-driven bean object.

The MessageDrivenContext interface is discussed next.

The javax.ejb.MessageDrivenContext Interface

The MessageDrivenContext interface provides access to the runtime message-driven context that the container provides for a message-driven enterprise bean instance. The container passes the MessageDrivenContext interface to an instance after the instance has been created. The message-driven context remains associated with the instance for the lifetime of the instance.

The MessageDrivenContext is derived from the EJBContext interface and has the following signature:

```
public interface MessageDrivenContext extends EJBContext
```

The MessageDrivenContext interface has the following methods:

- **getRollbackOnly**. Tests whether the transaction has been marked for rollback only. This method can be called only by a message-driven bean with container-managed transaction demarcation.
- **getUserTransaction**. Obtains the transaction demarcation interface. Only enterprise beans with bean-managed transactions can use the UserTransaction interface.
- **isCallerInRole**. Tests whether the caller has a given security role.
- **setRollbackOnly**. Marks the transaction for rollback only. This method can be called only by a message-driven bean with container-managed transaction demarcation.
- **getCallerPrincipal, getEJBHome, getEJBLocalHome**. These methods are inherited from the EJBContext interface and must not be called by an instance of a message-driven bean.

Accessing a Message-Driven Bean

A client application that wants to access a message-driven bean does so by retrieving a javax.jms.Queue object from a JNDI lookup. The following code illustrates how a reference to a queue called MyQueue can be obtained:

```
Context context = new InitialContext();
Queue queue = (Queue) context.lookup("java:com/env/jms/MyQueue");
```

Writing a Message-Driven Bean

The following example (in Listing 33.1) is a message-driven bean called MyMDB. It is a simple message-driven bean that listens to a queue and upon receiving a message, retrieves the message and sends a different TextMessage object to the queue. The example consists of five parts:

- Specifying the message-driven bean class
- Creating the deployment descriptor
- Configuring JBoss to deploy the message-driven bean
- Packaging the bean
- Writing the client application

These five parts are discussed in the following sections.

The Message-Driven Bean Class

Unlike session beans and entity beans, a message-driven bean has no home or remote interfaces. The only Java class that you need to write for the message-driven bean is the bean class itself. The code for the MyMDB message-driven bean is given in Listing 33.1.

Listing 33.1 **MyMDB Message-Driven Bean**

```
package com.brainysoftware.ejb;


import javax.ejb.MessageDrivenBean;
import javax.ejb.MessageDrivenContext;
import javax.ejb.EJBException;
import javax.jms.JMSException;
import javax.jms.Message;
import javax.jms.MessageListener;
import javax.jms.Queue;
import javax.jms.QueueConnection;
import javax.jms.QueueConnectionFactory;
import javax.jms.QueueSender;
import javax.jms.QueueSession;
import javax.jms.TextMessage;
import javax.naming.InitialContext;
import javax.naming.NamingException;


public class MyMDB implements MessageDrivenBean, MessageListener {
  MessageDrivenContext context = null;
  QueueConnection connection;
  QueueSession session;

  public MyMDB() {
```

```
    System.out.println("Constructing MyMDB");
  }

  public void setMessageDrivenContext(MessageDrivenContext context) {
    this.context = context;
    System.out.println("setMessageDrivenContext");
  }

  public void ejbCreate() throws EJBException {
    System.out.println("ejbCreate");
    try {
      InitialContext initContext = new InitialContext();
      QueueConnectionFactory qcf = (QueueConnectionFactory)
        initContext.lookup("java:comp/env/jms/QCF");
      connection = qcf.createQueueConnection();
      session = connection.createQueueSession(false,
➥QueueSession.AUTO_ACKNOWLEDGE);
      connection.start();
    }
    catch(Exception e) {
      throw new EJBException("Failed to initialize MyMDB", e);
    }
  }

  public void ejbRemove() {
    System.out.println("ejbRemove");
    context = null;
    try {
      if( session != null )
        session.close();
      if( connection != null )
        connection.close();
    }
    catch(JMSException e) {
      e.printStackTrace();
    }
  }

  public void onMessage(Message msg) {
    System.out.println("onMessage");
    try {
      TextMessage message = (TextMessage) msg;
      Queue queue = (Queue) msg.getJMSReplyTo();
      QueueSender sender = session.createSender(queue);
      TextMessage message2 = session.createTextMessage(message.getText());
      sender.send(message2);
      sender.close();
    }
    catch(Exception e) {
      e.printStackTrace();
    }
  }
}
```

Take a look at the ejbCreate method of the message-driven bean class. The first line of code after writing the method name to the Console is a try block that attempts to get a JNDI InitialContext object and perform a JNDI lookup to obtain a javax.jms.QueueConnectionFactory object, as follows:

```
try {
  InitialContext initContext = new InitialContext();
  QueueConnectionFactory qcf = (QueueConnectionFactory)
    initContext.lookup("java:comp/env/jms/QCF");
```

After you get the QueueConnectionFactory object, you use its createQueueConnection to construct a QueueConnection object, like this:

```
connection = qcf.createQueueConnection();
```

Then, you use the createQueueSession method of the QueueConnection interface to create a QueueSession object, as in the following code:

```
session = connection.createQueueSession(false,
➥QueueSession.AUTO_ACKNOWLEDGE);
```

Note that you pass false as the first argument to the createQueueSession method to indicate that you are not creating a transactional session object.

Finally, you start the QueueConnection object by invoking its start method with the following code:

```
connection.start();
```

Also important is the onMessage method that is inherited from the MessageListener interface. This method accepts a javax.jms.Message object representing the message that arrives, as you see here:

```
public void onMessage(Message msg) {
  .
  .
  .
}
```

The code assumes that the message is a TextMessage object and tries to cast the message to a TextMessage object:

```
try {
  TextMessage message = (TextMessage) msg;
```

The Message interface has the getJMSReplyTo method that returns a javax.jms.Destination object. Because it is a point-to-point domain, the Destination object should be a Queue object, as follows:

```
Queue queue = (Queue) msg.getJMSReplyTo();
```

Next, you can call the createSender method of the QueueSession interface, passing a Queue object. The return value of this method is a message producer, which is a QueueSender:

```
QueueSender sender = session.createSender(queue);
```

You then create a TextMessage object based on the message received by passing the text for the TextMessage to the createTextMessage method of the QueueSession object:

```
TextMessage message2 = session.createTextMessage(message.getText());
```

Now, you are ready to send the new message. You do this by calling the send method of the QueueSender object, as you see here:

```
sender.send(message2);
```

Finally, you call the close method to close the QueueSender object:

```
sender.close();
```

The Deployment Descriptor

Like other EJB applications incorporating session and entity beans, you need a deployment descriptor to deploy your message-driven bean. The deployment descriptor (ejb-jar.xml file) for this application is given in Listing 33.2.

Listing 33.2 **The Deployment Descriptor**

```
<?xml version="1.0"?>
<!DOCTYPE ejb-jar PUBLIC "-//Sun Microsystems, Inc.//DTD Enterprise
➥JavaBeans 2.0//EN" "http://java.sun.com/dtd/ejb-jar_2_0.dtd">

<ejb-jar>
  <enterprise-beans>
    <message-driven>
      <ejb-name>MyMDB</ejb-name>
      <ejb-class>com.brainysoftware.ejb.MyMDB</ejb-class>
      <transaction-type>Container</transaction-type>
      <acknowledge-mode>AUTO_ACKNOWLEDGE</acknowledge-mode>
      <message-driven-destination>
        <destination-type>javax.jms.Queue</destination-type>
      </message-driven-destination>
      <resource-ref>
        <res-ref-name>jms/QCF</res-ref-name>
        <res-type>javax.jms.QueueConnectionFactory</res-type>
        <res-auth>Container</res-auth>
      </resource-ref>
    </message-driven>
  </enterprise-beans>
</ejb-jar>
```

Note that under the <message-driven> element in Listing 33.2, you have the <acknowledge-mode> element that contains the value of AUTO_ACKNOWLEDGE.

Configuring the jboss.xml File

Specific to deploying the message-driven bean in JBoss, you need to configure the jboss.xml file with the file given in Listing 33.3.

Listing 33.3 **The jboss.xml File**

```
<?xml version="1.0" encoding="UTF-8"?>
<jboss>
  <enterprise-beans>
    <message-driven>
      <ejb-name>MyMDB</ejb-name>
      <destination-jndi-name>queue/MyQueue</destination-jndi-name>
      <resource-ref>
        <res-ref-name>jms/QCF</res-ref-name>
        <jndi-name>QueueConnectionFactory</jndi-name>
      </resource-ref>
    </message-driven>
  </enterprise-beans>
</jboss>
```

The reason you need a jboss.xml file is twofold.

First, the deployment descriptor does not specify the name of the queue the MyMDB bean listens to. Therefore, the queue must be specified by the bean deployer by incorporating this information in the jboss.xml file. Message-driven beans must always have a jboss.xml file for the specification of the destination name from which the beans are to receive messages.

The second reason you need a jboss.xml file is that you need to map the JMS QueueConnectionFactory reference in the deployment descriptor to the deployed JNDI name of the JBossMQ QueueConnectionFactory.

Packaging Your Message-Driven Bean

Now you are ready to package your entity bean. Do the following:

1. Compile all the .java class and place the .class files in the com/brainysoftware/ejb/ directory under your project directory.
2. Change directory to your project directory.
3. Type the following command:

```
jar cfv mdb.jar com/brainysoftware/ejb/MyMDB.class META-INF/
➥ejb-jar.xml
```

This command creates a .jar file called mdb.jar in the project directory. Copy this file into the deploy directory of JBoss. If JBoss is not running, start JBoss. If JBoss is already running, you don't need to do anything. JBoss's hot deploy feature will automatically try to deploy any package file saved into the deploy directory.

Writing the Client Application

To invoke the message-driven bean you deployed, you need a client application. You can use the application you developed in Chapter 32.

Summary

In this chapter, you learned how to write a message-driven bean by implementing the javax.ejb.MessageDrivenBean and the javax.jms.MessageListener interfaces. You also learned both how to develop an EJB application that uses a message-driven bean and how to deploy it in the JBoss application server.

IV

Appendixes

A Tomcat Installation and Configuration

TOMCAT IS THE MOST POPULAR REFERENCE implementation for servlets and JSP. At the time of this writing, the latest version of Tomcat at the time of this writing is 4.0.3, which implements the Servlet 2.3 and JSP 1.2 APIs. You need Tomcat or another reference implementation to run your servlets and JSP pages.

This appendix explains the installation and configuration of Tomcat in Windows NT/2000, UNIX, and Linux.

Tomcat Installation

Tomcat is written in Java. As such, it needs a Java compiler. Therefore, the first step in the installation is to download and install a JDK. Tomcat works with JDK 1.2 and later. The directory where you install the JDK is referred to as %JAVA_HOME%. The next steps vary, depending on the operating system on which you are installing Tomcat. The sections that follow explain the installation procedures for the different operating systems.

> **Note**
> If you have worked with previous versions of Tomcat, you'll see that installing Tomcat 4.0.x is much simpler than the previous versions.

Windows NT/2000 Installation

The key to installing Tomcat 4.0.x on Windows NT/2000 is the setting of the JAVA_HOME Environment variable. To install Tomcat on Windows NT/2000, follow these steps:

1. Download Tomcat binary from Apache Software Foundation's web site at `http://jakarta.apache.org/builds/jakarta-tomcat-4.0/release/`. Download the latest release version. For Windows installation, the easiest option for you may be to download the zip file. You can extract this file using your favorite zip program, such as WinZip. However, if you prefer, you can download any other file format.
2. Extract the compressed file into a directory. This directory is referred to as %CATALINA_HOME%.
3. Now you need to add the JAVA_HOME environment variable. Open the Control Panel and double-click the System applet.
4. Click the Advanced tab. You should see something similar to Figure A.1.

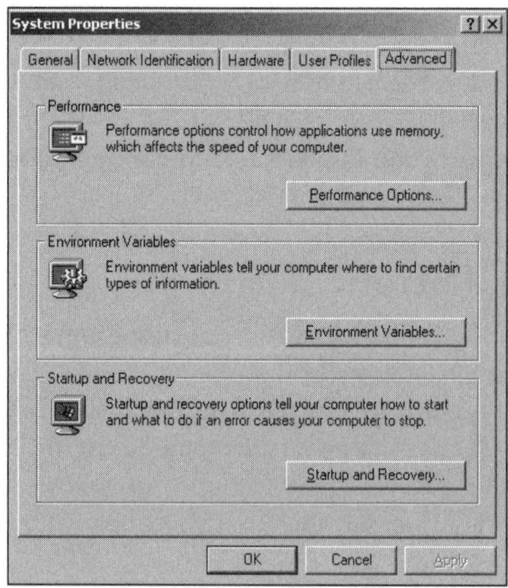

Figure A.1 The Advanced tab of the System applet in the Control Panel.

5. Click the Environment Variables button. You should see a screen similar to Figure A.2. You see two sections: the list of environment variables for the current user and the list of System environment variables. Add the new variable to the latter so that Tomcat can be used by other users.

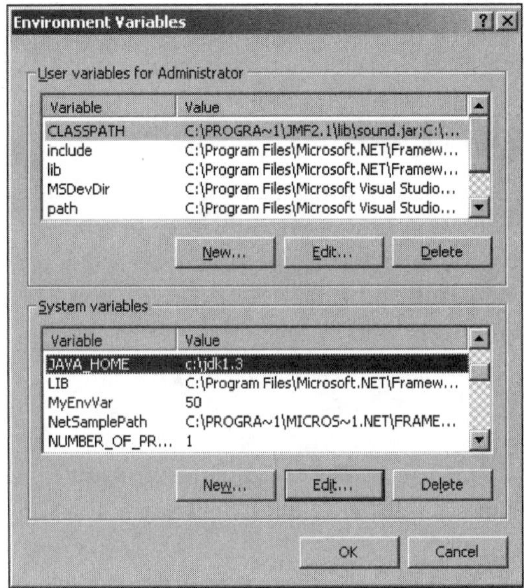

Figure A.2 The Environment Variables dialog box.

6. Click the New button in the System Variables section. The New System Variable dialog box appears (see Figure A.3).

New System Variable
Variable Name: JAVA_HOME
Variable Value: C:\jdk1.3
OK Cancel

Figure A.3 The New System Variable dialog box.

7. In the Variable Name box, type JAVA_HOME. In the Variable Value box, type the JDK installation directory. For example, if you installed the JDK in C:\jdk1.3 directory, enter C:\jdk1.3.
8. Click OK.

Now Tomcat is ready.

To run Tomcat, change the directory to the bin directory under %CATALINA_HOME%, and then type startup and press Enter.

Alternatively, you can use the following command:

```
%CATALINA_HOME%\bin\startup
```

Tomcat runs in a new console window. To stop Tomcat, simply close the console window.

In testing your servlet and JSP applications, you will need to start and stop Tomcat frequently. To help you run Tomcat quickly, you can create the following batch file and put in on the desktop:

```
cd C:\
cd InstallDirectory\bin
startup
```

In this code, InstallDirectory is the directory where you install Tomcat.

Now you can run Tomcat by double-clicking the batch file's icon.

To test whether Tomcat was installed properly, open your browser on the same computer you used to install Tomcat and direct it to the following URL:

```
http://localhost:8080
```

Warning

8080 is needed because Tomcat runs on port 8080 by default. Note you should not omit the http:// part of the URL.

You should see an image similar to Figure A.4.

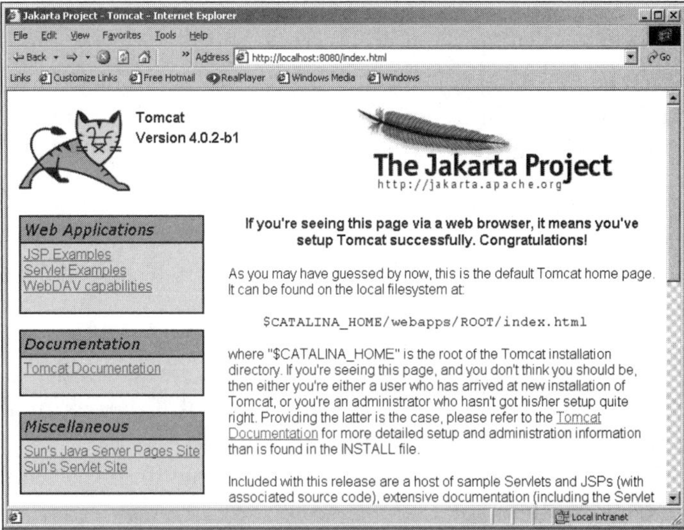

Figure A.4 Successful Tomcat installation.

If your computer is connected to a network, you can open the browser on a different computer and direct it to the following URL:

```
http://hostName:8080
```

In this line, hostName is the name of the computer on which Tomcat was installed.

UNIX/Linux Installation

Installation on UNIX/Linux is as simple as installation on Windows NT/2000, if not simpler. Again the key here is to create the: JAVA_HOME environment variable. In this example, it is assumed that JDK has been installed to the /usr/local/jdk1.3 directory. If you install the JDK and Tomcat in different directories, you need to change the code accordingly. The following steps show you how to install Tomcat on a UNIX/Linux computer:

1. Download Tomcat from the Apache Software Foundation's web site at `http://jakarta.apache.org`.
2. Extract the installation file to a directory. This directory will become %CATALINA_HOME%.
3. Add the JAVA_HOME environment variable. If you are using the bash shell, type the following command:

```
JAVA_HOME=/usr/local/jdk1.3
export JAVA_HOME
```

If you are using tcsh, type the following command:

```
setenv JAVA_HOME /usr/local/jdk1.3
```

Your Tomcat installation is now complete. To start Tomcat, run the startup.sh file in the bin directory under %CATALINA_HOME%. For example, from the bin directory, you can type ./startup.sh.

To stop Tomcat, run the shutdown.sh file in the bin directory under %CATALINA_HOME%. For example, from the bin directory, type ./shutdown.sh.

To test whether Tomcat was installed properly, open your browser on the computer on which you installed Tomcat and direct it to the following URL:

```
http://localhost:8080
```

Note that you should not omit the http:// part of the URL. You should see an image similar to the one shown in Figure A.4.

If your computer is connected to the network, you can open the browser in a different computer and direct it to the following URL:

```
http://hostName:8080
```

In this line, hostName is the computer name where Tomcat was installed.

Tomcat Directories

When you install Tomcat, the installation program creates a number of directories under %CATALINA_HOME%. Understanding the function of each subdirectory is important to configuring Tomcat and deploying your servlet and JSP applications.

The directories under %CATALINA_HOME% are shown in Table A.1.

Table A.1 **Subdirectories Under %CATALINA_HOME%**

Directory	**Description**
bin	Startup and shutdown scripts and other files.
classes	Unpacked classes global to web applications.
conf	Configuration files including server.xml (Tomcat's main configuration file) and the global web.xml (deployment descriptor) file.
server	Tomcat's archive files.
lib	Common classes in .jar files.
logs	Tomcat's log files.
common	Common classes for both Catalina and web applications.
webapps	Servlet and JSP applications.
work	Resulting servlets from the JSP pages translation.

Changing the Port

By default, Tomcat runs on port 8080. As a result, your users must always type the port number :8080 after the domain part in the URL. In fact, users must always type the port number unless Tomcat is run on port 80, the default port for HTTP.

You can change this by editing the Tomcat configuration file server.xml located in the conf directory under %CATALINA_HOME%.

First you need to find the following lines:

```
<!-- Define a non-SSL HTTP/1.1 Connector on port 8080 -->
<Connector className="org.apache.catalina.connector.http.HttpConnector"
  port="8080" minProcessors="5" maxProcessors="75"
  enableLookups="true" redirectPort="8443"
  acceptCount="10" debug="0" connectionTimeout="60000"
/>
```

You can see that in the third line there is the port attribute with a value of 8080. Change that value to 80 and save the file.

You need to restart Tomcat for this change to take effect. Now, you can call any page without including the port number in the URL.

On the UNIX/Linux platform, if you want to run a process using port numbers less than 1024, you must log in as the super user.

Note that you must not change Tomcat port to 80 if you are going to run Tomcat with other web servers, as discussed in the following sections.

Constructing a JSP Application

For each JSP application, you need a directory structure similar to that in Figure A.2, which shows a directory structure for an application called mail (highlighted). The mail directory is created under the webapps directory. In this example, there are other applications: admin, examples, ROOT, and test.

Underneath each JSP application are two important subdirectories: jsp and WEB-INF. Clearly, the jsp directory is for your JSP files, and it can contain subdirectories to organize your files. You also can place your static HTML files here.

WEB-INF holds two important subdirectories, classes and lib, and a configuration file called web.xml. For simple applications, you need only to copy the web.xml from the WEB-INF directory of one of the sample applications included with Tomcat installation and make modifications to this file.

The classes subdirectory is there for you to store classes such as JavaBeans that are needed by your application. The lib subdirectory is where you store archived Java class files that support your JSP application.

You also need to edit the server.xml file if you have placed your application outside the webapps directory. The Linux installation requires that you have the META-INF directory under your application even though you don't need to do anything to it.

B

The javax.servlet Package Reference

THE SERVLET 2.3 SPECIFICATION DEFINES TWO Java extension packages for developers who want to work with the servlet technology: the javax.servlet package and the javax.servlet.http package. The first package provides generic classes and interfaces that are protocol independent, and the second package, javax.servlet.http, contains classes and interfaces specific to HTTP.

This appendix presents the complete reference on the javax.servlet package. The javax.servlet.http package is presented in Appendix C, "javax.servlet.http PackageRefence." For brevity, a class or interface that belongs to the javax.servlet package is not written in its fully qualified name.

The javax.servlet package contains twelve interfaces, seven classes, and two exceptions. Figure B.1 shows the UML diagram for this package.

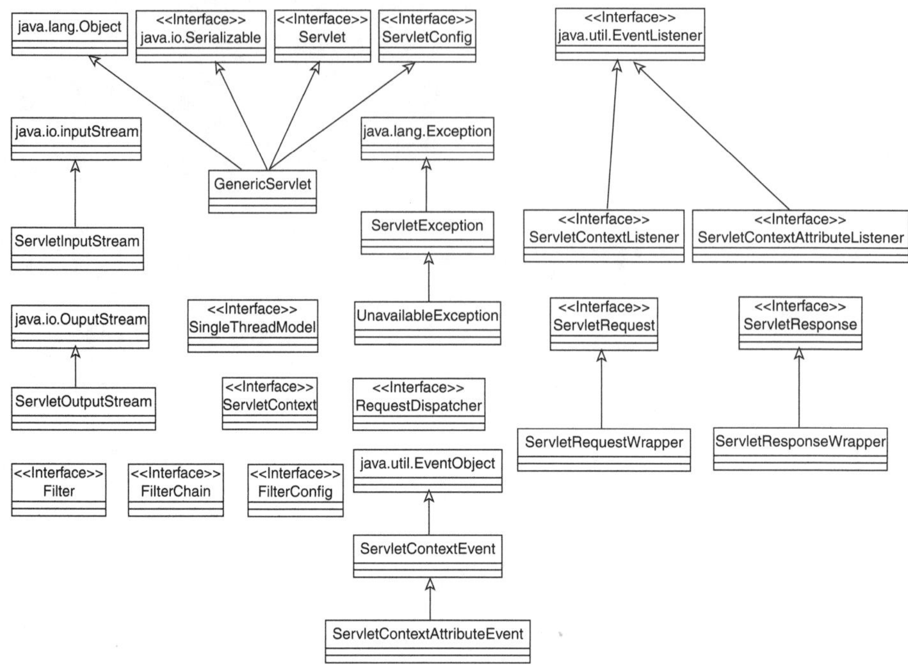

Figure B.1 The UML diagram for the javax.servlet package.

Tables B.1, B.2, and B.3 summarize the package interfaces, classes, and exceptions, respectively.

Table B.1 **The Interfaces in the javax.servlet Package**

Interface	Description
Filter	This interface represents a filter. A filter intercepts a request before the request is handled and can perform tasks on the request, the response, or both.
FilterChain	The servlet container creates a FilterChain object to provide a view into the invocation chain of a filtered request for a resource.
FilterConfig	The servlet container creates a FilterConfig object from which information, such as the filter name and initial parameters, can be obtained.
RequestDispatcher	Defines an object that dispatches a request to another dynamic resource, such as a servlet or a JSP page.
Servlet	The main interface that all servlets must implement either directly or indirectly.

Interface	Description
ServletConfig	Represents a servlet configuration object from which information, such as the servlet name, initial parameters, and the ServletContext object, can be obtained.
ServletContext	The ServletContext object is the interface between the servlet container and a servlet. One ServletContext object exists for each web application per Java Virtual Machine (JVM). In situations where the whole application resides in the same JVM, the ServletContext object can be used to share global information that will be available to any resource in the application.
ServletContext-AttributeListener	A class implementing this interface is used to receive notification of changes to the ServletContext object's attribute.
ServletContextListener	A class implementing this interface is used to receive notification of changes to the ServletContext object.
ServletRequest	Represents a request from a web client.
ServletResponse	Represents a response from the servlet to a web client.
SingleThreadModel	This interface is implemented by a servlet to guarantee that the servlet handles only one request at a time.

Table B.2 **The Classes in the javax.servlet Package**

Class	Description
GenericServlet	An abstract class that implements both the Servlet interface and the ServletConfig interface. You extend this class to create a protocol-independent servlet.
ServletContextAttributeEvent	The event class for notification of changes to the ServletContext object's attributes.
ServletContextEvent	The event class for notification of changes to the ServletContext object.
ServletInputStream	Represents an input stream for reading binary data from a client request.
ServletOutputStream	Represents an output stream for sending binary data to the client.
ServletRequestWrapper	Provides a wrapper to work conveniently with the ServletRequest interface.
ServletResponseWrapper	Provides a wrapper to work conveniently with the ServletResponse interface.

continues

Table B.2 **Continued**

Exception	Description
ServletException	A generic exception that a servlet can throw.
UnavailableException	An exception thrown when a servlet or filter is not available.

Interfaces

The following are the interfaces in the javax.servlet package. Each of the following sections describe an interface, its signature, and the interface's methods, if any.

Filter

The Filter interface represents a filter. You implement this interface to create a filter that intercepts a request and performs tasks on the request, the response to the request, or both.

Signature

```
public interface Filter
```

Methods

```
public void destroy()
```

The web container invokes this method when the filter is about to be taken out of service. The web container will wait until all threads within the filter's doFilter method have exited or after a timeout period has passed before calling this method. After this method is invoked, the web container will not call the doFilter method again upon this instance of the filter.

You can use this method to do some cleanup, such as releasing an object, closing a file, and so on.

```
public void doFilter(ServletRequest request, ServletResponse response,
➥FilterChain chain) throws java.io.IOException, ServletException
```

The web container invokes this method when a request/response pair is passed through the chain due to a client request for a resource path at the end of the chain:

```
public void init(FilterConfig filterConfig) throws ServletException
```

The web container calls this method when the filter is about to be put into service.

FilterChain

The servlet container creates a FilterChain object to provide a view into the invocation chain of a filtered request for a resource.

Signature

```
public interface FilterChain
```

Methods

```
public void doFilter(ServletRequest request, ServletResponse response) throws
➥java.io.IOException, ServletException
```

Causes the next filter in the chain to be invoked. If the calling filter is the last in the chain, it causes the resource at the end of the chain to be invoked.

FilterConfig

A filter configuration object that passes information from the web container to a filter.

Signature

```
public interface FilterConfig
```

Methods

```
public java.lang.String getFilterName()
```

Returns the name of the filter defined in the application's deployment descriptor.

```
public java.lang.String getInitParameter(java.lang.String name)
```

Returns the value of the specified initialization parameter, or returns null if the parameter does not exist.

```
public java.util.Enumeration getInitParameterNames()
```

Returns all the names of the filter's initialization parameter.

```
public ServletContext getServletContext()
```

Returns the ServletContext object.

RequestDispatcher

Defines an object that dispatches a request to another dynamic resource, such as a servlet or a JSP page.

Signature

```
public interface RequestDispatcher
```

Methods

```
public void forward(ServletRequest request, ServletResponse response)
throws java.io.IOException, ServletException
```

Forwards the servlet's request object to another static or dynamic resource.

```
public void include(ServletRequest request, ServletResponse response)
throws java.io.IOException, ServletException
```

Includes the processing output of another static or dynamic resource. In a nutshell, this has the same effect as a programmatic server-side include.

Servlet

The Servlet interface is the central abstraction of the Java servlet technology. All servlets must implement this interface either directly or indirectly.

Signature

```
public interface Servlet
```

Methods

```
public void destroy()
```

This is one of the life-cycle methods that is called by the servlet container when the servlet is being taken out of service.

```
public ServletConfig getServletConfig()
```

Returns the servlet's ServletConfig object containing initialization and startup parameters.

```
public java.lang.String getServletInfo()
```

Returns information about the current servlet.

```
public void init(ServletConfig config)
```

This is one of the life-cycle methods called by the servlet container when the servlet is being placed into service.

```
public void service(ServletRequest request, ServletResponse response)
throws java.io.IOException, ServletException
```

This is one of the life-cycle methods called by the servlet container when the servlet is requested, to allow the servlet to respond to a request.

ServletConfig

This interface represents a servlet configuration object that passes information from the servlet container to a servlet during the servlet initialization.

Signature

```
public interface ServletConfig
```

Methods

```
public java.lang.String getInitParameter(java.lang.String name)
```

Returns the value of the specified initialization parameter, or returns null if the parameter does not exist.

```
public java.util.Enumeration getInitParameterNames()
```

Returns an Enumeration containing all the parameter names of the servlet.

```
public ServletContext getServletContext()
```

Returns the ServletContext object.

```
public java.lang.String getServletName()
```

Returns the servlet name as specified in the application deployment descriptor.

ServletContext

The ServletContext object is the interface between the servlet container and a servlet. There is one ServletContext object for each web application per Java Virtual Machine (JVM). In those cases in which the whole application resides in the same JVM, the ServletContext object can be used to share global information that will be available to any resource in the application.

Signature

```
public interface ServletContext
```

Methods

```
public java.lang.Object getAttribute(java.lang.String name)
```

Returns the ServletContext object's attribute whose name is specified as the argument.

```
public java.util.Enumeration getAttributeNames()
```

Returns an Enumeration containing all the attribute names in the ServletContext object.

```
public ServletContext getContext(java.lang.String uri)
```

Returns the ServletContext object corresponding to the specified URI.

```
public java.lang.String getInitParameter(java.lang.String name)
```

Returns the value of the ServletContext's initial parameter for the specified parameter name.

```
public java.util.Enumeration getInitParameterNames()
```

Returns an Enumeration containing all the parameter names in the ServletContext object.

```
public int getMajorVersion()
```

Returns the major version of the Servlet API that the servlet container supports.

```
public java.lang.String getMimeType(java.lang.String file)
```

Returns the MIME type of file specified in the argument, or null if the MIME type is not known.

```
public int getMinorVersion()
```

Returns the minor version of the Servlet API that the servlet container supports.

```
public RequestDispatcher getNamedDispatcher(java.lang.String name)
```

Returns a wrapper RequestDispatcher object for the servlet whose name is specified in the argument.

```
public java.lang.String getRealPath(java.lang.String path)
```

Returns the real path for the virtual path specified as the argument.

```
public RequestDispatcher getRequestDispatcher(java.lang.String path)
```

Returns a wrapper RequestDispatcher object for the resource located at the path specified as the argument.

```
public java.net.URL getResource(java.lang.String path)
```

Returns a URL to the resource that is mapped to the path specified as the argument. The path must begin with a "/" and is interpreted as relative to the current context root.

```
public java.io.InputStream getResourceAsStream(java.lang.String path)
```

Returns the resource at the path specified as the argument.

```
public java.util.Set getResourcePaths(java.lang.String path)
```

Returns a listing containing all the paths to resources within the application whose longest subpath matches the path specified in the argument.

```
public java.lang.String getServerInfo()
```

Returns the servlet container's name and version number.

```
public Servlet getServlet(java.lang.String name) throws ServletException
```

This method is deprecated. In Servlet API 2.3, this method returns null. In previous versions, this method returns a servlet from a ServletContext object.

```
public java.lang.String getServletContextName()
```

Returns the value of the display-name element as specified in the deployment descriptor.

```
public java.util.Enumeration getServletNames()
```

This method is deprecated. In Servlet API 2.3, this method always returns an empty Enumeration object. It was originally used to retrieve all the servlet names.

```
public java.util.Enumeration getServlets()
```

This method is deprecated. Originally it retrieved all the servlets in the application. In Servlet API 2.3, it always returns an empty Enumeration object.

```
public void log(java.lang.Exception exception, java.lang.String message)
```

This method is deprecated. It was originally used to write an exception's stack trace and an error message to the servlet log file.

```
public void log(java.lang.String message)
```

Writes a message to the servlet log file.

```
public void log(java.lang.String message, java.lang.Throwable throwable)
```

Writes an error message and a stack trace for the Throwable object specified as the argument.

```
public void removeAttribute(java.lang.String name)
```

Removes the attribute whose name is specified as the argument from the ServletContext object.

```
public void setAttribute(java.lang.String name, java.lang.Object object)
```

Binds an object to a name in the ServletContext object. If an attribute with the same name already exists, the attribute value will be replaced with the new object.

ServletContextAttributeListener

A class implementing this interface is used to receive notification of changes to the ServletContext object's attribute.

Signature

```
public interface ServletContextAttributeListener extends
➥java.util.EventListener
```

Methods

```
public void attributeAdded(ServletContextAttributeEvent scae)
```

This method is called after an attribute is added to the ServletContext object.

```
public void attributeRemoved(ServletContextAttributeEvent scae)
```

This method is called after an attribute is removed from the ServletContext object.

```
public void attributeReplaced(ServletContextAttributeEvent scae)
```

This method is called after an attribute is replaced in the ServletContext object.

ServletContextListener

A class implementing this interface is used to receive notification of changes to the ServletContext object.

Signature

```
public interface ServletContextListener extends java.util.EventListener
```

Methods

```
public void contextDestroyed(ServletContextEvent sce)
```

This method is called as a notification that the ServletContext object is about to be destroyed; that is, the servlet container is about to be shut down.

```
public void contextInitialized(ServletContextEvent sce)
```

This method is called as a notification that the ServletContext object is about to be initialized; that is, the web application is ready to service clients' requests.

ServletRequest

Represents a request from a web client.

Signature

```
public interface ServletRequest
```

Methods

```
public java.lang.Object getAttribute(java.lang.String name)
```

Obtains the attribute whose name is specified in the argument from the ServletRequest object. This method returns null if there is no attribute having the specified name.

```
public java.lang.Enumeration getAttributeNames()
```

Returns all the attribute names from the ServletRequest object.

```
public java.lang.String getCharacterEncoding()
```

Returns the encoding used in the request body.

```
public int getContentLength()
```

Returns the length of the request body in bytes.

```
public java.lang.String getContentType()
```

Returns the MIME type of the request body, or returns null if the content type is not known.

```
public ServletInputStream getInputStream()
```

Returns the request body as binary data. The method must not be called if getReader has been called, and vice versa.

```
public java.util.Locale getLocale()
```

Returns the preferred Locale for the content that the client will accept.

```
public java.util.Enumeration getLocales()
```

Returns all the Locale objects starting from the more preferred locales that the client will accept. Locales are those specified in the Accept-Language header. If the request does not contain this header, this method returns the locale for the server.

```
public java.lang.String getParameter(java.lang.String name)
```

Returns the value of the parameter whose name is specified in the argument.

```
public java.util.Map getParameterMap()
```

Returns all the request parameters in a java.util.Map object.

```
public java.util.Enumeration getParameterNames()
```

Returns all the parameter names in the request.

```
public java.lang.String[] getParameterValues(java.lang.String name)
```

Returns the values of the parameter whose name is given as the argument.

```
public java.lang.String getProtocol()
```

Returns the name and version number of the protocol used to send the request.

```
public java.io.BufferedReader getReader()
```

Returns the request body as character data. This method must not be called after the getInputStream method is called, and vice versa.

```
public java.lang.String getRealPath(java.lang.String path)
```

This method is deprecated. You should use the getRealPath method of the ServletContext interface instead.

```
public java.lang.String getRemoteAddr()
```

Returns the IP address of the client computer.

```
public java.lang.String getRemoteHost()
```

Returns the DNS name of the client computer.

```
public RequestDispatcher getRequestDispatcher(java.lang.String path)
```

Returns a wrapper RequestDispatcher object for the resource whose path is given as the argument.

```
public java.lang.String getScheme()
```

Returns the protocol used for this request; for example, http, https, or ftp.

```
public java.lang.String getServerName()
```

Returns the host name of the server receiving the request.

```
public int getServerPort()
```

Returns the port number on which the request was received.

```
public boolean isSecure()
```

Indicates whether the request is sent using a secure channel, such as HTTPS.

```
public void removeAttribute(java.lang.String name)
```

Removes the attribute whose name is specified in the argument from the ServletRequest object.

```
public void setAttribute(java.lang.String name, java.lang.Object object)
```

Stores a name/object pair in the ServletRequest object.

```
public void setCharacterEncoding(java.lang.String env)
throws java.io.UnsupportedEncodingException
```

Sets a new character encoding for the request body.

ServletResponse

This interface represents the response from the servlet to a web client.

Signature

```
public interface ServletResponse
```

Methods

```
public void flushBuffer() throws java.io.IOException
```

Forces the content of the buffer to be sent to the client and clears the buffer.

```
public int getBufferSize()
```

Returns the buffer size for the response.

```
public java.lang.String getCharacterEncoding()
```

Returns the character set for the MIME body of the response.

```
public java.util.Locale getLocale()
```

Returns the locale for the response.

```
public ServletOutputStream getOutputStream() throws java.io.IOException
```

Returns a ServletOutputStream object to write binary data in the response. This method must not be called after the getWriter method is called, and vice versa.

```
public java.io.PrintWriter getWriter() throws java.io.IOException
```

Returns a PrintWriter object to write character text to be sent to the client.

```
public boolean isCommitted()
```

Indicates whether the response has been committed. A committed response has had its status code set and its headers written.

```
public void reset()
```

Clears the buffer content and the status code and headers.

```
public void resetBuffer()
```

Clears the buffer content without clearing the status code or headers.

```
public void setBufferSize(int size)
```

Sets the buffer size of the response.

```
public void setContentLength(int length)
```

Sets the length of the content body of the response in HTTP servlets by setting the HTTP Content-Length header.

```
public void setContentType(java.lang.String type)
```

Sets the response content type.

```
public void setLocale(java.util.Locale locale)
```

Sets the locale of the response.

SingleThreadModel

This interface is implemented by a servlet to guarantee that the servlet handles only one request at a time. This interface does not have any method.

Signature

```
public interface SingleThreadModel
```

Classes

The following are the classes in the javax.servlet package. Each of the following sections describes a class, its signature, and its methods, if any.

GenericServlet

An abstract class that implements both the Servlet interface and the ServletConfig interface. You extend this class to create a protocol-independent servlet.

Signature

```
public abstract class GenericServlet implements Servlet, ServletConfig,
➥java.io.Serializable
```

Methods

```
public void destroy()
```

The servlet container invokes this method to indicate to the servlet that it is being taken out of service.

```
public java.lang.String getInitParameter(java.lang.String name)
```

Returns the value of an initial parameter whose name is specified as the argument.

```
public java.util.Enumeration getInitParameterNames()
```

Returns all the initial parameter names.

```
public ServletConfig getServletConfig()
```

Sets the servlet's ServletConfig object.

```
public ServletContext getServletContext()
```

Returns the ServletContext object.

```
public java.lang.String getServletInfo()
```

Returns the information about the servlet.

```
public java.lang.String getServletName()
```

Returns the servlet's name.

```
public void init() throws ServletException
```

This method is provided for convenience so that the programmer does not have to call super.init(config).

```
public void init(ServletConfig config) throws ServletException
```

The servlet container invokes this method to indicate to the servlet that it is being put into service.

```
public void log(java.lang.String message)
```

Writes a message to the servlet log file.

```
public void log(java.lang.String message, java.lang.Throwable throwable)
```

Writes an error message and the stack trace of Throwable object passed in as an argument to the servlet log file.

```
public abstract void service(ServletRequest request, ServletResponse
response)
```

The servlet container invokes this method to allow the servlet to service a client.

ServletContextAttributeEvent

The event class for notification of changes to the ServletContext object's attributes.

Signature

```
public class ServletContextAttributeEvent extends ServletContextEvent
```

Methods

```
public java.lang.String getName()
```

Returns the name of the ServletContext attribute that changed.

```
public java.lang.Object getValue()
```

Returns the value of the ServletContext attribute that changed.

ServletContextEvent

The event class for notifications on changes to the ServletContext object.

Signature

```
public class ServletContextEvent extends java.util.EventObject
```

Methods

```
public ServletContext getServletContext()
```

Returns the ServletContext object that changed.

ServletInputStream

Represents an input stream for reading binary data from a client request.

Signature

```
public abstract class ServletInputStream extends java.io.InputStream
```

Methods

```
public int readLine(byte[] b, int off, int len) throws java.io.IOException
```

Reads the input stream, one line at a time. The bytes read are placed into the byte array. This method returns -1 if it reaches the end of the input stream before reading the maximum number of bytes.

ServletOutputStream

Represents an output stream for sending binary data to the client.

Signature

```
public abstract class ServletOutputStream extends java.io.OutputStream
```

Methods

```
public void print(boolean b) throws java.io.IOException
```

Sends a boolean to the client.

```
public void print(char c) throws java.io.IOException
```

Sends a character to the client.

```
public void print(double d) throws java.io.IOException
```

Sends a double to the client.

```
public void print(float f) throws java.io.IOException
```

Sends a float to the client.

```
public void print(int i) throws java.io.IOException
```

Sends an int to the client.

```
public void print(long l) throws java.io.IOException
```

Sends a long to the client.

```
public void print(String s) throws java.io.IOException
```

Sends a String to the client.

```
public void println(boolean b) throws java.io.IOException
```

Sends a boolean to the client followed by a carriage return-line feed.

```
public void println(char c) throws java.io.IOException
```

Sends a char to the client followed by a carriage-return linefeed.

```
public void println(double d) throws java.io.IOException
```

Sends a double to the client followed by a carriage-return linefeed.

```
public void println(float f) throws java.io.IOException
```

Sends a float to the client followed by a carriage-return linefeed.

```
public void println(int i) throws java.io.IOException
```

Sends an int to the client followed by a carriage–return linefeed.

```
public void println(long l) throws java.io.IOException
```

Sends a long to the client followed by a carriage-return linefeed.

```
public void println(String s) throws java.io.IOException
```

Sends a String to the client followed by a carriage-return linefeed.

ServletRequestWrapper

Provides a wrapper to work conveniently with the ServletRequest interface.

Signature

```
public class ServletRequestWrapper implements ServletRequest
```

Methods

```
public java.lang.Object getAttribute(java.lang.String name)
```

If not overridden, this method calls the getAttribute method on the wrapped request object.

```
public java.lang.Enumeration getAttributeNames()
```

If not overridden, this method calls the getAttributeNames method on the wrapped request object.

```
public java.lang.String getCharacterEncoding()
```

If not overridden, this method calls the getCharacterEncoding method on the wrapped request object.

```
public int getContentLength()
```

If not overridden, this method calls the getContentLength method on the wrapped request object.

```
public java.lang.String getContentType()
```

If not overridden, this method calls the getContentType method on the wrapped request object.

```
public ServletInputStream getInputStream()
```

If not overridden, this method calls the getInputStream method on the wrapped request object.

```
public java.util.Locale getLocale()
```

If not overridden, this method calls the getLocale method on the wrapped request object.

```
public java.util.Enumeration getLocales()
```

If not overridden, this method calls the getLocales method on the wrapped request object.

```
public java.lang.String getParameter(java.lang.String name)
```

If not overridden, this method calls the getParameter method on the wrapped request object.

```
public java.util.Map getParameterMap()
```

If not overridden, this method calls the getParameterMap method on the wrapped request object.

```
public java.util.Enumeration getParameterNames()
```

If not overridden, this method calls the getParameterNames method on the wrapped request object.

```
public java.lang.String[] getParameterValues(java.lang.String name)
```

If not overridden, this method calls the getParameterValues method on the wrapped request object.

```
public java.lang.String getProtocol()
```

If not overridden, this method calls the getProtocol method on the wrapped request object.

```
public java.io.BufferedReader getReader()
```

If not overridden, this method calls the getReader method on the wrapped request object.

```
public java.lang.String getRealPath(java.lang.String path)
```

If not overridden, this method calls the getRealPath method on the wrapped request object.

```
public java.lang.String getRemoteAddr()
```

If not overridden, this method calls the getRemoteAddr method on the wrapped request object.

```
public java.lang.String getRemoteHost()
```

If not overridden, this method calls the getRemoteHost method on the wrapped request object.

```
public ServletRequest getRequest()
```

Returns the wrapped request object.

```
public RequestDispatcher getRequestDispatcher(java.lang.String path)
```

If not overridden, this method calls the getRequestDispatcher method on the wrapped request object.

```
public java.lang.String getScheme()
```

If not overridden, this method calls the getScheme method on the wrapped request object.

```
public java.lang.String getServerName()
```

If not overridden, this method calls the getServerName method on the wrapped request object.

```
public int getServerPort()
```

If not overridden, this method calls the getServerPort method on the wrapped request object.

```
public boolean isSecure()
```

If not overridden, this method calls the isSecure method on the wrapped request object.

```
public void removeAttribute(java.lang.String name)
```

If not overridden, this method calls the removeAttribute method on the wrapped request object.

```
public void setAttribute(java.lang.String name, java.lang.Object object)
```

If not overridden, this method calls the setAttribute method on the wrapped request object.

```
public void setCharacterEncoding(java.lang.String env)
throws java.io.UnsupportedEncodingException
```

If not overridden, this method calls the setCharacterEncoding method on the wrapped request object.

```
public void setRequest(ServletRequest request) throws
➥java.lang.IllegalArgumentException
```

Set the request object being wrapped.

ServletResponseWrapper

Provides a wrapper to work conveniently with the ServletResponse interface.

Signature

```
public class ServletRequestWrapper implements ServletResponse
```

Methods

```
public void flushBuffer() throws java.io.IOException
```

If not overridden, this method calls the flushBuffer method on the wrapped response object.

```
public int getBufferSize()
```

If not overridden, this method calls the getBufferSize method on the wrapped response object.

```
public java.lang.String getCharacterEncoding()
```

If not overridden, this method calls the getCharacterEncoding method on the wrapped response object.

```
public java.util.Locale getLocale()
```

If not overridden, this method calls the getLocale method on the wrapped response object.

```
public ServletOutputStream getOutputStream() throws java.io.IOException
```

If not overridden, this method calls the getOutputStream method on the wrapped response object.

```
public ServletResponse getResponse() throws java.io.IOException
```

Returns the wrapped ServletResponse object.

```
public java.io.PrintWriter getWriter() throws java.io.IOException
```

If not overridden, this method calls the getWriter method on the wrapped response object.

```
public boolean isCommitted()
```

If not overridden, this method calls the isCommitted method on the wrapped response object.

```
public void reset()
```

If not overridden, this method calls the reset method on the wrapped response object.

```
public void resetBuffer()
```

If not overridden, this method calls the resetBuffer method on the wrapped response object.

```
public void setBufferSize(int size)
```

If not overridden, this method calls the setBufferSize method on the wrapped response object.

```
public void setContentLength(int length)
```

If not overridden, this method calls the setContentLength method on the wrapped response object.

```
public void setContentType(java.lang.String type)
```

If not overridden, this method calls the setContentType method on the wrapped response object.

```
public void setLocale(java.util.Locale locale)
```

If not overridden, this method calls the setLocale method on the wrapped response object.

```
public void setResponse(ServletResponse response)
```

Sets the response being wrapped.

Exceptions

The following are the exceptions in the javax.servlet package. Each of the following sections describe an exception, its signature, and its methods, if any.

ServletException

A generic exception that a servlet can throw.

Signature

```
public class ServletException extends java.lang.Exception.
```

Method

```
public java.lang.Throwable getRootCause()
```

Returns the exception that caused this ServletException.

UnavailableException

An exception thrown when a servlet or filter is not available.

Signature

```
public class UnavailableException extends ServletException.
```

Methods

```
public Servlet getServlet()
```

This method is deprecated. It returns the servlet that reported unavailability.

```
public int getUnavailableSeconds()
```

Returns the number of seconds the servlet expects to be temporarily unavailable. A negative number indicates that the servlet is unavailable permanently.

```
public boolean isPermanent()
```

Indicates whether the unavailability is permanent.

C

The javax.servlet.http Package Reference

THIS APPENDIX PRESENTS THE JAVAX.SERVLET.HTTP package as defined in the Servlet 2.3 Specification. This is the second of the two packages used in the servlet application development. The other package, javax.servlet, was given in Appendix B, "The javax.servlet Package Reference."

For brevity, in the description of each class and interface in this appendix, a type that belongs to the javax.servlet.http package is not written in its fully qualified name.

The javax.servlet.http package contains eight interfaces and seven classes. Figure C.1 shows the UML diagram for this package.

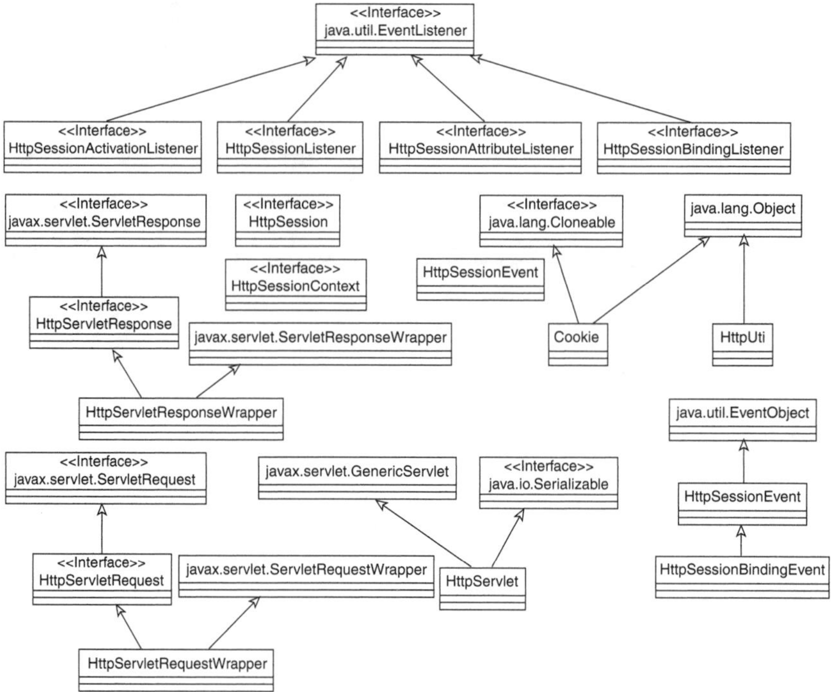

Figure C.1 The UML diagram for the javax.servlet.http package.

Tables C.1 and C.2 summarize the package interfaces and classes, respectively.

Table C.1 **The Interfaces in the javax.servlet.http Package**

Interface	Description
HttpServletRequest	Represents an HTTP client request.
HttpServletResponse	Represents an HTTP response from the server.
HttpSession	This interface defines a session specific to the user requesting the servlet.
HttpSessionActivationListener	A class implementing this interface is used to receive notification when the session will be passivated and activated.
HttpSessionAttributeListener	A class implementing this interface is used to receive notification of changes to the HttpSession object's attribute.
HttpSessionBindingListener	A class implementing this interface receives notification when it is bound to or unbound from a session.

Interface	Description
HttpSessionContext	This interface has been deprecated as of Servlet API 2.1 for security reasons.
HttpSessionListener	A class implementing this interface receives notification when there is a change to the list of active sessions.

Table C.2 **The Classes in the javax.servlet.http Package**

Class	Description
Cookie	Defines a cookie.
HttpServlet	An abstract class to be subclassed by an HTTP servlet.
HttpServletRequestWrapper	A wrapper class for working conveniently with the HttpServletRequest interface.
HttpServletResponseWrapper	A wrapper class for working conveniently with the HttpServletResponse interface.
HttpSessionBindingEvent	Events of this type are sent to an object implementing HttpSessionBindingListener when it is bound or unbound from a session, or to a HttpSessionAttributeListener that has been configured in the deployment descriptor when an attribute is bound, unbound, or replaced in a session.
HttpSessionEvent	Represents event notification for changes to session objects.
HttpUtils	This class has been deprecated as of Servlet API 2.3 and its methods have been moved to the request interfaces.

Interfaces

The following are the interfaces in the javax.servlet.http package. Each of the following sections describe an interface, its signature, and the interface's methods, if any.

HttpServletRequest

This interface represents an HTTP client request.

Signature

```
public interface HttpServletRequest extends javax.servlet.ServletRequest
```

Fields

```
public static final java.lang.String BASIC_AUTH
```

An identifier for the Basic authentication. The value of this field is "BASIC".

```
public static final java.lang.String CLIENT_CERT_AUTH
```

An identifier for the Basic authentication. The value of this field is "CLIENT_CERT".

```
public static final java.lang.String DIGEST_AUTH
```

An identifier for the Basic authentication. The value of this field is "DIGEST".

```
public static final java.lang.String FORM_AUTH
```

An identifier for the Basic authentication. The value of this field is "FORM".

Methods

```
public java.lang.String getAuthType()
```

Returns the type of the authentication scheme used to protect the servlet.

```
public java.lang.String getContextPath()
```

Returns the request context from the request URI.

```
public Cookie[] getCookies()
```

Returns the cookie collection of the request. If there is no cookie in this request, null is returned.

```
public long getDateHeader(java.lang.String name)
```

Returns the value of a header that contains a date. An example of a header that contains a date is If-Modified-Since.

```
public java.lang.String getHeader(java.lang.String name)
```

Returns the value of the header whose name is passed in as the argument.

```
public java.util.Enumeration getHeaderNames()
```

Returns all the header names in the request.

```
public java.util.Enumeration getHeaders(java.lang.String name)
```

Returns all the values of the header whose name is passed in as the argument.

```
public int getIntHeader(java.lang.String name) throws
java.lang.NumberFormatException
```

Returns the value of the header whose name is passed in as the argument. The method returns -1 if a header by the specified name does not exist. If the header value cannot be converted into an integer, the method throws a java.lang.NumberFormatException.

```
public java.lang.String getMethod()
```

Returns the method used to send the request. The most frequently used methods are GET and POST.

```
public java.lang.String getPathInfo()
```

Returns the information that follows the servlet path but precedes the query string.

```
public java.lang.String getPathTranslated()
```

Returns the path information after the servlet name but before the query string, and translates it to a real path.

```
public java.lang.String getQueryString()
```

Returns the query string in the request URL.

```
public java.lang.String getRemoteUser()
```

Returns the user login name.

```
public java.lang.String getRequestSessionId()
```

Returns the session identifier sent by the client. The session identifier returned by the client may not be the same as the identifier of the current session if the previous session has expired.

```
public java.lang.String getRequestURI()
```

Returns the part of the request's URL from the protocol name up to the query string in the first line of the request. For example, if the first line of the request is POST /app/page.jsp?name=ab HTTP/1.1, the getRequestURI method returns /app/page.jsp.

```
public java.lang.StringBuffer getRequestURL()
```

Returns the modified version of the client's URL so that the return value contains a protocol, server name, port number, and server path, but does not include the query string.

```
public java.lang.String getServletPath()
```

Returns the request URL that is used to call the servlet.

```
public HttpSession getSession()
```

Returns the session associated with this request. If the request does not have one, create a new HttpSession object for this user.

```
public HttpSession getSession(boolean create)
```

Returns the session associated with this request. If the request does not have one, create a new HttpSession object for this user if create is true.

```
public java.security.Principal getUserPrincipal()
```

Returns the Principal object containing the name of the current authenticated user, or returns null if the current user has not been authenticated.

```
public boolean isRequestedSessionIdFromCookie()
```

Indicates whether the session identifier from the request was sent as a cookie.

```
public boolean isRequestedSessionIdFromUrl()
```

Indicates whether the session identifier from the request was sent as part of the URL.

```
public boolean isRequestedSessionIdValid()
```

Indicates whether the session identifier from the request is associated with a valid HttpSession object.

```
public boolean isUserInRole(java.lang.String role)
```

Indicates whether the authenticated user is included in the specified role.

HttpServletResponse

This interface represents an HTTP response.

Signature

```
public interface HttpServletResponse extends javax.servlet.ServletResponse
```

Fields

```
public static final int SC_ACCEPTED
```

Status code (202) indicating that a request was accepted for processing, but was not completed.

```
public static final int SC_BAD_GATEWAY
```

Status code (502) indicating that the server received an invalid response from another server it consulted when acting as a proxy or gateway.

```
public static final int SC_BAD_REQUEST
```

Status code (400) indicating that the client sent a syntactically incorrect request.

```
public static final int SC_CONFLICT
```

Status code (409) indicating that there was a conflict with the current state of the resource so that the request could not be completed.

```
public static final int SC_CONTINUE
```

Status code (100) indicating that the client can continue.

```
public static final int SC_CREATED
```

Status code (201) indicating that the request succeeded and created a new resource on the server.

```
public static final int SC_EXPECTATION_FAILED
```

Status code (417) indicating that the server could not meet the expectation given in the Expect request header.

```
public static final int SC_FORBIDDEN
```

Status code (403) indicating that the server understood the request, but refused to fulfill it.

```
public static final int SC_GATEWAY_TIMEOUT
```

Status code (504) indicating that the server did not receive a timely response from the upstream server while acting as a gateway or proxy.

```
public static final int SC_GONE
```

Status code (410) indicating that the requested resource is no longer available on the server and there is no forwarding address.

```
public static final int SC_HTTP_VERSION_NOT_SUPPORTED
```

Status code (505) indicating that the server does not support the HTTP protocol used to send the request.

```
public static final int SC_INTERNAL_SERVER_ERROR
```

Status code (500) indicating that the server could not fulfill the request due to an internal error.

```
public static final int SC_LENGTH_REQUIRED
```

Status code (411) indicating that there is no defined Content-Length header and therefore the request cannot be processed.

```
public static final int SC_METHOD_NOT_ALLOWED
```

Status code (405) indicating that the method specified in the Request-Line is not allowed for the resource requested.

```
public static final int SC_MOVED_PERMANENTLY
```

Status code (301) indicating that the requested resource has been moved permanently to a new location.

```
public static final int SC_MOVED_TEMPORARILY
```

Status code (302) indicating that the requested resource has been moved temporarily to a new location.

```
public static final int SC_MULTIPLE_CHOICES
```

Status code (300) indicating that the requested resource corresponds to any one of a set of representations, each with its own specific location.

```
public static final int SC_NO_CONTENT
```

Status code (204) indicating that there is no information to send to the client.

```
public static final int SC_NON_AUTHORITATIVE_INFORMATION
```

Status code (203) indicating that the meta information sent by the client did not come from the server.

```
public static final int SC_NOT_ACCEPTABLE
```

Status code (406) indicating that the resource-generated response in the format is not acceptable, according to the client's accept header.

```
public static final int SC_NOT_FOUND
```

Status code (404) indicating that the requested resource cannot be found.

```
public static final int SC_NOT_IMPLEMENTED
```

Status code (501) indicating that the server does not implement the functionality requested by the client.

```
public static final int SC_NOT_MODIFIED
```

Status code (304) indicating that a conditional GET operation found that the resource was available and not modified.

```
public static final int SC_OK
```

Status code (200) indicating that the request succeeded normally.

```
public static final int SC_PARTIAL_CONTENT
```

Status code (206) indicating that the server could fulfill only part of the GET request.

```
public static final int SC_PAYMENT_REQUIRED
```

Status code (402), reserved for future use.

```
public static final int SC_PRECONDITION_FAILED
```

Status code (412) indicating that the precondition in at least one header evaluated to false when tested on the server.

```
public static final int SC_PROXY_AUTHENTICATION_REQUIRED
```

Status code (407) indicating that the client is required to first authenticate itself with the proxy.

```
public static final int SC_REQUEST_ENTITY_TOO_LARGE
```

Status code (413) indicating that the request cannot be processed because it is larger than what the server is willing to accept.

```
public static final int SC_REQUEST_TIMEOUT
```

Status code (408) indicating that the client did not complete the request within a specified time period.

```
public static final int SC_REQUEST_URI_TOO_LONG
```

Status code (414) indicating that the request cannot be processed because the URI is longer than what the server is willing to accept.

```
public static final int SC_REQUESTED_RANGE_NOT_SATISFIABLE
```

Status code (416) indicating that the requested byte range cannot be served.

```
public static final int SC_RESET_CONTENT
```

Status code (205) indicating that the agent should reset the document view, which caused the request to be sent.

```
public static final int SC_SEE_OTHER
```

Status code (303) indicating that the response to the request is available under a different URI.

```
public static final int SC_SERVICE_UNAVAILABLE
```

Status code (503) indicating that the server is overloaded and is temporarily unavailable.

```
public static final int SC_SWITCHING_PROTOCOLS
```

Status code (101) indicating that the server is switching protocols according to the Upgrade header.

```
public static final int SC_TEMPORARY_REDIRECT
```

Status code (307) indicating that the requested resource is temporarily available under a different URI.

```
public static final int SC_UNAUTHORIZED
```

Status code (401) indicating that the request came from an unauthorized user.

```
public static final int SC_UNSUPPORTED_MEDIA_TYPE
```

Status code (415) indicating that the request format is not supported by the requested resource for the requested method.

```
public static final int SC_USE_PROXY
```

Status code (305) indicating that the requested resource must be accessed through the proxy specified by the Location field.

Methods

```
public void addCookie(Cookie cookie)
```

Adds a cookie to the response.

```
public void addDateHeader(java.lang.String name, long date)
```

Adds a header with the specified name and a date value to the response.

```
public void addHeader(java.lang.String name, java.lang.String value)
```

Adds a header with the specified name and a String value to the response.

```
public void addIntHeader(java.lang.String name, int value)
```

Adds a header with the specified name and an integer value to the response.

```
public boolean containsHeader(java.lang.String name)
```

Indicates whether the response contains a specified header.

```
public java.lang.String encodeRedirectUrl(java.lang.String url)
```

This method is deprecated, use encodeRedirectURL instead.

```
public java.lang.String encodeRedirectURL(java.lang.String url)
```

Encodes a URL to be safely passed in to the sendRedirect method.

```
public java.lang.String encodeUrl(java.lang.String url)
```

This method is deprecated, use encodeURL instead.

```
public java.lang.String encodeURL(java.lang.String url)
```

Encodes the specified URL by adding the session identifier to it.

```
public void sendError(int sc) throws java.io.IOException
```

Sends an HTTP error message by specifying the status code. An IOException is thrown if the response has been committed.

```
public void sendError(int sc, java.lang.String message)
throws java.io.IOException
```

Sends an HTTP error message by specifying the status code and a descriptive message. An IOException is thrown if the response has been committed.

```
public void sendRedirect(java.lang.String location) throws
java.io.IOException
```

Forces the client to request a new location specified as the argument.

```
public void setDateHeader(java.lang.String name, long date)
```

Adds a header having a date value to the response. If the response already has a header by the specified name, the old value is overwritten.

```
public void setHeader(java.lang.String name, java.lang.String value)
```

Adds a header having a String value to the response. If the response already has a header by the specified name, the old value is overwritten.

```
public void setIntHeader(java.lang.String name, int value)
```

Adds a header having an integer value to the response. If the response already has a header by the specified name, the old value is overwritten.

```
public void setStatus(int sc)
```

Sets the status code of the response.

```
public void setStatus(int sc, java.lang.String message)
```

This method is deprecated, use sendError or setStatus instead.

HttpSession

This interface represents a user session.

Signature

```
public interface HttpSession
```

Methods

```
public java.lang.Object getAttribute(java.lang.String name)
```

Returns the attribute bound to the name given as the argument. If no attribute having the specified name is found, null is returned.

```
public java.util.Enumeration getAttributeNames()
```

Returns all the attribute names in the HttpSession object.

```
public long getCreationTime()
```

Returns a long representing the time the HttpSession object was created.

```
public java.lang.String getId()
```

Returns the session identifier.

```
public long getLastAccessedTime()
```

Returns the last time the client sent a request associated with this HttpSession object.

```
public int getMaxInactiveInterval()
```

Returns the number of seconds the server will wait after the last access from the client before invalidating this session.

```
public javax.servlet.ServletContext getServletContext()
```

Returns the ServletContext to which this HttpSession object belongs.

```
public HttpSessionContext getSessionContext()
```

This method is deprecated.

```
public java.lang.Object getValue(java.lang.String name) throws
java.lang.IllegalStateException
```

This method is deprecated; use getAttribute instead.

```
public java.lang.String[] getValueNames() throws
➥java.lang.IllegalStateException
```

This method is deprecated; use getAttributeNames instead.

```
public void invalidate() throws java.lang.IllegalStateException
```

Removes this HttpSession object.

```
public boolean isNew()throws java.lang.IllegalStateException
```

Indicates whether this session is created in the current request.

```
public void putValue(java.lang.String name, java.lang.Object value)
throws java.lang.IllegalStateException
```

This method is deprecated; use setAttribute instead.

```
public void removeAttribute(java.lang.String name) throws
➥java.lang.IllegalStateException
```

Removes the attribute bound to the specified name.

```
public void removeValue(java.lang.String name) throws
➥java.lang.IllegalStateException
```

This method is deprecated; use removeAttribute instead.

```
public void setAttribute(java.lang.String name, java.lang.Object value)
throws java.lang.IllegalStateException
```

Adds an attribute bound with the given name to the HttpSession object.

```
public void setMaxInactiveInterval(int interval)
```

Sets the number of seconds the server will wait after the last access from the client before invalidating the HttpSession object.

HttpSessionActivationListener

This interface is implemented by any class that needs to receive notification when the session will be passivated and activated.

Signature

```
public interface HttpSessionActivationListener extends
java.util.EventListener
```

Methods

```
public void sessionDidActivate(HttpSessionEvent he)
```

This method is invoked by the servlet container after the session has been activated.

```
public void sessionWillPassivate(HttpSessionEvent he)
```

This method is invoked by the servlet container before the session is passivated.

HttpSessionAttributeListener

This interface is implemented by any class that needs to receive notification on changes to the HttpSession object's attribute.

Signature

```
public interface HttpSessionAttributeListener extends java.util.EventListener
```

Methods

```
public void attributeAdded(HttpSessionBindingEvent he)
```

This method is invoked by the servlet container after an attribute has been added to a session.

```
public void attributeRemoved(HttpSessionBindingEvent he)
```

This method is invoked by the servlet container after an attribute is removed from a session.

```
public void attributeReplaced(HttpSessionBindingEvent he)
```

This method is invoked by the servlet container after an attribute is replaced in a session.

HttpSessionBindingListener

This interface is implemented by any class that needs to receive notification when it is bound to or unbound from a session.

Signature

```
public interface HttpSessionBindingListener extends java.util.EventListener
```

Methods

```
public void valueBound(HttpSessionBindingEvent he)
```

This method is invoked by the servlet container when the object is being bound to a session.

```
public void valueUnbound(HttpSessionBindingEvent he)
```

This method is invoked by the servlet container when the object is being unbound from a session.

HttpSessionContext

This interface is deprecated for security reasons.

HttpSessionListener

This interface is implemented by any class that needs to get notification when there is a change to the list of active sessions.

Signature

```
public interface HttpSessionListener extends java.util.EventListener
```

Methods

```
public void sessionCreated(HttpSessionEvent he)
```

This method is invoked by the servlet container after a session is created.

```
public void sessionDestroyed(HttpSessionEvent he)
```

This method is invoked by the servlet container after a session is destroyed.

Classes

The following are the classes in the javax.servlet.http package. The following sections describe each class, its signature, its fields, and its methods, if any.

Cookie

This class represents a cookie.

Signature

```
public class Cookie implements java.lang.Cloneable
```

Methods

```
public java.lang.Object clone()
```

Returns a copy of this cookie.

```
public java.lang.String getComment()
```

Returns the description of the cookie, or returns null if none is available.

```
public java.lang.String getDomain()
```

Returns the domain for this cookie.

```
public int getMaxAge()
```

Returns the number of seconds the cookie will persist. A return value of -1 indicates that the cookie will be destroyed when the user closes the browser.

```
public java.lang.String getName()
```

Returns the name of the cookie.

```
public java.lang.String getPath()
```

Returns the path on the server to which the browser returns this cookie.

```
public boolean getSecure()
```

Indicates whether the cookie is sent over a secure protocol.

```
public java.lang.String getValue()
```

Returns the cookie value.

```
public java.lang.String getVersion()
```

Returns the version number of the protocol with which the cookie complies. Version 0 complies with the original specification by Netscape and version 1 complies with RFC 2109.

```
public void setComment(java.lang.String comment)
```

Adds a description to the cookie.

```
public void setDomain(java.lang.String domain)
```

Defines a domain in which the cookie should be presented.

```
public void setMaxAge(int age)
```

Specifies the cookie's age in seconds.

```
public void setPath(java.lang.String path)
```

Specifies the cookie path.

```
public void setSecure(boolean secure)
```

Indicates to the browser whether the cookie should be sent only over a secure protocol.

```
public void setValue(java.lang.String value)
```

Replaces the old value with the one specified as the argument.

```
public void setVersion(int version)
```

Specifies the version of the protocol with which the cookie complies.

HttpServlet

An abstract class to be subclassed by an HTTP servlet.

Signature

```
public abstract class HttpServlet extends javax.servlet.GenericServlet
➥implements java.io.Serializable
```

Methods

```
protected void doDelete(HttpServletRequest request, HttpServletResponse
➥response) throws javax.servlet.ServletException, java.io.IOException
```

This method is invoked by the servlet container when a request is sent using the DELETE method.

```
protected void doGet(HttpServletRequest request, HttpServletResponse
response) throws javax.servlet.ServletException, java.io.IOException
```

This method is invoked by the servlet container when a request is sent using the GET method.

```
protected void doHead(HttpServletRequest request, HttpServletResponse
➥response) throws javax.servlet.ServletException, java.io.IOException
```

This method is invoked by the servlet container when a request is sent using the HEAD method.

```
protected void doOptions(HttpServletRequest request, HttpServletResponse
➥response) throws javax.servlet.ServletException, java.io.IOException
```

This method is invoked by the servlet container when a request is sent using the OPTIONS method.

```
protected void doPost(HttpServletRequest request, HttpServletResponse
➥response) throws javax.servlet.ServletException, java.io.IOException
```

This method is invoked by the servlet container when a request is sent using the POST method.

```
protected void doPut(HttpServletRequest request, HttpServletResponse
response) throws javax.servlet.ServletException, java.io.IOException
```

This method is invoked by the servlet container when a request is sent using the PUT method.

```
protected void doTrace(HttpServletRequest request, HttpServletResponse
➥response) throws javax.servlet.ServletException, java.io.IOException
```

This method is invoked by the servlet container when a request is sent using the TRACE method.

```
protected long getLastModified(HttpServletRequest request)
```

Returns the time the HttpServletRequest was last modified.

```
protected void service(HttpServletRequest request, HttpServletResponse
response) throws javax.servlet.ServletException, java.io.IOException
```

This method is called by the other service method to receive an HTTP request. This method will then dispatch the request to the corresponding do*XXX* method.

```
public void service(javax.servlet.ServletRequest request,
javax.servlet.ServletResponse response)
```

```
throws javax.servlet.ServletException, java.io.IOException
```

Dispatches client requests to the protected service method.

HttpServletRequestWrapper

A wrapper class for working conveniently with the HttpServletRequest interface.

Signature

```
public class HttpServletRequestWrapper extends
➥javax.servlet.ServletRequestWrapper implements
➥javax.servlet.http.HttpServletRequest
```

Methods

```
public java.lang.String getAuthType()
```

If not overridden, this method returns the similar method on the wrapped request object.

```
public java.lang.String getContextPath()
```

If not overridden, this method returns the similar method on the wrapped request object.

```
public Cookie[] getCookies()
```

If not overridden, this method returns the similar method on the wrapped request object.

```
public long getDateHeader(java.lang.String name)
```

If not overridden, this method returns the similar method on the wrapped request object.

```
public java.lang.String getHeader(java.lang.String name)
```

If not overridden, this method returns the similar method on the wrapped request object.

```
public java.util.Enumeration getHeaderNames()
```

If not overridden, this method returns the similar method on the wrapped request object.

```
public java.util.Enumeration getHeaders(java.lang.String name)
```

If not overridden, this method returns the similar method on the wrapped request object.

```
public int getIntHeader(java.lang.String name) throws
java.lang.NumberFormatException
```

If not overridden, this method returns the similar method on the wrapped request object.

```
public java.lang.String getMethod()
```

If not overridden, this method returns the similar method on the wrapped request object.

```
public java.lang.String getPathInfo()
```

If not overridden, this method returns the similar method on the wrapped request object.

```
public java.lang.String getPathTranslated()
```

If not overridden, this method returns the similar method on the wrapped request object.

```
public java.lang.String getQueryString()
```

If not overridden, this method returns the similar method on the wrapped request object.

```
public java.lang.String getRemoteUser()
```

If not overridden, this method returns the similar method on the wrapped request object.

```
public java.lang.String getRequestSessionId()
```

If not overridden, this method returns the similar method on the wrapped request object.

```
public java.lang.String getRequestURI()
```

If not overridden, this method returns the similar method on the wrapped request object.

```
public java.lang.StringBuffer getRequestURL()
```

If not overridden, this method returns the similar method on the wrapped request object.

```
public java.lang.String getServletPath()
```

If not overridden, this method returns the similar method on the wrapped request object.

```
public HttpSession getSession()
```

If not overridden, this method returns the similar method on the wrapped request object.

```
public HttpSession getSession(boolean create)
```

If not overridden, this method returns the similar method on the wrapped request object.

```
public java.security.Principal getUserPrincipal()
```

If not overridden, this method returns the similar method on the wrapped request object.

```
public boolean isRequestedSessionIdFromCookie()
```

If not overridden, this method returns the similar method on the wrapped request object.

```
public boolean isRequestedSessionIdFromUrl()
```

If not overridden, this method returns the similar method on the wrapped request object.

```
public boolean isRequestedSessionIdValid()
```

If not overridden, this method returns the similar method on the wrapped request object.

```
public boolean isUserInRole(java.lang.String role)
```

If not overridden, this method returns the similar method on the wrapped request object.

HttpServletResponseWrapper

A wrapper class for working conveniently with the HttpServletResponse interface.

Signature

```
public class HttpServletResponseWrapper extends
javax.servlet.ServletResponseWrapper implements
javax.servlet.http.HttpServletResponse
```

Methods

```
public void addCookie(Cookie cookie)
```

If not overridden, this method returns the similar method on the wrapped response object.

```
public void addDateHeader(java.lang.String name, long date)
```

If not overridden, this method returns the similar method on the wrapped response object.

```
public void addHeader(java.lang.String name, java.lang.String value)
```

If not overridden, this method returns the similar method on the wrapped response object.

```
public void addIntHeader(java.lang.String name, int value)
```

If not overridden, this method returns the similar method on the wrapped response object.

```
public boolean containsHeader(java.lang.String name)
```

If not overridden, this method returns the similar method on the wrapped response object.

```
public java.lang.String encodeRedirectUrl(java.lang.String url)
```

If not overridden, this method returns the similar method on the wrapped response object.

```
public java.lang.String encodeRedirectURL(java.lang.String url)
```

If not overridden, this method returns the similar method on the wrapped response object.

```
public java.lang.String encodeUrl(java.lang.String url)
```

If not overridden, this method returns the similar method on the wrapped response object.

```
public java.lang.String encodeURL(java.lang.String url)
```

If not overridden, this method returns the similar method on the wrapped response object.

```
public void sendError(int sc) throws java.io.IOException
```

If not overridden, this method returns the similar method on the wrapped response object.

```
public void sendError(int sc, java.lang.String message)
throws java.io.IOException
```

If not overridden, this method returns the similar method on the wrapped response object.

```
public void sendRedirect(java.lang.String location) throws
java.io.IOException
```

If not overridden, this method returns the similar method on the wrapped response object.

```
public void setDateHeader(java.lang.String name, long date)
```

If not overridden, this method returns the similar method on the wrapped response object.

```
public void setHeader(java.lang.String name, java.lang.String value)
```

If not overridden, this method returns the similar method on the wrapped response object.

```
public void setIntHeader(java.lang.String name, int value)
```

If not overridden, this method returns the similar method on the wrapped response object.

```
public void setStatus(int sc)
```

If not overridden, this method returns the similar method on the wrapped response object.

```
public void setStatus(int sc, java.lang.String message)
```

If not overridden, this method returns the similar method on the wrapped response object.

HttpSessionBindingEvent

Events of this type are sent to an object implementing HttpSessionBindingListener when it is bound or unbound from a session, or to a HttpSessionAttributeListener that has been configured in the deployment descriptor when an attribute is bound, unbound, or replaced in a session.

Signature

```
public class HttpSessionBindingEvent extends
javax.servlet.http.HttpSessionEvent
```

Methods

```
public java.lang.String getName()
```

Returns the name with which the session attribute is bound.

```
public HttpSession getSession()
```

Returns the changed session.

```
public java.lang.Object getValue()
```

Returns the session attribute that has been added, removed, or modified.

HttpSessionEvent

This class represents event notification for changes to session objects.

Signature

```
public class HttpSessionEvent extends java.util.EventObject
```

Methods

```
public HttpSession getSession()
```

Returns the changed session.

HttpUtils

This class is deprecated.

D

The javax.servlet.jsp Package Reference

THE JSP 1.2 SPECIFICATION DEFINES TWO Java extension packages for developers who want to work with the servlet technology: the javax.servlet.jsp package and the javax.servlet.jsp.tagext package. This appendix contains the complete reference of the javax.servlet.jsp package. The javax.servlet.jsp.tagext package is presented in Appendix E, "The javax.servlet.jsp.tagext Package Reference."

In this appendix, a type that belongs to the javax.servlet.jsp package is not written in its fully qualified name.

Tables D.1 and D.2 summarize the package interfaces and classes, respectively.

Table D.1 **The Interfaces in the javax.servlet.jsp Package**

Interface	Description
HttpJspPage	This interface defines a contract between a JSP page implementation class and a JSP container. Objects of this type are obtained from the JspFactory class.
JspPage	This interface is the superinterface of theHttpJspPage interface and defines a contract between a JSP page implementation class and a JSP container. JspPage objects are obtained from the JspFactory class.

Table D.2 **The Classes in the javax.servlet.jsp Package**

Class	Description
JspEngineInfo	Provides information on the JSP container.
JspException	The base class for all JSP exceptions.
JspFactory	An abstract class providing a number of methods from which various runtime objects for a JSP page can be obtained. An instance of the subclass of this class is created by the JSP container.
JspTagException	The exception to be thrown by a tag handler.
JspWriter	A JspWriter object corresponds to the implicit variable out in a JSP page, to which output to the client is written.
PageContext	An abstract class that needs to be subclassed so that the JSP container can provide implementation-dependent implementations.

Interfaces

The following are the interfaces in the javax.servlet.jsp package. Each of the following sections describes an interface, its signature, and its methods, if any.

HttpJspPage

This interface defines a contract between a JSP page implementation class and a JSP container. Objects of this type are obtained from the JspFactory class.

Signature

```
public interface HttpJspPage extends JspPage
```

Method

```
public void _jspService(javax.servlet.http.HttpServletRequest request,
➥javax.servlet.http.HttpServletResponse response)
throws javax.servlet.ServletException, java.io.IOException
```

This method is defined automatically by the JSP container and should not be defined by the JSP page author.

JspPage

This interface is the superinterface of the HttpJspPage interface and defines a contract between a JSP page implementation class and a JSP container. JspPage objects are obtained from the JspFactory class.

This interface has three methods, two of which are jspInit and jspDestroy. The third method, _jspService, depends on the specific protocol used. The signature of the _jspService method cannot be expressed in a generic way.

Signature

```
public interface JspPage extends javax.servlet.Servlet
```

Methods

```
public void jspDestroy()
```

This method is invoked when the JSP page is about to be destroyed.

```
public void jspInit()
```

This method is invoked when the JSP page is initialized.

Classes

The following are the classes in the javax.servlet.jsp package. Each of the following sections describes a class, its signature, its fields, and its methods, if any.

JspEngineInfo

This class provides information on the JSP container.

Signature

```
public abstract class JspEngineInfo
```

Method

```
public java.lang.String getSpecificationVersion()
```

Returns the JSP specification version number supported by the JSP container.

JspException

The base class for all JSP exceptions.

Signature

```
public class JspException extends java.lang.Exception
```

Method

```
public java.lang.Throwable getRootCause()
```

Returns the root exception that caused this exception.

JspFactory

An abstract class that provides a number of methods from which various run-time objects for a JSP page can be obtained. An instance of the subclass of this class is created by the JSP container.

Signature

```
public abstract class JspFactory
```

Methods

```
public static synchronized JspFactory getDefaultFactory()
```

Returns the default JspFactory object for this implementation.

```
public abstract PageContext getPageContext(javax.servlet.Servlet servlet,
➥javax.Servlet.ServletRequest request, javax.servlet.ServletResponse
➥response, java.lang.String errorPageUrl, boolean needsSession, int
➥buffer, boolean autoFlush)
```

Returns a PageContext object for the calling servlet and the current request and response.

```
public abstract void releasePageContext(PageContext pageContext)
```

This method is invoked to release a previously allocated PageContext object.

```
public static synchronized void setDefaultFactory(JspFactory defaultFactory)
```

This method is invoked by the JSP container to set the default JspFactory object for this implementation.

JspTagException

This is an exception to be thrown by a tag handler. This method does not define any method.

Signature

```
public class JspTagException extends JspException
```

JspWriter

A JspWriter object corresponds to the implicit variable out in a JSP page, to which output to the client is written.

Signature

```
public abstract class JspWriter extends java.io.Writer
```

Fields

```
protected boolean autoFlush
```

Indicates whether the content of the JspWriter object will be automatically flushed.

```
protected int bufferSize
```

The size of the buffer.

```
public static final int DEFAULT_BUFFER
```

A constant specifying the use of the implementation default size for the buffer.

```
public static final int NO_BUFFER
```

A constant specifying that no buffer is used.

```
public static final int UNBOUNDED_BUFFER
```

A constant specifying that the JspWriter is buffered and unbounded.

Methods

```
public abstract void clear() throws java.io.IOException
```

Clears the buffer. If the content of the buffer has been committed, a java.io.IOException is thrown.

```
public abstract void clearBuffer() throws java.io.IOException
```

Clears the buffer. If the content of the buffer has been committed, *no* exception is thrown.

```
public abstract void close() throws java.io.IOException
```

Flushes the buffer and closes the stream.

```
public abstract void flush() throws java.io.IOException
```

Flushes the buffer.

```
public int getBufferSize()
```

Returns the buffer size.

```
public abstract int getRemaining()
```

Returns the remaining unused number of bytes in the buffer.

```
public boolean isAutoFlush()
```

Indicates whether the autoflush feature is enabled.

```
public abstract void newLine() throws java.io.IOException
```

Sends a line separator character.

```
public abstract void print(boolean value) throws java.io.IOException
```

Prints a boolean.

```
public abstract void print(char value) throws java.io.IOException
```

Prints a char.

```
public abstract void print(char[] value) throws java.io.IOException
```

Prints an array of chars.

```
public abstract void print(double value) throws java.io.IOException
```

Prints a double.

```
public abstract void print(float value) throws java.io.IOException
```

Prints a float.

```
public abstract void print(int value) throws java.io.IOException
```

Prints an integer.

```
public abstract void print(long value) throws java.io.IOException
```

Prints a long.

```
public abstract void print(java.lang.Object object) throws
java.io.IOException
```

Prints an object.

```
public abstract void print(java.lang.String string) throws
java.io.IOException
```

Prints a String.

```
public abstract void println() throws java.io.IOException
```

Prints a line separator string.

```
public abstract void println(boolean value) throws java.io.IOException
```

Prints a boolean followed by a line separator string.

```
public abstract void println(char value) throws java.io.IOException
```

Prints a char followed by a line separator string.

```
public abstract void println(char[] value) throws java.io.IOException
```

Prints an array of chars followed by a line separator string.

```
public abstract void println(double value) throws java.io.IOException
```

Prints a double followed by a line separator string.

```
public abstract void println(float value) throws java.io.IOException
```

Prints a float followed by a line separator string.

```
public abstract void println(int value) throws java.io.IOException
```

Prints an integer followed by a line separator string.

```
public abstract void println(long value) throws java.io.IOException
```

Prints a long followed by a line separator string.

```
public abstract void println(java.lang.Object object) throws
java.io.IOException
```

Prints an object followed by a line separator string.

```
public abstract void println(java.lang.String string) throws
java.io.IOException
```

Prints a String followed by a line separator string.

PageContext

The PageContext class is an abstract class that needs to be subclassed so that the JSP container can provide implementation-dependent implementations.

Signature

```
public abstract class PageContext
```

Fields

```
public static final java.lang.String APPLICATION
```

Name to store the javax.servlet.ServletContext object in the current PageContext name table.

```
public static final int APPLICATION_SCOPE
```

An integer representing the application scope.

```
public static final java.lang.String CONFIG
```

The identifier used as the name to store the javax.servlet.ServletConfig object in the current PageContext name table.

```
public static final java.lang.String EXCEPTION
```

The identifier used as the name to store the uncaught exception in the ServletRequest attribute list and in the PageContext name table.

```
public static final java.lang.String OUT
```

The identifier used as the name to store the JspWriter object in the currnet PageContext name table.

```
public static final java.lang.String PAGE
```

The identifier used as the name to store the javax.servlet.Servlet object in the current PageContext name table.

```
public static final int PAGE_SCOPE
```

An integer representing the page scope.

```
public static final java.lang.String PAGE_CONTEXT
```

Name to store the current PageContext object in its own name table.

```
public static final java.lang.String REQUEST
```

Name to store the javax.servlet.ServletRequest object in the current PageContext name table.

```
public static final int REQUEST_SCOPE
```

An integer representing the request scope.

```
public static final java.lang.String RESPONSE
```

Name to store the javax.servlet.ServletResponse object in the current PageContext name table.

```
public static final java.lang.String SESSION
```

Name to store the javax.servlet.http.HttpSession object in the current PageContext name table.

```
public static final int SESSION_SCOPE
```

An integer representing the session scope.

Methods

```
public abstract java.lang.Object findAttribute(java.lang.String name)
```

Searches the attribute whose name is specified as the argument in the request, page, session (if valid), and application scopes.

```
public abstract void forward(java.lang.String localUrl)
throws javax.servlet.ServletException, java.io.IOException,
java.lang.IllegalArgumentException, java.lang.IllegalStateException,
java.lang.SecurityException
```

Forwards the request to another local resource.

```
public abstract java.lang.Object getAttribute(java.lang.String name)
```

Returns the attribute whose name is specified as the argument from the page scope.

```
public abstract java.lang.Object getAttribute(java.lang.String name, int
scope)
```

Returns the attribute whose name is specified as the argument from the specified scope.

```
public abstract java.util.Enumeration getAttributeNamesInScope(int scope)
```

Returns the names of attributes in the specified scope.

```
public abstract int getAttributesScope(java.lang.String name)
```

Returns the scope of the attribute whose name is specified as the argument.

```
public abstract java.lang.Exception getException()
```

Returns the current exception object.

```
public abstract JspWriter getOut()
```

Returns the current JspWriter object.

```
public abstract java.lang.Object getPage()
```

Returns the current page.

```
public abstract javax.servlet.ServletRequest getRequest()
```

Returns the current request object.

```
public abstract javax.servlet.ServletResponse getResponse()
```

Returns the current response object.

```
public abstract javax.servlet.ServletConfig getServletConfig()
```

Returns the current ServletConfig object.

```
public abstract javax.servlet.ServletContext getServletContext()
```

Returns the current ServletContext object.

```
public abstract javax.servlet.http.HttpSession getSession()
```

Returns the session object associated with the request.

```
public abstract void handlePageException(java.lang.Exception e)
throws javax.servlet.ServletException, java.io.IOException,
➥java.lang.NullPointerException, java.lang.SecurityException
```

Processes an unhandled page-level exception.

```
public abstract void handlePageException(java.lang.Throwable e)
throws javax.servlet.ServletException, java.io.IOException,
➥java.lang.NullPointerException, java.lang.SecurityException
```

Processes an unhandled page-level exception.

```
public abstract void include(java.lang.String relativeUrl)
throws javax.servlet.ServletException, java.io.IOException,
➥java.lang.IllegalArgumentException, java.lang.SecurityException
```

Processes an external resource and returns the command to the calling thread.

```
public abstract void initialize(javax.servlet.Servlet servlet,
➥javax.servlet.ServletRequest request, javax.servlet.ServletResponse
➥response, java.lang.String errorPageUrl, boolean needsSession, int
➥bufferSize, boolean autoFlush)
throws java.io.IOException, java.lang.IllegalStateException,
➥java.lang.IllegalArgumentException
```

This method is invoked by the JSP container to prepare the current page to service incoming requests.

```
public JspWriter popBody()
```

Returns the JspWriter saved by a previous pushBody method call.

```
public javax.servlet.jsp.tagext.BodyContent pushBody()
```

Returns a new BodyContent object, saves the current JspWriter object, and updates the "out" attribute value.

```
public void release()
```

This method is invoked by the JSP container to reset the internal state of the current PageContext object.

```
public abstract void removeAttribute(java.lang.String name)
```

Removes the first attribute found by searching the scopes.

```
public abstract void removeAttribute(java.lang.String name, int scope)
```

Removes the attribute in the specified scope.

```
public abstract void setAttribute(java.lang.String name, java.lang.Object
attribute) throws java.lang.NullPointerException
```

Adds an attribute to the page.

```
public abstract void setAttribute(java.lang.String name, java.lang.Object
attribute, int scope) throws java.lang.NullPointerException,
java.lang.IllegalArgumentException
```

Adds an attribute to the specified scope.

E

The javax.servlet.jsp.tagext Package Reference

THIS APPENDIX PRESENTS THE COMPLETE reference on the javax.servlet.jsp.tagext package—the second package specified in the JSP 1.2 Specification. The first package, javax.servlet.jsp, is shown in Appendix D, "The java.servlet.jsp Package Reference."

In this appendix, a type that belongs to the javax.servlet.jsp.tagext package is not written in its fully qualified name.

Tables E.1 and E.2 summarize the package interfaces and classes, respectively.

Table E.1 **The Interfaces in the javax.servlet.jsp.tagext Package**

Interface	Description
BodyTag	This interface is implemented by a tag handler that needs to manipulate its body.
IterationTag	This interface adds a method that deals with the re-evaluation of its body.
Tag	This interface needs to be implemented by a tag handler that does not need to manipulate its body.
TryCatchFinally	An auxiliary interface of the other interfaces to support additional hooks for managing resources.

Table E.2 **The Classes in the javax.servlet.jsp.tagext Package**

Class	Description
BodyContent	This class represents the body content of the tag.
BodyTagSupport	This is a base class that is subclassed by a tag handler that needs to manipulate its body.
PageData	This class provides information on a JSP page that is available at translation time.
TagAttributeInfo	This class provides information on the tag attributes.
TagData	This class provides information on the tag instance available at translation time.
TagExtraInfo	An optional class that provides additional translation-time information not available in the Tag Library Descriptor file.
TagInfo	This class provides the information for the tag in a tag library.
TagLibraryInfo	This class provides information time associated with a taglib directive and its TLD file that is available at translation time.
TagLibraryValidator	This class is a validator class for a JSP page that is available at translation time.
TagSupport	This class provides convenient methods and is a base class to be extended by new tag handlers.
TagVariableInfo	This class provides information for a tag in a Tag Library.
VariableInfo	This class provides information on the scripting variables.

Interfaces

The following are the interfaces in the javax.servlet.jsp.tagext package. Each of the following sections describes an interface, its signature, and its methods and fields, if any.

BodyTag

This interface is implemented by a tag handler that needs to manipulate its body.

Signature

```
public interface BodyTag extends IterationTag
```

Fields

```
public static final int EVAL_BODY_BUFFERED
```

A return value for the doStartTag method in a class that implements the BodyTag interface.

```
public static final int EVAL_BODY_TAG
```

This field is deprecated.

Methods

```
public void doInitBody()
throws javax.servlet.jsp.JspException
```

This method is invoked by the JSP container before the body is evaluated the first time.

```
public void setBodyContent(BodyContent bodyContent)
```

This method sets the BodyContent.

IterationTag

This interface adds a method that deals with the re-evaluation of its body.

Signature

```
public interface IterationTag extends Tag
```

Field

```
public static final int EVAL_BODY_AGAIN
```

A return value for the doAfterBody method, indicating that the container should evaluate the body again.

Method

```
public int doAfterBody() throws javax.servlet.jsp.JspException
```

This method is invoked by the JSP container to process body evaluation or body re-evaluation.

Tag

This interface is implemented by a tag handler that does not need to manipulate its body.

Signature

```
public interface Tag
```

Fields

```
public static final int EVAL_BODY_INCLUDE
```

A return value for the doStartBody method, indicating that the container should include the body into the existing out stream.

```
public static final int EVAL_PAGE
```

A return value for the doEndTag method, indicating that the container should continue evaluating the page.

```
public static final int SKIP_BODY
```

A return value for the doStartTag and doAfterBody methods, indicating that the container should skip the body.

```
public static final int SKIP_PAGE
```

A return value for the doEndTag method, indicating that the container should skip the remaining page.

Methods

```
public int doEndTag()
throws javax.servlet.jsp.JspException
```

This method is invoked by the JSP container to process the end tag for this tag instance.

```
public void doStartTag()
throws javax.servlet.jsp.JspException
```

This method is invoked by the JSP container to process the start tag for this tag instance.

```
public Tag getParent()
```

Returns the direct parent for this tag.

```
public void release()
```

This method is invoked to release a tag handler's state.

```
public void setPageContext(javax.servlet.jsp.PageContext pageContext)
```

Sets the current page context.

```
public void setParent(Tag parent)
```

This method is invoked by the JSP container to set the parent for the current tag handler.

TryCatchFinally

An auxiliary interface of the other interfaces to support additional hooks for managing resources.

Signature

```
public interface TryCatchFinally
```

Methods

```
public void doCatch(java.lang.Throwable t) throws java.lang.Throwable
```

This method is invoked if a Throwable is thrown while the JSP container is evaluating the BODY inside a tag or one of the following methods: Tag.doStartTag, Tag.doEndTag, IterationTag.doAfterBody, and BodyTag.doInitBody.

```
public void doFinally()
```

This method is invoked after doEndTag in any class implementing the Tag, IterationTag, or BodyTag interface.

Classes

The following are the classes in the javax.servlet.jsp.tagext package. Each of the following sections describes a class, its signature, its fields, and its methods, if any.

BodyContent

This class represents the body content of the tag.

Signature

```
public abstract class BodyContent extends javax.servlet.jsp.JspWriter
```

Methods

```
public void clearBody()
```

Clears the body.

```
public void flush() throws java.io.IOException
```

Redefines flush.

```
public javax.servlet.jsp.JspWriter getEnclosingWriter()
```

Returns the enclosing JspWriter object.

```
public abstract java.io.Reader getReader()
```

Returns this BodyContent as a Reader object.

```
public abstract java.lang.String getString()
```

Returns the string representation of this BodyContent.

```
public abstract void writeOut(java.io.Writer out) throws java.io.IOException
```

Writes this BodyContent to a Writer object.

BodyTagSupport

A base class that is subclassed by a tag handler that needs to manipulate its body.

Signature

```
public class BodyTagSupport extends TagSupport implements BodyTag
```

Methods

```
public int doAfterBody() throws http.servlet.jsp.JspException
```

This method is invoked after the evaluation of the body.

```
public int doEndTag() throws http.servlet.jsp.JspException
```

This method is invoked to process the end tag.

```
public int doInitBody() throws http.servlet.jsp.JspException
```

This method is invoked before the first body evaluation.

```
public int doStartTag() throws http.servlet.jsp.JspException
```

This method is invoked to process the start tag.

```
public BodyContent getBodyContent()
```

Returns the body content.

```
public javax.servlet.jsp.JspWriter getPreviousOut()
```

Returns the enclosing JspWriter.

```
public void release()
```

Releases the state.

```
public void setBodyContent(BodyContent bodyContent)
```

Sets the body content.

PageData

This class provides information on a JSP page that is available at translation time.

Signature

```
public abstract class PageData
```

Methods

```
public abstract java.io.InputStream getInputStream()
```

Returns the XML document of the JSP page.

TagAttributeInfo

This class provides information on the tag attributes.

Signature

```
public class TagAttributeInfo
```

Field

```
public static final java.lang.String ID
```

The identifier.

Methods

```
public boolean canBeRequestTime()
```

Indicates whether a request time value can be stored in this attribute.

```
public static TagAttributeInfo getIdAttribute(TagAttributeInfo[] tai)
```

Searches through the array of TagAttributeInfo objects and returns the TagAttributeInfo object containing the id.

```
public java.lang.String getName()
```

Returns the attribute name.

```
public java.lang.String getTypeName()
```

Returns the attribute type.

```
public boolean isRequired()
```

Indicates whether this attribute is required.

```
public java.lang.String toString()
```

Overrides the toString method of the java.lang.Object class.

TagData

This class provides information on the tag instance available at translation time.

Signature

```
public class TagData implements java.lang.Cloneable
```

Field

```
public static final java.lang.Object REQUEST_TIME_VALUE
```

A unique value for an attribute indicating that its value is only available at request time.

Methods

```
public java.lang.Object getAttribute(java.lang.String name)
```

Returns the attribute whose name is specified as the argument.

```
public java.util.Enumeration getAttributes()
```

Returns all the attributes.

```
public java.lang.String getAttributeString(java.lang.String name)
```

Returns the attribute whose name is specified as the argument.

```
public java.lang.String getId()
```

Returns the attribute identifier, if available.

```
public void setAttribute(java.lang.String name, java.lang.Object attribute)
```

Sets an attribute.

TagExtraInfo

An optional class that provides additional translation time information not available in the Tag Library Descriptor file.

Signature

```
public abstract class TagExtraInfo
```

Methods

```
public final TagInfo getTagInfo
```

Returns the TagInfo object for this class.

```
public VariableInfo[] getVariableInfo(TagData data)
```

Returns information on the scripting variables.

```
public boolean isValid(TagData data)
```

Indicates whether the tag instance is valid.

```
public final void setTagInfo(TagInfo tagInfo)
```

Sets the TagInfo for this class.

TagInfo

This class provides the information for the tag in a tag library.

Signature

```
public class TagInfo
```

Fields

```
public static final java.lang.String BODY_CONTENT_EMPTY
```

The value for the getBodyContent method when it's empty.

```
public static final java.lang.String BODY_CONTENT_JSP
```

The value for the getBodyContent method when it is JSP.

```
public static final java.lang.String BODY_CONTENT_TAG_DEPENDENT
```

The value for the getBodyContent method when it is tag dependent.

Methods

```
public TagAttributeInfo[] getAttributes()
```

Returns the attribute information on this tag.

```
public java.lang.String getBodyContent()
```

Returns the body content information for this tag.

```
public java.lang.String getDisplayName()
```

Returns the display name.

```
public java.lang.String getInfoString()
```

Returns the information string for this tag.

```
public java.lang.String getLargeIcon()
```

Returns the path to the large icon file.

```
public java.lang.String getSmallIcon()
```

Returns the path to the small icon file.

```
public java.lang.String getTagClassName()
```

Returns the class name that provides the handler for this tag.

```
public TagExtraInfo getTagExtraInfo()
```

Returns additional information for this tag.

```
public TagLibraryInfo getTagLibrary()
```

Returns the current tag library instance.

```
public java.lang.String getTagName()
```

Returns the tag short name.

```
public TagVariableInfo[] getTagVariableInfos()
```

Returns the TagVariableInfo objects associated with the current TagInfo.

```
public VariableInfo[] getVariableInfo(TagData tagData)
```

Returns the runtime information on scripting object.

```
public boolean isValid(TagData tagData)
```

Indicates whether the specified TagData is valid.

```
public void setTagExtraInfo(TagExtraInfo tei)
```

Sets the additional tag information.

```
public void setTagLibrary(TagLibraryInfo tli)
```

Sets the TagLibraryInfo property.

```
public java.lang.String toString()
```

This method overrides the toString method in the java.lang.Object class.

TagLibraryInfo

This class provides information time associated with a taglib directive and its TLD file that is available at translation time.

Signature

```
public abstract class TagLibraryInfo
```

Methods

```
public java.lang.String getInfoString()
```

Returns the information for this TLD.

```
public java.lang.String getPrefixString()
```

Returns the prefix for this taglib.

```
public java.lang.String getReliableURN()
```

Returns the reliable URN.

```
public java.lang.String getRequiredVersion()
```

Returns the required version number of the JSP container.

```
public java.lang.String getShortName()
```

Returns the short name described in the TLD.

```
public TagInfo getTag(java.lang.String shortName)
```

Returns the TagInfo instance for the specified short name.

```
public TagInfo[] getTags()
```

Returns all the TagInfo instances for this tag.

```
public java.lang.String getURI()
```

Returns the URI from the taglib directive.

TagLibraryValidator

This class is a validator class for a JSP page that is available at translation time.

Signature

```
public abstract class TagLibraryValidator
```

Methods

```
public java.util.Map getInitParameters()
```

Returns the initial parameters.

```
public void release()
```

Releases any kept data.

```
public void setInitParameters(java.util.Map initParameters)
```

Sets the initial parameters for this validator.

```
public java.lang.String validate(java.lang.String prefix, java.lang.String
➥uri, PageData pageData)
```

Validates a JSP page.

TagSupport

This class provides convenience methods and is a base class to be extended by new tag handlers.

Signature

```
public class TagSupport implements IterationTag, java.io.Serializable
```

Methods

```
public int doAfterBody throws javax.servlet.jsp.JspException
```

Processes a body.

```
public int doEndTag throws javax.servlet.jsp.JspException
```

Processes the end tag.

```
public int doStartTag throws javax.servlet.jsp.JspException
```

Processes the start tag.

```
public static final Tag findAncestorWithClass(Tag from, java.lang.Class
class)
```

Returns the instance of the closest type to the given class type, starting from the tag given as the from argument.

```
public java.langString getId()
```

Returns the id attribute.

```
public Tag getParent()
```

Returns the closest enclosing tag.

```
public java.lang.Object getValue(java.lang.String key)
```

Returns the value for the given key.

```
public java.util.Enumeration getValues()
```

Returns all the values in this tag.

```
public void release()
```

Releases the state.

```
public void removeValue(java.lang.String key)
```

Removes the value associated with the given key.

```
public void setId(java.lang.String id)
```

Sets the tag's id attribute.

```
public void setPageContext(javax.servlet.jsp.PageContext pageContext)
```

Sets the page context.

```
public void setParent(Tag parent)
```

Sets the enclosing tag for this tag.

```
public void setValue(java.lang.String key, java.lang.Object value)
```

Associates a key with a value.

TagVariableInfo

This class provides information for a tag in a Tag Library.

Signature

```
public class TagVariableInfo
```

Methods

```
public java.lang.String getClassName()
```

Returns the class name of the variable.

```
public boolean getDeclare()
```

Indicates whether the variable is to be declared.

```
public java.lang.String getNameFromAttribute()
```

Returns the attribute defining the variable name.

```
public java.lang.String getNameGiven()
```

Returns the variable name.

```
public int getScope()
```

Returns the scope of the variable.

VariableInfo

This class provides information on the scripting variables.

Signature

```
public class VariableInfo
```

Fields

```
public static final int AT_BEGIN
```

The scope indicator that the variable is visible after the start tag.

```
public static final int AT_END
```

The scope indicator that the variable is visible after the end tag.

```
public static final int NESTED
```

The scope indicator that the variable is visible only within the start/end tags.

Methods

```
public java.lang.String getClassName()
```

Returns the class name of this variable.

```
public boolean getDeclare()
```

Indicates whether the variable is to be declared.

```
public int getScope()
```

Returns the variable scope.

```
public java.lang.String getVarName()
```

Returns the variable name.

F

JBoss Installation and Configuration

THE JBOSS SERVER (`www.jboss.org`) is a J2EE-compliant application server that is implemented in 100 percent pure Java. Distributed under the GNU public license, JBoss is totally free. There is no per-CPU licensing scheme, and no fee for even commercial use.

The zero cost is not the only factor that differentiates JBoss from competitors, however. JBoss prides itself in having features such as "hot deploy," "dynamic proxies," and a JMX-based fully modular design that enables you to replace virtually every component of the server. That is something you can't find even in commercial products, no matter how deep you are willing to put your hand in your pocket. Also important is the fact that JBoss is relatively slim, consuming less memory and disk space, making it much faster to start up. Currently at version 2.4.4, JBoss also comes equipped with a built-in SQL database server for handling persistent beans. This addition makes installation easier because you don't need to download and install a separate product. This database server starts up automatically when you start the server, unlike some competing products where the database server has to be started separately. The "no cost for ownership" nature of JBoss does not mean performance is being compromised. There is a report in which JBoss outperforms some of the market leaders in this field.

Yes, sure, JBoss has some weaknesses, too. Like most open source products, JBoss lacks documentation. There are several how-to articles available; however, these are far from sufficient. And, of course, there is no technical support even though training and consulting are available from the JBoss Group (not free, of course). If you have a problem, basically you just have to rely on the mailing list to find your answers. Browsing through the archive before you start coding can be useful because at least you will then know what to expect.

System Requirements

Both Windows and Linux versions of JBoss require Java Development Kit (JDK) 1.3 to run.

Hardware-wise, you need a machine with at least 64 megabytes of RAM. I could not find any specification telling the lowest breed of CPU JBoss needs. When I install it on my Pentium 550MHz machine, however, I get satisfactory performance. Of course, like other server-based software, the more RAM and CPU power, the better. In terms of hard disk space, JBoss requires only a few megabytes of your hard disk.

Installing JBoss

JBoss installation is relatively simple and straightforward. In fact, ease of installation is one of JBoss's strong points. Before you do the installation, however, make sure that your JDK is working.

Windows Installations

To install JBoss on a Windows machine, do the following steps:

1. Download the binary package (in .zip format) from `http://www.jboss.org/binary.jsp` in the Download—Binary section. Save this zip file into a temporary directory.
2. Unzip the downloaded file using WinZip or a similar product and extract the compressed files into a directory, such as C:\jboss. This directory is called the JBOSS_HOME directory.

That's it.

Linux Installations

Follow these steps to install JBoss on Linux:

1. Download the binary file from `http://www.jboss.org/binary.jsp` into a temporary directory:

```
lynx -source http://www.jboss.org/bin/jboss-2.1.zip > jboss-2.1.zip
```

2. Select an install directory. In this example, assume that /usr/local is used as the install directory.
3. Change directory to this select directory
4. Decompress the binary file. If you have downloaded the binary as a zip file into the /tmp directory, the command to unzip it is unzip /tmp/jboss-2.x.zip. The files will be extracted into the jboss directory under your install directory. This is your JBOSS_HOME directory. If your install directory is /usr/local, your JBOSS_HOME directory is /usr/local/jboss.

If the installation goes smoothly, you should be able to see a directory structure like the one shown in Figure F.1.

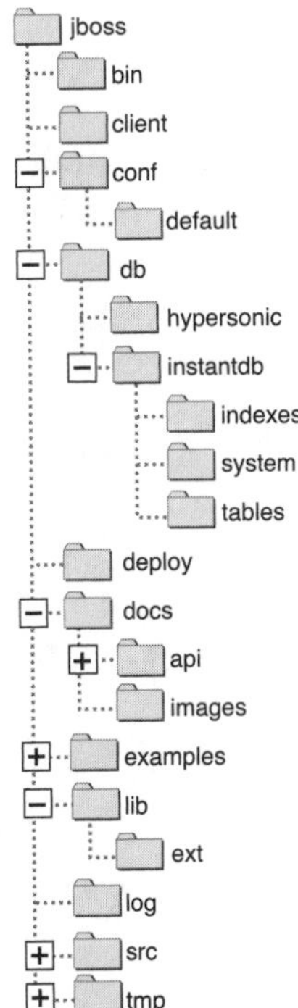

Figure F.1 JBoss directory structure.

Directory Structure

All directories referred to in the next sections are relative to JBOSS_HOME; that is, the top directory of the JBoss installation. The directories are described in the following sections.

bin

All the binaries included with JBoss distribution are located in this directory. Of most importance are the run.bat and the run.sh files that you use to start JBoss on Windows and Linux, respectively.

lib and lib/ext

These two directories contain Java libraries in the .jar and .zip formats that JBoss uses. There is a split between those libraries that had to be in the system classpath (that is, jars in lib directory) versus the ones in lib/ext directory, which are made available to the JBoss server MLet based classloader. If you need to add some Java libraries to JBoss—for example jdbc driver jars—you should drop the libraries in the lib/ext directory. These will be picked up by JBoss automatically.

db

Directory containing hypersonic and instantdb databases related files (configuration files, indexing tables, and so on) as well as JBossMQ—Java Messaging System (JMS) provider message queue files.

deploy

The deployment directory. Just drop your jars here and they will be deployed automatically.

log

The directory for log files. File logging is on by default.

conf

JBoss configuration set(s) are located here. By default there is only one configuration set: default. However, you can add one or more configuration sets if you like.

client

Libraries required for clients are in the client directory. A typical client requires jboss-client.jar, jbosssx-client.jar, jaas.jar, jnp-client.jar, ejb.jar, and jta-spec1_0_1.jar. If your client is not running JDK 1.3, it will require jndi.jar as well. If you are going to be using JBossMQ JMS provider, you also will need jbossmq-client.jar.

Configuration

There's basically nothing you need to do to get JBoss up and running. You might need to make minor configuration changes to support your specific applications, however. If you do make configuration changes, consult the Advanced Configuration section of the online documentation.

Running JBoss

To run JBoss on Linux, follow these steps:

- Make sure that you have write permission to the JBoss directory (needed for log files and deployment)
- Change to the bin directory under the JBoss directory and then type ./run.sh

Running JBoss on Windows is even easier: you need only to change the directory to the bin directory, and then run the run.bat file.

The server should start without any error messages or exceptions being thrown. It will produce several pages of output on startup.

Deployment

This is one of the nice features of JBoss. To deploy a bean, simply copy its .jar file into the deploy directory under the JBoss home directory. If you do this when the bean is already loaded, JBoss automatically unloads it, and then loads the new version.

JBoss and Tomcat

If your EJB client is a servlet or a JSP page, you surely need Tomcat, the servlet/JSP container, to execute your servlet/JSP. For better performance, you may want to run Tomcat in the same Virtual Machine as JBoss. The JBoss organization has finished integrating the JBoss server with Tomcat version 4.0.1. You can download this package and install it on your computer without any fuss.

In a typical web application, however, you normally have static HTML pages as well as dynamic pages. Allowing Tomcat to serve HTML pages as well is not an efficient approach. The solution is usually to install a scalable web server, such as Apache, at the front. Only requests for servlet/JSP pages are forwarded to Tomcat.

When Tomcat is integrated inside JBoss, running Tomcat as an Apache module makes the system installation more complex. In brief, there is not yet one single download installation that requires no configuration that can integrate JBoss with Tomcat and a web server. Hopefully, this will be available in not-too-distant future. When this is finished, JBoss can deliver much better system performance and still provides easy installation and configuration.

Summary

JBoss is free and has proven itself a high performer. Its strong features include easy installation and hot deployment.

G

Related Resources

THIS APPENDIX PROVIDES YOU WITH LINKS to various related topics that will help you develop your skills. These resources include a wealth of information from J2EE tutorials to specification information and application servers.

J2EE

Visit these sites to find additional resources for J2EE:

- `http://java.sun.com/j2ee/` Sun Microsystem's site for the Java 2 Platform Enterprise Edition.
- `http://java.sun.com/blueprints/enterprise/index.htm` Resources for Java Enterprise blueprints.
- `http://java.sun.com/j2ee/sdk_1.3/index.htm` The link to download the Java 2 SDK, Enterprise Edition.

- `http://java.sun.com/blueprints/patterns/j2ee_patterns/index.html` J2EE design patterns.
- `http://java.sun.com/j2ee/tutorial/1_3-fcs/index.html` J2EE tutorials.
- `http://java.sun.com/blueprints/code/index.html#java_pet_store_demo` A sample application that shows how to use the capabilities of the J2EE 1.3 platform to develop flexible, scalable, cross-platform enterprise applications.

Servlet

These sites can provide additional helpful information on servlet:

- `http://java.sun.com/products/servlet/index.html` The main site for the Java servlet technology.
- `http://www.jcp.org/aboutJava/communityprocess/final/jsr053/` The Servlet 2.3 specification.
- `http://java.sun.com/products/servlet/Filters.html` A white paper on servlet filters.

JSP

For more information on JSP, visit these sites:

- `http://java.sun.com/products/jsp/index.html` Sun Microsystem's site for JSP.
- `http://www.jcp.org/aboutJava/communityprocess/final/jsr053/` The JSP 1.2 specification.
- `http://jakarta.apache.org/struts/index.html` The open source framework for building web applications with servlets and JSP.

Tag Library

For tag library resources, go to the following site:

- `http://jakarta.apache.org/taglibs/index.html` The Jakarta Taglibs open source tag library.

Servlet/JSP Containers

These sites provide additional resources for servlet/JSP:

- `http://jakarta.apache.org/tomcat/index.html` The Jakarta Tomcat open source servlet/JSP container.
- `http://www.newatlanta.com/` New Atlanta Communicatons's ServletExec servlet/JSP container.
- `http://www.caucho.com/` Caucho Technology's Resin servlet/JSP container.

JDBC

Visit these sites to find out more about JDBC:

- `http://java.sun.com/products/jdbc/index.html` The main source for the JDBC technology.
- `http://java.sun.com/products/jdbc/index.html` JDBC download page.
- `http://java.sun.com/products/jdbc/index.html` The list of JDBC drivers.

JNDI

The following sites give you additional resources for JNDI:

- `http://java.sun.com/products/jndi/index.html` The source for JNDI.
- `http://java.sun.com/products/jndi/index.html#download` JNDI software download.
- `http://java.sun.com/products/jndi/tutorial/index.html` A JNDI tutorial.

JMS

The following sites give you additional resources for JMS:

- `http://java.sun.com/products/jms/index.html` Sun Microsystem's web site for JMS API.
- `http://java.sun.com/products/jms/tutorial/1_3-fcs/doc/jms_tutorialTOC.html` JMS tutorials.

EJB

These sites offer EJB extras:

- `http://java.sun.com/products/ejb/index.html` Sun Microsystem's main site for Enterprise JavaBeans.
- `http://java.sun.com/products/ejb/2.0.html` The EJB 2.0 specification.

J2EE Server

The following are J2EE Server resources:

- `http://www.jboss.org` The JBoss open source application server.
- `http://www.weblogic.com` BEA Systems' WebLogic application server.
- `http://www-4.ibm.com/software/webservers/appserv/` IBM's WebSphere application server.
- `http://www.bluestone.com/products/hp-as/default.htm` HP's HP-AS application server.
- `http://orion.evermind.net/` The Orion application server web site.
- `http://www.iplanet.com/` The iPlanet application server web site.
- `http://www.oracle.com/ip/deploy/ias/` Oracle's application server.
- `http://www.silverstream.com/Website/app/en_US/AppServer` Silverstream's eXtend application server.
- `http://www.gemstone.com/products/` Gemstone application server.
- `http://www.borland.com/bes/appserver/` Borland's application server.
- `http://www.persistence.com/products/powertier/index.php` Persistence's PowerTier application server.
- `http://www.trifork.com/` Trifork's application server.
- `http://www.macromedia.com/software/jrun/` Macromedia's JRun application server.
- `http://www.interstage.com/` Fujitsu's Interstage application server.
- `http://www.hitachi.co.jp/Prod/comp/soft1/open-e/Cosminexus/index/index.html` Hitachi's Cosminexus application server.
- `http://www.enterprisebeans.de/` In-Q-My's application server.
- `http://www.interactivebusiness.com/EASInfo/frameset1.html` IBS Enterprise application server.
- `http://www.iona.com/products/appserv.htm` Iona's Orbix E2A application server.

- `http://www.lutris.com/` Lutris application server.
- `http://www.pramati.com/` Pramati applicaton server.
- `http://www.secant.com/products/ES/index.html` Secant's ModelMethods Enterprise server.
- `http://www.sybase.com/products/easerver` Sybase's EA server.

H

What's On the CD-ROM?

THE ACCOMPANYING CD-ROM CONTAINS the code listings for the book, as well as software and project files for some of the chapters.

The following sections contain detailed descriptions of the CD's contents:

- The BrainySoftware.com Java File Upload Bean that is free for non-commercial use. For more information about the licensing, refer to the document in the software/FileUploadBean directory on the CD.
- The BrainySoftware.com Java File Download Bean that is free for non-commercial and commercial use for the purchaser of this book. For more information about the licensing, refer to the document in the software/FileDownloadBean directory on the CD.
- The StringUtil.jar file containing a library of functions.
- The Docman document management project.
- The Tassie project.
- The Burnaby project.
- The mmmysql JDBC Driver for MySql. Licensing information can be found in the ReadMe.txt in the software/mmmysql on the CD.
- The jboss application server.

Warning

For more information about the use of this CD, please review the ReadMe.txt file in the root directory. This file includes important disclaimer information, as well as information about installation, system requirements, troubleshooting, and technical support.

Technical Support Issues

If you have any difficulties with this CD, you can access our web site at `http://www.newriders.com`.

Read This Before Opening the Software

By opening the CD package, you agree to be bound by the following agreement:

You may not copy or redistribute the entire CD-ROM as a whole. Copying and redistribution of individual software programs on the CD-ROM is governed by terms set by individual copyright holders.

The installer, code, images, actions, and brushes from the author(s) are copyrighted by the publisher and the authors.

This software is sold as-is, without warranty of any kind, either expressed or implied, including but not limited to, the implied warranties of merchantability and fitness for a particular purpose. Neither the publisher nor its dealers or distributors assumes any liability for any alleged or actual damages arising from the use of this program. (Some states do not allow for the exclusion of implied warranties, so the exclusion may not apply to you.)

GNU LESSER GENERAL PUBLIC LICENSE

Version 2.1, February 1999

Copyright (C) 1991, 1999 Free Software Foundation, Inc.

59 Temple Place, Suite 330, Boston, MA 02111-1307 USA

Everyone is permitted to copy and distribute verbatim copies of this license document, but changing it is not allowed.

[This is the first released version of the Lesser GPL. It also counts as the successor of the GNU Library Public License, version 2, hence the version number 2.1.]

Preamble

The licenses for most software are designed to take away your freedom to share and change it. By contrast, the GNU General Public Licenses are intended to guarantee your freedom to share and change free software—to make sure the software is free for all its users.

This license, the Lesser General Public License, applies to some specially designated software packages—typically libraries—of the Free Software Foundation and other authors who decide to use it. You can use it too, but we suggest you first think carefully about whether this license or the ordinary General Public License is the better strategy to use in any particular case, based on the explanations below.

When we speak of free software, we are referring to freedom of use, not price. Our General Public Licenses are designed to make sure that you have the freedom to distribute copies of free software (and charge for this service if you wish); that you receive source code or can get it if you want it; that you can change the software and use pieces of it in new free programs; and that you are informed that you can do these things.

To protect your rights, we need to make restrictions that forbid distributors to deny you these rights or to ask you to surrender these rights. These restrictions translate to certain responsibilities for you if you distribute copies of the library or if you modify it.

For example, if you distribute copies of the library, whether gratis or for a fee, you must give the recipients all the rights that we gave you. You must make sure that they, too, receive or can get the source code. If you link other code with the library, you must provide complete object files to the recipients, so that they can relink them with the library after making changes to the library and recompiling it. And you must show them these terms so they know their rights.

We protect your rights with a two-step method: (1) we copyright the library, and (2) we offer you this license, which gives you legal permission to copy, distribute and/or modify the library.

To protect each distributor, we want to make it very clear that there is no warranty for the free library. Also, if the library is modified by someone else and passed on, the recipients should know that what they have is not the original version, so that the original author's reputation will not be affected by problems that might be introduced by others.

Finally, software patents pose a constant threat to the existence of any free program. We wish to make sure that a company cannot effectively restrict the users of a free program by obtaining a restrictive license from a patent holder.

Therefore, we insist that any patent license obtained for a version of the library must be consistent with the full freedom of use specified in this license.

Most GNU software, including some libraries, is covered by the ordinary GNU General Public License. This license, the GNU Lesser General Public License, applies to certain designated libraries, and is quite different from the ordinary General Public License. We use this license for certain libraries in order to permit linking those libraries into non-free programs.

When a program is linked with a library, whether statically or using a shared library, the combination of the two is legally speaking a combined work, a derivative of the original library. The ordinary General Public License therefore permits such linking only if the entire combination fits its criteria of freedom. The Lesser General Public License permits more lax criteria for linking other code with the library.

We call this license the "Lesser" General Public License because it does Less to protect the user's freedom than the ordinary General Public License. It also provides other free software developers Less of an advantage over competing non-free programs. These disadvantages are the reason we use the ordinary General Public License for many libraries. However, the Lesser license provides advantages in certain special circumstances.

For example, on rare occasions, there may be a special need to encourage the widest possible use of a certain library, so that it becomes a de-facto standard. To achieve this, non-free programs must be allowed to use the library. A more frequent case is that a free library does the same job as widely used non-free libraries. In this case, there is little to gain by limiting the free library to free oftware only, so we use the Lesser General Public License.

In other cases, permission to use a particular library in non-free programs enables a greater number of people to use a large body of free software. For example, permission to use the GNU C Library in non-free programs enables many more people to use the whole GNUoperating system, as well as its variant, the GNU/Linux operating system.

Although the Lesser General Public License is Less protective of the users' freedom, it does ensure that the user of a program that is linked with the Library has the freedom and the wherewithal to run that program using a modified version of the Library.

The precise terms and conditions for copying, distribution and modification follow. Pay close attention to the difference between "work based on the library" and a "work that uses the library". The former contains code derived from the library, whereas the latter must be combined with the library in order to run.

GNU LESSER GENERAL PUBLIC LICENSE

TERMS AND CONDITIONS FOR COPYING, DISTRIBUTION AND MODIFICATION

This License Agreement applies to any software library or other program which contains a notice placed by the copyright holder or other authorized party saying it may be distributed under the terms of this Lesser General Public License (also called "this License").

Each licensee is addressed as "you".

A "library" means a collection of software functions and/or data prepared so as to be conveniently linked with application programs (which use some of those functions and data) to form executables.

The "Library", below, refers to any such software library or work which has been distributed under these terms. A "work based on the Library" means either the Library or any derivative work under copyright law: that is to say, a work containing the Library or a portion of it, either verbatim or with modifications and/or translated straightforwardly into another language. (Hereinafter, translation is included without limitation in the term "modification".)

"Source code" for a work means the preferred form of the work for making modifications to it. For a library, complete source code means all the source code for all modules it contains, plus any associated interface definition files, plus the scripts used to control compilation and installation of the library.

Activities other than copying, distribution and modification are not covered by this License; they are outside its scope. The act of running a program using the Library is not restricted, and output from such a program is covered only if its contents constitute a work based on the Library (independent of the use of the Library in a tool for writing it). Whether that is true depends on what the Library does and what the program that uses the Library does.

1. You may copy and distribute verbatim copies of the Library's complete source code as you receive it, in any medium, provided that you conspicuously and appropriately publish on each copy an appropriate copyright notice and disclaimer of warranty; keep intact all the notices that refer to this License and to the absence of any warranty; and distribute a copy of this License along with the Library.

You may charge a fee for the physical act of transferring a copy, and you may at your option offer warranty protection in exchange for a fee.

2. You may modify your copy or copies of the Library or any portion of it, thus forming a work based on the Library, and copy and distribute such modifications or work under the terms of Section 1 above, provided that you also meet all of these conditions:

The modified work must itself be a software library.

You must cause the files modified to carry prominent notices stating that you changed the files and the date of any change.

c) You must cause the whole of the work to be licensed at no charge to all third parties under the terms of this License.

d) If a facility in the modified Library refers to a function or a table of data to be supplied by an application program that uses the facility, other than as an argument passed when the facility is invoked, then you must make a good faith effort to ensure that, in the event an application does not supply such function or table, the facility still operates, and performs whatever part of its purpose remains meaningful.

(For example, a function in a library to compute square roots has a purpose that is entirely well-defined independent of the application. Therefore, Subsection 2d requires that any application-supplied function or table used by this function must be optional: if the application does not supply it, the square root function must still compute square roots.)

These requirements apply to the modified work as a whole. If identifiable sections of that work are not derived from the Library, and can be reasonably considered independent and separate works in themselves, then this License, and its terms, do not apply to those sections when you distribute them as separate works. But when you distribute the same sections as part of a whole which is a work based on the Library, the distribution of the whole must be on the terms of this License, whose permissions for other licensees extend to the entire whole, and thus to each and every part regardless of who wrote it.

Thus, it is not the intent of this section to claim rights or contest your rights to work written entirely by you; rather, the intent is to exercise the right to control the distribution of derivative or collective works based on the Library.

In addition, mere aggregation of another work not based on the Library with the Library (or with a work based on the Library) on a volume of a storage or distribution medium does not bring the other work under the scope of this License.

3. You may opt to apply the terms of the ordinary GNU General Public License instead of this License to a given copy of the Library. To do this, you must alter all the notices that refer to this License, so that they refer to the ordinary GNU General Public License, version 2, instead of to this License. (If a newer version than version 2 of the ordinary GNU General Public License has appeared, then you can specify that version instead if you wish.) Do not make any other change in these notices.

Once this change is made in a given copy, it is irreversible for that copy, so the ordinary GNU General Public License applies to all subsequent copies and derivative works made from that copy.

This option is useful when you wish to copy part of the code of the Library into a program that is not a library.

4. You may copy and distribute the Library (or a portion or derivative of it, under Section 2) in object code or executable form under the terms of Sections 1 and 2 above provided that you accompany it with the complete corresponding machine-readable source code, which must be distributed under the terms of Sections 1 and 2 above on a medium customarily used for software interchange.

If distribution of object code is made by offering access to copy from a designated place, then offering equivalent access to copy the source code from the same place satisfies the requirement to distribute the source code, even though third parties are not compelled to copy the source along with the object code.

5. A program that contains no derivative of any portion of the Library, but is designed to work with the Library by being compiled or linked with it, is called a "work that uses the Library". Such a work, in isolation, is not a derivative work of the Library, and therefore falls outside the scope of this License.

However, linking a "work that uses the Library" with the Library creates an executable that is a derivative of the Library (because it contains portions of the Library), rather than a "work that uses the library". The executable is therefore covered by this License. Section 6 states terms for distribution of such executables.

When a "work that uses the Library" uses material from a header file that is part of the Library, the object code for the work may be a derivative work of the Library even though the source code is not. Whether this is true is especially significant if the work can be linked without the Library, or if the work is itself a library. The threshold for this to be true is not precisely defined by law. If such an object file uses only numerical parameters, data structure layouts and accessors, and small macros and small inline functions (ten lines or less in length), then the use of the object file is unrestricted, regardless of whether it is legally a derivative work. (Executables containing this object code plus portions of the Library will still fall under Section 6.) Otherwise, if the work is a derivative of the Library, you may distribute the object code for the work under the terms of Section 6. Any executables containing that work also fall under Section 6, whether or not they are linked directly with the Library itself.

6. As an exception to the Sections above, you may also combine or link a "work that uses the Library" with the Library to produce a work containing portions of the Library, and distribute that work under terms of your choice, provided that the terms permit modification of the work for the customer's own use and reverse engineering for debugging such modifications.

You must give prominent notice with each copy of the work that the Library is used in it and that the Library and its use are covered by this License. You must supply a copy of this License. If the work during execution displays copyright notices, you must include the copyright notice for the Library among them, as well as a reference directing the user to the copy of this License. Also, you must do one of these things:

Accompany the work with the complete corresponding machine-readable source code for the Library including whatever changes were used in the work (which must be distributed under Sections 1 and 2 above); and, if the work is an executable linked with the Library, with the complete machine-readable "work that uses the Library", as object code and/or source code, so that the user can modify the Library and then relink to produce a modified executable containing the modified Library. (It is understood that the user who changes the contents of definitions files in the Library will not necessarily be able to recompile the application to use the modified definitions.)

Use a suitable shared library mechanism for linking with the Library. A suitable mechanism is one that (1) uses at run time a copy of the library already present on the user's computer system, rather than copying library functions into the executable, and (2) will operate properly with a modified version of the library, if the user installs one, as long as the modified version is interface-compatible with the version that the work was made with.

Accompany the work with a written offer, valid for at least three years, to give the same user the materials specified in Subsection 6a, above, for a charge no more than the cost of performing this distribution.

If distribution of the work is made by offering access to copy from a designated place, offer equivalent access to copy the above specified materials from the same place.

e) Verify that the user has already received a copy of these materials or that you have already sent this user a copy.

For an executable, the required form of the "work that uses the Library" must include any data and utility programs needed for reproducing the executable from it. However, as a special exception, the materials to be distributed need not include anything that is normally distributed (in either source or binary form) with the major components (compiler, kernel, and so on) of the operating system on which the executable runs, unless that component itself accompanies the executable.

It may happen that this requirement contradicts the license restrictions of other proprietary libraries that do not normally accompany the operating system. Such a contradiction means you cannot use both them and the Library together in an executable that you distribute.

7.You may place library facilities that are a work based on the Library side-by-side in a single library together with other library facilities not covered by this License, and distribute such a combined library, provided that the separate distribution of the work based on the Library and of the other library facilities is otherwise permitted, and provided that you do these two things:

a) Accompany the combined library with a copy of the same work based on the Library, uncombined with any other library facilities. This must be distributed under the terms of the Sections above.

b) Give prominent notice with the combined library of the fact that part of it is a work based on the Library, and explaining where to find the accompanying uncombined form of the same work.

8.You may not copy, modify, sublicense, link with, or distribute the Library except as expressly provided under this License. Any attempt otherwise to copy, modify, sublicense, link with, or distribute the Library is void, and will automatically terminate your rights under this License. However, parties who have received copies, or rights, from you under this License will not have their licenses terminated so long as such parties remain in full compliance.

9.You are not required to accept this License, since you have not signed it. However, nothing else grants you permission to modify or distribute the Library or its derivative works. These actions are prohibited by law if you do not accept this License. Therefore, by modifying or distributing the Library (or any work based on the Library), you indicate your acceptance of this License to do so, and all its terms and conditions for copying, distributing or modifying the Library or works based on it.

10. Each time you redistribute the Library (or any work based on the Library), the recipient automatically receives a license from the original licensor to copy, distribute, link with or modify the Library subject to these terms and conditions. You may not impose any further restrictions on the recipients' exercise of the rights granted herein. You are not responsible for enforcing compliance by third parties with this License.

11. If, as a consequence of a court judgment or allegation of patent infringement or for any other reason (not limited to patent issues), conditions are imposed on you (whether by court order, agreement or otherwise) that contradict the conditions of this License, they do not excuse you from the conditions of this License. If you cannot distribute so as to satisfy simultaneously your obligations under this License and any other pertinent obligations, then as a consequence you may not distribute the Library at all. For example,

if a patent license would not permit royalty-free redistribution of the Library by all those who receive copies directly or indirectly through you, then the only way you could satisfy both it and this License would be to refrain entirely from distribution of the Library.

If any portion of this section is held invalid or unenforceable under any particular circumstance, the balance of the section is intended to apply, and the section as a whole is intended to apply in other circumstances. It is not the purpose of this section to induce you to infringe any patents or other property right claims or to contest validity of any such claims; this section has the sole purpose of protecting the integrity of the free software distribution system which is implemented by public license practices. Many people have made generous contributions to the wide range of software distributed through that system in reliance on consistent application of that system; it is up to the author/donor to decide if he or she is willing to distribute software through any other system and a licensee cannot impose that choice. This section is intended to make thoroughly clear what is believed to be a consequence of the rest of this License.

12. If the distribution and/or use of the Library is restricted in certain countries either by patents or by copyrighted interfaces, the original copyright holder who places the Library under this License may add an explicit geographical distribution limitation excluding those countries, so that distribution is permitted only in or among countries not thus excluded. In such case, this License incorporates the limitation as if written in the body of this License.

13. The Free Software Foundation may publish revised and/or new versions of the Lesser General Public License from time to time. Such new versions will be similar in spirit to the present version, but may differ in detail to address new problems or concerns. Each version is given a distinguishing version number. If the Library specifies a version number of this License which applies to it and "any later version", you have the option of following the terms and conditions either of that version or of any later version published by the Free Software Foundation. If the Library does not specify a license version number, you may choose any version ever published by the Free Software Foundation.

14. If you wish to incorporate parts of the Library into other free programs whose distribution conditions are incompatible with these, write to the author to ask for permission. For software which is copyrighted by the Free Software Foundation, write to the Free Software Foundation; we sometimes make exceptions for this. Our decision will be guided by the two goals of preserving the free status of all derivatives of our free software and of promoting the sharing and reuse of software generally.

NO WARRANTY

15. BECAUSE THE LIBRARY IS LICENSED FREE OF CHARGE, THERE IS NO WARRANTY FOR THE LIBRARY, TO THE EXTENT PERMITTED BY APPLICABLE LAW. EXCEPT WHEN OTHERWISE STATED IN WRITING THE COPYRIGHT HOLDERS AND/OR OTHER PARTIES PROVIDE THE LIBRARY "AS IS" WITHOUT WARRANTY OF ANY KIND, EITHER EXPRESSED OR IMPLIED, INCLUDING, BUT NOT LIMITED TO, THE IMPLIED WARRANTIES OF MERCHANTABILITY AND FITNESS FOR A PARTICULAR PURPOSE. THE ENTIRE RISK AS TO THE QUALITY AND PERFORMANCE OF THE LIBRARY IS WITH YOU. SHOULD THE LIBRARY PROVE DEFECTIVE, YOU ASSUME THE COST OF ALL NECESSARY SERVICING, REPAIR OR CORRECTION.

16. IN NO EVENT UNLESS REQUIRED BY APPLICABLE LAW OR AGREED TO IN WRITING WILL ANY COPYRIGHT HOLDER, OR ANY OTHER PARTY WHO MAY MODIFY AND/OR REDISTRIBUTE THE LIBRARY AS PERMITTED ABOVE, BE LIABLE TO YOU FOR DAMAGES, INCLUDING ANY GENERAL, SPECIAL, INCIDENTAL OR CONSEQUENTIAL DAMAGES ARISING OUT OF THE USE OR INABILITY TO USE THE LIBRARY (INCLUDING BUT NOT LIMITED TO LOSS OF DATA OR DATA BEING RENDERED INACCURATE OR LOSSES SUSTAINED BY YOU OR THIRD PARTIES OR A FAILURE OF THE LIBRARY TO OPERATE WITH ANY OTHER SOFTWARE), EVEN IF SUCH HOLDER OR OTHER PARTY HAS BEEN ADVISED OF THE POSSIBILITY OF SUCH DAMAGES.

END OF TERMS AND CONDITIONS

How to Apply These Terms to Your New Libraries

If you develop a new library, and you want it to be of the greatest possible use to the public, we recommend making it free software that everyone can redistribute and change. You can do so by permitting redistribution under these terms (or, alternatively, under the terms of the ordinary General Public License).

To apply these terms, attach the following notices to the library. It is safest to attach them to the start of each source file to most effectively convey the exclusion of warranty; and each file should have at least the "copyright" line and a pointer to where the full notice is found. <one line to give the library's name and a brief idea of what it does.> Copyright (C) <year> <name of author>

This library is free software; you can redistribute it and/or modify it under the terms of the GNU Lesser General Public License as published by the Free Software Foundation; either version 2.1 of the License, or (at your option) any later version.
This library is distributed in the hope that it will be useful, but WITHOUT ANY WARRANTY; without even the implied warranty of MERCHANTABILITY or FITNESS FOR A PARTICULAR PURPOSE. See the GNU Lesser General Public License for more details.
You should have received a copy of the GNU Lesser General Public License along with this library; if not, write to the Free Software
Foundation, Inc., 59 Temple Place, Suite 330, Boston, MA 02111-1307 USA
Also add information on how to contact you by electronic and paper mail.
You should also get your employer (if you work as a programmer) or your school, if any, to sign a "copyright disclaimer" for the library, if necessary. Here is a sample; alter the names:Yoyodyne, Inc., hereby disclaims all copyright interest in the library `Frob' (a library for tweaking knobs) written by James Random Hacker.
Ty Coon, President ofVice
That's all there is to it!

Index

Symbols

A

C

D

E

F

G

H

I

K-L

M

N

O

P

S

T

U

V

W

X-Z

HOW TO CONTACT US

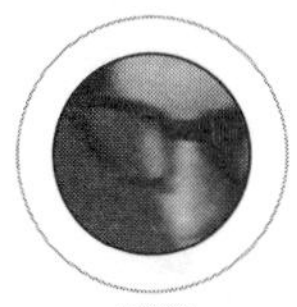
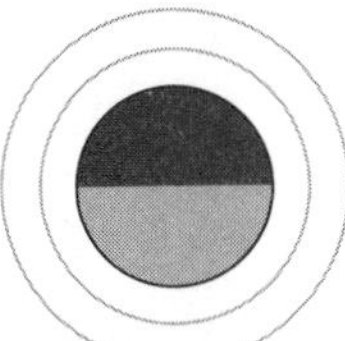

VISIT OUR WEB SITE

WWW.NEWRIDERS.COM

On our web site, you'll find information about our other books, authors, tables of contents, and book errata. You will also find information about book registration and how to purchase our books, both domestically and internationally.

EMAIL US

Contact us at: **nrfeedback@newriders.com**

- If you have comments or questions about this book
- To report errors that you have found in this book
- If you have a book proposal to submit or are interested in writing for New Riders
- If you are an expert in a computer topic or technology and are interested in being a technical editor who reviews manuscripts for technical accuracy

Contact us at: **nreducation@newriders.com**

- If you are an instructor from an educational institution who wants to preview New Riders books for classroom use. Email should include your name, title, school, department, address, phone number, office days/hours, text in use, and enrollment, along with your request for desk/examination copies and/or additional information.

Contact us at: **nrmedia@newriders.com**

- If you are a member of the media who is interested in reviewing copies of New Riders books. Send your name, mailing address, and email address, along with the name of the publication or web site you work for.

BULK PURCHASES/CORPORATE SALES

If you are interested in buying 10 or more copies of a title or want to set up an account for your company to purchase directly from the publisher at a substantial discount, contact us at 800-382-3419 or email your contact information to `corpsales@pearsontechgroup.com`. A sales representative will contact you with more information.

WRITE TO US

New Riders Publishing
201 W. 103rd St.
Indianapolis, IN 46290-1097

CALL/FAX US

Toll-free (800) 571-5840
If outside U.S. (317) 581-3500
Ask for New Riders
FAX: (317) 581-4663

VOICES THAT MATTER

WWW.NEWRIDERS.COM

RELATED NEW RIDERS TITLES

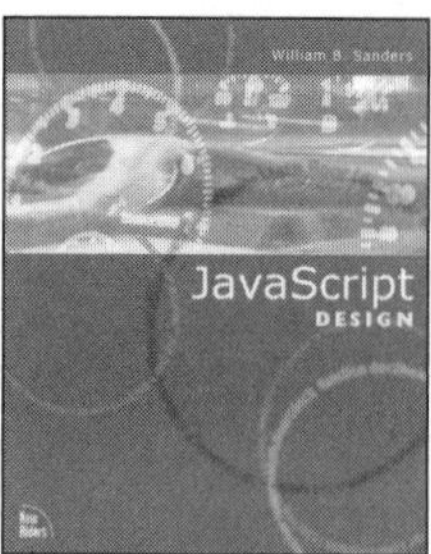

JavaScript Design

Bill Sanders

Designers need to understand how to apply developer tools to their work. *JavaScript Design* helps you do this by showing you how to create interactive JavaScript applications for the web.

ISBN: 0735711666
482 pages
US$39.99

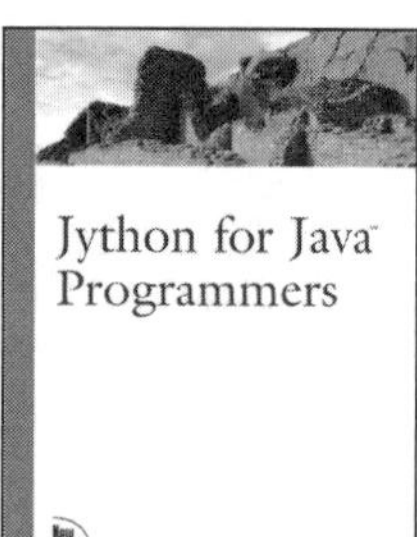

Jython for Java Programmers

Robert Bill

Delve into the new and exciting world of Jython, a speedy and efficient scripting language written in Java. After a brief introduction, the book utilizes examples to ensure that you increase your programming productivity and get the most from Jython.

ISBN: 0735711119
460 pages
US$49.99

JSP and Tag Libraries for Web Development

Wellington Silva

This book, with its explanation of tag library technology and examples of implementation, helps to bring the capabilities of tag libraries to the arsenals of current JSP programmers.

ISBN: 0735710953
464 pages
US$39.99

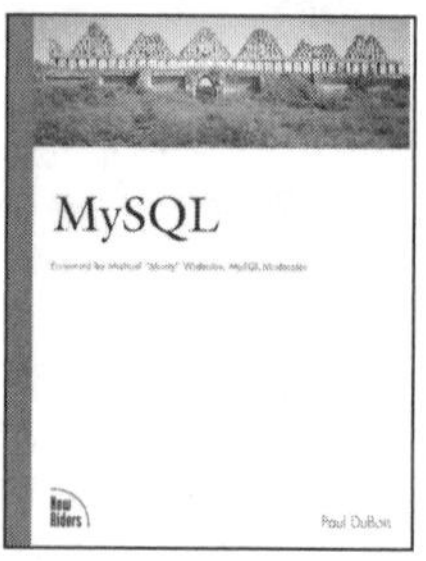

MySQL

Paul DuBois

MySQL teaches you how to use the tools provided by the MySQL distribution, by covering installation, setup, daily use, security, optimizatio maintenance, and troubleshooting. It also discusses important third-party tools, such as the Perl DBI and Apac PHP interfaces that provide access to MySQL.

ISBN: 0735709211
800 pages
US$49.99

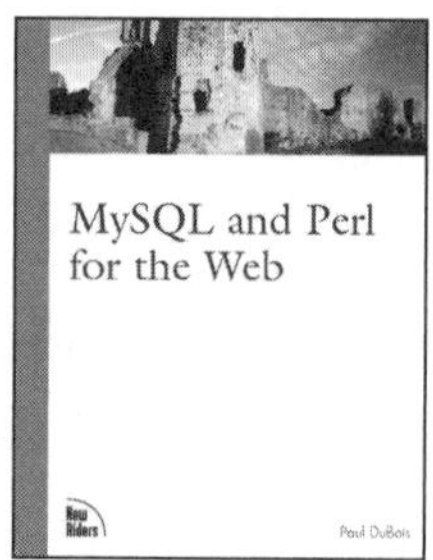

MySQL and Perl for the Web

Paul Dubois

Paul DuBois does it again with *MySQL and Perl for the Web*. Th time, he tells you how to bring your web site to life by using th powerful combination of Perl a MySQL.

ISBN: 0735710546
500 pages
US$44.99

Inside ASP.NET

Scott Worley, Budi Kurniawan

Discover the sheer power and flexibility of the ASP.NET development environment and prepare yourself for the future web development.

ISBN: 0735711356
736 pages
US$49.99

Colophon

Photographed on the cover is a picture of a Coral trout, otherwise known as the Plectropomus leopardus, by photographer Ian Cartwright. Coral trout are native to the Australian waters and can be located in places such as the Great Barrier Reef, where they dwell near outer reefs feasting on small fish. The Coral trout are considered to be an expensive and tasty treat and can be found on the mainland served up in some of Sydney's most popular restaurants.

These fish are a rather interesting species when it comes to their sex. They are called protogynous hermaphrodites, which means that they function during the first part of their lives as females and function in the latter part as males. They can easily be identified by their numerous round blue or red spots on their head and body.

Sydney, Austrailia is also home to author Budi Kurniawan.

This book was written and edited in Microsoft Word, and laid out in QuarkXPress. The font used for the body text is Bembo and Mono. It was printed on 50# Husky Offset Smooth paper at R.R. Donnelley & Sons in Crawfordsville, Indiana. Prepress consisted of PostScript computer-to-plate technology (filmless process). The cover was printed at Moore Langen Printing in Terre Haute, Indiana, on Carolina, coated on one side.